Third Edition

The Well-Managed Health Care Organization

Third Edition

The Well-Managed Health Care Organization

John R. Griffith

AUPHA Press/Health Administration Press
Ann Arbor, Michigan 1995

99 98 97 96 95   5 4 3 2 1

Library of Congress Cataloging-in-Publication Data

Griffith, John R.
    The well-managed health care organization / John R. Griffith. — 3rd ed.
        p.   cm.
    Includes bibliographical references and index.
    ISBN 1-56793-034-4 (hardbound : acid free)
    1. Health services administration. I. Title.
RA971.G77   1995   362.1'068—dc20   95-18402 CIP

The paper used in this publication meets the minimum requirements of American National Standard for Information Sciences—Permanence of Paper for Printed Library Materials, ANSI Z39.48-1984. ∞™

Health Administration Press
A division of the Foundation
    of the American College of
    Healthcare Executives
1021 East Huron Street
Ann Arbor, Michigan 48104
(313) 764-1380

Association of University Programs
    in Health Administration
1911 North Fort Myer Drive, Suite 503
Arlington, VA 22209
(703) 524-5500

Dedicated to my father, the late Richard R. Griffith, FACHE, and his colleagues. They were the first generation of hospital executives, who created the community hospital and laid the foundations for the well-managed health care organization.

CONTENTS

LIST OF FIGURES

PREFACE

THIS BOOK, now in its third edition, arises from a deep conviction in the worth of locally managed health care and a respect for the organizations that have emerged as central to that care. Originally community hospitals, these organizations have expanded to new roles, embracing more comprehensive services and broader commitments for the quality and cost. They have taken new names like "health systems" to reflect their expansion. The new organizations, supported in part by volunteered labor and charitable donations, continue a priceless tradition of neighbors helping one another in time of need. This tradition of Samaritanism is in itself an important contributor to the core concepts of community.

I believe local organizations to manage health care are inevitable, improvable, and inherently better than imaginable alternatives. The concepts of local control and Samaritan intent are ones which should be strengthened and expanded. Their most important strength is their commitment to their communities, and the loyalty which that commitment generates among their users. The most telling evidence of that strength is the rapid response of the community to any perceived threat. The depth of their support is sometimes only clear when there is a danger that the organization will disappear. The central measure of their performance, therefore, is their ability to satisfy local needs, to draw customers, and to bring them back again.

This book offers practical suggestions to strengthen and improve the community health care organization. These are based on observation of successful models, searching for the best practices for tasks which clearly must be done if the organization is to succeed. They are organized around a comprehensive and well-supported theory of management, outlined in Chapter 2, and expanded in terms of major systems of activities essential to the organization. I hope they are expressed in terms a beginner can understand, but they are increasingly rigorous and technical. Successful habits and traditions turn gradually to explicit policies, and these become more complex as they are adapted to broader and broader circumstances. What was a handshake for my father is a written, often quantitative procedure for me, and will be a dynamic computerized exchange for my sons and daughters. Simply put, as the world and medicine have become more complex, so has health care management.

As the editions mount, the list of people who have contributed to the work is ever growing. It is impossible to identify them all. Three deserve mention for the third edition: Albert F. Gilbert, Ph.D., President of Summa Health Systems of Akron, Ohio, has provided me with a vital, ongoing view of a real-world site. The people of Henry Ford Health System and Intermountain Health Care have given me hours of exposure to the problems and solutions involved in large-scale health care organizations. I am indebted to their chief executives, Gail L. Warden and Scott Parker (and Gail's predecessor, Stanley Nelson), for both the models and access to them. I am grateful, and I hope I have represented their work faithfully and wisely.

I am particularly grateful to Ms. Barbara Hiney, Chair of the Governing Board, Summa Health Systems, my colleague Jeffrey A. Alexander, the Richard C. Jelinek Professor of Health Management, and to several top students at Michigan—Mark Balsamo, David Cartwright, Jessica Graus, Cindy Ma, Amir Dan Rubin, and Ashley Shrader—who read and contributed to Chapter 3. Similarly, I appreciate the comments of Karole Heyrman, BSN, Ph.D., Deborah S. VandenBroek, MSN, MHSA, and Dorothy E. Deremo, MSN, MHSA, who reviewed Chapter 14. I am sure these readers improved the final result, but the final work, with any remaining errors, remains my responsibility. Gene Regenstreif helped substantially with fact finding and the preparation of the index. Kathleen S. Sodt spent many hours on the figures and tables for this work, vastly improving their readability and appearance.

EMERGENCE OF THE HEALTH CARE ORGANIZATION

Health Care Organizations in Transition

HEALTH CARE is the most universally used social service in America. Practically everyone uses health care, or has a close associate who uses health care, in any given year. It lengthens many of our lives, and it makes most of our lives more comfortable and more enjoyable. It is also very expensive. Many of us use several thousand dollars worth of health care in a single year. On the average, it consumes about one-sixth of our income, outpacing education, defense, welfare, pensions, and justice.

Forces for Health Care Reform

Health care is also one of the most rapidly changing services. "Reform" is simply a catchword for the need for change and the forces that shape its direction. The rate of change is faster now than it has ever been. A trip to the doctor's office is noticeably different from a few years ago; a trip to the hospital is even more strikingly changed. Technology, demography, economics, and politics have driven the change. New drugs, tests, and procedures emerge each year. The population is older and needs more services. But technological change in health care has been important for over a century, and the population has been aging since public health reforms and immunization campaigns around 1900.

The forces accelerating change in health care today are economic and political. The reform issues are *value*—service received for dollar spent—and *access*—who can count on and who is denied financial assistance. The cost of health care has been rising rapidly for more than two decades, substantially exceeding the general rate of inflation or the rate of growth of the economy.[1,2] The cost, largely managed through employment benefits, has become a burden for workers and businesses. It has risen to the point which taxes not just the resources of individuals, but those of the nation. As the cost mounted, more and more people were unable to obtain regular sources of health care finance, even through government programs like Medicaid.

Political pressures mounted from those dissatisfied with the price, and from the specter of growing numbers of uninsured citizens. The intervention of government, which pays almost one-third of the cost directly, is inevitable in an activity so vital and so expensive. The actions of Congress tying Medicare hospital prices to the federal budget increases[3] and restructuring Medicare doctors' fees were major events opening the era of accelerated change.[4] Despite the failure to agree on more extensive legislation, there is a consensus that cost must be considered in vital decisions.[5]

To implement the political agreement and meet the economic pressure, health care managers must increase the value of health care—that is, limit cost without raising the danger that care will be inaccessible, insensitive, or inadequate. The solution lies in extensive reorganization. Health care has been called the last cottage industry. Until just recently, it was mostly provided by physicians who worked alone or in small partnerships, and who charged a separate fee for each service they rendered. The doctors were supported by about 6,000 independent hospitals, mostly managed by citizens of local communities. There was little integration among doctors, among hospitals, or between doctors and hospitals. A disparate group of other professions and organizations—podiatrists, psychologists, drug stores, and home health agencies, for example—were even less integrated. The "non-system," as its critics called it, was financed by several thousand insurance companies, employers, and government agencies who for the most part paid the bills submitted with loud complaint but little or no effective intervention.

There is evidence that reorganization can be successful. Certain forms of health care organization have demonstrated that they can deliver care which is acceptable to large numbers of Americans, at a cost and a rate of cost increase significantly lower than the overall numbers. These organizations have a different style of relationship between the physician, the organization, and the patient, like Henry Ford

Health System of Detroit, Michigan, or the Mayo Clinic of Rochester, Minnesota, and Phoenix, Arizona. Reinforcing that relationship, they often have a different health insurance relationship with the patient or the employer, like Group Health Cooperative of Puget Sound or Kaiser Permanente. But these organizations and others like them have been in existence for 50 years or more. They have not been universally popular anywhere, and they have not always succeeded in new locations. They offer important guides to the future, but we will not meet our goals by cloning them indiscriminately.

The Premise of *The Well-Managed Health Care Organization*

Health care organizations will be in transition for the foreseeable future. The accelerated change, which began in the 1980s and was implicit in the national goals of the 1990s, will take several decades to reach stability. Two demands of the marketplace are central to the future development of health care organizations. The first is the ability to incorporate into a health insurance package most of the sources of primary care, including office and home care, preventive services, pharmacies, laboratories, and emergency services. The second is the ability to control cost and quality of those services.

Successful health care organizations must meet these demands. They will start from and improve upon historical models. Many will blend successful hospital organizations with new structures of medical organization and finance. Some will arise from other models, chiefly multispecialty group practices and governmental organizations. They will invent themselves as they respond to market pressures.

Similar transitions have occurred historically in many other industries. As the business historian Alfred Chandler has noted, the shift is frequently to greater value, not just to lower cost.[6] Greater value usually involves a transfer of responsibilities originally left to the market or the buyer to a more comprehensive organization better equipped to fulfill them. Often the new organization's contributions are in coordinating, integrating, or improving the uniformity of the product or service. It achieves the improvements by designing new technology or new applications.[7] So it will be in health care. Instead of individual arrangements with several different doctors and facilities, many Americans will choose health care organizations which deliver comprehensive services for competitive package prices.

The well-managed health care organizations will achieve that value by using new methods of organizing, designing, and assuring high-quality, cost-effective service. They will bear full responsibility for maintaining quality of service and share risk for meeting economic targets. They will be constantly changing, evolving accommodations to external pressures. Existing successes will provide important prototypes. New models are sure to be developed. Traditional models may have surprising longevity. But the winners will integrate a broad spectrum of prevention, health maintenance, ambulatory care, acute care, and chronic care, and they will work much more closely with insurance and health care financing agencies.

This book describes the well-managed health care organization in terms of issues it must solve rather than advocating a particular form of solution. It attempts to identify the external pressures the organization must meet, the functions which must be performed to meet those pressures, and how those functions are carried out in successful organizations. In the jargon of the continuous quality improvement movement, it is an effort to document "best practice" on the most critical elements of organization survival.

As such, it should be useful to people in any organization now providing health care. Whether the application is to integrated health care systems or traditional hospitals and medical groups, the processes described are ones that have to work for the organization to succeed. They are the processes that design services, allocate resources, attract patients, assure quality, and recruit health care professionals. These processes are described in terms of five major systems: *governance*—the executive and its components, planning, marketing, and information; *finance*; *clinical services*; *human resources*; and *plant*. The emphasis is on integrating these systems and the approach is to identify what each *must* do to allow the other four to work effectively. The governance, executive, and clinical service systems get heavy emphasis. Finance, human resources, and plant get less detailed attention. It is a fair statement that no system is fully described. Whole books—indeed libraries—of information relevant to each system are omitted by necessity. A modest start on the omissions is provided in the Suggested Readings at the end of each chapter.

The Building Blocks: Health Care Organizations of the 1990s

Health care organizations arise from two ancient and deeply valued social traditions. One is the hospital, the place of shelter for the sick or needy. The other is the physician, or healer, the individual who possesses special talents to promote health. These traditions have occurred in most civilized societies, changing over time and place as needs and opportunities changed. The new health care organization can be said to be only the latest implementation of the tradition; it is unique in that it goes further than almost any predecessor in intertwining both concepts. It also is evolving new relationships with the other two parts of modern health care, a group of associated industries providing services to patients, and health insurance organizations which are essential to finance such a large portion of personal expenditures.

Hospitals

The idea that a society or community should have a special place for care of the sick and needy is almost as ancient as the "healer" tradition. It is referenced in the earliest writings of major civilizations and is found in some form in every modern society. It found root in the United States before the Revolution, when Ben Franklin founded The Pennsylvania Hospital in 1760[8] and the new federal government constructed hospitals in several other cities. The initial role for these hospitals, and for other hospitals before the late nineteenth century, was to provide a safe place for the ill or impaired to live. Those who had homes did not use hospitals. The visit of the doctor was normally to the home. The doctor often volunteered his time to care for the sick who were poor, coming to the hospital only to make those visits.[9]

The Rise of Hospitals as Community Resources

Only after the explosion of medical knowledge began did the hospital become an essential partner for the physician. The hospital's ability to provide capital equipment and trained personnel made it important. By the twentieth century, advances in surgery required radiology and laboratory diagnostic facilities, operating theaters, trained nurse assistants, anesthesiologists, and postoperative care. Around the turn of the century, some doctors attempted to provide these on their own in proprietary hospitals. It soon became clear that not-for-profit **community hospitals** had both tax advantages and market advantages, since the facilities could be used by many surgeons without the necessity for organizing the surgeons themselves.

As health care became more complex, the not-for-profit hospital continued to finance the heavy capital investments, providing facilities and equipment which were paid for by the community and available to all qualified practitioners. It recruited or trained support staff, pooling demand from many doctors who affiliated with it to provide work for a growing number of health care professions and technician groups. After World War II its role was recognized in the Hill-Burton Act, federal legislation which assisted hundreds of communities to build not-for-profit hospitals. Also principally in the post war era, hospitals began to maintain procedures and systems which assure quality not just among the other health care professions, but among doctors themselves.[10] These three elements—capital, human capital, and quality assurance—constitute an organization of health care.

By the 1980s, 6,000 community hospitals were society's longest-standing commitment to organizing health care. At their peak, about one in ten citizens became inpatients every year, and many others visited emergency rooms or outpatient services. Hospitals are found in all but the smallest villages across the nation. In each community, they are the largest resource of facilities and equipment, far outstripping the investment of individual practitioners. They are the leading employers of many of the health care professions, including physicians, and they provide systems and procedures which are essential to high-technology medicine. Most important, both the courts and the national organization recognizing good management, the Joint Commission on Accreditation of Healthcare Organizations (JCAHO), have established the hospital as the principal vehicle to control the quality of the health care transaction.

Ownership of Community Hospitals

Hospitals in the United States are owned by a wide variety of groups and are even occasionally owned by individuals. Most hospitals are community hospitals, providing general acute care for a wide variety of diseases. There are three major types of ownership.

- *Government*—Hospitals are owned by federal, state, or local governments. Federal and state institutions tend to have special purposes, such as the care of special groups (military, mentally ill) or education (hospitals attached to state universities). Local government includes not only cities and counties, but also in several states, hospital authorities that have been created from smaller political units. Local government hospitals in large cities are principally for the care of the poor, but many in smaller cities and towns are indistinguishable from not-for-profit institutions. Both are counted as community hospitals. State mental hospitals and federal hospitals are not classed as community hospitals.

- *Not-for-profit*—Hospitals are owned by corporations established by private (nongovernmental) groups for the common good rather than for individual gain. As a result, they are granted broad federal, state, and local tax exemptions. Although they are frequently operated by organizations which have religious ties, secular, or nonreligious, not-for-profit hospitals constitute the largest single group of community hospitals both in number and in total volume of care, exceeding religious not-for-profit, government, and for-profit hospitals by a wide margin.

- *For-profit*—Hospitals are owned by private corporations, which are allowed to declare dividends or otherwise distribute profits to individuals. They pay taxes like other private corporations. These hospitals are also called *investor-owned*. They are usually community hospitals, although there has been rapid growth in private psychiatric hospitals. Historically, the owners were doctors and other individuals, but large-scale publicly held corporations now own most for-profit hospitals. Although the amount of care given by for-profit hospitals is smaller than that given by government or not-for-profit hospitals, it has grown rapidly since 1970.

Figure 1.1 shows community hospital statistics compiled by the American Hospital Association (AHA). Because the AHA plays a major role in collecting statistics about hospitals, its classification system is used for most purposes.[11] Several measures of volume are shown in the table, in addition to the number of institutions in each ownership class. Beds, admissions, and expenses can be used to classify hospitals by size. Discharges, which are virtually identical to admissions in the course of a year, and revenue, differing from expenses only by profit or loss, are also used.

Most U.S. community hospitals are small, but as Figure 1.2 shows, larger hospitals provide most of the service. The trend has been for smaller hospitals in urban areas to disappear. They either go out of business or are acquired by larger institutions. In rural areas, there is still a need for a convenient primary care facility, but the role of inpatient care in that facility has diminished. Many hospitals in rural areas provide outpatient services exclusively.[12]

Implications of Different Types of Ownership

Both for-profit and not-for-profit ownerships are sometimes referred to as private, to distinguish them from public or government hospitals. However, as a consequence of their commitment not to distribute profits or assets to any individual, not-for-profit hospitals are legally dedicated to the collective good. Thus for the vast majority of community hospitals in the United States, the owners, in the sense of beneficiaries, are the communities they serve. The owners of record hold the assets, including any accumulated profits, in trust for the citizens of the community.

In part because of the trust relationship, but perhaps in larger part because of the need to be responsive to the same market opportunities,

Figure 1.1 U.S. Community Hospitals by Ownership, 1993

Ownership	Number	Beds (000s)	Admissions (000s)	Expenses ($ 000,000)	Personnel (000s)
Nongovernment					
Not-for-profit	3,173	656	23,056	183.8	2,692
For-profit	723	99	2,969	22.5	285
State and local governments	1,396	166	5,008	41.8	643
Total	5,292	921	31,034	$248.1	3,620

	Number (%)	Beds (%)	Admissions (%)	Expenses (%)	Personnel (%)
Nongovernment					
Not-for-profit	60	71	74	74	74
For-profit	14	11	10	9	8
State and local governments	26	18	16	17	18
Total	100	100	100	100	100

SOURCE: American Hospital Association, *Hospital Statistics, 1933–94 Edition* (Chicago: AHA), Table 5A.

ownership of community hospitals is rarely critical in its overall management. Many hospitals owned by local governments are indistinguishable from not-for-profit hospitals in similar settings. Except for the obvious right to distribute dividends and the obligation to pay taxes, so are those of for-profit owners. In the courts, government hospitals are generally held to slightly higher standards of public accountability and conformity to the U.S. Constitution. Because they must honor any citizen's economic rights and religious freedom, they are obliged to provide abortions (if they provide related services),[13] to have open medical staffs, and to respect constitutional guarantees of freedom from participation in religious activities. Private hospitals are obliged simply to use due process and not to discriminate on grounds of age, sex, race, or creed. Other ownership distinctions make similarly minor differences. The only difference in the rights and obligations of religious versus nonreligious not-for-profit owners is that religious owners may favor persons having their own beliefs. (In practice this privilege is rarely exercised.)

Given the narrow range of these distinctions, it is not surprising that studies of the effectiveness of various types of ownership rarely reveal major differences.[14] How well a hospital carries out the process of market assessment and program development depends much more

Figure 1.2 U.S. Community Hospitals by Size, 1993

Bed Size	Number	Beds (000s)	Admissions (000s)	Expenses ($ 000,000)	Personnel (000s)
6–49	1,130	39	939	5.7	111
50–99	1,210	87	2,334	15.2	259
100–199	1,321	187	5,845	40.8	630
200–299	725	177	6277	46.5	679
300–399	412	141	5,263	42.0	598
400–499	201	89	3,260	26.7	386
500 or more	293	201	7,116	71.2	957
Total	5,292	921	31,034	$248.1	3,620

	Number (%)	Beds (%)	Admissions (%)	Expenses (%)	Personnel (%)
6–49	21	5	3	2	3
50–99	23	9	8	6	7
100–199	25	20	19	16	17
200–299	14	19	20	19	19
300–399	8	15	17	17	17
400–499	4	10	11	11	11
500 or more	6	22	23	29	26
Total	100	100	100	100	100

SOURCE: American Hospital Association, *Hospital Statistics, 1993–94 Edition* (Chicago: AHA), Table 5A.

on who manages it and how well than it does on who owns the property. A community hospital can be successful under any ownership if it is effectively managed. The most significant difference is that the results of that success accrue to a community in the case of not-for-profit hospitals and to the stockholders in the case of for-profit hospitals. Health care systems integrating several hospitals may have an advantage. The range of necessary skills and experience is much broader in a system, and if these virtues can be translated to more effective management, systems will thrive where individual institutions fail. But as in the comparison of for-profit and not-for-profit ownership, evidence of their superiority is not easy to develop.[15]

Health Care Systems

As Figure 1.3 shows, most hospitals, operating 48 percent of beds, are now part of health care systems. The nature of the association varies from wholly owned subsidiaries, to management contracts and loose affiliations. However, the tendency to aggregation is still continuing. Existing ties are being strengthened and extended, and the number of unaffiliated organizations continues to decline. Affiliation does not change the jobs to be done, or escape the need to meet the issues of cost control and access. It does increase the influence, capital, and human resources available to smaller institutions. Larger organizations have more clout in political and marketing arenas. They are better able to represent their needs, and their size allows them to command more attention. Economically, they can generate greater borrowing capacity. They can support greater expertise in both clinical and managerial activities. They can develop specialized solutions to problems like information systems, materials management, and plant and equipment maintenance.

Health care systems can be described in terms of two categories. Geographically scattered systems have a small market share in each of many different health care regions. Many of the Catholic health care systems follow this model. The original for-profit corporations also followed this model, building small hospitals in a large number of cities stretching across the Sun Belt. Geographically focused systems attempt to capture substantial market share in one or a small number of geographic areas. They are often formed by merger or acquisition of previously independent institutions. Many of the larger systems following this model are also closely affiliated with **health maintenance organizations** (HMOs). Their market dominance in a specific place makes it possible for them to sell and service large risk-sharing contracts, whereas the systems operating in geographically scattered sites have had difficulty meeting specific customer needs. Kaiser Permanente,

Figure 1.3   U.S. Health Care Systems

Ownership	Number of Systems	%	Beds* (000s)	%
Church-related	81	27	137	34
Other not-for-profit	164	56	181	33
For-profit	50	17	134	33
Total	295	100	452	100

* Includes beds owned, leased, managed by contract and sponsored.
SOURCE: American Hospital Association's *Guide to the Health Care Field, 1993–94 Edition* (Chicago: AHA, 1993), Tables 1 and 3 (p. B3).

by far the largest health care system in the nation, and many of the hospitals affiliated with large group practices are examples.

Focused systems have been thriving in recent years. Because of their power in local markets and their capital and human resource base, they are well-positioned to meet cost and quality control challenges. As a result, geographically scattered systems have been trying to capture more market share in their existing locations. They do this by merging entire systems (e.g., the Columbia Health System, formed by merger of Galen and Hospital Corporation of America, in 1993)[16] or by affiliating with other institutions or systems on a location by location basis (e.g., the actions of the Daughters of Charity).[17]

Along with the trend to health care systems, hospitals have recently moved to alliances to increase their political and economic influence and help them improve their cost and quality performance. Unlike systems, which generally involve merger of assets and permanent transfer of some governance decisions to a central organization, alliances are contractual arrangements which can be terminated on relatively short notice. Despite sound theory which suggests that they are inherently transient vehicles,[18] there are 15 of them serving 2,305 hospitals and systems.[19]

Physicians

The notion of the healer with special powers can be traced to prehistoric civilizations where it occurs as the witch doctor or shaman. Early healers provided herbal remedies, surgical intervention, and psychological support for patients and families. Their knowledge and skills were extensive, and some treatments remain in use today. Traditional medical knowledge occurs in the early writings of both eastern and western civilizations. Hippocrates began the codification of disease and treatment for western civilization in 260 B.C.E. A long line of clinical investigators added slowly to Hippocratic knowledge.

The Rise of Specialization

In the mid-nineteenth century, the discovery of anesthesia and the germ theory of disease greatly extended surgical opportunities. An explosion of surgical capability continued through the twentieth century. In addition, vastly more effective pharmaceuticals were discovered for anemia, diabetes, and a wide variety of infectious diseases. Similarly, immunizations for many serious epidemic diseases were developed, and oral contraceptives became available. Radiologic, chemical, and electronic diagnosis were perfected. Endoscopic diagnosis and treatment, direct visualization and manipulation of internal organs through small surgical incisions, became commonplace near the end of the twentieth century.

The rapid increase in knowledge was paralleled by a restructuring of medical education and the development of medical specialties. Although American physicians are licensed by state governments to practice any form of medicine or surgery, the vast majority now practice in only 1 or 2 of more than 30 different specialties. Certification for these specialties is provided by a system of specialty boards which supervise training programs, maintain life-long periodic examinations, encourage research and publication in their area, and stimulate continuing education for their members.[20] Specialty certification is rapidly becoming a condition for practice, especially in organized medical settings. About 88 percent are certified overall.[21]

The specialties can be grouped several ways, but the most useful for the purposes of health care organizations may be that which emphasizes four main divisions: primary care, medicine, surgery, and diagnosis. Primary care doctors hold themselves out as the first point of contact for the patient, doctors who can identify diagnoses, provide treatment directly for most problems, and select appropriate specialists for the balance. The latter three groups receive many or all of their patients on referral from other physicians. They are called the referral specialties. Figure 1.4 shows a list of specialty boards in the United States and their 1990 membership in active practice. It also shows the number of multiple specialties reported by individual doctors, and the number of doctors not certified by any board. Two important generalizations are supported by Figure 1.4. First, most physicians are now certified. A relatively small and declining fraction are in what used to be called "general practice." Second, many fewer are certified in primary care than in the referral specialties. It is generally believed that there are significant shortages in primary care, and surpluses in many referral specialties.[22]

The actual practice of these specialties is different on almost every dimension. Some doctors (e.g., rheumatologists) practice principally by evaluating and understanding the course of disease; some (orthopedists) make dramatic interventions with elaborate technology. Some (pathologists) rarely communicate with patients as individuals and others (anesthesiologists) relate to them almost incidentally in the course of treatment, while still others (psychiatrists) must establish an intimate ongoing relationship. Some (intensivists) cannot practice outside the hospital; others (family practice) rarely use the hospital themselves. There is also a substantial difference in earnings. Until the 1990s, primary care doctors earned less than half the income of those

Figure 1.4 Distribution of U.S. Physicians in Active Practice by Specialty Certification, 1990

Specialty	Number of Physicians (000s)
Primary Care	**245 (36%)**
Family practice	52
Emergency medicine	14
General internal medicine	77
General pediatrics	38
Obstetrics/gynecology	30
Psychiatry	34
Medicine	**67 (10%)**
Cardiology	16
Dermatology	8
Endocrinology	3
Gastroenterology	8
Geriatrics	1
Neonatology and pediatric sub-specialties	5
Neurology	9
Oncology	4
Physiatry	4
Pulmonary medicine and intensive care	6
Rheumatology	3
Surgery	**123 (18%)**
Anesthesiology	26
General surgery	33
Neurosurgery	4
Ophthalmology	16
Orthopedics	19
Otolaryngology	8
Plastic surgery	5
Radiation therapy	3
Urology	9
Diagnosis	**9 (1%)**
Pathology	1
Radiology	8
Other Specialties and Practicing without Certification	**257 (38%)**
Deduction for multiple board membership	17
Total	**685 (100%)**

SOURCE: American Medical Association's, *Physician Characteristics and Distribution in the Unites States*, 1992 ed. (Chicago: AMA, 1992), Tables B-8 and B-12; American Osteopathic Association's, *1991 Yearbook and Directory of Osteopathic Physicians*, 82d ed. (Chicago: AOA, 1991), Statistical Tables on the Osteopathic Profession, Numbers of Current (Active) Osteopathic Certifications.

who rely upon the most expensive technology. Not surprisingly, there are also substantial differences in temperament, life style, and values between specialties as well as between individuals.

Figure 1.5 shows the distribution of U.S. physicians by type of practice as of 1990. The vast majority were in small single specialty groups or independent practice, and most of the financial arrangement was in individual fees. While it would be wrong to say these forms are not organized, they are small organizations with limited capability. The larger, more organized models of medical practice included:

- Multispecialty group practices open to fee-for-service and HMO financing, such as the Mayo Clinic and Henry Ford Medical Group
- Group practices limited to HMO financing such as Kaiser Permanente
- **Independent physician associations** (IPAs) organized to allow doctors practicing independently for fee-for-service financing to collaborate to serve HMOs
- Expanded hospital-based practice organizations accepting both fee-for-service and HMO financing
- Government programs such as the Army and the Veterans' Administration
- University medical school faculties.

Other Health Care Providers

Hospitals and doctors provide about two-thirds of all health care. The balance is provided by a wide variety of other practitioners and organizations.

Figure 1.5 Practice Arrangements of Active U.S. Physicians, 1991

Practice Arrangement	Number (000s)	Percent
In solo practice or partnership arrangement	168	25
In single specialty groups	165	24
In multispecialty groups accepting fee-for-service	140	20
In federal service	20	3
In training programs	83	12
Not in patient care	43	6
Not accounted for	66	10
Total	685	100

SOURCES: American Medical Association's, *Medical Groups in the United States: A Survey of Practice Characteristics* (Chicago: AMA, 1992); American Medical Association's Department of Physician Data Services.

Health Care Professions

About 50 professions other than physicians provide health services to patients. The list of professions reported by the U.S. Department of Labor is shown in Figure 1.6. Most are licensed or certified by state agencies and have professional associations providing evidence of appropriate training. They work in corporate settings such as hospitals, clinics, and nursing homes, but many also practice independently under fee-for-service compensation. As insurance becomes more comprehensive, the trend is for these professions to move toward employment in health care corporations. The greater the interaction between the profession and other forms of care, the faster this movement is likely to be. For the patient, integration offers increased assurance of quality, greater convenience, and reduced danger of confusion or conflict between care givers. For the insurer or health care organization, integration improves cost, quality, and utilization control.

Other Provider Organizations

Also paralleling the growth of medical technology, many other sources of care emerged in the twentieth century. They include nursing homes, pharmacies, specialty hospitals, visiting nurse and home care programs,

Figure 1.6   Health Care Professions Other than Physicians

Providing General Care
Licensed practical nurses
Nurse practitioners
Registered nurses
Physician assistants

Providing Care Limited to Specific Organs or Diseases
Chiropractors
Dentists
Midwives
Psychologists
Social workers
Optometrists
Podiatrists

Providing Care Limited to Specific Modalities
Electroencephalograph technologists
Electrocardiograph technologists
Audiobiologists
Dieticians
Recreational therapists
Laboratory technologists
Pharmacists
Physical therapists
Occupational therapists
Medical technologists
Imaging technologists
Emergency medical technicians
Radiation therapists
Respiratory therapists
Speech pathologists

NOTE: List updated to include numbers and multiple sources with change in number and date of the Occupational Handbook.
SOURCE: U.S. Department of Labor's, *Occupational Outlook Handbook*, Bulletin 2400 (Washington, DC: U.S. Government Printing Office 1992).

home meal programs, hospices, and durable medical equipment suppliers. Many of these are affiliated with general hospitals and clinics, but many operate as independent entities. Most are small businesses operating in a single community. Some, such as the for-profit nursing home chains, are multistate corporations. In addition to these identifiable businesses, there are voluntary organizations and support groups which provide substantial health care. Alcoholics Anonymous is the oldest and one of the most successful.

Many of these care organizations became important industries in themselves, while remaining relatively small parts of the total expenditure for health care. The drug industry is a useful example. The amount spent per person per year mounted from $22 in the 1960s to $41 in 1970 to $210 in 1990. The increase paid for most of the antibiotics, oral contraceptives, anticoagulants, hypertensive agents, vaccines for polio, measles, and whooping cough, and cancer drugs. None of these existed in the 1930s, with the exception of the first sulfonamide antibiotics. Drugs are produced principally by a few large multinational companies, and distributed principally by hospitals and 50,000 licensed pharmacies. Although many pharmacies are independent small businesses, retail drug chains began rapid growth in the 1970s and by the 1980s provided 65 percent of the nonhospital market. Drugs provided in the hospital were insured in early private health insurance plans. Those for outpatient care were one of the last elements added to health insurance. Medicare and many private traditional health insurance programs did not cover outpatient drugs in the early 1990s.

The nursing home, home care, and hospice have important parallels to pharmacies. They generate commercial opportunities for small local businesses and national supply corporations. The local businesses are often acquired by larger, publicly listed stock companies. These seek economies of scale by mastering the details of care delivery and supporting local operations with training, supplies, and capital. Some community hospitals offer these services as well, but as of 1990, hospital availability was neither widespread nor important as a total share of the individual markets.[23]

Health Insurance Organizations

It is clear that modern health care can be financed only in the context of health insurance or related risk-sharing mechanisms. The unpredictable risk of very high-cost illness must be shared collectively. With individual episodes of care frequently exceeding average family income several-fold, it is impossible to consider other financing such as credit or cash payment. Most Americans have a mechanism to finance their health care. Most working families receive it as an employment benefit. The aged participate in **Medicare**, a mandatory government health insurance, and most of them have supplementary private insurance. Some, but not all, poor receive **Medicaid**, direct assistance from state governments. A few people purchase health insurance individually, or through groups other than employment. Coming from so many different sources, it is not surprising that the insurance varies widely in the details of the protection it provides, or that some people fall through the cracks. Through 1994 about 15 percent of the population had none of these mechanisms, and additional millions had insurance which was inadequate for their needs.

The coverage itself is administered by about 2,000 different companies. A much smaller number are economically important in geographically specific market places. These are mostly large Blue Cross and Blue Shield Plans and commercial insurance companies who administer many different kinds of programs for employers and government. Technically, many of these programs are not insurance, because the employer or the government accepts the financial risk for the group in question, and the administrator sees that care is provided according to the contracts and pays the providers. Medicare is the largest single example. The federal government holds the insurance risk, through the Medicare Trust Fund. Insurance companies, called intermediaries, administer the plan in each state. There are often two intermediaries, one for Part A, covering mostly hospital expenses, and one for Part B, covering medical and other practitioner expenses. Similar complexities describe the private market. Large employers often self-insure their groups. They frequently turn to intermediaries or third party administrators to administer the health care benefit.

Health insurance companies initially identified their function as bearing risk, marketing, subscriber billing and service, and claims payment. They often avoided any selection of providers and accepted the providers' judgment both as to appropriate treatment and fair price. The Medicare Act Preamble, which called for "reasonable costs" to pay hospitals and "usual, customary and reasonable" fees for physicians,[24] was widely accepted as a model. Traditional health insurance still fulfills these functions. Under pressure to improve cost performance, alternative structures developed. The large intermediaries offered these and even pioneered in their development, so that they now offer a range of products and services from traditional health insurance to benefit administration only, with several alternative forms of coverage.

What's the "inflationary consequence of the divorce?"

What are the 3 major categories of cost control?

However necessary it might be, insurance itself contributes to the increase in costs. Insurance divorces the payment mechanism from the point of service, and removes the economic consequence of decisions by both the caregivers and the patients. When the premium is paid by employers and is subject to tax preferences, the consequence is doubly or triply removed.[25] The issue is how to design insurance which simultaneously provides the necessary financial protection and minimizes the inflationary consequences of the divorce.

Devices to achieve cost control have become increasingly sophisticated in the past 20 years, since the passage of the HMO Act in 1973. They fall into three major categories.

1. Limits on payment
   - To patients—deductibles which delay payment until a specific amount has been spent by the patient and copayments which put the patient at some financial risk at each step of care. The deductible is a standard feature of catastrophic or major medical insurance contracts, where it serves to rule out routine medical expenses. Copayments are often a feature of indemnity insurance which pays actual costs up to a limited amount for each health care event.
   - To providers—fee-for-service payment to providers discounted below what is perceived to be the market rate. This approach has been routine in Medicaid and is used increasingly in preferred provider health care financing. It also is implicit in Medicare payment to both physicians and hospitals, where it is combined with other devices.

2. Limits on provider selection
   - Most advanced health care financing plans limit the patient to a panel of providers approved in advance. **Preferred provider organization (PPO)** and HMO contracts are designed around this feature. Point-of-service (POS) plans offer unlimited choice of provider with substantial financial incentives for the patient to use panel providers.

3. Provider risk-sharing
   - Risk-sharing plans use financial devices to encourage providers to eliminate unnecessary services. They include bundled prices such as diagnosis-related groups (DRGs), where payment is based on the patient's condition rather than what was done for each patient. They also include a variety of payment mechanisms, such as withholding a fraction of the payment

to distribute if utilization targets are met, or providing other incentives for meeting targets.

- In its most advanced form, risk sharing pays providers capitation, a fixed dollar amount for each month the patient remains under contract. This requires an explicit selection of provider by the patient, even though the patient may not seek care at all.

The most sophisticated insurance products use several of these devices simultaneously. HMOs frequently combine copayments, provider selection, bundled payment, and provider capitation. POS plans offer the patient a choice of provider for a price, but use copayments deliberately to channel care to selected providers with whom they have risk-sharing contracts. Even traditional contracts have increasingly elaborate devices to influence both patient and provider behavior. Because the individual customer or group of customers can select the product they want, each successful product must attract a reasonable share of the market. No product will be perfect; there are real choices in front of the customer. The most important choices center around the provider panel and price considerations. Obviously the more attractive the panel is, the larger market share it will attract at a given price, and the more effective at cost control the panel is the lower price it can offer. Panels which are both attractive and cost-effective will attract large numbers of patients and achieve further economies through their size.

The health insurance market has undergone significant changes in the 1980s and further rapid change is likely through the 1990s. All forms of cost-controlling products are growing in market share. Provider selection and provider risk-sharing, specifically HMOs and POS products, are growing most rapidly. In some cities they have achieved substantial market shares, and where this has occurred, health care organizations have been revolutionized. When providers must meet cost and quality standards in order to be selected, and when they share in the risk that costs will exceed premiums paid, strong incentives are established to change patterns of practice and seek new economies. The providers' energies are turned to devising lower-cost ways to achieve equivalent or better quality of care. They reorganize the array of existing hospitals, physician practices, other professionals, and other provider organizations to meet that challenge.

The Vision of the Well-Managed Health Care Organization

The well-managed health care organization described in this book is an evolving organization, building upon its predecessors, and continuously *what are the four ideals of the well managed HCO?*

striving for an ideal. One can summarize the ideal on four dimensions: access, technical quality, perceived quality, and cost. Simply stated, the ideal health care organization will provide access for all, sound, comprehensive and appropriate quality of care, please all its patients, and be affordable to its community. There are inevitable trade-offs between these four dimensions; no real institution will ever achieve the ideal. The well-managed organization must make the trade-offs in a manner that its customers will call satisfactory.

The customer voice for reform has intensified and clarified in the past decade. The four dimensions have become more clearly articulated. The feasible levels of performance have become more visible, and standards the well-managed organization must meet have emerged.

Access *how does ↑ access lead to lower costs?*

Customer demands for access have several important dimensions to the well-managed health care organization. First, the process of care will be **vertically integrated**. The ideal health care organization will strive for seamless service to the patient from the initial contact for preventive services and health promotion, through routine care to crisis episodes and the management of chronic illness. It will encourage healthy lifestyles through education and advertising. It will offer convenient access through organized primary care. It will integrate referral specialists, clinical support services, and inpatient care to make the most expensive episodes of care cost-effective. It will improve efficiency, and quality of other professions and provider organizations, integrating pharmacies, nursing homes, home care, hospices, and the professionals who work in them.

Primary care assumes a special prominence because of its intake position. The success of a specific insurance plan frequently rests on the panel of primary care providers available to the customer. People want providers who are sensitive, responsive to questions, and have convenient hours and parking. If the plan is to grow, some providers must be open to new patients. Many of the contacts must be for prevention of disease and promotion of health. Primary care practitioners must be able and willing to assist customers on smoking, contraception, immunization, child safety, diet, and emotional health. Effective cost control begins with programs to reduce illness and the need for health care.

Frequently used referral specialists and clinical support services like cardiology evaluations and imaging must also be convenient. Although people are willing to go further for hospital and less common referral care, they clearly prefer to stay in the community where they shop or work. Excessive delays, long drives, and multiple trips discourage customers and reduce re-enrollment. They also reduce word-of-mouth endorsement.

Second, the ideal health care organization will offer universal service. It will serve all patients and will strive to capture as large a share of each form of health insurance as it can. Because health care organizations and even individual physician providers have high fixed costs, high volumes lead to lower costs. Because much health care is highly specialized, large numbers of primary care patients are necessary to support each specialty. Both economies of operation and marketing advantages accrue to the organization which actively recruits all possible patients, even though some of them may be financed at less than full cost.

Various experimental programs suggest that most health care organizations will have specific programs for care of low-income groups. They will include emergency and walk-in care, and in urban areas will include outreach activities and convenient local clinics emphasizing early treatment and prevention. Rural areas will have less flexibility, but will still need specially designed programs to meet the needs of people whose health care costs must be minimized.

Third, the ideal health care organization will be **horizontally integrated**. Because several important health care services, like obstetrics, coronary care, emergency care, and expensive diagnostic services, and services supporting the care process, like education, marketing, information systems, and finance, are less costly when spread over larger bases, each organization will strive to be as large as it can within its geographic community. The more cost-effective organizations will tend to acquire or dominate less efficient ones. The trend to health care systems will continue.

Some advantages of centralized services depend upon geography. It is impossible to centralize obstetrics across several counties, for example, even though high-risk mothers and babies can be helicoptered long distances. Other advantages, like finance and information services, offer economies in any location. Locally oriented health care systems can capture both advantages; regional or national systems only the latter. Other things being equal, local systems would prevail. However, there are real concerns with monopolies. Although many small communities will continue to find all their health care eggs in one basket, medium-sized ones may prefer two or three competing systems. It is likely that large cities will have strong local, regional, and national systems, with many of the national systems oriented around national insurance vendors.

Quality of Care

What are the general principles of Quality? examples?

The ideal health care organization will provide and document uniformly high-quality care, as measured by conformity to standards for care processes and desirable outcomes. Considerable evidence suggests that the quality of the present health care is highly variable. Customer pressure for uniform high quality is mounting, matched by increasing sophistication in measurement.[26] Employers and insurers purchasing care and assembling panels of providers will insist on technical quality. Well-designed organizations can make major gains in quality, and they will do so in order to capture larger market shares.

The principles of quality management are now well documented and understood. They emphasize the importance of meeting customer demands, heavy reliance on measurement, and empowerment of workers directly involved in the care process to agree upon processes which will assure quality and implement them. When applied to clinical situations, these principles lead to protocols or guidelines for care, agreements between individual practitioners and different professions which optimize the overall quality. The very notion of agreement is radical to some concepts of individual professional integrity. Advanced organization and human relations skills are essential to achieve consensuses and implement them. Reward systems, including both monetary and nonmonetary rewards are essential to encourage compliance. A substantial portion of the administrative structure of the ideal health care system will be devoted to quality infrastructure—information systems, incentive systems, and continuous improvement processes.

Customer Satisfaction

The ideal health care system will emphasize customer satisfaction as the best way to build and retain market share. Direct measurement of satisfaction will be detailed, comprehensive, and commonplace. There will be high expectations for the simpler elements of customer satisfaction, like geographic convenience and waiting times. Physician and nurse primary care providers will be expected to be sensitive and compassionate in all their dealings with patients. Failures on this score will be as serious as departures from technical quality. Other professionals and provider organizations will find that they have two customers, the patient and the referring primary provider. Both will have substantial authority to dictate the terms of service.

Beyond the initial determinants of good service, customer satisfaction is likely to take on a deeper meaning. Much of medical care involves choices between alternatives, sometimes with enormous consequences. Through most of the twentieth century, responsibility for these choices was vested solely with physicians. The trend toward informing the patient about his disease and its management alternatives began with informed consent for surgery in the 1960s,[27] and has grown steadily since.

Where traditional medicine was likely to recommend or prescribe a certain course of action, managed care will present it as an option more or less strongly urged as the clinical situation suggests. Defensive medicine, the policy of protecting against rare but high-cost eventualities, will be replaced with watchful waiting approaches which reserve the more expensive and invasive actions for cases where clear threats develop, unless the patient expresses a clear and coherent desire for more. Patient choice is likely to become a major part of managing care of aging and chronically ill patients, resulting in the expanded use of hospice care and deaths outside the acute hospital.[28]

Affordable Cost

The ideal health care organization will deliver care at costs determined by the customer. For 25 years following the passage of Medicare and Medicaid, costs passed to the customer or payer were determined mostly by the providers. The Medicare guidelines, reasonable cost and usual customary and reasonable fees, turned out to be highly inflationary as interpreted by the providers. Health care costs mounted at double digit rates throughout the period. It is clear that these guidelines and rates are no longer acceptable.

Effective demands for cost control began in 1983, when Medicare established fixed prices for individual inpatient DRGs. The demand for non-Medicare cost control was expressed mainly by shifts to HMO and PPO insurance. It spread rapidly in some cities but hardly at all in others throughout the next decade. The health care reform movement begun by President Clinton in 1993 greatly accelerated the trend.

The traditional arrangement of independent hospitals, doctors, and health insurance had three glaring failures. First, and most easily corrected was the rapid rise in hospital costs. Second was its inability to control either cost or quality in outpatient environments such as doctors' offices or freestanding diagnostic and surgical centers. Third was its inability to provide comprehensive prevention and care, transferring the patient effectively to the site which held the highest value.

The ideal health care organization will be very good at all these jobs. Its hospitals will be efficient units just big enough to meet the needs of its insured population. It will encourage truly cost-effective medicine by selecting and rewarding physicians and other practitioners who practice it. It will stress health promotion and illness prevention, and will move patients easily across several sites for care, such as primary care offices, specialty treatment centers, hospitals, home care, rehabilitation, and long-term care. Doing all three jobs will require tight contracts between the various practitioners and agencies, with common rather than competing incentives. Some successful models will resemble Kaiser Permanente, with owned hospitals and largely employed practitioners, but others will achieve the cost control goals through other arrangements.

Using This Book

This book is a basic text on building and managing organizations which directly provide health care. It is deliberately designed to identify the major functions which any care-giving organization must perform, whether it is a traditional hospital, a small group practice, or a comprehensive system like Kaiser Permanente. The book attempts to identify all the functions which any successful health care organization must perform and to describe the ways the most successful organizations accomplish them. Where possible, it adds a commentary on known shortcomings of existing methods and discusses experimental solutions.

The book does not assume that any one model of solution will prevail. Rather, it assumes that in a country as large and complicated as the United States, many models will exist, just as they do today. Many existing organizations will be so transformed by health care reform that they will be unrecognizable in a few years, but some will survive in something near their traditional form. The essential for survival is that the function be accomplished to the satisfaction of the local marketplace, rather than that the solution follow some predetermined model.

Structure of the Book

The essential functions are organized into five major groups of activities. Each is discussed in a separate part of the book describing a system of the organization which accomplishes the necessary tasks. Each system and each task is described not as the insider performing the task would see it, but rather as the other systems require it. That is, each system is described in terms of what it must do to make the whole effective.

Governing: Making Health Care Organizations Responsive to Their Environment

Any successful organization must have a boundary-spanning function which relates it effectively to its environment.[29] The function is called governance, and in all but the smallest health care organizations it is carried out by a governing board. Part I examines what it means to relate to the environment, and how successful governing boards do it.

Executing: Supporting and Implementing Governance Decisions

Modern organizations execute policy decisions through an elaborate structure deliberately designed to encourage two way communications and to identify, evaluate, and resolve conflicting opportunities and opinions. The leadership of the executive system performs a critical function in coordinating the activities of the other four systems. In health care, the executive function rarely makes decisions, but it designs the way decisions are made, determining who participates in each decision, and how. Part II describes the functions the executive must perform, and the concepts which guide how to perform them effectively.

Learning: Meeting Planning, Marketing, Finance, and Information Needs

The modern organization is dynamic, constantly changing in response to new demands from its environment. Peter Senge has called it the "learning organization."[30] Elaborate fact-finding, performance measurement, and analytic activities support the learning organization. Information is used as a resource, like money. Part III describes the information which supports learning, and also describes two related functions, marketing and finance.

Caring: Building Quality of Clinical Service

The defining characteristic of health care organizations is the actual provision of health care; it is an individualized, deeply personal activity unlike any other in modern life. It is, and must remain, the responsibility of autonomous practitioners, but it must respond dynamically to customer needs. The mechanisms that reconcile autonomy and responsiveness are built upon a century of effort. Part IV describes how the **clinical system** works, beginning with the tested and proven approaches and distinguishing the structures for physicians, nurses, and other clinical support professions.

Sustaining: *Providing Human Resources and Plant Services*

Finally, the modern organization has a series of responsibilities to its members and its customers which it meets through its **human resources** activities and its **plant services**. Part V describes these in terms that reflect the needs of the organization as a whole.

How to Use the Book

The book is designed to be both a text and a reference. Beginners should read through it as it is written. Even if they choose to start with some part other than governance, there is value to seeing how the processes of managing a complex organization unfold. Starting at the beginning means starting with an understanding of the kinds of forces operating on the organization and the role of governance in identifying and responding to those forces. Even the most detailed study of another major system will be incomplete without that understanding.

Experienced executives should already understand the governance process, at least at an intuitive level. They might skip to whatever system is of interest to see what desirable practices are on a question of interest. The parts of the book are designed to be self-contained for the sophisticated reader. There is an index and a glossary to track important terms across the parts. Clinical practitioners who want to understand how the organization affects their lives directly can begin with Part IV, caring. But again, the issues of governance are essential to a well-grounded understanding.

Notes

1. K. R. Levit, H. C. Lazenby, C. A. Cowan, and S. W. Letsch, 1991, "National Health Expenditures, 1990," *Health Care Financing Review* 13 (1): 29–54, 46.
2. V. R. Fuchs, 1990, "The Health Sector's Share of the Gross National Product," *Science* 247 (2 February): 534–38.
3. Tax Equity and Fiscal Responsibility Act of 1982 (P.L. 97-248).
4. Omnibus Budget Reconciliation Act of 1989 (P.L. 101-239).
5. Ginzburg, E., ed., 1994, *Critical Issues in Health Reform* (Boulder, CO: Westview Press).
6. A. D. Chandler, 1977, *The Visible Hand: The Managerial Revolution in American Business* (Cambridge, MA: Belknap Press).
7. Ibid.
8. B. Franklin, quoted in L. B. Coker, ed., 1954, *Some Account of the Pennsylvania Hospital* (Baltimore, MD: Johns Hopkins Press).
9. C. E. Rosenberg, 1987, *The Care of Strangers: The Rise of America's Hospital System* (New York: Basic Books).

10. R. Stevens, 1989, *In Sickness and In Wealth: American Hospitals in the Twentieth Century* (New York: Basic Books).

11. *Hospital Statistics* (Chicago: American Hospital Association).

12. W. D. Helms, D. M. Campion, and I. Moscovice, 1991, *Delivering Essential Health Care Services in Rural Areas: An Analysis of Alternative Models* (Washington, DC: Alpha Center Health Policy and Planning, Inc.).

13. A. F. Southwick, 1988, *The Law of Hospital and Health Care Administration*, 2d ed. (Ann Arbor, MI: Health Administration Press), 455–56.

14. B. H. Gray, ed., 1986, *For-Profit Enterprise in Health Care* (Washington, DC: National Academy Press).

15. S. M. Shortell, 1988, "The Evolution of Hospital Systems: Unfulfilled Promises and Self-Fulfilling Prophecies," *Medical Care Review* 45 (2): 177–214.

16. *New York Times*, 1993, "Merger of Hospital Companies Approved," 1 September.

17. 1995 Annual Report, Daughters of Charity Health System, Evansville, IN.

18. H. S. Zuckerman and T. A. D'Aunno, 1990, "Hospital Alliances: Cooperative Strategy in a Competitive Environment," *Health Care Management Review* 15 (Spring): 21–30.

19. American Hospital Association, 1993, *Guide to the Health Care Field* (Chicago: AHA).

20. D. G. Langsley, ed., 1983, *Legal Aspects of Certification and Accreditation* (Evanston, IL: American Board of Medical Specialties), ix–x.

21. American Medical Association, 1992, *Physician Characteristics and Distribution in the U.S.* (Chicago: American Medical Association), Table A-2.

22. J. A. Schroeder, 1993, "Training an Appropriate Mix of Physicians to Meet the Nation's Needs," *Academic Medicine* 68 (2): 118–22.

23. American Hospital Association, 1993, *Hospital Statistics* 1993–94 ed. (Chicago: AHA); M. A. Davis, 1993, "Nursing Home Ownership Revisited," *Medical Care* 29 (November): 1062–68; A. J. Kania, 1993, "Hospital-Based Home Care: Integral to Seamless Service," *Health Care Strategic Management* 11 (August): 21.

24. Social Security Amendments of 1965 (P.L 89-97), Preamble.

25. P. J. Feldstein, 1993, *Health Care Economics*, 4th ed. (Albany, NY: Delmar Publishers, Inc.), 546.

26. *Health Plan Employer Data and Information Set (HEDIS)*, 1994 (Washington, DC: National Commission on Quality Assurance).

27. A. F. Southwick, 1988, *The Law of Hospital and Health Care Administration*, 2d ed. (Ann Arbor, MI: Health Administration Press), 361.

28. J. Arras, 1993, "Ethical Issues in Emergency Care," *Clinics in Geriatric Medicine* 9 (August): 655–64.

29. H. Mintzberg, 1979, *The Structuring of Organizations: A Synthesis of the Research* (Englewood Cliffs, NJ: Prentice-Hall).

30. P. Senge, 1990, *The Fifth Discipline: The Art and Practice of the Learning Organization* (New York: Doubleday/Currency).

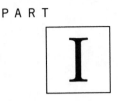
Governing: Making Health Care Organizations Responsive to Their Environment

I

Governing, Making Health Care
Organizations Responsive to
Their Environment

HOW HEALTH CARE ORGANIZATIONS RELATE TO THEIR ENVIRONMENT

ORGANIZATIONS ARE creations of and by human beings to accomplish goals they might otherwise be unable to reach. They emerged contemporaneous with civilization itself,[1] are often unsuccessful, and in the last century have become noticeably more complicated.[2] Health care organizations are no exceptions to these statements. This chapter outlines the vocabulary, taxonomy, and premises describing the relationship of the organization to its environment. It also

1. Develops a four-part theory of management selected to represent the actual activities of successful health care organizations, but consistent with general studies of organizations
2. Applies the theory to the modern health care organization, identifying the many individuals and groups it serves and illustrating its activities
3. Identifies the core motivations of people who use and work in health care organizations
4. Discusses the future agenda and the strategies that distinguish well-managed health care organizations.

Understanding the Forces Shaping Organizations

A large number of theories are useful to understand organizations and their activities.[3] The distinction between well-managed organizations and those not so successful appears to begin with the underlying theory

How can resource dependency cause a HCO to fail?

guiding the actions of their leaders.[4] This chapter develops a theory based upon four concepts that are widely accepted among the most successful health care organizations and that have been found useful in the study of organizations generally. The first is the concept of **resource dependency**, which suggests that organizations depend upon their ability to attract resources, such as financial support of customers and the effort of employees. They thrive only because they are successful at attracting these resources and fail when they are unable to attract one or more resources. The second concept is that of **community-focused strategic management**, the notion that the organization itself repeatedly asks the questions, What is our community's goal? Why? and How does the organization serve it? "We" is the community being served by the organization. The third concept, **continuous improvement**, suggests that the equilibrium will never be fully achieved, that the organization is, in fact, always striving toward a moving goal. The fourth, **scale**, implies that comprehensive organizations meeting a broad spectrum of health needs for large markets have the best chances for long-term success.

what is open system theory?

Open Systems

Open systems theory implies that any organization can be described in terms of processes which meet demand and earn income by transforming certain resources, basically labor, supplies, and equipment, into new products and services with added value. Any successful organization is dependent on all elements of the set—that is, demand, income, labor, supplies, and equipment, and limited by the element in shortest supply.

The transactions between the elements, such as hiring, buying, and selling, are exchanges. An **exchange** is a transfer of goods, services, or purchasing power that occurs legitimately when both parties believe themselves to benefit from it. Exchanges occur constantly in society, and in a certain sense they ultimately can occur only between individuals. As a practical matter, however, a great many exchanges occur through formal groups of people, such as governments and organizations that represent and have the commitment of their members. **Exchange partners** are individuals or groups who have an existing commitment to an organization, including at least customers, workers, and suppliers. Particularly important exchange partners are called **stakeholders**. Partners can be classified according to the nature of their exchange. One very useful classification of partners is between **customers** and **providers**. Customers are all those partners who use the services of the organization and generally compensate the organization for those services. Providers are all those who provide services and generally are compensated by the organization for their efforts. (Compensation in either case may be something other than money.)

A simple organization, say a hamburger stand, exists because it has cooks, meat, buns, and a grill, and because it has customers who perceive that there is value added (that is, they are willing to pay at least slightly more than the cost) for the service of transforming the raw materials into hamburgers. Although we tend to think of the original inputs as resources, the hamburgers as outputs, and the willingness to buy as demand, open systems theory says that all of these elements must be present, and that the size of the hamburger stand will depend exactly upon the capacity of the scarcest one. That is, the stand will sell as many hamburgers as customers want, or as many as it can make from the available meat or buns, or as many as the cooks can grill, whichever is smallest.

The concept of open systems is closely related to the theory of the firm in economics. Like the theory of the firm, it forces the system operator to consider prices, quality, and value for the customer; and a similar list for the supplier including employees, competitor performance, and the needs of the organization and its owners. The two sets must be integrated as a totality, seeking a solution that is acceptable to all. It is particularly useful in a market economy and a free society, because it reveals the importance of satisfying people who voluntarily supply the resources. That is, it teaches hamburger stand operators that they are always dependent on the customers, the cooks, the butcher, the baker and other exchange partners like the government agencies that permit the stand to sell hamburgers.

None of the exchange partners are forced to make their contribution; the operator must convince each of them to cooperate. Since convincing them will inevitably involve some compromise, they have **influence,**—that is, the ability to change or shift the organization. Influence is gained by controlling a resource. The more complete the control and the more critical the resource, the greater the influence. Those people who can affect the success of the organization are called **influentials.** Open systems management, then, is the constant search for the solution that is optimally attractive to the influentials.

Community-Focused Strategic Management

The concept of strategic management implies that the organization is deliberately guided toward an explicit purpose, and that one of the functions is to ask persistently three questions: (1) What is our purpose, or why are we here? (2) Why did we select that purpose and is it the best choice? (3) How do we best achieve our purpose?[5] The pursuit of these questions serves a dual purpose; it forces the organization to a continuing survey of its environment and its relation to it, and it provides a mechanism to promote consensus among the people supporting the organization. The "we" underlying these questions is the owners, but under open systems theory it becomes clear that the owners must answer in a broader context if their organization is to survive for a long time. A community focus including all influentials and stakeholders is essential to provide a broad base of continuing support.

The theory used in the book assumes that the organization's overriding goal is a mutually satisfactory long-term relationship with all the various groups on which it depends. Since environments are constantly changing, the search for equilibrium is an ongoing one. **Boundary-spanning** activities, those through which the organization selects its exchanges, look outward to define what the organization must do to thrive. The strategic management includes a deliberate effort to identify people, both providers and customers, whose needs are not met, and bring them into the consensus. The organization searches for ways to expand, and has a bias toward comprehensive services and mass markets.

The hamburger stand is set up where customers want to buy hamburgers and where the cooks are comfortable cooking them. It learns the price, quality, and service combinations that please the most customers, and trains and supports its workers to meet them. If the combinations change the organization will deliberately evaluate the change and adapt its operations in the direction that seems most fruitful. This means that if the customers express a desire for chicken nuggets, or if the owners decide the customers can be convinced to buy them at a profitable price, the organization will deliberately weigh a change which takes it outside its original hamburger mission and technology.

The **operating system** identifies specific **expectations** the organization must establish in order to complete the exchanges. Expectations must translate the desires of the external world, learned by boundary-spanning activities, into effective responses. Even in a very simple hamburger stand, there are a great many expectations. For example, the size of the burgers, the availability of condiments, the wrappers or utensils, the cooking methods, the number of burgers one cook can cook in one hour, the level of customer satisfaction anticipated, the sale price, the appearance of the finished order, and its bacterial content. The operating system specifies them, and makes them clear to the workers. (And recognizing the workers' status as influentials and stakeholders, it tries to gain worker acceptance, or consensus about them.) It also measures what actually happens, and compares that to the expectations. It strives to bring the two into agreement by manipulating various parts of the organization. Its success must be fed back to the open system as one consideration in the boundary-spanning acivities and selection of future exchanges. That is, if the stand is having trouble meeting some expectations, then either the expectations or the process must be changed.

Operating systems and expectations provide the data for the test of expansion possibilities. Obviously, the answer to expansion proposals is not automatic. Some missions (fried fish, for example) may not be feasible or profitable. The organization must maintain some kind of stability. It can change only so fast without confusing both its customers and its providers. A given proposal, such as chicken nuggets would be explored through a series of operating expectations covering technology, costs, quality, prices, supply sources, and so forth.

Both boundary-spanning activities and operations use systems of control and communications to seek equilibrium. In this book they are viewed as doubly linked. The outward-looking, broader reaching, more ambiguous boundary spanning identifies potential directions. These are translated into the more immediate, narrow, and precise expectations used by operations. The results of operations are fed back into boundary spanning for the next round of revisions.

Continuous Improvement

If influentials and exchange partners were unchanging in their needs, strategic management would lead to a stable, more or less permanent relationship. This actually happens occasionally, usually in smaller communities for limited periods of time. For most of the world it is unrealistic. The desires of the exchange partners change, the relative influence of various stakeholders change, and the goals of the organization must change in response. So pervasive is change in modern society that most successful organizations expect to change constantly. Homeostasis becomes a goal which is never reached. The organization is designed around a concept of **continuous improvement**, that the organization will set expectations which it can and will achieve, but which will be set at a better level each year. Continuous improvement concepts were developed in Japan[6] and became widely accepted in the United States during the 1980s and 1990s.[7] They add several important dimensions to the theory.

Customer Initiative

First, continuous improvement places the customer—that is, the one who starts with the money—in the position of defining the good or service the organization supplies. Without in any way ignoring the needs of the worker, it notes that success depends on convincing customers to use the service (and part with their money). That is, if customers want soy burgers instead of beef burgers, then that is what the stand will make. This concept has three advantages. It provides a focus for boundary spanning and expectation setting. It gives a rule for settling disputes. Most important, the focus and the rule are consistent with free market and democratic principles.

Worker Empowerment

Second, continuous improvement relies heavily on the worker. **Empowerment** empowers the workers, encouraging them to take control of the operating situation and revise it as necessary to meet or improve upon the expectations. Empowering workers requires an ability to translate the results of boundary spanning to specific expectations effectively. It also requires a reward system and a style of management that encourage consensus. This means that the forces supporting the workers' contribution are adequate training, effective logistics (supplies, tools, equipment), and response to questions. Management's responsibilities are derived from worker needs, rather than the other way around. In the hamburger stand, workers are free to act as they please, so long as the needs of the other influentials, including other workers, are met. In practice, this means management must explain the goals and coach about how to meet them, rather than give orders without explanation. It also means that management is responsible for the stand, the meat and bun supply, advertising, and answering any question the worker has.

Process Focus

Third, as a result of the authority accorded to customers and workers, the focus of improvement itself is on revision of **process**—that is, the series of actions or steps which transform inputs to outputs. If there is a gap between what the customer is willing to buy and what the operation can produce, the production process is the focus for revision. If the customer is willing to pay 49 cents for a burger, and it costs 50 to make one, the process must be changed. The ingredients must be obtained more cheaply, or prepared more cheaply. Considerable experimentation could go into finding a way to eliminate that one penny difference. New formulations of the burger, new ways of cooking it, wrapping it, or handling the condiments might all be considered. The possibilities to increase volume, such as faster service at peak hours, longer hours, advertising, and relocation, have to be evaluated. Other requirements like taste, appearance, and the food sanitation rules cannot be ignored.

The workers would be expected to come up with the solution if possible, but management must answer all their questions and provide appropriate logistics.

Process revision typically follows the **Shewhart cycle**, called **Plan-Do-Check-Act** (or PDCA) shown conceptually in Figure 2.1.[8] PDCA suggests that process revision is approached by careful study of the problem with a deliberate effort to uncover the most fundamental possible corrections (*plan*), an idea, or proposal for revision which is developed to attack the problem (*do*), a trial, where the idea is systematically field tested (*check*), and implementation (*act*). The cycle is a robust methodology for a team or an individual searching for a way to improve a process.

4 *Factual Basis*

Fourth, workers are guided in their search for improved processes by facts, and factual analysis. Facts—that is, measurements from the real world—define the specific goals of improvement, and factual analysis identifies the shape it might take. Facts are the arbiters for the inevitable disagreements, between and among the customers and workers. The search for facts is far-ranging. Science, the study of the factual world, is central. The organization will do what is factually sound and scientifically proven. Most applied activities, even including hamburgers,

How does the

Figure 2.1 Shewhart Cycle for Process Improvement *provide continuous improvement?*

ACT-Implement the best
solution and return
to Plan.

PLAN-Identify the real
problem.
Analyze causes.

CHECK-Test the solution.
Evaluate the result.
Consider further
improvements.

DO-Develop improved
systems.
Select the best
improvement.

integrate several different sciences in the creation and marketing of their product or service. The hamburger stand will fail without at least intuitive understanding of the relevant issues in nutrition, bacteriology, accounting, economics, and psychology. If the stand succeeds and grows larger, chemistry and statistics will be added to the list, and the depth of understanding must increase for all.

A team of empowered workers will do better if it gains skill at using facts in two applications—to analyze and understand actual performance, and to make choices between alternative goals and processes. Analyzing performance calls for measurement, data collection and recording, and data manipulation and display. For example, the hamburger stand striving for the essential 1 cent margin, might study how big a hamburger is satisfactory to its customers. Then, recognizing that smaller burgers can drive away customers and bigger ones erode profits, it might measure actual burgers to identify how many burgers are different than the minimum, and design a patty-making process which assured uniformly satisfactory size.

Statistics will figure heavily in this analysis. The major ones are shown in Figure 2.2. Samples of customers will be drawn to identify the satisfactory size. Since customer satisfaction is a complex matter, many dimensions will be measured simultaneously and multivariate regression analysis will be used to evaluate the contribution of burger size. Daily samples of actual burger size will measure the process. Since both the average size of the burger and the variation in size are important, both the mean and the standard deviation of the process sample must be analyzed. Further, since most of us are not statisticians, graphic devices will be necessary to show everyone what performance is. The graphs in Figure 2.2 show that the burger size is too big by about 5 percent, but the variation in the size is completely unsatisfactory. The hamburger-making process must be redesigned to get the size under control.

Using facts to make choices between alternative goals and processes is a philosophical commitment, as important as, and quite different from, the ability to analyze the facts themselves. There are competing philosophies, such as religion or ethics (which may forbid certain businesses entirely, or under certain circumstances), authority (whatever the boss says), power (a test of wills between management and union), and simply tradition ("we've always done it this way"). The theory of this book suggests that the more reliance is on facts, the greater the organization's chance of success. Most people are unwilling to make a complete commitment to follow facts blindly, and therefore make certain religious or ethical constraints. The successful organization

Figure 2.2 Use of Facts for Management Decisions: How Big Should a Hamburger Be?

Part I. Customer Wishes—Data from Customer Surveys

A. Known elements affecting overall satisfaction with product
Burger: price size, condiments, roll, cooking time
Wrapper: convenience
Service: server attitude, hours, location, parking, amenities
Other: other meal items, side orders, drinks.

B. Customer Survey

McDougal's Burgers
Overall, how would you rate this trip to McDougal's?

	Great	Good	OK	Poor	Awful

Now tell us about the details:

Wrapper	Great	Good	OK	Poor	Awful
Roll	Great	Good	OK	Poor	Awful
Burger size	Great	Good	OK	Poor	Awful
Burger cooking	Great	Good	OK	Poor	Awful
Condiments	Great	Good	OK	Poor	Awful
Fries	Great	Good	OK	Poor	Awful
Desserts	Great	Good	OK	Poor	Awful
Drinks	Great	Good	OK	Poor	Awful
Service	Great	Good	OK	Poor	Awful
Parking	Great	Good	OK	Poor	Awful
Location	Great	Good	OK	Poor	Awful
Hours	Great	Good	OK	Poor	Awful

Thank You! Come Back Soon!

C. Multi-variate Analysis
Customer satisfaction = β_1(Wrapper) + β_2(Roll) + β_3(Size) + β_4(Cook) + β_5(Cond) + β_6(Fries) + β_7(Desserts) + β_8(Drinks) + β_9(Service) + β_{10}(Parking) + β_{11}(Location) + β_{12}(Hours) + ϵ

Part II. Burger Size

A. Actual Burger Sizes Daily Burger Weight Sample

Burger #	Size (Lbs.)
3	.275
14	.243
27	.258
35	.260
49	.243

Continued

Burger #	Size (Lbs.)
•	
•	
•	
Average	.250
Std. dev.	.065

Control

Run Chart of Daily Weight Sample Means and Standard Deviations

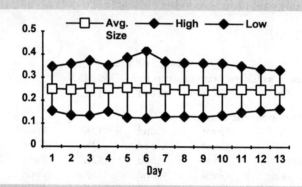

SIZE: .240 pounds, ± .06 pounds

B. Desired Burger

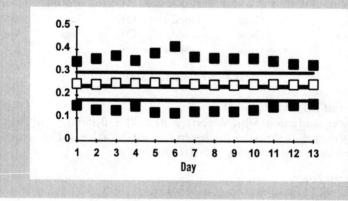

integrates these effectively into its search for solutions. The violation of widely accepted religious or ethical tenets will cause failure.

The hamburger stand might have these possibilities: buying a higher quality of beef, expanding its advertising, or improving its worker training. Each of these will add to costs. Profits will increase only if they also either expand markets or reduce costs, but the connection between the action and result is not immediately clear. Since all three options meet ethical and religious standards, the organization will use facts to assess them. It will survey customers and make trials of new advertising, revised beef specifications and training programs. It will finally select the opportunities that increase profit. If possible, it will not decide the question on the owner's opinion or the threat of a strike, and it will not allow inertia to stifle all three opportunities.

The use of facts as guidelines for improvement goes beyond the selection of alternatives to the design and promotion of alternatives. The organization which follows continuous improvement theory quickly comes to know more about its business than anyone else. It is likely to be the first to discover or invent new opportunities which go beyond the customers' range of knowledge, but which will fill customer needs. Sony's "Walkman" is the recent example most often cited, but Henry Ford's Model T is the most striking. After people saw these products, tried them, and became convinced that they worked, the market for them exploded. Only organizations deeply knowledgeable in the products and the markets involved can make these kinds of advances.

Scale

The three principles of resource dependence, community-focused strategic management, and continuous improvement taken in combination imply substantial size and scope of operations. Large, even very large, organizations are the rule in many fields, including hamburger stands. The modern organization has grown precisely because size has proven to be an asset in following the principles. How did McDonald's emerge from something so simple? The answer is that there is a large market for inexpensive hamburgers, and a not-so-simple technology that made them profitable. The technology is based rigorously in a broad range of science. The contribution of McDonald's—"over 100 billion sold"— is scale. Ray Kroc bought a hamburger stand and a name from the McDonald brothers. The company he built uses television to advertise to mass markets, sophisticated franchising and stock structures to gain capital, standardized equipment, and supplies to control cost and quality, concentrated purchasing power to gain price advantage, and central education to teach its franchisees and workers. These kinds of activities are not accessible to the small organization. When Kroc converted from a hamburger stand to McDonald's, he discovered how to put the advantages of scale to work. He copied the history of several other industries (transportation, petrochemical, communications, steel)[9] in inventing a new, larger-scale approach to hamburgers. McDonald's as an idea did

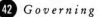

Figure 2.3 Major Exchange Partners

Customer Partners
Patients and families
  Payment partners
    Insurance carriers and intermediaries
      HMOs
      IPAs
      PPOs
      TPAs
      Medicare
      Medicaid
    Buyers
      Employing corporations
      Unions
      Federal, state, and local governments
    Regulatory partners
      Governmental regulatory agencies
      Peer review organizations
      JCAHO
    Community partners
      Police
      Social service agencies
      Local government
      Charitable, religious, educational, and cultural organizations
      Citizens at large
      Media

Provider Partners
Members
  Employees
  Medical staff members
  Trustees
  Volunteers
Member groups
  Unions
  Professional associations
Suppliers
Other providers
  Community clinics
  Mental health and substance abuse clinics
  Mental hospitals
  Home care agencies
  Drug stores
  Long-term care facilities
Government agencies representing members
  Occupational safety
  Professional licensure
  Environmental protection
  Equal employment opportunity

not exist before he created it, and it is obviously something much different from simply a collection of hamburger stands. Independent hamburger stands still exist, of course. They sell hamburgers that are several times more expensive, and they count their sales in thousands, not billions. They have become what is called a niche market.

It appears that the movement toward broad scale and scope of health care organizations will continue. Larger organizations have more flexibility, more influence over their environment, and generally greater access to capital than small ones. In health care, they can meet the broad range of market demand, from specialized cancer treatment and transplant surgery to routine obstetrics care more efficiently. As with other industries, niche providers will continue to exist, and even thrive, but they are not likely to be the dominant solution.

Applying the Theory to Health Care Organizations

This four-part theory of resource dependence, community-focused strategic management, continuous improvement, and large scale is far from the only one which explains health care organizations. It is used in this book because it works. Successful health care organizations aggressively follow the concepts. They are likely to become the dominant form of future health care delivery. They recognize their dependence on customers and workers, seek areas where an equilibrium can be built between the two, measure their performance against expectations, and strive for continuous improvement. They have built up consistent ways of implementing the theory through years of experimentation. Those solutions are the content of the book. The four concepts appear and reappear in methods these organizations use to solve the day-to-day issues which arise.

Open Systems

Exchanges and Exchange Partners

Health care organizations have a particularly complex set of exchange partners. The importance and cost of the service lead to both customer and the provider exchanges which are far more complicated than for hamburgers. Figure 2.3 summarizes the exchange partners.

Customer partners: Patients and families *Patients* are the most important exchange partners. Patients anticipate appropriate, high-quality medical care, and they hold the health care organization responsible for supplying it. Most patients are aided in their hospitalization by *friends and family.* In some cases, health care organizations must establish close and direct relations with friends and family (for example, with the fathers of newborn, the next-of-kin of the dying, and the family of chronically impaired patients). The health care organization is responsible for amenities, safety, parking, and on-site mobility for both patients and families.

Customer partners: Payment partners   In modern industrial societies, patients rely on a variety of insurance mechanisms to pay for care. **Insurance carriers** are essential exchange partners. The traditional *indemnity insurance carriers*, who offer cash compensation for health care expenses, differ by locale. The **Blue Cross–Blue Shield Plan** is usually important. Newer forms of insurance have created many alternative delivery systems. Most are commonly referred to by their initials:

- **HMOs,** health maintenance organizations, are usually broad-benefit health insurance plans that work through revised payment structures for providers.
- **IPAs,** independent practice associations, are one form of HMO.
- **PPOs,** preferred provider organizations, are health care financing plans that pay on a traditional basis, but only to selected providers that are presumably more economical.
- **TPAs, third-party administrators,** are organizations that process claims and sometimes also audit use for insurance companies or employers who are carrying their own insurance.

Two large governmental insurance programs are direct exchange partners with most health care organizations. Medicare deals with health care organizations through the **Medicare intermediary**, usually the local Blue Cross–Blue Shield Plan. Medicaid, a state-federal program financing care for the poor, is run through the state **Medicaid agency.**

Customer partners: Buyers   Much insurance is provided through employment. Since health care insurance is an increasingly expensive employment benefit, *employing corporations* have become important exchange partners. Historically, *unions* played a major role in establishing health insurance as an employee benefit. *Federal, state, and local governments* purchase insurance for special groups of citizens and also buy as employers. In the past decade, buyers have been concerned about the cost of health and hospital care and have taken action to restrict the growth of costs, with only partial success. They are almost certain to become both more aggressive and more effective in pursuing cost control.

Customer partners: Regulatory partners Health care is judged by society to require collective supervision via government regulation. As a result, **governmental regulatory agencies** are exchange partners. Licensing agencies and rate-regulating commissions are common. Many states have certificate-of-need laws requiring permission for hospital construction or expansion. *Peer review organizations* (*PROs*) led by doctors, do not insure or provide care, but audit the use of insurance benefits for Medicare and other insurers.

Most insurers mandate two outside audits of hospital performance, one by the **Joint Commission on Accreditation of Healthcare Organizations (JCAHO)** or its osteopathic counterpart, the **American Osteopathic Association**, and the other by a *public accounting firm* of the health care organization's choice. Health care organizations have exchange relationships with these agencies.

Customer partners: Community partners The health care organization makes certain exchanges with other organizations, governments, and informal groups. These are numerous, varied, and far-reaching. Taken as a whole, they constitute the **community**, the individuals, groups, and organizations who have or may have exchanges with the health care organization. Health care organizations provide babies for adoption; receive the victims of accidents, violent crimes, rape, and family abuse; and attract the homeless, the mentally incompetent, and the chronically alcoholic. These activities draw them into exchange relations with *police* and *social service agencies*.

Health care organizations require land and zoning permits; they use water, sewer, traffic, electronic communications, fire protection, and police services. In these areas, health care organizations often present special problems which must be negotiated with *local government*.

Health care organizations take United Fund charity; they facilitate baptisms, ritual circumcisions, group religious observances, and rites for the dying. They provide educational facilities and services to the community. These activities make them partners of *charitable, religious, educational, and cultural organizations*.

Health care organizations are frequently one of the largest employers in town, and they often occupy land that, if taxed, would add noticeably to local tax revenues. As a result, the *citizens at large* hold the health care organization to certain standards; they, too, can be viewed as exchange partners. Communication with these extended groups often involves the **media**, press, radio, and television coverage, as well as purchased advertising.

Provider partners: Members The second most fundamental exchange is between the health care organization and its **members,** those people who give their time and energy to the organization. Health care organization members are **employees, medical staff members, trustees,** and other **volunteers.** Employees are compensated by salary and wages; medical staff members (e.g., physicians, dentists, psychologists, podiatrists, etc.) may receive monetary compensation either through the health care organization or directly from patients or insurance carriers. Trustees and a great many others volunteer their time to the health care organization, their only compensation being the satisfaction they achieve from their work.

The compensation for doctors and employees must be economically competitive. Also, whether participation is vocational or volunteer, the individual must receive some satisfaction beyond earnings. Otherwise, volunteers will stop volunteering, and doctors and employees will leave for other organizations which can better fulfill their needs. Yet the health care organization cannot provide earnings for the doctors and employees unless it sells their services to patients.

Provider partners: Member groups Members are often organized into groups, and their groups manage their exchanges to some extent. There are *unions* and *professional associations* for members, and any subunit of the health care organization—the doctors specializing in neurology, for example—can become a group representing its members to the health care organization. Group membership is itself an exchange; it is fruitful for individuals because they can meet some needs that would otherwise go unmet. The success of the groups depends upon the set of exchanges that commits the individuals to their groups.

Provider partners: Suppliers Health care organizations use significant quantities of goods and services. The **suppliers** of these, from artificial implants to banking, are exchange partners. Suppliers of certain critical goods and services—such as electrical power, communications, and human blood—are particularly important exchange partners.

Provider partners: Other providers In the course of meeting patient needs, health care organizations have considerable contact with other providers, including competing health care organizations and agencies whose limited service lines may be either competitive or complementary, such as mental health and substance abuse clinics, mental hospitals, home care agencies, drug stores, and long-term care facilities. The **vertical integration** of health care providers, the tendency to cover the broadest possible spectrum of health care rather than a single service such as hospitalization, has led to increasingly formal relationships with these organizations, ranging from referral agreements through joint ventures to acquisition and operation of services. It is not uncommon for two health care organizations to collaborate for certain activities, such as medical education or care of the poor, and compete on others.

Provider partners: Government agencies representing members Government agencies of various kinds monitor the rights of member groups. **Occupational safety, licensure, environmental protection, and equal employment opportunity agencies** are among those entitled to access to the health care organization and its records. The health care organization is obligated to collect Social Security and federal income taxes. Records and taxes are examples of exchanges between health care organizations and government agencies.

Networking

Most individuals and organizations in a modern society are active in social, political, and economic groups which interact both with their members and other groups. Each of the exchange partners of the health care organization has relationships with exchange partners of their own. These interactions lead to **networks** of complex exchange relationships. The health care organization is always located in a web of such networks. Understanding and respect for these networks is one of the keys to success. Exchange partners can reward more generously services which do not require them to revise other important relationships. Figure 2.4 shows a greatly oversimplified network relationship of health care organization exchange partners. A healthy organization will make a great many network ties, and will act in such a way as to keep them intact whenever possible.

The most important of the networks are those providing patient care. Patients create exchanges with their families, with health education and promotion services, doctors, drug stores, hospitals, other care providers, and support groups. They visit doctors more frequently than most of the others. Both patients and doctors prize a relationship which encourages an intimate, collaborative approach to promoting and maintaining health. **Primary care practitioners**—are doctors in family practice, general internal medicine, pediatrics, obstetrics, and psychiatry; nurse practitioners and midwives specialize in carrying out that relationship effectively. **Referral specialists** tend to see patients referred by primary care doctors and to care for them on a more limited and transient basis. They are more likely to manage episodes of inpatient hospital care. Several diagnostic and treatment services, also

Figure 2.4 Network of Exchange Partners in a Community

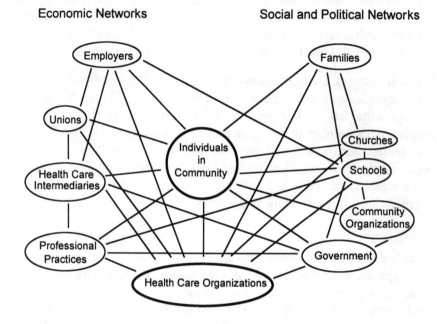

Economic Networks Social and Political Networks

called **clinical support services**, are used by both primary and referral doctors. They are available to patients at the most appropriate site, hospital, home, or office. Most people expect to get health care from several of these groups, and have several established relationships.

The network financing care is also important. Patients rarely pay directly for care and often do not pay directly for their own health insurance. They obtain insurance through their employer or some other group, sometimes represented by unions. For many health care organizations, direct relations with insurance carriers yield their largest single source of revenue. Yet the carrier is only the point of contact; carriers must meet the desires of employers, patients, and unions. The proliferation of new organizations for financing care and the decline of Blue Cross–Blue Shield in the marketplace was associated with profound shifts in the exchanges between these three groups. These, in turn, were driven by changes in the general economy, chiefly in the diminished ability of the United States to compete in world trade. Viewed from the perspective of the employment network, health care is important, but it's obviously only a small part of the total relationship.

A third important network is the one relating to government. Governments have multiple exchanges with health care organizations, as well as exchanges among themselves (for example, state and federal governments) and between units of government (such as Medicaid and the regulatory agencies). There are obvious relations among governments and employers, unions, and the citizenry. When people are dissatisfied with their exchange relationship with health care organizations, they can choose either governmental or nongovernmental routes to relief. The presssure for health care reform gains its strength from people's conviction that a new set of rules governing both the care networks and the employment networks is necessary. Government difficulty paying for Medicaid and Medicare costs has already led to a series of new rules aimed at finding more cost-effective solutions.

Influence

The complexity of the exchange networks is obvious from the list. The number of individual partners is much greater than the number of types; thousands of individuals and dozens of organizations are involved. The groups can be classified by their influence, that is, by their ability to affect the health care organization's success.

Member partners with critical skills, such as doctors, have considerable influence, as do partners with whom there are frequent exchanges, such as payment partners. Buyers also have developed considerable influence, usually through their role as trustees. Government regulation in some states may restrict the prices which can be charged or the investment in facilities and equipment. Some partners have very specific or temporary influence, but it may still be powerful. Public health licensure officials, for example, can close a health care organization for an emergency situation. A group or even an individual who relates to the institution only infrequently can sometimes acquire startling influence for a short period of time. Pickets or the media are examples.

Influence is relative among the partners and variable across time and place, although national, regional, and community trends and events dictate considerable similarity at any particular time. Change is driven by changes in the desires of the influentials, and changes in the relative importance, or **power**, of the influentials.

The history of the modern health care organization can generally be described as one of steadily increasing numbers of influentials and a gradual shift away from the dramatic curative episode. The "doctors' workshop" of the first decades of the twentieth century accurately captures the influence existing then—influence limited almost exclusively to physicians, particularly surgeons. The development of technology, the growth of health insurance, government subsidies through Hill-Burton and other legislative vehicles, and government finance through

Medicare and Medicaid led to demonstrable increases in the lists of influentials. But these programs also represented an era of wide-spread respect for professional judgment and medical technology. The money, and the influence went to high-tech medical services largely in acute general hospitals through 1970.

Over time dissenters to the high-tech consensus slowly gained more influence.[10,11] One of the obvious weaknesses of high-tech medicine was its cost. A large number of states investigated regulatory agencies to control of costs in the 1970s, and some states implemented them. They had only mixed effectiveness, so the pressure for cost control continued to grow.[12] In 1983, the federal government changed the hospital payment for Medicare from a "reasonable cost" concept to a fixed amount per discharge, with annual increases based upon the federal budget. Since Medicare revenue constituted 35 to 40 percent of most hospitals' income, the government's influence was unquestionable. Driven by some of the same underlying causes, some employers became more aggressive in addressing the cost of health insurance premiums. Many firms avoided providing insurance, creating a pool of uninsured persons. Others reduced the scope of coverage or demanded partial payment by the employee. Lack of health insurance, or the fear of it, became a political force in itself. Employee premium sharing generated opportunities for managed care insurance which could offer better financial protection for less cost. The net result of these actions was a significant rise in the influence of payment partners. At the same time, certain kinds of government regulatory agencies, particularly the health systems agencies, lost influence because they were not effective.

This change in the influence structure established the grounds for health care reform. Well-managed health care organizations responded to it as it emerged, making substantial changes to control costs. Hospitals set to work on improving the efficiency of inpatient services. Since the costs of hospital care also involves the clinical decisions about what services to use, reorganizations soon began to focus heavily upon the medical staff. Well-managed hospitals were in a position to respond to the new needs more rapidly and more effectively than less effective ones. They entered the period of extreme change with three assets: First, they had the resources which accrued to successful institutions prior to the change; second, they had a background of goodwill and effective communications with their exchange partners; and third, they had better sensing and forecasting mechanisms which allowed them to see the extent and permanence of the change faster.

Community-Focused Strategic Management

With so many exchange partners and influentials, the construction of a strategy becomes a difficult task. It is often argued that America's current health care system does not do it very well. Not only are costs not controlled, but the system spends a large amount of money on an infrastructure which does not deliver care, but facilitates equilibrium between the demands of the participants.[13] Yet given the diversity of the country, and the difficulty of gaining consensus on issues such as health care, a local approach may be the most feasible. At least the decision-makers are accessible. Political, social, and economic avenues are open to those who wish to change the system.

The Contribution of Community Focus

The terms community focus and customer initiative imply a point of view about the strategic management, that priority belongs to the patient and the community as a whole, rather than a select group of owners or workers. That perspective is adopted deliberately by many health care organizations. They are not-for-profit, legally incorporated for the benefit of the public, and their strategies are deliberately responsible to a specific geographic community. Their mission is usually stated as improving the health of that community, rather than simply providing health care to it.

Broader mission statements incorporate perspectives of prevention and health promotion that until recently were rarely emphasized by hospitals or medical group practices. These perspectives hold great promise for cost reduction, particularly among poor and disadvantaged populations. Counseling on child-rearing, safety, smoking, alcohol and other substance abuse, safe sex, and nutrition can reduce the cost of care itself and improving health and productivity. Among the elderly, management of disease is intermingled with social needs—housing, nutrition, and assistance with daily living.

These perspectives have led to a new concept of an integrated health system, an organization that strives deliberately to meet all the needs of its community at minimum cost. As Figure 2.5 shows, services of the organization begin with those aimed at keeping the community well, and continue through several levels of disease or condition management. At each stage, the objective is to return the patient to the well population at the lowest possible cost. Thus the bulk of disease is treated on an ambulatory basis. The services of the health care organization extend through continuing nursing home care, where the goal is to maintain as much independence as possible, to the end of life, where the patient is encouraged to determine the outcome as much as possible.

For-profit health care organizations cannot ignore community focus. They must satisfy the same customer requirements, including cost control, and the preventive and health promotion activities have the same return for them.

The Role of the Organization

The organization, the superstructure beyond the intimate health care transaction itself, has a role which is harder to understand than the

Figure 2.5 How the Health Care Organization Sustains Its Community at Minimum Cost

Condition or Disease State	Kind of Health Care	Management Objective	Example
Well population ↓	Health promotion/disease prevention	Promotion of healthy lifestyles	Immunization, environmental safety, nutrition, exercise
Disease or condition risk ↓	Detection & secondary prevention	Encourage effective use of care	Smoking cessation, prenatal, well-baby care
Ambulatory management (acute or chronic condition) ↓	Health maintenance	Maximum functioning	Infectious disease, AIDS, asthma, trauma, arthritis
Acute management ↓	Episodic care	Cure, repair, limit disability	Surgery, radiation, ICU, Obstetrics delivery
Rehabilitation management ↓	Restoration	Prompt, full return to function	Exercise, retraining, prostheses
Continuing care ↓	Support	Maximum independence	Nursing home, home care
Death	Assistance	Most satisfactory end of life	Hospice, self-determination

doctor's or the patient's. It must carry out a series of functions which identify and maintain the equilibrium. These are clearly functions different from the activities of doctoring or nursing.

- The organization must conduct an ongoing search and evaluation process that identifies mutually acceptable exchanges between customers and providers.[14] The best exchanges are those that society wants most, as measured by its willingness to commit resources, and those that the health care organization can deliver better than any other source. All objectives, goals, or purposes, even the mission of the health care organization are set as a result of this search.
- The organization acquires the necessary resources. That is, it markets services, recruits people, purchases supplies, and collects revenue. (These are often called logistic functions.)
- The organization facilitates solutions. That is, it supports communications, clarifies responsibilities, assists in building consensus, encourages performance, and resolves conflicts.
- The organization controls the environment and its providers so that it usually meets the customers' expectations. Control is achieved via agreement with empowered workers, about designed processes and detailed expectations. The agreements are used constantly to steer the organization. That is to say control is achieved by building consensus with providers, not by enforcing compliance.

These functions remain secondary to the exchanges of medical care itself. Success for the organization is the reward for fulfilling the exchanges society sees as most useful, and society gets little benefit from the organizational activities per se. On the other hand, the organization is essential, because it provides services direct care givers cannot do by themselves.

Organizational failure can occur in four ways:

1. The organization can misread society's desires and select the wrong exchanges.
2. The translation of exchanges into expectations can contain errors.
3. The delivery units can fail to meet their expectations.
4. The demands of society can move away from those the organization can fulfill.

Limits on the Strategies

Some people would argue that this view of the health care organization is too broad. They would contend that the theory gives the health care organization very few limits; the health care organization could try to do anything society wants. If society wanted the health care organization to operate a bank, for example, it could try. This statement is literally correct. The theory encourages health care organizations to contemplate such ideas, but to do them only when they would be successful. There are tricks to every trade, and health care organizations know the tricks of health care. They do not know the tricks of banking and would probably fail at it. In practice, there are limits on what society will actually request and even more on what the health care organization can deliver. One function of the organization is to find those limits.

Other people suggest that the community-focused concept ignores the wishes of owners. This is actually a misreading of the theory, which only says that the health care organization should seek mutually satisfactory exchanges. Does a traditional hospital have to become a health care organization? The theory gives the organization the right and obligation to decide. It might choose to remain an inpatient facility, and contract with other organizations which provided the other services. The mission can be decided on economic, moral, or even esthetic grounds. However, if the organization is not successful at its chosen mission, it faces a more serious choice—meet the demands of the customers and providers, or disband. A mission based on extensive review of real and perceived community needs obviously has greater chances for success than one which is the whim of a small set of owners. But owners who can back their whim with substantial resources or a rational plan can improve their odds. A specialty hospital for children, for example, might succeed because it offers unique services and attracts a substantial endowment.

Continuous Improvement

The concepts of continuous improvement are the most recent additions to the theory of health care organizations. The individual components of customer initiative, worker empowerment, process focus, and factual basis have long histories and were both scientifically and practically supported before what is called "the quality movement" began. The movement reinvigorated the elements, and tied them together effectively.[15]

Patients, the primary customers of health care, were historically viewed as passive recipients of treatment they did not understand and could not evaluate.[16] They have emerged under continuous improvement and health care reform as the final arbiters of both cost and quality. Leading health care institutions survey their patients constantly, seeking evidence of satisfaction with the care process, the amenities surrounding it, and the results.[17] Documented outcomes of treatment and efforts at prevention and health promotion are now required by employers.[18] The financial realities of health care delivery enhances the power of relatively small customers. High fixed costs, particularly the training of specialists and capital equipment they require, must be supported by large patient volumes. Each specialist and specialty service, therefore, must optimize income by attracting the largest possible group of patients. Few can afford the luxury of limiting their market.

Health care may have the largest number of different professional skills of any industry. Specialization has provided great benefits, but it has created a world in which many professions compete for power. Effective integration of several dozen specialists (several may be involved even in a single case) has not been easy. The creation of multispecialty teams, focused around specific diseases has been important. It coordinates specialties around scientifically defensible objectives. It replaces both authoritarian bureaucracies and the dominant voice of the physician.

The quality movement stresses the importance of empowered workers who can modify their jobs to meet customer needs. The approach of analyzing patterns of care and devising general guidelines often called protocols has proven effective. It allows workers to review factual and scientific evidence, debate alternatives, and reach agreement about processes of care. As they do, they learn and implement new approaches. It is rarely necessary to criticize them for noncompliance; they have committed themselves to compliance in advance.

The methods used to implement continuous improvement in health care have used factual data and scientific evidence at every step. As a result, information has been transformed into a strategic resource for the organization.[19] Its importance is recognized among leading health care organizations, as evidenced both by survey of management[20] and capital expenditure plans.[21] The capture, archiving, analysis, and communication of information has become a major element in the contribution of the health care organization.

Scale

Health care organizations have traditionally been small, as Chapter 1 illustrates, but in the future, well-managed health care organizations are likely to be large in size (number of patients or annual dollar volume) and scope (variety of services). Large organizations supported by large markets generate returns to scale, the ability to finance technology of all kinds which smaller firms cannot afford. The emerging health care organization requires technological resources for clinical and business operations. The integration of several different sciences and technologies to produce patient care—the list is much longer than for hamburgers—calls for large, diverse worker groups and physical facilities. The technology to process facts also provides returns to scale.

If payment mechanisms are available to support it, the health care organization which adopts a community focus ends up with a broader scale in two respects. First, it is driven to capture as much of the market as possible, and encouraged to capture groups who were previously disadvantaged. Second, capitation and similar payment schemes encourage it to pursue prevention and health promotion aggressively.

At the same time, health care remains a uniquely personal service delivered by one human being to another. The technological imperative is to invent the larger-scale approach that retains the personal touch. There will be a role for niche providers, small independent hospitals and medical practices. If they are well managed, they will follow all the major parts of the theory, but they will trade the returns to scale for specific advantages in specific markets.

Important Customer Motivations

Benjamin Franklin, conducting the fund drive for the first community hospital in North America (The Pennsylvania Hospital, founded in 1760), eloquently built his case on five arguments:

- We need a refuge for the unfortunate, and Christianity will reward you for your generosity to this cause. [Although Franklin did not say so, Judaism, Islam, and Buddhism also praise charitable behavior.]
- You might need it yourself this very night.
- Among other things, we can keep contagious people off the streets.
- We can certainly handle this better as a community than as individuals.
- Grants from the Crown and the Commonwealth will lower the out-of-pocket costs. [He might have added that the grants were "new money" that would eventually end up in Philadelphians' purses.][22]

Little has changed in 200 years except the language. Four of these arguments appear in most twentieth-century fund-raising literature. The fifth, control of contagious disease, is a contribution of health care organizations to public health. It was reduced in importance when antibiotics came into widespread use, but it has received increased attention recently.

If the open systems concept is correct, health care organizations have grown in importance because customers perceived that they fulfilled certain needs more effectively than did the available alternatives. Organizations as widespread as these must respond to needs that are nearly universal, and it ought to be possible to identify what they are.

In fact, the history of hospitals clearly reveals multiple and powerful motivations in the communities that built them.[23,24] Although other taxonomies could be created, it is useful to think of these motivations in Franklin's five groups:

1. *Samaritanism and support of the poor*, a desire to aid the sick and needy because the aid itself has value or intrinsic merit. In advanced industrial nations, Samaritanism has two forms: the larger part consists of government programs supported by tax dollars; the smaller is personal, voluntary charity.
2. *Personal health*, a desire to improve the health of oneself and one's loved ones, to be able to deal more effectively with disease, disability, and death.
3. *Public health*, a desire for health as a collective or social benefit, to reduce contagion, assure a healthy work force and military force, and reduce the tax burdens associated with disease, disability, and death.
4. *Economic gain for the community*, a desire to use the health care organization as a source of income and employment to make the community as a whole economically successful.
5. *Control of costs and quality of health care*, a desire to make collective decisions which assure certain levels of quality or control the costs of the health care endeavor. The health care organization is used as a device to make collective decisions about health services, analogous to the use of elected councils and school boards to make similar decisions about city services and education.

These five motivations are long-standing, and the current arguments appear to be more about the relative importance of each than to introduce new ones. It appears reasonable that the same five motivations will stimulate action and debate 20 years from now.

Samaritanism and Support of the Poor

Whether Samaritanism deserves first place in a list of motivations for health care organizations is debatable, but a claim for prominence can be based on the long history and diversity of examples. The urge to help one's fellow man is widespread, although it appears to wax and wane at various times and places. It is one of the characteristics that distinguishes man from animals. "It is more blessed to give than to receive" is an important principle in most major religions and ethical systems. A world without charity would be palpably less civilized.

The word *hospital* has the same root as the words *host* and *hospitality* and *hotel*, reflecting the ancient role of places called hospitals as refuges. In the twentieth century, places called hospitals range from simple refuges in emerging nations, to citadels of high technology where refuge is not often considered. Samaritanism occurs in both, however. Charity to the sick and injured is particularly appealing to many citizens of the community. The sick have an obvious need, and concerns with the worth of the recipients can be set aside more easily than they can, for example, in the case of criminals or unwed mothers.[25]

Samaritanism often includes contributions of service. Volunteers provide important amenities and assistance in most community health care organizations. Although real value exists for the health care organization, it is not the full measure of the exchange. The opportunity to serve is also important. The service of trustees is almost entirely volunteered; tax law for not-for-profit corporations requires that they receive no direct profit from their efforts. Many hours of medical staff activity are unpaid as well. Although one can argue that doctors are compensated by the privilege of using the organization in caring for patients or other economic advantage, it is clear that many doctors contribute their time just because they want to. Often overlooked is the charitable impulse of employees at all levels in health care organizations. Aiding the sick is in itself a reward of their job, a compensation that sometimes offsets low wages. Whenever a health care organization employee or doctor spends time at activities that would be better compensated elsewhere, a charitable donation has occurred.

Not all charitable motives are altruistic. Donations to health care organizations are a way to relieve feelings of guilt about wealth, advertise the better characteristics of the donor, and since 1913, reduce income taxes. Donors seek health care organizations to meet needs that could be more those of the giver than of the recipient. For example, children's hospitals are more appealing to donors than an objective observer might expect. Donor satisfaction is as important to the exchange as the use to which the gift is put; if donors are not satisfied, gifts will not continue. It is easy to be cynical about the power of Samaritanism, but it may be unwise. Donated funds amount to less than 2 percent of all income, but they are important in research, education, and buildings. Added to an earned surplus, they allow levels of flexibility and amenities that might otherwise be impossible. They are important sources of unrestricted capital. The contributions of time and effort are not easily measured, but they probably exceed monetary gifts by several times when the efforts of providers are included.

The burden of care for the poor has been increasingly assumed by government programs. The United States has a tradition of local tax support for health care which still exists in most states but is no longer a major revenue source. State and federal funds are combined in the Medicaid program, now the largest source of funds for care of the poor. These programs are distinguished from governmental insurance programs because the citizen must demonstrate poverty (pass a "means test") to qualify. They can also be viewed as Samaritanism; in fact, they are often justified politically in that way. They also have more mundane motives. Government funds distributed through a community's health care organization create jobs, simultaneously fulfilling the economic gain motivation.

Personal Health

Most Americans would say that the purpose of health care organizations is to provide personal health care, but until a century ago, hospitals and doctors had almost no contribution to make toward restoring health, and the actual lifesaving abilities of a health care organization are probably still less than most people think. Personal health care comes from several sources; the individual, family and friends, and doctors are all important. Personal health services that they either cannot or prefer not to provide are what the health care organization supplies. What the community expects of the health care organization, therefore, is the difference between what the community wants in total and what it is willing to provide elsewhere. It is the change in this expectation that drives much of the current revisions. There is some evidence that the perceived value of high technology has declined, while that of organized preventive and supportive services like ambulatory care and home care has increased.

High-Tech Health Care

The health care organization's contribution to personal health care became more complicated, expensive, and high-tech as its services became available and valuable. The hospital operating room was the first such service to emerge. By 1870, new technology was providing safe and-pain-free surgery, greatly improving the patient's chance of surviving what are today's routine procedures. Cesarean section ceased to be immediately fatal to the mother. Hernia repairs, trauma repairs, and removal of diseased organs in the abdominal cavity became dramatically safer. The cost, difficulty, and need for trained personnel put this technology out of reach of most individual doctors. The new opportunities for truly valuable care via the hospital led to the first great growth period for American hospitals.[26]

After a new service leaves the research stage, it often becomes an activity that occurs solely in the hospital on an inpatient basis. As the technology is improved and its limitations understood, the service gradually moves to the outpatient clinic, before finally migrating to the doctor's office, at least for the less complicated cases. Many of the surgical procedures responsible for the rise in the hospital's importance a century ago are now done without overnight hospitalization. Some are done in doctors' offices, and some have been replaced by nonsurgical treatment.

A community's investment in health care organizations and costs of hospital care is dramatically affected by attitudes toward the desirability of new technology. A community that is slow to adopt the fruits of research may invest little or nothing in early stage, hospital-centered technology. A community with a bias toward rapid adoption of technology will invest much more in hospitals and will pay much more for hospital care. Within surprisingly broad ranges, the level of technology chosen is not reflected in measurable differences in health. One reason is that health care benefits are difficult to measure. Another is that patients can usually go to another hospital that has the necessary technology, if it is not provided in the local community.

Technology is attractive because it provides comfort, convenience, reassurance, or some other important, but less than vital, benefit. Thus, when communities bias their health care organization plans toward or away from high-tech investment, they are dealing with matters below the threshold of differences in personal health. It may be less convenient to drive Grandmother to the state university health care organization for care; it does not measurably affect her health, and it clearly does not affect her longevity.

The High-Touch Alternative

The hospital is usually portrayed as high-tech. Dramatic conquests over disease, death, and disability are real and important. Stopped hearts are restarted, airways are reopened, arteries are sewn, babies are rescued, rampant infection is overcome. People are snatched from the shadow of death dozens of times each day. What is important to understand is that this is only a part of health care activity. The popular raison d'etre of the hospital may be dramatic lifesaving, but the day-to-day reality is relief of distress that is not life-threatening. The patient with cardiovascular disease is much more often in the hospital for continuing support of an impaired heart than immediate treatment of a heart attack. Chronic lung disease is more common than the occasional dramatic stoppage of breathing. Alcoholism, a principal cause of accidents, remains after the artery is sewn. Prenatal care and prevention of unwanted pregnancy are both cheaper and more effective than dramatic interventions at birth.

Increasingly, health care services are part of a "high-touch" program of care emphasizing prevention, health maintenance, and management of chronic illness, rather than interventions to cure a specific disease. Not only are few patients at death's door when they seek care, few are cured when they leave. Most are better off in some important ways, and a very small percentage leave dead. Many will return in months or years with a new manifestation of a continuing underlying disease.

Much of this continuing care has been carried on in the doctor's office, but the nature of the care and the economics of delivering it have led to a proliferation of other mechanisms for care—multispecialty facilities for outpatient diagnosis and treatment; increased use of psychologists, nurse practitioners, social workers, and other nonphysicians; group educational activities for prevention and case management; services and equipment delivered to the home; hospices; and long-term care facilities.

Public Health

The distinction between public and personal health is conceptually clear but sometimes hard to trace in real situations. Personal health care is that given directly to the individual, while public health emphasizes activity for groups, such as maintaining a pure water supply. A public benefit also occurs, however, when care is given to individuals, and maintenance of a healthy workforce and a healthy army are important public health goals.

The historical example of hospitals' public health role was care of contagious disease. Quarantine of persons with a contagious disease was one of the important exchange contributions of hospitals until this century. Hospitals were relied upon for care of persons with a long list of contagious diseases, beginning with tuberculosis and leprosy and including scarlet fever, polio, and infant diarrheal diseases. These diseases have now been nearly eliminated by vaccines or reduced greatly in severity by antibiotics.

Today, AIDS (acquired immune deficiency syndrome) is one of the few numerically important infectious diseases, and, once again, the health care organization is expected to provide public health support.

Tuberculosis (TB) is recurring as an antibiotic-resistant disease. Management of contagion is part of the job of the health care organization. Both AIDS and TB as public health problems relate to people's risk and treatment habits. The new issues of public health are related to behavioral issues. Laws, regulations, education, taxation, and subsidies remain important vehicles for containing or eliminating these diseases, as they were for TB, pneumonia, and syphilis a century ago. Modifications of personal health care are also important, and they are the domain of health care organizations.

Health care organizations contribute to public health by providing personal health services for these diseases. They also have an important role in prevention, because they normally reach people when they are especially receptive to learning better health habits, improved nutrition, and the best care for their continuing disease or disability. Many health care organizations also provide preventive education for parents: safe pregnancy, avoidance of drugs injurious to the infant, nutrition and breast feeding, psychological aspects of child rearing, the importance of immunization, and family planning are topics frequently covered. They also assist the aged and chronic sick with blood pressure control, substance abuse, nutritional habits, exercise programs, and rehabilitation. Each preventive success eliminates a potential financial burden on the state.

Economic Gain for the Community

Funds spent on health care organizations generate nonhealth-related economic gains for their communities both directly and indirectly. Directly, health care organizations create jobs, particularly for unskilled workers, who are difficult to employ in modern society. Health care organizations also generate income for some local suppliers. If the money that pays for these expenditures comes from outside the community, the community as a whole benefits. Indirectly, the recipients of these funds spend them within the community on more goods and services. It is estimated that each dollar of hospital expenditure generates two dollars of total community wealth.[27]

A health care organization can attract outside dollars in four basic ways:

- By selling services to patients from other communities
- By attracting federal and state funds and donations from "foreign" foundations
- By providing service to local people whose insurance is paid by others
- By attracting new industry to a community.

Sale of service to "foreigners" brings revenue to the local community that would otherwise have been spent elsewhere. Hospital care can be sold as interstate or even foreign exchange. Rochester, Minnesota, and Boston, Massachusetts, are extreme examples of communities which attract dollars through hospital operation. Even sales to local customers bring in new money when the funding comes from a larger pool. For example, if a community provides more treatment to Medicare patients than other communities do, it earns more than it pays in Social Security tax. These dollars create jobs and other desirable results. A similar example exists where a plant or division of a large corporation shares a common health insurance cost with other units in other communities.

The fourth case is more complicated. When employers locate new plants or expand old ones, they examine the resources that each competing site offers. Indirectly, health care organizations help local economies by making it much easier to recruit doctors; in addition, a well-staffed health care organization is one of the assets of an attractive community. Many U.S. communities have aggressive programs to recruit new industry. New industry brings new people and new wealth to town, but the new people want satisfactory health care organizations and doctors. Concerned industrialists are now seeking economy more than attractiveness, but both goals will remain important.

Health care organizations also provide training opportunities. Although few are associated with medical schools, many assist in the training of other clinical specialists. As such, they open vocational opportunities within the community for young people who would otherwise move away.

The Health Care Organization as a Control Organization

One function of organizations is to insure uniformity of performance—that is, to control. A few organizations do nothing but control, serving as advisers, auditors, and brokers to assist the buyer as exchange partner. Trade and professional associations also have a control function; they differentiate qualified sellers by their recognition. Many other organizations assume responsibility for maintaining cost and quality as part of the provision of goods and services, through contracts, guarantees, service commitments, and the like.

Quality of Service

When hospital service had little effect on illness, quality tended to be viewed as less important; but when success became the rule, concerns about quality developed and resulted in three types of control mechanisms. First, licensure was adopted by some states to control the quality of hospitals. Second, day-to-day measurement and control of quality came to be provided by peer review, a system whereby doctors and nurses evaluate one another's work. The Joint Commission on Accreditation of Healthcare Organizations became the principal vehicle for the development of peer review, and the complexity and rigor of the system have increased steadily. Third, the malpractice lawsuit became the vehicle for gaining compensation when poor quality had been delivered, causing the threat of malpractice suits to become an important pressure to maintain quality.

While licensing programs have the appeal of democratic control, their record is unattractive. Many states did not attempt to license hospitals until they were forced to by Medicare law. Under Medicare, the states wrote different standards and adopted different approaches to enforcement. Licensure focuses heavily on fire safety and sanitation. While these are important in hospitals, as they are in other dormitory settings, the major risks in hospitals lie in the practice of medicine and nursing. Only the Joint Commission and its members have systematically addressed those risks.

The notion of peer review, that a group of doctors can assist themselves in improving quality, received strong impetus from the American College of Surgeons (ACS) shortly after World War I.[28] The ACS, a voluntary association of surgeons seeking to improve their profession, began to certify hospitals whose activities included keeping adequate records and routinely reviewing at least the more serious results of care. Not incidentally, certification also required that surgical practice be limited to qualified surgeons. Membership in the ACS was not the sole measure of qualification, but it certainly was an acceptable one. Much is made of the self-serving character of the ACS concepts. On the other hand, it was the only group providing guidance on the qualifications of surgeons. Nonsurgical specialists (internists) were few in number and had no formal program for this task. Also, the ACS program was successful. Hospitals became steadily safer places, and under ACS leadership much surgery by unqualified surgeons was eliminated.

By 1951 it had become clear that the ACS was not big enough to manage the certification program. At ACS's invitation, a joint commission made up of the American Medical Association, the American Hospital Association, and the American College of Physicians was formed to accredit hospitals. A process of extending and improving the criteria for accreditation was begun, and the program assumed considerable importance when Blue Cross included accreditation as a condition for payment of insurance benefits. By the late 1950s, Blue Cross had become the dominant private insurance carrier, and its endorsement of accreditation meant that few hospitals could do without it. The vast majority of community hospitals were accredited by the time Medicare was enacted, and the act recognized the voluntary system of accreditation as one of two ways in which a hospital could be certified to receive Medicare funds. It is almost impossible for a community hospital to survive without Medicare certification, and well over 95 percent are accredited.

The accrediting organization broadened its scope to other kinds of delivery organizations and changed its name in the 1980s to the Joint Commission on Accreditation of Healthcare Organizations (JCAHO). The standards for accreditation grow steadily more complex, reflecting JCAHO's consensus of exchange relationships relating to quality of care. Arguments that the commission was biased toward providers led to the appointment of consumer representatives in the early 1970s, although the practical impact of that action is unclear. The Commission represents the view of the leadership of the health care world, and it has the influence to enforce that view on every community hospital. It is clear that unresponsive behavior on the part of this leadership would lead to replacement of the Commission, for example, by a federal licensing program.

A strong public interest has been expressed in protection of individuals who might have received injury through the health care system. Relief is provided through the courts, where suit can be brought against both the health care organization and the doctor for malpractice. The trend of malpractice decisions has been steadily toward increased responsibility for the community hospital. Charitable immunity and governmental immunity protected hospitals from malpractice liability through World War II. Beginning about 1950, the courts began holding hospitals financially responsible for the consequences of their negligent acts. The number of suits won by former patients increased, but the number instituted rose even more spectacularly. By 1980, community hospitals were clearly responsible not only for any negligence of their employees, but also for any negligence of their physicians, and monetary judgments were increasingly levied against the hospital as well as the doctor. These changes in the legal exchange relationships had profound implications for the organization of hospitals. They forced the development of means for controlling physician behavior and encouraged consensus on standards of practice for diagnosis and treatment. Most hospitals chose to respond by using peer review, reinforcing the JCAHO quality assurance structures.

Cost Control

When the government chooses tax-subsidized financing; directly subsidizes technological development, education, and expansion; insists on minimum levels of quality and access; and demands high-tech services, one would expect the resulting system to be expensive. It is not surprising, therefore, that the U.S. health care system is among the most expensive in the world. The final decision on how much to pay is quite beyond the scope of health care organization management or even health care management. The amount of money to be devoted to health care is a function of income and the desire for health care relative to the desire for other services, such as food, defense, and education. This means that many characteristics of the system—its rules for charity, fascination with technology, and attitude toward malpractice liability, for example—are statements from the environment rather than issues to be debated in community hospital management.

At the same time, one repeatedly hears a demand for economy. Advocates of economy have a serious political problem: the economy they seek involves the loss of somebody's job in some local community. By 1970, it was becoming clear that the price for the American way was not going to be cheap, and concerns for economy began to be expressed under the guise of efficiency. (From a politician's point of view it is wise to blur the distinction between economy and efficiency, so as not to appear in favor of cutting back or removing local gains. Managers, however, cannot afford to be confused.)

Planning regulation   One important early expression of concern over costs was that for planning capital expansion and facility construction. Public Law 89-749, the Community Health Planning Act, was passed in 1966, only a year after Medicare and Medicaid. It established a set of locally oriented review boards for hospital capital expansion. Public Law 93-641 and Public Law 93-602, enacted eight years later, reinforced local review board decisions by requiring state **certificates of need** (CON) for construction and federal approval for Medicare and Medicaid payments. Thus, in most states, hospitals could not construct additional facilities or open new services without approval.

Utilization review   Public Law 93-602 took an additional step: it established *professional standards review organizations* (PSROs), local physician-controlled groups responsible for monitoring both the quality and the appropriateness of hospital care under the Medicare program. The activity was called utilization review. The notion that economy in hospital care might relate to the doctor's actions in admitting, discharging, and designing specific treatments had attracted state insurance commissioners more than a decade before, and prototypes of PSROs existed in western states. The fundamental contribution of PSROs was to extend the concept of peer review beyond quality to the efficiency of medical and hospital care. In 1983, the PSROs were reorganized into **professional review organizations** (PROs).

Unfortunately, neither planning nor PSROs worked particularly well. Repeated studies had trouble demonstrating that gains exceeded program costs.[29] Thus, while the drive for economy was blunted temporarily, the motivation became stronger as costs continued to mount.

Rate regulation After 1975, the states developed a strong interest in hospital economy, not only because of the views of their citizens, but more directly because of difficulties in funding their share of the Medicaid program. Over half the states had rate regulation programs by 1980, and they differed markedly. By far the most rigorous as well as the oldest was New York's. After several modifications, the New York program was structured so that it was one of the few that measurably achieved its stated purpose. It actually reduced real dollar expenditures. Many others were apparently designed more to slow rather than stop the increase in costs. Using persuasion, public disclosure, reviews of budgets, limits on price increases, and other methods, the public made clear its diminishing appetite for the very rapid expansion that had prevailed from 1967 to 1977.

It is noteworthy that the places which had most enthusiastically supported expansion had the highest costs and most enthusiastically supported regulation. New York City had built a large public hospital system in the 1930s, and the State of New York wrote one of the broadest interpretations of Medicaid benefits. Massachusetts, another state which adopted rigorous rate regulation, had developed a broad spectrum of tax-supported benefits for its citizens, including Medicaid. It ended the 1970s with one of the highest tax burdens of the 50 states, as well as one of the heaviest burdens of hospital costs. Similarly, New Jersey and Maryland developed elaborate cost-control programs. Rate regulation in most other states was a less pressing issue. As a result, legislation gathered less widespread support, and the programs were weaker in design and less effective in controlling costs. It is tempting to conclude that these programs failed because they did not reduce costs, but such value judgments are dangerous. Another perspective might be that they more effectively represented the collective will of the people, who in the main did not want cost reduction.

The competitive movement   The most striking change in the expression of motivation for economy came after 1980, with the rapid growth of interest in organizations directly controlling the cost of care and guaranteeing a certain insurance premium. These were marketplace expressions of motivation, as opposed to regulatory approaches. Prepaid group practices, the first model for such activity, had existed since World War II, but had not been popular except in the western states. They were relabeled "health maintenance organizations" in the late 1960s. A limited total cost per person per year, or capitation, is central to the concept. Efforts by several states and the federal government to stimulate HMO growth had modest success.

The recession of 1981–1983, combined with the implications of international manufacturing competition, stimulated significant market demand for controlled mechanisms of care delivery. The original HMO capitation concept, plus the newer ones of IPAs and PPOs, became the talk of the marketplace. In addition, difficulties in funding the Social Security Trust Fund for Medicare led the federal government to limit payment to hospitals by means of the **prospective payment system** (PPS) in Public Law 98-21, Social Security Amendments of 1983. The federal program was a payment program, not rate regulation. It differed from the capitation approach by focusing on each hospitalization, setting a price based upon categories of illness called **diagnosis-related groups** (DRGs).

The Clinton administration's reform movement emphasized the importance of local control of health care under the label managed competition. It sought devices which might strengthen local organizations striving to deliver high-quality, cost-effective care. A contrary theory, the single payer plan emphasized the role of government in setting the overall cost limit, as is done in Canada. Despite vigorous efforts by its advocates, the single payer concept never captured widespread congressional attention; the debate moved the original Clinton proposals away from regulatory approaches towards increased reliance on private enterprise. Which would work best in an absolute sense will never be known, but it is unlikely that the United States will change this basic direction in the next several decades. Only a massive failure of the newly emerging system would create political pressures strong enough to revise the consensus.

Important Member Motivations

No one is forced to work for a specific institution.[30] Health care organization members, whether volunteers, physicians, or employees, voluntarily exchange their services to fulfill their personal needs. This is true in two senses. Any member can legally (though perhaps not conveniently) leave, but more important, members' enthusiasm and commitment determine the amount of effort they contribute to the organization's goals. The well-managed institution attracts and keeps the best members because it understands what members seek from their work and provides those rewards copiously enough to gain enthusiastic participation.

Member rewards are both psychological and monetary. Although most members require a competitive monetary compensation, the extra enthusiasm and commitment that makes the difference between excellence and mediocrity tends to come from psychological rewards. These may also be more difficult to provide, and only a well-run institution can offer extensive psychological rewards. As a result, they should come first in any analysis of member motivation. While the list can be arranged in different ways,[31] the following is a convenient summary of the psychological and monetary rewards many members seek. (There is further discussion of incentives and programs for building an effective work force in Chapter 15.)

1. *Samaritan satisfactions in treating the sick.* Both the caring role and the curing role are intrinsically enjoyable, and they are also recognized and respected in human societies. Religious recognition is particularly strong. A surprising number of health care organization workers feel that God will reward them for their efforts, but many others simply believe that their work is part of a good life and, therefore, wish to do their jobs well. This satisfaction is not limited to professional caregivers; unskilled workers also enjoy knowing that they are contributing to the Samaritan motive.

2. *Acceptance by the work group.* Work is an important social event for most people, and the comradeship of the work group is an important reward. To use this reward for the benefit of the organization as a whole requires careful control of the corporate culture, but it is not impossible. Health care organizations have advantages over many kinds of commerce in that their professional groups already share a common socialization and they can attract people who share belief in a Samaritan motive.

3. *Professional or craftsmanship rewards.* Similar to the Samaritan motive is the intrinsic reward offered by the power and technology of modern medicine. At a very fundamental level, it is rewarding to do a surgical procedure or see a patient get well. Craftsmanship applies as well even to menial jobs, which can be a source of pride if well done. Proper training, tools, work plans, and supervisory attitudes are supplied by management, and they allow workers to take pride in their work.

4. *Personal and public recognition.* Recognition of satisfactory performance is an essential psychological reward in organizations. The member's immediate superior must recognize the member's effort and show a discriminating appreciation for it. The approval of peers is also important and stems from the socialization of the work group. Beyond this personal recognition, public acknowledgment can be achieved in a variety of ways, as appropriate to the service, such as recognition of the achievements by professional organizations.

5. *Compensation, incentive compensation, and promotions.* These constitute the tangible rewards of health care work. The possibilities of using compensation as a reward for extra effort are limited because each member's base compensation must be at a competitive level. Theoretically, additional rewards can be given to individuals who help units achieve their expectations. Relatively small bonuses or annual increases based on merit, rather than time in grade, are common ways to do this. However, elaborate incentive compensation systems are difficult to use and have not been proven effective.

The health care organization rewards the member and completes the exchange agreement by fulfilling these needs. Well-managed operation can be understood as fulfilling the largest possible set of exchanges, simultaneously meeting the members' needs and customer partners' needs described above. The well-managed health care organization must fulfill more member needs than its competitors. Reviewing the list shows several opportunities, but simultaneously reveals the complexity of the task.

Health care organizations that have difficulty motivating their personnel often have problems with the second, third, and fourth incentive groups. They lack the kind of complex systems necessary to provide comfortable environments, pride of profession and craft, and explicit recognition of good performance. Lack of clear expectations and consensus on goals are probably the most common causes of disincentive. A feeling that the real rewards will be handed out on a basis other than achievement of the publicly stated goals may be the most destructive counter incentive. Boards and executive officers whose actions are unpredictable or inconsistent are in danger of generating this result. Cynical statements such as, "It's not what you do, but who you know" or "The doctors (or the surgeons, or the unions, or any other special-interest group) really run this place; they get what they want, and the rest of us get leftovers," reflect the alienation that causes failure. To correct these problems, one must look to the organization structure and management technology as well as to the incentives.

Emerging Motivations and Future Strategic Responses

The immediate future in health care is exciting. Opportunities abound to find new solutions that meet customer needs and offer increased satisfaction to providers. The risk of failure is also real. Many of the solutions are untested and they demand sophisticated organizations dedicated to making them work. American health care has faced such challenges at least twice before, when aseptic surgery and the germ theory of disease were discovered in the nineteenth century, and after antibiotics and laboratory diagnosis were introduced in the mid-twentieth century.[32] Each time, the solutions were found, improvements were made, and a new equilibrium was struck. Progress is time-consuming, irregular, and occasionally painful, but it does occur. Here is the agenda which will drive the third revolution.

Community Focus

Finding and building a community focus is a complex challenge. Like most human endeavors and desires, the underlying motivations of customers and providers can easily be incompatible. There are contradictions within each group and between the two. The motivations of any real community are likely to be even more complex, deeply rooted in community and individual histories, and economically competing. People express their motivations through specific demands for services or compensation, selection of providers, endorsement of legislative positions, and donations. Their normal expressions are self-centered and even greedy. Implementing such potentially antagonistic motives is clearly not simple. The chances for misunderstanding, argument, and exploitation are very real.

Small, niche organizations are well equipped to deal with these problems. They exist by finding and serving limited groups, meeting their specific needs better than comprehensive service, mass market organizations. The health care marketplace has been a niche provider industry. Solo medical practitioners, or those working in small specialty-oriented groups, small groups of other clinical professions, independent drug stores, outpatient clinics, and home care agencies consume a large portion of national health care expenditures. Hospitals consume only a little, about 40 percent, and large integrated clinics are rare enough to be a minor factor in the balance.[33]

The trend is shifting away from niche provision and the shift is likely to accelerate. These are the forces supporting comprehensive, community-focused health care organizations.

- Aging of the U.S. population: Older people tend to have multiple conditions and overlapping medical needs. The comprehensive provider can meet the full set, winning an advantage.
- Health insurance: As health insurance covers a broader spectrum of services, its cost-control problems mount. The comprehensive provider can accept the risk of managing care better than niche providers.
- Clinical technology: Much new clinical technology is for relatively rare diseases. It is expensive and requires large patient populations to support it.
- Marketing technology: The ability to identify customer desires through polling, focus groups, and similar devices has been more effectively applied to health care in recent years. As a result, large health care organizations have a new ability to monitor and improve their service. The technology allows them to overcome some of the face-to-face advantage of niche providers.
- Managerial technology: Information processing technology allows larger organizations to operate more effectively. Computerized medical records have opened a variety of communication possibilities that were previously advantages to small providers who could rely on direct conversation. More complex environments require more managerial skill, and large organizations can support specialists in areas such as finance, law, human resources, and marketing.
- Capital: All forms of technology tend to increase capital requirements, and large organizations have more access to capital.

Ethical Values

The best-managed health care organizations begin with ethical concepts that minimize conflicts between customers and providers. They seek members who share certain ethical values:

- A love of human life and dignity, which is expressed as a willingness to give service and to respect each patient's rights and desires. Love and respect extend to members of the organization as well. Members are accepted as individuals and are respected for their contributions.
- Quality of service to the patient or customer is taken as primary and inviolate. The well-run health care organization satisfies all reasonable expectations of quality and requires adequate quality as the immutable foundation of any activity it undertakes.
- Quality of service is multidimensional and must include access, satisfaction, continuity, comprehensiveness, prevention, and

compliance, as well as the narrow technical issues of accurate diagnosis and treatment.[34] Since all of the dimensions of quality of service are important to the patient, the well-managed health care organizations attempts to consider them all in its mission, plans, and expectations.

- Members of the organization are expected to search for improvements which serve both customers and members, and to derive satisfaction from identifying and achieving these improvements.

Well-managed health care organizations strive to attract and encourage people who share these values. They announce their ethical commitment through their mission and their public statements, and reinforce it through their actions. They praise acts of kindness and foster a caring environment. They avoid and discourage those who disagree, particularly those who are unable to express love and respect for individual dignity. A broad spectrum of incentives, including recognition, encouragement, praise, promotion and monetary compensation, rewards dedication to these values. Sanctions are used rarely, in cases where the individual's behavior threatens the quality of care or the continued effectiveness of the work group.[35]

A More Comprehensive View of Control

The central issue in the third revolution is cost control. It is cost and the threat of increased costs that drew the attention of Congress dealing with the Clinton administration reform. Cost makes it difficult to cover the uninsured. Cost is the issue driving employer concerns. A great consensus that health care is an affordable, cost-effective service which should be the right of all swept the North Atlantic nations after World War II. That consensus, a major part of the second revolution, has significantly weakened under the pressures of inflation, deficits, slowed economic growth, and taxation, but most of all it is weakened by the continued rapid growth of health care cost itself. The 1990s exchange problem can be summarized as the need to balance four competing demands for

- Expanding control of cost and quality
- Extending care to those who are denied financial coverage for it
- Continued expansion of both high-tech and high-touch services
- Expanded prevention programs.

Extending care and expanding technology will drive costs up. Control and prevention may, if correctly implemented, hold them down.

The well-managed health care organizations will be those that successfully balance those conflicting forces at the level desired by their
communities.

Efforts to solve the problem will emphasize control elements first,
leading to a restructuring of the health care organization's clinical
organization and its physician relationships. As Stevens has speculated,
the health care organization of the future either becomes the control
mechanism where the balance is struck, or its identity will be assumed
by the institution which does this job.[36] Restructuring efforts are already underway in well-managed health care organizations, as indicated
throughout this book. As they progress, it will become clear that
underlying attitudes must change among both customer and provider
partners. The following examples show the diversity and complexity of
the personal health service motives and suggest the extent of changes
which will be necessary.

- Care of the dying must undergo fundamental review. About 15
  percent of health care organization expenditures go for the care of
  people who will not survive a year.[37] Often the terminal nature of
  their illness is known. Although the amount and kind of care given
  by hospitals to the dying has recently opened to debate, a pattern
  of maximal response, sometimes well past the point where quality
  of life remained, was widespread. The hospital has been assigned
  an important role because people believe that it will prolong life, if
  possible, and reduce the burden on the family. This responsibility
  must now be resolved so that futile care is avoided and funds that
  could be more usefully spent on other patients are not wasted.

- Obstetrics and newborn care provide another numerically
  important example. Well over 99 percent of births in this country
  occur in hospitals, and nearly one-third of them are by cesarean
  section. It appears that both facts represent potentially reducible
  costs. Evidence for the reduction of cesarean sections appears in
  the clinical literature. International comparisons reveal that home
  birthing with midwives, when properly organized, can be as safe as
  hospital births. Attitudes determine the need to use the hospital,
  not technology or safety.

- Communities and, as a result, health care organizations differ in
  their views of the importance of integrated services for chronic
  disease. Nursing homes are frequently associated directly with
  community hospitals in Wisconsin, though they rarely are in other
  states. Home and outpatient support for the elderly also vary.
  Comprehensive programs for care under controlled circumstances
  are rare, but appear to hold promise for both cost and quality
  improvements.

- Cigarettes, alcohol, and other substance abuse consume about one-fifth of all health care expenses, over $100 billion dollars a year, and cost about as much in loss of productive work.[38] There is still extensive argument over the effectiveness of treatment programs. Many communities have begun to emphasize prevention and health promotion, but the vigor of their pursuit has differed.

- Although most patients still select their physicians directly, in some circumstances the doctor is an employee or contractual affiliate of the health care organization. In such cases, the organization and the economic incentives support the individual physician in control of costs and quality. The evidence suggests that such arrangements can be substantially more cost effective than the traditional approaches.[39]

- Much of the medical care for the poor has been provided in clinics and emergency rooms. Neither of these sources is likely to emphasize the continuous, comprehensive care necessary to support prevention and health promotion, or to provide optimal treatment of chronic or behaviorally oriented diseases. Important cost-saving opportunities are available through improved delivery systems, but progress depends upon improved financial structures. Medicaid HMOs have recently been adopted by many states as a first step.

- Health care organizations must provide a level of comfort and convenience matching the lifestyle of the community. With modern transportation, hospitals can be 30 miles or more from some patients. In the postwar decades, as Americans grew rapidly wealthier, hospitals were pressured to provide levels of amenities which, in some cases, exceeded what is available to patients in their homes. Other advanced nations have made other choices, with no loss of health.

Values that communities place on benefits such as these clearly differ by time and place. The priorities and directions they choose will differ, as will their solutions. The constants will be change itself, and the elements of the theory—open systems, community-focused strategic management, continuous improvement, and scale.

Suggested Readings

On Organization Theory

Aldrich, H. E. 1979. *Organizations and Environments.* Englewood Cliffs, NJ: Prentice-Hall.

Ginn, G. O. 1990. "Strategic Change in Hospitals: An Examination of the Response of the Acute Care Hospital to the Turbulent Environment of the 1980s." *Health Services Research* 25 (October): 565–91.

Katz, D., and R. L. Kahn. 1966. *The Social Psychology of Organizations*. New York: Wiley.

Laumann, E., and F. Pappi. 1976. *Networks of Collective Action: A Perspective on Community Influence Systems*. New York: Academic Press.

Pfeffer, J., and G. R. Salancik. 1978. *The External Control of Organizations: A Resource Dependence Perspective*. New York: Harper & Row.

Scott, W. R. 1993. "The Organization of Medical Care Services: Toward an Integrated Theoretical Model." *Medical Care Review* 50 (Fall): 271–303.

Thompson, J. D. 1967. *Organizations in Action*. New York: McGraw-Hill.

On the History of Hospitals and Health Care

Rosenberg, C. E. 1987. *The Care of Strangers: The Rise of America's Hospital System*. New York: Basic Books.

Starr, P. 1982. *The Social Transformation of American Medicine*. New York: Basic Books.

Stevens, R. 1989. *In Sickness and In Wealth: American Hospitals in the Twentieth Century*. New York: Basic Books.

Notes

1. W. H. McNeill, 1963, *The Rise of the West: A History of the Human Community* (Chicago: University of Chicago Press), 53–58.
2. A. D. Chandler, 1977, *The Visible Hand: The Managerial Revolution in American Business* (Cambridge, MA: Belknap Press).
3. W. R. Scott, 1993, "The Organization of Medical Care Services: Toward an Integrated Theoretical Model," *Medical Care Review* 50 (Fall): 271–303.
4. M. Arndt and B. Bigelow, 1992, "Vertical Integration in Hospitals: A Framework for Analysis," *Medical Care Review* 49 (Spring): 93–115.
5. Scott, "The Organization of Medical Care Services," 293.
6. M. Imai, 1986, *Kaizen: The Key to Japan's Competitive Success* (New York: Random House).
7. W. E. Deming, 1986, *Out of the Crisis* (Cambridge: Massachusetts Institute of Technology, Center for Advanced Engineering Study); J. M. Juran, 1989, *On Leadership for Quality: An Executive Handbook* (New York: Free Press).
8. Deming, *Out of the Crisis*, 88.
9. Chandler, *The Visible Hand*.
10. I. Illich, 1976, *Medical Nemesis: The Expropriation of Health* (New York: Pantheon Books).
11. P. Starr, 1982, *The Social Transformation of American Medicine* (New York: Basic Books), 379–88.
12. C. C. Havighurst, 1982, *Deregulating the Health Care Industry: Planning for Competition* (Cambridge, MA: Ballinger Publishing Co.).
13. S. Woolhandler and D. U. Himmelstein, 1991, "The Deteriorating Adminstrative Efficiency of the U.S. Health Care System," *New England Journal of Medicine* 324 (18): 1253–58; D. U. Himmelstein and S. Woolhandler, 1986, "Cost without

Benefit: Administrative Waste in U.S. Health Care," *New England Journal of Medicine* 314 (7): 441–45.

14. G. O. Ginn, 1990, "Strategic Change in Hospitals: An Examination of the Response of the Acute Care Hospital to the Turbulent Environment of the 1980s," *Health Services Research* 25 (October): 565–91.

15. J. R. Griffith, V. K. Sahney, and R. A. Mohr, 1995, *Reengineering Health Care: Building on CQI* (Ann Arbor, MI: Health Administration Press).

16. R. L. Coser, 1963, "Alienation and Social Structure," in *The Hospital in Modern Society*, ed. E. Freidson (Glencoe, IL: Free Press), 231–65.

17. R. A. Carr-Hill, 1992, "The Measurement of Patient Satisfaction," *Journal of Public Health Medicine* 14 (September): 236–49.

18. *QRC Advisor*, 1993, "HEDIS (Health Plan Employer Data and Information Set) 2.0 To Provide Standard Performance Data for Health Plans," 9 (July): 6–7.

19. J. R. Griffith, 1994, "Reengineering Health Care: Management Systems for Survivors," *Hospital & Health Services Administration* 39 (Winter): 451–70.

20. R. R. Gillies, S. M. Shortell, D. A. Anderson, J. B. Mitchell, and K. L. Morgan, 1993, "Conceptualizing and Measuring Integration: Findings from the Health Systems Integration Study," *Hospital & Health Services Administration* 38 (Winter): 467–89.

21. Griffith et al., *Reengineering Health Care*, Chapter 5.

22. B. Franklin, quoted in L. B. Coker, ed., 1954, *Some Account of the Pennsylvania Hospital* (Baltimore, MD: Johns Hopkins Press).

23. C. E. Rosenberg, 1987, *The Care of Strangers: The Rise of America's Health Care System* (New York: Basic Books).

24. R. Stevens, 1989, *In Sickness and In Wealth: American Hospitals in the Twentieth Century* (New York: Basic Books).

25. Rosenberg, *The Care of Strangers*, 337–52.

26. Ibid, 142–65.

27. J. R. C. Wheeler and D. G. Smith, 1986, "Multiplier Estimation for Local Economic Impact Analysis," *Journal of Business Forecasting* 5 (Spring): 20–21.

28. P. A. Lembcke, 1967, "The Evolution of the Medical Audit," *Journal of the American Medical Association* 199: 543–50.

29. R. Lohr and R. H. Brook, 1984, *Quality Assurance in Medicine: Experience in the Public Sector* (Santa Monica, CA: RAND).

30. C. L. Bamard, 1938, *The Functions of the Executive* (Cambridge, MA: Harvard University Press).

31. R. M. Steers and L. W. Porter, 1983, *Motivation and Work Behavior* (New York: McGraw-Hill).

32. G. Rosen, 1963, "The Hospital: Historical Sociology of a Community Institution," in *The Hospital in Modern Society*, ed. E. Freidson (New York: Free Press).

33. S. W. Letsch, H. C. Lazenby, K. R. Levit, and C. A. Cowan, "National Health Expenditures, 1991," *Health Care Financing Review* 14 (Winter): 1.

34. A. Donabedian, 1980, *Explorations in Quality Assessment and Monitoring*, Vol. 1 in *The Definition of Quality and Approaches to its Assessment* (Ann Arbor, MI: Health Administration Press).

35. C. C. Haddock, 1989, "Transformational Leadership and the Employee Discipline Process," *Hospital & Health Services Administration* 34 (Summer): 185–94.

36. Stevens, *In Sickness and In Wealth*, Chapter 13.

37. M. Scitovsky, 1984, "The High Cost of Dying: What Do the Data Show?" *Milbank Memorial Fund Quarterly* 62 (Fall): 591–608.

38. W. G. Manning, E. B. Keeler, J. P. Newhouse, E. M. Sloss, and J. D. Wasserman, 1989, "The Taxes of Sin: Do Smokers and Drinkers Pay their Way?" *Journal of the American Medical Association* 26 (17 March): 1604–9.

39. W. G. Manning, A. Leibowitz, G. A. Goldberg, W. H. Rogers, and J. P. Newhouse, 1984, "A Controlled Trial of the Effect of a Prepaid Group Practice on Use of Services," *New England Journal of Medicine* 310 (7 June): 1505–10.

THE GOVERNING BOARD

BECAUSE THEIR responsibilities are so important and because most people have only infrequent contact with them, governing boards tend to be surrounded with mystery. In fact, however, they are units of bureaucratic organization and are more similar to than different from the other units. They are committees by design—individual board members have no authority per se—and they are subject to all the usual problems of committees. Like the simplest manufacturing unit, the governing board can be described in terms of its purposes, functions, membership, and internal organization and the measures by which its performance is judged. In addition, the chapter discusses some of the strategies pursued to maintain excellence at the board level.

Society has established, through law and tradition, two basic criteria for the actions of governing boards. The first is that the yardstick of action is prudence and reasonableness rather than the looser one of well intentioned or the stronger one of successful. Board members should be careful, thoughtful, and judicious in decision making. They need not always be right. The second is that the board members hold a position of trust for the owners. They must not take unfair advantage of their membership and must to the best of their ability direct their actions to the benefit of the whole ownership. In for-profit corporations, this means avoiding situations that give special advantage to some owners, particularly the directors themselves. In not-for-profit corporations, this means the board members must attempt to reflect the needs of all individuals in the community who depend upon the institution for care.

The topics addressed by board members are complex, ambiguous, multidimensional issues which demand both knowledge and judgment. Boards rarely act alone; the fact-finding and analysis required usually comes from the executive management and the organization at large. The executives themselves spend a great deal of time assisting boards to understand the content of the issues before them. Executive staffs in finance, planning, marketing, and information also support the board as well as other organization members. This chapter tries to illuminate the decisions the board must make. The following two sections, on the executive and the staff organizations, detail the kind of support which is required.

Purpose

The basic purpose of the governing board has already been stated: the board is accountable to the owners and must attempt to identify and carry out their wishes as effectively as possible. Two long and relatively clear traditions, one for-profit and the other not-for-profit, amplify this deceptively simple statement. It is fair to say that the differences between the two forms of organization are clearer at the governing board level than anywhere else.

In the for-profit tradition, the focus is upon maximizing profit. Board members, usually called directors, are compensated for their efforts and are usually given strong financial incentives for success. Subject to legal restrictions designed to protect the owners, directors may choose to maximize profit in either the long or the short run. They should select among opportunities for expansion on the basis of the profit expected. They may sell all or part of the assets whenever that is the most profitable course of action. They may discontinue all parts of the business and liquidate the assets when profit can be enhanced by investment in some other area or activity.

In the not-for-profit tradition, the owners are the members of the community served. Although this is a less precise concept, it is assumed that assets should be protected, although not necessarily enhanced through profit making, and used for the health care needs of the community.[1] The governing board members are often called **trustees**, rather than directors, reflecting their acceptance of the assets in trust for the community. They are rarely compensated except for out-of-pocket expenses. It is illegal and unethical for them to benefit financially as individuals. They should expand the organization in directions that best fulfill community health care needs. They may sell assets or discontinue services only when these are no longer necessary, and there are important legal barriers to their liquidating or transferring the entire assets of the health care organization.

The governance functions, that is the responsibilities that the governing board normally assumes, must always be met, but the growth of multiunit health care systems has opened a variety of structural solutions. Some have centralized the governance functions, while others have divided the governance functions in various ways between subsidiary boards and a central corporation. The structural forms are still evolving, but there appear to be two keys to their success: completeness and total clarity in the division of responsibility. No governance function may be omitted or left ambiguously to more than one group.[2]

Functions

In both legal and organization theory, responsibility can never be completely delegated. Thus one statement of the governing board's responsibilities is that the board is responsible for everything that goes on in the hospital, as well as things that did not go on but might reasonably have. Under this theory, the board is responsible for the decision and its consequences. Whether the organization thrives or fails, the board is responsible. In fundamental and inescapable ways, these statements are true. No one active in health care organizations should ever forget the ultimate, all-inclusive responsibility of the governing board.

On the other hand, the all-inclusive viewpoint seems to contradict the foundation of bureaucratic organization, which is to subdivide tasks to allow for many participants and to gain the benefits of specialization. While the board may be responsible for delivering babies safely, the plain fact is that most board members know nothing about delivering babies. This dilemma can be resolved by looking at responsibility as a multidimensional concept and finding those elements which can be done best by each participant. Then the list of functions of the governing board is the list of things it can do best. With the governing board and many other units, the list of functions begins with those activities *only* it can do.

Many writers have tried to list unique or appropriate board functions. Their lists reflect the diversity of opinion across the nation, the developments of thinking over time, and the subtlety of the question. At least three perspectives on the functions of boards exist. Managerial functions trace activities or decisions necessary by the board to support the organization as a whole. Political functions view the organization as a source of largesse, and establish rules for the distribution of resources.

A third view establishes the board's function as the contributor of critical resources.

Most real organizations probably balance all three functional approaches. This chapter examines all three. The order of emphasis begins with managerial functions, under the theory that without successful discharge of these functions, the organization will collapse, and the other functions become moot. Like the theory adopted in Chapter 2, this approach parallels that of the most successful health care organizations. The dynamic appears to be that winning organizations tend to attract the resources they need and generate sufficient resources for all, so that contribution and distribution becomes less significant.

There is now little or no disagreement about the following list of essential managerial functions[3]:

1. Appoint the chief executive
2. Establish the mission and vision
3. Approve the long-range plans and the annual budget
4. Assure quality of medical care
5. Monitor performance against plans and budgets

1. Appoint the Chief Executive

Typical board members have full-time occupations, volunteer their services, and have only limited time for the organization. They will serve only a few years and will be replaced by others. Board decisions are made by committee, whereas implementation requires an individual. All of these factors—the competing obligations of board members, the lack of continuity, and the need for an individual to implement the will of the majority—demand an executive. The **chief executive officer** (CEO) is a full-time paid executive. In larger health care organizations, an executive office supports the CEO with up to several dozen deputies and staff.

The functions of the CEO are developed in detail in Chapter 4. They are far-reaching and critical, making the selection of the CEO an extraordinarily demanding board decision. In summary, the CEO selects and supervises all other employees of the hospitals, coordinates the design and operation of the governance system and the other four systems, and represents the board internally and externally. CEOs act for the board in all emergencies and countless small, unforeseen events, where they must divine and do what the board would have wanted. The CEO generates almost all the internal facts the board sees and influences what external facts are brought to the board's attention. Finally, the members of the executive staff are often the only people in the community professionally trained in health care delivery. That training covers technical questions of need, demand, finance, quality, efficiency, law, and government regulation that are not included in the training of doctors, lawyers, or business persons. As such, the executive staff is the sole routine source of information in this complex and rapidly changing area.

Appointing the chief executive is actually a two-part function: it involves the selection of the CEO and the development and maintenance of a sound working relationship later.

Selecting the CEO

Many persons would say selecting the CEO is the most important decision a board will make, principally because of the impact the CEO has on other board decisions. The decision is also exceptionally difficult. It involves judging the future skills of individuals, always a hazardous undertaking. It is made without the assistance of a CEO, whereas other decisions have the benefit of the CEO's counsel. It is made infrequently, and the people who make it may never have selected a CEO before.

How does a board make such a difficult decision? The best way is to follow with extra thoroughness and care the rules that improve all high-level personnel decisions. There should be a description of duties and responsibilities, even though for this job they are ambiguous. The job description should be translated into selection criteria identifying the desired skills and attributes of the individual. The priority or importance of these criteria and the ways in which these skills will be measured in specific applicants should be specified.

The job description should include typical CEO functions (see Chapter 4), but it should also be tailored to the mission, vision, and long-range plan, because these identify directions the board believes are important. Selection criteria are derived from the available personnel pool (also discussed in Chapter 4) and the needs developed in the long-range plan. Sometimes the board is seeking a CEO because it is dissatisfied with the long-range plan, so a key part of the new CEO's job would be to develop a plan. The criteria in such a case would emphasize planning skill.

A wide-ranging search for applicants should be undertaken. Large health care organizations usually search nationally, or over large regions. "The best possible training and experience" is now preferred as a criterion over "knowledge of local customs." For most U.S. organizations, the law requires not only equal opportunity on the basis of race, age, sex, and handicap, but affirmative action in seeking candidates disadvantaged on those grounds. An unbiased procedure relying on the judgment of several people should be used to select among the applicants. Formal reporting of independent opinions is often sought, both to encourage conformation to the selection criteria and to avoid bias. The interviews and activities used to acquaint the board with the candidates must also be used to acquaint the candidates with the job opportunity and convince them to accept it if offered.

Given the rigor and complexity of these procedures, it is not surprising that many boards fail to follow them completely. To the extent that they fail, they rely on good luck to find the executive they need. Increasing numbers of boards have found that using consultants trained in executive recruitment is effective. Consultants have substantial experience with the process, knowledge of how to complete the procedures efficiently, objectivity regarding local history, and familiarity with candidates and their demands. They lack knowledge of local needs. Like any other group of people they differ in skill and motivation, but their record can be assessed by talking to previous clients. Evaluating consultants is easier by far than evaluating executives.

CEO Evaluation and Retention

One way to minimize the difficulties and risk of CEO selection is to keep a sound relationship with the current CEO. While this is obviously a complex matter, there are four guidelines for improving the effectiveness and prolonging the tenure of CEOs. Not surprisingly, these are similar to the guidelines for all participants in bureaucratic organizations.

- The board and the CEO should have a mutual understanding of the employment contract. There is always a contract between the board and the chief executive. The formality of that contract depends upon the situation, but more formal, written contracts have become popular in recent years.[4] The contract should specify any departures from the usual duties of the CEO, mechanisms for review of performance, and compensation and ways in which it can be changed. It also should state the procedures for terminating the relationship, including appropriate protection for both the hospital and the CEO. Properly performed, the hospital CEO's job is now and always has been a high-risk one.[5] Thus even handshake agreements should include appropriate protection if the CEO must leave the institution.

- The board and the chief executive should agree upon short-term (usually one-year) goals and expectations and should review progress toward them at the end of the period. The expectations for the CEO are more ambiguous than those for others in the organization, and they are also more subject to unexpected outside influences. They must occasionally be revised radically in midcourse. Even in extreme cases, however, it is far easier to evaluate the accomplishments of the CEO when the desired directions have been established in advance. The expectations for the CEO are related to the goals of the institution as a whole. They emerge from other activities of the governing board, particularly establishing the long-range plan and approving the annual budget.

- Compensation should be based upon market conditions. As a general rule, the only fair and reasonable guideline for designing a compensation package is the marketplace, that is, what the institution would have to pay a similarly prepared person and what the person could earn in similar employment elsewhere. This statement is true for all employees, but particularly for CEOs. The high visibility of CEOs in the community and their relatively high income tempt unsophisticated board members to use other criteria, but these are likely to encounter difficulty. The marketplace used to determine pay should be the same one used in the selection procedure. For almost all large hospitals, and for increasing numbers of small hospitals, this is the national market for people trained and experienced in hospital management.

  Incentive compensation is increasingly common for CEOs of larger health care organizations. The incentive should be based on the overall achievement of the organization, and can be based either on a previously agreed formula or an annual evaluation against previously agreed criteria.

  Compensation includes payments in addition to salary that frequently are unique to the CEO. A compensation package can consist of a salary, the employment benefits offered to all employees, special benefits offered the chief executive, the terms under which bonuses and merit increases will be paid, an agreement on the disposition of any incidental income the CEO might earn as a result of related professional activity, and an agreement on both voluntary and involuntary termination compensation. Special benefits usually exploit both the mutual interests of the hospital and of the CEO and the income tax laws. Many different items can be included, such as payment of housing, transportation, education, association, and club membership costs and deferred income provisions. Bonuses and achievement incentives are more common in for-profit hospitals, but they are spreading among not-for-profit institutions.

- Annual performance and compensation reviews are now routine, and often include incentive payment. Such reviews are properly the function of a compensation committee of the board, but the committee should look broadly for evidence of performance. CEOs are rewarded for their efforts toward the agreed-upon goals, and goals for the coming year are established. The compensation committee can determine the amount based upon the overall success of the institution and the contributions of others. The incentive payment can be either from a predetermined formula or an individual evaluation. Specific incentives carry the danger of being incomplete or biased. They may inadvertently distract the executive's efforts from the real goals of the organization toward partial ones. Individual evaluation is harder to document and may be more subject to bias. The payment can be quite large, on the order of 50 percent of total compensation. It may be better to minimize base salary and use performance-based compensation both to motivate the executive and to provide an convincing explanation of the total compensation. Incentive-based compensation may be more palatable to the general public than high salary.

2. Establish the Mission and Vision

Modern corporations work by a process of goal setting, assessment, adjustment, and achievement. They repeat this process many times and in many ways, striving for three ideal conditions derived from open systems theory, strategic management, and continuous improvement:

1. The goals of the organization as a whole are those which the larger society of customers and providers will appreciate and reward.
2. A clear corporate strategy is consistently translated to a readily visible goal for each unit of the organization.
3. The goals and achievements of the organization are assessed and amended at frequent intervals.

No organization ever achieves the ideal. Good organizations spend more thought and effort determining what society will appreciate, and more time communicating and coordinating goals among units. They assess and adjust more frequently at all levels.

The goal-setting process for a large corporation begins with the establishment of the mission and vision, continues through the amplification of the mission into a strategic plan, tests the reality of the plan with a carefully developed financial plan, and uses the plans to guide annual budgeting exercises, which establish all the closed systems parameters for individual work units.

The first step toward these ideals is the identification of explicit mission for the health care organization, and a vision of how it will be carried out. The mission and vision are widely disseminated public statements which are only infrequently changed. They are core beliefs about the organization which serve as moral and practical guides to many decisions. The mission and vision allow customers and providers to visualize and identify with the underlying goals of the organization. Properly developed and written, the mission and vision serve as an expression of the common beliefs which bind the members together. They are symbolic statements designed to extract an emotional commitment. They advertise beliefs to potential customers and providers, serve as guides for evaluating practical alternatives, and are frequently used to test ideas about future directions. They should suggest commitment to moral standards, and they should also suggest the directions in which the business is headed.

The **mission** statement is a statement of the basic purposes and activities of the organization. Most people tend to think of the **vision statement** as broader, more emotionally and morally based, and more difficult to achieve than the mission.[6] Both perspectives are essential, but terminology differs. Some combine mission and vision into a single document, and others make slightly different assignments between the terms. Taken together, they express not only what the organization is committed to do (here called the mission), but what it hopes to do (here called the vision). Examples of missions and visions are shown in Figures 3.1 and 3.2, from two very large and successful health care organizations.

The Organizational Mission

The mission statement should specify three things:

1. *Community.* What geographic, demographic, religious, or financial group is to be served? Under free choice of physician and hospital, the hospital often indicates an offer or an intent to serve a community. The measure of how well it actually serves that community is represented by its market share. A broad statement would be, "All the citizens of XYZ County and those who seek our care from elsewhere." A narrow statement would be, "All children (or some other limited population) who live in XYZ County."

2. *Service.* The full scope of potential services of health care organizations is shown in Figure 3.3. A strong base in traditional acute care, almost always including acute inpatient care and at least some outpatient care, is the usual starting point. Larger health care organizations (HCOs) are expanding outpatient activity, mental health and substance abuse programs, chronic care, and prevention and health education. Some are also extending their

Figure 3.1   Henry Ford Health System: Redefining Who We Are

"Our growth from Henry Ford Hospital into Henry Ford Health System has placed communication demands on us that no one could have foreseen," Gail Warden, President and Chief Executive Officer, said. "If we hope to continue leading, it is essential that we improve our ability to share our mission more effectively with each other and with our customers."

Mission

Henry Ford Health System is a national leader in health care. Our essential priority is to provide exceptional quality, cost-effective care, strengthened by excellence in education and research. We work together to improve health and the quality of life in the communities of Southeastern Michigan and the neighboring regions.

Vision

We are expanding the health care delivery system concept through our pioneering vision and leadership's commitment to innovation, always striving to improve access, cost effectiveness, and quality of care:

- We are designing our services and programs around the needs of our patients and the communities we serve.
- We are integrating our services to provide complete, lifelong health care in ways our customers find easy to use.
- We are enhancing the value of our services through innovative partnerships, managed care, and health education programs.
- To continually improve our services, we measure patient satisfaction and community health.

Values

The following values are fundamental to us:

- Patients come first. We exist to serve those who need our services. Our patients deserve our best work delivered in ways respectful of community diversity.
- People are our strength. Our work defines our success and determines our reputation. As each of us is perceived, so is Henry Ford Health System.
- We practice continuous improvement. We are each responsible for maintaining an environment that encourages learning and creative thinking, and helps us to develop and apply new knowledge and skills to everything we do.
- We support our communities. We advocate improved community health by getting involved. We volunteer our time, expertise, and facilities as a responsible corporate citizen and a good neighbor.
- We are all in this together. We embrace the dignity of our diverse workforce as one of our greatest human assets. We respect the people of our communities as ourselves, and we welcome their volunteer activities in supplementing our services.
- We serve with compassion. To build trust and understanding, we listen. To help, we act on our understanding.
- We have a social conscience. Our presence counts. We want our doors to be open to everyone.

Used with permission of Henry Ford Health System, Detroit, MI. © 1994.

Figure 3.2   Mission Statement of Intermountain Health Care

Our Mission
Excellence in the provision of health care services to communities in the Intermountain region.

Our Commitments
- *Excellent service* to our patients, customers, and physicians is our most important consideration.
- We will provide our services with *integrity*. Our actions will enhance our reputation and reflect the trust placed in us by those we serve.
- *Our employees are our most important resource.* We will attract exceptional individuals at all levels of the organization and provide fair compensation and opportunities for personal and professional growth. We recognize and reward employees who achieve excellence in their work.
- We are committed to *serving diverse needs* of the young and old, the rich and poor, and those living in urban and rural communities.
- We will reflect the *caring and noble* nature of our mission in all that we do. Our services must be high quality, cost-effective, and accessible, achieving a balance between community needs and available resources.
- It is our intent to be a *model health care system.* We will strive to be a national leader in nonprofit health care delivery.
- We will maintain the *financial strength* necessary to fulfill our mission.

The mission of Intermountain Health Care includes a commitment to provide care to those with a medical need, regardless of ability to pay. For more information about qualifying for financial assistance, call the business office of any Intermountain Health Care hospital.

services beyond health-related issues to include residential care and social services, particularly for the aged. Some health care organizations identify specialized missions or services such as teaching and research. Some include health insurance and health care financing activities. Multi-institutional systems operating over broad markets, like Henry Ford and Intermountain Health Care (IHC), generally have the most comprehensive mission statements.

Smaller organizations are usually constrained by resources or market size from undertaking a broad mission. They focus on a niche among the potential services, usually acute ambulatory or inpatient care. A narrow statement, typical of the only hospital in a small community, might be: *"Acute inpatient care for diseases routinely encountered and for procedures routinely undertaken*

Figure 3.3 Integrated Delivery Network

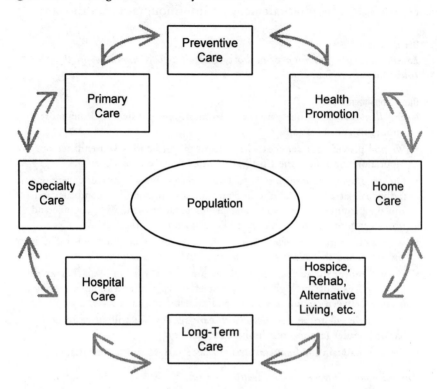

Reprinted with permission of the Catholic Health Association and Lewin-VHI, as it appeared in *A Handbook for Planning and Developing Integrated Delivery,* © 1993.

by primary care physicians and general and orthopedic surgeons, referral arrangements for diseases requiring more specialized resource, ambulatory surgical and emergency services, and assistance to private primary care physicians." Even this statement is broader than simply an inpatient hospital. Small health care organizations are also providing long-term care in nursing homes, and expanding their missions toward nonhealth services for the aged.

3. *Financing.* Financial constraints should be explicitly stated. Breadth of mission is determined by the amount of unfunded or underfunded work the institution is willing to undertake, and it is often wise to set that amount annually. Thus a broad mission would be, "*Provide services to the paying public at the lowest price consistent with long-term financial needs and provide charity care to the identified community to the extent resources permit. The board of trustees will establish eligibility criteria for financial need and*

charitable care annually." A narrow mission might be, "*Services will be priced competitively but must earn the return on equity required by market conditions. Service will be offered to all those who can demonstrate sufficient resources.*"

Too broad a mission makes planning decisions difficult and potentially inconsistent. A more serious problem is that it can dilute limited resources to the point where no job is done well. Too narrow a mission can cause the hospital to overlook important community needs and opportunities. These usually are met by the competition, which may then supplant the original institution in other areas as well.

Extending the Mission to a Vision

The vision should make clear what the organization hopes to achieve, what constraints it recognizes, and how it does business. It typically includes:

* *How the organization should be viewed by members and outsiders.* Concepts such as "caring," "charitable," "customer-oriented," "friendly," "reliable" are often used to convey a patient-centered focus. Many not-for-profit organizations emphasize their effort to embrace all members of the community. Religious organizations frequently state their spiritual commitments explicitly.
* *The organizational philosophy that guides operations.* Most organizations state their commitment to high-quality care. They emphasize equal rights for all employees and the dignity of work. They may recognize the importance of diversity, freedom of speech or opinion, or a spirit of tolerance. Some "strive to be best."
* *The organization's concept of its strengths and weaknesses.*[7] Many recognize a need to be cost-effective, prompt, and convenient. Some state a certain business strategy, such as a medical group practice, or a commitment to research and the most advanced technology.

Vision statements often rely on religious or moral commitments. They deliberately emphasize the ideals of democratic societies. They deal with hopes as much as with realities, but they must stay close enough to the possible to be perceived as sincere. A vision which is seen as pious or hypocritical can trigger a cynical response opposite from the one desired. The vision imposes an obligation upon the board members and corporate leadership. Their actions speak louder than words; if they often act contrary to the spirit of the vision, the other stakeholders see the statement as phony.

Developing the Mission and Vision

Writing the vision is difficult because of the need to be credible. Obviously the process of setting the mission and vision is complex and political. There are obvious conflicts, for example between the scope of service and the need for financial constraint. A good mission-setting procedure is based upon an accurate and comprehensive view of the desires of the exchange environment and the interests of stakeholders. The unique responsibility of directors or trustees is to pick, from all the possible things the organization might do, those that society will appreciate and reward most. The perspective they bring to the task is more that of an outsider than an insider. They rely on the CEO and the planning staff to provide alternate formulations of mission and vision, and to amplify the selected phrases into exchange needs and resources. In the end, the trustees must balance what is wanted with what is practical.

Although final responsibility for the mission and vision rests almost exclusively with the governing board, the purpose of mission and vision development process is twofold: (1) To establish a mission and vision which is consistent with the community needs and desires, so that customers and providers will prefer the organization over other alternatives; and (2) To educate as many members of the organization as possible about the mission and vision, encourage them to consider the choices they represent, and to come to a full understanding and acceptance of them. Corporations like Henry Ford and Intermountain use their missions and visions as a central educational device. They are prominently displayed and periodically reviewed by large numbers of managers to promote consensus and commitment. They are referenced in debate about future alternatives, and become the starting point for the development of long-range plans.

3. Approve the Long-Range Plans and the Annual Budget

The mission and vision are translated into plans which express the commitments of the organization in increasingly specific terms as time horizons grow shorter. The first step, **strategic planning**, translates the mission and vision into broad general directions or strategies that sketch important initiatives in terms of technology, markets, products, or affiliates—for example, to be the largest provider in an area, to offer nursing home care, to expand into health care finance, to achieve technological excellence in certain services, to collaborate with other organizations. The strategies in turn are accomplished through plans—to merge with competitors, purchase land, build buildings, acquire equipment, recruit personnel—which take several years to implement. The plans finally are translated to budgets which specify expectations for individual work groups for the next year or two.

These are **resource allocation decisions,** distinguished from the mission and vision by the commitment to expend resources in certain directions. Resources are finite; no organization can do everything. Selecting the opportunities to pursue means foreclosing others. The board shapes the evolution of the corporation through the series of planning activities shown in Figure 3.4. As the decisions get more specific, the involvement of the board becomes more general; the board is usually directly and deeply involved in strategic decisions, but provides only general oversight of the annual budget.

Strategic Planning

A dynamic, successful enterprise will develop dozens, even hundreds of new business opportunities and ways of meeting old goals. The board concentrates on maintaining consistency, responding to short-term changes in the environment without losing sight of the mission and vision. Governing boards are legally obligated to protect the assets of the firm. They do this by retaining final authority over major decisions which disburse or obligate the organization's assets, such as long-term borrowing, sale of land and buildings, and changes in the mission.

Figure 3.4 The Process of Plan Development

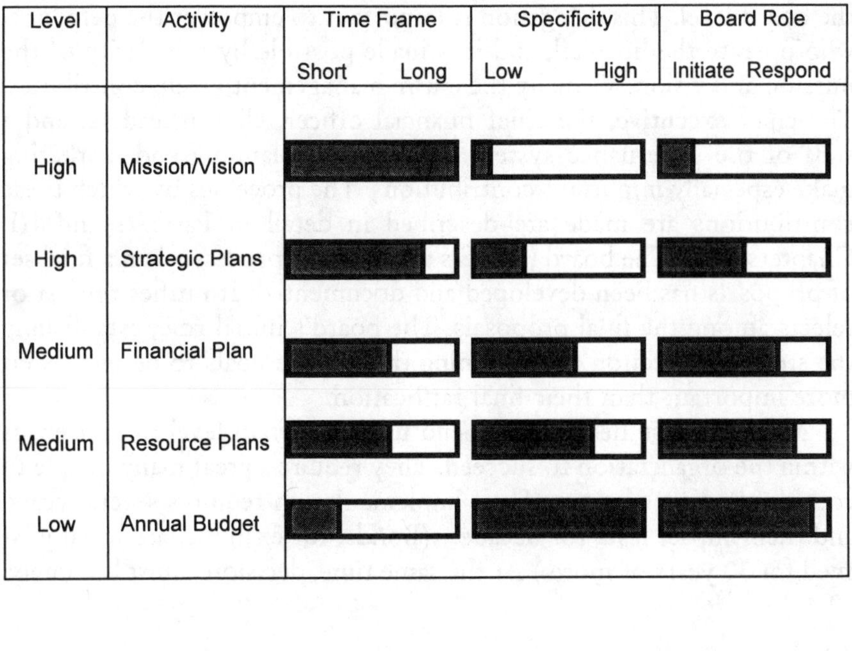

Level	Activity	Time Frame		Specificity		Board Role	
		Short	Long	Low	High	Initiate	Respond
High	Mission/Vision						
High	Strategic Plans						
Medium	Financial Plan						
Medium	Resource Plans						
Low	Annual Budget						

Strategic decisions are best approached by developing several scenarios. Scenarios often begin with sketches of various outcomes for the community: Several of the common topics for these scenarios are shown in Figure 3.5. The scenarios can be quite abstract and ambiguous, but they evaluate alternative **strategic opportunities**. These generally involve quantum shifts in service capabilities or market share, usually by mergers, acquisitions, and joint ventures or by very large-scale capital investments. Strategic opportunities require careful evaluation. Since they often are triggered by events external to the hospital, and since they often require rapid decisions, the governing board of the well-run hospital quietly but thoroughly evaluates the more probable strategic scenarios in advance and is therefore prepared for prompt action when required.

Strategy is successful when it meets market needs. Thus there is no blueprint for strategies, other than the brief checklist of recurring possibilities shown in Figure 3.5. The initiative for identifying strategic opportunities comes from **environmental assessment,** the formal and informal review of the trends occurring in the local area, from community health needs to competitor activities. The more thorough the assessment is, and the more people consider its implications, the more scenarios will be suggested. The most realistic of these should be developed and evaluated.

Long-Range Plans

Once strategies and priorities are set, the planning effort largely leaves the board level. This delegation is important to empower the personnel who operate the hospital, and it is made possible by the clarity of the mission and vision. Virtually the entire management group contributes. The chief executive, the chief financial officer, clinical leaders, and a staff of the governance system dedicated to planning and marketing make especially important contributions. The processes by which these contributions are made are described in detail in Parts II and III, Chapters 4–10. The board reenters the decision process when a final set of proposals has been developed and documented. It ratifies the list or selects among the final proposals. The board's initial role, establishing the strategic direction and outlining the specific goals to be met, is far more important than their final ratification.

Most of these decisions depend upon a certain level of consensus within the organization to succeed. They require a great many people to consider the implications. Their implementation requires several years, and their impact lasts for decades. (Bonds, for example, are usually issued for 30 years or more.) At the same time, decisions must be timely.

Figure 3.5 Illustrative Scenario Questions for Health Care Organizations

Issue	Scenarios	Critical Questions
Local affiliations	Specific affiliation opportunities	Size and strength of competitors Impact on cost and quality Ability to support high-tech specialties Existing physician affiliations Antitrust considerations Regional affiliation opportunities
Regional affiliations	Specific affiliation opportunities	Impact on local market share Total cost to patients and insurers Scope of services and medical specialization Total local expenditures Likely size of local HCOs Local political issues
Relation to insurers	Contract Joint venture Own	Market response Retention cash flow Variety of plans available to local buyers
Physician organization	Contract with: Physician organization Medical service organization Physician-hospital organization Foundation	Extent of HMO coverage Primary care physician preferences Specialist preferences Existing group practices

Real opportunities arise and disappear; once lost they may never return again. The management of these decisions must accommodate their complexity. This is done through a **planning** process which specifies how the board and others will make strategic decisions and implement them through **long-range plans.** The process establishes orderly review of opportunities, details the kinds of information which will be collected, and specifies who will be involved. Because the issues are so specific and so different, well-managed organizations have general guidelines on these questions which they adapt to the needs of each issue. The plans are documents which record decisions made, usually in the form of actions or events which are expected to occur at specific future times.

Long-Range Financial Plans

The test of the strategic and long-range planning activities comes when the financial impact is assessed. This involves realistic assumptions about future market share, prices, and costs which are used to build a *long-range financial plan* showing earnings, debt, and capitalization for at least the next seven years. The plan is actually a sophisticated financial model which can quickly calculate the implications of major decisions.

The plan tests the reality of the planning process. It accepts estimates of the cost and demand for various strategic opportunities, and shows the impact upon profit and debt structure under the market and price assumptions. The alternatives which generate the most favorable combination of market share and capital structure can be identified. The interactions are complex, because all the elements are interrelated. A new service affects cost, prices, market share, and profits, and the planner can structure it various ways to change the effects. Figure 3.6 shows the relationships built into the financial plan.

Approve the Annual Budget

The budget is the final step through which the mission, vision, and plan are translated into reality. Like the long-range plan, the budget is a detailed, complicated construction that requires substantial staff work and several months to complete. The budget includes both operating and capital expenditures. In well-managed organizations it is being broadened to incorporate an expanded array of measures reflecting the multiple dimensions of corporate success (discussed below in "Measures of Board Effectiveness"), including quality, demand, efficiency, revenue and profit, as well as costs. (The details of preparing the annual budget are described in Chapter 8, because in most organizations they are coordinated by the finance group.)

Quality and scope of service and cost are determined by the annual budget. For example, hours of operation affect access to care; number and type of staff affect waiting time; expenditures on supplies and maintenance affect amenities offered; and investments in education, capital equipment, and information systems affect the technical quality of many aspects of care. Well-run organizations use the budget exercise as a way to improve quality, market share, and productivity. The board's insistence on quality forces management to seek innovations which

Figure 3.6 Relationships Shaping Strategic Plans

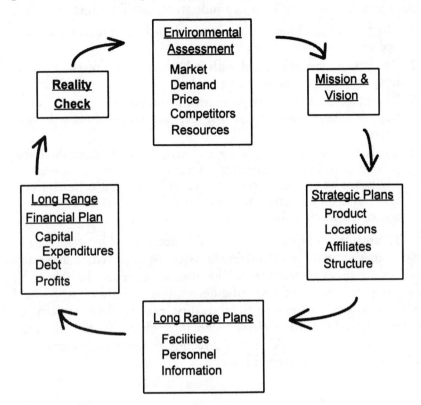

often improve both quality and productivity. Its insistence on productivity forces innovations which increase quality and market share.

The board is involved at two critical points in the budget development. At the outset, board committees are deeply involved in establishing guidelines. At the conclusion, board makes the final choices among competing opportunities, and approves the finished budget. Final approval should be anticlimactic; a well-managed budget process conforms to the guidelines and settles most questions before the board's approval.

Budget Guidelines

The budget requires effort by almost every member of the well-run hospital. The board's role is often implemented through its planning and finance committees. There will be important decisions among strongly defended alternatives which the board must resolve as the community's or stockholders' agent. To coordinate such widespread activity, the board sets desirable levels of key indicators, called **budget guidelines**:

1. The total expenditures of the hospital, including total employment and compensation of employees.
2. The pricing structure, and with it both the total revenue of the hospital and the amount to be paid out-of-pocket by local citizens.
3. The expenditure on new programs, plant, and capital equipment, and with these much of the cost increases that will occur in future years.
4. Goals for measures of quality and patient satisfaction, including programs to improve specific deficiencies. (These are a recent addition to the budget process. As well-managed organizations rely more on objective measures, the desired values are being translated to guidelines.)

The profit or surplus to be earned is determined by items one and two, and the amount of indebtedness to be incurred is determined by items one, two, and three. The alternatives must be selected by weighing the impact of a specific decision—say higher costs—on the other measures, including prices, quality, profits, debt capacity, and market share. All of these elements are interrelated, as shown in Figure 3.7. The guidelines provide initial direction to the management, which will develop a budget within them.

Figure 3.7 Relationships Shaping Annual Budget Guidelines

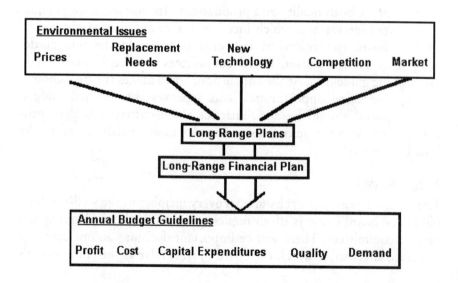

The operating budget prepared by management is a book-sized document which starts with global summaries and establishes expectations for every unit of the organization. A companion capital budget lists all major capital expenditures (Chapter 8). They normally meet the guidelines, but the board finance committee may wish to understand where the greatest difficulties were encountered, and what the trade-offs were. Capital projects are normally ranked in the priority recommended by management; the board may wish to debate the priorities as well as revisit its capital expenditure guideline. In general, however, the final review is a fine-tuning exercise within the guideline intentions.

4. Assure Quality of Medical Care

The fourth essential duty of the governing board is unique to health care organizations. The governing board is legally responsible for assuring the quality of medical care.[8] In carrying out this function, the board implements the community's specific desires and capabilities for quality of care and makes an important positive statement about the "corporate culture."[9] The board is liable for failing to exercise due care on behalf of the patients and the community and on behalf of physicians desiring to participate. The duty is normally discharged by a five-step process:

1. Approval of the **medical staff bylaws**, a formal statement of the governance procedures of the medical staff
2. Appointment of medical executives and specialty chiefs
3. Approval of the plan for medical staff recruitment and development, a part of the long-range plans
4. Approval of **privileges**, that is, the appointments of individual physicians, after review according to the bylaws
5. Review of available information on the quality of care and reports of outside agencies evaluating quality.

The board's role in these functions is limited. The core concept is one of **peer review**, that the care of all patients is subject to review by a group of similarly trained physicians. The initial development of all five steps is carried on by groups of peer physicians, whose work is integrated by the medical staff organization and the executive. The board assures itself that the result is consistent with the mission, vision, and plans. A well-run board will review the documentation and ask enough questions to protect its interests and the public's. As continuous improvement principles are applied, the board's role in monitoring quality will change. Stronger consensus among caregivers and better measures of performance should mean higher quality, but also less need for board intervention.[10] The board also serves as a final arbiter in case of disputes, but these should be rare.

Some basic facts heighten the importance of the board's medical staff activities. First, the health care organization is an expensive capital resource made available to the doctors by the owners in return for either profit or community health care. The board has an obligation to see that the owners receive fair value for the use of the resource. The courts have interpreted that obligation to include limiting privileges to the competence of each doctor.[11] Second, doctors are a uniquely expensive and critical resource for the community. A shortage of doctors in a community can be as serious as giving privileges beyond a safe level of competence. A surplus may encourage marginally necessary treatment which is both costly and dangerous. Third, most doctors would find their income severely reduced without participation in a health care organization. Doctors deserve fair treatment and equitable opportunities to participate. Fourth, many specialties require expensive capital and trained support personnel. If community demand is low, costs will mount drastically, and lack of practice may impair quality. Fifth, all doctors stand to lose income if there are too many doctors in a specialty. In short, the issues involve a sensitive balance of community and professional needs on both quality and economic dimensions.

Approval of Medical Staff Bylaws

In each hospital, the procedures of medical staff governance are written into bylaws. These documents have central legal importance.[12] Most lawyers believe that sound, well-implemented bylaws are the best protection against litigation, either for malpractice or for unjustifiable denial of privileges. The CEO frequently serves as coordinator for the maintenance of the bylaws and is the board's authority on the issues involved.

Although bylaws are procedural rather than substantive documents, certain procedural issues have profound substantive content, and the trustee relies primarily upon the chief executive and the medical staff leadership to identify these issues and their implications. Such issues arise frequently in questions of departmentalization, which indicates the groupings and the levels that must undertake peer review; membership representation on medical staff committees; methods of selecting, evaluating, and compensating medical staff leadership; medical staff participation in planning and governance activities, including staff representation on the governing board; and the authority of management to collect and report measures of quality and utilization. The direction these decisions take determines the institutional emphasis on primary versus specialty care, the level of specialized services that will be supported, and the kinds of physicians who will be attracted to the organization. These factors in turn affect cost and quality.

Approval of Medical Staff Recruitment Plan

One of the areas most likely to distinguish the well-managed health care organization is sophisticated medical staff planning and recruitment. The appropriate numbers and specialties of doctors are based on careful forecasts of community demand. The **medical staff recruitment plan** is a fundamental element of the long-range plans which establishes both the size of the medical staff and the services the organization must provide. Each medical specialty requires certain kinds and quantities of clinical support services, and, conversely, most hospital services require certain specialties on the medical staff. Each service must attract sufficient volume to support its fixed costs at a price the community can afford. Individual doctors must have enough work to maintain their skills, and the group must generate enough demand upon support personnel that they too remain proficient.

The plan is normally developed by the planning staff, with extensive consultation from the medical staff. (A medical staff of physicians in independent, competing practice should not approve the plan, because that action might constitute a potential antitrust violation: the doctors can be voting collectively to restrain entry of other doctors into the local community.) It is submitted to the governing board for approval along with the general plan, but because of its central position it usually receives individual attention.

Trustees must weigh four questions in adopting the plan:

1. Whether sufficient volume will exist to maintain skill levels of doctors and support personnel
2. Whether the proposed services are compatible with each other
3. Whether the estimated cost of the proposed scope of service is consistent with community desires
4. Whether the community's funds can better be spent by a different scope of service.

The first two questions are of quality. Infrequently used skills and services with small demand tend to have poorer results than high-volume activities.[13] Many high-tech services impose complex demands on clinical and cardiopulmonary laboratories, anesthesia, and imaging, for example. Similarly, cardiovascular surgery requires strong capabilities in cardiology, a nonsurgical specialty. The second pair of questions relates to optimal use of resources. With modern transportation, any specialized service is available to any patient. It is not a question of access, but one of convenience. The price paid for convenience must come from something else. It is the board's job to weigh when having an expensive service in town is worth the convenience, and to select the profile of services that best meets the community's desires and resources.

The plan adopted guides the recruitment efforts of the medical staff and the executive. The best organizations always recruit, recognizing that the first step to effective medical staff relations and to quality of medical care is to attract good doctors who are sympathetic with the mission and vision. Being competitive in recruitment usually requires significant financial investments. Doctors are financially assisted in a variety of ways at various times in their careers. Funds for this support become part of the financial plan and are approved by the board as part of the recruitment plan.

Annual Appointment of Physicians

Good practice now limits the appointment of each physician to a 12-month term. Appointment includes privileges to treat patients which are limited to the physician's demonstrated areas of competence. Annual reappointment follows a review of all areas of contribution to the hospital's goals, but the emphasis is on the quality of care given individual patients. (Hospitals owned by governments must appoint any licensed physician but may restrict privileges based upon competence.[14] Certain states have similar requirements on HMO participation, called "willing provider" laws.[15])

The board role is the final review and reappointment. The board should assure itself that review has been appropriately thorough on grounds of quality, but also that it has followed due process. Due process means adherence to the hospital's own bylaws, assurance of adequate supporting facilities and trained personnel, avoidance of discrimination based upon race, age, sex, or (in most cases) religion, and avoidance of restraint of trade.

Appointment of Medical Staff Leadership

Medical staffs are organized according to the various specialties. Each specialty (or group of similar specialties comprising an adequate number) has a leader and reports upward through a formal hierarchy. Medical staff leaders play an increasingly direct role in assessment and control of quality. Through risk management, utilization review, and outcomes quality concerns, sophisticated information systems are being developed. One role of staff leaders, for which they may be held accountable, is the setting and achieving of expectations on these measures.

At the same time, the medical staff organization can be viewed as a collective bargaining organization for doctors. From that perspective, the best leader may be the person who represents the doctors' viewpoint best. Thus members of the medical staff and the board may disagree not only on the specific people who should lead, but also on the criteria for leadership. In practice, successful organizations resolve this disagreement in two ways. They seek people who meet both criteria (and there are usually many), and they identify other opportunities for representation of and communication with the medical staff. Boards of successful organizations have steadily increased their influence in selecting medical staff leadership within this framework: many key clinical leaders are appointed by the board, serve at the board's pleasure rather than for a fixed term, and are employed by the hospital for this service. Boards must rely on the CEO and previously appointed leadership to ensure that well-qualified nominees arise from the medical staff, but board approval increases the authority of medical staff leaders and protects against misuse.

5. Monitor Performance against Plans and Budgets

The well-managed health care organization is future-oriented. It stresses discussion and agreement about future events, expressed in scenarios, plans, guidelines, and expectations, and works on the theory that carefully developed agreements about what *should* be done *will* be done. Monitoring becomes principally an activity to find insights for the next round of future agreements. The board's monitor role in that context is built into the annual environmental assessment, identifying the gaps between actual and desired that should be priorities for action. Only rarely is it necessary to correct or discipline, activities which are inherently historically oriented.

Two traditional monitoring functions remain important. The first is routine surveillance of performance data to detect unacceptably severe departures from plan. The second is acceptance of reports from outside agencies.

The board should routinely survey data reflecting the performance of the organization against its expectations. The measures used are discussed below in "Measures of Board Effectiveness." The norm is that the expectations will be met. When variations occur, it is important to give management the time and freedom to correct them. Board entry should not occur unless the variation is drastic, or it has gone on for several periods. Even then the first question is, What does the executive plan to do about the variation? Anything else draws the board into details of management it is not equipped to handle. Worse, it draws the board away from the future-oriented tasks it can do better than any other part of the organization.

Several outside agencies monitor performance from a public perspective, and report directly to the board. The most important are the financial auditor and the Joint Commission on Accreditation of Healthcare Organizations. The financial auditor attests that the accounting practices followed by the organization are sound, and that the financial reports fairly represent the state of the business. A **management letter** is directed to a board level officer. It points out real or potential problems which might impair either of these two statements in the future. The management letter is the board's best protection against misrepresentation, fraud or misappropriation of funds by employees. The JCAHO reviews the medical staff process and other elements of the hospital promoting quality of care. Its recent emphasis has been upon identifying specific measures of quality and productivity useful in improving performance in the various areas of hospitals. As of 1994, JCAHO accredits the components of integrated health care organizations—hospitals, mental hospitals, ambulatory surgical facilities, long-term care and rehabilitation units—rather than the parent organizations.[16]

These are activities designed as much to prevent misdoing as to detect it. Many boards establish an Audit Committee to receive and review such reports. Well-managed organizations expect "clean" reports; exceptions must be treated in proportion to their seriousness.

Resource Distribution Functions of the Board

The list of board functions can be lengthened by adding duties otherwise assigned to the executive, but more fruitfully by adopting different perspectives on the board's role. Alexander has argued that the five functions above represent a managerial perspective on board function. An alternative perspective sees the board not as a strategically-oriented body, but as a "political arena wherein competing interest groups vie for control of resources." Under such a model, "the satisfaction of critical constituencies such as the medical staff management and the community in terms of their involvement in the resource allocation process, becomes a more appropriate effectiveness outcome."[17]

Board Members as Interest Group Spokespersons

If board members are viewed as resource distributors, questions of equity of expenditures are highlighted vis à vis questions of patient service. Most of the organization's expenditures are income to various members of the community. The structure of the board relative to the socio-economic character of the community becomes important. Physician, supplier, and employee representation must be considered. The issues here are complex. Without question, the health care organization represents an important economic resource to the community. In many communities it will be among the largest employers, and a large share of its income will come from outside the community (see Chapter 2).

There is much about this model which is realistic and important. Distributional equity is a matter of constant concern, and politics is chiefly devoted to it. In health care it clearly takes two forms—who gets the care itself, and who gets the income generated by it.[18] Relocating a hospital to the suburbs makes care more accessible to the rich, and less to the poor. For the large number of low-income workers, it also means more travel time and costs, more work for less pay. Similarly, an emphasis on high-tech specialties moves both income and service away from the pressing needs of the disadvantaged, toward the more marginal ones of the wealthy. (The income of some specialist physicians is more than 20 times minimum wage).

From a resource distribution perspective, health care organizations are clearly suspect. Most board memberships are heavily weighted toward higher social strata. Physician members automatically represent the highest income group in health care, and nonphysicians tend to be drawn from corporate executives.[19] They are chosen for their exceptional skill at the managerial functions, and skillful people in U.S. society almost always earn comfortable incomes. If they exploit their position, they will pull resources toward the "haves," away from the "have-nots."

Accommodating the Political Model

Well-managed health care organizations use three strategies to accommodate the realities of the political model.

1. *Reliance on open systems and community-based strategic management theory.* One problem with the resource distribution model is its emphasis on distribution. It is clear that equity in dividing the pie is not the only factor determining how big a piece each group gets. The size of the pie is also important. Open systems and strategic management suggest that the better managed the institution is, the greater the rewards in total. If my slice of pie is enough for me, I will be less concerned with somebody else's piece. What supports the continued appointment of corporate executives and physicians to governing boards is their ability to make the organization successful.

2. *Deliberate identification and correction of dissatisfaction.* Well-managed organizations deliberately monitor satisfaction of all social groups. Patient and family satisfaction measures can easily be stratified by proxies for social class. Employee satisfaction can be monitored by skill and income level. Spokespersons from disadvantaged groups can be added to the board itself. Focus groups can explore attitudes of specific groups in depth. Specific problems can be identified and corrected. Strategies can be developed which deliberately redress important inequities. Affirmative action programs in employment, and community clinics for care of the poor are examples. These targeted programs can have striking results, and win considerable support.[20]

3. *A commitment to Samaritanism.* The underlying motive of Samaritanism is important here. It implies, as Franklin did (see Chapter 2), a universal, rather than a class, concern. These programs can easily deteriorate to tokenism or be ignored if that motive is allowed to die out. It is often the task of individual leaders, particularly including the chair and the CEO, to make sure Samaritanism and equity get appropriate attention.

Resource Contribution Functions of the Governing Board

Yet a third perspective views board members as contributors of resources to the organization. This is in contrast to Alexander's perspective, which views the organization as a source of resources. The resource-contributor model emphasizes the funds or services the board members may donate, or the influence they can bring to bear on critical external relations. Naming the richest family in town to the board, or the mayor's spouse, are examples of resource-contributor approaches. So is the appointment of a leading lawyer in the hope of reduced legal fees. There is evidence that organizations that can gain support from various parts of their communities do better than those that cannot.[21]

Board Members as Resource Contributors

If board members are viewed as resource contributors, three functions must be added to the initial list. Although each of the additional functions has merit and many board members perform them well, they have to be ranked as less important than the five decision-making functions. Among the three, board members as influentials is probably the most important.

1. *Board members as influentials.* Open systems theory holds that the board represents access to resources the hospital must acquire in order to succeed. Thus, board members must know people who

can give large sums of money, have entry to political offices where the hospital can be helped or hurt, and be able to speak for the hospital at other centers of community power, such as the boards of major employers. In short, board members are influential people who use their influence to help the hospital achieve its mission.

2. *Board members as figureheads and donors.* Board members are expected to exhibit loyalty to their organization and to speak well of it whenever possible. In that sense, all board members participate in public relations. Some individuals are so well known that the use of their names is in itself an endorsement; thus their first service to the hospital is simply the lending of their names. Similarly, some board members can afford to make major gifts to the hospital.

3. *Board members as specialists.* A slightly different theory of resource contribution holds that board members are selected for their particular skills—in law, finance, medicine, and so on. Such people are expected to contribute their professional perspectives to board deliberations rather than or in addition to a general understanding of community needs and values and broad experience making complex decisions.

Accommodating Resource Contribution Perspectives

The resource-oriented perspectives obviously have both theoretical merit and practical application. Many board members are in fact selected because they can contribute and others are chosen to represent differing perspectives in the community.

The theoretical case against the resource perspectives is simple: the five managerial functions are more important. Influence and resources should come from success of the organization, not be borrowed from board members. If the organization is managed well, it won't need to solicit help; if it is not, no amount of help will matter.

The theory seems to be correct in general, but not necessarily in the specifics. Organizations that are diligent at environmental assessment and strategic planning tend to identify specific resources which they can gain by selective board representation. Thus some members are selected because they have the ability to deliver a critical resource. Resource contribution becomes a secondary criterion of membership.

Membership

The capability of the board of directors or trustees may be the central factor in a health care organization's success or failure. Well-qualified boards tend to make more effective decisions, and they encounter less difficulty when they present their case to others in the community. They attract well-qualified hospital executives and doctors, as well as other well-qualified board members. Thus success feeds upon itself.

The issue of board membership is a continuing search for qualified, interested members, followed by ongoing programs to help those members make the biggest possible contribution. This section discusses board selection criteria, selection processes, compensation, education and support. It also addresses two special issues of membership: conflicts of interest for board members, and roles for doctors and CEOs on boards.

Membership Criteria

Skill and Character Criteria

The first criterion for board membership should be ability to carry out the five managerial functions. If the board is well chosen by this criterion, the community will have a health care organization closely tailored to its needs and wants. Without question, such excellent organizations exist. Their doctors and managers are capable, and their board members bring to each meeting good judgment based upon an acute sense of the directions the community as a whole would feel were appropriate. What characteristics predict these critical skills?

- *Familiarity with the community.* The raison d'être of community boards is their ability to relate health care decisions to local conditions. This means insight into how much money the community should pay for care, how to recruit professionals to the community, how to attract volunteers and donations, how to make community members feel comfortable in their organization, and how to influence local opinion and leadership. Most communities are comprised of many different groups whose views on these questions differ. A board can accommodate differing viewpoints both by having representatives of different groups as members and by having members whose grasp includes the diversity of the community. Desirable board members are those whose understandings transcend their own sex, race, and social group. (See the discussion of the representation criterion below.)
- *Familiarity with business decisions.* Most board decisions are multimillion-dollar commitments. They are measured and described in business terms. Health care organizations are part of the commerce of the community and therefore must communicate in the common languages of accounting, business law, finance, and marketing. Techniques for evaluating decisions use these

languages and incorporate increasingly sophisticated forecasting and statistical analyses. The hospital board room, like other board rooms, is a place where technical language is frequently used to communicate complex concepts. Thus board members need to be familiar with the languages and styles used to make these decisions.

There is also an emotional component to multimillion-dollar decisions. Although concepts from household management are important, and householders can make excellent board members, moving from hundred-dollar decisions to million-dollar decisions takes some practice. Both for familiarity with the languages and for psychological preparation, previous experience at decision making is important.

- *A record of success.* Candid managers will confess that selecting people for any job is difficult, and selecting them for jobs like board membership is exceptionally risky. The best predictor is a record of success. More important than general experience or formal education is how well the person has done on similar assignments. This indicator is important after the individual has joined the board, as well. Becoming familiar with the community and with business decisions takes both time and access to opportunity, so boards selected solely on those criteria will be heavily middle-class and middle-aged. They will tend to bring the prejudices of their group with them.

  Effective members should be promoted to higher board offices. Reliance on achievement is a way of overcoming biases in selecting board officers. Objective criteria open opportunities for capable females and members of minority groups.

- *Reputation.* The general reputation or character of an individual is important in two senses. First, like the record of success, it is an indication of what the individual will do in the future. Second, it serves to enhance the credibility of the individual. Persons with reputations for probity frequently gain influence because of that reputation. What they say is received more positively. Boards have a legal obligation for prudence. The appointment of people whose reputation is suspect could be construed as imprudent.

Representation Criteria

Representation criteria stem from the resource distribution functions of the board. As noted above, these functions are important. By law and tradition, the health care organization is an institution for persons of all races, creeds, and incomes. Many people support the political argument that only a member of a certain constituency can understand truly how the hospital treats that group. And constituencies are usually pleased by recognition at the board level. They believe a good board should have representation from women, the poor, important ethnic groups, labor, and so forth. The concept of representation can be extended to include hospital employees, doctors, religious bodies involved in ownership, and other groups.

Several caveats must be attached to the representation criterion. Most important is that representatives who lack the necessary skills and character are unlikely to help either their constituency or the community at large. Second, the board acts *by* consensus *for* the community as a whole. The concept of resource distribution tends to foster adversarial positions and compromise instead of consensus—and the compromise process may be inferior to consensus. Third is the problem of tokenism. A seat on a board, particularly a single seat, does not necessarily mean influence in the decisions. Finally, the appointment itself changes the individual. The lessons of the board room are not available to their constituents, and over a period of time, the board members are coopted from the view for which they were selected. Tokenism and co-optation can be deliberate adversarial strategies to diminish a group's influence.

Affirmative action to ensure that competent individuals are not excluded from board membership is encouraged under the law and seems likely to make organizations more successful. A balance can best be struck if two points are kept in mind:

1. Board members are appointed as individuals, not as representatives. They should be competent to serve in their own right, regardless of their position in the community.
2. Board members act on behalf of the community as a whole. This does not rule out special considerations of groups with unusual needs, but it places those considerations in a context—they are appropriate to the extent that they improve the community as a whole.

Selection Processes

Selecting board members involves issues of eligibility, terms, offices, committees, and the size of the board as well as the actual choice of individuals. Officers and committee chairs have more power than individual members, so their selection is equally important.

Appointment to Membership and Office

Most health care organizations have **self-perpetuating boards**. That is, the board itself selects new members and successors. Other methods include election by stockholders, the prescribed procedure in stock corporations, and election by members of the corporation who sometimes are simply interested members of the community. Boards of government institutions are frequently appointed by supporting jurisdictions or, rarely, through popular votes. Boards of subsidiaries in multicorporate systems are usually appointed by the parent corporation, with local nomination or advice. Boards generally elect their own officers. In addition to the officers, there are a number of committee members and chairs to be appointed, a job usually left to the chair, but sometimes subject to discussion or approval.

Role of the Nominating Committee

Nominees are usually asked beforehand if they will serve, and the best candidates frequently must be convinced. Keeping the job within limits that make it attractive is an important consideration. On most boards and similar social structures, truly contested elections and overt campaigning are rare. Many organizations nominate only one slate for boards and board offices. The existence of formal provisions for write-in candidates and nominations from the floor is an important safeguard in the corporate structure. They are rarely utilized. In the normal course of events, selection occurs in the **nominating committee**. The committee often proposes not only board members, but also corporate and board officers and occasionally chairs of standing committees.

The nominating committee is usually a standing committee with membership at least partially determined by the bylaws. It is common to put former officers on the nominating committee. Such a strategy emphasizes continuation of the status quo in the organization, so organizations wishing fresh ideas broaden nominating committee membership and charge it with searching more widely for nominees. It is typically in the confidential discussions of the nominating committee that individuals are suggested or overlooked, compared against criteria, and accepted or rejected. This makes the nominating committee one of the most powerful groups in an organization. Sophisticated leaders generally seek membership in it, or at least a voice in it. A key test of power in an organization is, who nominates the nominating committee? While the formal answer may be found in the corporate bylaws, the real answer reveals the most influential people in a well-run organization.

Size, Eligibility, and Length of Terms

The number of nominations to be made each year is a function of the number of board members and the length of their terms. There is little consensus on these issues. Board sizes range from a handful to a hundred, although between 10 and 20 members are most common.[22] The size of not-for-profit hospital boards has dropped,[23] although perhaps not as much as the demands for downsizing to make the board more efficient would suggest.[24] Terms are generally three or four years, and there are usually limits on the number of terms which can be served successively. Lengthy terms or unlimited renewal of terms can lead to stagnation; it is difficult for the nominating committee to pass over a faithful member who wants to serve another term unless the rules forbid it. Terms that are too short reduce the experience of officers as well as members. (It is possible to allow officers to extend their service beyond the normal limits.) Inexperienced officers rely more heavily on CEOs, thereby increasing their power, but the entire board is more prone to error because of its inexperience.

If there are 15 members, three-year terms, and a two-term limit, there will be five nominations each year, but many of these will be pro forma nominations for second terms. Only two or three new people will be added in most years. The median experience of board members will be about three years. (Some members will not serve two terms, of course.)

In addition to a length-of-service eligibility limit, many organizations have eligibility clauses related to the owning corporation. For-profit boards can require stock ownership. Church-sponsored organizations, even when they are operated as secular community institutions, can require that board members be from the religious group. Some government and voluntary not-for-profit institutions require residence in the political jurisdiction for board membership. Other eligibility clauses include phrases like "good moral character," although so much judgment is implied that they are more selection than eligibility criteria.

Compensation

Board compensation is rare among leading health care organizations. About 20 percent of all nongovernment hospitals compensate members. For-profit and not-for-profit hospitals do not differ; about one-third of government hospitals provide compensation. The dominant form of compensation is a per-meeting fee, apparently to cover costs of attending. Although there has been discussion of the importance of compensation to attract members and to allow lower-income participants,[25] the concept has not spread. Rates of compensation declined between 1985 and 1989.[26]

The rewards for serving on health care organization boards are complex. They include the satisfaction of a Samaritan need, pride in professional achievement, public recognition, association with community leaders, and some commercial opportunities which relate indirectly to recognition and association. They do not include significant direct financial reward. People serve on health care organization boards because they want to, because they enjoy the work.

Education and Support for Board Members

Successful organizations have both formal and informal programs for the education of board members. Even if new members meet the selection criteria perfectly, there are several unique aspects of health care management in general that they should be taught. There are also issues unique to the particular institution. While new members should bring fresh perspectives, they should not operate in ignorance of history. Evidence from California voluntary hospital boards shows that educated boards achieve greater financial success.[27]

Formal programs are limited principally by the time available to incoming members. They include tours, introductions to key personnel, conveyance of written documents and texts, and planned conversations and presentations. A typical list of subjects is shown in Figure 3.8.

To be effective, formal programs for board members should follow certain rules. Brevity is essential. Small segments should be scheduled for each specific topic. Most important, the member should be a participant. Questions should be encouraged, the style should be conversational, and the discussion should be extended over several sessions.

Most of the education board members receive is on the job. Well-organized boards make committee appointments carefully, allowing new members to become acquainted with the organization in less demanding assignments. They fill chairs with experienced members. They use chairs and organization executives to help members learn as they serve. The three critical committees, executive, finance, and long-range planning, should be composed of the more seasoned board members, and their chairs should be members nearing the end of service. The nominating committee is frequently the last service of a board member.

Board members are supported by the executive, who has responsibility for developing facts and arguments about issues, making recommendations, answering questions, and achieving expectations. In a larger organization, a substantial staff is committed to this work. The board member of a well-managed organization can expect accurate, thorough documentation and a reliable discussion of the alternatives as background for most important issues.

Board members can be sued as individuals, although such suits are rare. They are technically liable for failing to take due care, for deliberate self-serving, and for unnecessarily risky behavior. By definition, these events cannot occur in well-managed institutions, and they

Figure 3.8 Outline for Orientation of Trustees

Mission, Role, and History of Health Care Organizations
Difference between for-profit, not-for-profit, and government ownership
What health care organizations give to the community

How Health Care Organizations are Financed
Operating funds
    Private insurance
    Government insurance
    Uninsured patients
Capital funds
    Donations
    Use of earned surplus
    Sources of long-term debt

Health Care Organizations–Physician Relations
Nature of contract between doctors and health care organizations
Concept of peer review
Trustee responsibilities for the medical staff
    Approving bylaws
    Annual appointments
    Maintaining communication with the medical staff
        Need for communication
        Why communication should go through channels

Duties of Trustees
Appoint the CEO
Approve the long-range plan
Approve the annual budget
Appoint the medical staff
Monitor performance

Legal Issues in Trusteeship
Trustee liability
Trustee compensation
Conflict of interest

are very rare. The corporation should maintain directors' and officers' liability insurance, which provides legal and financial assistance against suits which might be placed.

Special Issues of Board Membership

Three issues of board membership have become prominent in many communities. They are issues on which there is room for substantial difference of opinion, but in each case a national consensus appears to be emerging. The latter two, doctor and CEO membership on boards, are philosophically related to the first, conflict of interest.

Conflict of Interest

The law and society assume that members of governing boards are serving on behalf of owners and that they should not serve when their personal interests conflict with the owners'. Conceptually, this is clear enough. In practice, difficulties crop up quickly. The local banker meets all other criteria for board membership—should the community deny the bank the profits of the organization account, or deny itself the benefit of the banker's volunteered service? The mayor's wife is knowledgeable, popular, and successful. It happens that she and her husband own a tract of land critical to the organization's future expansion. Should she be invited to serve on the board?

Unfortunately, the criteria for board membership make it likely that situations analogous to these will arise frequently. It is hard to find people who meet the skill, character, and influence criteria but have not also become involved in activities that eventually will conflict. Most board members will themselves have analogous conflicts. They would tend to invite these individuals to serve. Those who want broader representation on health care organization boards would disagree. The banks and the powerful are represented too well, and the poor and the disadvantaged are overlooked, they feel. One way to advance their cause is to argue that people serving on boards should be free of identifiable conflict. They would say the banker and the mayor's wife should not serve on the board. At its heart, this is often a special-interest position, the special interest being the poor or some other identifiable group.

Conflict of interest is inherent in any democratic structure, and it cannot be permanently resolved. (Totalitarian structures resolve it by giving the rulers special rights.) Law and good practice allow persons with conflicts to serve, but require that potential conflicts of interest be recognized, and that the individual not participate in the specific decision where a conflict may exist. Well-run boards solicit a list of each member's major activities and holdings annually, and make the list available for inspection. Individuals are expected to disqualify themselves, but they may be encouraged to do so by the chair or another member. Most organizations find practical solutions to the selection problem on a case-by-case basis, judging whether the benefits to the community outweigh the possible cost of self-interest. Individuals with such extensive conflicts that their service to the organization would be impaired are not appointed.

CEO Membership

The CEO is always an active participant in board deliberations of well-managed health care organizations. Because their principal livelihood is from employment at the organization, most CEOs have fundamental conflicts of interest in serving on the board. The conflict is particularly apparent when possibilities for merger or closure of the institution are considered. It also occurs when other employees or doctors present grievances against the CEO. Although less obvious, CEOs can influence the board by controlling the information it receives, (including the minutes) and by their role in suggesting the agenda.

Most hospital boards make the CEO an *ex officio* member, and there has been a steady trend toward giving them the right to vote.[28] In some cases, they hold prominent offices, such as chair of the executive committee or president of the corporation. The justification lies in the same rule governing other conflicts, that the community's potential benefit exceeds its potential loss. It appears to be correct; organizations which deeply involve the CEO in strategic decisions seem to succeed.

Physician Membership

Physicians practicing at the health care organization, also have clear conflicts of interest. The national consensus, however, is even clearer for physician than for CEO board membership; in fact, the JCAHO recommends it. There is empirical evidence that hospitals which have physicians in board roles have better mortality and morbidity performance, that is, their scores on important measures of quality of care are superior.[29] The arguments generally cited in support of physician membership involve representation. The board needs to hear the viewpoint of doctors, and doctors need to know their views are being expressed. It is sometimes argued that the board needs the expertise of doctors (their knowledge, as opposed to their viewpoint). This argument is dubious, because a board can and does invite any experts it requires into its deliberations.

As in other cases of special-interest representation, a health care organization may face serious competitive pressures if it does not appoint doctors to its board. Also, there is no clear evidence of harm to the thousands of hospitals that have made such appointments. In many cases, seats are set aside for doctors and nominations solicited from the medical staff. It is not uncommon for the medical staff to elect its representatives to the board. Usually only a few seats are available to doctors, however.[30]

The resolution leaves behind some new problems. One or two doctors cannot reasonably represent the view of all doctors on important issues. Their technical, economic and political views are influenced by their specialties. Family practitioners generally earn more of their income outside the hospital than surgeons, are paid less overall, collect less from health insurance and more from patients directly, and are paid more on the basis of day-to-day services than on episodes of illness. It is unlikely that a surgeon would effectively represent a family practitioner on important board issues, or that any family practitioner would feel reassured being represented by a surgeon. Other mechanisms must still be found to ensure communication across the broad spectrum of medical skills and interests.

Recent developments in medical staff relations (Chapter 12) have raised the possibility of much higher physician representation fractions, approaching 50 per cent. Not-for-profit corporations actively including physicians are subject to three different and often conflicting legal concepts. **Inurement** rules protect against the distribution of assets of a community corporation to individuals or small groups within the community. Regulations for these call for no more than 20 percent physician membership. Antitrust considerations forbid doctors (or other vendors) from collusion in restraint of trade. Independent practitioners (those who are not employed by the organization) cannot use the organization board to further their economic advantage. Medical practice acts in some states forbid "corporate practice of medicine," which can be construed to mean that a majority of the board of any organization employing physicians for direct medical care. Health care organizations seem to be using hierarchies of subsidiary and affiliated corporations to resolve these issues.[31]

The direction for the future is quite clear, but the details are not. Physicians will have a strong decision-making role, up to and including mission and strategy. They will be more prominent on governing boards. How it's done, by voting membership, subsidiaries, committees, will differ between organizations. Most successful organizations will probably use all those devices.

IV Organization of the Board

Board organization involves two major questions—how the governing board of the corporation as a whole organizes to assure effective completion of its functions, and how governance structures are arranged for subsidiaries.

Structure for an Effective Corporate Board

An effective board must be thorough in its environmental assessment, imaginative in its search for solutions, and deliberate in its eventual actions. It must also be timely, responding to issues in a time frame the exchange partners can accept, and efficient, not wasting the time of its own members and other participants in the decision process. Well-managed organizations meet these criteria better than their competition. They do so by a strategy of prioritization, preparation, focus, and delegation. The strategy generates the structure of the board.

Prioritization

A board fails if it mishandles the managerial, resource allocation, or resource distribution functions. These are essential to the boundary-spanning and leadership roles the board alone can fulfill. Ineffective boards fail to set clear missions, or back them with practical plans. They allow political dissatisfaction to fester and grow, rather than dealing with it. The first step in a successful board organization, therefore, is one which assigns priority to these functions.

The managerial functions are generally handled by a permanent calendar. As suggested in Figure 3.9, a systematic annual progression through them will occupy much of the board's available time.

The schedule should not be inflexible. Reports of political dissatisfaction or strategic opportunities will frequently draw the board off schedule, but a well-managed board returns to it rigorously. On the other hand, the calendar encourages the aggregation of similar and interrelated topics. One response to any proposed agenda item is: "Would that fit well into our forthcoming discussion on _____? Is there anything we should do to prepare for a discussion then?"

The actual agenda management falls heavily to board chair and CEO. Both topics and allotted time are developed in advance. Specific outcomes of board discussion are identified. These include action, delegation to committee, discussion and clarification, and information. Informing the board about issues under discussion is a critical part of the political process; a group can only defend its rights when it knows the issues.

Preparation

CEOs and their staffs are responsible for preparing appropriate backup for every agenda item. They have heavy responsibility for the environmental assessment and ongoing surveillance of the environment, for identifying issues, for analysis and development of proposals, and for understanding the needs of the community. Staff are also used extensively in disputes, both to gather and disseminate facts and to negotiate or eliminate conflicts. The CEO may be criticized for failing to identify an issue in time for appropriate action, for failing to develop the background properly, and for failing to identify potential conflict.

Figure 3.9 Calendar for Managerial Functions of Governing Boards

Quarter	Activity	Involvement
1*	Final review of performance	Finance, whole
	Executive review and compensation	Compensation
	Medical staff leadership appointments	Medical staff, executive staff
	Special projects assigned to ad hoc committees	Planning, ad hoc
	Matters arising	As indicated
2	Audit committee report	Audit, whole
	Monitor performance to date	Finance
	Environmental assessment	Planning, executive staff
	Review of strategic plans	Planning, executive staff
	Reports from special projects	Ad hoc, planning
	Initial update of long-range financial plan	Finance
	Matters arising	As indicated
3	Annual review of mission, vision, strategic plans, long-range plans	Whole plus guests
	Monitor performance to date	Finance
	Revise long-range financial plan	Finance, whole
	Establish budget guidelines	Finance, whole
	Matters arising	As indicated
4	Monitor performance to date	Finance
	Nominations for coming year	Nominations, whole
	Approve final budget	Finance, whole
	Matters arising	As indicated

*Quarters start with fiscal year.

The other aspect to preparation is general rather than specific to the issues at hand. Most issues take meaning from context; the better the environment and the usual processes are understood, the better the specific decision is likely to be. Thus, board selection and education are important preparation. Well-managed boards pursue these matters diligently. In addition, they are careful to balance the importance of the issue to the team managing it. They frequently pair inexperienced and experienced members to facilitate on-the-job learning.

Focus

Somewhat different from the issue of prioritization, successful boards focus on major issues one at a time, attempting to comprehend all aspects of the single issue and reach a consensus understanding of it. Such an understanding is prelude to an effective decision; even if a minority is opposed to the final outcome, they understand the logic that determined it and are convinced that the process was appropriate.

Retreats are effective as devices to focus board attention. They can be held in comfortable off-site settings, emphasizing the departure from usual practice. Longer sessions allow fuller presentation of issues and background. Additional representatives of medical staff and management can be invited, facilitating understanding, acceptance, and implementation of the final decision. Consultants and guests from the community can be used to expand knowledge of factual and political issues.

Delegation

Successful institutions are delegating more and better, to gain the benefits of broader intelligence, participation, and political consensus. Board committees serve several functions. They prioritize by weighing the importance of various issues, identifying interrelationships and combining or separating issues, and dispensing with issues which do not require full board attention. They prepare by fact-finding and educating board members and others with special interests. They focus by developing an expertise in a given area, such as finance. They often expand representation, routinely including staff not invited to the board itself. They solicit and evaluate differing political perspectives, a job employed staff may find difficult. Finally, they can take on especially sensitive issues, such as medical staff membership, compensation, nomination, and auditing, in a more discreet setting.

Well-managed boards delegate routinely to standing finance, planning, compensation, audit, and nominations committees as shown in Figure 3.10. The use of an executive committee appears to be diminishing. Boards have become smaller, making routine use of an executive committee unnecessary. The overall tendency is toward a small, active board, with a few important standing committees and heavy reliance on ad hoc committees.

Beyond the few standing committees, well-managed boards use ad hoc committees, formed as appropriate to the issue at hand. This results in an *accountable delegation,* deliberately passing authority down to the lowest relevant level, using broad representation and clear goals or acceptable solution parameters. "Accountable" protects the right to have one's view heard if necessary. Stakeholders understand that they have a reliable mechanism to a fair hearing on any question, at their discretion. "Delegation" assigns decisions to the people most important

Figure 3.10 Typical Standing Committees of the Governing Board

Committee	Function	Membership
Finance	Long-range financial plan, debt structure, initial budget guidelines, monitor budget performance	Treasurer, chief financial officer, potential future chairs
Planning	Environmental assessment, strategic plans, long-range plans	Chief planning officer, potential future chairs, medical staff representatives
Compensation	Review executive performance, award increases and bonuses	Officers, former officers
Audit	Review financial audit, JCAHO audit	Officers, former officers, medical staff representatives
Nominations	Nominate new board members, board officers	Senior board officers

to their implementation. Within accountability limits, delegation is complete. The boundaries of an acceptable decision are established in advance, and decisions within the boundaries are accepted without debate. The decisions are not "micro managed" by meddling or ritualistic reviews. The committee receiving the delegation knows it must produce a solution within the parameters if possible, and report back for further instructions if it cannot.[32] An effort is made to limit the number of committee levels. Ad hoc committees can report to standing committees or the board as a whole; they should not report to each other. A given issue should go through no more than one ad hoc committee.

Subsidiary Boards and Their Roles

The original concept of a governing board was of the ultimate authority for an independent corporate unit. The managerial and resource functions identified above derive from that concept. They must be referred to the most central level to be properly coordinated. The nature of hierarchical organizations is such that one can affiliate several such units, and establish governance functions for the affiliates, setting up boards which report to boards. For example, a health care organization which operated two hospitals, a medical group practice, and a health insurance company as subsidiaries would have to have at least one board, as shown in Figure 3.11A over the whole organization, but it might have five, four, or three, as shown in Figure 3.11B–3.11D.

Subsidiary boards make three contributions that have made them popular in regional health care organizations.

1. They expand geographic representation, allowing local preferences to be reflected in operating decisions and local leaders to retain a sense of influence over their institution.

2. They expand the time and resources important to manage complex ventures like health maintenance organizations more effectively, permitting the appointment of outside specialists, and also

Figure 3.11 Board Possibilites for a Multi-Unit Health Care Organization

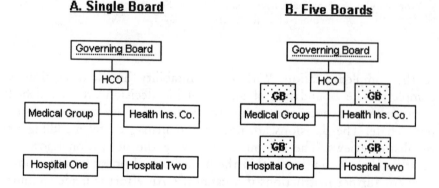

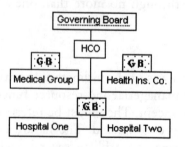

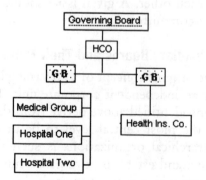

recognition of inside operating executives who would normally have board access if their corporation were freestanding.

3. They permit joint ventures with other corporations and partnerships with the medical staff.
4. They allow identification of taxable endeavors and protect the exemption of activities qualifying under the Internal Revenue Code.

Subsidiary boards operate under the concepts of "reserved powers" and "accountability." **Reserved powers** are held permanently by the corporate board. They include enough specific power to make sure the subsidiary continues to follow the mission and vision, and to resolve conflicts between subsidiaries. These usually include the rights to buy or sell other corporations and real estate; issue stock or debt; approve long-range plans, financial plans, and budgets; appoint or approve board members and the chief executive, and approve bylaws. Within the limits imposed by reserved powers and accountable delegation, subsidiary boards tend to work as corporate boards do. They carry out the managerial and resource-related functions for their organization, making recommendations to the parent board on the reserved matters.

Figure 3.12 shows the board structure of Henry Ford Health System. The several boards allow several dozen people to participate in the activity of the corporation, which serves about 20 percent of the metropolitan Detroit market of 4.5 million people. It is sufficiently flexible to allow the System to participate in a variety of partnership activities with several other large health care providers and insurers in the area, as well as to operate health care organizations oriented to specific local communities and reflecting their histories and preferences.

Alliances and Affiliations

The search for sufficient scale of operations and the ability to address specific problems has led to a variety of organization forms short of parent-subsidiary relationships. These are called alliances, and are implemented in general by contracts, rather than corporate charters or bylaws. The distinction is less a matter of corporate form than of the strength of the reserved powers. Alliances have inherent difficulties which appear to make them unstable. They must continually balance local with common needs, and they expend some energies in that process which more centralized forms can avoid.[33] Despite their limitations, they are popular devices to achieve lower prices on purchased supplies, provide certain services that are easily supplied to remote geographical areas, represent similar organization in state and national lobbying,

Figure 3.12 Henry Ford Health System Governance Structure

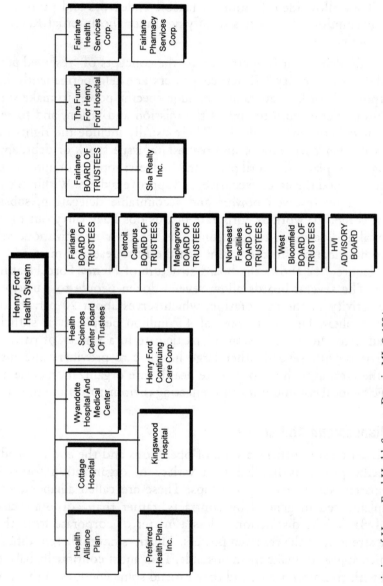

Used with permission of Henry Ford Health System, Detroit, MI. © 1994.

and negotiate contracts with national and regional health insurance providers. About 1,300 institutions are affiliated with the two largest alliances, Voluntary Hospitals of America and Premier Alliance. Over 2,900 hospitals belong to alliances in total.[34]

Regional affiliations are also popular. They provide opportunities to market health insurance to companies with regional distribution of workers and to arrange comprehensive coverage of services under managed care insurance. Large teaching hospitals in central urban areas affiliate with suburban and more remote institutions. The affiliation formalizes referral relationships, providing convenient specialty services to the hinterland and higher volumes to the central institution. Affiliations between regional systems and insurance carriers are becoming more common. These amount to contracts specifying cost, quality, and volumes health care organizations are expected to provide. The carriers handle subscriber services and marketing.

It is important to understand competition, even in hotly contested local markets, as a form of cooperation. For health care, competition is regulated by federal and state law, which generally encourages rivalry to win customers under specified conditions such as licensure, fair advertising, and avoidance of collusion or discrimination. The law permits a variety of kinds of collaboration. Health care organizations are learning to exploit both aspects of regulated markets. Thus, they can and do compete and collaborate with each other simultaneously. In Detroit, for example, Henry Ford Health System, Mercy Health Services and Blue Cross–Blue Shield of Michigan formed a "Community Care Partnership" to offer an advanced form of HMO insurance. They compete steadily in other lines of business, but Henry Ford and Mercy also operate two hospitals in a joint venture. It is probably true that in the long run these arrangements are unstable, but they are none the less real while they exist, which is already a period of several years. They are formed because they offer routes to market advantages which are more practical than other available alternatives.

Measures of Board Effectiveness

The board is to a large extent self-governing. Other than financial audits and inspection by licensing and accrediting agencies, there is no routine surveillance. It is therefore incumbent upon the board to have a rigorous program of self-assessment. The essential question in assessing the board's performance is whether owners' wants have been satisfied as well as other realistic alternatives would permit. The board's performance is the corporation's performance. When the corporation

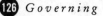

is for-profit, performance is the long-term potential profit. When the owner is the community at large, as is the case for not-for-profit corporations, performance is measured in terms of the effectiveness of the interaction between the organization and its exchange partners. Conceptually, the health care organization must find the balance equitably satisfying all. Realistically, such a balance is as hard to measure as it is to achieve. The first step is to understand the kinds of measurement necessary. As Kaplan and Norton have noted, these go well beyond simply accounting and financial reports, even for for-profit firms.[35]

Scope of Corporate Performance

Following the multidimensional concepts introduced by Kaplan and Norton restated in health care terms, one might begin with four major categories of satisfaction measures. Figure 3.13 shows several different measures of satisfaction, reflecting differences in their meaning to different stakeholders. The goal of board reporting is to cover all influential perspectives, so that no important perspective goes unreported. The omission of a perspective is potentially destructive, but the list of numbers should be as short as comprehensive coverage permits. The categories and labels are not likely to be critical so long as everything is reported and understood. It is frequently useful to present the values graphically to allow quick detection of changes, successes and potential problems.

Profit, market share, cost, and staffing, the first-listed measures in each category of Figure 3.13, are direct reflections of the acceptability of the organization to important stakeholders. While these constitute an acid test of the exchange relationships, they also may be slow and insensitive to important changes occurring in the environment. Additional measures are used to provide more diagnostic information on stakeholder demands, and to improve the speed of response. Put another way, by the time profit, market share, cost, or staffing shows a clear deterioration, it may be too late.

It is practical to measure many of the Figure 3.13 concepts, and health care organizations are beginning to do so. Figure 3.14 shows the measures in use by the corporate board of Henry Ford Health System, and Figure 3.15 those proposed by Intermountain Health Care.

These reports are designed to give the governing board a current assessment of overall performance. Chapter 9 covers the actual techniques of measurement and the relationships between these global measures and specific ones appropriate to subordinate units.

Figure 3.13 Dimensions of Satisfactory Corporate Performance

Dimension	Major Concepts
Financial performance	Adequate profit to sustain long-term growth or viability Satisfactory credit rating and financial structure
Patient and family satisfaction	Market share Positive responses to unbiased surveys Acceptable levels of positive outcomes Appropriate coverage of specialized and chronic needs Satisfactory access for disadvantaged groups Approval of appropriate regulatory agencies
Buyer satisfaction	Competitive costs of care Satisfactory claims and membership services
Provider satisfaction	Acceptable staffing levels and recruitment success Positive responses to worker and physician surveys

Guidelines for Evaluating Performance

In addition to current reports of values for the measures, the board needs referents or standards by which to evaluate them. There are four conceptual referents, listed here in increasing rigor or difficulty.

1. *Trends.* Last year's value or a time series of several years provides an initial baseline and allows judgment on the direction of the measure.
2. *Competitor and industry comparisons.* What other similar organizations are achieving provides crude guidelines, even if the available information is not strictly from competitors.
3. *Expectations.* A formally developed, agreed-upon expectation of an achievable goal allows integration of trends and comparisons with an analysis and improvement of process. Expectations for many of the measures should arise from the budget process discussed in Chapter 8.
4. *Benchmarks.* "Best practice" is the best value reported by any organization using the measure. The benchmark value may be from an organization entirely different from the governing

Figure 3.14 Henry Ford Health System Balanced Scorecard Performance Measures

1. **External Customer Satisfaction**
   A. Percent of patient dissatisfied or very dissatisfied
   B. Percent of voluntary disenrollment
   C. Access indicators
   D. Physician satisfaction survey
   E. Business attitude evaluation

2. **Clinical Process—Outcomes**
   A. Accreditation and regulatory approvals
   B. Health status (SF-36)
   C. Number of claims and litigations
   D. Patient falls
   E. Nosocomial infection rates
   F. HCFA—derived disease specific-mortality rates

3. **Financial Performance**
   A. Net operating income
   B. Cost/enrollee or cost/case (case-mix adjusted)
   C. Patient days/1,000 members
   D. DRG margin
   E. Bond rating

4. **Philanthropy**
   A. Total donations received (including commitments)
   B. Net philanthropic collections (net of expenses)
   C. Philanthropic expense ratio

5. **Community Dividend**
   A. Uncompensated care
   B. Contribution in voluntary efforts including such activities as community education (man-hours, $ value)

6. **Growth**
   A. Equivalent population served
   B. Market share

7. **Business Strategic Advantage**
   A. Cost leadership
   B. Distribution system
   C. Product offerings
   D. Process improvement teams— accomplishments

8. **Innovation**
   A. Percentage revenue from new products
   B. Percentage revenue from new markets

9. **Internal Customer Satisfaction**
   A. Employee satisfaction surveys
   B. Labor turnover
   C. Diversity goals

10. **Academic (education and research)**
    A. NIH grants received
    B. Total external funding
    C. Resident match results
    D. Student satisfaction with educational programs

Used with permission of Henry Ford Health System, Detroit, MI.

board's, as for example, the standards for financial ratios which are driven by the total bond market, not simply health care bonds, or the health care cost levels of a country with a different system.

Most boards use all four, but well-managed organizations are moving toward expectations and benchmarks.

Figure 3.15 Intermountain Health Care Board Quality
Assessment Report

1994	1Q '94	2Q '94	3Q '94	4Q '94	Yr. Mean
Measures of Clinical Outcomes					
1. Surgical wound infection rate:	1.61%	1.95%	2.09%		1.88%
2. Severe drug reactions	0.02%	0.05%	0.010%		0.03%
3. Returns to surgery	1.13%	0.62%	0.65%		0.80%
4. Mortality (exclude NBs, ER, DOA)	1.75%	1.44%	1.68%		1.62%
5. C-section rate Total	15.36%	15.39%	16.18%		15.64%
Primary	8.67%	8.43%	9.39%		8.83%
6. Readmissions within 30 days	6.89%	2.22%	3.02%		4.04%
Measures of Patient Satisfaction					
Patient perception of:					
7. Service quality, on a scale of 5	4.16	4.18	4.17		4.17
8. Clinical quality, on a scale of 5	4.66	4.68	4.63		4.66
Measures of Financial Outcomes					
9. Net operating income (000s)	$16,290	$11,767	$7,393		$11,817
System Demographics					
10. Inpatient admissions	26,409	24,330	23,874		24,871
11. Outpatient revenues (000s)	$102,734	$107,206	$107,153		$105,698
12. Average length of stay	4.10	3.93	3.79		3.94
13. Case-mix index	1.03	1.00	1.02		1.02

Definitions of Indicators

Measures of Clinical Outcomes

1. Surgical wound infection rate
Centers for Disease Control definitions for incisional surgical site and deep surgical site infections will be used to identify surgical wound infections.

2. Severe adverse drug reactions
A reaction that is life-threatening or contributes to death, or is permanently disabling, and/or requires intensive medical care. Number of adverse drug reactions/patient days.

3. Returns to surgery
Each hospital QM department will report all *unplanned* reopening of an operative site for any surgical patient. Number of unplanned surgical returns/total surgeries.

4. Mortality
Number of deaths/100% inpatient admissions (excluding DOAs and newborns).

Continued

Figure 3.15 Continued

5. C-section rate

Number of C-sections/total deliveries. Data manager will confirm C-section and primary/repeat rates from each hospital, comparing results with data from case-mix system. Number of Primary C-sections/total deliveries.

6. Readmissions within 30 days

All unplanned readmissions within 30 days of discharge/admissions.

7. Patient perception of service quality

Based on 15 questions related to nonclinical aspects of the patient's hospital stay. In computing the service quality scale, individual questions were weighted to reflect their relative importance in the patient's overall perception of hospital quality.

8. Patient perception of clinical quality

Based on four items from the questionnaire that represent different aspects of clinical care. The clinical scale score is the average of these four items.

Measures of Financial Outcomes

9. Net operating income

Net operating income is a traditional measure of overall financial performance. The measure represents net revenue less total expenses. Net operating income is highly dependent on volumes, and does not effectively measure changes in efficiency or utilization.

System Demographics

10. Inpatient admissions

Number of inpatients admitted on all acute medical/surgical, psychiatric and rehabilitation services.

11. Outpatient revenues

Revenues for all outpatient services.

12. Average length of stay

Average of length of stay for all acute medical/surgical, psychiatric and rehabilitation patients.

13. Case-mix index

This measure represents the average case-mix level for all patients. Each case is grouped by DRG. Each DRG has weight relative to other DRGs. The weights were developed based upon actual charge data for all IHC hospitals. The charges for all cases are totaled for a given time period, the average of the total charges is assigned a weight of 1. The sum of the number of cases by DRG multiplied by the weights by DRG is divided by the total number of cases to give the case-mix index. The index starts at 0 and has no upper limit. The scale for IHC hospitals ranges from 0.5 to 2.0. An index of 1 compared to an index of 2 means that a patient with an index of 2 uses twice as many resources as a patient with an index of 1.

Continued

Figure 3.15 Continued

Future Measurements
- Charge/case (adjusted for case mix and rate increases)
- Severity level (CSI)
- Functional status
- Deep vein thrombosis
- Cost per case

Used with permission of Intermountain Health Care.

Annual Performance Review

It is desirable for governing boards to set expectations for themselves on their performance. An annual report on the measures, including historic trends, would provide a basis for setting expectations. The process is likely to be more rigorous and more effective if an effort is made to quantify improvements anticipated in the coming year. Well-managed organizations undertake such reviews with increasingly thorough staff preparation and increasingly specific expectations. Properly, such a review is done at the start of the organization's annual budget cycle. For the annual review, the executive will supplement the measures themselves with a narrative of achievements, departures from plans, and opportunities for the future. Introspective review of this information and other information from environmental surveillance identifies necessary revisions to the mission and long-range plan and identifies the general goals guiding the organization's budget activity.

In well-run organizations, the annual review of board performance, like other monitoring activities, is mostly confirmations of planned progress.

Failures of Governance and Their Prevention

Well-managed organizations encourage board performance by pursuing the time schedules and procedural matters identified in the preceding section and by foreseeing and forestalling difficulties. Despite their best efforts, they occasionally encounter problems; less well run organizations tend to encounter the same kinds of problems more frequently and in more serious forms. There are no easy solutions, but several common causes of these failures can be identified.

Membership Failures

- *Representation.* The views of the board drift toward some groups in the community, such as the current medical staff and board members, or families under age 65, or families with health insurance. Adequate management must represent all the legitimate owners and meet the needs of a sufficient market to permit efficient operation.
- *Judgment.* Because of excessive turnover or poor selection, board members lack the knowledge and experience for their roles.
- *Motivation.* From lack of training or poor selection, board members fail to recognize the seriousness of the decisions.
- *Attendance.* From unrealistic assessment of time commitments, board members, particularly committee chairs, are absent from key meetings.

Structural Failures

- *Overcentralization.* Because there are too few subsidiary boards or effective committees, power becomes concentrated in a small group within the larger body.
- *Overdelegation.* Too many committees debating each question involves so many people that peripheral views get excessive attention and decisions are no longer made expeditiously.
- *Individualism.* Board members forget that their authority derives only from consensus and that they serve all owners rather than a special-interest group. (When board members act as individuals, they automatically become executives; conflict with the appointed executive is an immediate danger.)
- *Insufficient reserved powers.* The balance of power between the subsidiaries or affiliates and the central organization can impair performance. Too much power in the subsidiaries is reflected in conflicts, delays on critical corporatewide decisions, and general loss of market share, provider satisfaction, or profitability.
- *Excessive reserved powers.* Too little power in the subsidiaries is often reflected in some subsidiaries earlier than others, or can be traced to specific actions that were disappointing.

Process Failures

- *Identification of issues.* Critical trends are not identified quickly enough to deal with them satisfactorily. It is the chief executive's obligation to identify critical issues, but a badly managed board can ignore the executive's warning. Board members are also able to identify issues, and the well-managed organization encourages them to do so.

- *Inadequate staff preparation.* The CEO and executive staff fail to present concise, complete descriptions of problems and analysis of facts.
- *Poor control of agenda.* Ineffective management of agendas omits key viewpoints, fails to specify the opinions solicited, or allows committees to delay projects by inaction or by spending excessive time on less critical functions.
- *Repetition.* The board unnecessarily recapitulates debates and decisions of subcommittees and subsidiaries.

Well-managed organizations devote considerable attention to preventing these kinds of problems and to containing them when they occur. Troublefree performance is an ideal, achieved only by rigorous attention from the chief executive and the board leadership. The various difficulties and their corrections are interrelated. If motivation is weak, an extra effort to clarify the question and present the background concisely may help. If a standing committee has exercised questionable judgment, an ad hoc supplement may be in order. If recapitulation of debate has no other benefit than to ease the pain of defeat for a major constituency, it may be the right action.

Suggested Readings

Kovner, A. R. 1990. "Effective Governance for 1990 and Beyond." *Frontiers of Health Services Management* 6 (Spring): 3–27. See also in that issue commentaries by W. M. Hageman/R. J. Umbdenstock, J. A. Alexander, and H. S. Zuckerman.

Seay, J. D., and B. C. Vladeck. 1988. *In Sickness and In Health: The Mission of Voluntary Health Care Institutions.* New York: McGraw-Hill.

Shortell, S. M., and A. D. Kaluzny. 1988. *Health Care Management: A Text in Organization Theory and Behavior.* New York: Wiley. See especially L. R. Burns and S. W. Becker, "Leadership and Decision Making," 142–86; R. D. Luke and B. Kurowski, "Strategic Management," 463–91.

Shortell, S. M., E. M. Morrison, and B. Friedman. 1990. *Strategic Choices for America's Hospitals: Managing Change in Turbulent Times.* San Francisco: Jossey-Bass.

Notes

1. J. D. Seay and B. C. Vladeck, 1988, "Mission Matters," in *In Sickness and In Health: The Mission of Voluntary Health Care Institutions*, eds. J. D. Seay and B. C. Vladeck (New York: McGraw-Hill), 1–34.
2. Sisters of Mercy Health Corporation, 1980, *Integrated Governance and Management Process, Conceptual Design* (Farmington Hills, MI: SMHC).
3. A. R. Kovner, 1985, "Improving the Effectiveness of Hospital Governing Boards," *Frontiers of Health Services Management* 2 (August): 4–33. See also commentaries by R. F. Allison, R. M. Cunningham, Jr., and D. S. Peters.
4. Witt Associates, Inc., 1984, *Contracts for Health Care Executives* (Oakbrook, IL: Witt).

5. D. M. Kinzer, 1982, "Turnover of Hospital Chief Executive Officers: A Hospital Association Perspective," *Hospital & Health Services Administration* 27 (May–June): 11–33.

6. R. L. Ackoff, 1987, "Mission Statements," *Planning Preview* 15 (4): 30–31.

7. C. K. Gibson, D. J. Newton, and D. S. Cochrane, 1987, "An Empirical Investigation of the Nature of Hospital Mission Statements." *Health Care Management Review* 15 (3): 35–45.

8. A. F. Southwick, 1988, *The Law of Hospital and Health Care Administration*, 2d ed. (Ann Arbor, MI: Health Administration Press), 597.

9. M. R. Greenlick, 1988, "Profit and Nonprofit Organizations in Health Care: A Sociological Perspective," in *In Sickness and in Health, The Mission of Voluntary Health Care Institutions*, eds. J. D. Seay and B. C. Vladeck (New York: McGraw-Hill), 155–76.

10. B. J. Weiner and J. A. Alexander, 1993, "Hospital Governance and Quality of Care: A Critical Review of Transitional Roles," *Medical Care Review* 50 (Winter): 375–410.

11. Southwick, *The Law*, 585–89.

12. Ibid., Chapter 14.

13. D. Bayta and M. Bos, 1991, "The Relationship between Quantity and Quality with Coronary Artery Bypass Graft (CABG) Surgery," *Health Policy* 18 (June): 1–10.

14. Southwick, *The Law*, 589–98.

15. J. Anderson, 1994, "Perspectives: Any Willing Provider Battles Heat Up in States," *Faulkner & Gray's Medicine and Health* 48 (2 May): Supplement 4.

16. Joint Commission on Accreditation of Healthcare Organizations, 1990, *Quality Assurance in Ambulatory Care*, 2d ed. (Oakbrook Terrace, IL: JCAHO).

17. J. A. Alexander, 1990, "Governance for Whom? The Dilemmas of Change and Effectiveness in Hospital Boards," *Frontiers of Health Services Management* 6 (Spring): 39.

18. B. Ehrenreich and J. Ehrenreich, 1970, *The American Health Empire: Power, Profits, and Politics* (New York: Random House).

19. J. A. Alexander, 1990, *The Changing Character of Hospital Governance* (Chicago: Hospital Research and Educational Trust), 5–6.

20. Henry Ford Health System Department of Community Development, 1994, "Partners in the Community," quarterly newsletter (Detroit, MI): Summer.

21. I. Belknap and J. Steinle, 1963, *The Community and Its Hospitals* (Syracuse, NY: Syracuse University Press).

22. J. A. Alexander, 1986, *Current Issues in Governance*, Hospital Research and Educational Trust, Hospital Survey Series (Chicago, AHA).

23. Ibid., 220.

24. R. C. Coile, Jr., 1994, *The New Governance: Strategies for an Era of Health Reform* (Ann Arbor, MI: Health Administration Press), 27–44.

25. R. Umbdenstock, and W. Hageman, 1984, *Hospital Corporate Leadership: The Board and Chief Executive Officer Relationship* (Chicago: American Hospital Publishing Company).

26. Alexander, *Current Issues in Governance*, 25.

27. C. Molinari, L. Morlock, J. A. Alexander, and C. A. Lyles, 1992, "Hospital Board Effectiveness: Relationships between Board Training and Hospital Financial Viability." *Health Care Management Review* 17 (Summer): 43–49.

28. Alexander, *Current Issues in Governance*, 12–13.

29. S. M. Shortell and J. P. LoGerfo, 1981, "Hospital Medical Staff Organization and the Quality of Care," *Medical Care* 19 (10): 1041–52.

30. Alexander, *Current Issues in Governance*, 15–18.

31. L. R. Burns and D. P. Thorpe, 1994, "Trends and Models in Physician-Hospital Organization," *Health Care Management Review* 18 (Fall): 7–20.

32. J. R. Griffith, 1994, "Reengineering Health Care: Management Systems for Survivors," *Hospital & Health Services Administration* 39 (Winter): 451–70.

33. H. S. Zuckerman and T. A. D'Aunno, 1990, "Hospital Alliances: Cooperative Strategy in a Competitive Environment," *Health Care Management Review* 15 (Spring): 21–30.

34. American Hospital Association, 1993, *Guide to the Health Care Field* (Chicago: AHA).

35. R. S. Kaplan and D. P. Norton, 1992, "The Balanced Scorecard—Measures That Drive Performance," *Harvard Business Review* 72 (January–February): 71–79.

Executing: Supporting and Implementing Governance Decisions

11

THE EXECUTIVE OFFICE

THE EXECUTIVE office supports the governance system both in facilitating the decisions of the governing board and in seeing that the board decisions and plans are effectively implemented. As a result, it relates to every part of the enterprise, and is an inescapable part of any bureaucratic organization. It is a major contributor to the processes described in Part I, Governing, and it works intimately with the staff functions described in Part III, Learning. This chapter describes the purpose, functions, personnel, design, and evaluation of the executive office. The following chapter describes developments in one function which falls inescapably to the executive office, organizing the enterprise as a whole.

The executive office is led by the chief executive officer who is supported by an operations team. Although the team does not make a large number of decisions itself, it acquires considerable influence through its focal position in so many important communications. In larger health care organizations the team includes key line executives who manage the clinical activities, leaders of the major staff functions described in Part III, and leaders of corporate support such as the general counsel, development, human resources and plant. Smaller organizations may contract executive functions in whole or in part to outside firms. In very small health care organizations, the job of CEO can be part-time, either with other organizations or with other jobs such as chief nursing officer or CFO. Rarely, and usually ineffectively, executive functions are performed by volunteer board officers formally designated for the task.

Purpose

The purpose of the executive office is implementation. (The word executive itself comes from a Latin root meaning to carry out.) Implementation rests on three kinds of two-way exchange shown in Figure 4.1. The executive maintains effective commerce to and from the external world, the governing board, and the systems that support the care process. Effective commerce in this context must include whatever steps are necessary to achieve successful exchange relationships. Communication must occur in both directions; environmental assessment must report changing needs; and agreements must bring necessary resources. The executive office is responsible for almost all information formally supplied to the board, for all implementation of board decisions, and for all relationships with the medical staff and the employees. It is also responsible for a number of outreach and boundary-spanning functions, such as public relations, government relations, and fund raising.

Two conflicting stereotypes may confuse persons trying to understand what executives do. One is that the executive is a communicator, bringing people together to discuss their problems. While this stereotype is an excellent beginning in defining the executive function, it is incomplete. Discussion is not enough to create "effective commerce." Action must result, and it must be constructive in terms of the exchange relationships. Executive responsibilities do not end until constructive action occurs. The other stereotype is that the executive is the chief decision maker. In reality, decisions of great importance are made at every level of the organization; the most far-reaching are

Figure 4.1   Channels of Executive Implementation

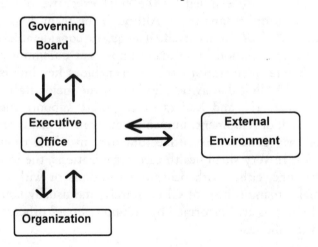

influenced by large numbers of stakeholders. The character of executive decisions is different as well. Rather than dealing directly with actions, they tend to deal with the structures and processes that support good action decisions.

The success of the executive function lies in decisions understood, accepted, and implemented in the organization. It lies in helping many people outside the executive office to participate in making the decisions. It lies in changes foreseen far enough in advance to allow a smooth transition—crises avoided rather than crises resolved. The best executive offices (though not necessarily the people in them) become almost invisible. So smoothly does the organization respond to the pressures of the outside world that the hand of the executive office is noticed by only the most observant. For most members of well-managed organizations, the front office is not a source of authority; it is a resource and a guide.

Functions

The executive function in bureaucratic organizations has proven quite difficult to describe, although many texts have striven to clarify it (see, for example, the introductory chapters to Shortell and Kaluzny[1] and their bibliography, in the Suggested Readings). The unlimited scope of executive responsibilities is a major source of the difficulty: the executive can be held responsible by the board for almost anything the board chooses. A second source of difficulty is the collaborative nature of executive behavior. The commerce between many groups indicated in Figure 4.1 requires prodigious flexibility. On the other hand, that same effective commerce requires that the general functions of the executive office be clear to other members of the organization and to the outside world. The functions discussed in this chapter delineate what an outsider, a doctor, an employee, or a board member should expect from the executive office. They can be summarized under the headings, lead, support, represent, and organize, as shown in Figure 4.2.

Leadership

Leadership can be understood as cognitive, moral, and inspirational. All three are important.

Cognitive Leadership

Like lawyers, engineers, and managers in other fields, health care executives exercise leadership by virtue of an intellectual area of study. The executive team, and particularly the CEO, have unique training in the

Figure 4.2 Functions of the Executive Office

 🏳	**Lead**	Identify trends and implications. Provide the initiative for action. Emphasize the importance of an issue. Provide or reward examples of ethical behavior. Encourage, reassure, motivate.
 ☎	**Support**	Provide training, supplies and facilities. Provide information. Provide special counsel or outside funding or both.
 🧍	**Represent**	Form alliances with like-minded organizations. Affiliate with organizations providing supplementary services. Form joint ventures with potential competitors. Contract with financing intermediaries.
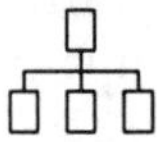 🗂	**Organize**	Assign accountability for operations. Form ad hoc committees, task forces, and work groups. Reconcile conflicts.

world of health care finance, economics, marketing, and measurement which allows them to understand the needs of various stakeholders and the implications of alternatives. They are important as observers and commentators on the external environment, and as sources of ideas, perspectives, suggestions, and solutions. The importance of this contribution cannot be overlooked; there is rarely any local source for a substitute.

Cognitive leadership activities include identifying trends, articulating visions, designing responses, clarifying alternatives, developing criteria and measures, and answering questions. These often are introduced as seeds for discussion and collaborative development, often unrecognized and sometimes unrecognizable in the final product. They are critical to effective commerce because they provide starting points for agreement. Cognitive leadership also includes developing and presenting educational programs. Examples include developing education programs for board members and other managers, providing examples from other institutions, bringing outside consultants and guests, and explaining the implications of legislation, regulation, and market developments.

As an illustration of cognitive leadership, the concepts of the "balanced scorecard" measures (Chapter 3) do not spring to the minds of doctors or board members. Formal education is necessary to establish a consensus as to their value. The concepts are not useful until specific measures have been found, tested, and installed. The measures do not collect themselves; elaborate systems are necessary for most of them. When faced with the cost of measurement, governing boards ask why the cost is justified, and the executive office is the only point in the organization equipped to give a comprehensive answer. The skills involved in the balanced scorecard include heavy doses of statistics, measurement, economics, accounting, finance, and marketing, all in the context of health care.

Moral Leadership

The chief executive and the executive office are highly visible. Their behavior is widely copied and admired. Their character eventually colors the organization as a whole. The *organization culture*, the style of its daily interactions at levels ranging from honesty and mutual respect to dress and etiquette, is strongly influenced by the executive office.[2]

Serious problems in areas such as ethnic, religious, and gender discrimination, theft and conversion of assets, fraud and misrepresentation, and even unnecessary death and disfiguration of patients is known to be related to moral leadership failures.[3] Conversely, many health care organizations have maintained admirable records. Intermountain Health Care, founded by the Mormon Church and now operated as a secular institution, is an example. Values which run counter to the Mormon tradition of communal support and mutual respect simply do not flourish in the Intermountain culture. An etiquette of respect and politeness pervades the organization, but at the same time its leaders emphasize the need for rigorous response to economic reality.[4]

The executive office establishes moral leadership by profession, in written and oral statements of all kinds, and by actions. Among the actions, the selection of other leaders who clearly agree with the professed moral positions is one of the most telling. The personal behavior of the team is always important. The often-subtle signals to discourage unwanted moral behavior are also influential. For example, candor and gender equality are reflected frequently in many small actions. Moral leaders try to be candid and non-sexist in all their own actions, but they also deliberately encourage those traits in others and discourage their opposites. Many people test the sincerity of the organization's public ethical professions. Their initial tests are tentative and limited, and they are sensitive to appropriately limited responses. From the consistent small responses of the executive office, a culture is built where most people simply conform without thinking about it. The dramatic, serious challenge does not often arise.

Inspirational Leadership

Leaders also inspire by charisma and personal example.[5] Separate from the cognitive and moral aspects of organizational life, there is an emotional component, whether the work is, satisfying or stultifying, important or trivial, invigorating or daunting; and whether the work place is enjoyable or unpleasant, comforting or threatening, collaborative or contentious. Leaders not only understand that open systems, strategic management, and continuous improvement models call for constant change in the organization, they also understand that many people find the change itself frightening. Leaders not only trace the cognitive aspects of response, they spend time helping people overcome their fears. They present change, like the work itself, as a rewarding challenge. Rhetoric and attitude are as important as the cognitive content in many ventures that test the mettle of organizations and their members.

Support

In a sense, the three forms of leadership support the organization, but there are other essential activities. The executive office provides support to all the other systems of the organization, and it is responsible for several activities undertaken for the good of the whole.

Functions Supporting Other Systems

The executive office is accountable to each of the other systems of the organization for their workplace, tools, and supplies. It is accountable for the information necessary to do the job, including some of the specific training. If any of these elements fail, workers cannot do their best. Figure 4.3 shows the major support services reporting to the executive office, and the important needs of the board, the medical staff, and the clinical services. The provision of these services is so complex that entire sections of the organization must be devoted to them, or alternatively, if they are purchased from outside, explicit steps must be taken to assure effective delivery. They are accountable to, and coordinated by, the executive.

Most patient and customer support comes from physician and clinical services, but the organization as a whole, and therefore the executive office, is directly responsible for several elements patients and families feel is important. These include a comprehensible bill reporting services rendered, access to and protection of confidentiality of medical records, a safe, convenient, and pleasant physical plant, and other amenities such as meals for visitors.

The executive office is staff to the governing board. It supplies all the formal information of the environmental assessment, as well as detailed analysis of all major proposals. It prepares accounting and financial reports in sufficient depth to permit the board to make realistic financial plans and to monitor progress. The board does not often

---

Figure 4.3 Major Support Functions Reporting to the Executive Office

Unique Needs of Special Importance

Function	Patients and Customers	Governing Board	Medical Staff	Clinical Services
Strategic				
Planning		✔	✔	✔
Marketing	✔		✔	✔
Financial				
Accounting	✔	✔	✔	✔
Finance		✔	✔	✔
Information				
Clinical	✔		✔	✔
Management	✔		✔	✔
Human Resources				
Recruitment			✔	✔
Training	✔		✔	✔
Compensation			✔	✔
Plant				
Amenities*	✔			
Supplies			✔	✔
Facilities and equipment			✔	✔

*Amenities include food services, safety, public areas, transportation, etc.

access the actual clinical records, but they require measures of quality and effective utilization derived from them. Like other members of the organization, they need education to the unique issues of health care management.

The medical staff and clinical services require comprehensive, direct support. To do their jobs, they need assistance managing human resources and plant services. Human resources facilitates recruitment, manages compensation and incentives, and supports continuing education for professionals and specific skill training for nonprofessional personnel. Caregivers need the same amenities as patients and board members, but they use a large variety of highly technical, often dangerous supplies, and require elaborate specialized plant services for many clinical areas. Rapid access to clinical information is essential to high-quality, cost-effective treatment. To maintain continuous improvement, caregivers must have accurate management and accounting information, often in formats not routinely reported to others. They participate actively in the planning process, usually in preparing, evaluating, and prioritizing specific proposals for board review. Carrying out these tasks requires access to environmental assessment and strategic information. They also participate actively in marketing, including product design, pricing, and promotion, and need in-depth, service-specific marketing analyses and programs.

Functions Supporting the Organization as a Whole

Legal counsel   Legal advice has become increasingly important in preventing law suits and reducing settlements for damages. Most large health care organizations have an office of the general counsel available to assist in difficult issues of patient care, employment, medical staff relations, affiliations, and supplier contracts. Smaller ones usually have a retainer arrangement with a private law firm. When necessary, specialist firms are employed on a fee basis.

Public relations and fund-raising   The CEO and members of the executive staff are normally the public spokespersons for the health care organization. They routinely present its mission, vision, achievements, and needs to the community through speeches, meetings, and interviews. They also identify and establish communications with key individuals in the community—political leaders, business leaders, major donors, and important figures in religious, charitable, and cultural activities. Often the most successful individual relationships are established with potential leaders in each of these activities. Although much important public relations is based on individual contact, it is also necessary to manage the presentation of the organization in the media. This is done through formal releases, designated spokespersons, and planned advertising.

Funds for expanding health care organization activities come from loans and gifts as well as past operations. The newer forms of corporate structure involve equity capital (stock and partnership agreements) as well. The CEO is generally expected to present the case for major new capital from any of these sources. Success frequently depends upon earlier general communication and individual relationships.

Larger health care organizations appoint professional staff for public relations and fund raising. This staff is part of the executive office. Although it handles routine communications and relations with the news media and provides essential support for fund raising, it does not eliminate the need for direct participation of the CEO and other ranking officers.

Legislative and regulatory representation   Local, state, and national governments all directly affect health care delivery.[6] Their activities include laws restricting and encouraging different forms of activity, licensure of facilities and personnel, taxes and subsidies of various kinds. There are laws and administrative regulations that

- *Govern caregivers and facilities*, such as federal education programs, state licenses, and local building permits
- *Shape health insurance*, such as federal ERISA legislation and state enabling acts for HMOs and PPOs
- *Define patient rights*, such as federal civil rights laws, drug and medical device regulation, and state laws governing liability and patient self-determination
- *Protect employee rights*, such as federal social security, unionization and equal opportunity laws, state employment security, and workers' compensation requirements
- *Offer subsidies for certain activities and taxing others*, such as federal and state subsidies for certain services, long-term finance, and certain construction sites, and federal income, state sales, and local property tax exemptions
- *Pay directly for patient care*, such as the federal Medicare, and federal employee programs, state Medicaid, and local support.

Health care organizations are important parts of political constituencies, entitled and obligated to represent their views in the legislative environment, and to seek the most favorable possible decisions in regulatory activities. (The obligation is twofold. First, legislators and regulators depend upon the health care organizations to protect their interests; they cannot be expert in all the implications of their actions. Second, the organization owes it to its owners to take full advantage of all opportunities.) Larger organizations often support lobbyists who monitor government activities. Smaller ones rely on trade associations and alliances. In either case, understanding the implications of actions and supplying information useful in presenting positions is an executive responsibility.

Accreditation Although accreditation by the Joint Commission on Accreditation of Healthcare Organizations (or the American Osteopathic Association) is technically voluntary, it is closely related to certification for Medicare payment and thus essential to most institutions. The JCAHO survey every three years is the most rigorous inspection the institution undergoes at the hands of an outside agency. Preparing the documentation and coordinating team visit, which usually spans several days is the responsibility of the executive.

Disaster planning Providing care during civil disaster is an important and respected function of community health care organizations. When disaster strikes, people turn instinctively to the hospital. Victims are brought by rescue vehicles, in private cars, or by other means. Even a large emergency service can face 20 times its normal peak load with very little warning. Word of disaster spreads quickly, particularly under the stimulus of television and radio. The hospital may be inundated with visitors, families, and well-meaning volunteers in addition to the sick and injured. Warning, medical needs, and severity of injuries differ greatly, depending on the disaster. The most common disasters are storms and large-scale accidents, such as fires and mass transport crashes. Fortunately, in many cases the larger the number of injured, the lower the percentage of very serious or fatal injuries.

Response to civil disaster requires a detailed plan that must be rehearsed periodically to comply with JCAHO regulations.[7] The design of the plan is a major project requiring the coordinated efforts of all management except members of the finance system.[8] The elements of the response include

- Rapid assembly of clinical and other personnel
- Reassignment of tasks, space, and equipment
- Establishment of supplementary telephone and radio communication
- Triage of arriving injured
- Provision of information to press, television, volunteers, and families.

Representation

The executive office is responsible for negotiating, monitoring, and maintaining relationships with other organizations which complement, supplement or compete with the mission. With the vertical integration of health care services, the representation function of the executive has greatly expanded. For larger organizations, each relationship begins with a make or buy decision: the organization can employ individuals or acquire subsidiaries skilled in the activity, "making" it as part of the core capability, or it can negotiate contract arrangements of various sorts relying on the collaboration of an independent corporation, effectively if not actually "buying" the service in question. The profile of makes and buys is a set of key strategic decisions. No known organization can make everything, and one which buys too much ends up with no core capability. Neither extreme is feasible. The executive office manages a panoply of relationships with outside corporations. (It is possible to view the relationship with the medical staff as a form of representation, but this text will treat it as part of the core capabilities, discussed in depth in Chapter 12.)

Alliances with Similar Noncompeting Organizations

As noted in Chapter 2, many well-run health care organizations now have relations with similar corporations through contractual membership in alliances. These relations are designed to accomplish important goals the participants could not do as well on their own. They are with similar organizations in other geographic markets, so the members do not compete directly. The services tend to expand the capability of the executive office itself, rather than increasing the scope of services or directly affecting market share. Important activities include

- *Joint purchasing agreements*, using the leverage of many buyers to obtain favorable prices
- *Educational and consulting programs*, where several organizations can collectively support highly trained and specialized skills
- *Medical research*, where a consortium of organizations can provide statistically reliable samples of patients specific diseases or conditions
- *General public relations*, as is common with trade associations
- *Legislative and regulatory representation*, where the participants must all be in the same governmental unit.

Alliances of this type are reasonably stable and provide useful services. The form of affiliation is usually an annual contract. The contract is normally undertaken with a longer term expectation, and involves substantial financial commitments, both to pay significant fees and to commit participation volume. General trade associations such as the American Hospital Association also perform some of these activities for members, but generally for lower fees and less commitment. The more recent growth of alliances such as Premier or Voluntary Hospitals of America has shown the increased power of grouping organizations with comparable missions and less danger of direct competition.

Affiliations with Competing Health Care Organizations

It is more difficult to maintain collaborative relationships with organizations which are directly competing in the same geographic market, but important opportunities exist. They include

- *Post-graduate medical education*, where several institutions can support specialty training
- *Highly specialized clinical services*, where neither of the partners can support the volumes necessary, such as programs for the disadvantaged, or in smaller communities, shared expensive diagnostic facilities
- *Collaboration to capture markets*, where two competing health care organizations agree to combine provider lists to attract employer groups.

The form of collaboration is usually contract for medical education, and joint venture for other activities. The relationships may be prelude to merger or acquisition.

Affiliations with Complementary Health Care Organizations

Vertical integration calls for service across all health care needs. Hospitals and doctors, the largest two groups of providers, historically avoided several services important to patients, including nursing homes, assisted living facilities, home care agencies, mental health and substance abuse services, medical equipment suppliers, and hospices. Separate, usually small organizations sprang up in many communities to fill these needs. As insurance and financing mechanisms improve, ownership of these facilities will become more attractive. Not surprisingly, the better financed services, chiefly home care and medical equipment have attracted ownership by acute care organizations. In the meantime, there are important advantages to affiliations by contracts.

The largest health care organizations now have at least token ownership in all of these services, but smaller organizations often choose affiliation. The goal of the contract is to assure customers seamless access to all necessary services, and to maintain control of cost and quality. The affiliation contract needs to include explicit programs to monitor all three dimensions of customer satisfaction, and it must be placed with agencies capable of meeting market goals. Otherwise, it becomes preferable for the health care organization to provide the service itself.

Alliances with Health Care Insurers

The majority of all patient care is financed through insurance carriers and intermediaries. The ability of the provider organization to increase or maintain market volumes depends directly upon the success of intermediary relationships. Under managed care, the intermediaries are increasingly selective in their contracts. Some intermediaries deliberately separate hospital from physician contracting, but many prefer to contract with a **common provider entity** making comprehensive services available. The federal government is apparently moving the Medicare program, the largest purchaser for most hospitals and many doctors, toward common provider contracts.[9]

Because there are large potential savings under managed care by reducing inpatient hospital, medical specialist, and clinical support services, contracts are increasingly restrictive on these items. In order to win the contracts, most provider organizations must restructure at lower volumes, and reduce resources for these services. Negotiation of the contracts requires an ability to commit the organization to effective restructuring.

Organization

The relationship of the parts of the organization to each other, and the rules and incentives which bind them to a common goal, are an area of decision making requiring knowledge, skills and experience rarely possessed by clinicians or trustees. The design of the organization is one of the very few areas where the executive office normally takes an authoritative position. Because of the complexity and technicality of the issues involved, it is the subject of the following chapter.

Selecting Executive Personnel

Large health care organizations now have several levels of health care executives, clinical executives, and specialists in the support services. Chief executives lead a team, hiring or promoting individuals as they mature. Clearly the quality of the team is a major determinant of the organization's success. Since it also determines the experience of future CEOs, it may be critical to the success of its members as individual professionals, as well. Issues in the selection and development of that team are the subject of this section. While the experience and skill required are discussed from the perspective of a younger executive planning a career, the same perspective should be useful to a superior seeking a subordinate executive.

Career Opportunities

The management of large health care organizations presents substantial opportunities. There are about 22,000 members of the leading professional association, the **American College of Healthcare Executives** (ACHE),[10] and an unknown but not insignificant number of others. Master's programs now produce about 2,000 graduates per year, suggesting a total pool of about 60,000. While many professional executives work in government, health insurance companies, and other activities not directly involved with patient care, about three times as many are in care-giving organizations.

A career in health care management, like other management careers, should present an opportunity for continuous growth and for personal and psychological rewards through a lifetime of personal growth. Financial rewards should reflect the increasing skill and contribution of the individual, with major increases in compensation reserved for those few who wish to be and are capable of being successful CEOs. Health care management supplies both of these needs. There are opportunities for limited responsibility, specialization, and demanding senior executive roles reachable only after 25 years of learning. The financial rewards are commensurate, reaching annual compensation about 15 times entry level professional salaries.[11]

The evolution of the industry from rapid growth to controlled growth and from small provider organizations to large integrated ones can be expected to produce major changes in both the number and roles of executives. Executive positions for clinicians will unquestionably increase, and there will be a shortage of qualified doctor and nurse executives for some time to come. The steadily increasing sophistication of the field has led to a continuing demand for accountants, lawyers, information specialists, and planning personnel. As corporations grow larger, opportunities for highly skilled and well-compensated general executives will increase. On the other hand, restructuring in the early 1990s emphasized elimination of management layers, reducing lower-level opportunities for both clinical and general managers.

Careers in health care management are generally an end in themselves; people come into health care management at various ages from various prior roles much more often than they leave the field for some other activity. Entry from senior clinical levels is much more common, for example, than return to clinical practice. Lawyers and accountants who come to specialize in health care applications tend to stay with the specialty, either improving their specialty skills or moving into general health care management as they are promoted.

Career Education

Graduate Education

Graduate education is increasingly the norm for all but the lowest levels of executive activity. Although exceptional individuals occasionally arrive through other routes, successful completion of graduate education is evidence of general intellectual ability, energy, and perseverance. High class standing or a degree from a particularly competitive school is usually a predictor of future success. Entry to health care management is from one of three sources. Many young people enter by way of a masters program in the field, gaining experience before and after their degree in junior management positions. Others enter from established careers in care-giving professions, chiefly medicine and nursing. The third, and probably smallest group, enter from general business, law, accounting, or other specialties. All develop their skills by continuing education and experience.

The kind of graduate education influences the knowledge and skills acquired. Clinical education and legal education emphasize skills other than management, and the knowledge these educational specialties impart is only partly relevant to health care. Finance, marketing, organizational design, and human relations are topics dealt with only in management-oriented graduate programs. A factual and analytic review of the health care system is generally available only in health care administration programs. The odds for young persons seeking a career in health care management favor those with graduate education in the field at the most selective school they can get into. For those who possess other graduate education, an alternate strategy would be to acquire missing skills through experience and missing knowledge through continuing education.

Additional formal education is particularly important for physicians and nurses transferring from patient care to management roles. It is useful for people whose prior work has been outside health care. General health care managers often seek additional learning from the fields and professions of business. A few master clinical professions after beginning a general career. Both degree programs, usually at the master's level, and formal continuing education programs are available to expand formal education.

Continuing Education

Regular participation in formal continuing education programs is a requirement for membership in the ACHE, as it is for many professional associations. Continuing education has three roles in an executive career; remedial, complementary, and supplementary. Remedial education addresses oversights in previous formal education. Evening courses, weekend programs, extended summer conferences, and study on one's own can do much to expand skills and knowledge. The diligent student can acquire or expand important concepts and skills in medicine, law, finance, management engineering, statistics, marketing, and other important skills through programs available at local colleges and books in nearby libraries.

Complementary education often consists of factual knowledge of new developments. The most common examples are factual presentations on various new laws, regulations and business opportunities. New analytic techniques can also be learned. Forecasting, using discounted cash flows, or installing patient-scheduling systems are examples. Most complementary education is in the form of one- or two-day conferences, but home study and participation via electronic media are becoming more common. The ACHE has developed an extensive series of conferences, home study programs, and publications.

Supplementary education is the least formal of the three forms, but not necessarily the least important. It broadens perspectives beyond the normal professional limits. Study of the health care systems of other nations is relatively popular. Some universities offer summer courses in comparative health care. Religious and liberal arts studies are important supplementary education. Some executives read literature, history, biography, and philosophy. The broader perspectives gained from these pursuits are useful in evaluating the changes in the environment and the opportunities they suggest. They are also useful in coping with the frustrations inherent in management. Among executives fully qualified in professional knowledge and skill, a broad perspective distinguishes the exceptional from the adequate.

Career Experience

Those seeking an executive want both formal education and the skills that are the distillate of successful experience, but these are harder to appraise. Decision-oriented experiences include information systems, planning, marketing, board, and medical staff; and decision-implementation experience includes organization design and direction of successful units or corporations. Skills include technical areas such as construction or finance, as well as leadership and human relations, and ethics, emotional strength, and commitment.

Decision-Oriented Experience

Ambitious executives should seek a wide variety of experience as well as a record of increasingly demanding responsibility. One way of viewing a professional record is to consider it in terms of decision-oriented and implementation-oriented experience. These concepts are similar to the older terms of staff and line, but they provide a more meaningful dichotomy, for several reasons. They suggest, correctly, that the two categories of experience are inseparable, complementary, and equal. They hint at the mind-set and skill requirements involved in executive performance, which must recognize and deal with the inseparability. Finally, they reflect the realities of modern health care organizations. Few real jobs are truly "staff" in the traditional concept of being without authority, and even fewer are "line" in the sense of implementing, but not making, decisions. Different jobs have different balances between the two, and advancing executives seek a cumulative profile which matches their interests and the needs of the positions to which they aspire.

Decision-oriented experience relates to the processes by which the organization sets its expectations, from environmental surveillance, planning, and marketing analyses to support of the board, medical staff, and middle management. Beginners often do fact-finding and preliminary work on budgets and long-range plans. These exercises are particularly fruitful because they show the range of possibilities and restrictions of the organization so well. They also are not sensitive; the inevitable beginners' mistakes will almost certainly be caught in subsequent reviews.

More seasoned executives move to activities closer to final decisions: negotiating expectations with middle management and primary monitors, ranking new program activities, developing plans to implement broad goals, specifying information requirements, and designing systems to produce them. Mature executives, often CEOs, address the most sensitive and difficult decisions: weighing the importance and permanence of environmental changes, recommending budget guidelines, and resolving serious disputes. As executives progress, the cost of error mounts, but so do their skills, wisdom, and emotional maturity.

Implementation-Oriented Experience

Implementation experience focuses more clearly on the ability to convince others and to gain their cooperation. The skills involving implementation transcend human relations, although they require effective interpersonal abilities. In the health care world, where little gets done without a team, implementation requires getting things done through a team, and implementation experience is learning how to make it happen. It begins with the recognition of open systems needs; getting the work done depends on people, and people accomplish goals because they see it as in their own best interest. One famous textbook puts it: "The essential task of management is to arrange organization conditions and methods of operation so that people can achieve their own goals best by directing their own efforts toward organizational objectives."[12]

Implementation skill is almost impossible to teach in formal settings. (Efforts like this book can lead people away from the wrong ideas, but they cannot build skills at the right ones.) What does seem reliable is that implementation skills are apparent early in most leaders and that they are improved by practice. Experience for health care executives can appropriately begin before the professional career, with college activities, for example, and can include experience outside health care, if time permits. Smaller voluntary organizations, local government, and charitable fund drives are common examples. So are state and national professional organizations.

Implementation skills are developed through direct supervisory experience but also through leading cross-functional teams and task forces. For CEO-level skills, the composition of the group led is probably more important than its size. Opportunities to lead groups containing doctors and other extensively educated individuals or groups of leaders, such as trustees, are valuable. It is important to understand that several jobs traditionally labeled staff—especially consulting, planning, and board and medical staff support—can include all of the experience opportunities of line positions, except that of routine supervision of large numbers of people. Certainly good staff work requires both decision-making and implementation skills. The final skill, the ability to project values and describe goals so that they are attractive to large numbers, is the characteristic that distinguishes the highest ranks of executives. The opportunities to practice it in advance are rare; the chance comes as the individual reaches the ranks just below the top.

Mentoring

An important aspect of experiential education is guidance and feedback. Ideally, senior executives coach junior ones, giving them guidance on how to approach problems, evaluations of performance, insights into hidden complexities, reassurance, and encouragement. It is generally wise for beginning executives to seek not one but several mentors, shifting among them as their situations change.[13]

Assessment of Professional Skills

Honest assessment of one's skills is a powerful tool. Maturing executives should develop profiles of their personal skills and knowledge, along with their professional goals. The profile, together with an effort to identify and analyze the requirements of jobs desired in the future, helps set learning goals and priorities. The ACHE offers an instrument to assist in self-evaluation, but it is a better beginning than final guide.[14] A realistic test of the profile is to compare it with actual job descriptions of open positions.

In the final analysis, skillful executives are those whose groups do a good job. In addition to personal profiles, executives should have an ongoing sense of how well they are doing their job. Well-managed organizations include an annual round of expectation setting and a review of performance based upon performance data. (See Measures of Executive Performance section below.) Good executives monitor their own performance continuously. If the information conveyed at an annual review is a surprise, that in itself is a symptom which needs to be explored. Good mentors can offer tips about potential growth and improvement, as part of the annual review and when indicated throughout the year.

Recruiting Effective Executives

Executive level personnel are mostly recruited through search firms, consulting companies which specialize in locating and evaluating executive talent. A good firm helps articulate job descriptions and selection criteria, advises on compensation and relevant experience, pursues affirmative action policies, develops the richest possible list of candidates, and conducts initial selection using interviews, references and biographical information. The health care organization usually makes the final selection from a small panel of persons found qualified by the search firm. Probably more important than the final selection are the organization's actions to describe the job and the selection criteria. It is impossible for the search firm to know the details of the local needs, and easier to find a good candidate for the wrong job than vice versa.

Most chief executives are now offered written contracts specifying the terms of employment.[15] These include a general description of the work obligations (it is almost impossible to describe an executive job specifically), salary compensation, incentive compensation, employment benefits, rights to products developed on the job, and extension and termination arrangements. Executives below the CEO are often covered under the organization's general supervisory level employment agreements, with letters confirming verbal contracts unique to the position. Although service of executives is at the pleasure of the CEO, or the board for the CEO position, it is increasingly common to have clauses protecting the executive against unexpected termination.

Executive compensation is determined by competitive markets. The usual domain of comparison is the national market place of organizations of similar size and type. Compensation in general parallels the earning opportunities of the lower-paid medical specialties. The opportunity to acquire equity, commonplace as an element of compensation among for-profit firms, is not available in health care organizations with a nonprofit structure. Thus although salaries tend to parallel comparable responsibility in other industries, total compensation is lower.

Because of the specialization of executive office personnel, health care organizations are often forced to recruit from outside. The largest health care organizations often follow a policy of promoting to the executive office from within. This reduces the risk associated with hiring outsiders and provides opportunities and incentives for lower managers in the organization. It also builds an executive office with detailed familiarity with the organization. The disadvantages are the dangers of inbreeding and complacency. An organization composed solely of people who have worked there all their lives can easily lose touch with innovations occurring elsewhere. It also can become willing to accept local compromises which others would reject, and in the worst cases, can build a culture of deference to its more persuasive or powerful members that obscures the important resource dependencies and market trends. The disadvantage can be overcome by an explicit policy of seeking outside education, consultation, comparison, and advice.

Organization of the Executive Office

The executive office is small relative to other units of the health care organizations. In small organizations it may be only one or two people; even in large ones the office accounts for only a small percent of total payroll costs. Despite its size, it presents several important design problems, principally because of its role in integrating the other systems and the complexities of being the focal point of commerce, as indicated in Figure 4.1. This section discusses representative examples of executive office organization and the responsibilities of key executives, with special attention to the accountability of the CEO and the COO.

Design of the Executive Office

Organization charts for executive units depict reality poorly, largely because they show only formal accountability, while many activities take place in committees and informal relationships. Figure 4.4 shows the elements which must relate through the executive office of a large health care organization operating a broad scope of services and in several geographic locations. The nine support activities represent common groupings of the executive office functions described above. Intermediary marketing might mean operating a health insurance or financing plan, but it also includes affiliation contracts with freestanding managed care and traditional insurance intermediaries, such as Blue Cross. It is the newest entry on the list, and its activities are expanded in Chapter 7.

Figure 4.4 as it stands almost certainly would not be effective. Assuming a vice president for each box, CEOs would have 11 or 12 people reporting to them directly, an unmanageable load given the complexity and importance of the issues. What is worse, the caregivers are isolated

Figure 4.4 The Relationship Problem of a Large HCO

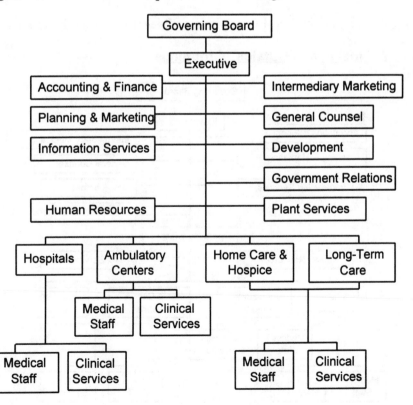

by the line structures of the subsidiary organizations. They would have no direct, face-to-face communication with the administrative support units or the chief executive, or the governing board. This problem, how to bring a very large number of activities together into decision-making groups that are effective both in size and in representation, is the core of the modern health care organization.

Real organizations are learning to solve the problems of Figure 4.4. The test is the organization's ability to respond to the changes in the marketplace. The winners succeed because they can effectively deliver the administrative services to their caregivers, enabling them to be more desirable in the marketplace than the earlier forms. It is clear from market trends that some organizations are winning, but the solutions they use are not simple or easy to describe.

At the level of the executive office, two major solution approaches are emerging. One, shown in Figure 4.5, establishes hierarchies within the support functions, grouping similar ones under group vice presidents to ease the reporting problem at the top. This approach creates natural groupings of people who frequently work on the same prob-

Figure 4.5   Hierarchical Groupings of Executive Office Functions

A. "Inside and Outside" Groupings

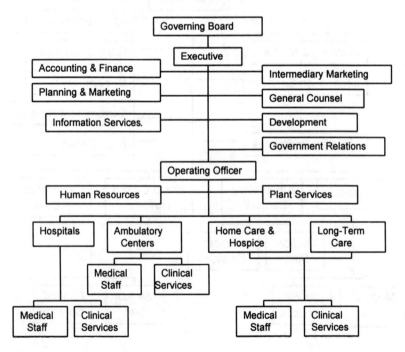

lem under a leader who can hold accountability for progress. Figure 4.5A emphasizes an inside/outside split, focusing those activities with a principally external orientation under the CEO, and those with a principally patient care orientation under a COO. Figure 4.5B establishes functional groupings. The nine support functions have been reduced to three, although of course other reasonable sets exist. The second approach, using operational teams, is illustrated in Figure 4.6. Permanent or ad hoc teams are established to address important issues. The teams must accept accountability; it is understood that effective solutions will be reached on timely schedules.

The solution approaches are not mutually exclusive. The leading institutions appear to use them both, creating fluid organizations which pass authority easily from one executive to another, depending upon the issue. The result is a different perspective on leadership and new roles for the members of the executive office. The traditional concept of the executive implied great power stemming from the office itself. The

Figure 4.5 Continued

B. Functional Groupings

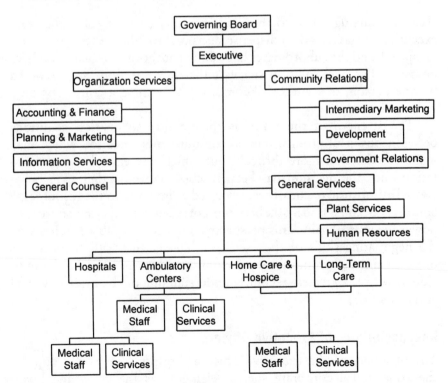

Figure 4.6 Operational Teams of Executive Office Functions

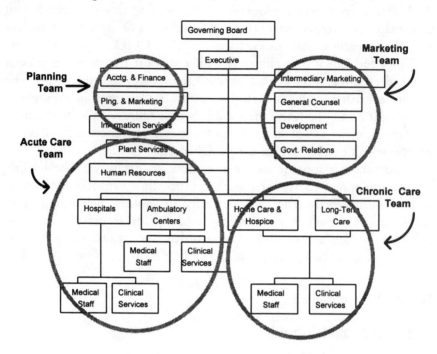

classical thinking reflected the rigid formality of Figure 4.4; the chief executive was assumed to dispense decisions to which there often was no appeal, and the subordinates held similar authority in their respective domains. The new solution suggests that few questions are answered by one person, that authority comes from reaching a consensus on a viable solution.

The strength of the teams is their ability to develop coalitions between powerful groups, mutual commitments to action which may make the decision more difficult, but which will ease the implementation once the decision has been reached. Power, rather than being viewed as intrinsic to the office, is viewed as intrinsic to the resources.[16] Solutions become trade-offs between potentially competing sources of power for mutual gain. This perspective puts considerable emphasis on the negotiating skills of the executive. Those who lead teams to the biggest gains get promotion opportunities. They may not be the individuals with the greatest technical understanding or the most powerful entry position.

Responsibilities of Executive Officers

The members of the executive office are responsible as a group for the same global corporate success elements as the governing board (see Chapter 3). The emphasis moves from identification of issues and solutions to implementation and actual performance. Several of the executive office members have specific duties as well These are shown in Figure 4.7. Several of them may be given dual titles and positions on the board of trustees in recognition of these responsibilities. Titles such as president and CEO or executive vice president and COO are increasingly common. The office of the general counsel can serve as secretary of the corporation, managing bylaws, charters, corporate reports, minutes, and other formal documentation. Chief financial officers commonly report to both the CEO and the finance committee of the board. They may hold the office of treasurer, although it is normally a volunteer board member in not-for-profit organizations. The chief medical officer usually has a board seat as well. Conversely, several of the lower ranking positions can be designated as directors rather than vice president or chief, and represented on board committees by higher ranking officers.

Unique Responsibilities of the CEO

The CEO is uniquely responsible for leadership of the executive office, for representing the organization to the outside world, for relations with the governing board, and for leadership of the organization as a whole. Leadership of the executive office is exercised through intellectual superiority, gained through experience and education, and through coaching and encouraging other members of the team. The best CEOs are often surprisingly non-directive. They frame issues, build teams, applaud successful proposals, and raise questions about less promising ones. By acting in this way, they promote true delegation. A non-directive approach allows alternative opinions, dialogue, and innovation, when more assertive stances would have the subordinates simply agreeing to the CEO's view. Their directive statements are at the most strategic level, such as proposals for initial budget targets, strategies for crucial negotiations, major restructuring, and stimulation of task forces to study new ideas.

CEOs are usually the principal spokespersons for the organization, representing it to the other organizations and forces in the community, in regional and state associations and to its own members. The direct CEO contact is often critical to a certain level of exchange relationships. Their accessibility to community business, charitable, political and financial leaders determines how comfortable those leaders are sharing their views about important issues. When they lose comfort, the stage has been set for actions not in the organization's interest. Such actions might include aiding competing institutions, denying access to funds or real estate resources, and taking restrictive political steps.

Figure 4.7 Duties of Executive Staff Members

Officer	Governing Board Committee Assignment	Major Duties
Chief executive officer	Executive, ex officio on all	External relations, governing board, leadership, ceremonial functions
Chief operating officer	Executive, Planning	Operations, selection and support of other line officers, coordination of staff support
Chief financial officer	Finance, Executive, Planning	Finance, accounting, protection of assets
Chief medical officer	Executive, Medical Staff Relations, Planning	Medical staff relations, medical education, medical staff recruitment, physician-hospital organization
Chief nursing officer	Planning	Nursing staff planning and recruitment, inpatient care, outpatient facilities management
Chief information officer	Planning	Information services, information planning, medical records
Vice president for planning and marketing	Planning, Finance	Planning support, marketing to intermediaries and buyers
General counsel	Executive, Finance	Bylaws, major contracts, risk management
Vice president for human resources	Compensation, Planning	Workforce planning, recruitment, benefits management, training programs, compensation programs
Vice president for plant services	Planning	Facilities planning, space allocation, plant operations, plant services

External relations now include a variety of agreements and contracts with other agencies. The CEO often initiates and finalizes these contracts, even though the detailed negotiation is left to others The CEO remains active in most joint venture, merger, and acquisition discussions. The negotiation of contracts specifying privileges and responsibilities between subsidiaries and parent or between partner organizations must involve the chief executive.

Successful chief executives also always play an active role in the affairs of the governing board. CEOs usually have voting membership on the board, but these activities are much more influential than a single vote. They monitor the agenda, making sure it is complete but not inefficient. They provide full factual support for all agenda items, almost always including a recommendation. They brief the chairs of the major committees on likely debate and its management. They maintain profiles of board members, suggest new board members, and provide criteria for selection. They guide orientation and training programs. They identify promising members and develop them through committee assignments. They make themselves available for informal discussion at the instigation of members, and they facilitate direct communication with their own subordinates and leaders of the other systems. Many of these duties cannot be delegated, but the most effective CEOs find ways to use board members and lower executives in these activities, both to save themselves time and to increase training opportunities.

The CEO is also spokesperson to, and leader of, the organization at large. The meaning, implications, and importance of major directions should be explained to the organization at large by the CEO, but the process of expanding the ideas into specific expectations is left to the rest of the executive office. The continuous improvement concept is one example. Enthusiastic support from the CEO is generally felt to be essential. The CEO is also sometimes the final point of appeal for dissatisfied members, but this role increasingly falls to other members of the executive office.

The best CEOs seem to lead their organizations in an ongoing, three-part process. First, they establish themselves and then their subordinates as respected sources of problem solving. That is, they make the management structure responsive to its employees, doctors, trustees, and patients. Beginning in the front office, but spread as rapidly as possible to all management, they emphasize the concept of service. This improves performance, but equally important, it raises the confidence of members and exchange partners. Second, CEOs work to open and expand conversations about the organization so all ideas can be discussed; they put a premium on useful innovations. This climate results from candor and objectivity, virtues that are themselves achieved by effective staff support and information systems. It also results from CEOs who share credit for progress with others. Third, the CEO uses the momentum of growing confidence and achievement to explore external threats to and opportunities for the organization—issues too frightening to debate openly in poorly run organizations—in ways that allow innovative and rewarding responses. The CEO's sound relationships and personal grasp of external issues are essential to completing this process.

Unique Responsibilities of the COO

The role of the COO is less specific than that of the other officers, and some organizations operate without a designated COO. The traditional COO role is an inside, implementation focus complementing the CEO's external one. In this model, the COOs are accountable to deliver on the short-term expectations for cost, demand, quality of care, and quality of work life. They are accountable for any failure of structure or process in medical staff organization, clinical care, recruitment, collective bargaining, nonfinancial records, and plant safety. In addition to these obligations, traditional COOs perform a "linking" function; they participate actively in strategic processes and are the main source of information about future performance and potential operating problems. They must maintain close relationships with information services, finance, and intermediary contracting, because these services directly affect operations.

Traditional COOs will participate directly in the recruitment of executive personnel other than the CEO. They will coordinate all issues of formal organizational design and work to overcome the inevitable design weaknesses. Finally, COOs will want to play the central role in both the design and the administration of compensation and reward systems. Management of the reward system is a logical extension of the COO's role in providing direction and control, and it also provides an opportunity to increase the loyalty of subordinates.

Properly understood, the traditional COO role is a focal point in the executive office almost as significant as the CEO, differing more in internal versus external focus than scope. It is hard to see how such a crucial role could ever disappear, but some institutions have had success with an operations team. The team would form anyway around the implementation issues and would be comprised of the major contributors to operational success, as shown in Figure 4.8. To succeed, the team must be able to work as effectively without a COO as it could with one.

Three elements are likely to be important in the success of the "No COO" operations team. First, the chief medical and nursing officers must be compatible, so that conflicts between them rarely reach the

Figure 4.8 Members and Agenda of the Operations Team

Members
Chief operating officer, if named
Chief medical officer
Chief nursing officer
Director of ambulatory services
Director of human resources
Director of plant services

Agenda
Communicate budget guidelines to individual units
Establish improvement priorities
Commission improvement teams
Establish clinical guideline teams
Supervise preparation of capital budget
Work with planning team on facilities and human resources plans
Work with information services on new information systems
Recruit new management personnel
Coach managers
Review compensation scales
Coordinate renovations, expansions, and major new equipment

level where mediation is required. Second, the support staff in information, accounting, and intermediary contracting must be effective, so that team energies are not depleted in fact-finding, analyzing, and contract development. Third, the overall scale must be such that the CEO can handle the linking functions to external questions, so that the team is not drawn excessively from their implementation function. In short, the "No COO" operating team is more likely to succeed in smaller organizations that are richly staffed. The best examples may be hospitals and clinics that are subsidiaries of larger integrated systems.

Measures of Executive Performance

It is important that no one in the organization be exempt from the process of expectation setting and performance review. There should be explicit expectations, reviews, and rewards for all executives, from the CEO to the beginning assistant. The measures should relate to the long-term survival of the enterprise. The performance review process should be fair in the sense that the judgments are objective and outcomes-oriented. The measures should be quantitative wherever possible.

The higher the rank of the executive, the greater importance should be placed upon response to and management of external issues. At the CEO level, and for the vice president of intermediary marketing, external issues could be considered more important than current operating performance. Evaluation of external issues can be based upon objective measures, but subjective assessment of what is feasible is inescapable.

Outcomes Performance Measures

Figure 4.9 shows the measures developed in Chapter 3 for judging the performance of the board and the corporation as a whole. Most of these items are now measured routinely by well-managed institutions. They are outcomes, or external measures which can be individually compared to ideal goals and quantitative expectations agreed upon at the start of each budget year. Taken as a whole, they constitute an overall measure of the executive office. Figure 4.10 shows a hypothetical profile of performance. It reflects a common problem—a shortfall in marketing goals led to a decrease in demand, and a drop in profits. Offsetting that, satisfaction scores for both patients and workers exceeded expectations. Clinical outcomes and financial position remained strong. To say the performance was good or unacceptable, or any other judgment, depends on a weighting of the various elements of the figure. The judgment should be at the board level; it must be consistent with the market realities and the mission or vision.

Well-managed institutions use an annual process like the following:

1. They use the measures suggested by Figure 4.9, with expectations and goals for each.
2. They develop actual comparisons such as those reflected in Figure 4.10.
3. They use board committees (usually Finance and Compensation) to evaluate the overall results, pronouncing them excellent or acceptable or worse.
4. They use the judgment and the specifics as input for next year's expectation setting.
5. They use the overall judgment and the comparisons for the individual areas to evaluate performance of individuals in the executive office.
6. The executive office members repeat the process for their subordinates. It spreads through the organization, using progressively more detailed measures, but retaining the emphasis on the overall achievement.

The central concepts here are the use of objective measures, the use of the governing board to make the judgment, and the application of

Figure 4.9   Measures of Executive Performance

Dimension*	Concepts	Emphasis**
Financial performance	Profit	CEO, CFO
	Credit rating	CEO, CFO
	Financial structure	CFO
Patient and family satisfaction	Market share	CEO, Int. Mktg., Plng.
	Survey scores	COO, CMO, CNO, Plant
	Clinical outcomes	CMO
	Scope of services	CEO, Plng.
	Access for disadvantaged	CEO, Plng.
	Regulatory approvals	COO
Buyer satisfaction	Costs	COO
	Intermediary and member service	Int. Mktg., CIO
Provider satisfaction	Staffing and recruitment	HR, COO
	Employee and physician surveys	COO, CMO CNO

*See Chapter 3 and Table 3.7 for concepts of dimensions.
**Executive office members having increased direct responsibility.
NOTE: CEO = chief executive officer; CFO = chief financial officer; Int. Mktg. = intermediary marketing; Plng. = planning; COO = chief operating officer; CMO = chief medical officer; CNO = chief nursing officer; Plant = plant services; CIO = chief information officer; HR = human resources.

the results both for feedback to the next round of expectations and the evaluation of individuals. Objective measures permit detail, precision and reliability which cannot be approached by subjective assessments. The governing board role is central to the board's power to carry out the functions it must. It is by interpreting performance that the board illustrates the mission and vision and puts reality into the planning process. Often the board makes explicit statements about what will or will not be acceptable. Rules conditioning the assessment on the most global measures, such as outcomes quality, patient satisfaction, or profit, help organization members understand the real priorities of the board. Finally, using the assessment both as feedback and for individual performance evaluation closes the loop. It shows priorities for next year's improvement, and it makes clear that individuals must first contribute to the success of the whole. Without this message, it is easy for individuals and units to optimize their own needs at the expense of the whole. This is an important way to encourage the opposite behavior.

Figure 4.10   Hypothetical Profile of Performance

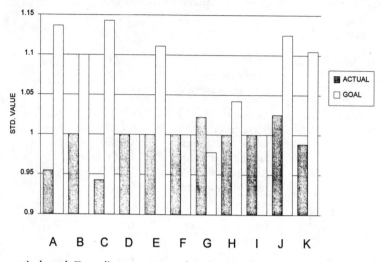

Measures A through K are diverse measures of quality, satisfaction, cost, etc. They are indexed to their own mean to allow visual comparison.

(It is sometimes stated very strongly: No department or individual bonuses unless the corporation as a whole does well.)

Other Performance Measures

Process Measures

Particularly at levels below the CEO, there are numerous measures of individual processes which contribute to global outcomes measures. These are useful in several ways. They permit diagnosis of trouble spots, assist in designing improvements, and allow assessment of individuals and activities that are only components of the whole. They can be used to supplement outcomes measures in evaluating the executive office and its members. They do not replace outcomes measures. The association between good process and good outcomes is usually imperfectly understood, and to omit direct measures of critical success elements is imprudent.

Statements describing professional quality of work can be found in textbooks for many areas of executive activity, such as planning, community relations, advertising, information systems, and law. Where these standards exist, a series of questions or criteria can be developed to indicate acceptable practice, and actual practice compared against it. However, there are few published commentaries on the CEO's obligations to represent the organization, to maintain contact with influential persons in the community, and to assist in board selection and development.[17]

Goal Achievement Measures

Another approach to measurement uses agreement between the executive and the reviewer as to the goals to be achieved or projects to be completed within the period. This technique, often called **management by objective** (MBO), is particularly suited to difficult and ambiguous work. It involves explicit expectations, and a more or less formal contract between workers and their superiors on what is to be accomplished and, in some cases, how. The performance measure compares actual achievement to the initial agreement. The approach is useful but is subject to a number of weaknesses. The expectations are of process or tasks to be done, not outcomes or actual behavioral change. Setting them is a burdensome task, and there is a strong tendency to keep them too vague to be useful. Once set, it is difficult to handle unforeseen contingencies that arise. In the worst case, they may be used as excuses for ignoring critical problems.

Despite its weaknesses, goal achievement seems to be a useful supplement to outcomes measures. Its application in the executive office is best for relatively specific tasks achievable in a year or less, and explicitly related to a strategic initiative. Thus "move to establish productive communications with XYZ Company" is fruitful if XYZ relations fit into an accepted strategic plan, the moves are well understood, and the results will occur promptly, while "develop a plan for an HMO" or "improve relations with the media" are dubious. (The first sounds like the strategy itself and should be broken into specific steps with clear end points. The second is hopelessly vague.)

The Process of Evaluating Executives

The reality is that executive worlds are ambiguous and executive behavior is complex. The central question in evaluating performance of the office and its members is how to use the measures most effectively. A single score could be constructed from the data in Figure 4.10, by weighting each element. (A simple average assigns a weight of one to each element.) Assigning weights is almost impossible, and the weights may change radically over time. A profile may be more useful. It leads to an analysis and specific plans for improvement which provide more insights than a batting average. It discourages competitive ranking against peers, a practice which is destructive in the executive office, where constant collaboration is essential.

Often the board compensation committee and one or two top executives guide the evaluation of the executive office; afterwards, the committee evaluates the remaining executives. Self-evaluation is essential, and an executive should have the opportunity to prepare it before a conference with superiors. The inevitable overall judgment should play a minor part in the process, with the emphasis on the setting of next year's expectations. The evaluation can be used for merit pay increases and bonuses. A retrospective evaluation of this type is probably preferable to more mechanistic reward systems which pick a few of the many measures in advance and automatically reward achievement on those measures. Prospective systems are open to gaming. If the reward is for profits, but not provider satisfaction, the executive team can increase profits by reducing services to doctors and employees. Such an action will be dysfunctional in the long run. The richness of subjective evaluation, profiling, and retrospective review add information and perspective missing in prospective schemes.

Encouraging Effective Executive Office Performance

The issues an organization deals with come and go rather quickly. The organization makes appropriate responses and thrives, or inappropriate ones and declines. However important the issues of today, they will be replaced by others tomorrow. It is the structure for dealing with this stream of transient issues that is the constant and the key to success. Although the executives of well-run organizations are always deeply involved in the issues of the day, it is their ability to focus upon the underlying structure and improve it that makes them exceptional. Using the specific issues as opportunities, they work tirelessly to achieve certain characteristics of structure. These criteria for excellence are like the organization's vision statement. They are never fully met; the continuous effort brings the organization closer to the ideal. Three important elements of this "Executive Vision" are the appropriate use of power, effective timing, and the development of a supporting culture or style.

Using Power

Alexander and Morlock have pointed out that many health care executives have serious and possibly disabling ambivalences about power, recognizing its existence and importance, but fearing it will subvert official goals.[18] Alexander and Morlock agree with Pfeffer, who argues for the deliberate use of politics and power to advance the goals of organizations of all kinds.[19] This perspective calls for an intimate familiarity with the needs and viewpoints of all the stakeholders. Positions are made explicit, needs and rights are recognized, conflicts are identified and resolved as feasible. In some cases, power of individual stakeholders is accepted, and the vision of others is trimmed to the political reality. The organization accepts openly what it would accept tacitly in a more traditional structure.

Well-managed organizations do as these authors suggest. Their assessments identify individual and group goals, and their strategic plans recognize realities stemming from technical, economic, and regulatory advantages. They build coalitions, make deals, and compromise collective goals to achieve as much as possible within feasible limits. They are in short political in the deepest sense of the word, politics as a method of resolving conflict within a group.

One implication of this perspective is that external events drive improvement, rather than the view of the governing board or the vision of leadership. On some of the most critical issues of the day, such as the extent of managed care, the treatment available to the disadvantaged, or the centralization of management, the prevailing view of the community is accepted. In the absence of persuasive pressure for change, the status quo remains. The topics which are selected for change are those where the largest forces can be assembled, or in some cases, where the weakest defenses lie. The power that drives change is the power of the marketplace. The executives of well-managed organizations say, "The customer is demanding these changes." They do not say, "The board wants this done," or worse yet, "The boss wants this." The legitimacy of any issue and the criteria for its solution are defined by the customer.

Timing the Response

A consequence of the pragmatic use of power is that the ultimate control of the agenda passes to the customer. But this approach naively pursued could lead to a chaotic expediency, rather than effective response to customer needs. The American marketplace is a babel of conflicting demands. It would literally be impossible to respond to them all. So well-managed organizations not only listen to the marketplace, they weigh and filter what they hear, responding to that set which they believe will be optimally satisfactory in the long run. Finding the optimum is a difficult, time-consuming challenge. Well-managed organizations identify the issues far enough in advance to allow full exploration.

Ideally, an organization should perceive each new external or exchange demand before it becomes a serious concern, in order to respond as it is articulated rather than when it becomes critical. The well-managed organization is rarely surprised or unprepared, and its members are relieved of a major source of stress. Farsightedness results from extensive environmental surveillance and a willingness to face and resolve power conflicts. Desirable characteristics are eroded quickly under crisis management. An organization which has drifted toward crisis management must concentrate on environmental surveillance and the education of important decision makers and stakeholders to regain farsightedness. The farsighted organization can afford the time to educate, debate, and innovate in formulating its response. The special skills and knowledge of the CEO and the executive office are vital to the farsightedness of the organization.

Management Style

The attitude of the executive group in well-run health care organizations seems to be different from that of less successful ones. The executive office members are more positive, more helpful, more open, and more encouraging in their relations with others. A participative, rather than an authoritarian, style of management is permanently embedded. The best executives coach; they don't order. They praise before they criticize. In the end, there is more to praise and less to criticize because the executives have established a system that helps people do well.

Six elements of style that are repeatedly cited as important in organizational literature are predictability, candor, responsiveness, persuasiveness, conflict resolution, and participation.

1. *Predictability.* Much of an organization's success depends upon teamwork, and teamwork depends upon knowing the role of others. Thus, an organization which handles similar decisions in similar ways and follows predictable cycles of behavior reduces stress and enhances the contribution of its members. An organization which is unpredictable is harder to deal with than one that is predictably dysfunctional.

2. *Candor.* An ever-present temptation in organizations is to tell people what they want to hear rather than the truth. Unfortunately, they all want to hear something different, and the practical result of lack of candor is chaos. The withholding of information is as self-defeating as overt distortion; yet many poor managers do it, whether accidentally or deliberately. Ignorance leads first to guesswork and surprises and shortly thereafter to suspicions and paranoia. In well-managed organizations, one can easily find out what one wants to know and rely on what one hears. Good executives encourage this characteristic by personal action, repeated reference to its importance, and reward for its practice.

3. *Responsiveness.* One obligation of management is to respond to subordinates' questions and concerns. It is clear that the more effectively the superior responds, the greater the productivity and performance of the subordinate will be.

4. *Persuasiveness.* An ability to articulate objectives, describe potential rewards, explain how difficulties can be overcome, and inspire confidence is a valuable tool in building consensus and motivation. The impact is enhanced by predictability, candor, and responsiveness. Persuasiveness is often based less on rhetoric than on a thorough understanding of both people and concepts, backed by a record of success.

5. *Conflict resolution.* Closely related to responsiveness is the ability to resolve conflicts in ways that are predictable and reasonable, but also as constructive as possible. Predictability applies both to the method of conflict resolution and the result. Understanding the likely outcome tends to minimize the conflicts. "Reasonable" is a better criterion than "fair," because many conflicts must be resolved in the organization's favor rather than in that of an individual. Polzer and Neale offer a typology of conflicts applicable to health care organizations, and a discussion of how to resolve many kinds of conflicts.[20]

6. *Participation.* Generally speaking, an organization that solicits the opinion of its members, both formally and informally, as a matter of course will do better than one that discourages member participation. This is especially true in hospitals, where the constant variation in patient needs places a great many decisions at the bedside or at lower levels of the organization.

Suggested Readings

Kovner, A. R., and D. Neuhauser. 1990. *Health Services Management: Readings and Commentary*, 4th ed. Ann Arbor, MI: Health Administration Press, especially pp. 21–113.

Mick, S. S., ed. 1990. *Innovations in Health Care Delivery*. San Francisco: Jossey-Bass.

Pfeffer, J. 1992. *Managing with Power: Politics and Influence in Organizations*. Boston: Harvard Business School Press.

Shortell, S. M., and A. D. Kaluzny. 1994. *Health Care Management: Organization Design and Behavior*, 3d ed. Albany, NY: Delmar Publications.

Steers, R. M., and L. W. Porter. 1987. *Motivation and Work Behavior*. New York: McGraw-Hill.

Notes

1. H. S. Zuckerman and W. L. Dowling, 1994, "The Managerial Role," and S. M. Shortell and A. D. Kaluzny, "Organization Theory and Health Services

Management," in *Health Care Management: Organization Design and Behavior*, eds. S. M. Shortell and A. D. Kaluzny (Albany, NY: Delmar Publishers), 3–53.

2. M. Alveson, 1993, *Cultural Perspectives on Organizations* (New York: Cambridge University Press).

3. J. R. Griffith, 1993, *The Moral Challenges of Health Care Management*, (Ann Arbor, MI: Health Administration Press), 95–148.

4. J. R. Griffith, V. K. Sahney, and R. A. Mohr, 1995, *Reengineering Health Care: Building on CQI* (Ann Arbor, MI: Health Administration Press), Chapter 6.

5. D. D. Pointer and J. P. Sanchez, 1994, "Leadership: A Framework for Thinking and Acting," in *Health Care Management: Organization Design and Behavior*, eds. S. M. Shortell and A. D. Kaluzny, 85–112.

6. G. Anderson, R. Heyssel, and R. Dickler, 1993, "Competition versus Regulation: Its Effect on Hospitals," *Health Affairs* 12 (Spring): 70–80.

7. Joint Commission on Accreditation of Healthcare Organizations, 1995, *Accreditation Manual for Hospitals* (Oakbrook Terrace, IL: JCAHO).

8. Joint Commission on Accreditation of Healthcare Organizations, 1990, *Emergency Preparedness: When the Disaster Strikes* (Oakbrook Terrace, IL: JCAHO).

9. G. C. Faja, 1992, "Package Pricing Project Improves Hospital-Physician Relations," interview by D. E. L. Johnson, *Health Care Strategic Management* 10 (October): 14–19.

10. American College of Healthcare Executives, 1992 Bibliographical Directory of the Membership (Chicago: ACHE), v.

11. L. Scott, 1993, "Facilities Spread the Cash Around," *Modern Healthcare* 23 (14 June): 39.

12. D. A. McGregor, 1960, *The Human Side of Enterprise* (New York: McGraw-Hill).

13. T. C. Dolan, 1993, "Mentoring in the 1990s," *Healthcare Executive* 8 (November–December): 3.

14. M. B. Silberm, 1992, "CEO-ship: Avoiding the Rocks of Self-Malpractice," *Healthcare Executive* 7 (November–December): 26–27.

15. American College of Hospital Administration, 1982, *Report on the Committee on Contracts for Hospital Chief Executive Officers (Chicago: ACHA)*.

16. *J. A. Alexander and L. L. Morlock, 1994, "Power and Politics in Health Services Organizations," in Health Care Management: Organization Design and Behavior*, eds. S. M. Shortell and A. D. Kaluzny, 212–338.

17. American College of Healthcare Executives, 1993, *Evaluating the Performance of the Hospital in a Total Quality Management Environment* (Chicago: ACHE).

18. Alexander and Morlock, "Power and Politics," 215.

19. J. Pfeffer, 1992, *Managing with Power: Politics and Influence in Organizations* (Boston: Harvard Business School Press).

20. J. T. Polzer and M. A. Neale, 1994, "Conflict Management and Negotiation," in *Health Care Management*, 113–33.

DESIGNING THE HEALTH CARE ORGANIZATION

> *Organize: . . . provide with the structure and*
> *interdependence of parts which subserves vital*
> *processes. . . . Oxford English Dictionary*[1]

A HEALTH CARE delivery organization creates a whole from several hundred or thousand well-intentioned individuals. It provides a structure called a **bureaucratic organization**, which recognizes and capitalizes upon their interdependence, using specialization to enhance the individual contributions, so that the whole is substantially more valuable than what they could achieve on their own.[2] Most of the economic activity of modern society is carried out by bureaucratic organizations (as is most religious, artistic, and social activity: the Catholic Church, the New York Philharmonic Orchestra, and the Boy Scouts of America are bureaucratic organizations). Although the term bureaucratic is often used pejoratively, this term is purely descriptive, coined by researchers to describe a form of human endeavor in which individuals and groups bring different skills to bear on an objective in accordance with a formal structure of authority and responsibility.

Organizing the health care delivery enterprise is one of the four functions that must be performed by the executive office. The purpose of bureaucratic structure is to facilitate responsiveness to the environment. The structure allows the enterprise to gain the benefits of specialized labor and capital, understand its resource dependencies, establish strategies to deal with them, and undertake continuous improvement.

Structure is provided in several ways. First, in social behaviors common to any group of people, people learn to respect the power if not the rights of others, to share information and gratification, to make partnerships and friendships, and finally to divide and specialize the work. Any group develops an **informal organization** as a result of these processes. Second, in what is called the **formal (or hierarchical) organization**, people are granted authority over certain activities, held accountable for certain results, and given incentives for exceeding them. Third, to operate in a dynamic environment the hierarchical organization must specify rules for collaboration to solve arising problems and reach certain decisions. These rules create a **collateral organization** of group activities, committees, task forces and work groups with assignments and methods of operating different from the formal organization. All three of these are ongoing, evolving parts of even a small health care operation.

Beyond these interactions of people, it is possible to organize organizations. If a number of people are organized effectively to be a medical group, and a second set is organized to be a hospital, the two can affiliate with each other and then with a second, similar pair, and so forth. *Multi-unit organizations* interrelate several organizations of similar or complementary services. A variety of structures have emerged, differing in the geography and scope of services of their components, but also in their formality, and the way they distribute power and authority among their members.

This chapter reviews how well-managed health care providers build and use their organizations. It starts with the organization of people into groups, beginning with the informal organization, and proceeds to the hierarchical organization and the collateral organization of a single provider unit such as a hospital or clinic. Following the history of well-managed health care organizations, the chapter then reviews the organization of single provider units into the larger and more recent health care systems. It concludes with a review of the steps appropriate to redesign a traditional health care organization to a broader and more effective one.

The goals of the chapter are modest. The subject of organization is easily a lifetime's study. The Suggested Readings, at the end of the chapter, are themselves condensations of dozens of other works. Despite a century packed with major milestones of understanding, it is clear that there is much still to be learned. The chapter will provide a framework that describes what successful health care organizations are doing. The framework should provide health care managers with a useful beginning, and allow health care providers and others who work within organizations an understanding of what lies behind the structures of daily work life.

✓The Informal Organization

All groups of people working together develop informal organizations. They consist of the network of communications the members establish for their own reasons. The informal organizations of health care organizations are exceptionally important. Health care requires great latitude to doctors and nurses dealing directly with patients, because patients' needs vary. Much of the interaction of caregivers is the result of informal organization. The three-shift operation of hospitals is another factor encouraging informal organization. The night crew is almost certain to encounter situations in which it must devise its own answers. Among large numbers of people of similar rank, such as doctors, informal structures can exert powerful forces where formal ones would be intolerable.[3] In smaller organizations informal structures are often more important than the formal ones. As size, distance, and complexity grow, informal organizations lose some of their power, but they never disappear and should never be ignored.

Although it is usually impossible to describe the informal structure in detail, the best formal organizations not only recognize their informal shadows, but also exploit their strengths and overcome their weaknesses.[4] In other words, the formal organization strengthens the informal one and does what the informal one cannot. Simultaneously, it relies on the informal organization to do what it cannot. Informal organizations are powerful, if not always reliable, communications links. They spread facts, falsehoods, and opinions quickly. They encourage and discourage selected behaviors, setting both high and low limits on work output in certain situations, rigidly defining job roles in others. They can cause consensus around important ideas, such as how patients are approached, what can be said to a person of higher formal rank, who the leaders are, and who can be trusted.

The informal organization is used in several ways by well-managed health care enterprises. Direct participation in the communication provides a view of what is important to organization members. Potentially troublesome information can be "leaked" so that reactions can be judged without attribution or confrontation. Informal leaders can be identified.[5] Recognized leaders can be kept abreast of issues as way of keeping the "rumor mill" accurate. They can be brought into critical decisions, so that the outcome adequately reflects member needs, and so that they can convey resource dependency realities to their colleagues. A number of important issues of management style get translated through the informal organization. Peters and Waterman have documented its power in several case studies.[6]

2. The Accountability Hierarchy or Formal Organization

The Accountable Work Group

Responsibility Centers

The smallest aggregate of formal organizational activity modeled is usually the first level at which a formal, monitored accountability appears. That unit has several labels, **responsibility center (RC)** probably being the clearest. **Primary work group** is also used. Health care RCs can be formed around similar skills, such as a nursing station staff, or around patient needs, such as a primary care practice. Even a modest hospital will have upwards of 50 RCs. Very large health care organizations will have several hundred.

Several examples of RCs are shown in Figure 5.1. Hospitals and large clinics will typically have an RC for each care unit, such as a nursing floor or clinic. They aggregate similar RCs into **departments** on the basis of technical function (for example, the laboratory is divided into chemistry, hematology, bacteriology, and histology RCs). They may organize a 24-hour service, such as security, into shifts. They divide a dispersed activity, such as housekeeping, into geographic areas. Laundries and operating rooms are organized around equipment—wash wheels and irons, heart pumps and lasers.

The Accountability Commitment

The RC (and by extension, larger units of the formal organization) makes certain commitments to the central organization and receives certain assurances in return. These commitments are called **expectations** throughout this text . They describe the nature of the relationship with the larger group. The expectations cover several dimensions traced directly from the balanced scorecard concepts describing the overall corporate accountability (see Chapter 3). Under the continuous improvement concept of empowerment, the expectation agreement is negotiated to reflect a mutual understanding of what must be done to fill resource dependency needs and carry out the strategic management (see Chapter 2). The group is empowered in the sense that it has authority to change its work condition to fulfill the expectations.

In traditional management, an accountable leader for the group was always designated, called generically the **responsibility center manager (RCM), primary monitor** or **first-line supervisor**. Often the RCM has a title like head nurse, or foreman related to the type of work the group does. Under continuous improvement, it is not always necessary for the group to have a formally designated leader. A trend has grown to

Figure 5.1 Examples of Health Care Responsibility Centers

Inpatient Nursing Unit
Head nurse (BSN)
Clinical specialist (BSN)
Staff nurses (RN)
Licensed practical nurses
Nurse aids
Clerks

Primary Care Office
Primary care physician (M.D.)
Nurse practitioner (MSN)
Office nurse (RN or LPN)
Clerks

Clinical Laboratory
Chief pathologist (M.D.)
Laboratory Manager (M.S. or Ph.D.)
Certified technicians (B.S.)
Assistant technicians
Clerks

Intensive Care Unit
Physician manager (M.D.)
Head nurse (BSN)
Clinical specialists (BSN)
Staff nurses (RN)
Licensed practical nurses (LPN)

Housekeeping
Supervisor
Housekeeping personnel

Physical Therapy
Chief physical therapist (BS, RPT)
Physical therapists (BS, RPT)
Therapy aids
Clerks

team or group accountability, sharing negotiation of the expectations, design of the work, and rewards of achievement. Large groups working in dynamic environments such as patient care usually need some designated spokesperson. The practical result is that the leader remains, but the group becomes more participative and democratic. The leader's role now emphasizes coordination, coaching, and external communications.

This structure has proven successful for a number of leading health care organizations.[7,8] It is important to understand how it differs from traditional thought about accountability. Figure 5.2 emphasizes the key distinctions. The agreement is negotiated, not imposed. The leader coaches, not commands. The measures of performance reflect the full range of resource dependencies, not simply output and cost. The team is encouraged, not threatened. It is expected to understand both the origin and validity of the goals, and the ways to manipulate the work environment to improve goal achievement. In short, it is dramatically different from the traditional view of organizations as top-down, authoritatively driven structures.[9,10,11] This view is not only prevalent among leading health care organizations, it is highly consistent with what has been learned about organizations and the motivation of people in them during the twentieth century.[12]

Figure 5.2 New and Traditional Accountability Approaches

New	Traditional
Shared Vision Management and workers understand their mutual dependence upon customers, and share a common vision of how they will succeed.	**Adversarial Competition** Management and workers view themselves as dividing a fixed set of resources and competing for shares.
Negotiated Agreement RC workers participate in analyzing resource dependency needs and work processes, commit themselves to a realistic level of achievement.	**Imposed Decision** Superiors in organization use authority to tell RC workers what production goals must be.
Coaching RCM provides information, answers questions, makes suggestions to workers who design new processes.	**Commanding** "The boss tells you what to do."
Full-Performance Measures Technical quality, patient/customer satisfaction, worker satisfaction, output, cost, and contribution to overall profit all considered in designing process, assessing performance.	**Partial-Performance Measures** Usually just cost and output. RC team could "game" by cutting quality and satisfaction.
Encouragement Workers trained to solve problems, encouraged to try, praised for success, and often given monetary incentives for meeting goals.	**Threats** Workers punished for failures, sometimes even when they weren't at fault.

Criteria for RC Design

Design of RCs is one of the organizing tasks. It is usually carried out under the supervision of the executive office, with each level designing its subordinate groups. The design criteria for each responsibility center are:

1. *To assign every necessary task to a single RC.* If tasks are assigned to more than one RC or to no RC, there is no way of ensuring accountability.

2. *To assign related tasks to the same RC.* If related tasks are assigned to different RCs, problems of continuity and coordination may arise.

3. *To assign tasks requiring similar skills to the same RC.* A work group and a manager with a common background can communicate with each other more easily.

4. *To limit each RC to a reasonable overall set of tasks.* The RC must be able to maintain control of the activity by direct communication of group members, imposing time, geographic, technical, and size limits on RCs.

These criteria are more difficult in reality than they sound on paper. The design of RCs is clearly related to the identification of tasks. Certain potential tasks, such as updating patient record will have to be subdivided into types of entries and possibly shifts, so that entries are made by every patient care RC, and the record is updated in the middle of the night, when necessary. Scrupulous attention to task definition and accountability assignment will complete the first criterion. The second and third are harder. At a conceptual level, all care of each patient is interrelated, suggesting that the unit of organization should be the patient. At the same time, it is impossible for one person, or even one team, to master all the skills necessary to care for seriously ill patients, suggesting that the unit of organization should be skill or function. Figure 5.3, a partial list of routine needs of a recovering surgical patient, illustrates the problem. In the real world of health care, criterion 2, relating tasks, and criterion 3, relating skills, are intrinsically in conflict. One calls for an organization around patients with similar needs (as exist in ICUs, nurseries, primary care clinics, etc.). The other calls for organization around similar skills (as also exist in therapy departments, pharmacies, diagnostic services).

Figure 5.3 Patient Need and Professional Skill Conflicts

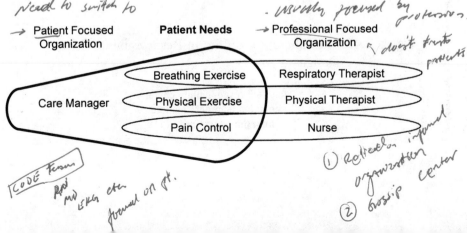

Similar conflicts exist with geography and function. Is it better to put all the therapists in one place, or one in each care site? Should the pharmacists be located on the floors, more convenient to the users, or in the pharmacy, where a smaller number might do the same amount of work? Finally, as health care organizations grow larger, conflicts arise over the final criterion, the span of control. Should there be a pharmacy organization in each hospital, or a single one serving the whole? The design criteria (tasks, relationships, skills, and span) are inherently in conflict. There are frequently two geographic units with similar functions, or two functions in the same geographic area, or two skills required for the same function. Many large organizations have several laboratories. Emergency rooms require almost every clinical profession, plus housekeeping and other plant services. Even the task assignment of the nursing unit RC is slightly ambiguous, because housekeeping, dietary, several diagnostic and treatment services, and medical staff are all important to the function of the nursing unit.

As a result, there is no such thing as a perfect accountability hierarchy. The conflicts arise again and again, and must be met with supplementary arrangements to assure an acceptable overall quality and cost. And, because conditions change, there is no permanent solution (Figure 5.4).

Implementing the Criteria

In every case where these conflicts arise, trade-offs must be made to resolve them. Well-run hospitals consider the next two steps of organization design—setting the reporting hierarchy of middle management and building collateral communications—as ways of overcoming the weaknesses of a specific set of RCs. When the RC design process is properly done, it generates three results:

1. It specifies the RCs and the RCMs.
2. It identifies the trade-offs, or departures from criteria, that were made to resolve particular conflicts.

Figure 5.4 The Inherent Conflict in Responsibility Center Design

Any real responsibility center contains inherent conflicts from the design criteria.

3. It suggests hierarchical and collateral relationships that will optimize these trade-offs.

In other words, there are always three avenues to organizational improvement—changing the RCs, revising the middle management structure, and strengthening collateral relationships.

Grouping RCs

The Traditional Pyramid

The accountability structure allows the division of labor both between and within groups, and it permits a hierarchy to be formed using the group leaders as linking elements in a chain which can start at a relatively simple set of related tasks and reach to the balanced scorecard accountability of the governing board. Monitors of aggregates such as nursing departments are often identified as **middle managers,** or, at the highest level, **executives.** It is the core concept of formal organization, the frame on which the real structure is built. The linking of progressively larger groups of RCs creates the traditional pyramidal structure of formal organizations, as shown in Figure 5.5.

The groups within the traditional pyramid are formed using the same criteria as the RCs. They are typically formed around functional (nursing, medicine, laboratory, etc.) activities, geographic sites (hospitals, large clinics, etc.), and specific markets or patient groups (HMO

Figure 5.5 Linking Work Groups into the Accountability Hierarchy

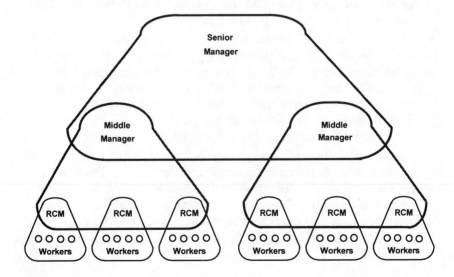

clients, children, mental health, etc.) Unfortunately, the inherent conflicts continue, and the rule in Figure 5.3 applies. There is never a
perfect solution.

The function of middle management is to facilitate the effective
performance of the RCs. Middle managers ensure that each of their
RCs receives the resources it needs and meets the demands for service
anticipated in the expectations. They communicate open systems needs
downward and subordinates' views upward. They are accountable upward for adherence to agreed-upon expectations, downward for resolving issues their subordinates cannot, and both ways for negotiating the
expectations. That is to say, middle managers have an explicit obligation
to respond to their subordinates as well as to their superiors.

Mintzberg notes that, in addition to the accountability hierarchy,
the parts of the pyramid all have boundary-spanning activities with each
other and often with the external environment. In addition, he notes
that some of the accountability hierarchies serve the central purpose
of the organization and are traditionally called **line units**, while others
serve technical and logistic support activities, sometimes called **staff
units**, and still others constitute the **strategic apex**.[13]

Mintzberg's model fits health care organizations well. It is expanded
in this text to five major systems Figure 5.6:

- *Governance:* The top of the strategic apex of Mintzberg's model,
  is responsible for external relations, surveillance, and strategic
  responses.
- *Executive:* Part of the strategic apex responsible for the effective
  operation of governance and the maintenance of effective technical
  and support functions for the clinical system
- *Clinical:* The "line" of the health care organization, delivering
  service to the ultimate customer or patient. The clinical system
  includes all the professional caregivers. The emergence of
  the health care organization from its predecessor hospitals
  and independent physician offices is marked by the formal
  incorporation of physicians, although there are a variety of
  mechanisms for accomplishing the linkage.
- *Finance, Planning, Marketing, and Information Services:* Technical
  services that support the strategic and line units. These units
  are essential to the operation of large-scale organizations. Their
  growth is directly related to the organization's ability to handle
  more complex problems and to replace smaller enterprises.
- *Human Resources and Plant Services:* The logistic support activities
  for all the other units.

Information Flows and Accountability

The formal organization hierarchy is made real by two elements of information flow and a third of authority and accountability. First, it is the designated channel by which expectations are negotiated, exchanging information in both directions until the external needs and governing board strategies are matched by commitments on the part of divisions and individual work groups. Second, it is the channel for the distribution of performance information, with the reports of actual performance and comparison to expectation reflecting the accountability of each level. A specific measure, such as patient satisfaction scores, can be reported to an individual RC, an aggregate of several similar RCs, an individual caregiving unit, and a health care system as a whole, as indicated in Figure 5.7. At each level, the routine report gives the individual values and the average of the units directly accountable. That is, the lines of information dissemination actually define the formal organization. Third, should a pair of levels fail to agree upon expectations, or a unit consistently fail to meet them, the superior unit is responsible for analyzing and resolving the problem. That is, while the emphasis

Figure 5.6 Traditional Health Care Pyramid, after Mintzberg

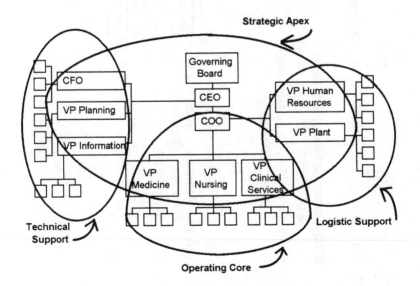

Adapted from H. Mintzberg, *The Structuring of Organizations: A Synthesis of Research* (Englewood Cliffs, NJ: Prentice-Hall), pp. 18–35.

Figure 5.7 Vertical Information Flows in an Accountability Hierarchy

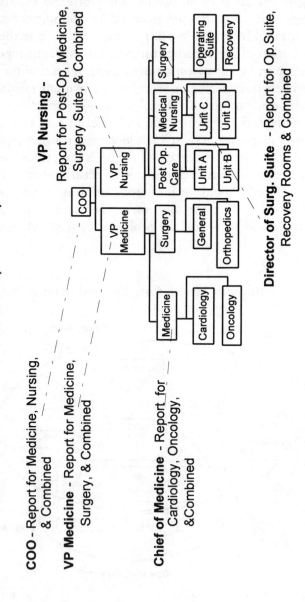

COO - Report for Medicine, Nursing, & Combined

VP Medicine - Report for Medicine, Surgery, & Combined

VP Nursing - Report for Post-Op, Medicine, Surgery Suite, & Combined

Chief of Medicine - Report for Cardiology, Oncology, &Combined

Director of Surg. Suite - Report for Op.Suite, Recovery Rooms & Combined is always on negotiation of solutions and prevention of problems, the ultimate authority and responsibility of the formal organization to meet external conditions remains.

As Mintzberg suggests, it is relatively easy to tie elements of the organization horizontally as well as vertically. The information flows for negotiation and monitoring can specify as many ties to the technical and support activities as necessary.[14] Figure 5.8 shows a formal relationship between a line unit, a technical unit, and a support unit. Such an association allows the technical and support units to subdivide their work according to line clients.

Formal Organization of the Clinical System

The inherent conflicts in grouping people and RCs are most serious in the clinical system. The problems of patient (task)-oriented or professional (skill)-oriented groupings are severe. Geography and time are both important. (The organization that fits during peak hours may be absurd in slack.) Overshadowing these are the history of physicians' independence from the accountability hierarchy, and differences in relative status between physicians and other caregivers. Together, they make clinical organization design a formidable challenge. Three major approaches have been used: separate medical and nonmedical hierarchies, integrated clinical organizations, and matrix organizations. Well-run health care organizations appear to succeed not so much because they have picked a specific structure as because they identify and correct problems as they arise within the structure they have selected.

Figure 5.8 Horizontal Information Flows in an Accountability Hierarchy

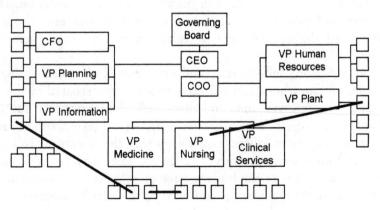

Separate Medical and Nonmedical Hierarchies

Hospitals traditionally emphasized similar skills or professional knowledge in establishing separate clinical hierarchies, one for their employees and the other for attending physicians. The result is an organization such as that shown in Figure 5.5, which emphasizes the distinctiveness of the medical staff and of the various clinical support activities. The physician hierarchy was severely limited in scope. The expectations consisted of limited agreements covering general qualifications, basic quality of care and adherence to a few standard procedures.

The organization of Figure 5.9 has one great strength and a number of potentially disabling weaknesses. Its strength is that the hierarchical chains—medicine, nursing, and the clinical support services—have strong professional content. Participants in each group share similar training, usually regulated by licensure or certification. The RCs can make use of their staff's professional knowledge, skills, and socialization to define and control activities. As a result, peers confer about highly technical matters, and consensus about a new practice can be reached quickly, unless it crosses hierarchical lines.

Conversely, the Figure 5.9 organization creates a large number of hierarchies with a tendency to concern themselves with their own objectives rather than the organization's. They all pressure the executive office to give them equal recognition, regardless of their relative contributions. This results in many short hierarchies, such as social services and cardiopulmonology, and a few long and complex ones, such as nursing or laboratory. As a result, some RCs have short chains to the strategic apex, while others are insulated by several layers of middle management. Middle managers on the same level have vastly different hierarchies reporting to them. The tendency of the professions to proliferate, driven by the increasing specialization of science, has emphasized the weaknesses of the conventional organization. There are more professions, more hierarchies, and more concerns about the weakness of the conventional organization in 1990 than there were in 1960.

The isolation, self-interest, and competition that can spring up between, say, anesthesia and operating rooms is exacerbated by the split between the employee units and their medical counterparts, surgeons and anesthesiologists. While these four units (and several others) must cooperate to complete surgery on any patient, the structure gives them poor mechanisms and incentives to do so. The surgeons, who might think of themselves as the leaders, have only limited accountability to the medical staff organization, and none to the anesthesiologists or the managers of the employee services.

Figure 5.9 Traditional Clinical Relationships

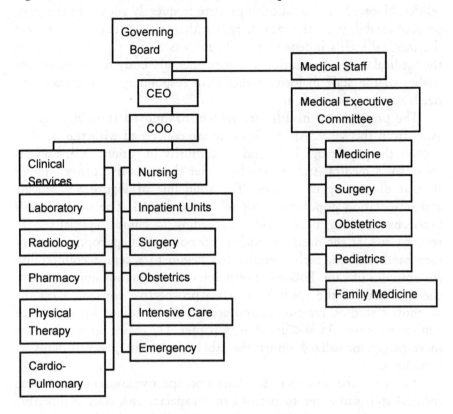

Communication between these chains usually occurs through informal or collateral structures. Informal communications among individuals treating the same patient tend to die out as the organization becomes larger. Deliberate efforts to stimulate the collateral organization and the informal organization become necessary. The most up-to-date version of the conventional organization is supplemented by a great variety of collateral committees, task forces, work groups, networks, and affiliations, all aimed at integrating the various hierarchies effectively. Examples include discharge planning committees, budget committees, ethics committees, operating room committees, and a number of ad hoc planning teams and task forces, and work groups.

Extending Accountability to the Medical Staff

For many years it was common to indicate the medical staff as a separate and distinct organization. Varieties of reporting relationships were used, many of them deliberately ambiguous, to explain how the medical staff, executive office, and governing board shared responsibilities. "Dotted line" relationships were frequently shown in the past, or accountability to the board, rather than the executive, to reflect the medical staff's independence. There was also a tendency to treat the medical staff organization as a parliamentary body representing the wishes of the staff majority rather than responding to the exchange needs of the organization.

The pressure for health care reform has moved thinking steadily away from this view. Although many are concerned with the need to protect the physician's independent authority in patient care, there is room for a medical staff hierarchy under the executive office, similar to that of nursing or finance. The solid line of Figure 5.9 reflects a representation popular in hospitals around 1985. The medical staff hierarchy has long been divided according to clinical specialties. In recent years, as the need for quality, economy, and appropriateness of care has increased, each specialty has begun to accept accountability for episodes of care. Following principles of continuous improvement, the members of the specialty reach a prospective consensus on the diagnostic studies, treatment, and acceptable outcomes for groups of similar patients. As discussed in Chapter 11, these agreements are increasingly formalized under the label of patient care protocols or guidelines.

As part of the process of reaching a prospective consensus, a strong medical staff can agree to performance expectations, thus completing the accountability commitment of the formal hierarchy. Many doctors are now employed as RCMs and middle managers in clinical organizations. (They are usually called chiefs.) Their obligations in these roles are no different from those of other RCMs, but more than any one else, they must follow continuous improvement principles and the new approaches to accountability shown in Figure 5.2.[15] In the transformation, a whole new dimension is added to information needs. The data originally collected by RCs and organized around the accountability hierarchy must now be presented by patient type to allow the medical specialty to evaluate its practices. Figure 5.10 shows the translation required.

This approach has been rewarding, but it is not without flaws. Gaining support, designing, and implementing protocols are all difficult steps; their success is not proven in more than a few situations. Close collaboration across the formal organization is required to achieve improvements. All of the clinical specialties involved in care must participate to gain full value from the protocols.

Figure 5.10 Translating from Hierarchical (Input) to Clinical (Output) Measurement

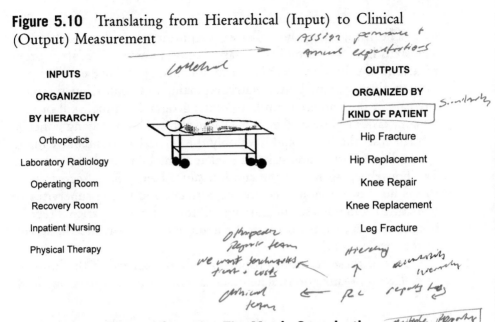

INPUTS	OUTPUTS
ORGANIZED	ORGANIZED BY
BY HIERARCHY	KIND OF PATIENT
Orthopedics	Hip Fracture
Laboratory Radiology	Hip Replacement
Operating Room	Knee Repair
Recovery Room	Knee Replacement
Inpatient Nursing	Leg Fracture
Physical Therapy	

Extending the Formal Hierarchy: The Matrix Organization

Formal hierarchies are powerful but limited devices which comprise only part of any real organization. Six approaches help overcome their intrinsic problems:

1. Build upon the informal organization and the professional commitment of health care workers to do a good job. A culture encouraging cooperation and reinforcing the need to succeed as a whole will help people collaborate. Leadership example and formal incentives can help.[16]

2. Deliberately design performance measures, information systems, and incentives to encourage collaboration. If an RC has expectations that can only be met by collaboration, it will collaborate. Conversely, if its expectations cover only things it can do on its own, it will resist collaboration.[17]

3. Use designated "liaison positions" to encourage information transfer.[18] These are particularly useful in relating line to technical and logistic support units. They also appear in routine interfacing tasks, such as patient scheduling positions.

4. Rely upon line managers in a position to negotiate integration.[19] The middle manager or executives can be the intermediaries for two or more of the units reporting to them.

5. Develop parts of the collateral organization to design expectations and work processes optimizing the whole.[20]

6. Formalize multiple accountabilities in a matrix structure.

Successful health care organizations rely constantly on the first four. The fifth, using the collateral organization, is discussed below. The sixth has had a long history as a tempting device.[21] **Matrix organizations** are those where RCs or middle managers have explicit, permanent, dual accountability. Matrix reporting can be developed around any pair of the potential conflict points: geography, time, skill or profession, task or patient. Figure 5.11 illustrates the underlying concept. In each case, the RC would have only the vertical accountability under the traditional structure; it has a dual accountability under the matrix. The housekeeping RC in the surgical suite, Figure 5.11, reports both to the head of the housekeeping department and to the supervisor of operating room nurses. The nursing RC for orthopedic patients reports both to the supervisor for surgical nursing and to the orthopedic service of the medical staff.

Most of these relationships are already recognized in the informal or collateral organizations. The practical effect of the matrix organiza-

Figure 5.11   Elementary Models of Matrix Relationships

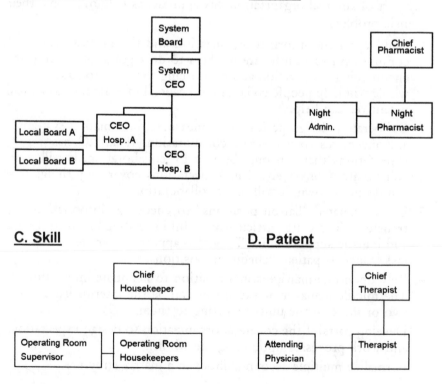

tion is to emphasize the most important ones by making them permanent and adding them to the conventional reporting relationships. It has intuitive appeal as a description of hospital organization, because many RCMs have a subordinate relationship to another profession in addition to their hierarchical one. As the examples in the preceding paragraph suggest, these relationships are frequently between parallel chains in the clinical hierarchies, such as nursing or medicine. Under the conventional organization, the cross-chain obligations can be overlooked, even though the result impairs quality of care. Matrix organization explicitly defines the most important obligation outside the RCM's own profession or trade.

The matrix organization has proven more difficult to implement in health care than it might at first appear,[22] for two reasons. First, although the communications difficulties of the conventional organization frequently involve several professions or hierarchies, it is impractical to consider more than a dual reporting matrix. Thus, all the intrinsic conflicts with the units *not* formalized in the matrix remain; indeed, they can be exacerbated. Second, the dual reporting structure can easily deteriorate into a competitive relationship among three people, the RCMs and their two supervisors. Three-person relationships are notoriously unstable in general, and those in hospital matrix organizations are exacerbated by conflicts involving professional groups and status. (For example, consider the opportunities to form two-on-one adversarial pairs in Figure 5.11 among the orthopedic head nurse, the orthopedists, and a nursing supervisor whose specialty is surgical nursing.[23])

Despite their difficulties, some forms of matrix organization appear to be a permanent part of health care organization design. Matrix organizations between the professional functions of the traditional clinical hierarchy and the market-oriented service lines or business units hold great promise. Other matrix designs balancing relationships which are less directly market-oriented appear to be useful in specific kinds of health care organizations.

The Service Line Matrix—Market by Function

Market-oriented analyses quickly recognize that patient and buyer populations are not homogeneous in their needs, and must be segmented into groups to be approached effectively.[24] Common examples include segmentation by geography (e.g., Northside Clinic); demography (Women's Health); or disease (Mental Health) or treatment resources (Children's Hospital, Nursing Home). Health care organizations frequently create separate hierarchies for various markets called **service**

lines or **business units.** The lines can also include nonhealth care activities, such as health insurance.

If these divisions are organized only according to their market segment, they must rely on collateral communications to receive services from conventionally organized departments. For example, a long-term care division would have no direct accountability to professional units providing clinical services in an acute inpatient division. As a result, it might depart from the standards of quality expected in the rest of the organization. Conversely, if the traditional clinical organization is followed, nursing and medicine in long-term care have no accountability for the cost or quality of overall service provided the long-term care patients. They might give long-term care patients lower priority, or even ignore them.

Figure 5.12 shows a service line matrix structure for a small facility offering acute inpatient, outpatient, and long-term care. Within each division, individuals or RCs have a dual reporting responsibility—to the division director, and to the clinical supervisor. As indicated, a formal relationship might be omitted where an informal agreement, occasional committee meeting, or even a purchase contract were sufficient.

As the whole organization grows larger, this form of matrix organization expands into what are called multidivisional organizations.[25] The matrix concept may or may not be carried out to all levels. Usually it is not when the subsidiaries reach sufficient size to be competitive on their own. That is, a nursing RC might have a dual reporting relationship in a small rural facility. Only the service line nursing

Figure 5.12 Small Service Line Matrix Structure

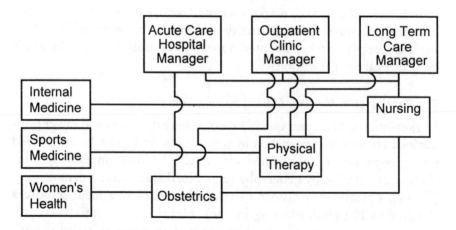

director might report dually in a medium-sized clinic, and only the chief executive might report dually in a large multihospital chain.

Other Matrix Organizations

The most common variant of multidivisional organization now in place is the multihospital system. For-profit systems tend to use traditional hierarchical structures shown in Figure 5.9. Not-for-profit systems have tended to decentralize the governance function, centralizing only some elements of strategic planning and finance, but at least the CEO holds an explicit dual accountability, as shown in Figure 5.13.[26]

Another variant of the matrix organization has emerged in academic medical centers. It assigns authority and accountability to physician chiefs who also chair medical departments. This explicitly establishes a formal hierarchy for medical staff organization on the basis of medical specialty. Other units, including clinical services like nursing, laboratories, imaging and technical or logistic support like finance and plant services, have a dual reporting relationship to their professional hierarchy as well as to the medical hierarchy.[27] The matrix is responsible for resources—cost, efficiency, and revenue—as well as quality of care. In the constrained revenue situation that exists under reform, they must seek efficiencies and improved quality. The management team of the Johns Hopkins Hospital argues that their organization has done so more successfully than a conventional organization would have.[28]

The Collateral Organization or Decision-Making Structure

The accountability hierarchy is good at giving care. It starts stopped hearts, replaces organs, cures infections, delivers babies, and carries out thousands of specific tasks in the process. The collateral organization is good at making decisions. It sets goals, identifies alternatives, resolves priorities, builds consensus, and settles conflicts covering thousands of specific activities. Its processes—who decides what, when, and how—define the organizational culture and determine the success of stakeholder negotiations.

No real organization could function without one. The technical and logistic support sections are useless without mechanisms for effective communication with the line. Without the means of relating between the line accountability chains, the conflict, confusion, and tension would soon stop any health care organization from functioning. The inventions that permit the growth of large organizations outside

Figure 5.13 Traditional and Matrix Hierarchies in Multi-Institutional Systems

A. Traditional Structure

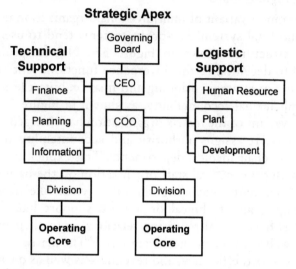

Note: Support groups frequently designate liaison individuals.

B. Matrix Structure

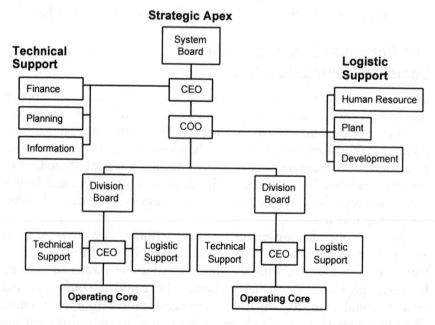

Note: Support groups are frequently linked in addition.

of health care, like the nineteenth century railroads and the twentieth century chemical and automobile industries, are largely in the collateral organization.[29,30]

The collateral organization always involves two or more units of the formal hierarchy. It spans units in different hierarchies for understanding and communicating perceptions about the outside environment and the daily work. It is a network of committees, task forces, and work groups linking managers at several different levels. Most managers are involved in several collateral activities.

Figure 5.14 gives some common examples. Collateral relationships are either permanent or ad hoc, in general they shift much more often than hierarchical ones. Most institutions have several planning committees operating simultaneously at various levels of the organization. Many are formed as issues arise and disbanded after a single decision. The well-designed hospital attempts to move the consensus as quickly as possible into the formal accountability hierarchy where quantitative expectations can be negotiated to encourage efficient responses. A capital budget committee is needed at least annually, and is usually permanent, like the credentials committee of the medical staff. At operational levels, groups such as the pharmacy committee and the medical data committee are permanent resources.

Yet because it does not actually give care, the entire collateral organization is overhead, a cost burden on the line. As the market gets more demanding, hospital decision processes must yield more difficult decisions better and faster, just as the line must learn to give higher quality, more efficient care. Control of the collateral organization can be a problem. Establishing the processes is the unique domain of managers; nobody else thinks about them much. Improving decision processes calls for understanding the kinds of decisions to be made, developing new patterns of delegation, and supporting the decision structure effectively.

Classifying Decisions

As it resolves the problems of resource dependency, develops management strategy, and pursues continuous improvement, any firm or organization faces four kinds of decisions: mission or vision (what the business is and why); resource allocation (products, quality, volume, price, method, and profit); organizational design (decision procedures, communication, authority), and implementation (recruiting, selecting, and training personnel, plus specific, detailed procedures and technology). It must reach these continually and collaboratively among both

Figure 5.14 Examples of the Collateral Organization

Committee Title	Purpose	Membership	Principal Technical Support	Duration
Strategic Planning	Develop and evaluate strategic options	Board members, CEO, COO, CFO, VP of planning	Planning	Permanent
Programmatic Planning	Develop and evaluate specific programs and implementation options	Managers of units directly involved, planning staff, finance staff	Planning	Ad hoc (one for each important project)
Pharmacy and Therapeutics	Decide drugs for hospital use, study and improve drug costs	Physicians representing several specialties, nurses, chief pharmacist	Pharmacy	Permanent
Capital Budget Request	Prioritize competing requests for capital funds	Medical staff leaders, executive office, clinical service representatives, CFO	Finance	Annual
Outpatient Scheduling Study	Improve patient service in outpatient areas	Medical, nursing, clinical service managers directly involved	Management engineering	Ad hoc
Clinical Protocol Development	Develop care plan for specific diagnosis	Medical leaders from involved specialties, nursing, clinical support services	Medical records, information services, finance	Ad hoc

worker and customer stakeholders, building new consensuses as needs, power relationships, and technologies change.[31,32]

The four classes can be expanded into the processes which are now accepted as good practice in health care. Figure 5.15 shows this relationship.[33] (Admittedly, real life processes are iterative and overlapping compared to the neat rows and columns of the figure.) Mission and vision setting rest upon environmental assessment and are implemented by deliberate strategies relating to a specific market. Resource allocation begins with long-range planning of services and finances, which define plans for facilities and human resources and in turn, operating and capital budgets. Implementation begins with personnel selection and continues with detailed operational procedures, training, performance evaluation and rewards. Organization design establishes the formal structure of accountability and the roles and membership of standing and ad hoc committees. Policies for information access, conflict resolution, and performance evaluation should support the design.

Achieving Effective Delegation

Criteria for Effective Decision Processes

The issue is how to improve these processes so that they support continuous improvement of line activities. Improvement involves making economically viable and timely decisions, designing new processes, and getting widespread agreement and support within the empowerment concept. The twin tests of the decisions and processes that result are realism in the marketplace and conviction among those who must implement them. Realism means they will lead to a successful future for the enterprise. They will meet the test of competition. Conviction means that they are persuasive; that is, most members of the organization will believe that the processes are sound, the decisions are realistic, and they as individuals will have a successful future.

Recognizing Mutual Stakeholder Rights

Modern health care organizations operate in an environment where all stakeholders have opinions and expect their opinions to receive serious attention. The hospitals of the twentieth century were a different environment where traditional treaties assigned authority for decisions and rigidly divided the organization "turf" among the stakeholders.[34] The doctor knew best, the nurse was "his handmaiden," and the patient followed orders rather than participating in care. Trustees felt they handled the business matters, and often thought of themselves as beholden to the institution, rather than the constituencies it serves.[35] Managers

Figure 5.15 A Classification of Decision Processes

Type	Level Strategic	Programmatic
Mission/vision	Environmental assessment Strategic plans	Marketing plans Specific joint ventures

Resource allocation	Services plan
	
	Financial plan
	
	Technology selection
		Facilities plan,
		  Human resources plan
		Operating budget,
		  Capital budget
		Equipment selection

Implementation	Personnel selection
	
	Human resource policies
	Process design
		Individual credentialing,
		  recruitment, and
		  development
		Incentive programs
		Patient care protocols,
		  policies, and procedures

Organizational	Accountability hierarchy Management system	Information plan Participation in care teams Conflict resolution mechanism Appeals mechanism

thought of themselves as the third leg of a (wobbly) three legged-stool with the physicians and the trustees.[36]

Ideas like these fail both realism and conviction tests. (Few will regret their passing; they are beginning to sound sexist and even absurd.) Today's world requires a much more democratic and dynamic structure of decision-making authority. This means that people from a variety of backgrounds must learn to share decisions they once considered their professional prerogatives, and also that they must learn to make decisions outside their professional areas. People will have both cognitive and emotional difficulties with the transition. At a cognitive level, training can overcome ignorance of outsiders' values and lack of technical knowledge. A broader fact base in the presentation of each decision will help people reach beyond their field. The education will be specific rather than general. Successful organizations will teach people how to choose between trans-plasminogen activase (TPA) and streptokinase, not how to be cardiologists and health economists. This expanded cognitive requirement is a major force in the growth of information systems, discussed in Chapters 9 and 10.

The continuous improvement focus on a shared vision and emphasis on coaching and leadership helps the emotional adjustment to new decision roles. Revising the mission and vision starts a process of reeducation because it focuses all stakeholders' attention on what the organization in fact is—the best device available to the stakeholders to achieve common goals. It is reviewed annually partially to reinforce everybody's adjustment to new ways. The initial years particularly require leadership skills, patience, and sensitivity from health care managers. Beyond revisiting the vision, it is important to reinforce the new style with examples and cases showing its advantages. That is, the decision system must advertise its successes. So the first problems attacked are easy ones where most people agree improvement is possible. The capital and operating budget programs evolve over several years as people become comfortable with the accountability involved. Pilot programs test next steps, provide visible examples, and develop coaches. At each step, victories are deliberately identified and celebrated.

Building Effective Delegation

New rules must replace the old turf domains for delegating decisions. The realism criterion demands continuous improvement of both cost and quality. The conviction criterion must assure all stakeholders that their individual interests will not be subverted by decisions beyond their immediate surveillance.[37] The processes to meet these criteria must integrate complex patient and customer values with extensive technical knowledge from a wide span of professions. The integration should be complete, timely, and efficient. A missing or misstated stakeholder or technical viewpoint may lead to failure. Decisions should be prompt, if only to clear the field for the next problem. Stakeholder gridlock will be fatal. Finally, the decisions should be efficient, optimizing the scarce time of the decision makers.

Dynamic accountable delegation is used to meet these criteria. "Dynamic" means that the topics are selected by the central governance structure according to stakeholder needs related to the topic itself, rather than unvarying treaties. There are no sacred cows or private domains. "Accountable" protects the right to have one's view heard if necessary. Each stakeholder group understands that it has a reliable mechanism to a fair hearing on any question, at its discretion. Such a mechanism rarely existed under the old treaties. "Delegation" assigns decisions to the stakeholders most important to their implementation. Within accountability limits, delegation is complete. The boundaries of an acceptable decision are established in advance, and decisions within the boundaries are accepted without debate. The decisions are not micromanaged by meddling or ritualistic reviews.

The most widespread model of accountable delegation is the medical staff credentialling system, where decisions about individual physicians are made by physicians professionally competent to do so, but the criteria, process, and result are subject to review by a governing board representing a much broader constituency.

Dynamic accountability allows special committees to negotiate specific conflicts, or direct representation of a minority position, such as placing physicians on governing boards. At the same time, it allows a reversibility the old rules never had. A specific decision or a class of decisions can always be reviewed if some stakeholders feel aggrieved enough. In practice a very small fraction of the delegated decisions is challenged. This is because the delegates understand the guidelines they receive from the other stakeholders, and understand that it is in their interest to make the right to review moot by accommodating others' needs in the initial decision.

Under accountable delegation, the governing board sets the mission and vision on behalf of the customer stakeholders. Doctors and employees buy into the mission by making suggestions, but ultimately by signing on. Broad participation, understanding, and acceptance are essential. Beyond the mission and vision, the more abstract, global, or central the decision, generally toward the top and left of Figure 5.15, the greater the need for direct customer participation. Trustees focus on the scope of services, long-range financial plan, and budget guidelines. These decisions provide landmarks for insider delegation of the balance of the resource allocation and implementation decisions.

The larger the contribution of clinical knowledge to the solution, generally toward the bottom and right of Figure 5.15, the more authority to propose solutions is delegated to the inside stakeholders. Most budget detail, care plan, and implementation decisions are delegated to insiders held accountable to the mission and vision and overall cost constraints. Cross-functional teams are also accountable delegation. In the case of clinical guidelines the delegation is actually from individual physicians to the team. It involves admitting the realism of customer input.

Supporting the Decision System

The executive office is the accountable delegate for the organizational decisions of Figure 5.15. It designs the processes and suggests the accountable delegation in accordance with the stakeholder demands and the criteria of realism and conviction. Conversely, it generally plays a supporting, rather than a direct role, for the rest of Figure 5.15, the mission and vision, resource allocation, and implementation decisions.

Designing the Decision Process

There are four parts to designing an effective decision process. First the rules must have recognized authorities.[38] Decision-making rules tend to be easy to forget and even easier to attack when the decision itself is not what the stakeholder hoped for. Conflicts about the rules can disable the entire continuous improvement effort. The bylaws for the board and medical staff constitute the major authorities, documenting agreements which are historically tested and formally recognized. Procedure manuals and memoranda from accountable individuals define less important ones. Well-written rules develop authority as they are used. Decisions reached and conflicts resolved become a body of "case law" which is accepted by all. As good rules become accepted, they legitimate the process and diminish conflict.

Second, good design must include appeals mechanisms for both the specific decision and the decision process. To meet the conviction criterion, any stakeholder who feels aggrieved enough must be able to appeal either process or result. If the appeal generates a sufficient constituency for change, change can occur. If not, the individual can accept the decision or leave the organization. The decision system can do no more than provide an avenue for prompt and fair hearing, but it must do that much. The board and its major committees will be important as the final appeals bodies.

Third, the rules are supported by appointing and charging committees, setting agendas, keeping minutes, training people to follow procedures, and supplying information and coaches. Leaders in all parts of the organization must know what the relevant bylaws and procedures say, or how to find out. A beginning doctor, worker or trustee is not expected to memorize the decision-making rules, but rather to know and trust someone who does. Knowing or finding the answer is properly the role of every first line supervisor and medical division chief. Training these people in decision making is an obvious step, already incorporated in the continuous improvement programs of well-managed institutions.[39]

Fourth, the decision system must be enforced. A few flagrant departures can destroy it. Exceptions to the rules and special pleadings beyond the appeals process must be strongly and promptly resisted. Enforcement means that behavior is redirected according to the rules. Punishment is not involved. Except in the rare case of deliberately

Figure 5.16 Structuring the Collateral Organization

Decision	Committee	Delegation From	Delegation To	Accountability	Authority
Financial guidelines	Finance	Governing board	Finance committee, finance, CEO	Strategic and financial plans	Bylaws
New program evaluation	Ad hoc	Executive office	Caregivers and managers directly involved	Mission, cost, quality	Budget procedure manual
Drug selection and use	Pharmacy and thera-peutics	Medical executive committee	Designated physician and nursing representatives, pharmacist	Quality, cost, physician satisfaction	Medical staff bylaws
Outpatient scheduling	Ad hoc	Executive office	Caregivers and managers directly involved	Cost, output, patient and physician satisfaction	Traditionally accepted
Clinical protocol	Ad hoc	Medical staff department	Involved specialists, nurses	Quality, cost, patient, physician, and nurse satisfaction	Medical staff bylaws

destructive behavior, the individuals are simply shown that following procedures is the effective path.

Figure 5.16 shows some examples of decisions which can be made through the delegation process. The committee membership represents the sector to which the decision is delegated. Their accountability is reflected in the charges and the authorities. Ideally, the charge should reflect the limits of the acceptable decisions and the authorities the rules governing process. In reality, many of these messages are implicit, taken for granted in the organization culture. Others are vague or ambiguous, because the various stakeholders have not fully formulated their own views. As organization members become familiar with delegated decision making, they learn to overcome these difficulties. The enterprise as a whole learns ways to address tough questions fairly and effectively, and moves ahead of its competitors as a result.

Using Middle Management Effectively

Middle managers constitute much of the collateral organization. The questions referred to them by the RCs are such that they must communicate across reporting hierarchies as well as within them. Meeting the expectations for the RCs reporting to them will usually be a matter of improving the fit of inputs, outputs, and demands with those of other units. Health care managers are usually professionally trained people with unique insights into the trends of specific technology. Thus, their views are also important to issues of environmental assessment. As a result, middle managers are members and leaders of most of the committees, task forces, and work groups that constitute the collateral structure.

In the ideal organization, middle management would be a small cadre of experts working on planning, budgeting, and recruitment for occasional RCM vacancies. In poorly designed organizations, middle managers are so consumed by daily problems that they have no time for planning, budgeting, or recruitment. A catch-22 is involved: middle managers are overworked, so they are tempted to add more middle managers; but adding more middle managers intensifies the communication problem without necessarily improving productivity or quality. Recent trends have been in the opposite direction: empowering RCs and RCMs to solve their own problems, controlling the activities and effectiveness of the collateral organization, and reducing the middle management structure.

Middle managers often lack training in management, because they are promoted from clinical professions. They sometimes come with dysfunctional accountability perspectives learned from community stereotypes. They must be taught their responsibilities, with emphasis upon their obligations to subordinates, and trained in collateral organization skills including problem analysis, coaching, and meeting management. One of the tasks of senior management is to help middle managers by coaching, by graduated experience opportunities, and by example.

Multi-Unit Organizations

A single health care facility might begin as an informal organization of less than a dozen people. By the time it reached 50 people, it would have a formal hierarchy and some established collateral activities. By developing these three parts of the organization, it could grow to a few thousand members, the size of a large hospital or very large clinic. But if it then decided to acquire a second health care organization, particularly one in a different geographic or product market, new organizational questions would arise. The health care industry has been moving rapidly toward that situation. As noted in Chapter 1, over half of all hospitals are now in multi-unit organizations. The largest and most structured of these arrangements, integrated health care systems, have been thriving. Multi-organizational arrangements tie together formal units capable of independent existence and often having independent competitors. They constitute a new and rapidly evolving level of organization in health care. Three issues contribute to understanding the new level: why multi-organization systems are formed, what their components can be, and how they are structured.

Why Multi-Unit Organizations Are Created

Conceptually, from the theories of open systems and strategic management, organizations grow in ways that increase the satisfaction of their stakeholders, and they stop growing when the next increment would represent a net decrease in satisfaction.[40] A certain amount of trial and error, and variation around the prevailing level of achievement is predictable. People will try an organization too ambitious, and fail. Others will delay, and be overtaken by successful larger and more innovative models.[41] Success will be widely copied, and soon embedded in the prevailing practice. Organizations in general have become larger and more diverse as the management learned skills to make larger units more effective.

Large organizations have several advantages that make them attractive.

- *Returns to size.* A larger organization of a single limited type is potentially more efficient and more responsive to a specific customer need than a small one. For example, an obstetrical delivery unit as it grows in size almost automatically encounters the following advantages:

- The demand for services, while always randomly varying, becomes more stable, so that idle periods waiting for patients are reduced, and average loads get much closer to peak loads. Thus caregivers and facilities are more efficient.
- Volumes of activity permit several skill levels of personnel. Assistants with less training can multiply the services of expensive professionals without impairing quality.
- The volume of purchases allows the organization to negotiate better prices.
- *Returns to scope of service.* Larger organizations can afford a wider array of services, making themselves more attractive to the market.
  - The small obstetrical unit might add prenatal care because it helps attract patients, reduces complications of childbirth (and therefor costs), and generates activities which can be done in the slack times when there are no deliveries.
  - It might then add other women's health services and well-child care because its market demanded them.
  - At larger volumes, the unit can support its own educational programs for patients and staff.
  - As it grows, the unit can afford to add specialty services, such as intensive neonatal care and services for high-risk mothers, that are used only rarely.
- *Improved control of the environment.* Larger units can be more effective in negotiating prices and conditions, allowing them to attract more patients and personnel.
  - As it grows, the obstetrical unit can attract the attention of powerful organizations which can be convinced to assist in meeting mutual goals. A large unit could approach the school system, the local government, and local industry to address problems of inadequate prenatal care and teenaged pregnancies.
  - Representing a large number of influentials who are also voters, the organization can lobby more effectively, and protect itself from adverse law and regulation. Licensure laws, government health insurance coverage, taxation, and employment regulation would all be important to the obstetrical unit.
  - Controlling a large share of the market, the organization can affect the price it receives for services. It can lobby

for increased Medicaid prices for obstetrical services. It can advertise to support demand at a profitable price. (Controlling the price of services sold is illegal under antitrust law in certain circumstances, but the proscription is not automatic until the seller approaches half of the total provider capability, is deliberately predatory, or colludes with other providers.)

- *Improved opportunities for capital.* Multiple organization structures open new financial opportunities which expand the available funds or in some cases, protect existing fund sources from risk or damage. The financial aspects of multiple corporate structures are discussed in Chapter 8.

Conversely, there are two forces which keep organizations from growing:

- *Market limitations.* Geography, wealth, and taste cause both customers and caregivers to choose other organizations. For the obstetrics unit, there are only a certain number of patients within a reasonable travel time for obstetrical services. A fraction of these women may prefer a smaller competitor. Similarly, doctors and nurses may look on the organization as impersonal, rigid, or out-of-date, and choose other employment.

- *Organizational limitations.* All organizations are prey to failure in their accountability hierarchy, where the subordinate units substitute their own goals for those of the collective, and in their collateral structures, where decisions get delayed, stalled, or diverted to special interests. In either case, the ability of the organization to satisfy its customers and workers declines. Large organizations represent large consensuses which may be difficult to build and even harder to hold together. The obstetric unit, having added units in several cities, may discover that those units run better by themselves than with a formal relationship.

Forms of Multi-Unit Organizations

There are two major forms of multi-unit organization. **Alliances** are interorganizational relations that are entered into primarily for strategic purposes.[42] They stop short of creating new corporations or changing ownership and allow members to disaffiliate relatively easily and quickly. As a result, the central organization must spend considerable energy sustaining the internal relationships. It can undertake only activities which the entire body consents to, even though all members do not participate, thus severely restricting its scope and flexibility. There is reason to think alliances are inherently transient; they either evolve toward more centralized structures or they disappear.[43]

Multi-corporate organizations involve separate corporate charters, with control expressed through ownership positions. Although the variations are limitless, three underlying schemes of multi-corporate structures can be detected either alone or in combination in specific examples:

1. *Parent-subsidiary.* A corporation may establish or acquire a wholly owned subsidiary which is usually dedicated to a specific activity. The most common example may be the creation of separate corporations, usually called *foundations* for managing endowment and frequently also for stimulating teaching and research. The foundation is usually tax-exempt; the parent may or may not be. Alternatively, the subsidiary could be for-profit for a particularly risky activity or protection of existing tax advantages. It would either use its for-profit status to reward private investors or it would be engaging in an activity categorized as taxable unrelated income by the IRS.

2. *Holding company.* This common model consists of one parent and a variety of subsidiaries that may differ in tax structure, purpose, location, or other parameters. The holding company model retains certain central control, specified in the reserved powers discussed in Chapter 5, but offers great flexibility in protecting assets and tax advantages, developing partnerships, and expanding sources of capital.

3. *Joint venture.* Two or more parent corporations invest in a subsidiary. The reasons for separate incorporation may include risk in tax, but they are also likely to include the advantages of having additional investors. The most common form of partnership activity is a joint venture partnership. Shared service organizations constitute one form of joint venture. The parents are frequently otherwise competing hospital corporations. Another common form is a joint venture with individuals in the hospital's medical staff or with a corporate structure of the staff itself.

How Components of Multi-Unit Organizations Are Described

Four distinct dimensions describe multi-unit organizations.

- *Size* is most often measured by dollar volumes flowing through a corporate entity, but it can also be measured by numbers of customers, employees, or affiliated units.

- *Geography* is the extent to which the units are in the same or different health care markets. Two systems equal in size, uniformity, and formality, are different if one is concentrated in a single geographic market, and the other operates in several markets. (Henry Ford Health System, concentrated in southeast Michigan, and The Mayo Clinics, operating in Minnesota, Florida, and Arizona, for example)
- *Uniformity* is the extent to which the units produce the same, complementary, or disparate scope of services. Structures which combine similar organizations (a chain of obstetrical delivery units, for example) are said to be **horizontally integrated**. Those combining complementary organizations (a prenatal care unit, a delivery unit, a well-baby and postpartum unit, women's services, and child and adolescent services, for example) are said to be **vertically integrated**. The ultimate vertical integration combines most ambulatory and inpatient acute care services and health insurance (Kaiser-Permanente, for example). **Diversified** organizations are composed of disparate services which are neither complementary or competing. Diversification is rare in health care. A few hospitals own diverse businesses such as food and laundry services, for example.
- *Formality* is measured by the degree to which the central or parent organization retains control. Structures which retain much control in the parent are said to be **centralized**. Those which allow much power in the subsidiary are **decentralized**.

How Multi-Unit Organizations Are Designed

The design of multi-unit organizations is an extension of the concepts of informal organization, formal hierarchy, collateral organization to a new level of complexity, since each of the units carries out these concepts already. Clearly, design must follow market realities; a focused organization of similar small clinics will not look like Kaiser-Permanente. The design process in use at present tends to accept as given the size, geography, and uniformity of the units, and adjust the formality to get optimal results from that configuration. Given the record to date, it is not surprising that there is no science of multi-organization design.[44]

Size of Multi-Unit Organizations

The average size of comparable health care corporations has grown steadily in the past quarter century. Hospitals, nursing home chains, HMOs all tend to be larger as corporate units. Even physician services, where the smallest possible unit, the solo practitioner, still remains, are organized into bigger units now than they were at the start of Medicare in 1967. The trend is clearly toward oligopolistic competition: a few competitors in each scope of service set competing in a single geographic area.

Geography

Many of the existing multi-unit organizations affiliate units that operate in separate geographic markets. Each unit competes with different corporations, under different laws and health insurance arrangements. Most of the religious hospital chains are examples. Before the 1990s, only a minority of multi-unit organizations pursued a strategy of growth within a single market. Vertically integrated models like Group Health of Puget Sound were relatively rare. Horizontally integrated models became more common as stronger hospitals in most larger cities acquired weaker competitors. There are now examples in most large cities.

U.S. cities differ significantly in many characteristics, including the incidence of disease and the quantities and costs of health care. They evolve at different rates, and have different market interests at any one time. A central corporation which tries to impose a single approach (the use of HMO physician panels, for example) must find locations receptive to its philosophy. Conversely, an organization like a religious hospital chain which inherits its geographic locations will need more decentralization to succeed. However, there is a competing model—if the service is narrowly defined and standardized to be optimally efficient, the central organization may compete successfully in many markets. Thus, fancy restaurants tend to be individually owned, but McDonald's sells worldwide. So far, there is no health care version of McDonald's.

Uniformity

Although horizontal integration continues at a rapid pace within and across geographic markets, the trend of the 1990s is to vertical integration. The traditional hospital represents a kind of vertical integration, and a number of its components are copied by single service competitors like freestanding laboratories, drug stores, and clinics. In general, the hospitals are winning the competition against these entities, but the victory is less than decisive. Organizations integrating physician services are growing rapidly, and many of these are allied with hospitals.[45] Health care systems, which generally incorporate hospitals, medical organizations, and insurance intermediaries, have grown steadily since the passage of the HMO act in 1972, and are growing rapidly in the 1990s. The trend suggests that the most common organization of the future will be integrated across all acute care services, and that they will have close ties to health insurance intermediaries.

Formality

No multi-unit organization is completely centralized or completely decentralized. (The former would be a single organization, and the latter would not be an organization at all.) More decentralized, looser affiliations rely on alliances rather than ownership arrangements. Alliances tend to exist among organizations not competing in the same geographic or service market, because direct competition tends to destroy consensus.[46] Alliances among similar hospitals in different geographic markets are common, as noted in Chapter 1. Alliances between competitors in adjacent markets are increasing. Regional affiliations link organizations which compete in adjacent geographic markets. Certain levels of hospital-physician relations, without formal ownership arrangements, can be understood as alliances in adjacent service markets. Contracts between hospitals and long-term care units are similar. These alliances may be interim stages, presaging future centralization by merger or acquisition.

At the same time, overly centralized organizations encounter serious difficulties as well. Particularly when the parent has subsidiaries in several different markets, responding to local needs becomes a problem, and carrying out empowerment concepts becomes more difficult. The successful centralized institutions have followed the model of the U.S. Constitution, centralizing certain decisions, called **reserved powers**, and deliberately decentralizing all decisions not specifically centralized. Reserved powers tend to be the core elements that define the central corporation—the mission, particular values of the owners, financial security, and the right to acquire or divest units. They are implemented by specific bylaws requirements for central authorization. The following reserved powers are common:

- Appointment of the subsidiary governance board and chief executive
- Approval of the strategic plan of the subsidiary
- Approval of the financial plan and annual budget
- Issuance of long-term debt
- Sale or purchase of any corporation or subsidiary, or the entry into any contract which might impair the authority of the central body in one of the preceding four.

This approach has allowed many for-profit and religious not-for-profit chains to operate in diverse geographic environments. It also is used in large vertically integrated systems, such as Intermountain and Henry Ford Health System.[47] It tends to succeed where a clear and attractive mission can be articulated and the central organization demonstrates its ability to achieve that mission.

Hospitals that are part of geographically diverse systems still look much like their independent competitors. They have better resources in governance, finance, training, information systems, and recruitment which they are still learning to exploit. It can be argued that these central resources give the systems significant advantages, but the only available evidence suggests that decision making has actually been decentralized in response to the severe environmental pressures of the early 1980s.[48]

Examples of Multi-Unit Organization

Figure 5.17 describes four multi-unit organizations, Premier Alliance, Mercy Health Services, Henry Ford Health System, and Healthtrust, Inc. They are representative examples of the diversity and strength of the concept. One of them, Premier, does not provide health care. Its purpose is to support large health care systems which are effective in their own markets. Mercy Health Services was one of the first reorganizations of Catholic hospitals. Like many of the Catholic systems, it was founded as a chain of hospitals serving independent communities. Over almost 20 years, it has grown both vertically and horizontally. Ford started as an integrated health system with salaried physicians. It is now a major force in southeast Michigan, providing comprehensive medical care under all forms of insurance, medical education, and research. HealthTrust, Inc. was part of HCA, one of the earliest and most successful chains of for-profit hospitals. It continues to operate facilities in a number of markets, and is working to become more vertically integrated.

Redesigning a Traditional Organization

Many existing health care organizations face extensive programs of redesign to transform themselves from traditional hospitals to at least comprehensive acute care services. They must organize their medical practices, change the relation of physicians and hospitals, tighten control of clinical services, and make substantial reductions in cost without impairing quality. To achieve this, they must revise their accountability hierarchies, expand their decision-making capability, improve their productivity, and evaluate an array of multi-unit organization opportunities, all within a relatively short time frame. One path to

Figure 5.17 Representative Multi-Unit Organizations

Organization	Type	History	Services	Size	Structure
Premier Alliance	Alliance	Founded 1983 Original members were Jewish hospitals	Supports members with purchasing, education, research funding	110 member and affiliate hospitals*	Decentralized. Affiliates have only a contract relationship
Mercy Health Services†	Vertically integrated, geographically diverse, religious chain	Founded 1976, by Detroit Province, Sisters of Mercy	Hospitals, affiliated physician organizations, HMO, PPO, long-term care facilities, home and hospice care	31 hospitals in 5 states.	Moderately centralized. Mission, plans, CEO, and financial powers reserved, but MHS has been innovative in arrangements to meet local needs.
Henry Ford Health System†	Vertically integrated not-for-profit system serving southeast Michigan	Founded 1917 by Henry Ford as an innovative health care organization	Ambulatory care, hospitals, employed and affiliated physician groups, HMO, PPO, some community clinics and long-term care	5 hospitals, 33 outpatient care sites	Centralized. Mission, plans, CEO, financial, and acquisition powers reserved. Local units have boards, but their strategic authority is limited.
Health Trust	For-profit hospital chain	Founded 1985 as a spin-off from another chain	Principally traditional hospital services	117 hospitals	Centralized. Mission, plans, CEO, financial, and acquisition powers reserved. Local units have boards, but their strategic authority is limited.

*Revenues for Premier are funds earned by the corporation, not the revenues of its members.
†Mercy Health Services and Henry Ford Health System have engaged in several collaborative ventures, including the contract management of two facilities and a point-of-service HMO product.

making the transition lies with organizational redesign. It begins by making the design the focus of participative discussion, and continues through a specific program of annual improvement in both line and collateral functioning.

Organization Design as a Process of Collaboration

The organization is designed through three interrelated actions:

1. Specifying the tasks and the accountability for each small work group
2. Establishing the reporting and supervisory responsibilities of middle management, which constitutes the accountability hierarchy
3. Building collateral relationships between hierarchies, thereby allowing them to coordinate and integrate their expectations toward a common goal.

The responsibility for successful organization design falls more heavily on the executive office than on any other unit of the organization. The governing board is rarely involved in the design process, although it sometimes approves the final plan. The executive office controls the design process and its outcome. It stimulates and guides the participation of a variety of people in an ongoing process of designing and amending both the accountability hierarchy and the collateral organization itself.

A critical part of redesign is deciding who else will participate in the design decision at hand. Design decisions require much detailed information that no individual is likely to possess. On the other hand, breadth of vision and an understanding of relationships among activities are important to successful organization design. It is the job of the executive office to stimulate individuals to contribute the various viewpoints, and see that they are all considered carefully. The executive office often outlines the major elements of the hierarchy and the permanent collateral organization, adapts these to improve realism and conviction, helps the participants resolve the details, and approves the result.

Steps in a Major Reorganization

Step 0: Planning the Process

Most major redesigns start with a small managing team, composed of one or two persons from the medical staff, governing board, and executive office. A consultant and a project staff manager are frequently included. This group is usually highly informal. It consists of leaders who are committed to the need for redesign. Its first job is to plan the redesign process, including identifying goals and participants. Its second is to keep the process on track and on time. The managing team remains active to the end of the project, focusing mostly on process issues which arise. It finds needed resources, resolves conflicts, and devises ways around roadblocks. Ideally, it concentrates on implications of what is being considered, endeavoring to identify problems early and move to prevent their slowing group progress.

The managing team should not mastermind. The best redesigns will be those that arise from thorough discussion of the issues, because the dialogue will improve both conviction and reality.

Step 1: Building Awareness

A participative redesign process begins with a deliberate effort to make most trustees, managers and medical leaders aware of the need. Multiple committees and task forces assess the magnitude and urgency of the new public concern involving the costs associated with health care. It is not uncommon to have more than 100 people involved; the target audience is on the order of 10 percent of the hospital's members, including physicians. Consultants, visitors, trips, and formal education programs are used to help people understand the opportunities and requirements of the changing environment. The objective is to have a cadre of people capable of explaining the new situation, and comfortable with the organization's strategic response, to any interested member, or person whose job will be affected.

The awareness building process cannot be secret. The hospital's competitors will gain a clear picture of the direction in which the institution is moving, but this is believed to be less costly than the opposite, where members do not understand either the need or the direction. Because of the competitive implications, the institution must maintain steady progress once the process begins.

Step 2: Formulating the Overall Strategy

Constraints and guidelines suggested by the hospital's history and mission are evaluated and incorporated into a revised mission. These often include assessment of major needs perceived by customers; potentially desirable affiliations, acquisitions, and mergers; identification of the needs of loyal physicians; programs to protect the employment and rights of workers; and religious and other concerns unique to the particular institution. The activity continues to be participative; a deliberate effort is made to hear and respond to member as well as customer needs. Much of the effort lies in crafting strategies which are rewarding to all. Discussion and debate frequently spill over into the informal organization, subcommittees and ad hoc study groups addressing specific questions.

Step 3: Checking Resources and Requirements

Staff and task forces outline the long-range plans implied by the strategy. The finance system revises the long-range financial plan to compare financial resources with needs. Since the resources must be projected to an uncertain future, and the costs of many strategies are unclear, both sides of the equation are highly ambiguous. The uncertainty is both emotionally and intellectually disconcerting; many members of the team have difficulty with the decisions.

The concepts of Step 2 must be translated to realistic possibilities. Success often depends upon imaginative solutions, ways to get more from existing resources or find new financial sources. The discussion is often technical and challenging. Difficulties are met with careful analysis, deliberate pursuit of specific concerns to determine their likelihood and magnitude, search for revealing examples among other institutions, and patient, solicitous discussion. The number of participants is reduced. Specific problems which arise are taken back to people directly affected by the result to resolve, resulting in a large number of ad hoc groups.

The result of Step 3 is a clearer and more formally stated strategy which usually requires specific applications of funds. It should be formally approved by the governing board, and its major components should be clear to all the Step 1 participants. Although some details may be deliberately concealed to protect against competitive response, the plan is not secret. The needs for conviction and realism outweigh the advantages of secrecy.

Step 4: Implementing the Design

The results of Step 3 must be translated to specific actions. New processes must be written, people must be trained, equipment and supplies must be obtained, measures of success must be installed. In many cases, trials are necessary to adjust final details. The process can take several years, particularly when construction is involved. Progress towards implementation is maintained by charges and timelines to specific ad hoc committees and groups, and by deliberate time planning. Special accountability units may be established for large projects. These will have time-related milestones as their principle expectations. The executive office is ultimately accountable for progress.

The endpoint of redesign comes when the anticipated changes are built into annual budget expectations and achieved by the RC teams.

Suggested Readings

Griffith, J. R., V. K. Sahney, and R. A. Mohr. 1994. *Reengineering Health Care: Building on CQI.* Ann Arbor, MI: Health Administration Press.

Mick, S. S., ed. 1990. *Innovations in Health Care Delivery: Insights of Organization Theory.* San Francisco: Jossey-Bass.

Mintzberg, H. 1979. *The Structuring of Organizations: A Synthesis of Research.* Englewood Cliffs, NJ: Prentice-Hall.

Peters, T. J., and R. H. Waterman, Jr. 1982. *In Search of Excellence: Lessons from America's Best-Run Companies.* New York: Harper & Row, Inc.

Shortell, S. M., and A. D. Kaluzny. 1994. *Health Care Management: Organization Design and Behavior,* 3d ed. New York: Delmar Publications.

Notes

1. *The New Shorter Oxford English Dictionary on Historic Principles,* Vol. II, 1993 (Oxford, UK: Clarendon Press), 2020.

2. M. Weber, 1967, *The Theory of Social and Economic Organizations* (Glencoe, IL: Free Press).

3. E. Freidson, 1980, *Doctoring Together: A Study of Professional and Social Control* (Chicago: University of Chicago Press).

4. H. Mintzberg, 1979, *The Structuring of Organizations: A Synthesis of the Research* (Englewood Cliffs, NJ: Prentice-Hall), 46–53.

5. J. K. Stross and W. R. Harian, 1979, "The Dissemination of New Medical Information," *Journal of American Medical Association* 241 (15 June): 2622–24.

6. T. J. Peters and R. H. Waterman, Jr., 1982, *In Search of Excellence: Lessons from America's Best-Run Companies* (New York: Harper & Row, Inc.).

7. J. R. Griffith, V. K. Sahney, and R. A. Mohr, 1995, *Reengineering Health Care: Building on CQI* (Ann Arbor, MI: Health Administration Press).

8. M. M. Melum and M. K. Sinorius, 1992, *Total Quality Management: The Health Care Pioneers* (Chicago: American Hospital Publishing, Inc.).

9. N. Machiavelli, 1913, *The Prince,* 2d ed. (Oxford: Clarendon Press).

10. H. Fayol, 1949, *General and Industrial Management* (London: Pitman).

11. F. W. Taylor, 1911, *Principles of Scientific Management* (New York: Harper and Brothers).

12. T. A. D'Aunno and M. D. Fottler, 1994, "Motivating People," in *Health Care Management: Organization Design and Behavior,* eds. S. M. Shortell and A. D. Kaluzny, 57–84. Also see F. J. Roethlisberger and W. J. Dixon, 1939, *Management and the Worker: An Account of a Research Program Conducted by the Western Electric Company and Hawthorne Works, Chicago* (Cambridge, MA: Harvard University Press); R. E. Likert, 1967, *The Human Organization* (New York: McGraw Hill); E. Katz and R. Kahn, 1978, *The Social Psychology of Organizations,* 2d ed. (New York: John Wiley & Sons).

13. Mintzberg, *The Structuring of Organizations*, 18–34.

14. Ibid., 148–60.

15. J. M. Eisenberg, 1980, *The Physician's Practice* (New York: John Wiley & Sons).

16. Peters and Waterman, *In Search of Excellence.*

17. Mintzberg, *The Structuring of Organizations*, 148–60.

18. Ibid., 162–63.

19. Ibid., 165–67.

20. P. Leatt, S. M. Shortell, and J. R. Kimberly, 1994, "Organization Design," in *Health Care Management*, 256–58.

21. D. Neuhauser, 1972, "The Hospital as a Matrix Organization," *Hospital Administration* 17 (Fall): 8–25.

22. L. R. Bums, 1989, "Matrix Management in Hospitals: Testing Theories of Matrix Structure and Development." *Administrative Science Quarterly* 34 (September): 349–68.

23. L. F. McMahon, Jr., R. B. Fettler, J. L. Freeman, and J. D. Thompson, 1986, "Hospital Matrix Management in DRGBased Prospective Payment," *Hospital & Health Services Administration* 31 (January–February): 62–74.

24. P. Kotler and R. N. Clarke, 1987, *Marketing for Health Care Organizations* (Englewood Cliffs, NJ: Prentice-Hall), 233–51.

25. J. P. Clement, 1988, "Vertical Integration and Diversification of Acute Care Hospitals: Conceptual Definitions." *Hospital & Health Services Administration* 33 (Spring): 99–110.

26. Sisters of Mercy Health Corporation, 1980, *Integrated Governance and Management Process: Conceptual Design* (Farmington Hills, MI: SMHC).

27. Leatt et al., "Organization Design," 252–54.

28. R. M. Heyssel, J. R. Gainter, I. W. Kues, M. Jones, and S. H. Lipstein, 1984, "Decentralized Management in a Teaching Hospital," *New England Journal of Medicine,* 310 (31 May): 1477–80.

29. A. D. Chandler, 1977, *The Visible Hand: The Managerial Revolution in American Business* (Cambridge, MA: Belknap Press).

30. A. P. Sloan, 1964, *My Years with General Motors* (Garden City, NY: Doubleday).

31. H. A. Simon, 1976, *Administrative Behavior: A Study of the Decision-Making Process in Administrative Organizations,* 3d ed. (New York: Free Press).

32. Mintzberg, *The Structuring of Organizations*, 58–64.

33. J. R. Griffith, 1994, "Reengineering Health Care: Management Systems for Survivors," *Hospital & Health Services Administration,* 39 (Winter): 451–70.

34. P. Starr, 1982, *The Social Transformation of American Medicine* (New York: Basic Books), 145–78.

35. C. Perrow, 1963, "Goals and Power Structures: A Historical Case Study," in *Hospitals in Modern Society,* ed. E. Freidson (Glencoe, IL: Free Press).

36. R. L. Johnson, 1979, "Revisiting the Wobbly Three-Legged Stool," *Health Care Management Review* 4 (Summer): 15–22.

37. A. L. Delbecq and S. L. Gill, 1985, "Justice as a Prelude to Teamwork in Medical Centers," *Health Care Management Review* 10 (Winter): 45–51.

38. S. L. Gill, E. W. Springer, and A. L. Delbecq, 1987, "Commitment and Discipline in Hospitals: Leadership Protocols and Legal Precedents," *Health Care Management Review* 12 (Summer): 75–82.

39. Melum and Sinioris, *Total Quality Management*, 93–128.

40. S. S. Mick, 1990, "Explaining Vertical Integration in Health Care: An Analysis and Synthesis of Transaction-Cost Economics and Strategic Management Theory," in *Innovations in Health Care Delivery: Insights of Organization Theory*, ed. S. S. Mick (San Francisco: Jossey-Bass Publishers), 207–40.

41. S. M. Shortell, 1988, "The Evolution of Hospital Systems: Unfulfilled Promises and Self-Fulfilling Prophecies," *Medical Care Review* 45 (2): 177–214.

42. B. B. Longest, 1990, "Interorganizational Linkages in the Health Care Sector," *Health Care Management Review* 15 (1): 17–28.

43. H. S. Zuckerman and T. A. D'Aunno, 1990, "Hospital Alliances: Cooperative Strategy in a Competitive Environment," *Health Care Management Review* 15 (Spring): 21–30.

44. S. M. Shortell, "The Evolution of Hospital Systems."

45. S. M. Shortell, R. R. Gillies, D. A. Anderson, J. B. Mitchell, and K. L. Morgan, 1993, "Creating Organized Delivery Systems: The Barriers and Facilitators," *Hospital & Health Services Administration* 38 (Winter): 447–66.

46. E. J. Zajac and T. A. D'Aunno, "Managing Strategic Alliances," in *Health Care Management: Organization Design and Behavior*, eds. S. M. Shortell and A. D. Kaluzny, 274–93.

47. Griffith et al., *Reengineering Health Care*.

48. J. A. Alexander, 1991, "Adaptive Changes in Corporate Control Practices," *Academy of Management Journal* 34 (January): 162–93.

Learning: Meeting Planning, Marketing, Finance, and Information Needs

PLANNING THE HEALTH CARE ORGANIZATION

PLANNING AND marketing define the health care organization's basic response to its environment. They are resource allocation decision processes which must meet the twin tests of realism (fit with the realities of the customer and provider markets) and conviction (convincing individual patients and workers that the decisions are in their personal best interests) (See Chapter 5). Excellent planning and marketing must not only lead to rewarding exchanges between the organization and its community, but also encourage a timely, responsive, consistent, and even-handed process for resource allocations resolving many potentially conflicting interests. In the context of the theory of open systems, community-oriented strategic management, and continuous improvement (See Chapter 2), they must be *proactive*, emphasizing foresight and placing the thinking of management in the future compared to the present. They are always **market oriented**; that is, they assess the real interests of the community and search for ways to meet them.

Planning and marketing are such extensive activities that it is difficult to develop uniform definitions. Different authors use different, sometimes conflicting terminology. **Planning** often refers to the process of making resource allocation decisions about the future, particularly the process of involving organization members and selecting among alternative courses of action. The term **marketing** has an unfortunate sharp distinction between its technical and common usage. In common usage, as the term might be understood by doctors, nurses, and some trustees, marketing generally implies sales, promotional or advertising activity. In contrast, as it appears in professional texts and journals,[1] marketing also incorporates the entire set of activities and processes normally ascribed to planning plus those relating to sales and promotion.

Both of these concepts are important. The text will identify planning as a resource allocation activity, and marketing as an activity deliberately oriented to the management (usually enhancement) of customer demand. Recognizing the importance of marketing, in the sense of establishing fruitful relationships with patients, intermediaries, and other stakeholders, Chapter 7 is devoted to that subject. This chapter covers planning, making decisions about mission, vision, alliances, services, products, locations, and prices. It covers purpose, functions, measures of planning effectiveness, organization for planning, issues in programmatic proposal evaluation, and issues in strategic positioning.

Purpose

The purpose of planning is to optimize the organization's future exchange relationships. Only the word future distinguishes this purpose from the purpose of the entire governance system. Planning includes analysis of future community needs and interests, response to external threats and opportunities, design and promotion of new programs, assembly and recruitment of necessary resources, and acquisition of required permits and certificates. Compounding planning's broad scope, the subtlety of the concepts that lie behind the word optimize makes planning one of the most fascinating activities in health care management.

Optimize implies finding the best possible achievement of some good or benefit through decisions allocating scarce resources. One optimizes the benefits of a specific activity relative to its costs, but in the final analysis, both benefits and costs are in the eye of the beholder. Especially for the not-for-profit health care organization, a key part of the planning process consists of understanding and reaching consensus on the benefits to be achieved. This understanding is embodied in the mission, a statement of the preferred good or benefit couched in terms of community, service, and finance. (See below, and Chapter 3.) The mission provides a guide which is used routinely and consistently to make resource allocation decisions.

The first stage in optimizing is to design each health care project to have the greatest possible benefit to cost ratio, and to rank order possible projects, identifying and implementing the ones which have the greatest ratio of benefits to costs, as shown in the center box of Figure 6.1. Conceptually, one finds a project, evaluates it in terms of the mission, and, if the benefits exceed the costs by more than any other project, adopts it. Practically, the process is almost never so simple. Selection is less critical than discovery; the best projects often require laborious and frustrating search. Neither the benefits nor the costs are easy to measure. They are even less easy to compare against one another and against other projects.

The first stage leaves two formidable questions, shown in the upper and lower boxes of Figure 6.1: "How much is a health care benefit worth in terms of nonhealth care opportunities?" and "Given that the future is always uncertain, how do I deal with the risk that my forecasts are incorrect?" These questions are outside the control of the organization. The value of the benefit is set by market and regulatory pricing mechanisms; it is worth what the customer is willing to pay

Figure 6.1 Optimization Concept

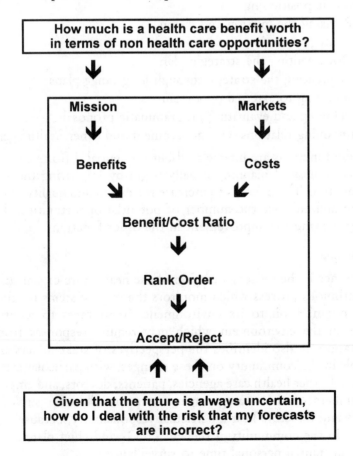

for it. Risk is what cannot be foreseen. Whenever a given proposal is accepted, a decision is made that the risk is tolerable and that the objective can be reached within the customer's price limit. The ideal is to make these decisions in such a way that even with complete hindsight, none would be changed. Real organizations fall substantially short of the ideal, but well-managed organizations come close enough that the corrections are usually minor. In other words, they thrive because they plan well, choosing and delivering health care that the customer is comfortable buying and they can comfortably deliver.

Functions

Achieving optimal planning decisions is the result of a six-step process:

1. Surveillance
   a. Environmental assessment
   b. Community-based epidemiologic planning
2. Strategic positioning
   a. Revising the mission and vision
   b. Strategy selection
   c. Documenting the strategic plan
3. Implementing the strategy through long-range plans
4. Responding to external opportunities
5. Developing and evaluating programmatic proposals
6. Maintaining relations with government and other health agencies

These functions are interrelated but sequential. Efforts to enhance the effectiveness of planning usually begin by improving the surveillance function. The intent is to increase the extent and quality of understanding and enhance the number of potential opportunities, thereby creating demand for improvement in the other functions.

Surveillance

Surveillance is the sensory function of the health care organization. It is a continuous process which monitors the open systems relationship of the organization to its environment. It attempts to identify all changes in the environment which may require responses from the organization. It also identifies the perspectives of stakeholders and influentials in the community on these changes, with particular attention to those of other health care agencies, patients, doctors, and employees. All members of the strategic apex are responsible for surveillance. Trustees and directors bear a particular responsibility, because of their contacts in the community. Excellent CEOs and chief planners often devote substantial personal time to surveillance.

Surveillance should be both broad and timely. No risk is as great as the risk of the unnoticed idea. Thorough surveillance opens opportunities for revision and compromise that might otherwise be overlooked. The missed trend away from an old product or service, the overlooked interest in a new one, the too-narrow perception of capability underlie many wrong investments and the demise of entire industries. The earlier a change is identified, the longer the organization has to respond. As a result, good surveillance includes large amounts of vague, rapidly changing information. (It can include deliberately misleading information placed by competitors.) Evaluating the information to decide what to act upon, what to monitor, and what to ignore, is part of the process. There is a danger of too-rapid response, of over-reacting to a transient variation. Yet, perversely, this danger often arises from incomplete surveillance. The transient fad is more likely to be identified as such when one's knowledge is broad.

Environmental Assessment

Environmental assessment is a formal surveillance review of the organization and its environment. It is undertaken annually by the planning unit, and supported by detailed factual and quantitative analysis. As much as possible should be quantified, but the appeal of numbers should not overshadow the importance of changes in unmeasurable topics, particularly attitudes, beliefs, and technology. Good environmental assessment takes into account the following:

- *Community demography, epidemiology, and economy.* (See Community-Based Planning below.) A thorough description of the market being served, identification of all major trends, and forecasts to the future are essential to the environmental assessment.

- *Patient and health insurance buyer attitudes.* Trends in total purchases of health care, selection of form or site of care, and market share should be described and quantified if data can be obtained at a reasonable cost. Particular attention should be paid to the attitudes of unions, employers, and governments, whose decisions affect large groups of individual consumers. While state and national trends are important, the view of local groups on key matters such as service, debt, price, and amenities is often the final determinant of planning and financial strategy. Communities vary substantially within a single state. Household surveys are a useful, although expensive, vehicle for assessing attitudes and behavior, and their popularity is growing rapidly. Focus groups can provide in-depth understanding of customer perspectives, although it is difficult to get complete representation.

- *Trends in insurance intermediary activity.* Insurer and intermediary arrangements such as the development of capitation, preferred provider contracts, and limits on payment are important influences on strategy. The rapid growth of managed care has resulted in radical revisions in strategies of many providers. Payment limits imposed by Medicare, Blue Cross, and Medicaid have important financial and managerial consequences. The trends in market share of the various insurance products and the payment policies of the larger intermediaries must be examined and forecast.

- *Trends in clinical practice.* Technology and the attitudes of practitioners and patients interact to create demands for new services and new modes of delivery. (In the 1980s, for example, patients began to prefer outpatient over inpatient care. At the same time, technology supported rapid growth in organ transplantation.) While clinical trends are difficult to forecast quantitatively, describing them improves decision making.

- *Member attitudes and capabilities.* Trends in the skills and attitudes of current employees, physicians, and volunteers are important background to planning decisions. Formal surveys are frequently used, but additional insights can be gained through focus groups and informal discussion.

- *Trends in physician availability and organization.* The number of physicians in practice, by specialty and other characteristics, is a critical indicator of both cost and quality of care. Both surpluses and shortages of physicians can increase cost and decrease quality of care.

- *Trends in other health worker availability.* Supplies of other health workers sometimes become critically short. Well-managed institutions adapt quickly to these shortages, protecting their staff. They also deal effectively with surpluses, using advance warning to plan workforce reduction and make it less painful for workers.

- *Role of other provider organizations.* Other provider organizations can complement the mission, be competitors, or allies. Any given organization must choose between avoidance, competition, or collaboration modes of interacting with all others serving its population. To make these decisions, it needs accurate descriptions. Mission, ownership, location, and services are usually public information. Trends in market shares and finances reflect changes in the relative strength of organizations. Population surveys and historic use data are the sources for market share information. Financial strength of competitors is frequently available from public sources. Since detailed data are often kept secret, quantitative forecasts are not always available and subjective observations become important in their absence. Strategic positioning, discussed below, identifies the mode of interacting with each other provider.

The planning unit is accountable for a thorough data base of all of these elements and a written annual review highlighting important trends and developments. It should also be accountable for reporting and, where possible, integrating insights or beliefs regarding future trends offered by other members of governance. It maintains this data base during the year as a resource for ongoing resource allocation decisions.

Community-Based Epidemiologic Planning

Health care systems now identify geographic communities, or markets, whose health care needs they will meet. The demographic, economic, and epidemiological characteristics of these communities are a fundamental data set for planning decisions of all kinds. The general model to estimate local demand for a given service is an equation which accommodates the fact that most conditions for which people seek health care differ by age, sex, income, and other factors.[2]

$$\left\{\begin{matrix} \text{Demand for} \\ \text{a service} \end{matrix}\right\} = \left\{\begin{matrix} \text{Population} \\ \text{at risk} \end{matrix}\right\} \times \left\{\begin{matrix} \text{Incidence} \\ \text{rate} \end{matrix}\right\} \times \left\{\begin{matrix} \text{Average use} \\ \text{per incident} \end{matrix}\right\} \times \left\{\begin{matrix} \text{Market} \\ \text{share} \end{matrix}\right\}$$

Examples of the use of the model are shown in Figure 6.2. Obstetrics is the easiest to understand. It also has the best supporting data, allowing great refinement in the estimate. Obstetrical deliveries occur only to young women. The population at risk and the anticipated fertility rates are frequently available for each year of age. The use per incident for deliveries is essentially one. Market share can be measured from history. All of these data must be forecast into the future. State agencies now prepare detailed population forecasts. The fertility rates and market share can be forecast from history or by survey of childbearing intentions.

The remaining examples of Figure 6.2 show the application of the model in other areas. Post-partum care days in obstetrics resemble the forecast for deliveries, but each mother uses about two days, a number that differs by locale. Well-baby visits are planned events important to provide immunizations, instruction to the mother, and early detection of developmental problems. The population at risk is all babies born in the last year; the incidence and the number of visits per baby are set by policy; and the market share closely related to the obstetrics share. The forecast would be used not only to estimate demand, but

Figure 6.2 Examples of Planning Decisions

Example	Population at Risk	Incidence Rate	Use per Incident	Market Share
Obstetrics deliveries	Fertile women	Births/fertile woman-year	1 deliveries/ woman	% of all births to women in community
Postpartum care	Delivered women	Births/fertile woman-year	2.0 days/ delivery	% of all births to women in community
Well-baby visits	Infants < 1 year	Births/fertile woman-year	4.0 visits/ year	% of all well-baby visits in community
Emergency department visits	Economic, geographic subsets of population	ED visits/person for each subset	1.0 visits/ arrival	% of community visits seeking this ED
Hip replacements	Population aged 50–65, over 65	Hip replacement/ person for each subset	1.0 surgeries/ patient	% of candidates seeking this institution

as a quality standard—a well-managed health insurance program will strive to achieve 100 percent of scheduled visits.

Emergency department visits are expensive, and managed care strategies call for minimizing them. They are a function of availability of health insurance, other primary care sources, and life style. As a result, the population at risk would be segregated economically or geographically to identify different incidence rates. For many purposes, it would also be necessary to adjust for time of day and day of week. This would be done by using several different incident rates. The use term could be set at one, yielding a forecast of visits, or the average number of hours of use, yielding an estimate of use of facilities. Hip replacement surgery occurs almost exclusively among the elderly, and the use term can be adjusted to forecast either procedures or expected days of inpatient stay.

Using the incidence of disease, as well as services, the model can forecast much health care activity. Epidemiologic studies have developed the incidence of most common and expensive illness, and analyzed the population characteristics associated with it. Estimates can be compared to actual values for diseases reducible by prevention or management, such as cancer, heart disease, and AIDS, to reveal unique risks or treatment practices in the community. These are useful in identifying cost-improvement possibilities. A simple example is births to very young single mothers. These are associated with high-cost problems in infant care. Programs to reduce these births by discouraging teenaged pregnancy are cost-effective. Programs to reach young mothers early in their pregnancies reduce the risk and cost of problems. Under capitation insurance contracts, these gains work directly to reduce overall cost of care.

No forecast is ever completely reliable. There are possible errors in the model design, such as the omission of some low-risk populations. There will be occasional cases from outside the age range or geographic area of the population at risk for all of these models. Simple multipliers are usually used to adjust for these. Almost any term of the obstetrics example can change. There can be sudden shifts in the population (for example, if a major employer opens or closes) in fertility (it fell by about 24 percent in the years 1960–1965, as women's views of desirable family size changed), and the market share, if another provider closes. The number of days of postpartum care has dropped almost 50 percent in the last decade. The reliability of the forecast must be evaluated using several alternative assumptions about the forecast parameters, a process called **sensitivity analysis**.

The planning department routinely produces short- and long-run forecasts for a number of important demand measures. It maintains a data base which allows generations of forecasts for almost any service demand on request. These are used in strategic positioning, the development of facility and service plans, and the construction of expectations for the next budget year. The reliability of the forecasts, the advice available from the planning department, and the speed with which the request can be serviced are critical elements in long-term success of the organization. The data for incidence rates, advice on segmentation of the population, and ranges of current practice on use are frequently available form national consulting services. Calculation and presentation software are also available to make construction of forecasts, sensitivity analysis, and exploration of alternative scenarios quick and easy.

Strategic Positioning

The mission, ownership, scope of activity, location, and partners of the organization define its **strategic position**. Surveillance information and the environmental assessment are used to review the strategic position at least annually but also as opportunities arise. Many of the opportunities arise from the actions of others—changes of service, closures, offers to partner, changes in health care financing, partnering strategies of competitors—at times outside local control. Being able to respond to those opportunities requires a thorough knowledge of internal and environmental realities.

Hoshin *Perspective*

The continuous improvement approach to strategic planning has been called *hoshin* planning, an effort to link all levels of resource allocation closely to customer needs.[3] *Hoshin* means a core belief, an intellectual pole star or reference point. In continuous improvement, the *hoshin* is customer needs. The best examples of *hoshin* perspective go far beyond meeting immediate customer requests to anticipate and even implant ideas customers would never have thought of on their own. Examples abound in the high-tech Japanese companies, Sony's Walkman being one of the most dramatic. The *hoshin* perspective involves a sophisticated interplay of market analysis, technology analysis, creativity, and role-playing leading to breakthrough inventions and fundamental redesigns.

In *hoshin* planning, both existing and proposed activities are modeled in business plans against market and price trends.[4] Quality measures establish minimums for acceptable performance, and the costs of meeting those minimums are tested against market price realities. The long-range financial plan provides the acid test for the enterprise as a whole. The achievable cost trend will be plotted against an outsider-determined price trend. The difference must generate the capital the organization needs for survival. That set of services or products that passes the acid test becomes the services plan. Realism centers on the assumptions for the models. Benchmarking information on the performance of competitors and market leaders becomes essential to achieve realism.

Health care organizations have a long way to go to reach a true *hoshin* perspective.[5] They may be no different from organizations generally in that respect; Hamel and Prahalad point out that corporations which thrive in competitive markets have greater ambition, and follow a rigorous program of focused, complementary innovation.[6] In health care, provider logic, rather than customer logic, has traditionally driven innovation. That is, new products and services are often driven from the perspective of a technological challenge, rather than one of what the customer might want given a full understanding of the options.

(Cesarean sections, circumcisions, prostatectomies, and executive physicals are among the more glaring examples.) What is missing, so far, is creativity, role-playing, and break-through innovation oriented around customer realities. There are methods and styles of delivering health care we have not dreamed of yet.

Revising the Mission and Vision

The mission set by the governing board (Chapter 3) identifies the community to be served, the level of service, and the financial limits. A vision statement often adds the philosophic goals and style by which the mission will be achieved. Together, these statements represent the most central desire of the owners and stakeholders and, as such, become the benchmark for all subsequent planning decisions. To fulfill the benchmark function, they should be as permanent as possible. But in a dynamic environment, even the most carefully set mission may lose its relevance. Acquisitions and divestitures may change the community. Changes in demography, technology, and the competitive environment make certain services essential and others redundant. Growth of effective community concern about cost forces revision of financing statements.

Even though major change is infrequent in the mission and even rarer in the vision, well-run organizations review the need for change annually. They contemplate mission revision far more often than they actually revise, since it is wise to consider many scenarios that in the end do not materialize. Given the mission's central role of setting values and directing the optimization process, it is important to deal decisively with possible changes. The governing board planning committee should review each year's environmental assessment for mission consequences. Actual revisions of mission require formal board action. The planning staff marshals the arguments for and against revision, and suggests appropriate wording.

Strategy Selection

Strategy selection begins with a review of the organization's strategic options and responses, utilizing a framework such as the strengths, weaknesses, opportunities, and threats (or SWOT) analysis.[7,8] The SWOT analysis uses the environmental assessment and the *hoshin* principle, but makes judgments about the implications of the data. In SWOT analyses, strengths and weaknesses describe internal characteristics, and threats and opportunities external ones. These are described briefly, but as realistically as possible. Figure 6.3 shows a SWOT analysis for a successful health care organization serving about half of a community of 750,000 persons in 1994. The community has not expressed strong interest in managed care and has resisted past efforts at cost control, but the organization, here called Excalibur Health System, expects that attitude to change. The mission and vision commit the organization to retaining local service, income, and control with a nearly comprehensive scope of services and the use of managed care insurance to stimulate high-quality, cost-effective care.

The resulting display is checked against the mission and vision and used to identify broad goals or strategic directions for the institution. A key part of the exercise is the study of overall patterns, raising the questions shown in Figure 6.4. The answers to these questions will determine the strategic direction. Various ways to improve the SWOT, usually called **scenarios**, will be proposed and evaluated against the environmental assessment. Some will die quickly, as major flaws appear. Others will receive detailed and quantitative review, even constructing market and financial forecasts of their implications. The SWOT description is used to test the scenarios for realism—consistency, fit with the environment, fit with accessible resources, and conviction—acceptance and support of members and stakeholders.[9] Those with the best fit will carry forward, perhaps to reality.

The institution's scope of services is part of the strategic decision set. Many organizations review their service profile by using a matrix allowing consideration of two dimensions of desirability. There are several alternatives for defining the axes. The versions of the Boston Consulting Group[10] or General Electric[11] are popular. Both lead to a display such as that illustrated in Figure 6.5, where the axes are market attractiveness (opportunities for growth or profit) versus market advantage (internal resources required for expansion). Such displays are useful in selecting the optimum portfolio of services. For example, a small rural hospital, noting that there was a high demand for home care and respite care in its community and recognizing that it had a geographic advantage for such services (Situation A), would include them in its plans. Obstetrics, where the hospital has a strong geographic advantage, is not attractive for expansion because the need is already met. (Situation B) It would be retained. A high-tech service requiring specialists who would be difficult to recruit and only infrequently needed (Situation C) would be avoided. Presumably all the entries meet quality and cost standards before they are entered.

The strategic direction which emerges from a health care organization's decisions reflects an attitude or business philosophy. The philosophy should be consistent with the mission and vision. It is important to communicate the philosophy to organization members. Members and potential members know what the organization stands

Figure 6.3 SWOT Analysis for Excalibur Health System

Strengths
Merger of two facilities now completed
Single governance and medical staff established for system
Strong medical staff support
Recent reduction of 400 personnel, 200 more in view
$50 million available cash, plus $30 million to correct existing deficiencies
Rapidly developing information system
Owns small HMO
Medical school affiliation, strong primary care program
Loyal and satisfied personnel

Weaknesses
No COO or visible second-in-command
Ineffective physician-hospital organization
Dissatisfaction among primary care physicians
Low volume, high costs at smaller facility
Poor ambulatory patient amenities at larger facility
Serious OR shortages/deficiencies at larger facility
Despite cost reduction, Medicare patients are served at a small financial loss
Some aggressive HMO/PPO contracts are served at a loss

Opportunities
Strong community support, 50 percent market share
Community loyal to local care, doctors, and traditional health care finance
Recent alliance with leading institutions in region
Possible link with large regional HMO/PPO
Generally favorable patient attitudes
Several smaller hospitals in region are in marginal condition
Primary care doctors seeking organization help

Threats
Major competitor in city gained market share during merger years
Largest intermediary in region has linked with competitor
Regional competitors in adjacent city to north threaten northern edge of
    primary market and several specialties
State reform may require new low-income/Medicaid HMO
Federal reform may cause severe Medicare losses
Shortage of primary care physicians
Probable oversupply of referral specialists and specialty residency training

SOURCE: Based upon a real organization, in 1993. Identity concealed.

for, and what kinds of proposals for change are likely to gain support. If EHS's strategy continues to emphasize local control, notions of sale or merger with health care organizations in other cities need not

> **Figure 6.4** Questions Arising from the Excalibur Health System SWOT
>
> **Service Position**
> Affiliate with regional HMO/PPO? Sell or expand own HMO?
> Build a low-income/Medicaid HMO?
> Attempt to recover link to largest intermediary?
> Provide primary care organization support?
> Defend traditional medicine and health care finance?
> Promote local specialty capability?
>
> **Geographic Position**
> Close or find new uses for smaller facility? Use as OR/ambulatory site?
> Develop alliances with smaller hospitals in area?
> Pursue regional alliance?
> Affiliate with strong competitor from adjacent city to north?
> Acquire or affiliate with leading local competitor?
>
> **Operating Position**
> Continue aggressive personnel reduction?
> Develop program to change clinical behavior, break even in Medicare, HMO
>   patients?
> Correct ambulatory care amenities at larger facility?
> Correct OR deficiencies at larger facility?
> Expand primary care physician supply?
> Refocus medical training program to primary care?
> Continue information system development?

be considered. If it continues to encourage managed care, partnering with established HMOs who can market effectively must be weighed against expansion of the owned HMO. If developing primary care continues to be an important goal, proposing a new transplant surgery program is probably a waste of time. Proposing a service corporation to support owned and affiliated primary care practices will be much better received.

The strategic direction of an institution can always be described by the specific proposals selected to improve its SWOT. It is also possible to describe strategy according to one of several available paradigms. Miles and Snow have characterized strategies according to risk and aggressiveness, describing four archetypes, "prospector, analyzer, reactor, and defender."[12] Eastaugh has modified the archtypes based on actual characteristics of hospitals.[13] The differences between the archtypes are two dimensional, as shown in Figure 6.6. One dimension is external,

Figure 6.5 Matrix of Market Attractiveness and Advantage

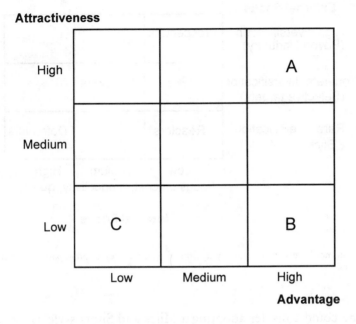

Service A, where the market is attractive and the organization has a strong advantage is one which would be selected for further investment.

B, where the attractiveness is low, but the organization has an advantage would be supported but not expanded.

C, where both market and advantage are low would be phased out or avoided.

or market oriented, the willingness to seek new lines of business, even outside health care. The other is internal, the concentration on meeting quality and cost standards in the core business.

The Miles and Snow taxonomy is probably the most useful for health care organizations. Other strategic philosophies include Porter's "cost leadership versus [quality] differentiation,"[14] and Miller and Friesen's "adaptive, dominant, giant, conglomerate, and niche innovator."[15] Shortell, Morrison, and Friedman note that the effectiveness of the Miles and Snow strategies depends upon the environment, and that among health care systems prospectors and analyzers have the advantage in the current health care environment.[16] Eastaugh notes that single hospital prospectors have not fared as well as analyzers, and defenders have done better than either.[17] Reactors fare badly in both studies.

Figure 6.6 Miles and Snow Typology of Strategic Types

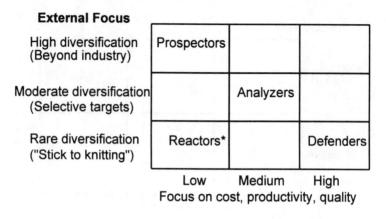

*Reactors do not have a strong strategy in either direction. They respond passively to actions of competitors.

One could consider adopting a Miles and Snow style as a strategy: "We want to be an analyzer health care organization." This is dangerous because it substitutes labels and generalities for a set of specific actions which are realistic and convincing in the specific setting. As the study by Shortell and others suggests, the critical issues in strategic direction are realistic appraisal and response to external forces, consistency in application, and congruence with internal resources. Saying, "We are analyzers," is less important than doing the analysis and selecting some actions. The lesson from the research is that a willingness to change is essential when the environment around you is changing.

The strategic direction of most successful organizations is toward integrated acute care services, financially supported by HMOs which are either owned or closely affiliated. The leading organizations are convinced that comprehensive control of acute care is essential to meet customer demands for economy and quality. The success of examples such as Henry Ford Health System and Intermountain Health Care have reinforced that belief. Shortell, Gillies, Anderson, Mitchell, and Morgan, labeling this outcome "Organized Delivery System," have identified eight barriers limiting the success of the strategy.[18] These are shown in Figure 6.7. Generally, the barriers and reactions to them can be understood in three groups. Failures to win internal conviction about the new strategy are addressed with education and consensus building techniques, plus efforts to stimulate a more articulate customer market. Failures to progress with the implementation are addressed by specific actions to strengthen critical resources. Finally, internal resistance or prolonged inability to meet critical new goals is met with the deliberate use of power. Rules and procedures are changed, and obstructing personnel are replaced. The list of barriers and what has to be done about them is instructive for organizations which want to move in this direction. It is also important as a model of strategic positioning generally. Positioning comes close to the core of the organization itself, where decisions are translated into action. Implementation is a thread that runs conspicuously through the facilitators; clearly selecting the strategy is only the beginning.

The alternative to the integrated service strategy is a niche strategy, deliberately seeking highly specialized services that can be delivered to a receptive market. Specialty hospitals serving children, mentally ill, cancer patients, and the like are following niche strategies. Small rural health care organizations offering primary care and limited hospitalization are also niche strategists. Although both the label and reality suggest that niche strategies are associated with smaller organizations, some niche strategies can be quite large. Some for-profit chains pursue niches in several markets simultaneously. HealthTrust, Inc., has acute care hospital facilities in several dozen different cities. National Medical Enterprises attempted a niche strategy with a for-profit chain of mental health facilities. Each holding of these companies is relatively small, but in total they generate two substantial publicly listed companies. Several for-profit chains pursue similar niches in chronic care.

One variant on niche strategies is currently pursued by large commercial insurance companies. The companies target several large communities where they have high sales of all their insurance products, including health insurance. They then develop HMO insurance which they support with networks of primary care physicians under rigorous cost incentives and contracts with hospitals at bargain prices. It does not appear likely that they will develop large market shares in any city. Their attractiveness lies in their ability to serve all the insurance needs of large companies (which may have workers to insure in several cities) and to control costs by a limited access primary care network and hard negotiating on price of services.

The strength of niche strategies is the ability to respond quickly and excellently within the limited service. Niches tend to emerge around new services and to sustain themselves when unique factors in the service are difficult for competitors to copy. The problem with niche strategies is the risk that the comparative advantage will disappear. The

Figure 6.7   Barriers and Facilitators of Organized Delivery Systems

Barrier	Facilitator
Understanding and Acceptance	
Failure to understand primary care and wellness as the new core business	Invest in educational programs and consultants emphasizing new core.
	Deliberately involve "naysayers" in strategic discussions.
	Change the incentive of key managers.
	Seek new appointments experienced in new core.
Inability to overcome the hospital paradigm	Revise mission and vision
	Limit capital expenditure toward old uses, expand it toward ambulatory care.
	Increase influence of primary care physicians.
	Stimulate growth of managed care insurance.
Implementation	
Lack of strategic alignment	Expand performance measures
	Centralization of planning effort and planning staff
	Develop realistic and convincing strategies for each subsidiary
	Close or divest subsidiaries not fitting new core business
Ambiguous roles and responsibilities	Expansion and clarification of roles
	Strengthen incentive system and relate to performance measures
	Elimination of redundant managers
Inability to manage managed care	Expand/revise quality improvement activities
	Improve cost data
	Hire experienced manager
	Partner with experienced, effective HMO
Inability to execute the strategy	Replace/reassign middle management
	Revise the strategic position
	Replace the CEO
Resistance	
Resistance by system board members	Selection of committees, committee chairs
	Deliberate confrontation and resolution of board ambivalence
	Replacement of board members
	Board restructuring

Continued

Figure 6.7 Continued

Barrier	Facilitator
Resistance by subsidiary units	Centralization of capital budget, budget authority
	Replacement of local board members
	Expansion of subsidiary CEO responsibilities
	Removal of uncooperative executives

Adapted and reprinted with permission from *Hospital & Health Services Administration* © 1993, as it appeared in S. M. Shortell, R. R. Gillies, D. A. Anderson, J. B. Mitchell, and K. L. Morgan's "Creating Organized Delivery Systems: The Barriers and Facilitators," Volume 38, No. 4, p. 447.

technology may change, making it possible for every integrated health system to achieve results as good as the niche specialists. The financing may change, making the niche company prey to expanded competition if it improves, and insufficient funds if it diminishes. Customer judgments may change, so that people who were willing to travel for a specialized service decide not to, or in the case of rural institutions, decide the trip to the big city is worth the effort. The result is that niche strategy institutions are a relatively small part of the total; integrated comprehensive strategies prevail.

Validating the Strategic Plan

The strategic position must meet the two tests of realism and conviction. First, it must represent a broadly accepted consensus about what should be done, incorporating not just the customer *hoshin*, but also the needs of providers and organization members. Second, it must be financially realistic.

Consensus about the strategic direction is usually documented by the actions taken. When a direction is selected, it usually requires a specific program of implementation. The program must be described in detail in order to implement it; the documentation grows with the implementation decisions. It is usually recorded in plans for revisions of services and facilities. New programs require funds, and thus appear quickly in the long-range financial plan. For this reason there is no strategic plan document in many organizations, yet a large number of people know the organization's direction in considerable detail. They should. If they do not, the strategy fails the test of conviction and is difficult or impossible to implement.

People learn the strategic direction by participating in the annual environmental assessment and some of the strategic discussions which arise then and during the year. Iteration of the mission and vision and the environmental assessment over several years helps physicians and middle managers understand both the strategy and the supporting need. The best organizations encourage all their members to think in terms of SWOT analysis. Not only does the exercise strengthen continuing improvement programs, it also teaches the usefulness of the analysis, and makes it easier to understand that the organization as a whole faces a profile of needs and achievements. The result is that the strategic plan is not secret. In the words of the Intermountain planner Greg Poulsen, "It's in our competitors' portfolio tomorrow morning."[19] The Intermountain approach is to win not on secrecy but on sound implementation.

Financial realism is tested repeatedly, using the long-range financial plan. Strategies are tested against the plan, which measures the organization's financial resources, as soon as they are clear enough to indicate the changes they require in expenditures and the advantages they bring in revenue. The process is iterative. The first check is almost intuitive, "Do we have, or can we get, the resources to do this?" The final check incorporates the details of specific plans into the financial plan, and shows the capital required and the impact on measures of financial strength, as described in Chapter 8.

Implementing the Strategy Through Long-Range Plans

The decisions associated with planning tend to be in environmental assessment, strategic positioning, and a large number of proposals which are very specific and limited in scope. Some mechanism must exist to coordinate between the strategic goals and the projects, between the projects themselves, and between last year's decisions and next year's. The mechanism is usually called **long-range planning**. Long-range planning does three things:

1. It rolls the strategic agenda forward to a level of detail permitting it to be checked for financial reality against the long-range financial plan.
2. It provides a central body of documentation which supports funding requests, makes clear the commitments the organization has made, and identifies the benefits anticipated from them.
3. It guides teams developing implementation plans at all levels, down to those working on continuous improvement projects for the next annual budget.

All well-run health care organizations now do long-range planning; they have a mission, a vision, a strategic direction, and an agenda of goals to implement that direction. Their current planning efforts, therefore, are addressed to revision, rather than preparation de novo. They conduct an annual review, revising as necessary and extending the plan an additional year with each review with special action in between reviews as required. Achieving this level took most of them several years. The time is spent building the data base for surveillance and building consensus around the vision and the strategic agenda. Each annual revision strengthens the organization by improving the available information, clarifying the agenda, and spreading or at least reaffirming commitment about it.

One can conceptualize long-range planning in three parts: a process, a book, and a library. The process is the ongoing activity of collecting, disseminating, testing, and evaluating possibilities for the future. The book is usually referred to as the long-range plan, which expands the mission by specifying the broad outlines of the major actions the health care organization intends, and records the specific decisions which have been made but not yet implemented. (The long-range plan is usually several volumes in length.) The library consists of the detailed files supporting these decisions. It includes the data bases on operations, the competition, and the environment. It also includes the documentation of future actions, which in large projects, such as replacement of a facility, can grow to rooms full of plans and documentation.

The Long-Range Plan as a Coordinating Process

Long-range planning is the process which builds a set of shared decisions implementing community-focused strategic management. It identifies alternatives, debates their merits, and eventually reaches conclusions which must be accepted by all for the organization to succeed. (Members often express and continue to hold reservations. They must be willing to act in support of the agreed-upon direction.) In terms of Chapter 5, the planning process relies heavily on the collateral organization to explore alternatives and reach conclusions. It uses accountable delegation to gain the perspective of the members most directly involved. It requires strong technical support, not only from planning, but also from finance and information services.

The long-range plan has to be understood to fulfill its coordinating function. The broad concepts of the plan should be familiar to every manager. Summaries of the plan are widely distributed, not just to anyone in the organization who needs them, but to anyone who might need them or even might do a better job if he or she understood them. Certain elements of the long-range plan may be kept confidential. These generally include all cases in which knowledge of the organization's interest would adversely affect achievement of the goals. The organization's interest in a piece of real estate often increases its price, for example. Mergers, acquisitions, and entry into new markets can be hurt by untimely public recognition.

Well-managed health care organizations use all the tools of consensus building in developing widespread conviction about the plan. Discussion deliberately seeks contrary views, and deals with them thoroughly. Although innovation and candor are encouraged, incentives to accept the group position are also kept strong. Individual persuasion is common. Conflict resolution techniques are used frequently. It is generally better to seek a mutually acceptable solution than to force acceptance, but the overriding need to respond to the customer is never overlooked.

The planning unit is responsible for widespread distribution of the concepts, identification of parties potentially interested in specific questions, reviewing the ongoing debate for potential conflict or omission, and serving as a resource on process and history. It facilitates coordination of plans at a detailed level when necessary. It supports the line, the executive and governance in conducting the discussion. Scenarios, illustrations, fact bases, and forecasts are supplied as necessary.

The Long-Range Plan as a Document

The decisions which result from the planning process are incorporated in a set of documents called the long-range or *strategic plan*. The plan for a well-run organization is organized to parallel the accountability for implementation, and includes the following parts:

- *Mission and vision.*
- *Environmental description and forecasts*—These are derived from the environmental assessment, cover about five years, and identify potential directions of change for a second five years. They include
  - age, sex, health insurance, and income characteristics of the community
  - demand and market share for major service groups
  - major competing organizations by service, size, and announced intentions
  - important uncertainties, identifiable risks of failure to achieve mission, and unmet community needs.

- *Services plan*—specifying the clinical services and other major activities in which the institution will engage.
- *Long-range financial plan*—summarizing the expected financial impact upon income statements, cash flow, long-term debt, and balance sheets (see Chapter 8).
- *Facilities plan*—detailing the construction and renovation activities (see Chapter 16).
- *Human resources plan*—showing the expected personnel needs, terminations, and recruitment requirements (see Chapter 15).
- *Medical staff plan*—a part of the Human Resources Plan focusing on physician replacement and recruitment (see Chapter 12).
- *Information services plan*—describing the future capability and hardware array of information service, including plans for collection, standardization, communication, and archiving of data (see Chapter 10).

Although the plans may be separate documents, the processes generating the decisions must be integrated. In general, mission and vision drive services and finances, and these, in turn, drive facilities, human resources, and information needs. Thus, the plans can be portrayed in a hierarchical relationship as shown in Figure 6.8.

The planning unit is responsible for maintaining the long-range plans as a set and preparing the annual environmental assessment with its required forecasts. The other technical and logistic support services are responsible for their components. The finance unit normally maintains the financial plan. Information services develops the information plan, plant services the facilities plan, and human resources the

Figure 6.8   Hierarchical Relationship of Long-Range Plans

human resources plan. The services plan, which identifies much of the strategic agenda, is directly supported by the planning staff, as is the medical staff plan. All the decisions going into the plans require broad participation. The supporting unit must see that participation occurs, appropriate data are provided, decisions are documented, and appropriate approvals are obtained. Major outlines of the plans are approved by the governing board, and more detailed elements by appropriate line and staff officers.

Responding to External Opportunities

Many strategic opportunities arise from external events. Chances to change partnership arrangements arise from changes in competitors' status. Major buyers and intermediaries announce programs and request responses. Laws are passed, and governmental agencies seek new arrangements. These opportunities have a number of potentially troublesome characteristics. They tend to be unique, so prior experience is not directly applicable. The timetable by which they arise and must be evaluated is usually outside the organization's control. They often involve sums of money several times the normal operating and capital budgets. They imply disruption of the lives of many members of the organization. They also may require secrecy, because premature public knowledge would substantially change the nature of the transaction. And, they are usually irreversible.

External strategic opportunities generally require high-risk decisions that test the governance structure and the skills of its leaders as no other activity does. The uniqueness of each opportunity makes rules impractical, but there are some characteristics common to successful responses:

- Surveillance of market and political trends gives advance warning on many changes in customer needs. Many opportunities can be predicted some years in advance.
- Surveillance of competitors' activity can alert the organization to many partnership opportunities. Who is growing, failing, buying, selling, or approaching a critical organizational juncture can usually be detected in advance.
- The general opportunities can be debated in advance and broad positions established as part of the strategic position. A well-written mission statement, long-range plan, and fiscal plan, plus the history of discussion surrounding them, provide the criteria for evaluating most specific strategic opportunities.
- Well-run organizations can assemble a knowledgeable response

team for each specific opportunity. The team is limited in size if necessary and its membership emphasizes maturity in business decisions. The CEO is usually team leader, although a senior board officer occasionally assumes this role. Trusted senior physicians should be included. Senior line officers often contribute. Planning, marketing, and finance staff make up the workforce. Outside consultants are frequently useful, particularly in situations without parallels in the organization's history.

- Response teams may be accountable only to the executive committee or senior governance officers until the project has undergone initial review. This arrangement preserves confidentiality where that is necessary. It also introduces all the dangers associated with secrecy, including opportunities for improper personal gain. However, since formal action always requires governing board approval, secrecy can, at best, be temporary. The costs of secrecy are such that well-run organizations formalize and reveal strategic options as quickly as possible.

In short, preparation allows the well-managed institution to make prudent evaluations of opportunities within externally imposed time frames.

Developing and Evaluating Programmatic Proposals

Much of the implementation of strategy is in the form of detailed projects specifying resources and processes for RCs and groups of related RCs. Many proposals come from line sources. The redesign and revision of existing programs arising from continuous improvement often requires new equipment and facilities. These projects are usually called **programmatic proposals**. Other programmatic proposals arise as strategies are implemented. They have to be justified, compared against alternative uses of funds, approved, and implemented. Large ventures like new facilities or products are often made up of many smaller projects. While these would follow a different approval process, the same sort of analysis and justification are in order. Figure 6.9 gives examples.

Well-managed organizations encourage programmatic proposals, because they reflect an alert, flexible work attitude and because they provide an opportunity for continuous improvement. An abundant supply of programmatic proposals minimizes the danger that the best solution will be overlooked. Hundreds of programmatic proposals origi-nate each year in large health care organizations. Dozens survive initial review and are formally documented. Perhaps a third of those docu-mented are funded.

Figure 6.9 Examples of Programmatic Proposals

Proposal	Description	Approximate Cost	Possible Justification
Renovate ORs	Enlarge operating suite into adjacent inpatient unit, modernize	$10,000,000	Increase attractiveness to ambulatory surgery patients
Replace flat work ironer	Replace old ironer with faster machine less likely to break down	$50,000	Essential to laundry operation; more reliable service; lower unit cost
Laser surgery equipment	Specially designed laser for gyneco-logical surgery	$50,000	Match competitor's investment
Expand parking lot	Add 50 spaces for visitors	$1,000,000	Relieve crowding for ambulatory patient visits

Developing Programmatic Proposals

An important part of the planning role is to support line managers as they develop proposals for continuous improvement or to implement agreed-upon strategies. Planning staff are a source of knowledge about the plans in existence and the discussion which surrounded the decisions. They also are expert in the data available to analyze specific issues or opportunities, analytic techniques to use the data effectively, and the processes by which decisions are made. The proposals which survive initial, informal review are usually evaluated by a line and planning team which begins as a simple consultation between two people. In complex projects, the team can grow to a formal planning structure bringing in experts from other line areas and other technical and logistic support areas as needed. For a major project, the proposal development team would include outside consultants and dozens of organization members, with a still larger number called in periodically on specific questions.

Marketing textbooks note that introducing a new product or service successfully requires a comprehensive approach to its design summarized by the four P's.[20]

- *Place* is the segment of the market to be served and the issues of style, location, and amenities that make the service maximally attractive to the customer.

- *Product* is the exact definition and design of service to be offered.
- *Price* is the total cost the customer is willing to pay for given services, including transaction costs such as travel time, and in health care including an analysis of the insured and out-of-pocket portions of costs.
- *Promotion* is the advertising, public relations, and communications that make customers aware of the service and its desirability.

While this approach may seem grandiose for some of the smaller and more mundane proposals, it is quite valuable. It is better to consider every aspect cursorily than to leave one out. A replacement flatwork ironer in the hospital laundry looks simple, but it should prompt a thorough review of the laundry's future demand, the price of competitive laundry services, the desirability of closing the laundry and purchasing the service elsewhere, and the possibility of actually expanding laundry volume by selling the service to others. For a proposal like a new primary care clinic, the comprehensive approach suggested by the mnemonic may spell the difference between success and failure.

The initial role of planning is to help the proposal maker to reach a quick and approximate idea of the project's value. If the first review step is an inexpensive but effective test against reality, unpromising ideas can be abandoned quickly. Many proposals die at this point, withdrawn by their originator. The remaining set of programmatic proposals must be evaluated thoroughly, involving significant time, effort, and cost. Figure 6.10 shows a standard list of review questions. The experience, analytic skill, and information base in planning are important to answering these questions.

The evaluation method places great responsibility on line management which must implement the proposal if it is accepted. Line involvement helps ensure that the benefits claimed are actually achieved. The RC or group which originated the proposal continues to control its destiny. It is important to note that the planning staff does not judge the proposals themselves. Planning staff assists the line managers to assure a thorough, accurate, and persuasive presentation. They help the line managers to articulate benefits in the light of the plan and mission, to specify the market as precisely as possible, and to forecast demand. They also review the protocol for developing proposals uniformly, in order to permit fair competitive evaluation.

Preparing a large proposal, particularly in its later, more precise stages, requires collaboration of many units of the organization. Demand is forecast from planning surveys. Considering the need and availability of specific resources usually requires assistance from the human resources and plant systems. Health care benefits are often derived from scientific literature and clinical opinion. Revenue or profit

Figure 6.10 Issues in Evaluating a Programmatic Proposal

The assistance provided by the Planning/Marketing Department to line supervisors considering programmatic proposals begins with a thorough checklist of the likely issues to be involved. There is no perfect list, but a schema such as the one below tends to reveal the important questions in an order which identifies those most likely to be disabling early, when the idea can easily be modified, deferred or abandoned.

Mission, Vision, and Plan

- What is the relationship of this proposal to the mission and vision?
- Is this proposal essential to implement a strategic goal in the long-range plan?
- If the proposal arises outside the current strategic goals, can it be designed to enhance or improve the current plan?

Benefit

- In the most specific terms possible, what does this project contribute to health care? If possible, state:
  - the nature of the contribution, the probability of success, and the associated risk for each individual benefiting; and
  - the kinds and numbers of persons benefiting.
- If the organization were unable to adopt the proposal, what would be the implication? Are there alternative sources of care? What costs are associated with using these sources?
- If the proposal contributes to some additional or secondary objectives, what are these contributions and what is their value?

Market and Demand

- What size and segment of the community will this proposal serve? What fraction of this group is likely to seek care at this organization?
- What is the trend in the size of this group and its tendency to seek care here? How will the proposal affect this trend?
- To what extent is the demand dependent upon insurance or finance incentives? What is the likely trend for these provisions?
- What impact will the proposal have on the organization's general market share or on other specific services?
- What implications does the project have for the recruitment of physicians and other key health care personnel?
- What response or initiatives does this proposal suggest for competing hospitals or health care organizations?
- What are the promotional requirements of the proposal?

Continued

Figure 6.10 Continued

Costs and Resources

- What are the marginal operating and capital costs of the proposal, including start-up costs and possible revenue losses from other services?
- Are there cost implications for other services or overhead activities?
- Are there special or critical resource requirements?
- Are there identifiable opportunity costs associated with the proposal, or other proposals or opportunities which are facilitated by this proposal?
- Are there other intangible elements (positive or negative) associated with this proposal?

Finance

- What are the capital requirements, project life, and finance costs associated with the proposal?
- What is the competitive price and anticipated net revenue?
- What is the demand elasticity and profit sensitivity?
- What are the insurance or finance sources of revenue, and what implications do these sources raise?
- What is the net cash flow associated with the proposal over its life, and the discounted value of that flow?

Other Factors

- What are the opportunities to enhance this proposal or others by combination?
- Are there any specific risks or benefits associated with the proposal not elsewhere identified?
- Does the proposal suggest a strategic opportunity, such as a joint venture or the purchase or sale of a major service?

Timing, Implementation, and Evaluation

- What are the critical path components of the installation process, and how long will they take?
- What are the problems or advantages associated with deferring or speeding the implementation?
- What are the anticipated changes in the operating budget of the units accountable for the proposal? What changes are required in supporting units?

benefits require careful analysis of pricing and service contracts. The marginal costs used in evaluation are rarely available from routine accounting data and must often be developed through special studies.

Opportunity costs, the costs of committing a specific resource such as space, and thereby making it unavailable to an alternative use, require a thorough review of possible alternatives. All future costs and revenues should be discounted to a common time so they can be compared. Determining risks and ranges for expectations requires experience and statistical skills. Planning staff should be prepared to carry out many of the specific calculations. Their role is to coordinate the process, collect the necessary knowledge efficiently, and make sure appropriate technical procedures are followed.

The key to effective assistance is to encourage iterative evaluation aimed at identifying promising ideas early. Although each element of the closed system model must be considered, the rigor and precision of each expectation should be reduced in the early stage of proposal development. This technique allows the well-run organization to consider many proposals and to select the best from a large pool. Iterative evaluation requires a willingness to work with imprecise estimates and an ability to make sound initial judgments. The longer and more completely a proposal is considered, the more is invested in it. A proposal abandoned after much work represents a hidden cost that can be avoided by good initial judgment.

Evaluating Programmatic Proposals

The development team strives to make the project as attractive as possible, and does not evaluate it against other opportunities. The originator of the proposal can judge the project ineffective and withdraw it, but evaluation beyond that should be done by committees of line officers in a process designed to give each proposal fair hearing against others in similar line areas, and then against others from the entire organization. The issues listed in Figure 6.9 are designed to generate a thorough review of costs and benefits. The categories of the figure provide a good outline for summarizing projects uniformly. Most projects are summarized by a title or sentence, a one- to two-page executive summary, and many pages of documentation and detail.

A good system for handling programmatic proposals is shown in the flow chart, Figure 6.11. Following are some important concepts for the individual steps.

Prior to the direct entry of planning and the construction of a formal proposal:

- The planning unit is responsible for broad communication of the strategic direction via distribution of the environmental assessment and appropriate sections of the mission and long-range plan.

- A supportive management environment encourages line supervisors to look within their own areas for imaginative ideas.
- Individuals and informal line groups develop ideas in terms of their closed system parameters, but in a subjective, nonquantitative, inexpensive way.

The most promising ideas pass the first review in Figure 6.11 and formal analysis and documentation is undertaken:

- A planning staff member is assigned to the project. That person and the line advocate comprise a line and staff team for initial formal development of the proposal.
- The line and staff team develops more precise costs and benefits. Depending on the magnitude of the proposal, this step may include several additional reviews by line and planning groups. The proposal may be integrated with others and a larger team created. A member from finance is usually added to large projects. The completed proposal must be fully specified in terms of detailed procedures, resources required, and revised operating expectations.

The proposal then undergoes a series of competitive reviews:

- Annually, completed proposals are grouped by accountability hierarchy and ranked by line management teams. Large sections may have several rounds of internal ranking. A programmatic proposal in the laboratory would be ranked against other laboratory proposals, then other clinical support service proposals, and finally other clinical proposals. Proposals are judged in light of the mission, environmental assessment, and long-range plan. The fate of low-ranking proposals becomes increasingly clear; they are often withdrawn by mutual consent. (The withdrawn proposals are often reworked; the impact of competitive review improves them.)
- Ranked lists of proposals from the sections are then integrated into a single list for the division, and the final committee review ranks projects for the system board.
- The governing board acts upon the individual elements of the capital budget request, authorizing expenditure, conditional expenditure, deferral, or rejection. This action is part of the annual budget approval. Projects are normally approved in rank order. Decisions involving the total amount of funds to be committed are based not only on mission, environment, and plan, but also on financial considerations.
- Detailed implementation plans and schedules for approved proposals are developed by the line-staff team. A project manager is appointed and held accountable for conformance to both plans and schedules. Progress is usually monitored by an appropriate

Figure 6.11   Flow Chart of Programmatic Proposal Review

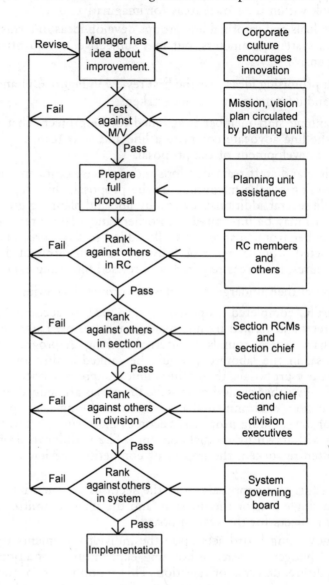

line manager, with the aid of the line-staff team. The planning staff is responsible for all outside negotiations for permits and approvals. Special teams are usually assembled when negotiations with competitors are involved.

• Unfunded proposals are returned to the line systems, which can resubmit them the next year, improve them, or abandon them.

These steps are easier to describe than to follow in the real world; processes described here as discrete are really continuous and intertwined. The basic structure has several important advantages. Its iterative, expanding approach to evaluation and its insistence on competitively ranked recommendations promote efficiency. The integrated line and staff roles encourage thorough competitive review and limit expensive governing board time without diminishing board influence. Broad employee, and medical staff participation promotes development of realistic expectations, but also enhances a sense of involvement. Finally, the development of specific implementation plans and schedules smoothes the process of change.

Maintaining Relations with Government and Other Health Agencies

Health care organizations have ongoing relationships even though they may be competing directly. They also are obligated to gain certain planning approvals and to comply with other laws affecting the planning process.

Assist in Negotiations with Competing or Collaborating Organizations

As noted above, strategic positioning should be based on thorough, ongoing surveillance of institutions with related or potentially related missions. This surveillance frequently includes considerable direct communication, and this in turn leads to collaborative relationships of various kinds (Chapter 5, Mulit-Unit Organizations).

There is a long-standing tradition that community hospitals should collaborate with one another, principally because they share a common obligation to the same community and because such collaboration appears to be more economical. However, in the era of unlimited financial support and significant subsidization for growth, the tradition was exceptionally difficult to implement. In the newer, more restrictive and more competitive environment, collaboration appears, ironically, to be more successful, even as competition is more common.

Even bitterly competing health care organizations tend to communicate frequently. Any collaborative activity which is not a violation of the antitrust laws is a fair topic of conversation. Ad hoc allegiances to market-specific products, such as health insurance plans, or to meet specific needs, such as clinical training programs, or serve specific populations, such as programs for the disadvantaged, are common.

Within a framework of competition, communication and collaboration are used constantly.

The antitrust implications of dialogue between competitors are difficult to describe. The law on per se violations is clear: conversations between competitors cannot include collusion to set prices, divide or establish markets, or exclude other competitors. Such actions are criminal, and individuals have been prosecuted for them. On the other hand, exploration of merger or shared service possibilities is neither a criminal nor a civil violation of the acts if it can be defended as being in the public interest. A practical suggestion is that dialogue is necessary, but that the per se topics should be avoided in action, implication, and intent. Legal counsel is frequently necessary; many actions depend on details of presentation and content.

Activities other than the per se violations which tend to increase the services available for patients are generally defensible under antitrust, and are also important between health care organizations not directly competing, such as hospitals and nursing homes. Competitors can often improve services by mergers and affiliations. Legal counsel is indicated to keep the discussion consistent with the law. The actual negotiation of mergers and affiliations is usually reserved to the CEO and selected members of the governing board, but the planning executive is a member of the well-run organization's strategic response teams, and planning data are the appropriate bases for many of the decisions. As a result, the planning executive is frequently a participant.

Obtaining Regulatory Approvals

National laws enacted in 1966 and 1974 encouraged the states to develop regulation of hospital investments. As a result, many states issue **certificates of need** (CONs) for new services and construction or renovation. State approval of construction as a requirement for reimbursement by Medicare is more uniform; no new capital cost can be recovered from Medicare unless section 1122 approval is obtained. These laws are enforced with varying degrees of vigor, and their importance is diminishing. (The federal law terminated in 1988). When the law is enforced, CONs represent franchises which have economic value in themselves. Winning CONs or blocking opponents' can become an important competitive arena.

Success in winning CONs depends upon timing, well-designed and attractive services, technically well-prepared proposals, and the support of influential persons in the community. One individual should be accountable for the management of applications. The planning executive, is often designated, although the task can be retained by the

CEO or delegated to government relations staff. Strategies for dealing with HSAs and certificates of need vary. The influence of these laws is arguable.[21] Most well-run organizations have developed strategies and tactics for gaining the approval of all or nearly all their important options and proposals.

In some communities there are voluntary or other regulatory bodies, and in most cities, hospital construction requires zoning board approval, or construction permits, or both. These negotiations are clearly the responsibility of planning units.

Measures of Planning Effectiveness

The planning activity, like every other part of the well-run organization, should have established performance measures, short-term expectations, and regular reporting of achievement against these. The unit's scope, demand, output quality, cost, and human resources should be measured as quantitatively and objectively as possible, and specific expectations should be set. Those important expectations not quantifiable, such as the unit's contribution to overall success, must be covered by discussion and agreement. A set of measures for a planning unit is shown in Figure 6.12.

Demand, Output, and Productivity Measures

The demand for planning is the amount of service expected by other units. Demand can be assessed by a log of the routine reports, special reports or projects, committee meetings and assignments, and other activities anticipated during the forthcoming year. These items can rarely be fully quantified, and the dimensions are not additive. In addition, planning plays an important standby role, which cannot be foreseen. As a result, demand expectations are best described by a measure of satisfaction with service. Two are suggested in Figure 6.11. One is collected by survey of planning unit users, and the other can be developed from a log of requests and dispositions.

It is also difficult to specify expectations for planning output, although there are exceptions for certain parts of the total activity. As a result, few organizations rely on quantitative output expectations; instead, they emphasize an understanding of the kinds of services anticipated and agreement on the quality of service anticipated. Because of the difficulties of quantifying output, productivity has little meaning in planning. The term is occasionally confused with promptness, which is a dimension of quality.

Figure 6.12 Performance Measures for Planning Services

Dimension Measured	Measure
Demand for planning services	User satisfaction with response time Activity log Delays to respond to service requests
Outcomes quality Demand and market share forecasts	Variations from annual forecasts of major measures of market share and demand for service Comparisons of rates of growth of demand and revenue for new services implemented with forecasts from programmatic proposals
Programmatic project forecasts	Actual project implementation costs against forecast Actual project operating costs and profit against forecast Project implementation timetables against forecast
Regulatory agency relations	Percentage of applications successfully submitted
Patient and buyer influence	Attitudes of patients and buyers toward institutional mission and specific programs, with particular attention to attitudes of influentials
Member satisfaction	Attitudes toward overall planning service Attitudes toward timely recognition of opportunities and potential problems Attitudes toward timely completion of projects relative to community and market needs and opportunities
Cost measures	Total direct costs Labor costs Consultant costs Data and information acquisition costs
Human resources satisfaction	Satisfaction scores of planning personnel Vacancy, turnover, and recruitment effectiveness
Contribution measure	Evaluation of strategic position by governing board

Quality Measures

Quality of planning includes outcomes measures on how accurate, timely, and effective the planning contribution was and process measures on the methods and approaches used. A well-run planning unit will have expectations and routine measurement involving at least the topics listed in Figure 6.12. Unfortunately, major projects involve the entire organization, and take several years to complete. The difficulties of measuring and isolating the planning contribution to the results suggest strongly that these measures must be considered subjectively. Often, evaluation must be limited to the events that are complete and self-contained enough to yield lessons for the future. These anecdotes are still enough for beneficial review and evaluation. In addition, there are accessible outcomes and process quality measures.

Resource Measures for Planning

The planning activity should have an explicit cost budget, like any other unit in the organization. The budget must be fixed rather than flexible, and established subjectively, based upon the scope and quality of service desired. The principle costs are labor costs, and consultant services are often separately accounted. Costs of data and information are also important. Some information must now be purchased from outside sources and computer hardware and software is essential to effective service.

Satisfaction of planning personnel is a valid human resources measure for this unit, as it is for all others. Evidence of respect by peers, such as publications or presentations, is sometimes used.

The planning activity has no direct revenue or profit. It can be evaluated indirectly by the revenue from specific projects, as noted in Figure 6.12, but the line contributes to this achievement. It is probably better to evaluate planning on the most direct measure, that is, changes in market share, than on the more remote, profits. It is also possible to specify a strategic objective—for example, that the unit must identify and develop several appropriate new sources of market share. Such an objective is probably more appropriate to a five-year horizon than to an annual one, but it could be included in the long-range plan and used to support more specific annual expectations.

It is possible to evaluate planning units according to the technical proficiency of their work, such as the completeness of data, availability of analytic software, and the use of correct analytic technique. These evaluations all require judgments and are difficult to reduce to numerical scores. Periodic evaluation by outside consultants and review against JCAHO criteria are useful. The ultimate judgment of planning, that the organization is or is not positioned where it should be in the community, is based upon the environmental surveillance itself. The evaluation planning is inevitably bound up with that of the chief executive and the governing board. The final assessment of planning is the board's function, exercised through the planning committee or the compensation committee.

Organization for Planning

Personnel Requirements

Even a large health care organization will employ only a few people in its planning activity. Other members of the governance system, particularly the CEO and CFO, will have important planning functions, and outside consultants are often used. Very small hospitals must assign planning and marketing responsibilities directly to the chief executive or one deputy. A small professional staff with an identified chief (usually called Vice President for Planning) is common even in smaller organizations and can often be justified by reduced expenditures for outside consultants.

Professional Skills of Planning Executives

Effective institutional planning requires an ability to build consensus by negotiation, together with mastery of a growing body of professional knowledge and skill. Professional requirements include techniques for analysis, knowledge of health care administration, and understanding of community and individual opinion formation. Analytic techniques should include practical skills in cost accounting, present value analysis, statistics, forecasting, and business plan modeling. The complexity of health care also requires detailed knowledge: current status and trends in health insurance, government financial programs, health personnel availability, health care technology, sources of capital funds, the role of regulatory bodies, and prevention of disease. Finally, the planning executive must understand community power structures and decision processes, methods of information dissemination, and the uses of advertising and public relations.

Most of the professional subject matter is covered in an accredited master's degree program in health care administration. A graduate degree in business also covers many of the topics, although with important omissions in the specifics of the health care field. Competent individuals with a degree in either of these fields can improve their skill through continuing education and reading. The combination of both business and health administration degrees is increasingly relevant and becoming more popular.

Negotiating skills are learned by practice. Certainly the mature planning executive should be able to conduct fruitful meetings, identify and assist in the resolution of disputes, and present information clearly and convincingly, both orally and in writing. Beginners must learn those skills by observation and supervised experience, although community and extramural collegiate activities are useful.

Planning personnel are recruited in national markets. Deputies and beginners are often selected from among recent graduates. Planning executives are promoted from within, attracted from consulting firms, or hired from other organizations. Although experience and maturity are important, it is not uncommon to rely upon the experience of the CEO to overcome immaturity in the planning unit. The centrality, breadth of scope, and requirements for planning suggest it as an excellent background for CEOs and COOs.

Outside Consultants

The variety and extent of skills required in planning make it a fruitful area for the use of consultants. Many activities of planning can be assigned to outside firms. These include:

- *Surveillance.* Demographic and economic forecasts, trends in technology and personnel availability, evaluation of future plant and equipment needs, consumer demand and market surveys, and surveys of competitor's behavior.
- *Strategic responses.* Investigation of competitor's interests and positions, evaluation of expansion and acquisition options, advice on entering new markets or offering new services, and experience in strategic procedures and negotiations.
- *Proposal development and evaluation.* Suggestions for new products and services, feasibility and cost-benefit analyses, and design of response evaluation protocol.
- *Communication and consensus building.* Assistance starting and maintaining a planning oriented dialogue among organization influentials.

Consultants can specialize in understanding demographic, economic, and underlying attitudinal trends; act as extra hands; impart technical skills for specialized responses; bring knowledge of what others facing the same problem are doing; and mediate entrenched conflicts over the nature of the mission, the objectives, or a specific response. The possible uses of outside consultants are so extensive that specifying what they *cannot* do may be the easiest way to identify their contribution. Consultants cannot replace the judgment of either operating personnel or governing board members, and, of course, they cannot and do not accept accountability for the mission, vision, long-range plan objectives, or selection of specific programs. Thus, any consultant's recommendation must be carefully and fully evaluated by those responsible for the institution. Consultants cannot provide the continuity of an ongoing executive presence.

The keys to successful use of consultants are as follows:

1. The assignment should be clearly specified in terms of process, timing, and result. As a general rule, the clearer the assignment and the more details of the work specified in advance, the better the chances for success. It is occasionally wise to use consultants to gain fresh insights into vague, ill-defined problems, but such use should be limited to very short-term assignments.

2. To be cost-effective, topics assigned to consultants should require skills or quantities of effort not available locally. Using consultants as neutral third parties is essentially correcting a failure of the local process, and this should not occur often.

3. Consultant firms should be selected on the basis of relevant prior experience. In the absence of direct experience with a consultant, opinions of other clients should be solicited before any major assignment is made.

4. Consultant activities should be carefully monitored against the specifications throughout the project. This job is often assigned to the planning executive.

Organization

Most planning units in health care organizations are small enough that the internal organization is simply an RC team. In larger units, deputy planner-marketers can be held accountable for specifics along the lines of surveillance, mission, and strategic options, and programmatic proposal development and implementation. Planning activities are sometimes merged with marketing, and two RCs covering planning and marketing under one vice president is not uncommon. A functional view designates individuals responsible for maintaining relations between planning and major clinical units. This suggests that a practical organization of a planning unit follows matrix organization principles, with each deputy of the planning executive accountable for a functional area and relations with specific line units.

The supervision of consultants should also be explicitly assigned to individuals, with accountability running through the planning executive. Failure to identify a point of contact slows the consultants, adds to their costs, and defeats the possibility of continuous monitoring during the contract period.

Well-run organizations keep planning activities very close to the CEO and the governing board. Split reporting of planning functions, some to the CEO and some to the COO, may cause some aspects to get less attention than they should. Assignment of planning to the COO risks an undesirably short-term focus and may result in insufficient attention to strategic options and community needs. Assignment of planning to the CFO increases the dominance of the financial aspect of decisions; in the long run, responsiveness to community need should determine the decisions more than financial implications.

Larger health care systems frequently centralize some aspects of planning to improve the technical skills of personnel, to provide economies of scale, and to ensure consistency when appropriate. On the other hand, health care remains a locally generated and locally delivered product. Many leading not-for-profit chains deliberately retain local planning staffs at least in each of their geographical communities.

Management Issues

Success in planning occurs when the organization is led into fruitful endeavors. Failure comes in two ways, when weaker ventures are selected and when better ones are overlooked. From that perspective, a formal planning activity must justify its existence by being prompt and thorough: it must uncover the obscure and have new detail about the obvious. From one viewpoint, planning is an intelligence activity, uncovering hidden risks and overlooked opportunities. From another, it is a service to expedite a decision-making process. The conventional model for success emphasizes surveillance, mission setting, and long-range planning as the background and guide to decisions that must be made on strategic opportunities and programmatic proposals. Experience with this model has revealed some areas in which special attention is useful. These issues are reviewed in two groups: (1) technical foundations within the planning unit and (2) premises for evaluating opportunities and proposals in not-for-profit organizations.

Technical Foundations

Successful planning units seem to excel in four technical areas: (1) they take extra pains to guard against oversights; (2) they use the most objective forecasts they can obtain; (3) they are rigorous in their evaluation of costs and benefits; and (4) they follow procedures that deliberately use comparison and competition to debate the best course of action.

Guarding against Oversight

The first step in avoiding overlooking the best ideas is in recognizing the danger of doing so. Most planning and forecasting is done by extrapolating from past history, often assuming *ceteris paribus* (other things being equal). No other approach is practical or prudent as a mainstay of a planning unit, or of a governance activity generally. Truly radical departures are rare; the past is usually prologue to the present. Thus, most of the time this approach is both the least expensive and the most likely to be correct. Success lies in discovering those few cases in which the future will depart radically from the past. There are several ways to check for this possibility.

- Radical change often occurs at different times in different places. A check of conditions elsewhere may show trends not yet evident in the local community.
- The *hoshin* concept is useful. It leads to a search for the ideal way to meet customer needs, perhaps using technology the customer could never think of on his own.
- Radical change often arises from individuals with different views from the rest of the group, sometimes to the point of being outcasts. Careful study of the opinions of critics of the status quo can suggest practical improvements.
- Imagination can be prompted by deliberately trying to think the unthinkable. The most successful planners deliberately insert a step in major forecasting or planning exercises which asks two questions: What could occur that would make this forecast totally wrong? and Is there any other scenario, however improbable, that would be significantly more attractive than this one, and what might make such a scenario more probable?

An environment in which ideas can be openly expressed promotes discovery of the rare radical departure. Many successful institutions promote such an environment by periodically inviting consultants and speakers known for their unconventional views; making sure that those who express unusual views are protected from personal insult or injury, such as losing promotions or salary increases; and opening their plans to widespread debate and discussion, with the intention of finding conflicting views and evaluating them.

Using Objective Forecasts

Subjective forecasts, those prepared intuitively by people working in the area under study, can be very accurate for periods of less than two years, if they are carefully prepared. Their accuracy deteriorates rapidly over longer terms and in unfamiliar applications. Successful organizations take pains to find independent sources of forecasts, to use several different sources, and to use rigorously unbiased methods to describe the future and to evaluate a range of possible scenarios.

Such cold-blooded realism improves planning in two ways: it reveals projects based on fantasy soon enough to avoid them, and it develops a climate of credibility, in which the surviving proposals can be effectively evaluated. It requires a sophisticated, well-thought-out system of data management to carry it out. Data bases and forecasting models must be readily available, easy to use, and easy to understand. An important contribution of planning personnel is in knowing and using these tools, and bringing them to bear in ways the line originators of the proposal can appreciate.

Exogenous factors influencing demand must be forecast as accurately as possible. These include community population, age and sex distribution, birth rate, income, insurance coverage, and the need for goods and services other than health care. Most of these are forecast by several independent sources, and well-run organizations use these forecasts rather than their own. They discard predictions by groups with vested interests (such as the local power companies and the Chamber of Commerce), and use the remaining ones to project both an expectation and a range of possibilities. They then explore costs and benefits of proposed responses across the range of values, showing the sensitivity of the conclusion to forecasting assumptions. Graphic displays are important in helping people understand alternatives and their consequences.

Using Cost-Benefit Measures Effectively

The costs and benefits of many different proposals must be assessed quickly and inexpensively. The iterative evaluation described above is one step toward this goal. Some others that well-run organizations adopt include:

- Adhering to a formal protocol that prompts recognition of obscure costs and hidden risks. The protocol should strongly encourage investigation of several areas known to be overlooked in less rigorous approaches:
  - Costs of borrowing or leasing
  - Costs of obsolescence, or unduly optimistic estimates of project life
  - Opportunity costs in committing irreplaceable resources
  - Overhead costs or burdens on other units
  - Promotional costs and the implications of competition for limited demand
  - Intangible costs, including possible political repercussions, member dissatisfaction, and malpractice liability.

- Searching for combinations of projects which increase the attractiveness of all of the individual projects. Often a project that is too costly to be undertaken on its own is valuable when it is included in a package with others. Renovations, for example, create conditions in which many previously impractical revisions become cost-effective. They also represent windows in time. When the renovation is complete, overlooked projects may be forever lost. The well-run organization sees more possible combinations because it looks for them.

- Encouraging complete identification and description of benefits which cannot be assigned precise dollar valuation. Most benefits, particularly those related to health, are difficult to evaluate and impossible to measure in dollar terms. They can be identified and described, and the number of people likely to receive them can be forecast. These estimates are much less expensive than imprecise dollar estimates and probably as useful.

- Using staff experts, individuals from other health care systems, and outside consultants to enhance the accuracy of cost and benefit estimates. Physicians, industrial engineers, purchasing agents, finance department staff, and plant department staff can improve the reliability and the credibility of estimates. Outside consultants bring objectivity and broader experience to bear.

- Using examples from other health care organizations. The most convincing evidence of accurate cost-benefit estimates is the existence of a smoothly operating example elsewhere. Few organizations have the resources to pioneer; those that do, do so in only a few areas. Many poorly run organizations are trapped by delusions of uniqueness or unrealistic visions of leadership.

Maintaining Objectivity in the Evaluation Process

Objectivity and realism must extend beyond the exogenous forecasts and the development of cost-benefit measures to the entire process of response evaluation and selection. There are natural human tendencies not only to overstate the ratio of benefits to costs, but also to distort it in favor of one's personal desires. The well-run organization must use accountable delegation processes for evaluating response that minimize both these risks. The following are specific steps:

- Use line-staff teams to develop projects, because their dual contribution tends to reduce bias.

- Group programmatic proposals together with an annual timetable tied to the budget cycle, and start comparative review as far down the accountability hierarchy as possible, even within a single responsibility center.

- Provide sequential review against broadening competition and at higher levels of the accountability hierarchy.
- Keep a broadly representative membership on the planning committee or the capital budget committee. The committee that makes the final recommendation to the board frequently must weigh several expensive, strongly advocated projects, each of which has considerable merit. The credibility of this committee is essential to continued generation of proposals.
- Encourage candid discussion of proposals by minimizing the negative consequences of honesty. Influential people must visibly respect the opinions of individuals who are less powerful. Power should not be rewarded in the planning process. Helpful techniques for encouraging candor include
  - adhering to the established protocol for all proposals;
  - selecting planning committee members so that powerful people are balanced against one another rather than against groups of less powerful people;
  - chairing meetings competently, so that all can be heard;
  - using outside consultants to counterbalance local experts; and
  - instructing or sanctioning individuals who endanger the process of development and evaluation.

Evaluating Opportunities in Not-for-Profit Health Care Organizations

It sometimes happens that very similar opportunities are attractive to one organization but not another. Assuming that both are well run, considerations other than the opportunity itself must lead to this result. There are five premises about planning decisions that are independent of the individual proposal or opportunity and related to the values or beliefs of the decision makers:

1. Community mission
2. Community values
3. Time horizon used for decision making
4. Willingness to accept risk
5. Willingness to assume debt

Well-managed health care organizations have consensus positions on these elements. Each position involves a set of trade-offs in which certain proposals will face diminished chances of acceptance, while others will face enhanced chances. The trade-offs are by definition intangible (that is, impractical to measure in dollar terms in most situations), and they are implicitly decided by any action taken, even an action to defer or delay. An institution's profile on the premises, reflected in its actual decisions, constitutes part of its style or corporate culture.

Community Mission

The motivations for operating community health care organizations are classified in Chapter 2 as Samaritanism, personal health, public health, community economic gain, and health care economy. All of these but personal health, and especially Samaritanism and public health, are goals which make communities attractive as a whole, rather than direct benefits to individuals.[22] For-profit organizations are justified in ignoring these benefits unless they contribute directly to profit; they are not expected to contribute to these values, and they can be penalized for diverting funds away from their owners. Not-for-profit organizations are explicitly rewarded by their tax exemptions. The justification for these exemptions is often criticized by people who say that the true owners are the doctors and employees, who take the value of the exemption in enhanced salaries.[23] Leaders of not-for-profit health care have responded by increased emphasis on community values.[24,25]

It is possible to measure the community contribution indirectly by accounting data such as bad debts, uncompensated care, and investment in health education. It is also assessed by the existence or commitment to certain programs such as the willingness to meet needs of the disadvantaged. Evidence from California hospitals by Clement, Smith, and Wheeler suggests that the amount of community contribution declined during the 1980s, but in 1987 it remained more valuable than the tax exemption itself, or alternative investments.[26]

The leadership of voluntary health care is strongly committed to the concept of returning the value of the tax advantage and more to the community. It is one of the unique contributions that justify the existence of these corporate structures. Thus projects which meet community needs have advantages over those that do not in not-for-profit health care organizations. This does not mean they will always be adopted, but it does mean that they need not show profits or personal health market share as their main or sole justification.

Community Values

Closely related to the concept of community mission, a not-for-profit organization may protect certain assets, or resources, which will never have a precise accounting definition. The organization's religious commitment, or achievement of a certain mission, such as care of the poor, are assets to the community that never appear on any balance sheet. These must remain intangible, but they also must figure into decisions. Often one can conceptualize a value, but the problems of estimating it are so complex that the answer is left in intangible form. One might say, for example, that the value of a new inner city program for the poor is equivalent to the saving in high-cost emergency room treatment, or the value of the number of jobs that would be lost to the local economy if no one took care of the poor. (Presumably employers and workers would prefer communities that do a better job.) Unfortunately, the first value is difficult and the second impossible to determine.

Beyond the empirical difficulty, there are many more philosophical issues than one would at first think. For example, what is the value of affiliation with a medical school or a religious organization? What is the importance of remaining in a certain location, such as a downtown site near the homes of poor patients and unskilled workers? How much is it appropriate to spend on aesthetics, such as a statue or a traditional building? (The Johns Hopkins Hospital has kept its nineteenth-century entrance with the large marble statue of Christ and the famous dome over it at very high cost. How can one decide whether the cost is worthwhile? One cannot, except by voting yes or no on the specific proposal. Those who vote to save the entrance consider tradition, viable expression of a Samaritan commitment, and aesthetics to be more important than the benefits which might have accrued from alternative use of the space and funds.)

It is generally believed that not-for-profit organizations should place higher values on intangible assets. That is, one of the social functions of hospitals, Blue Cross Plans, universities, and private foundations is to uphold the values that may be overlooked in purely commercial transactions. There is by definition no evidence that this policy is correct, but it is widely accepted. The converse can be more convincingly stated: if health care organizations do not protect intangibles, they lose an important characteristic distinguishing them from for-profit organizations. Sooner or later, people will ask why they should continue to exist.

Time Horizon Used for Decision Making

The benefits of different proposals have different time horizons. Most of the community-oriented motivations have long time horizons. Samaritanism, public health, and health care economy, which are concerned directly with the well-being of the community, have the longest horizons, in the sense that only a small fraction of the total benefit is recovered in the short term. Preventive personal health care also tends to have long horizons; preventive care for children, for example, produces benefits throughout their lives. High-tech care and care of the dying tend to produce much shorter-range benefits. Thus, a short-term style will emphasize proposals whose benefits lie in high-tech personal health care and community economic benefits (such as employment). An extreme short-term orientation ignores facility replacement cost and focuses on the status quo in health care financing. An extreme long-term view puts cost burdens on short-term proposals to protect longer-term values.

The correct time horizon depends on time and place, but well-run health care organizations emphasize the long term. Actions which only yield immediate benefits are considered expedient, and usually avoided. Organizations which are in trouble tend to shorter horizons, but a sign of their recovery is a movement to longer perspectives.

Risk

All proposals and strategies involve risks, but the amount and kind of risk can differ. In an oversimplified example, two projects are proposed. One may save thousands of lives if it works, but it is difficult to estimate the chances that it will work. The other is virtually certain to save 200 lives. If both cost exactly the same, and only one can be adopted, which should the organization choose? At very high risk of failure for the first project, the certain project will be selected without much disagreement. As the risk of failure diminishes, more decision makers will opt for the first proposal. There is an underlying bias toward prudence, expressed in the law and tradition of not-for-profit organizations, which favor risk avoidance. Yet prudence itself must be defined. Time and place determine what is acceptable risk. In the example, a research hospital might accept much higher levels of risk than a community hospital, and hospitals in a wealthy nation would take more risk than those in a poor one.

In real health care organizations, the odds are never clear, costs are never exactly the same, and projects are rarely directly comparable. Each year the institution makes a series of specific decisions which reflect what the governance structure feels to be acceptable levels of risk. The accepted role of not-for-profit organizations emphasizes prudence; very high risks must be placed in organizations specially designed to deal with them, and to limit losses of community funds. Higher risks should be matched by higher potential gains. Consistency is important.

The institution should not be risk averse, unwilling to accept risk on one decision and risk taking on a similar opportunity.

Liquidity

The issue of liquidity and borrowing is inseparably related to risk. Resources in their liquid form are usually invested in readily salable instruments earning a tangible return. When funded, strategic and programmatic proposals always have some opportunity cost. The funds transferred from liquid to illiquid assets are no longer available for spending. A decision to wait, or to remain liquid, is a decision that the benefits of the project will not overcome the loss of flexibility. It implies that a better, as yet unforeseen, opportunity will arise. A decision to spend is the opposite, and a decision to borrow, which itself carries a tangible cost, is a decision that the value of the project exceeds the cost of borrowing. The tangible costs and benefits of borrowing are handled by competent technical analysis. What complicates the decision is that borrowing has intangible costs that apply to all projects rather than to any specific opportunity. Borrowing reduces the future ability of the organization to borrow and, as a result, its ability to respond to unforeseen trouble. That is to say, the opportunity cost of borrowing is increased risk.

It is also important to understand the relationship of liquidity to expansion and to economical health care. Borrowing permits rapid expansion, which for health care organizations means increased costs to the community. A strong motivation for economy discourages borrowing. The cost of borrowing, and to a certain extent the risk, is set by the interest rate. The organization may add to the interest rate the intangible cost of borrowing, or preference for liquidity, sometimes called the *hurdle rate*. Organizations that prefer liquidity generally set a high hurdle rate: they expect any successful proposal to repay not only the interest, but also the hurdle. The result is that fewer projects are accepted; those that are tend to have short-term benefits and lower risks.

Well-managed not-for-profit health care organizations tend toward higher liquidity. They use hurdle rates either explicitly or implicitly to avoid projects of limited return.

Importance of Community Representation in Decisions

As major alternatives are debated at the governing board level, positions on these premises are identified by specific resource allocation decisions. The profile which emerges will ultimately reflect the relative weight placed on representation of different perspectives within the community. A representative profile of well-managed not-for-profit health care organizations is shown in Figure 6.13. Individual organizations and communities will differ, but in general, the not-for-profit vision is one of community support, community values, longer terms, prudence, and liquidity.

Many classifications of the community can be used. The consumer-provider dichotomy is an important but simplistic one. Whether decision makers are poor or rich, influential or not, religious or secular, male or female, or white or black also influences the final values placed on the premises. The ability to accommodate the views of others, however, appears more important than actual affiliation. Wise decision makers not only transcend their own self-interest and background, but they also recognize the need for compromise and the importance of understanding specifics in order to compromise effectively. One characteristic of well-run health care organizations is that they recognize when special interests are important and accommodate them in specific, rather than general, terms.

The subtleties of the question begin to emerge if one considers the issue of customer versus provider orientation. Customers and providers may have legitimately conflicting interests. Optimization will call for finding the balance that maximizes the totality of interests met. If too

Figure 6.13 Profile of Not-for-Profit Values

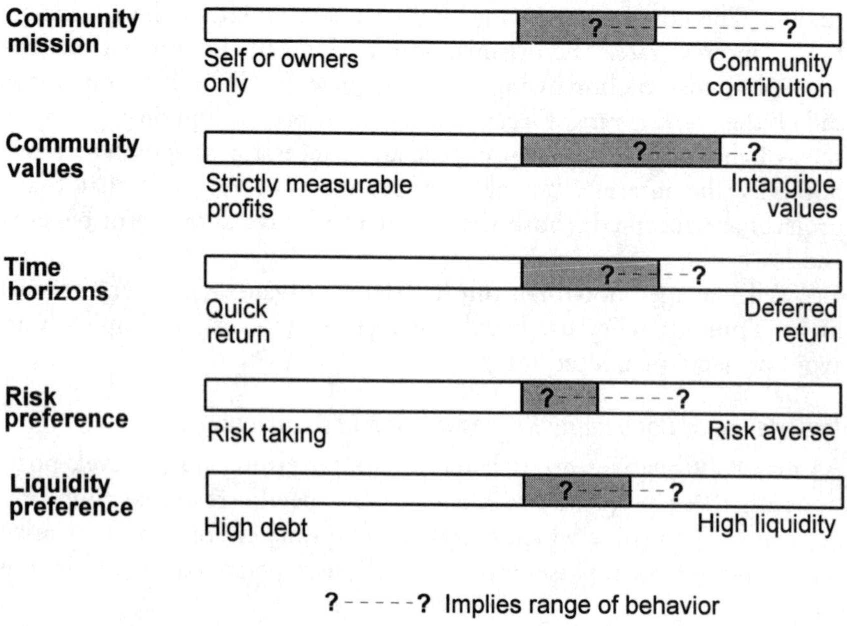

Community mission	Self or owners only — Community contribution
Community values	Strictly measurable profits — Intangible values
Time horizons	Quick return — Deferred return
Risk preference	Risk taking — Risk averse
Liquidity preference	High debt — High liquidity

? - - - - - ? Implies range of behavior

much is conceded to the providers, some community goals may not be achieved, and the community may seek service elsewhere or seek to change the representation; if too little, the members may leave, strike, or otherwise resist. Conflicts often result in failure to achieve either member or community goals. Through its planning decisions, a health care organization inevitably places itself on the community versus member continuum. That is, it implicitly trades off the values of the decision makers on questions such as the importance of hospital employment and the attractiveness of the community to other commerce.

The consistency, wisdom, and effectiveness that decisions such as these reflect distinguish the well-run health care organization. The predisposition of the governing board toward short or long term, high or low risk, greater or less liquidity, and for or against certain missions and values, will determine the eventual shape of the organization.

Suggested Readings

Kotler, P. 1991. *Strategic Marketing for Non-Profit Organizations*, 4th ed. Englewood Cliffs, NJ: Prentice-Hall.

Kotler, P., and R. N. Clark. 1987. *Marketing for Health Care Organizations.* Englewood Cliffs, NJ: Prentice-Hall.

Porter, M. E. 1980. *Competitive Strategy: Techniques for Analyzing Industries and Competitors.* New York: Free Press.

Spiegel, S. E., and H. H. Hyman. 1991. *Strategic Health Planning: Methods and Techniques Applied to Marketing and Management.* Norwood, NJ: Ablex Publishing Corporation.

Shortell, S. M., E. M. Morrison, and B. Friedman. 1990. *Strategic Choices for America's Hospitals: Managing Change in Turbulent Times.* San Francisco: Jossey-Bass.

Veney, J. E., and A. D. Kaluzny. 1992. *Evaluation and Decision Making for Health Services*, 2d ed. Ann Arbor, MI: Health Administration Press.

Notes

1. P. Kotler, 1991, *Strategic Marketing for Non-Profit Organizations*, 4th ed. (Englewood Cliffs, NJ: Prentice-Hall).

2. J. R. Griffith, W. M. Hancock, and F. C. Munson, 1976, *Cost Control in Hospitals* (Ann Arbor, MI: Health Administration Press), 23–89.

3. See *Quality Management in Health Care* 1993, 1 (Summer). The issue is devoted to strategic quality planning and includes articles based on five different health care systems.

4. D. M. Demers, 1993, "Implementing Hoshin Planning at the Vermont Medical Center," *Quality Management in Health Care*, 1 (Summer): 64–72. See especially p. 69.

5. See *Quality Management in Health Care*, 1993, 1 (Summer).

6. G. Hamel and C. K. Prahalad, 1993, "Strategy as Stretch and Leverage," *Harvard Business Review* 71 (March–April): 75–84.

7. T. Proctor and P. Ruocco, 1992, "Generating Marketing Strategies: A Structured Creative Decision Support Method (Matching Organizational Strengths and Weaknesses with Opportunities and Threats)," *Management Decision* 30 (5): 50–53.

8. J. Peters, 1993, "On Audits," *Management Decision* 31 (6): 26–27.

9. M. E. Porter, 1980, *Competitive Strategy: Techniques for Analyzing Industries and Competitors* (New York: Free Press), xvi–xx.

10. D. F. Abell and J. S. Hammond, 1979, *Strategic Market Planning: Problems and Analytic Approaches* (Englewood Cliffs, NJ: Prentice-Hall).

11. H. Thomas and D. Gardner, 1985, *Strategic Marketing and Management* (New York: Wiley).

12. R. E. Miles and C. C. Snow, 1978, *Organizational Strategy, Structure, and Process* (New York: McGraw-Hill).

13. S. R. Eastaugh, 1992, "Hospital Strategy and Financial Performance," *Health Care Management Review* 17 (3): 19–31.

14. M. E. Porter, 1980, *Competitive Strategy* (New York: Free Press).

15. D. Miller and P. H. Friesen, 1984, *Organizations: A Quantum View* (Englewood Cliffs, NJ: Prentice-Hall).

16. S. M. Shortell, E. M. Morrison, and B. Friedman, 1990, *Strategic Choices for America's Hospitals: Managing Change in Turbulent Times* (San Francisco: Jossey-Bass).

17. Eastaugh, "Hospital Strategy and Financial Performance," 27.

18. S. M. Shortell, R. R. Gillies, D. A. Anderson, J. B. Mitchell, and K. L. Morgan, 1993, "Creating Organized Delivery Systems: The Barriers and Facilitators" *Hospital & Health Services Administration* 38 (Winter): 447–60.

19. J. R. Griffith, V. Sahney, and R. Mohr, 1995, *Reengineering Health Care: Building on CQI* (Ann Arbor, MI: Health Administration Press), Chapter 4.

20. P. Kotler, 1982, *Marketing for Non-Profit Organizations*, 2d ed. (Englewood Cliffs, NJ: Prentice-Hall).

21. U. S. General Accounting Office, 1981, "Health Systems Plans: A Poor Framework for Promoting Health Care Improvements," Report to Congress by the Controller General of the United States (Washington, DC: U.S. Government Printing Office).

22. H. Long, 1976, "Valuation as a Criterion in Not-For-Profit Decision-Making," 1 (Summer): 34–52.

23. B. Arrington and C. C. Haddock, 1990, "Who Really Profits from Non-Profits," *Health Services Research* 25 (June): 291–304.

24. J. D. Seay and B. C. Vladeck, eds., 1988, *In Sickness and in Health: The Mission of Voluntary Health Institutions* (New York: McGraw-Hill).

25. A. R. Kovner, 1994, "The Hospital Community Benefits Standards Program and Health Reform," *Hospital & Health Services Administration* 39 (Summer): 143–57.

26. J. P. Clement, D. G. Smith, and J. R. C. Wheeler, 1994, "What Do We Want and What Do We Get from Not-for-Profit Hospitals?" *Hospital & Health Services Administration* 39 (Summer): 159–78.

MARKETING THE HEALTH CARE ORGANIZATION

THE PLANNING activity discussed in the previous chapter is designed to produce health care the customer wants and deliver it where the customer wants at a price the customer is willing to pay. Kotler and Clarke define marketing as:

> the analysis, planning, implementation, and control of carefully formulated programs designed to bring about voluntary exchanges of values with target markets for the purpose of achieving organizational objectives.[1]

Proper planning is inescapable with that definition, or in any other situation where voluntary exchanges drive the end result. Yet even assuming that planning is highly customer-oriented and results in an attractive product, placement, and price, there is still a need for the fourth P, following the marketing mnemonic, to promote—to inform customers, convince them, and assist them to buy. As Kotler implies, target markets are the key to this activity. The organization must identify specific **markets**, groups of people seeking to make exchanges of value, and present its opportunities. **Marketing** is the deliberate effort to establish fruitful relationships with exchange partners. It applies not just to customers, but to all exchanges, including employees and other community agencies.

Marketing has become more important to health care organizations with the growth of managed care and price-oriented competition. Health care organizations today work steadily on attracting patients to their doctors, linking doctors to the organization, winning contracts with intermediaries which will be profitable, and persuading employers and insured groups of their advantages. Seventy percent of hospitals were reported to have moderate to high marketing orientations in 1991. Larger hospitals reported an average of about 15 people in marketing, public relations and planning activity, with seven devoted to marketing, five to public relations, and only three to planning.[2] In a different survey, about a third of the expenditures were for advertising, and only one in four marketing people reported responsibility for planning. Most of the funds went for consumer marketing. Physician marketing received 20 percent of the funds, and employer marketing about 10 percent.[3]

This chapter will identify the purpose and functions of marketing, provide measures of marketing performance, and discuss the organization of marketing functions. Because extensive marketing activity is so recent, there is a limited body of knowledge about marketing. Many of the concepts are new and untested, and patterns of successful market management have not yet emerged. Leading institutions are taking assertive actions to bring patients to the primary care doctors' offices, and from there into the other services. They are working directly to build relationships with insurance carriers, intermediaries, and employers. Well-run institutions market themselves to their employees as well; it gives them the opportunity to select the best and to attract professionals in short supply. This chapter will identify those jobs, and describe what must be done about them, taking the outsider's perspective and stating what marketing must do for the organization as a whole to succeed.

Purpose

The purpose of marketing, as Kotler and Clarke suggest, is to build exchange relationships which forward the organization's mission and strategic position. Bluntly, it is the critical link that brings patients and providers together. It completes the tasks of representation described in Chapter 3, identifying initial perspectives, emphasizing commonalities, and encouraging consummation. It brings to fruition the external portions of the strategic position developed as a planning activity in Chapter 6. Under community-based epidemiologic planning, marketing must have as its goal the delivery of all necessary care, that is, care that if left undone would substantially impair the patient's functioning. Under managed care concepts, marketing must not result in the delivery of unnecessary care, because such care wastes resources and drives up costs. The purpose of marketing, then, must be to bring patients and providers together in such a way that the optimum level of care is reached.

Several difficulties complicate this purpose, and overcoming them is an intrinsic part of health care marketing. Marketing health care must deal with

- An intimate, life-shaping service about which people have strong and sometimes irrational feelings.
- Differences of opinion among patients, buyers, providers, and society at large about what is appropriate care. Optimum treatment is only imprecisely known, and there may be serious disagreements about what is necessary.
- Expenses which are often unpredictable and which fall disproportionately on a few people. These must be financed by insurance, bringing a third party into the transaction. The insurance mechanism raises the need for agreement about what is necessary.
- Expenses which are among the largest elements of most personal budgets. The cost of insurance is met through payroll deductions and employer contributions, bringing a fourth party into the transaction.
- Very serious consequences, including loss of life, associated with poor quality and omitted care. These are morally unacceptable; they have become economically unacceptable under health care reform.
- Delivery mechanisms which are highly capital intensive, and as a result have high fixed costs. This requires careful adjustment of supply and demand and opens the possibility of differential pricing.
- Interests of other organizations and their members which may be in direct conflict with those of the organization represented.

There is no other industry or service that combines all these characteristics. They mean that health care marketing must accommodate not only the differences between individuals, but simultaneously those between many groups and organizations with contradictory goals.

Functions

In such a complex environment it would be disastrous to think of marketing as a simple or limited activity. It has five major functions, as shown in Figure 7.1.

Identifying Markets of Health Care Organizations

Marketing deals with complexity by **segmentation**, the deliberate effort to separate target audiences by the message to which they will respond.

Figure 7.1 Marketing Functions

Function	Description
1. Identifying markets	Marketing must begin with a solid understanding of the market structure with emphasis on recognizing target markets, groups of participants with similar goals.
2. Promoting the organization	Marketing must make the organization as a whole attractive to the entire community by finding and emphasizing the goals broadly shared and by identifying and meeting those unique but critical to particular groups.
3. Managing external relationships	Marketing must establish constructive relationships with other organizations, such as insurance intermediaries, employers, and providers of competing or noncompeting services.
4. Convincing patients to select the organization	Marketing must make potential patients aware of the service and persuade them to select the organization over its competitors.
5. Attracting capable workers	Marketing must assure a steady stream of personnel seeking to join the organization. The successful organization will market itself so that it has a choice of qualified applicants, even in areas of personnel shortages.

The first marketing function is to identify, describe, and understand the exchange partners of the community being served. Following the outline in Chapter 2, the general categories are patients and families; insurance carriers and intermediaries; employers, unions, governments and other buyers; physicians and employees; and a variety of community organizations which can affect mission achievement.

The market segmentation data base begins with the epidemiological planning data described in Chapter 6. The content tends to expand over time in the number of segments and combinations which can be examined and the amount of knowledge in each. The data base becomes a rich resource for the well-managed organization. It can be used for fact-finding, analysis, promotion, and negotiation. It supports both the strategic planning and the marketing activities, making it possible to identify specific groups of people and organizations in the community with specific needs, interests, talents, and affiliations.

Counts, descriptions, and information about leadership and ways to reach members of specific segments are available to the designers and implementers of proposals.

Purposes of Segmentation

Each group of individual exchange partners must be understood in terms of its wants and needs, but also in terms of how it can be reached with information and how its opinions can be influenced. Exchange groups like patients or buyers are not homogeneous within themselves; they must be segmented further to understand them fully. The first goal of segmentation is to identify all segments of a market in terms of their interests, emphasizing the homogeneity of each segment, and identifying how it differs from others. The second goal is to understand how each target group will respond to specific health care alternatives. Understanding supports quantitative estimates of the four parameters of the planning equation in Chapter 6 for each of the dozens of unique services a health care organization offers:

$$\left\{ \begin{matrix} \text{Demand for} \\ \text{a service} \end{matrix} \right\} = \left\{ \begin{matrix} \text{Population} \\ \text{at risk} \end{matrix} \right\} \times \left\{ \begin{matrix} \text{Incidence} \\ \text{rate} \end{matrix} \right\} \times \left\{ \begin{matrix} \text{Average use} \\ \text{per incident} \end{matrix} \right\} \times \left\{ \begin{matrix} \text{Market} \\ \text{share} \end{matrix} \right\}$$

The third goal of segmentation is to understand for each segment how changes in product, place, price, and promotion will affect the demand. That is, to predict the effect of changes on the four parameters, and from them upon demand for the service.

The answers to these questions determine the customer demand and the required provider supply simultaneously. The need for providers is directly related to the demand for their services. Many answers involve groups other than the patients or potential patients involved. Taking a relatively simple service, well-baby care, it is possible to reach an initial estimate of the demand relatively quickly. Using the parameters suggested in Figure 7.2 an initial forecast of well-baby visits can be constructed:

$$\left\{ \begin{matrix} \text{Well-baby} \\ \text{visits} \end{matrix} \right\} = \left\{ \begin{matrix} \text{Number of} \\ \text{births/year} \end{matrix} \right\} \times \left\{ \begin{matrix} \text{Number of} \\ \text{visits/baby} \end{matrix} \right\} \times \left\{ \begin{matrix} \text{Pct. of all} \\ \text{well-baby visits} \end{matrix} \right\}$$

The initial estimate treats the well-baby market as homogeneous, that is, it assumes all babies and mothers are alike. This is a doubtful assumption; it is possible to identify a series of questions based on differences in the baby and mother market:

- What fraction of babies now receive care from any provider? Would they move from their present provider to a new service?

What would make them move? More comprehensive service? Better hours or amenities? Lower price? Advertising or other promotion?

- What fraction of babies now do not receive care? Why? What would bring these mothers to a new service?

- Is there any condition which might discourage mothers from using well-baby care? How can it be avoided?

- Is there any condition which might strongly encourage mothers to use this service? How can it be incorporated into the well-baby program?

- How will well-baby care be financed? What price is practical for the patient? What are the chances of insurance coverage? Will employers and unions support well-baby care as an employment benefit? What is the price sensitivity for insurance or employment coverage?

- What agencies and individuals now provide well-baby care? What are the opportunities to collaborate with them? What collaboration mechanisms are likely to be rewarding? What will the terms of competition be? What will be the cost of meeting those terms?

The answers to these questions will lead to multiple market segments as shown in Figure 7.2. Some of the segments will be unique to the problem at hand, but all will be related to the identification of useful subgroups of exchanges. Out of the repeated segmentation of the market comes differentiated programs reflecting the needs of the segments. These have their own solutions of price, placement, and promotion even though the product, well-baby care, is the same.

As answers to the questions are developed the well-baby proposal may change shape several times depending on the specific circumstances of the community. The fraction of babies not now receiving care (the right-hand group of Figure 7.2) will be much higher in certain rural and inner city locations, for example. An extensive program of clinics to reach babies now missed may have substantial value to Medicaid and local government public health activities. To keep costs low, the clinics may emphasize nurse practitioner care. To reach an audience not already sold on the product, special outreach activities may be useful. Joint finance or collaborative relationships may emerge. Even direct competitors may wish to collaborate on a program if it reduces their costs and does not impair their market share. Schools, day care centers, and churches may be willing to advocate use of the well-baby service. A low-cost promotional campaign may be designed among these groups. "New Program 1" of Figure 7.2 would meet this combination of needs.

Figure 7.2   Segmenting the Well-Baby Care Market

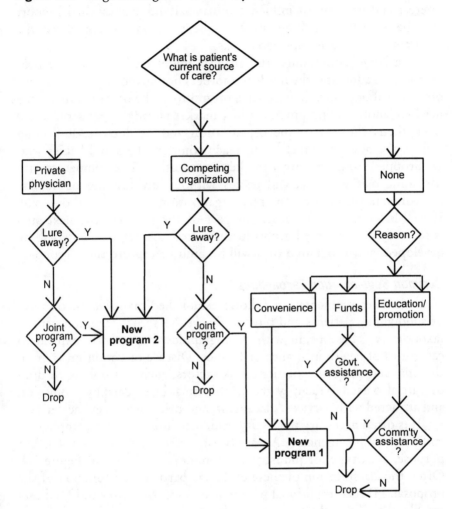

Other babies (the left of Figure 7.2) will have their need met by family practitioners and pediatricians in independent practice or by existing programs operated by competitors. Aggressively luring mothers away from their current physicians may be very costly, since these are primary care doctors who may be critical to the organization in other ways. A proposal to collaborate with current providers to support their current activities and fill the remaining unmet need by attracting it to existing sources may emerge. This pattern of market interest leads to "New Program 2" of Figure 7.2. Organizations normally peripheral to health care, such as schools and churches may still have an important interest and position of influence. Financial and promotional support may be available for Program 2, if the partners are convinced the program will achieve important goals.

In a larger community, the analysis might lead to two new programs. One addresses the needs of mothers not now being reached with broad collaboration and innovative promotion. The other addresses the needs of mothers and providers in a market already being served, and strengthens the ties to the organization and its doctors. Reflecting reality, the new programs fail to reach some mothers and babies who are dropped from one target market or the other. The competitor still has some market share, and babies without any funding or outside the contacts through community organizations are still without care. If well-baby care is an important part of the mission, the next step is to study the unserved group further. New market segments will be developed, and Program 3 or 4 will be built to capture these groups.

Common Segmentation Taxonomies

Much market segmentation follows established taxonomies, or ways of subdividing patients and buyers. Figure 7.3 shows common patient taxonomies. These begin with demographics, but quickly expand to categories of health insurance or finance. Disease or condition is often the final stage of segmentation. Risk factors, such as smoking or drug use, are also used to identify groups that must be reached by promotion and attracted with services, placement, and price that meet their needs.

It is often necessary to classify insurance intermediaries, employers, and community agencies. A variety of approaches can be used, but purpose, size, type, or industry are common, as shown in Figure 7.4. Often the classification of these exchange partners is a function of the proposal. HMOs, traditional private insurance, Medicare and Medicaid are likely to offer different prices for a given service, have different criteria for necessity, and different rules to enforce those criteria.

Providers and Members as Markets

Market segmentation techniques can be applied to relationships with physicians, employees, volunteers, and charitable donors. In open systems theory, these too are voluntary exchanges contributing to organizational objectives. Since most successful proposals must fit both customer and provider needs, negotiation and promotion are likely to be necessary with both groups. Many health care organizations invest in promotional material to attract donors, recruit clinical specialists in short supply, and encourage volunteers. These markets are segmented

Figure 7.3 Patient-Oriented Taxonomies

Category	Classifications
Demographic	Age Sex Race Education
Economic	Income Employment Social class
Geographic	Zip code of residence Census tract Political subdivision
Health care finance	Managed vs. traditional insurance Private vs. government insurance
Diagnosis	Disease classification Procedure Diagnosis-related group (DRG) Ambulatory visit group
Risk	Health behavior attribute Preexisting condition Chronic or high-cost disease

by profession or type of work, and in the case of donors, by type and dollar level of giving.

The post-reform health care organization is likely to include within its formal structures a much larger array of people and services than the traditional hospital or freestanding medical clinic. Competitors will become partners, co-owners, and in some cases subsidiaries. Techniques of market segmentation apply here as well. Competitors and complementary organizations will fulfill a continuum of relationships ranging from collaborative to adversarial. As shown in Figure 7.5, they are classed by type of service, size, market served, financial strength, and type of relationship, where the last is understood to be flexible and subject to change.

The marketing role of physicians is unique, and is discussed in Chapter 12. Segmentation is still important. It is possible to segment physicians by specialty, age, location, and by their organizational affiliation. The last is not necessarily permanent; proposals may involve

Figure 7.4 Insurance Intermediary and Employer Taxonomies

Category	Classifications
Employers	Size
	Geographic location
	Industry
	Ownership
	Income level
	Union organization
	Health insurance benefit
	Health insurance type
Intermediary	Health insurance type
	Ownership or corporate structure
	Size
	Number of health insurance subscribers
	Employer groups covered

winning physicians over to your organization in order to capture the demand they represent. Particularly primary care physicians exercising their gatekeeper role have an important influence on demand, as the well-baby example suggests.

Market Segmentation as an Organization Framework

MacStravic has proposed market segment administration as an alternative to product line organization in health care organizations. He suggests that a limited set of segments, such as young adults, older adults, seniors, physicians, and businesses, be identified. A strategy for developing familiarity, attractiveness, and market share within the segment is developed, implemented, and assessed. Data monitoring performance and profitability are developed, and accountability is assigned. He notes that segment administration is time-consuming, difficult, and has a heavy front end investment compared to product line management. However, it builds broader support than most product-oriented strategies, and is more focused than a general stance toward the market.[4]

Promoting the Organization

One function of marketing is to maintain the overall reputation or **image** of the organization so that it remains attractive to most members of the community at large. The twentieth century has seen a major

Figure 7.5 Health Care Provider Taxonomies

Category	Classification
Individual providers	Training, certification, or licensure Organizational affiliation Age
Organized providers	Scope of service Geographic location Ownership Size Market share Financial strength Competititve position

expansion of the public's right to know. The well-run health care organization must respond affirmatively to this trend, using the obligations to inform the public as an opportunity to promote broader support. Image building usually begins as a communitywide effort, reflecting the mission of most health care organizations. The activities include public and community relations, image advertising and promotion, and media relations. As certain groups in the community articulate special needs or are identified as important market segments, image building may be tailored to those groups. The message to those groups emphasizes both the general contribution of the organization and its ability to meet particular needs.

Public and Community Relations

Well-managed organizations continually describe themselves to their communities through a deliberate program of public and community relations. Public and community relations includes descriptive information such as annual reports, personal appearances by management and caregivers, and deliberate contacts with influentials and opinion leaders. It is one of several sources from which people derive a positive image of the hospital. Obviously success begins with having a good story to tell. Although the information is slanted to emphasize the positive aspects, ability to be candid about weaknesses is recognized and respected. Public information should be coordinated with advertising. Both may deliberately promote use of organization services. It relates indirectly to lobbying (Chapter 4), because grass-roots support depends upon a favorable response by individuals in the community.

Most members of strategic management are involved in public and community relations activity. Speeches, personal contacts and participation in community affairs are important. The CEO has a uniquely important role. Specific accountability for coordinating public information and promotion should be assigned, and marketing has strong claims to the assignment. Coordination of themes, logos, and printing styles are important. The organization often issues material such as newsletters, annual reports, and regular mailings which describe the organization in general terms and highlight specific events.

The goal of image building activity is to increase two dimensions of recognition of the institution, familiarity and attractiveness. Well-established scales and survey techniques allow the organization to monitor how familiar members of the community are with the organization, usually measured by ability to recall the name without prompting and ability to recognize the name in a list. Similarly, well-designed questionnaires allow profiling of what people think of the organization, how they compare it to competitors, and which attributes they like most or least.[5]

Segmentation is effective in public relations. A successful program identifies both goals and audiences. Specific strategies to communicate concepts about the organization strengthen the familiarity built by general releases. Special community relations efforts may be directed to certain groups, such as people living in the local neighborhood, people with special interests, or people who are influential with the organization's target markets.[6] Community relations relates to media relations; the activities are often chosen with an eye to attracting coverage in local media.

Image Advertising and Promotion

Image advertising and promotion has also become commonplace in recent years. It includes purchased media exposure which is not related to a specific sales objectives, or which share a specific and a general goal. It also includes association of the institution with various activities, such as athletic events or public services, and distribution of products bearing the name and logo of the organization. Most well-managed organizations try to establish their name, mission, and an image of warmth and supportiveness. Some also emphasize their technological proficiency or convenience. Often the image message is combined with a specific promotion. Advertising techniques easily support dual concepts like, "Bring your baby for care while he's well to keep him well," and "Excalibur Health System cares about you and your family."

Image promotion is far from a panacea. It takes a large number of exposures even to increase name recognition, and changing attractiveness is harder. Kotler and Clarke note:

> Health care organizations seeking to change their images must have great patience, because images tend to last long after the reality of an organization has changed. . . . Image persistence is explained by the fact that once people have a certain image of an object, they tend to be selective perceivers of further data; their perceptions are oriented toward seeing what they expect to see.[7]

Media Relations

Media relations is an element of image development that may be overrated in importance. Most organizations are acutely aware of what is said about them in the media, but the evidence suggests that the public at large is quite resistive to media statements. None the less, the media can portray the organization favorably or unfavorably, and the result often depends on the quality of information supplied by the organization. There are two types of media communication. One is the planned release of information, where the organization wishes to have its story told by print or electronic media. Attractive, thorough releases, identification of visual elements for photos and television, access to knowledgeable, articulate spokespersons, and identification of newsworthy elements all assist in improving the coverage. A deliberate program of regular information releases and efforts to draw media attention to favorable events promotes a positive image. The more information released, the greater the familiarity and attractiveness of the community is likely to be.

The second type of communication is response to media initiatives. These are often related to major news events such as health care to prominent personages or general disasters. In the worst case, they come as a result of unfavorable events such as lowered bond ratings, civil lawsuits, or criminal behavior. They can be quite hostile when journalists sense or assume something is wrong. Investigative journalism is an aggressive effort to dig out all the public might want to know, with emphasis on what the organization might want to hide. Effective handling of media initiatives is largely preventive. The organization should prevent or minimize events which will draw investigation. It should maintain a strong program of releasing newsworthy, positive information about itself. It should attempt to deal fully and candidly with issues, anticipating reporters' questions and preparing detailed responses. It should establish its spokespersons and equip them to give thorough, convincing replies to questions. Training and experience are necessary to handle the functions of media relations well.[8]

Managing External Relationships

A fully vertically integrated organization would offer all of the array of patient services is suggested by Figure 2.1 of Chapter 2 under one corporate umbrella. Few health care organizations even come close to this goal. Health insurance and intermediary functions are often arranged by others. Nursing home care, mental health and substance abuse programs, hospices, and home care are often provided by other organizations. The medical staff itself may be a separate corporation, several corporations, or even a series of unincorporated units. Drugs and medical equipment are often supplied to ambulatory patients through independent organizations. The fourth parties of the health insurance transaction, employers and government, rarely provide care directly but they exert substantial influence on the care itself.

Patients need all of these services. None can be omitted from a comprehensive program of care, and from the patient's perspective, the entire program should be seamless. Services should depend upon patient needs, not organizational barriers. The health care organization must deal with the conflict between patient perspective and organizational reality.

The goal of well-managed organizations must be to meet the customer needs with barrier free relationships that encourage transfers as soon as they are clinically indicated and make the mechanics of transfer virtually invisible to patients. The goal requires minimizing **transfer costs**, that is the costs of maintaining the relationship, including the costs of moving patients geographically or between corporations.[9] Only two possibilities exist to fulfill the goal. One is ownership of the necessary services; the other is collaboration with other organizations, some of which will inevitably be competitors. Few organizations, if any, will own all services. Almost all organizations will collaborate for at least some services; it now appears likely that most organizations will collaborate on several major services, of which insurance may be the most important. The management of relationships between the components of health care and health care financing has become one of the major functions of the modern health care organization. Paradoxically, the implications of ownership lead back to issues of collaboration, as the following example shows. That is, the issues involved in reducing transfer costs tend to be operational questions reflecting needs of participants more than the ownership or formal relationship between the units.

Analyzing the Health Care Marketplace

The first step to a strategy of organizational positioning is a review of all services customers need, and where they get them. A simplified version of this review is given in the following example.

Modern Health Services (MHS) is an integrated health system serving a large metropolitan area (called Metropolis to protect the actual identity). It has adopted a special mission to serve the poor, and does more than its share of charity and under-financed care. As shown in Figure 7.6, MHS in Metropolis owns an unusually broad range of services—acute inpatient facilities, mental health and substance abuse services, nursing homes, home care, hospices, and medical equipment services for the aging. It owns an HMO and PPOs, and several local organizations relating it to its physicians. The corporation is doing well, but not dramatically so. It has a stable to slowly growing market share, positive net income and a reasonable balance sheet. So do several other large health care organizations representing an array from comparable integration to single purpose competitors. The fact that there are no clear competitive winners suggests that simple models like total integration or arms-length collaboration have market and organizational limitations.

Here are a few of the strategic problems facing MHS:

1. Geography
   - The Metropolis market, shown in Figure 7.7, is about 4 million people, stretched over a seven-county land area which takes about ninety minutes to cross either north-south or east-west. Travel times between points are longer if freeways are not convenient.
   - Central City, the geographic and historic center of Metropolis, is only one of many residential, work or shopping destinations.

Figure 7.6 Organization of an Integrated Health System

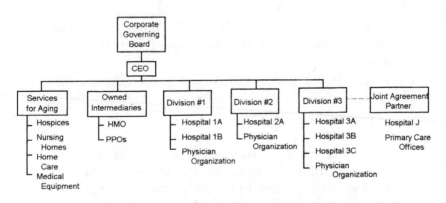

Many units have their own advisory boards, composed of members of local communities, physicians, and representatives of other units.

Figure 7.7 The Metropolitan Health Care Market

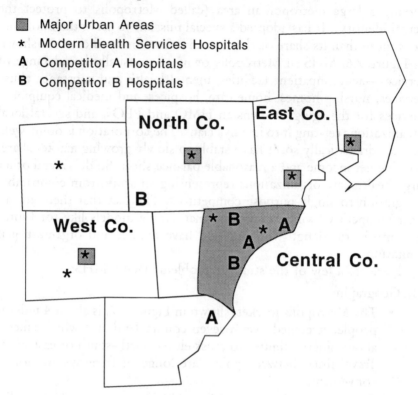

    Each family has a constellation of destinations which it views as convenient, but the constellations tend to be idiosyncratic.

- In contrast to their employees, many large employers operate in several geographic locations and view the market as a single entity.

2. Health insurance markets
   - Blue Cross and Blue Shield (BCBS) dominates traditional insurance, which in total covers about 50 percent of the market.
   - Edison Health System (EHS) and BCBS dominate the HMO market, which is about 25 percent of the total. The MHS HMO has only 10 percent of the HMO market, or 2 percent of the total.
   - Oldmount Health Service and several other acute care providers and their physicians have linked to form the largest of several PPOs, but PPOs are relatively insignificant at around 10 percent of the total.

- Medicare subscribers are broadly distributed geographically and are almost exclusively served by traditional coverage. They constitute 10 percent of the insured, but a much larger percent of the expenditures.
- Medicaid and uninsured populations are about 10 percent of the total market but are concentrated in a few specific locations. The largest is Central City.

3. Health care markets
   - There are four multihospital providers, MHS, EHS, Oldmount and the Central City Medical Center. Several other large hospitals have formed alliances with Oldmount. The remaining competition is scattered and for the most part ineffectual.
   - Smaller, focused organizations can move quickly to develop specific market strategies and high-quality operations in mental health, substance abuse, long-term care, home care, and hospices. These "independents" form the primary competition for MHS in these markets.
   - Physician organizations are relatively rare and untested, although EHS employs about two-thirds of its medical staff. MHS is a leader in developing these structures among independent physicians, but its own organizations differ in commitment, maturity and effectiveness.

The pressures of conflicting marketplaces that MHS faces in Metropolis are unique only in the details. Although the example is from the perspective of one health care organization, the analysis would be similar for its major competitors. Most metropolitan areas hold the same combinations of diverse geographies, overlapping markets, and varying competitors. The underlying array of complementary, competing, and collaborating organizations will be present in all, and will change over time. In Central City, for example, most employer-insured business flows through BCBS. In other cities it might be dispersed through third party administrators or smaller PPOs relating to subsets of the providers. Under health reform, it will migrate toward managed care solutions of various kinds.

Unified responses to this environment simply will not work. What it takes to build market share for a hospice in the northern suburbs has nothing to do with the tasks of expanding the HMO in the west. Target markets for various MHS products are readily identified: cancer and AIDS patients in the northern county for the hospice, regionally oriented employers for the HMO. MHS must "formulate programs designed to bring about exchanges of values" with these markets. There are three consequences to this reality. First, there is a strong need to decentralize and delegate so that MHS subsidiaries are effective in various geographic and service markets. The result is that each subsidiary develops its own strategies, oriented around its market and explicitly different from others. Second, tensions develop between the subsidiaries which must be solved by essentially the devices used to relate freestanding corporations. That is, a significant portion of the corporate effort must go to transfer costs, settling internal boundary disputes and in some cases making sure the subsidiaries do not become independent. The core is weakened as a result of the delegation and transfer costs. It tends to look more like an alliance, and less like an integrated organization. Third, tensions also develop between MHS, its subsidiaries and other organizations. Even an organization as large as MHS cannot ignore the possibilities of collaboration with other organizations. Effective abilities to deal with other large organizations tend to strengthen the core. But to be effective, MHS must be able to speak for all its subsidiaries.

Developing a Strategy of Internal Relationships

Internal opportunities MHS has pursued a decentralized vision, with local boards for each of its major geographic areas, and separate boards for its aging services and its HMO/PPO. Each of these subsidiaries is charged with building market share, but it is also expected to work closely with other MHS corporations and to earn a small surplus. Some predictable tension lines emerge:

- The HMO, fighting aggressively for market share against external regional competitors, wants effective cost and quality control from the health care providers. The providers, operating in local markets, are more responsive to local demands for service and employment.
- Physicians, even more locally focused than MHS provider organizations, resist integration of medical and hospital care. As primary care grows in importance, tensions between primary and referral physicians mount.
- The acute care hospitals are forced to support managed care concepts even though managed care is only 25 percent of the market. Major reductions in cost and use of hospital and specialty services are likely to occur as a result.
- The hospitals are forced to mediate primary/referral physician conflicts. They start at this task with stronger ties to the specialists than to primary care.

- Relationships between acute care and aging services are remote. The locations and market shares of the aging services are such that it is frequently difficult to encourage transfers within MHS.
- Perspectives of major competitors are far from uniform. For example, EHS is a friend to some MHS subsidiaries and a threat to others. BCBS is a major source of revenue to all acute care subsidiaries and physicians, but clearly a threat to the HMO.

The strength of these tensions is such that members of MHS subsidiaries not infrequently wonder whether they belong to the central organization or would be better on their own. The central organization spends much, possibly most, of its time trying to align interests of various subsidiaries in order to meet market opportunities. The advantage of MHS over separate organizations is constantly in doubt.

To understand the marketing opportunities and devise a successful strategy for MHS, it is necessary to search aggressively for shared advantages. One way to identify these is to ask what would happen if all the subsidiaries of Figure 7.6 were granted immediate independence. The results would be something like this:

- The shared HMO would be as independent as its competitors. As an independent organization, the HMO becomes a distant third in a competitive marketplace, without the capital reserves or market contacts of the two leaders. It could have more difficulty implementing a successful strategy than it does now.
- Each health care subsidiary would face the task of negotiating new relationships with insurers and intermediaries. An advantage of collective negotiation would be lost, and most subsidiaries would move to replace it with new collective relationships.
- The physician organization problems would remain. The subsidiaries would lose the impetus for organization provided by the HMO, and might be separated from their physicians by some HMO strategies. Since no subsidiary is large enough to operate a successful HMO, they would probably move to form new allegiances protecting their physician relations.
- The aging services units would see little change from independence. They would lose referral sources and would move to replace these on a geographically convenient basis.
- The fund-raising capability of the central organization would be lost. The subsidiaries as independents would have difficulty raising equivalent amounts of capital. Capital shortages would make it difficult to implement long-range plans. Some might be forced to seek new affiliations to meet capital needs.

- The opportunity to serve the poor would be substantially diminished. Much of the service to the poor is geographically specific and relies upon subsidies from the earning of other areas.

The results of MHS dissolution in most cases would find the former subsidiaries making new allegiances. It is predictable that these allegiances would present problems very like those of the current MHS structure. The advantages that keep MHS in existence are

- The ability to address regional markets
- The ability to raise capital
- The ability to negotiate collectively with entities taking a regional perspective
- The ability to sustain experimental and developmental programs which provide examples and incentives for continuous improvement
- The ability to serve the poor.

An internal strategy An MHS strategy must capitalize upon these advantages and avoid exacerbating the existing tensions. Such a strategy might be based on the following tenets:

- Emphasize financial stability and protection of the capital base. The central office would prescribe acceptable limits for long-range financial plans and annual budget guidelines. It would authorize and obtain capital funds.
- Encourage independent actions by subsidiaries within a framework of centralized capital generation and a market trend toward centralized health care finance dominated by managed care.
- Establish capital fund priorities for programs that enhance managed care capability, such as the expansion of managed care insurance, the development of information systems, or the organization of physician services.
- Support care of the disadvantaged, with explicit assignment of funds earned by the subsidiaries.
- Provide central planning and marketing data bases and technical support specialists to assist subsidiaries in developing locally effective strategies.
- Use regional media to promote an MHS image with public relations, advertising, and coordinated support for local efforts.
- Assign accountability to the central office for relations with the other large organizations and regionally oriented employers and for developing regional markets.

The most critical element of the strategy is the maintenance of healthy subsidiaries. This demands certain reserved powers enforcing capital and other performance and effective measurement systems for the central unit. It also demands decentralization, allowing the subsidiaries to act as though they were independent entities in their specific markets wherever possible. Since most of the direct competitors are independent, any strategy which ties the hands of local subsidiaries will fail.

Developing an External Strategy

If the first part of the MHS strategy is to decentralize within explicit limits and encourage independent response to local markets, the second must be to deal centrally with the common forces of the regional market. As noted in Chapter 4, other organizations can be classified as those that compete for market share (competitors), those with whom formal agreements have been reached (allies), and those which offer noncompeting services (complementary organizations). As the complexity of MHS relationships and the Metropolis market suggest, large regional organizations tend to be all three.

External analysis Figure 7.8 shows the major current ties between Metropolitan health care providers and health insurance organizations, as of 1994. Figure 7.8 is considerably simpler than reality. It illustrates the kinds of relationships which can exist and shows some important examples. Collaborative relationships between insurance intermediaries and providers and competitive relations between similar organizations are inevitable. The reality of Figure 7.8 is that most competing organizations also collaborate.

There are several levels of relationships between the organizations in Figure 7.8. Strictly speaking, all are forms of collaboration.

- Competition emphasizes independence, but the organizations are forced by tradition and by law to compete within a framework of rules. Products and services must be comparable, for example. Price is an important basis for comparison; quality is becoming one. Many sales are made in response to customer requests for proposals; in these, the customer outlines major parameters of the service rather than the vendor. Laws forbid collusion over price and markets, and require truth in advertising.

- Contracts are defined agreements between parties who may be competitors in other areas to accomplish specific considerations important to each of the parties. BCBS's participating hospital agreement is an example. It sets the terms under which the hospital will provide inpatient and outpatient care to members and the price that will be paid.

Figure 7.8 Relationships of Major Metropolitan Health Care Organizations

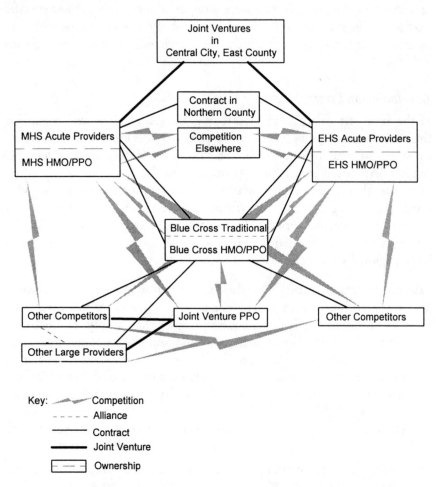

- Alliances involve an agreement to collaborate on undefined activities such as problem-solving. They permit wider ranging considerations than can be specified in contracts, but like contracts, they are still subject to laws governing competition and can be terminated by the parties. They are often supplemented by letters of agreement and contracts on specific activities.
- Joint ventures are longer-term contracts committing assets to specific goals and specific governance structures. Thus EHS and MHS have agreed to run provider facilities in the eastern suburbs through shared governance and executive activities. Termination of the agreement would be difficult, but neither party is committed to loss of autonomy outside the specific venture.

- Joint-operating agreements are contracts of long-term affiliation just short of merger. Like mergers, they establish a new entity, but they reserve certain rights, such as the ability to dissolve the agreement or the ability to appoint certain officers, to the original participants.
- Mergers and acquisitions are irreversible combinations of assets and operations. Normally in a merger neither of the original parties survives; in an acquisition only one party survives.

It is easy to explain how a situation such as Figure 7.8 develops. In each collaboration, the participants seek first to meet market need, and thereby improve their own performance, and second to minimize transfer costs. Thus relationships between competitors such as the alliance between Oldmount and other providers to run a PPO or the management contracts and joint ventures to link EHS and MHS make perfect sense. Each relationship was the lowest transfer cost opportunity the participants could find to meet specific market goals. Oldmount and its allies were seeking a managed care vehicle to keep control of markets they saw moving to the three insurance intermediaries. MHS was seeking ways to reduce costs and support specialty services in the northern suburb where a major corporation needed facilities to match its growing sales. A contract serves the purpose. The MHS/EHS joint venture allowed them to serve eastern markets neither had been able to penetrate on their own.

It is likely that the Figure 7.8 relationships will change steadily as the market changes. Organizations like the Central City Medical Center, which has no affiliation except contracts with insurance intermediaries may be forced to seek stronger ties. Even ownership arrangements can be created or dissolved. Alliances like the one between Oldmount and others may grow to ownership relations or be replaced by other affiliations. (One participant in the PPO joint venture has announced a joint operating agreement with an MHS subsidiary.)

An external strategy   One important contribution of the central unit of large organizations like MHS is to monitor and pursue opportunities for collaboration with other organizations. These opportunities require substantial planning and analysis, as indicated in Chapter 6. They also require extensive negotiation and exploratory discussion. Identifying and pursuing regional opportunities is an ongoing marketing function of the MHS central organization, occupying much of the time of its executives and employing a sophisticated data base and several analysts. The opportunities for MHS include:

- Joint ventures with other large provider systems. Acquisition is unlikely, but other collaborative efforts have been rewarding in the past. The test of these relationships is their ability to increase or protect market share while maintaining financial stability. The implications of agreements between the other systems which might threaten MHS share has to be considered.

- Collaborative actions with other insurers and intermediaries. These might include sale of the HMO, although the price would have to be very attractive. Short of that, they might include acquisitions and joint ventures designed to increase both the overall HMO market and the MHS share.

- New relationships with providers not now affiliated with any of the four large systems. These might include acquisition of new members or sale of existing units, and a variety of collaborative possibilities short of those. Implications of unaffiliated providers joining competitor systems must be considered. Since provider markets must be segmented by service and geography, it is possible to delegate specific segments to specific subsidiaries, but a central review would be useful.

- Improved collaboration with physicians. As managed care grows, MHS will need to reduce its affiliations with referral specialists and increase those with primary care physicians. Models for collaboration are discussed in detail in Chapter 12. The central organization can supply consultation, educational programs, and capital for these activities.

- Monitoring interests of regional insurance buyers. To date, the Metropolitan employers and unions have been loyal to intermediaries often selected decades ago. Should that loyalty diminish, large market shares would suddenly open for competitors. MHS can consider new products which might be attractive to those markets, and should monitor opinions of various segments of buyer markets assiduously.

Marketing the Organization to Patients

Promotion of health care services was considered unethical by physicians and inappropriate by not-for-profit hospitals until 1978 when a ruling of the U.S. Supreme Court held the proscription to be in violation of antitrust laws.[10] A second problem is that promotion of health care risks unnecessary demand for services. While providing unnecessary services is highly profitable for providers under traditional insurance mechanisms, it is certainly unethical because it is dangerous for the patient. It is also self-defeating under managed care insurance because it increases cost without adding to revenue. These complexities limited direct marketing to patients to issues of product, price, and place until about the last 10 years.[11]

The growth of managed care and the antitrust decision clarified direct patient marketing. It is an area of increasing importance, and one where health care organizations will grow in skill and sophistication in the future. Issues of product, price, and place will continue to be solved by careful planning activities, but deliberate efforts to make patients aware of choices and to influence their behavior will be critical to success. They will take three principal forms. First, promotional activities will be used to convince patients to select insurance intermediaries and provider panels. Second, they will be used to encourage wellness and disease prevention. Third, they will be used to adjust patient expectations about care.

Influencing Patient Selection of Providers and Insurers

As health care moves from atomistic markets of individual providers to oligopolistic markets with large integrated providers, the maintenance of broader customer allegiance becomes essential. Three major thrusts toward winning and keeping allegiance have emerged. They are oriented around attractive provider panels, customer satisfaction, and advertising.

As managed care replaces traditional insurance, the selection of physician moves from point of service to choice of insurance plan, and the choice is of a panel rather than an individual provider. The issues in patient selection are largely those of product and placement, but patients have a strong loyalty to providers who have served them well in the past.

Product issues A chain of market decision makers develops, as shown in Figure 7.9. The employer role is moving toward offering alternative insurance plans, with initial screening of price and quality.[12] There is a strong tendency for the insurance plan to offer coverage of a broad spectrum of service. An integrated health care organization gains a marketing advantage because it can serve all or most of the spectrum, but some insurance plans apparently deliberately divide panel construction, separating primary care from specialists and hospitals. Transaction costs mount for the insurer if it must use a variety of panels. The employee and spouse select between plans based on out-of-pocket premium share or copayment costs, panel image, and placement. Women influence more of the decision than men. Consumers value loyalty to their historic providers, convenience, certain amenities such as waiting time and parking, alternatives in primary care, and reputation or credentials of specialists.[13]

An attractive primary care panel is crucial for an integrated health care organization. Patients want easy and prompt access for care, and

Figure 7.9 Chain of Buyer Selections and Provider Feedback

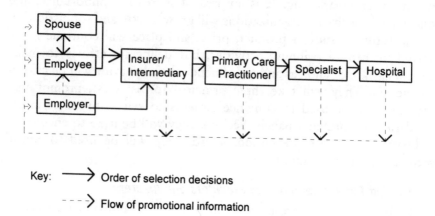

Key: ⟶ Order of selection decisions

- - -> Flow of promotional information

minimal waiting time. They also want choice of gender, age and ethnic background, confidence in provider judgment, and prompt referral to specialists when required. Emergency coverage and off-hours access are important. Although many patients prefer physicians, there are growing roles for nurse practitioners and midwives. The larger the panel, the fewer patients will have to be lured from their historic relationship. At the same time, the panel must be willing to accept risk for cost and quality of care. Only competent and well-oriented physicians will be able to operate effectively under risk contracts. One job of the integrated health care organization becomes building and maintaining this panel. Its skills are a major factor in cost, quality and patient satisfaction.

Specialists are typically selected by primary care physicians under managed care, but are often selected directly by patients under traditional insurance. Patients judge specialists on credentials and placement amenities.[14] Employers judge them on cost and measurable quality outcomes. Primary care physicians judge specialists on cost, a broader range of outcomes and process quality, and patient satisfaction. Much care requires at least periodic consultation by a specialist, even if the primary care provider keeps control. Integrated health care organizations must balance the number of specialists to need, avoiding either shortages or surpluses, and provide the necessary support in equipment and staff. The inpatient hospital and large ambulatory services are increasingly the domain of the specialist. Effective management of the specialist and hospital services is a major support function appreciated by primary care physicians. Thus an integrated health care organization will work to maintain a high-quality, cost-effective specialty and hospital service that is attractive to primary care doctors.

Stable volumes of patients are essential to support both quality and price of specialty and hospital services. Strategies for specialists and hospitals encourage maintaining as broad a range of contracts as possible, and discounting some prices when necessary. High fixed costs make significant discounts possible, but only in the short run and only to the extent that variable costs are covered. There is strong pressure on the hospital to remove physicians who cannot meet cost or quality standards and to lure physicians or services which are broadly attractive.[15]

Promotion issues Panels of referral specialists, like inpatient hospital services, are in excess supply and heavily competitive environments. Promoting use of the panel to patients becomes essential. Most organizations strive to capture market share from all payment sources, since high overall demand lowers average cost. Public relations and direct patient advertising are important vehicles to sustain demand. There is growing emphasis on promotion to specific segments with material directly related to their medical need.[16] Promotion can be oriented around social class[17] and health attitudes,[18,19] and as noted in the well-baby example, collaboration can reduce or spread the cost of promotion. It is possible to share promotional expenses with suppliers when the service generates a demand for a specific product.[20] "Service recovery" approaches can reduce dissatisfaction with service and enhance efforts to improve quality.[21]

Television, direct mail, billboards, print and radio media are used in promotion. Television advertising is the most expensive. In metropolitan areas, many print media are also expensive.[22] As in the southeast Metropolis example, daily newspapers and television reach a population much larger than that served by a singly hospital or physician group. Only the larger systems serving several counties can efficiently advertise in these media. Radio and local print media are more geographically targeted. The cost of promotion in metropolitan areas is one advantage of integrated systems; they serve a higher fraction of the market and get more gain from expensive advertising.

Influencing Patient Behavior

Certain life styles or behaviors can substantially increase the risk of high-cost illness. Prominent among these are smoking, alcohol and narcotics abuse, teen pregnancy, child safety, and unprotected sex. Health care costs can be reduced if these activities are prevented by education and motivational programs. Certain health care activities can significantly reduce the risk of high-cost illness. These include immunizations, early detection of disease, and careful management of chronic illness. Very costly diseases such as polio and complications of measles and whooping cough can be prevented by immunization. Health care cost can be reduced by early detection and careful management of high blood pressure, some cancers, pregnancy and fetal development problems, and some behavioral problems. Under managed care, effective management of these disease risks works directly to improve both member health and health care cost. Integrated health care systems are moving to address these needs.

Promoting wellness Two approaches are now being followed to encourage people to avoid health risks and to seek valuable preventive care. First, general promotional campaigns are used to encourage safe behavior among the membership at large. These include direct mail, media advertising, print and video material in doctors offices and other sites such as schools and work. The content of these messages reflects health concerns shared by well members of the population. It can include image advertising, and can be linked to direct appeals to select certain insurance plans or primary care panels. Wellness behavior promotion has become an ongoing part of media advertising and is an important public health function. Governments have a strong interest in it, because they cover two groups with exceptional risk, the aged, and the poor.

General promotion requires very high frequency of contact. Effective strategies must overcome complex motivations to pursue the unhealthy behavior.[23] They repeat the message over and over, and use a variety of vehicles to convey and reinforce it. Wellness promotion becomes an ongoing activity, consuming a specific budget and constantly studied for opportunities to improve cost-effectiveness.

Managing high-risk members The second approach to influencing patient behavior identifies groups or individuals at particular risk for targeted efforts. Risk identification may focus on a specific demographic group, such as teenagers for safe sex and pregnancy prevention, or middle-aged women for Pap smears and breast examinations. Media promotions may focus on media known to reach the target audience. Because the audience is targeted, the message may be more specific and the frequency of contact increased. High-risk prevention may include direct contact, such as home visits to new parents, when home safety, child care, and child-rearing issues can be discussed directly.

It is possible to segment still further, seeking individuals with clear risk factors for high-cost health care, such as known alcohol or drug abuse, genetic predisposition, or existing disease. Risk factors can be identified by surveys, interviews (including initial medical examinations) and from medical records. Members of the risk group can be encouraged to use certain providers specializing in the care of the disease or problem in question. These providers may be skilled at gaining rapid recovery, reducing complications, or encouraging more effective patient responses.

Managing Patient Care Expectations

Patient satisfaction is essential to retain market share and is useful in attracting new customers. It is routinely and closely monitored, providing data at the level of individual care sites and identifying causes of low scores. Patient satisfaction is also important in malpractice claim management.[24] Clearly the improvement of patient satisfaction relates heavily to staff performance and amenities. One way to manage patient expectations is to identify and meet them. Programs exist to analyze shortfalls in depth, pinpointing specific responses.[25] Programs have also been designed to recover from serious dissatisfaction.[26] It is also true that expectations can be unrealistic, and that marketing techniques can modify them. As in the case of wellness behavior and risk prevention, efforts can be either general or targeted.

Media reports frequently emphasize dramatic, curative medical intervention, and some public opinion may overstate the power and value of high-tech care. It is important to counter these and restore realistic expectations. Wellness themes counter these perspectives and condition patients to think in terms of prevention and cost-effective management. Full understanding of the procedures for using available services is important. Patients will be less likely to be dissatisfied if they have a clear picture of how the system is supposed to work. Restrictions on after hours access and direct contact with referral physicians are likely to be causes of dissatisfaction; the right thing to do can be clearly stated, explained, and made as simple as possible. The use of nurse practitioners in place of physicians offers certain advantages in both cost and effectiveness.[27] Promotion may overcome some of the lack of confidence in nurses among customers. Similar promotion may be useful in reducing the customer demand for specialist care.

General efforts might include availability of alternative care services, such as the provision of telephone response for emergency night calls. In these systems, nurses work from manuals or computerized screens to evaluate patient symptoms and suggest safe, low-cost responses. Prompted to question for risks that the patient or a parent might overlook, they can provide reassurance and recommend simple treatments when these are indicated. If the patient desires, or the clinical situation indicates, they can refer the patient to appropriate care site and even arrange transportation. Expensive trips to emergency rooms are avoided and primary care physicians are saved unnecessary meetings.

Targeted activities focus on the expectations of specific patient groups. Advance description of elective procedures can identify many common complications or variations in the recovery pattern and provide instructions or reassurance about them. It can prepare the patient to accept the usual outcomes. It is known in advertising that customers tend to perceive what they have been conditioned to expect.[28] Clinical problems associated with a high level of dissatisfaction can be identified and studied to devise more satisfactory treatment patterns. These may deliberately emphasize activities which are designed to provide symptomatic relief, such as the deliberate use of chiropractors in certain cases of low-back pain.[29]

Specific high-cost problems may be addressed through complex strategies. The cost of care at the end of life, estimated to be more than 25 percent of all Medicare expenses, can be reduced without substantial change in the outcome through the use of fewer heroic measures.[30] Avoiding unnecessary heroics requires prior understanding and acceptance by patient and family, and reassurance to caregivers. A comprehensive strategy would reach patients well before their life end, allow close relatives to understand the issues and participate in the decisions, offer alternatives to heroic intervention, and build consensus and acceptance among caregivers. Every hospital admission and HMO enrollee must by law be given the opportunity to complete an advance directive informing his or her caregivers on managing the end of life.[31] The organization can stress the desirability of completing the directive, without bias toward a particular solution. If patients consider the issue, it seems likely they will improve their understanding and many will have greater comfort with lower cost measures.

The use of sites and agencies other than health care may allow more complete and candid discussion of the end-of-life issues, allowing patients and families to become comfortable in advance. Churches, congregate living centers, and senior recreational facilities can hold educational discussions on the question of dying. Promotion which reaches both patients and staff will improve staff understanding and acceptance as well.[32] Hospices provide not only an alternate form of treatment appropriate to specific patients; they also exemplify a philosophy of how to die. Ethics committees can be established both to supervise the strategy itself and to provide consultation to staff in complex cases. Finally, bereavement counseling can assist both families and staff with the painful emotions involved.

Marketing the Organization to Providers

Employees, physicians, donors, and volunteers enter into voluntary exchange relationships with health care organizations that have many similarities with customer relations. The organization wants ideally to be attractive in all these relationships; it can deal with an oversupply by being selective.

The effort to market the organization to providers begins by deliberately incorporating their viewpoint in all the various levels of decisions (Chapter 5). The opinions of current members will be an important predictor for those who may join in the future. Thus well managed organizations seek broad participation in decisions like the mission, vision, and strategic positioning. These statements of intent attract like-minded people and discourage those whose values are not supportive of the group's. As the goals are translated to operations, the operations themselves reveal the intent and capability of the organization. Operational realities reinforce or belie commitment to community values, and providers will seek organizations whose real values parallel their own.

The effect of specific promotional activities upon providers is carefully considered in well-managed organizations. Several common public relations documents are used as much to recruit and inform members as customers. The mission and vision are usually promoted aggressively among the members. The annual report and periodic newsletters, and press releases used by local media reaches providers as well as customers. Much of the customer-oriented promotion also reaches provider groups. Because of their interest, they are likely to be particularly sensitive to the messages. Some messages, like "Excalibur Health System is a caring organization," may be as powerful as tools to reach providers as they are to convince customers.

Most large health care organizations also promote themselves directly to provider groups. Promotional packets for potential house officers and physicians seeking primary care locations are commonplace; considerable care and expense is justified in the light of the importance of the decision on both sides. Various promotional devices are used to attract clinical professionals in short supply. Many organizations advertise routinely in nursing, physical therapy and pharmacy journals to attract new professionals.

Strategic affiliations to recruit personnel are also common. Affiliation with teaching programs increases the familiarity of graduating students. Programs to assist students with summer and part-time work affect not only the students directly involved, but their classmates who learn by word-of-mouth. Some institutions reach several years below graduation. Working with inner city high schools to encourage young people to enter healing professions is popular. Like many promotional activities, it reaches two audiences, the students and the community at large.

Measures of Marketing Performance

Global Measures of Marketing

Although the measures available are incomplete, a marketing program can be assessed by five of the six dimensions used in other programs. Output can be counted in terms of specific activities, although the counts are an incomplete representation of the whole activity. Some activities, like advertising, can be tracked with productivity measures such as cost per contact. Quality of marketing programs can be assessed in both outcomes and process contexts. Costs can be captured in conventional accounting systems, with emphasis on labor, surveys and special data acquisition, and advertising costs. Although the marketing staff is small, satisfaction remains an important performance measure. Contribution can sometimes be measured in terms of profit and market share. Demand for marketing services is obscure and probably cannot be assessed. Figure 7.10 shows a set of measures for the marketing program of a large health care organization. Expectations are set about these measures in the annual budget exercise, and performance is assessed against expectations.

Campaign-Oriented Measures of Marketing

The central measures of contribution or value of a marketing program are market share and profitability. It is difficult to construct a single global assessment, because both are the result not simply of marketing but the successful management of all parts of the organization. The usual solution is to identify gains or losses among target markets and specific campaigns. Expectations can be set about changes in target market shares and the profitability of specific programs. These are reasonably free of interactions with the rest of the institution, so

Figure 7.10   Possible Measures for a Marketing Program

Dimension	Measure
Output	Advertising expenditure, reach, frequency
	Cost per media exposure
	Presentations, speeches
	Media references
	Negotitations conducted
Quality	Survey and focus group responses to media releases
	Independent evaluation of content and design
Cost	Personnel
	Data acquisition
	Advertising
Human resources	Departmental employee satisfaction
Contribution	Changes in demand or market share
	Changes in familiarity, attractiveness
	Estimates of changes in profitability

that marketing can be accountable for the results. Performance of the program as a whole can be based upon the sum or average of these measures. Thus an organization might identify 35 percent of a large market as generally preferring its services, and might identify several strategies to expand this share, such as a Medicare HMO, centers of excellence in certain referral specialties, and an expanded availability of primary care physicians. Each of these has specific measures of profitability and patient demand. Expectations for improvement in these measures can be established in the budget negotiations, as shown in Figure 7.11.

The global measures for a program of all three activities would be based on statistical aggregates of the activities, such as:

- Sum of increase in demand resulting from each activity, and sum of profit contribution of each activity
- Percentage of expectation met in market share improvement, and percentage of expectation met in profitability

Either of these approaches is preferable to using the actual change overall market share because it is more sensitive and more free of outside influences.

More specific measures are available for components of the marketing program. Advertising and public relations campaigns can be

Figure 7.11 Measures for Specific Campaigns

Campaign	Actions	Measures
Medicare HMO.	Advertising in local papers, TV, radio shows Billboards on major traffic arteries Appearances in senior centers, churches, union halls Direct mail to lists of former HMO members discontinued on retirement Direct sales to seniors indicating interest Prizes for subscribers bringing new members	Number of exposures; exposures/target audience member; cost/exposure by medium Number of public relations appearances, audience size Number of responses by phone, letter Survey of awareness and attractiveness* Number of subscribers, percent of total market, cost per subscriber Surveys of subscriber satisfaction and estimate of continued subscription
Centers of excellence in orthopedics, cardiology	Preparation of data on cost per case and quality of results Publication of original research in peer-reviewed journals, distribution of reprints, feature stories in local media Direct sales to managers of local HMOs, PPOs Competitive bid for Medicare, Medicaid contracts Presentations to primary care physicians	Increase in listings on contracts for referrals from HMOs, PPOs, government programs Increased referrals of traditional insurance patients Change in total demand, cost per case Cost of campaign per new case Cost of campaign/change in profit per case
Increased primary care access	Direct mailing to physicians in primary care fellowships Coordination with presently affiliated physicians Senior executive meetings with local physicians affiliated with competitors Program of practice acquisition, expansion Introduction of nurse practitioners, with media advertising and public relations Program of office support to increase physician productivity	Number of new responses Number of new physicians recruited Number of nurse practitioners placed, demand for nurse practitioner services Patient visits/physician Delay for emergency, routine, and preventive office visits Patient satisfaction Program cost per new physician, per new visit

*See Kotler and Clarke's *Marketing for Health Care Organizations*, pp. 440–41.

measured by **reach**, an estimate of the number of people who will see or hear a specific advertisement, and **frequency**, the average number of times each person is reached. Efficiency measures are useful in these situations; it is common to calculate cost per exposure, where exposure equals reach times frequency. These are useful in guiding decisions about specific campaigns, but it is important to remember that they have no direct relation to the overall goals of increasing exchanges.

Surveys and direct consumer evaluations are important in assessing marketing activity, and provide both procedural and outcomes quality indicators. Major promotional objectives should have pre- and post-campaign evaluations built in. Advertising material can be pretested on focus groups to assess its effectiveness in changing customer attitudes and expectations, for example. Surveys can assess name familiarity, attitudes, and several stages of acceptability up to actual changes in behavior. Focus group approaches use smaller samples but allow in-depth discussions with individuals. They will sacrifice precision in estimating specific attitudes, but expand details of the dynamics of the exchange. For example, surveys can identify how many items in wellness programs actually changed health risk behavior, while focus groups and individual interviews might reveal specific items the customer liked or did not like. The latter are more useful in designing improvements to the program. They can be conducted by an independent agency, without identifying the sponsoring organization if desired.

Surveys and focus groups can be quite costly. The cost of obtaining the information must be weighed against the cost of not having it, which are also high. Misjudging patient needs or potential demand can endanger the institution; the cost of a survey to learn these needs is never that high. Maintaining objectivity is important; professional sampling techniques, questionnaire design and administration are costly, but not as costly as an error in assessing a program. It is possible to reduce costs by combining surveys which require similar samples. Thus a general marketing program adds expertise in assessing customer needs and exchange opportunities. It also offers opportunities to reduce costs by tying similar assessments together.[33]

Organizing the Marketing Activity

The contribution of a specialized marketing unit is technical and professional expertise; the steps involved in marketing are increasingly elaborate. Thus recruitment of trained personnel, or special training for those already with the organization, is appropriate. Masters degrees in business or health administration are useful beginnings, but neither program emphasizes the details of advertising or public relations. Experience with a commercial agency or a large health care–oriented team is highly desirable for the senior marketing people.

Consultants are available for most marketing functions. Advertising particularly is purchased from agencies with experience in design, campaign development, and media contracts. Market studies and customer surveys are often contracted to consultants. They benefit from advanced technical knowledge, and a consultant with a detailed knowledge of a geographic area can achieve better results at lower costs. Unfortunately, the history of health care marketing is too short for the development of clear standards of performance. Neither clients nor agencies have the broad base of knowledge and experience that characterizes marketing in consumer products. The data base which results from continuing study of a market is a valuable proprietary resource. Even if much of the data collection is delegated to planning or marketing consultants, the organization should make an effort to retain the data in their entirety.

Strategic marketing is rarely contracted to consultants. Negotiation is often retained as an activity of the CEO or senior staff. Consultants can be used as intermediaries or mediators, but local leaders may be as effective in these roles.

Given the small size of most marketing activities, it seems likely that internal organization is a team, perhaps with designated leadership based on seniority or professional experience. Internal organization by market segment is useful, particularly when there is little overlap in specific actions. For example, the group marketing to insurance intermediaries and employers is likely to be different from that concentrating on marketing to patients. It could be established as a separate responsibility center.

The important organizational questions are the scope of the marketing activity and its relation to other units. There is apparently some tendency to separate public relations from the marketing activity, and a stronger one to separate marketing from planning.[34] There are inescapable ties between these activities. Marketing and planning share a data base which is a major resource for the organization. The evaluation of many strategic and some programmatic opportunities requires both a marketing and a planning perspective. Marketing and public relations for a specific project or for image building should be integrated. Thus even in larger organizations with three separate functions and accountabilities, coordination under one executive appears desirable. The three functions affect the future of the organization as a whole, and should be close to the strategic core. Reporting to the chief executive officer is most common, and most appropriate.

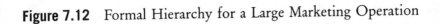

Figure 7.12 Formal Hierarchy for a Large Marketing Operation

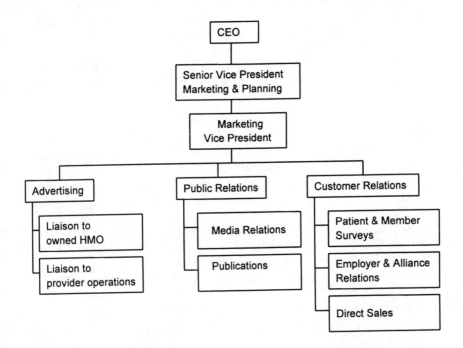

Figure 7.12 suggests the formal marketing accountability hierarchy for a large organization. Duties in most smaller organizations are probably a team responsibility, and most of the specific responsibility centers disappear. Members of either structure might have formal ties to specific subsidiaries, in a matrix organization as is sometimes used in planning. In the very largest organizations, marketing may be decentralized to subsidiaries. Alternatively, a central marketing unit can consider itself an in-house consultant service to all parts of the organization which seek its help. It is possible to establish charges and transfer payments for consultant services, permitting better cost allocation between subsidiaries and promoting a professional relationship between the units.

Suggested Readings

Cooper, P. D. 1994. *Health Care Marketing: A Foundation for Managed Quality.* Gaithersburg, MD: Aspen Publishers.

Kotler, P., and R. N. Clarke. 1987. *Marketing for Health Care Organizations.* Englewood Cliffs, NJ: Prentice-Hall.

Lewton, K. L. 1991. *Public Relations in Health Care.* Chicago: American Hospital Association.

Simon, R. 1994. *Levers of Control: How Managers Use Innovative Control Systems to Drive Strategic Renewal.* Cambridge, MA: Harvard Business School Press.

Zajac, E. J., and T. A. D'Aunno. 1994. "Managing Strategic Alliances." In *Health Care Management: Organization, Design, and Behavior,* 3d ed., eds. S. M. Shortell and A. D. Kaluzny, 274–93. New York: Delmar Publishers.

Zuckerman, H. S., and A. D. Kaluzny. 1991. "Strategic Alliances in Health Care: The Challenges of Cooperation." *Frontiers of Health Services Management* 7 (Spring): 3–23, 35.

Notes

1. P. Kotler, and R. N. Clarke, 1987, *Marketing for Health Care Organizations* (Englewood Cliffs, NJ: Prentice-Hall), 5.
2. G. M. Naidu, A. Kleimenhagen, and G. D. Pilari, 1992, "Organization of Marketing in U.S. Hospitals: An Empirical Investigation," *Health Care Management Review* 17 (4): 29–32.
3. J. A. Boscarino and S. R. Stieber, 1994, "The Future of Marketing Health Care Services," in *Health Care Marketing: A Foundation for Managed Quality,* ed. P. D. Cooper (Gaithersburg, MD: Aspen Publishers), 71–83.
4. S. MacStravic, 1989, "Market Administration in Health Care Delivery," *Health Care Management Review* 14 (1): 41–48.
5. Kotler and Clarke, *Marketing for Health Care Organizations,* 61–67.
6. K. L. Lewton, 1991, *Public Relations in Health Care* (Chicago: American Hospital Association), 133–62.
7. Kotler and Clarke, *Marketing for Health Care Organizations,* 66–67.
8. R. Frasca and M. Schneider, 1988, "Press Relations: A 14-Point Plan for Enhancing the Public Image of Health Care Institutions," *Health Care Management Review* 13 (4): 49–57.
9. S. S. Mick, 1990, *Innovations in Health Care Delivery: Insights of Organization Theory* (San Francisco: Jossey-Bass), 207–40.
10. American Medical Association, 3 Trade Req. Rep. CCH.
11. Kotler and Clarke, *Marketing for Health Care Organizations,* 25–27.
12. National Committee for Quality Assurance, 1993, *Health Plan Employer Data and Information Set and Users' Manual* (Washington, DC: NCQA).
13. J. R. Galagher, 1989, "Listening to the Consumer: Implications of a Statewide Study of North Carolinians," *Journal of Health Care Marketing* 9 (4): 56–60.
14. P. M. Lane and J. D. Lindquist, 1988, "Hospital Choice: A Summary of the Key Empirical and Hypothetical Findings of the 1980s," *Journal of Health Care Marketing* 8 (4): 5–20.
15. J. A. Chilingerian, 1988, "New Directions for Hospital Strategic Management: The Market for Efficient Care," *Health Care Management Review* 17 (4): 73–80.
16. MacStravic, "Market Administration in Health Care Delivery," 41–48.
17. S. Dawson, 1989, "Health Care Consumption and Consumer Social Class: A Different Look at the Patient," *Journal of Health Care Marketing* 9 (3): 15–25.
18. J. John and G. Miaoulis, 1992, "A Model for Understandinq Benefit Segmentation in Preventive Health Care," *Health Care Management Review* 17 (2): 21–32.

19. A. G. Woodside, R. L. Nielsen, F. Walters, and G. D. Muller, 1988, "Preference Segmentation of Health Care Services: The Old-Fashioneds, Value Conscious, Affluents, and Professional Want-It-Alls," *Journal of Health Care Marketing* 8 (2): 14–24.

20. S. MacStravic, 1993, "Reverse and Double-Reverse Marketing for Health Care Organizations," *Health Care Management Review* 18 (3): 53–58.

21. S. B. Schweikhart, S. Strasser, and M. R. Kennedy, 1993, "Service Recovery in Health Services Organizations," *Hospital & Health Services Administration* 38 (Spring): 3–21.

22. Kotler and Clarke, *Marketing for Health Care Organizations*, 428–63.

23. R. P. Hill, 1989, "The Growing Threat of AIDS: How Marketers Must Respond," *Journal of Health Care Marketing* 9 (2): 9–12.

24. S. MacStravic, 1989, "Use Marketing to Reduce Malpractice Costs in Health Care," *Health Care Management Review* 14 (4): 51–56.

25. L. R. Burns and L. R. Beach, 1994, "The Quality Improvement Strategy," *Health Care Management Review* 19 (2): 21–31.

26. Schwiekhart et al., "Service Recovery in Health Services Organizations," 3–21.

27. S. Barger and P. Rosenfeld, 1993, "Models in Community Health Care: Findings from a National Study of Community Nursing Centers," *Nursing and Health Care* 14 (October): 426–31.

28. MacStravic, "Use Marketing to Reduce Malpractice Costs," 54.

29. P. Curtis and G. Bove, 1992, "Family Physicians, Chiropractors, and Back Pain," *Journal of Family Practice* 35 (November): 551–55.

30. J. D. Lubitz and G. F. Riley, 1993, "Trends in Medicare Payments in the Last Year of Life," *New England Journal of Medicine* 328 (15 April): 1092–96.

31. *Hastings Center Report*, 1991, "Practicing the PSDA [Patient Self-Determination Act]," Special Supplement, 21 (September-October): S1–S16.

32. MacStravic, "Use Marketing to Reduce Malpractice Costs," 55.

33. Kotler and Clarke, *Marketing for Health Care Organizations*, 428–63.

34. Naidu et al., "Organization of Marketing in U.S. Hospitals," 29–32.

THE FINANCE SYSTEM

THE FINANCE system of the modern health care organization controls all the assets, collects all the revenue, arranges all the funding, settles all the financial obligations, and makes a major contribution to information collection and cost control. It includes accounting as well as finance and is headed by a professional with training and experience in both fields who is usually the second or third most powerful person in the organization. The extensive role of finance of health care organizations is no different in purpose or function from other industries, although some of the approaches are modified to accommodate not-for-profit structures and health insurance contracts.

This chapter describes the contribution finance makes to other systems, those tasks which it must do to make the whole succeed. Finance and accounting are subject to much study, regulation, and standardization. Comprehensive texts describe the overall operation of the system. Laws, regulations, contracts, and standard practice control what is done in countless specific situations. Much of this is effectively monitored by the processes themselves and by a unique characteristic of the financial system, the annual outside audit. The audit itself, almost always conducted by one of a few national firms, is a major force toward standardization. The chapter will assume that these standards have been met, and emphasize the activities that distinguish the most successful health care organizations, principally strategic financial planning, provision of capital, and cost monitoring and reporting. The chapter outline follows the usual pattern of purpose and function, performance measures, personnel and organization.

Purpose

The purposes of the finance system are to support the enterprise by

1. Recording and reporting transactions that change the value of the firm
2. Guarding assets and resources against theft, waste, or loss
3. Assisting operations in setting and achieving cost and revenue improvements
4. Assisting governance in short- and long-term planning
5. Arranging capital funding to implement governance decisions.

These five purposes are accomplished through two general functions—controllership, incorporating the first three, and financial management, incorporating the last two. The activities supporting these functions are shown in Figure 8.1. Although the list is lengthy and complex, most of the activities can be easily associated with one or two of the five purposes.

Controllership Functions

Financial Accounting

Accounting fulfills a direct obligation to the owners and the public, to record and report all transactions affecting the value of the firm. It establishes the number and value of all financial exchanges. The activity itself is organized by purpose into financial accounting and managerial accounting. Most of the data recording occurs in financial accounting. Completing these two functions keeps finance personnel involved in most areas of the organization.

The purpose of financial accounting is to state as accurately as possible the position of the firm in terms of the value of its assets, the equity residual to its owners, and the change in value occurring in each accounting period. Financial accounting generates the familiar balance sheet, operating statement, and cash flow statement which are basic management information for all corporations and are required public documents for most. It records each financial transaction of the organization and its subsidiaries.

Revenue Accounting

Revenue accounting records all the health care organization's cash acquisition. In the United States patient care revenue is almost universally organized by individual **patient ledger**, a detailed record of the individual charges for each service or supply rendered to each patient.

Figure 8.1 Functions of the Financial System

Function	Activity	Purpose
Controllership		
Accounting	Financial accounting	Establish value of organization
	Managerial accounting	Report to management
	Disclosure of financial information	Report to owners and external stakeholders
Protection of assets	Inurement physical assets audits	Guard against loss and diversion of property
Budgeting	Budget guidelines	Assist line management to meet market needs
	Operating, financial, and capital budgets	
Reporting and control	Routine reports on operations	Support line management in monitoring
	Special studies for planning and evaluation	Support continuous improvement
Financial Management		
Financial planning	Long-range financial plan	Test mission and vision against market reality
		Establish budget guidelines
Financial structures	Multiple corporate structures	Increase investment
		Contain risk
Securing long-term funds	Management of borrowing	Minimize cost of capital
	Management of stock and equity accounts	Maximize return on assets
Managing short-term assets and liabilities	Working capital Management	Minimize cost of working capital

Additional revenue categories are established for nonpatient-related sources. The charges within the patient ledger are organized by the profession or type of provider. Only some government hospitals and a few providers employed by HMOs do not maintain patient ledgers.

The detailed patient ledger is expensive, but it provides extensive, reliable, patient-specific data on the quantities of services rendered. Modern computer programs permit virtually limitless specification of the patient ledger; they also support a clinical abstract containing summaries of diagnosis and treatment. The ledger is routinely carried to detail of individual doses of drugs and hours or minutes of professional service. It is closely related to the medical record data processing systems described in Chapter 10 and has emerged as the principal source of data for achieving clinical economy and quality control. It also supports analysis for long-range planning, strategic decisions, marketing campaigns, and new program proposals.

The custom of individual ledger entry began in an era when patients and insurers paid fee-for-service charges established by the provider for each item. Many insurers, led by the federal Medicare program, moved to cost-based, rather than charge-based revenue structures for hospitals in the 1960s and 1970s. That system failed to control costs, and was abandoned beginning in 1983 in favor of prospective payment systems which unilaterally established prices for inpatient care. Payments for hospitals were based upon larger aggregates representing episodes of care—the disease-specific discharge, or diagnosis-related group (DRG) for inpatients, and global payments for some outpatient care. HMOs moved to per diem payments (a lump sum per day of care, including all services) or capitation, a monthly payment for each patient at risk entirely separate from the number or identity of individual patients receiving care.[1]

The movement away from fee-for-service payment divorced actual revenue from individual items of care. In most cases paid by DRG or capitation, the individual patient ledger no longer records anything relevant to revenue, but it remained useful as a control tool because it allowed the provider to understand exactly what services each patient received. It also remained the method of charging patients and insurers who paid amounts related to the posted charge. In the mid 1990s, about a quarter of all inpatient care and most outpatient care was still paid on a fee-related basis. The ledger was also built into many aggregate payment schemes to identify catastrophically expensive cases called "outliers," which qualified for special additional payments.

The following are the major components of revenue accounting under a mixture of fee-for-service, aggregate episodes of care, and capitated contracts:

- *Patient accounts receivable.* The quantity of services rendered and the fee requested for each service are posted to individual patient ledgers. The sum of all posted charges is called **gross revenue.**

Gross revenue is available for all individual items charged, and can be summed across items, yielding detailed data for services, such as operating rooms, physical therapy, or drugs. It is available for many responsibility centers under the formal accountability hierarchy. It can also be summed by patient or patient group, such as disease or payment group.

- *Revenue adjustments.* The differences between gross revenue and what is actually received are posted at the level of detail supported by the payment. Specific items can be adjusted under some discounted fee payments. Individual patient ledgers are adjusted for a discount applied to the whole episode of care but not to the specific items. Write-offs for charity and bad debts are also handled at the patient level. In the case of capitation payment, the discount cannot be calculated for the individual patient, but must be applied to the group of ledgers covered by the HMO contract.

- *Net revenue.* The income actually received, as opposed to what is initially posted; it is equal to gross revenue minus adjustments. The level of detail for which net revenue is available depends upon the kind of insurance contract. For those paying fees or specified discounts, net revenue is available at the individual ledger. For those paying episode aggregates, net revenue is available at the episode. For those paying capitation, net revenue is only available for the month or year, for all patients treated under the contract. Net revenue usually cannot be calculated for the specific item or the service group because a net revenue value is not available for every patient.

- *Nonoperating revenue.* Income generated from non–patient care activities, including investments in securities and earnings from unrelated businesses. It is an important contribution to overall profit for many health care organizations.

The structure of revenue accounting and the information available at various levels of aggregation are shown in Figure 8.2.

Expenditures Accounting

Accounting for expenditures reports all disbursement of funds and simultaneously generates basic information on costs. Cost ledgers show the quantities and prices of items purchased or disbursed. Thus the payroll system generates paychecks, records of hours worked by employee, and data on labor costs; the accounts payable system issues checks for purchased goods and services, and provides counts of quantities used, and data on cost of supplies.

Expenditures accounting is organized according to the formal accountability hierarchy, down to the level of responsibility centers

Figure 8.2 Revenue Account Organization and Availability of Information

Ledger Level	Activity Counts	Gross Revenue	Aggregate Payment Adjustment	Capitation Payment Adjustment	Net Revenue
Individual item	Yes	Yes	No	No	No
Patient	Yes	Yes	Yes	No	No
Responsibility center	Yes	Yes	No	No	No
Disease group	Yes	Yes	Yes	No	Yes
Payer group	Yes	Yes	Yes	Yes	Yes
Accounting period	Yes	Yes	Yes	Yes	Yes

(Chapter 5). Within each RC, expenditures are classified by **natural accounts**, the kind of resource purchased, principally labor, supplies, equipment and facilities, and other. Aggregates of cost or quantity are available for each natural account under automated recording schemes.

Some transactions are internal rather than external exchanges. These are called **general ledger transactions.** General ledger entries are usually expense adjustments, although revenue adjustments are possible. They adjust inventory values, assign capital costs through depreciation, and recognize other long-term transactions. They tend to reflect costs which are incurred by the organization as a whole rather than items clearly assigned to individual responsibility centers and to deal with resources that last considerably longer than one budget or financial cycle. As a result, they are available by natural account, but must be estimated with limited accuracy at accountability hierarchy levels below that at which they occur. For example, depreciation can be accounted to individual capital items, but these range from multipurpose buildings to equipment used only for one billed service.

Figure 8.3 shows the organization and availability of expenditures accounting information. As the footnotes indicate, the precision of expenditures accounting can be expanded. Many costs are directly accounted to specific patients and care activities in areas like the operating rooms and primary care offices. They add to the accounting expense, but improve its accuracy. Unfortunately, they can never be entirely complete. Important costs, such as the environmental sanitation of the operating rooms and the liability insurance of the primary care office, are inescapably joint, that is, the costs incurred are largely unrelated to the individual services rendered or patients treated.

Disclosure of Financial Information

Financial accounting provides a basic set of data about all the transactions of the health care organization which supports managerial accounting and which generates financial reports for owners, lenders, payers, and other exchange partners. Three main reports have become standard for health care organizations and most other nongovernmental enterprises.[2] They are the balance sheet; the income, or profit and loss statement; and the statement of sources and uses of funds. A fourth, the statement of changes in fund balances, was added in 1990.[3] These summarize the financial activities and situation of the organization in a form now almost universal in the business world. They are usually issued monthly or quarterly to the board and monthly to the executive office.

The financial statements are a critical report to the governing board, which is obligated to monitor performance and protection of assets on behalf of the owners. Each board member should receive a copy, and should be assisted to understand them. Annually, the board receives

Figure 8.3 Expenditures Account Organization and Availability of Information

Ledger Level	Labor Quantities and Costs	Supplies Quantities and Costs	Equipment Quantities and Costs	General Ledger Transactions
Individual item	Partial*	Yes**	No	No
Patient	Partial*	Yes	No	No
Responsibility center	Yes	Yes	Yes	Yes
Disease group	Partial*	Yes	No	No
Payer group	Partial*	Yes	No	No
Accounting period	Yes	Yes	Yes	Yes

*Certain high-cost labor, such as physician and nurse practitioner time can be accounted to the individual patient. General staff, such as clerical support, cannot practically be accounted in this way.
**Certain general supplies, such as inpatient linen, cannot practically be accounted to individual items. Most higher-cost supplies, including drugs and appliances, are directly accounted.

the audited, final versions of these statements. They constitute the record of the board's own financial management and the discharge of its obligation to exercise fiscal prudence.

The audited annual statements are also the basis for most of the organization's financial communication with the outside world. HMOs and intermediaries often demand access to provider organization finances as a condition of payment. Audited income statements and balance sheets for hospitals must be reported to the federal government as a condition of participation in Medicare. Once filed, they are accessible to the public under the Freedom of Information Act. Several states now require public release of financial reports as well. Health care organizations issuing bonds on public markets are also required to reveal standard financial information, plus pro formas forecasting their performance in future years. They make these public to support sale of bonds.

As a result, financial disclosure is inescapable for most organizations. Most other private corporations are required to make such disclosures to the public, so nondisclosure can arouse suspicion. Well-managed health care organizations deliberately publish their financial reports as part of their program of community relations. Governing boards have some flexibility in reporting, stemming from their ability to form foundations and subsidiary corporations. Subsidiaries of integrated systems, both for-profit and not-for-profit, are not automatically required to disclose their financial information, but many multihospital organizations operating in several communities make them public as a basic community relations gesture.

Managerial Accounting

Managerial accounting is a deliberate effort to relate revenue and expenditures to individual services and the activities of responsibility centers. Its purpose is to assist management in optimization of results with data useful in planning, setting expectations, and improving performance.[4] Opposite to financial accounting, it is oriented to produce information for internal organization uses, allowing management decisions about costs, profitability, revision, continuation and discontinuation of services. As Figures 8.2 and 8.3 suggest, managerial accounting is complicated in health care organizations because revenue is no longer received in aggregates paralleling the way services are produced. There are two theoretical solutions to the problem, either accumulate the costs from individual services to revenue aggregates, or disaggregate the revenue. Serious technical problems exist for each alternative, but aggregation of costs to revenue units is clearly the preferable choice. It is supported by the patient ledger accounting system, which captures a large part of the necessary data, and it permits systematic review of total costs against the patient's clinical needs.

The management question answered by managerial accounting is whether the individual service or the responsibility center rendering it operated at an acceptable level of cost. The service must simultaneously meet standards of quality and patient satisfaction, but these are not at issue in the managerial accounting data. Given a service acceptable in quality and patient satisfaction, cost must meet three tests:

1. At the level of aggregation at which payment is received, cost plus an allowance for the long-run strategic goals of the organization must be less than or equal to the amount paid. (Certain services may be deliberately subsidized; this amounts to a negative allowance for strategic purposes.)
2. At the level of aggregation at which control is achieved, usually the responsibility center, cost must be less or equal to the amount management is willing to distribute to that activity relative to others comprising the revenue aggregate.
3. At the level of the production unit, cost must be less than or equal to benchmark or best practice values. (An organization with several unit costs failing this test would concentrate on the biggest possible improvements.)

The source of data for these tests is the financial accounting system, but because of the differences in organization of accounts and level of aggregation between expenditures and revenue accounting, substantial manipulations and adjustments are necessary to translate the data to managerially useful forms.[5] The process for the translation involves identification of costs by variability and by accountability and identification of revenue by level of aggregation.

Variable, Semivariable, and Fixed Costs

Natural cost accounts are classified into variable, semivariable and fixed costs, where the category depends upon the relationship of costs to output, the number of units of service produced. Variable costs are those directly proportional to output, such as meals or supplies. Semivariable costs are related to output, but in a nonlinear way. The most common is a step function, where certain levels of output require additional costs, such as the hiring of another professional provider. Fixed costs are those independent of output; usually costs which must be incurred to produce even a single unit of output, such as facilities and equipment essential to a quality service. The algebraic and graphic relationships of cost to volume are shown in Figure 8.4.

Figure 8.4 Variable, Semi-Variable, and Fixed-Cost Relationships

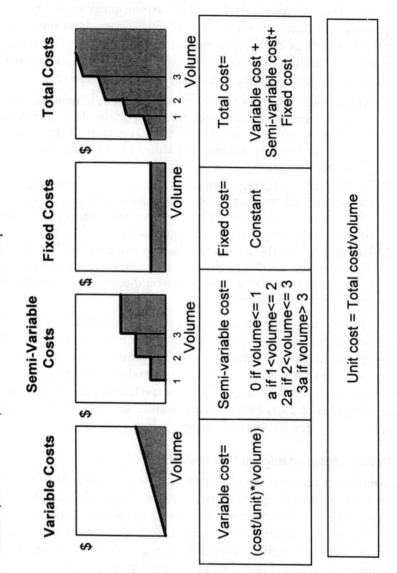

Marginal Costs

Marginal costs are the unit costs of an additional or eliminated unit of service. They are closely related to variable direct costs, but when a capacity limit of a semivariable resource is reached, there can be a sudden shift in the unit cost, as the total cost graph of Figure 8.4 reflects. Whenever a fixed or semivariable resource is used at less than capacity, the marginal unit cost is exactly equal to the variable costs. Whenever the fixed or semivariable resource must be adjusted to accommodate a change in volume, the marginal cost must be specifically calculated. Marginal costs can range from near zero to very large numbers.

Marginal costs figure in marketing and operations management. The economic rules for accepting new business or discontinuing existing business can be simply stated: (1) Accept additional volume if marginal revenue exceeds marginal costs; and (2) Discontinue existing volume if marginal revenue is less than marginal costs. A line manager seeking to optimize the overall cost performance of a responsibility center would concentrate on reducing volumes of items with the highest marginal costs, that is those which are near a semivariable or fixed resource limit, or those which have very high variable costs.

Direct and Indirect Costs

Some costs are incurred at the point of service, and are accounted directly through the natural accounts of the responsibility center or even smaller elements. The cost of supplies used directly in patient care, such as drugs or appliances, can be accounted through the RC to the patient using them. These are called **direct costs**. Other costs are incurred for large aggregates of the organization, even for the organization as a whole. Insurance, debt service, expenses of the executive office, and the operation of central services like parking and security are examples. These are called **indirect costs**, or **overhead**. Only direct costs can be controlled by the responsibility center. There are two ways to handle indirect costs. One, popular in hospitals under cost-based reimbursement, was to allocate indirect costs back to responsibility centers using complex formulas based on assumed relations between these costs and measures of output or resource consumption. Indirect costs were frequently allocated on the basis of facility space, number of employees, total direct costs, or gross revenues.[6] The allocation is frequently arbitrary, and it is impossible to hold the responsibility center accountable for allocated costs. The other approach is to establish transfer pricing.

Transfer Pricing

When the basic accounting of resources is in place, it becomes possible to view some responsibility centers as independent businesses, buying and selling services to each other as well as selling them to the patient or customer. The price for these internally purchased services is called a **transfer price**, which must be set by the finance activity, working with the selling RC. Conceptually, the transfer price allows the buying RC to look on the purchase as a variable cost resource to be used as effectively as possible. It also allows the buying RC to evaluate inside against outside sources. Presumably it will pay no more than competitive outside prices. Simultaneously, it forces the selling RC to compare its production costs against outside prices. It may recover an **implicit profit**, the difference between revenues at the transfer price and costs. If the producing unit cannot match the external price for an equivalent service, questions arise. The organization can presumably purchase the service from outside for a more advantageous price.

Transfer prices are desirable whenever they can be established, but many services cannot be rationally priced. Usually the problem lies with measuring the quantity of service, as in the case of governing board and executive office expenses. Problems with price comparisons are often raised by RCs reluctant to face market rigor, but there are few services for which some outside vendor cannot be found. Often the transfer price should be based on the lowest bid offered by a qualified contractor. Those services which cannot be priced must be allocated as overhead.[7]

Achieving Accountability

To improve performance, line managers must accept accountability for meeting the three tests of managerial accounting. These can be algebraically stated as shown in Figure 8.5. The responsibility of the finance system is to produce the data for all three tests. The normal process in well-managed organizations is to develop forecasts of each test, refine these into expectations which are incorporated into the budget process, and monitor actual performance against expectations. The emphasis is on continuous improvement, a better fit overall to market expectations each year.

The third test is used to establish goals for continuous improvement. It requires the deliberate search for comparative data revealing best practices. Identifying best practices and benchmark costs is a shared activity between accounting and line management. Accounting can assist in obtaining information from other companies, and in understanding the managerial accounting assumptions involved in the

Figure 8.5 Managerial Accounting Tests of Costs and Revenue

Test	Concept	Application Level	Algebraic Statement
1.	Profitability	Smallest unit of payment	Unit cost + allowance for strategic goals ≤ unit payment
2.	Control	RC or lowest level of accountability	Unit cost ≤ management allowance or budget guideline
3.	Improvement	Unit of production or payment	Unit cost ≤ benchmark or best practice

benchmark. Any real organization will always have an agenda of areas where it falls short of best practice. It will set priorities for shortfalls according to their contribution to overall profit, and work on as many as it can each year.

It is important to note that the tests call for two separate managerial accounting systems. The control test is organized around the traditional accountability hierarchy, and focuses on costs of individual services, sometimes called **intermediate products**. The profitability test must be at the level of the revenue contracts and is organized around episodes of care and patient groups, sometimes called **final products**. The accounting system must aggregate intermediate product costs to the level of final products. The third, the improvement test, applies to each form of organization. Benchmarks and best practices are relevant to both the traditional hierarchy and the final product evaluations of profit.

A final product in health care almost always involves several different services, from several different responsibility centers. It has traditionally been managed by each attending physician, who acted in what he or she perceived to be the patient's best interests, often without specific knowledge of the costs of the actions. The customer insistence upon cost limits requires that the attending physician now consider costs specifically. Each test and treatment must be weighed in the light of its contribution to the outcome; ideally only those essential to the outcome should be ordered. The attending physician, a role now held by the primary care physician, is held accountable for costs, and must now have final product data showing actual costs of treatment alternatives.

The complexity of modern treatment makes the attending physician mechanism, while vitally important, insufficient. Many patients are treated by several physicians and an even larger number of clinical support services, each of which brings new professional skills and perspectives. Cross-functional teams have been identified as the vehicle to assist attending physicians in achieving control.[8] The teams are organized around groups of patients with similar needs and bring together the several medical and clinical support providers, usually caring for the group. A substantial number of teams is necessary to cover the major patient groups, and many responsibility centers must be represented on several teams. Each team must be supplied with data allowing a comparison of total costs against total revenues.

The final product management team is concerned with the quality, patient satisfaction, and profitability of the product. All three must be maintained in order to succeed. (Declines in quality and satisfaction may lead to reduced volumes; where many costs are fixed these produce drastic changes in profitability.) From the cost accounting perspective alone, the team is concerned with appropriate volumes of services and competitive costs. Figure 8.6 shows the assembly of final product costs from managerial accounting data initially organized by responsibility center. Part A of Figure 8.6 shows total direct and indirect costs, but conceptually, each final product team should have data on fixed and variable direct cost components, and estimates of marginal costs arising from its actions. These are shown in Part B. The cost savings the final product team will achieve with various reductions will be closer to the variable costs. Reducing laboratory tests from 25 to 20 will save only $2.50, not worth the effort to discuss it. Sending mother and baby home a day early will save only $130, not the $1800 per day of total direct costs. Part B also shows that if there is room to expand the number of deliveries without encountering any semivariable boundaries, the marginal cost of an additional delivery will also be $642.50. Strategically, an effort to build market share might be much more rewarding than an effort to cut costs, and additional market share might be desirable at a reduced price per delivery. However, in the long run, the institution as a whole will be forced to get total costs below revenues. Otherwise, there will be no funds for replacement of equipment and facilities.

In reality, there are several unsolved problems in providing Figure 8.6 data.[9] Well-managed organizations can provide estimates of current direct and indirect costs, with commentary on the likely impact of changes in quantities of services upon the total cost. The estimates of direct costs are often questionable for small, high-volume services, like the laboratory tests in Figure 8.6. True marginal costs remain unknown in most situations.

Figure 8.6 Estimating Final Product Cost from Responsibility Center Data

A. General Model

RC unit direct cost × Volume used in final product = Final product direct cost element

RC unit indirect cost × Volume used in final product = Final product indirect cost element

Central and governance indirect costs = Allocated indirect costs

Sum of all final product cost elements = Final product cost

Obstetrics Example

Delivery room cost per use*	$1,250	×	1	=	$1,250.00
Postpartum care cost per day*	550	×	2 days	=	1,100.00
Nursery care cost per day*	300	×	2 days	=	600.00
Laboratory cost per test*	4.50	×	25 tests	=	112.50
Drug (1) cost per dose*	5.75	×	12 doses	=	69.00
Drug (2) cost per dose*	18.50	×	4 doses	=	74.00
Indirect costs	Allocated				1,200.00
Total				=	$4,405.50

*Includes RC indirect costs.

B. Variable Cost Model

RC unit variable cost × Volume used in final product = Final product variable cost element

Allocated RC fixed cost for each service = Fixed cost elements

Central and governance indirect costs (fixed) = Allocated indirect costs

Sum of all final product cost elements = Final product cost

Obstetrics Example

Delivery room cost per use	$ 250	×	1	=	$ 250.00
Postpartum care cost per day	100	×	2 days	=	200.00
Nursery care cost per day	30	×	2 days	=	60.00
Laboratory cost per test	.50	×	25 tests	=	12.50
Drug (1) cost per dose	5.00	×	12 doses	=	60.00
Drug (2) cost per dose	15.00	×	4 doses	=	60.00
Total variable costs			Delivery		$642.50
Fixed costs	Allocated				
Delivery	$1,000.00				
Postpartum	900.00				
Nursery	540.00				
Laboratory	100.00				
Pharmacy	23.00				$2,563.00
Indirect costs	Allocated				$1,200.00
Total				=	$4,405.50

The final product team concentrates on the areas where important cost savings or quality improvements appear likely, rather than rigorously applying the economic rules involving marginal costs. It endeavors to reach consensus on the most appropriate way to treat the typical patient in the group, and applies the Figure 8.5 tests of profitability, control, and improvement against that consensus. At the present time, this approach has proven highly productive.[10]

Budgeting

Budgeting and reporting deal with expectation setting and achievement, the basic engine for continuous improvement and competitive operation. They rest upon effective managerial accounting and financial planning. At present, leading organizations are expanding the budget to include expectations on several dimensions of performance discussed in Chapters 9 and 10, but cost budgeting remains a central part of the annual exercise. Reporting to responsibility center managers is being strengthened by improving the reliability and specificity of cost data, developing more accurate forecasts of demand and output, and providing historic data to support the expectation setting process. Budgeting of final products and accountability of final product teams, the action that creates a formal matrix organization, has just begun in the leading institutions. It can be expected to become widespread in the next few years.

The finance system provides the cost and revenue data and sometimes assists with other measures. A section of the finance system, the budget office, generally coordinates budget development. The development and approval process is usually called budgeting; the monitoring process includes cost accounting and reporting. The two parts are actually intertwined.

Budget Components

The budget for a health care organization is a full, detailed description of expected financial transactions, by accounting period, for at least an entire year. Because it takes time to develop, the forecast must cover about 18 months into the future. Some well-run hospitals budget a second or even a third year in preliminary terms as part of their yearly budget cycle. The review of future expectations is useful to them in making smooth progress toward their financial goals.

The major parts of the annual budget address both operational and financial planning needs. The **operating budgets** are made up of the following:

- Responsibility center **expenditure budgets**, or **cost budgets**, that is, costs anticipated by reporting period, responsibility center, and natural account. Costs are often identified as fixed, semivariable or variable. Anticipated volumes of demand or output are now incorporated into cost budgets. Indirect costs are sometimes shown, but the emphasis is on direct costs controllable by the responsibility center or unit.

- Aggregate expenditures budgets, successive "roll-ups," or aggregates, summarize larger sections of the organization paralleling the accountability hierarchy.

- **Revenue budgets** at aggregate levels reflecting the receipt of income. With the increase in aggregated revenue, revenue budgets are less useful at RC levels. Only gross revenues are available. Profit figures are particularly misleading at the responsibility center level. Under aggregate payments higher volumes of services decrease profits; standard gross revenue accounting reports a profit increase to the RC creating at least an implied incentive to counterproductive activity. For that reason, leading institutions are now reporting revenues only at aggregates that can be held accountable.

- **Final product budgets** of cost and revenue for DRGs and capitated costs per member per month. These are the first step in holding cross-functional teams accountable.

The **financial budgets** are composed of the following:

- **Income and expense budget**, sometimes called a "profit plan,"[11] expected net income and expenses incurred by the organization as a whole.

- **Financial budgets**, sometimes called "pro formas," establishing the financial position of the organization.

- **Cash flow budget**, estimates of cash income and outgo by period, used by finance in cash and liability management.

- **New programs and capital budget**, lists of proposed capital expenditures and new or significantly revised programs, with their implications for the operating and cash budgets by period and responsibility center. The new programs and capital budget includes all anticipated expenditures for facilities and equipment, as well as sources of funds for them. New programs and revisions of services are considered as part of the capital budget, even though they involve revenue and operating costs as well as capital. This permits initial consideration of a status quo operating budget and more rigorous evaluation of both existing and proposed components.

Figure 8.7 shows the major budgets and their relationship to the finance system purposes of operational improvement, planning, and funds acquisition.

Primary Unit Operating Budgets

Expenditures budgets are developed for each responsibility center and accountable cross functional team. The primary unit budgets specify expectations in enough detail to serve as an unambiguous guide to the RC or team managing the activity; for each month of the coming fiscal year, by natural account. Leading institutions now include expectations for quality, patient satisfaction, employee and physician satisfaction developed from non-accounting data as well as demand, output, and efficiency expectations developed largely from accounting data. Revenue is budgeted if it is within the control of the reporting unit. One advantage of the matrix organization with cross functional teams is that the teams can be held directly to market-based revenue guidelines. Teams working on specific inpatient groups can meet the Medicare DRG prices, for example. When revenue is not available, the case for most traditional RCs, a managerially established cost guideline must substitute for it to indicate acceptable performance.

Both physical and dollar measures are budgeted for many natural accounts, at the level of detail needed by the line unit to achieve control. Demand and output are forecast in terms of counts and contribution

Figure 8.7 Major Budgets and Their Relation to Financial Goals

Budget	Contents	Use
RC operating budget	RC expense budget RC revenues when applicable Nonfinancial performance expectations	One- or two-year plan of acceptable RC operation
Final product (FP) operating budget	FP expense and revenue budget Nonfinancial performance expectations	One- or two-year plan of acceptable FP operation
Financial budget	Detailed pro forma of corporate income, expense, and balance sheet	Verify budget guidelines and confirm LRFP
Cash budget	Projection of monthly cash flows	Manage working capital

to revenue if relevant. The counts are frequently subdivided to specific kinds of patients or specific services within the accountable unit. Expectations are developed for labor hours and costs by pay class, and major supply items are budgeted in counts as well as dollars.

The budget can be **flexible**, that is based upon changing variable costs to meet an expectation for a a steady unit cost, called a **standard cost**, or **forecast**, based upon prior demand forecasts for the period and meeting an expected total cost. The concept of a standard cost is useful in analyzing variation; part of the variation can be attributed to changes in demand or output, and part to changes in the use of resources. Flexible budgets require the line manager to predict volume changes and adjust staffing and other resources.[12] When demand is not under RC control and cannot be managed, flexible budgets cannot be used effectively. There are few RCs where they are feasible in health care organizations, because of the difficulty of accurate day-to-day forecasting. The concept of standard cost is useful in reporting, however, to isolate variations in cost caused by random shifts in demand.

The major sources of budget expectations are as follows:

- Demand is forecast for major elements such as managed care members, primary care contacts, emergency visits, hospitalizations, births, and surgeries. These events can be accurately forecast in most large operations by statistical analysis of market trends, combined with judgments of executive personnel. Forecasts for more detailed care elements are derived from those for major elements. They are developed first by the budget office and then refined for each unit by line personnel. The initial forecast is for continuation of past activities; it is then modified by actions taken on new programs and capital.

- Output forecasts are derived from the demand forecast by the RC. The usual expectation is that 100 percent of demand will be met, so that the two numbers are equal. Demand may be turned away in some situations, such as an appropriateness review or unexpected changes in the patient's condition. In other situations, output may exceed demand because of repeated work or additional services conditional on the initial results.

- Costs are forecast by historic unit costs, by natural account, with independent assessment of trends in prices of purchased goods and services. The price analysis is usually prepared by purchasing for supplies, human resources for personnel, and finance for indirect cost items. The initial cost forecast is based on a continuation of past activities. The RC is responsible for changes in unit costs and volumes developed by study of operations during the year. These may depend upon new programs and capital actions. These are part of continuous improvement activities and are frequently necessary to meet constraints on the total increase for the entire institution.

It is sometimes useful to reconsider the entire operation of a unit, in an effort to establish an optimally efficient operation which can be used as a benchmark or as the basis for a new program request. One of the questions properly addressed in this review is whether the unit can be replaced by purchase of service from outside vendors. (A related question is whether the operation can be improved by acquisitions of services now rendered elsewhere.) This process, called zero-based budgeting, does not appear fruitful as a routine approach.[13] External benchmarks and market needs are usually a more effective way to gain continuous improvement.

- Efficiency or productivity, is calculated mechanically as the ratios of costs to output. Both physical and dollar values are important. Productivity estimates are often compared to benchmarks and historical values, and used to identify improvement opportunities.

- Revenue, when applicable, is forecast from the output forecasts and anticipated prices. Prices are set at the executive level, reflecting both market realities and financial needs. Prices are generally established for each major payer group, with attention to the actual price (net revenue) as well as the posted charge. (There are still some payers willing to support cost-based prices, and even costs shifted from those accounts paying less than costs.) Smaller service units are generally priced in blocks, retaining a fixed ratio to each other. These ratios, used for each of the many different types of laboratory tests, for example, are called **relative value scales**. Transfer prices are established in the same way.

- Cost guidelines, used when revenue is not available at the primary level, are statements of allowable levels of cost performance. They may be used in addition to revenue guidelines as well.

Budget Guidelines

Each primary unit budget is developed subject to guidelines derived from the long-range financial plan. The guidelines are controlled by market conditions and are expressed first for the organization as a whole, and then for progressively smaller aggregates. They address the survival requirements of the organization, and are expressed in terms of expected revenue, necessary profit, and allowable costs. Where market-based revenue estimates are available, the guidelines for smaller aggregates can address all three items. It is not necessary to hold each aggregate to the same profit margin; some units can be deliberately subsidized and others held to higher standards. Many religious health care organizations subsidize units meeting the needs of the poor, for example.

When revenue estimates are not available, a cost guideline must still be used to keep the unit from absorbing unnecessary resources. The guideline cannot be set directly upon market considerations, but it should realistically reflect these. Benchmarks, historic trends, and overall institutional needs are used to set the cost guideline. Often the unit is involved in the process, and incentives are established for exceptional effort. Some organizations use two guidelines, one for minimally acceptable performance, and a second stretch guideline for exceptional achievement. Typical cost guidelines in the 1990s are, "No increase in unit cost," "Decrease by x percent each year to reach benchmark unit cost in three years."

Developing the Operating Budget

The budget development process is supported by the finance system, which is responsible for reaching an acceptable solution within a specified time frame. It follows an annual cycle which develops information from the environment down to the RC or cross-functional team. The cycle is shown in Figure 8.8. Completing the cycle takes about six months, and demands substantial effort by every manager and executive, as well as members of the governing board. During the remainder of the year, managers can focus on the analysis of operations and development of improved methods, so that these are ready for implementation with the next cycle.

The process is managed by "packages," specific bundles of information that are transferred from one unit or level to another, and timetables, which set deadlines for package transfers.[14] The package concept allows the budget office to route information to the correct location, permitting many different teams in the hospital to work at once. Figure 8.9 shows the major steps, although the process is usually more complex than the figure indicates. As a general rule, there is a specific information package for each RC or unit at each step, although later rounds of revision tend to focus on only a few unresolved areas.

The actual calculation is now computerized. Units have direct access to their own electronic files, and can change physical cost and some demand elements at will up to the package deadlines. At that time, they must submit the packages to central control, where aggregates are calculated and values checked against historic records for errors or potential difficulties.

Much of the effort for the revenue budget is carried out by finance, in collaboration with marketing and planning. The budget is developed

Figure 8.8 Annual Budget Cycle

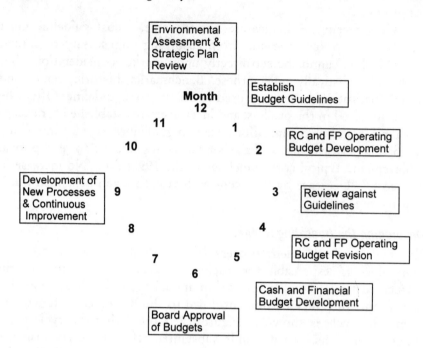

from volume forecasts, prices, and price adjustments. Pricing is moving to higher aggregates and becoming an increasingly market driven. Capitation prices are available only for the provider organization as a whole. Employers now often indicate the acceptable limit of prices to the insurance intermediary, who translates it to provider payments. The federal government promulgates Medicare prices. Preparation of transfer prices for imputing revenue to units serving only other RCs is also principally an accounting responsibility. Both cost analysis and market surveys are required.

The following are guidelines for a well-run budget process:

1. The parts of the budget must constitute an integral whole. The planned activities must be consistent with each other, the strategic plan and long-range financial plan, and the annual environmental survey.

2. Budget guidelines are developed by the governing board at the outset of each budget cycle, and are a major force in gaining consistency and timely progress. These include
   • market-based forecasts of revenue
   • a minimum acceptable return from operations established from the strategic plan and the long-range financial plan

Figure 8.9 Major Steps in Developing Operations Budgets

Month	Finance Activity	Line Activity	Intent
1. Establish budget guidelines	Set volume forecasts, cost changes	Distribute instructions, forms, and timetables	Provide targets and information for line managers' guidance
2. Develop RC and FP budget	Provide more detailed forecasts, historical, and comparative information to RCs and FPs Answer questions and requests for advice	Develop budgets within guidelines	Specify realistic operational expectations for coming year
3. Review against guidelines	Tally proposed operating budgets and check against LRFP	Consider possible improvements or "stretch" budgets	Assure competitive operation
4. Revise to improve compliance	Suggest areas for revision	Reconsider guidelines	Improve competitive position Accommodate late changes in external environment
5. Develop cash and financial budgets	Develop complete budget for board review Double check financial implications		Prepare integrated package for board action
6. Board approves of budgets	Recommend final budget to board		Final review
7–11. Develop new processes and continuous improvement	Report on performance against budget Provide benchmark information and guidance on improvement opportunities Assist in evaluating new processes	Develop improved processes Execute plan-do-check-act of Shewhart cycle	Find opportunities to improve competitive position
12. Assess environmental and review strategic plan	Present long-range forecasts, market analysis, evaluation of current mission and vision	Review and understand competitive environment	Develop consensus on organization needs, environmental conditions Reiterate relevant policy on quality, human resources, and operations

- a limit on increase in total cost
- a maximum allowable capital expenditure.

3. The budget for capital expenses and new programs is separately developed and approved. It simplifies the dialogue for the expense budget and
   - permits ad hoc debate on the relative value of programs
   - allows the approval of new programs and even replacement capital to be adjusted quickly as conditions change
   - encourages deletion proposals for obsolete or uneconomical programs
   - permits the use of new programs as rewards for achieving cost and efficiency goals.

4. Line managers receive training in advance covering the budget philosophy, the importance of the outcomes expectations, the reasons for being given the opportunity to propose expectations rather than being forced to accept those of others, and the value of incorporating the viewpoints of work group members.

5. Continuous improvement is the norm. An RC can assume that, if nothing else changed, next year's budget would redo last year's work with slightly fewer resources because its people would have the advantage of practice and study of improvement possibilities. Well-run organizations often focus on a ceteris paribus budget in the initial discussion in order to identify the improvement in efficiency. Subsequently, adjustments can be made for minor volume, intensity, and process changes. Major changes are treated as new services and separately justified in the new programs and capital budget.

6. The quality of data and the preparation of information by the budget office are important contributions to success, measured both by time to completion and usefulness of result. These should be improved from year to year, building upon past work.

7. The budget process itself is subject to continuous improvement. It should be made more rigorous over time. An organization having difficulty establishing or meeting its budget is well advised to limit its attention to elementary concepts, concentrating on getting guidelines, forecasts, and improvement processes established and accepted. A well-run organization with many years' budgeting experience will accommodate fluctuating demand, fixed, variable, and semivariable expenses, transfer prices, and stretch scenarios. It also would have extended the detail of its reporting, both by type of resource and number of RCs. Similar growth in sophistication would occur in the capital and new programs budget.

8. RCs and cross-functional teams must participate in budget development. They should fully understand the market forces and

planning processes leading to the budget guidelines. They should be able to anticipate the guidelines for at least two years in the future. They should be trained in process analysis and continuous improvement, and encouraged to work throughout the year in preparation for next year's budget needs.

9. Line managers must accept the final decisions and be convinced of their realism.[15] Executive staff and senior managers are responsible for resolving conflicts. If finance or other technical support groups impose solutions, the stage is set for failure, continued dissent and dissatisfaction.

10. An organizationwide dialogue should go on about the market, the guidelines, and the continuous improvement program. Such a dialogue is probably essential to allow the matrix approach, and gain effective collaboration between the traditional RCs and the newer cross-functional teams. The effectiveness of the dialogue is more important than issues of data quality or process sophistication. When an effective dialogue exists, quality and sophistication often improve as a result. Without effective dialogue, there is a constant danger of having the RCs adopt an adversarial or destructive approach to the budget.[16]

Developing the New Programs and Capital Budget

New programs and capital requests, even equipment replacement, are authorized by the governing board through the new programs and capital budget. Each potential investment is developed as a programmatic proposal (See Chapter 6). Proposals are ranked competitively by line teams, as shown in Figure 6.11, and the final approval must accommodate the capital expenditure budget guideline. The approved proposals will constitute the budget for new programs and capital expenditures and as such will affect the revenue, cost, and cash flow budgets.

The criterion for all capital investment is optimization of long-term exchange relationships between the hospital and its community. For the organization to thrive, new projects, expansions, and replacement of old investments must always be selected on the basis of this criterion, which must balance both member (internal) needs and patient (external) needs. The nature of professional behavior is such that the best managers and clinicians will always have proposals which cannot be funded, so considerable tension surrounds the selection process. The process must not only identify the best proposals, but also seem equitable to organization members.

Finance is a good choice to manage the competitive review process. Their technical skills prevent distortion of costs or benefits, and they are relatively unbiased. The following steps are helpful:

1. Proposals accumulated during the year are submitted to ad hoc committees within each of the major operating systems. The task of these committees is to rank the proposals submitted. That is, clinical proposals are ranked in the clinical system, accounting proposals in the finance system, and so on. Within the larger systems, subcommittees may rank sets of related proposals.

2. Ranking should follow established guidelines for both process and criteria:

   a. A process which allows each committee member a secret vote on the rank is preferable, because it reduces recrimination, collusion, and status differentials.

   b. Membership on the committee should reflect contribution to the hospital's mission, but it should also offer broad opportunity to reward successful managers. High turnover of individuals is desirable, as long as the representation of various groups is kept constant.

   c. Discussion and debate should be focused upon the criterion of optimizing the organization's exchange relationships, rather than the gain of a particular group or unit.

3. Second review by an executive-level committee with representation weighted to clinical systems should integrate the rankings of the initial committees. The board planning committee may accept the initial rankings as advisory or may refer back for reconsideration. In rare cases, it may revise the original rankings, but it should do this only after discussion with the proposal supporters. It may also revise the capital budget guideline up or down, depending upon the opportunities in the proposals and environmental needs. (For example, sudden changes in interest rates often cause a reevaluation of capital plans.)

4. Final recommendation for acceptance should be taken from the combined ranking by the finance committee. Disagreement between the finance committee and the second review may be referred to the full board in rare cases.

5. Acceptance by the board is normally at the time of adoption of the operating budget. Contingent acceptance is possible and often desirable. Thus a proposal may be accepted if cash flows at midyear reach a specified level, or if demand for certain services exceeds expectations.

The capital budget process requires extensive automation. There are a large number of proposals, and they are frequently combined or modified. While full descriptions are not easily computerized, a brief summary and a business plan can be entered for each. The competitive process is rigorous, and many proposals are withdrawn for further study. When the proposals are approved and implemented they often affect operating budgets. Even after approval, the details of implementation can change. Automation facilitates management of the active list of proposals, the approved budget, implementation, and modification of operating budgets.

Reporting and Control

Several kinds of cost and revenue details are reported to other systems by finance, including reports on budget performance, cost studies, and special or ad hoc analyses.

Routine Reports to Accountable Units

The controller provides monthly reports to general management, from the RC to the governing board, to assist them in achieving expectations. The purpose of the reports is to allow management to identify and correct any deviation from the budget expectations. When deviations occur, they are normally corrected by the lowest level of management affected. Higher levels enter only if the first efforts are ineffective. Finance personnel are involved only if there are questions of accounting or forecasts. Deviations are normally very rare. Several tens of thousands of expectations are set in the budgets of a moderate-sized health care organization and compared to performance monthly. More than one or two deviations per RC per month would be dysfunctional, because it diverts RC energies from continuous improvement to correcting past mistakes.

The design, content, and delivery of these reports are a major part of the controller's job. The reports should

- Correspond exactly to the expectations set in budgets, both in definition and time. (A common error is to report accrued rather than actual data for calendar months, creating a noticeable distortion because of varying numbers of weekend days. One solution is to avoid accruals; another is to use a 13-month year.)
- Be delivered promptly, within a few days of actual events.
- Be clearly and usefully presented. (A common problem is excess information, confusing the control purpose of the report with an archival one. Line managers who request a copy of the archive should receive it, but the control report focuses on material elements.)
- Present both physical and dollar measures on labor and other major costs.
- Be available to each person in the formal organization for his or her exact area of accountability.

- Condense information so that it is both automatically summarized from lower hierarchies and presented with equal economy at all levels. (This means that the COO's report is about the same length as a typical RC's. It usually follows very similar design.)
- Emphasize financially important variation so that major problems can be identified quickly.

Reports on Product Costs

The accounting for final product cost follows the process outlined in Figure 8.6, above. The reports should contain expectation and actual values for the following:

- Counts of individual services for homogeneous groups of patients, usually available from the patient ledgers
- Total net revenues and unit revenues by group
- Direct costs of the intermediate products. These must be obtained from the cost data for the revenue-producing responsibility centers
- An indirect allocation for costs of central services
- Profit
- A method for identifying marginal costs so that the relationship between cost and changes in volume of each final product can be determined.

Each of these presents serious challenges to the accounting system. First, final product costs require software capable of correctly grouping patients by final product and handling numerically burdensome calculations. (One must not overlook the scale of the activity. There are several hundred final products and several thousand intermediate products.) This problem is now largely met with expanded clinical information on the patient ledger and data base management systems.

Second, as indicated above, calculations of indirect and marginal costs are complex and subjective. The burden of indirect costs can be shifted to various final products; no rule requires it to be divided in any specific way. As a result, profit calculations are also subjective. Semivariable costs make the estimation of marginal costs potentially treacherous. Considerable dialogue must accompany final product reports if the limitations of the reports are to be understood by the cross-functional teams. Such an understanding is necessary to gain their acceptance and motivate them towards continuous improvement.

Thus, final product costing becomes a matter of preparing estimates or approximations using the best available data and methods, and improving upon accuracy with time. Because of the difficulties, costs are prepared only for selected products, routinely for those which make large contributions to revenue, or on a special study basis for those potentially affected by some proposed change. Most health care organizations are taking a gradual approach to both the accuracy of product cost estimates and the scope of reporting. At the outset, even crude approximations serve to identify important avenues of efficiency and economy.[17] As time passes, the approximations will be improved and substantial extensions of the accounting system will accompany those improvements.

Reports on Planning and Special Studies

Financial data are also essential to analyze operations, constructing estimates for new or revised activities, and evaluate capital investment opportunities. Both RC and product-oriented estimates are required for careful exploration of the strategic possibilities discussed in chapter 7, that is, opportunities to reconfigure the services of the organization by adding or dropping certain activities or by merger, divestiture, acquisition, or joint venture. Common uses include:

- Developing new budget expectations, particularly when the operating conditions have changed
- Establishing prices of intermediate products in situations where these are sold directly, and negotiating prices of final products with third parties
- Comparing local production with outside purchase, often called *make or buy decisions*
- Comparing alternative methods, particularly those substituting capital for labor
- Ranking cost-saving opportunities to identify promising areas in which to eliminate or reduce use
- Estimating the impact on costs of expanding or contracting a product or service.

Information for these purposes is produced on demand, rather than by a routine schedule. The accounting function includes the maintenance of a cost data archive to explore specific questions, retrieval of relevant information, consultation on the limitations and applications of the data, and assistance in developing forecasts and expectations for new equipment and new operational processes. The level of detail required by specific proposals often calls for specific supplementary cost studies and extrapolation beyond normally recorded levels.

A well-managed accounting operation produces information as required by line management and cross-functional teams using an automated archive of financial and managerial accounting information. It also offers consultative assistance in understanding both accounting and financial implications of specific decisions. Ideally, finance personnel work directly with RCs and teams, helping them identify fruitful avenues of investigation, develop useful proposals, and translate operational changes to accounting and financial implications.

Protection of Assets

The health care organization as a corporate entity is required to maintain control of all its properties for its owners. The governing board and members of management are individually and severally responsible for prudent protection of assets, including avoidance of inurement.

Physical Assets

Generally, the protection of the physical assets is considered part of the function of the plant system, assigned to security, maintenance, and materials management. Prudent purchasing practices are included in the responsibilities of materials management. The risk of misappropriation of assets is probably greater than the risks of theft or destruction by outside sources. The finance system is responsible for prudent protection against both. The responsibility extends to the physical protection of cash, securities, and receivables, and for assuring that plant and equipment were used as anticipated. The major risks it guards against are

- Unjustified free or unbilled service to patients
- Embezzlement of cash in the collections process
- Bribes and kickbacks in purchasing arrangements
- Supervision of financial conflicts of interest among governing board members and officers
- Diversion or theft of supplies and equipment
- Falsified employment and hours
- Purchase of supplies or equipment without appropriate authorization.

All organizations face continuing real losses of assets, and acceptable performance requires continuing diligence. Most well-run health care organizations find that control of assets can safely be delegated to the finance system with only brief annual review. This is because a sound and well-understood program has been developed for the purpose; it has five parts:

1. Detailed, written procedures govern the handling of the various assets and transactions. These procedures primarily rely on the division of functions between two or more individuals and the routine reporting of checks and balances to protect assets. It is

common to assign responsibility for authorizing the transaction (a payment or a charge) to line managers and to responsibility for collecting or disbursing funds to accounting personnel.

2. Adequate written records and accounting systems document the actual use of assets.

3. Special attention to collections and cashiering. Significant efforts must be made to assure that third parties and individuals pay promptly and fully. Payment in cash and checks must be protected against embezzlement. Carefully designed systems to assure prompt payment and protect both receivables and cash rely heavily on the principle of division of tasks between two or more individuals, minimizing the opportunity for any single individual to reduce income by accident or by diversion.

4. Adherence to risk control procedures and documentation requirements is monitored through a small group of internal auditors, who usually report directly to the CFO.

5. Annual outside audits verify both adherence to procedure and validity of reported outcome.

Inurement

Inurement is the diversion of funds to persons in governance or management as a result of their position of trust. Not-for-profit structure requires that no individual benefit from service to the corporation beyond any stipulated salary or compensation. For-profit structure has an analogous protection against exploitation of stockholders by directors. Under these rules, directors, managers, or trustees may not engage in business which allows them to derive financial advantage from their governing board role. The rule applies as well to physicians, but its application is more complex. The corporation is not enjoined from doing business with a board member, if such business and board membership are in the owners' interests. Thus the key word is "advantage."

To protect against inurement, the hospital must establish, and the CFO must enforce, policies that reduce financial conflict of interest. These policies have two parts. First, every governing board member and officer is required to file an annual disclosure statement identifying all their financial interests and potentially conflicting commitments, including membership on other voluntary boards. Second, members are expected to divorce themselves from any specific decision or action which involves their interests or conflicting affiliations. Well-run organizations achieve this by making the point well in advance of any specific application and by selecting members who understand both the law and the ethics.

Auditing

Programs to protect against loss, diversion, and inurement are audited routinely, first by an internal audit group and second by outside auditors.

Internal auditors use a variety of monitoring devices to detect changes in physical assets and cash, or departure from accepted practice. They pay particular attention to known areas of high risk, such as receivables and collections, payrolls, prices of purchased items, and supplies with street value. Internal auditors also review accounting practices and procedures, and monitor compliance.

Outside auditors certify the financial statements to be correct, usually on a fiscal year basis. The federal government requires an audit as a condition of participation for Medicare, and many intermediaries have similar requirements. Lenders require annual audits before and during the period of any loan. The audit emphasizes areas of known high risk. They are expected to maintain a deliberate distance from internal employees being audited, including the internal auditors, and to use objective methods to ascertain the accuracy of reported values for balance sheet items. They are also expected to review accounting processes and to suggest changes which will improve accounting accuracy.

Berman, Kukla, and Weeks note that the external auditor's "primary concern is not the needs of internal management but rather the needs of external agencies and organizations."[18] In addition, "The value and usefulness of an independent auditor lie as much in business convention as they do in operational control."[19] Their point is well taken. External auditors make a prudent survey of the accuracy of records. Although this includes review of protection of assets, it does not in any sense include either budgeting or financial management. For protection of assets as well as for cost control, the hospital's best control systems are continuous and internal rather than episodic and external. The external controls imposed by the auditor are secondary and designed to assure that the primary systems are working.

The governing board's role is to select the outside auditors, receive their report and review it carefully, and take action to correct any deficiencies noted.

Considerable care in selecting and instructing the auditor is justified. The auditor should be accountable directly to the board's finance committee. The firm should be free of any other financial relationship to the organization. Technically, this means that any consultants should be hired from a different firm than the one handling the audit. While sound, this rule is frequently breached. It is unacceptable, however, to use a firm represented on the hospital's governing board. The accountants' code of ethics states:

> Any direct financial interest or material indirect financial interest is prohibited as is any relationship to the client, such as . . . voting trustee, director, officer, or key employee.[20]

While the hospital board might override the conflict of interest for banking, groceries, or the practice of medicine, it seems both unwise and unnecessary to do so for the audit. The distance and independence of the auditor are an integral part of the audit's success.

Instructions to the auditor should be formulated by the audit committee of the governing board, usually including only the outside directors who serve as chair, finance chair, treasurer or secretary. The instructions for audits of protection of assets should be reviewed and revised annually. It is common to use sampling techniques, with attention focused in proportion to the risk involved. This means that certain high-risk activities will be scrutinized annually, others less frequently. The revisions can bring different aspects of the asset protection system under scrutiny each year. The instructions should be based in part on advice from the CEO and CFO but should be confidential between the finance committee and the auditor. Most firms offer an oral summary and discussion of the management letter, which the board should accept.

The report goes directly to the audit committee. Thus the auditors are free to comment upon the CEO and CFO as well as others. The auditors' comments on both problems with the accounts and weaknesses identified in the asset protection policies are included in a document called the **management letter**, which accompanies the audited financial reports. Well-run health care organizations have little trouble with this system. The expectation for the management letter is "no deficiencies," and it is usually achieved. The success of this system means that governance groups and CFOs of well-run organizations need spend little time on asset protection activity, despite its complexity and importance.

Financial Management Functions

The financial management function projects future financial needs, arranges to meet them, and manages the assets and liabilities of the health care organization in ways which increase its profitability. Financial management in this sense is relatively recent, arising from the increased revenue base created by Medicare, Medicaid, and widespread private health insurance, and from the opportunities for obtaining credit and equity which these created. Before 1970, hospitals had two sources of funds, retained earnings and gifts. The growth of public corporations, extended series of bonds issued and reissued to minimize interest costs, and deliberate investment in joint ventures for profit is as telling a story of the health care industry as the development of heart transplants. Even traditionally not-for-profit organizations now engage in a broad spectrum of financing opportunities. The four components of financial management—financial planning, management of intercorporate transfers, long-term capital acquisition, and management of short-term assets and liabilities—are now essential to survival.

Financial Planning

Financial management is a forward-looking activity with a long time horizon. It begins with the generation of a *long-range financial plan* (LRFP) which incorporates the expected income and expense for every element of the strategic plan, specifying the amount and the time of its occurrence. Although the accuracy of the estimates deteriorates in distant future years because of the uncertainty involved, large financial requirements must be accommodated even though they are many years distant. Some activities of the LRFP such as bond repayments and major facility replacement require financial planning horizons up to 30 years. Discounting techniques reduce their relative impact on the near term.

Financial planning is now commonly done on computers. A financial planning model generates pro forma statements of income, asset and liability position, and cash flow for each of the future years. Pro forma plans show not only the amounts of cash the organization will need, but also the sources of available funds. The first step of financial planning is generally undertaken by the CFO and his or her immediate staff, possibly with members of the finance committee of the governing board.[21] For as many scenarios as can be practically accommodated, the computer program will produce pro forma statements. These can be evaluated by means of ratio analysis,[22] which compares various aspects of the financial statements, such as the ratio of debt to equity, debt service to cash flow, debt service to income, and so on. These can be subjectively assessed or compared to published data to judge

- The cost and reasonableness of borrowing from various sources
- The cost improvements required to meet market constraints on revenue
- The cash flow required to support debt service
- The identity and magnitude of various financial risks

- The overall prudence of the financial management.

Good financial planning will consider as many alternate assumptions as possible in terms of their impact upon the long-range plan. Various assumptions might address

- The impact of the business cycle
- Proposed federal and state legislation
- Trends in health insurance coverage and benefits
- Donation, grant, and subsidized funding sources
- Alternative debt structures and timing
- Opportunities for joint ventures and equity capitalization.

LRFP development will also accommodate the widest possible variety of assumptions about the long-range plan itself. These might include operational changes speeding up or slowing down some programs, combining programs, and even abandoning some. They might also include financing changes revising debt structure, changing profit margin requirements, acquiring new equity investors. They may even include closure or divestiture of some units or the merger or closure of the institution. The objective is to identify the optimum operating condition consistent with the mission and strategic plan, and to evaluate that condition in terms of its acceptability. Unacceptable results at any step can force a complete reevaluation of the strategic plan.

The LRFP is used to establish the budget guidelines. Each year's guidelines translate the LRFP to operational requirements. Substantial departure from the plan threatens the financial security of hospital and cannot be accepted as prudent management. The keys to success are similar to those of planning generally: thorough and imaginative search for opportunities and consequences, careful factual analysis and forecasting, and sufficient lead time to permit unhurried decision making. Good general accounting systems and sufficient automated support substantially reduce the required lead time. As is so often the case, success feeds upon itself; the hospital which falls behind is tempted by shortcuts and risks that erode its position further.

As indicated in Chapter 3, the financial plan is a critical reality check for the organization. It tests the practicality of the mission, vision and strategic plan. Given that prices are set by customers, the financial plan estimates the costs of services, including capital costs, and shows whether the organization will thrive. Figure 8.10 shows the tests and the kinds of rethinking necessary to make the strategic plan fit financial realities. Obviously, the ideal is a strategic plan that generates operating costs substantially below available prices; when that occurs the organization has a steady stream of profits which it can amplify with borrowed or invested capital. It can invest the funds in growth, capturing an increasing market share. The ideal is not often achieved. Much more likely are the scenarios where early losses are necessary and growth leads to a deferred income stream, or where the plan can never earn money, or cannot earn sufficient funds to attract capital at reasonable prices. The well-managed organization recognizes these danger signals, and makes the necessary adjustment. The poorly managed organization ignores the financial planning step, or convinces itself that miracles will happen.

Financial Management of Multicorporate Structures

As noted in Chapter 5, many health care organizations are now multicorporate structures taking advantage of legal, market, and financial advantages. Both for-profit and not-for-profit corporations as general legal entities are permitted to form new corporations, invest in other corporations, and reverse these actions by sale or liquidation. Except for the restrictions of antitrust, there is no limit on the amount or percentage of the investment involved; it can range from negligible to wholly owned. Any combination of for-profit and not-for-profit entities is possible. The tax obligations of each corporation are considered individually as the structures develop.

The major financial benefits of multiple corporate structures are

- *Capital opportunities.* Separate corporations offer opportunities not only to dedicate capital, but also to raise new capital, either through

Figure 8.10 Tests and Adjustments in Financial Planning

Test	External Source	Adjustment Required
Debt ratios	Bond market	Keep debt within bond rating limits
Price	Buyers and intermediaries	Keep price competitive
Earnings	Bond market	Keep cash flow within bond rating limits
Demand and market share	Competitor analysis	Keep volume forecast consistent with competitor and market conditions
Cost	Benchmarks	Keep cost at or below (revenue − profit)

borrowing or equity, as discussed below. These advantages can be obtained even within the not-for-profit structure; affiliation of several hospitals operating in different marketplaces is considered by bondholders to be more diversified and therefore less risky. As a result, they will accept lower interest. Some activities are attractive to equity capital; these can be pursued only through a for-profit structure. If the parent corporation is not-for-profit, a for-profit subsidiary can be formed.

- *Reward.* Separate for-profit corporations allow various groups to invest in activities of interest to them, and to receive financial reward for the success of those activities.
- *Risk.* The liabilities and obligations of the owned or subsidiary corporation cannot generally be transferred to the parent. (There are certain exceptions, and the law in this area is changing.) Thus the parent risks only those assets actually invested in the subsidiary.
- *Taxation.* Not-for-profit corporations can be taxed on certain activities, and for-profit corporations can respond to incentives built into the tax law with nontaxable actions. It is frequently desirable to support this line of reasoning with separate corporations. These clarify the tax position and are eligible for explicit Internal Revenue Service (IRS) rulings. In addition, they can frequently be designed with a view toward minimizing the overall tax obligation.

Well-managed health care organizations use multicorporate structures as tools to achieve specific ends. There is no theoretical or demonstrated general advantage to one structure over another. In fact, operational differences between organizations depend more upon how the structure is implemented than the specific form. Thus new corporate relationships arise because they offer improved ways to meet strategic objectives or implement specific plans. The finance system has the obligation of identifying, evaluating, and recommending these opportunities.

When a multicorporate structure exists, unique opportunities are created to allocate costs and profits. Within limits of accepted accounting practice and IRS regulation, funds can be transferred between corporations by transfer of earnings or by charges for services. In multicorporate situations, the parent institution may participate in equity funding and receive rewards from it. It may also sell or buy services from the subsidiary at a negotiated price. A relatively common example has a hospital that is exempt from taxes under Section 501(C)(3) of the Internal Revenue Code forming a for-profit corporation with outside investors and then contracting with that corporation to carry out certain activities. Thus the hospital invests some of its own funds to the for-profit corporation as equity, buys services through the contract, and expects to earn profits from its ownership position.

Charges for the contractual services between affiliated corporations are a form of transfer pricing.[23] The transfer price is clearly important to the hospital, the partner, and the IRS. It is usually possible to make substantial impact upon subsidiary financial reports by carefully adjusting charges. Many integrated health care organizations pursue these manipulations as a tax avoidance strategy. Unfortunately, the best tax strategy may not fairly reflect operational conditions, and may establish negative incentives for management. Strategies based on accurate assessment of costs and profits have more long-run potential.[24] These attempt to reflect the operation of each subsidiary as if it were a freestanding organization in a competitive market with others.

Securing and Managing Long-Term Funds

Finance is responsible for all loans, bonds, and equity capital. It evaluates alternative financing means, develops a financial strategy to implement the strategic plan, and recommends the best solution to the governing board. It arranges placement of debt and prepares supporting financial information and pro formas, and it manages repayment schedules, mandatory reserves, and other elements of debt obligation. It monitors the financial markets for opportunities to restructure financing. It manages endowments of not-for-profit health care organizations.

The LRFP is used to develop capital needs and sources, including prospectuses for borrowing and equity funding and plans for soliciting capital donations. Most changes in the long-term funds involve large sums of money and are done through bond issues or new corporations with equity financing. Hospitals relied largely on donated capital from both government and private sources prior to 1970. Borrowing became the overwhelming source of capitalization under cost-based reimbursement through the early 1980s. The stimulus of competition promoted a number of innovative financial solutions, including equity funding and the development of multicorporate structures. It is possible for a tax-paying corporation to own a not-for-profit corporation and vice versa, opening the possibility of almost limitless combinations and variations.[25]

Debt and Equity Capitalization

It appears likely that borrowing, principally long-term, tax-exempt bonds, will remain an important form of capital finance for conservative not-for-profit health care organizations. Many well-managed organizations will choose to be in this group, and will deliberately manage their LRFP and operations to attract funds at advantageous rates. Lenders require extensive documentation of assets, income, and net profit. Interest rates and the availability of funds depend upon an effective presentation. Lenders prefer and reward low risk. Thus the organization which demonstrates good results in finance and quality is preferred in the financial marketplace. However, it can maintain that favored position in the long run only to the extent that it invests prudently to enhance its own customer base. Either excess borrowing or insufficient investment can diminish the chance of success in the long run.

Equity finance is generally appropriate for working capital and the support of developmental operating expenses, whereas debt tends to be used to finance real property and long-term assets. Equity is also useful in joint ventures, allowing the partners to be rewarded for successful risk-taking. In general the riskier the enterprise, the more likely and appropriate is capital finance. Investors generally expect returns commensurate with their risk. Venture capitalists, willing to support new and untested ideas, do so in the expectation of returns substantially in excess of anything available in lending markets. Tax laws are quite important in equity finance, both from the point of view of the corporation and that of the investor.

Well-managed health care organizations exercise extreme prudence in the use of both debt and new equity finance. Evidence suggests that there are a great many dangers. Half of all newly formed for-profit corporations are bankrupt within 12 months; it is said that half of the balance fail to survive the next economic downturn. Leverage, the ratio of debt to equity finance, is critical. If debt costs are not covered by revenue, the investors' equity is used. A great many corporations of substantial size and reputation have foundered because they incurred excessive debt. Health care experience is almost all from the period before intense price competition; it has not stood the test of an industry-wide recession. Thus prudence demands small, diversified investments limited to amounts which the organization could lose without seriously impairing its mission.

An example might clarify the complex financial and operational issues involved in capital funds acquisition. Figure 8.11 shows a simplified situation. A certain health care organization might plan to spend $50 million over the next three years to expand primary care and outpatient services. It anticipates a handsome increase in net income of $10 million per year from the new service (20 percent return on investment), with relatively small risk that income will fall below that level. It has several sources for the $50 million. It could use reserves from prior earnings. These are currently earning about 10 percent per year from investments in securities. It could seek tax-exempt bonds, in which case it would pay about 8 percent interest. It could create a for-profit joint venture with its physicians or with another corporation, and raise part of the money from equity investment. Finally, it could combine any or all of these approaches.

The number of questions and assumptions required even in this simple example indicates the complexity and challenge of the exercise. Obviously, accurate forecasts of volume, costs, revenues, and effects on other services are essential, even though opening is several years away. These matters must be addressed in the proposal for the venture, as discussed in Chapters 6 and 7. In addition, financial assumptions must be made about the following:

- *Price and volume interactions for the new service.* Careful understanding of the market tolerance for prices and the risks involved if demand or output does not meet expectations are essential to evaluate the project and the financing mechanisms. In general, current earnings are largely reserved to meet capital replacement costs, debt financing is used for secure, low-risk activities, and equity financing is used where risk and potential reward are high. The joint venture with physicians, for example, would provide strong incentives to exceed volume forecasts.

Figure 8.11 Implications of Alternative Funding Sources for Ambulatory Care Project at HCO, Inc. (millions of dollars)

Scenario	Bond Interest	Physician Income	HCO Investment	HCO Income Gain*	Loss**	Net	ROI***
I. From HCO retained earnings	0	0	$50	$10	$5	$5	10%
II. 50% bonds, 50% retained earnings	$2	0	$25	$8	$2.5	$5.5	22%
III. 50% bonds, 25% retained earn, 25% physician equity	$2	$4	$12.5	$4	$1.25	$2.75	22%

*Earnings from project.
**Losses from earnings on invested funds.
***Net earnings from project as percent of HCO investment.

- *Costs of alternative sources of capital.* Each of the sources has different costs and obligations built into it. The use of retained earnings may impair the organization's ability to meet other needs, such as the replacement of equipment or increase in market share by other means, such as the acquisition of competitors. Bonds will have an interest rate dependent on the market at the time of sale, the organization's overall financial position, and federal tax policy. Organizations which have been prudently managed in the past will have advantages for all kinds of capital. They will have more retained earnings, lower bond interest and more debt capacity, and will be more attractive to outside investors.

- *Impact of the new service on other strategic goals.* The financing may affect competitors in ways advantageous to the organization. A joint venture with primary care physicians may provide an avenue to affiliate them more closely with the organization, and may improve the ability to recruit. A joint venture with a potential competitor may reduce risk and expand resources simultaneously.

- *Tax implications.* If ordinary income taxes apply, they will be approximately 40 percent of earnings, enough to make substantial differences in the results. A tax adviser may be able to find precedents that establish the tax obligations of the various structures, or it may be necessary to seek a letter from the IRS.

The LRFP financial model will be employed to test outcomes not only for the expected conditions but for a range of possible futures. Each major funding avenue will be explored several times, under varying assumptions. Consultants will advise on approaches, assumptions, and implications. The financial results will be evaluated against the marketing and operational considerations. The final solution is likely to draw on all three sources of funds. Scenario III looks attractive, because it allows the institution to limit its capital investment, allows physician participation, and still yields a handsome return of over 20 percent. It can be recommended to the board with widespread support from the participants.

Managing Endowments

Most not-for-profit health care organizations have acquired endowments or permanent charitable funds. These must be invested, and the well-managed hospital invests them in a manner which is consistent with its strategic plan. The funds can be invested for growth or income, or they can be invested in hospital activities, such as malpractice insurance reserves or physical facilities, which return income through leases. The assistance of professional investment managers is advisable. Larger organizations use several different managers. The organization must evaluate its overall investment strategy itself; professional managers cannot make these basic decisions.

Managing Short-Term Assets and Liabilities

Any operation requires **working capital,** funds that are used to cover expenses made in advance of payment for services. The finance system manages these transactions to maximum advantage for the organization. The process is generally called working capital management.

Short-term financial management deals in terms of days. Income can be obtained by moving assets rapidly. Cash is never left in non-interest-bearing accounts. Other liquid assets are placed where they will obtain the highest return consistent with risk and the length of time available. (Large sums of money can be invested for small interest returns on an overnight basis.) Accounts receivable and inventories are minimized because they earn no return. Accounts payable and other debts are settled exactly when due, allowing the organization to use the funds involved as long as possible.

Short-term borrowing is available to health care organizations. Bank loans are the most common source. Short-term borrowing is minimized because it costs money. At the same time, however, costs of borrowing need to be compared to opportunity costs of liquidating assets or failing to meet liabilities in a timely fashion. The objective is to reduce total costs of working capital, rather than to avoid borrowing per se.

Issues in Financial Management

The objective of financial management is to acquire sufficient capital to implement the mission and vision at minimum cost. The trick to doing well lies in financial planning. As usual, it is the farsighted institution which can take advantage of the environment rather than being totally submissive to it. Good financial leadership, through the appointment of an experienced, able CFO and the use of knowledgeable consultants and board members, is obviously essential. But many questions demand the judgment of nonfinancial people, including physicians, the CEO and the governing board.

Maintaining a Realistic Plan

Financial planning starts with the current financial position and some strategic preferences. It develops several ways in which the preferences can be financed, using combinations of cash from operations, borrowing, equity, and gifts. Well-managed institutions select among these using the following principles:

- The bias should be toward liquidity and, as a result, flexibility. Well-run organizations keep the horizon of the plans short, adopt no proposal in the absence of compelling benefit, and maintain options rather than commitments as long as possible.
- The criteria for investment decisions must weigh risk as well as cost against benefit to the community. The result of increased risk is that the total cost of all of the proposals in the plan will rise, thus requiring greater benefits to make them desirable. (Usually this is expressed through an increase in the borrowing interest rate.) There are three basic causes of increased risk: (1) prior actions of the organization have reduced its financial capacity; (2) individual proposals that are inherently risky; and (3) too large a total set of proposals. Well-run organizations minimize their exposure by careful attention to all three. Their bias is against risk in most situations.
- It is helpful to earmark portions of the available funds for various purposes in the strategic plan, such as maintenance of current operations, development of new markets, expansion of primary care affiliations, or development of information systems.
- Timing is frequently important in the price of capital. Well-run organizations allow themselves sufficient flexibility to take advantage of low interest rates and to avoid borrowing at peak rates.
- The recurring question addressed is what profit, or return from operations, the organization should seek. Where competition establishes prices and revenues, this establishes the maximum cost the hospital can incur. Well-run not-for-profit hospitals have tended to seek returns in the range of 5 percent of total costs. For-profit organizations seek before-tax returns two to three times that high. Health care organizations should seek to maintain similar levels.

Pricing and Transfer Pricing

In the new environment, the well-run health care organization operates in a sufficiently attractive and efficient manner to attract satisfactory volumes at prices available in the marketplace. However, depending on the competitive strength of the buyer, individual services may be priced higher or lower than the prevailing market. Both options represent cross subsidies from some patients and their insurers to others, but they also represent ways of attracting necessary volumes and profits. Minimum acceptable prices are theoretically set by the variable cost of the service—if net revenue exceeds marginal cost, the offer should be accepted, assuming a better one cannot be had. Theoretically there is no maximum either to profits or prices, but as a practical matter attention must be paid to the political implications of cross subsidization. The group paying the premium may take the argument into the political arena on its own terms, which may be quite disadvantageous to the hospital.

The organization has some luxury of choice, both to decline offers at unacceptably low prices and to subsidize some services, such as care of the poor. The choice is limited and fragile, however. The role of the governing board in the new environment is to

- Set the desired overall margin from operations as part of financial planning
- Establish pricing guidelines that require board approval for any major cross subsidization
- Support information systems and management capability which will improve the organization's ability to compete by improving variable cost efficiency and by attracting high demand for fixed assets
- Evaluate the political and mission-related aspects of subsidies, charity, or other major departures from desired prices in a political or influence context.

Use of Reserves and Debt

The most general and far-reaching fiscal policy decision facing the governing board is the relative use of debt or reserves. The typical community hospital held long-term debt amounting to close to 50 percent of its assets.[26] Most of this indebtedness was incurred to finance capital for the 15 to 18 percent annual growth hospitals experienced before 1983.

A critical function of the finance committee and the governing board is to set the desired degree of liquidity or leverage. The decision is made via the long-range plan and financial plan, and the results are measured by the ratios of debt to equity and debt service costs to earnings. There are no general guidelines on the "right" values of these ratios, except that it is unwise to impair the bond rating without extremely good justification. The values for other communities and other organizations can be misleading; the appropriate response must be developed out of an understanding of the local community. The following observations may be helpful:

- Many well-run organizations have operated from conservative, or highly liquid, positions in the past. They will probably continue to do so and will be even more successful. The general bias or predisposition of the well-run health care organization is toward liquidity.

- The buyer's movement toward price competition is an expression of real concern with costs. It therefore represents strong pressure for liquidity.

- Serious threat to actual loss of market share is the most compelling reason to sacrifice liquidity.

- Extreme positions of either liquidity or debt require justification. They are probably best justified as temporary phenomena and any organization at such an extreme is generally well advised to be moving back toward a more usual position.

- Health care reform demands extensive capital, in areas that are new for most organizations. Large-scale funding is required to reorganize medical practices, build information systems, and support cost-effective operational changes.

- Health care organizations in highly liquid positions will be presented with substantial opportunities for growth by acquisition.

Personnel and Organization

Various skilled and unskilled personnel work in the finance system of even a small health care organization. Many of these people perform tasks that are indistinguishable from those in any other corporation, while others perform tasks that require extensive familiarity with health care. The chief financial officer and her or his staff develop specifications for these jobs, sometimes in consultation with the outside auditor. On-the-job training is often practical at lower levels, but supervisory people now usually have advanced degrees in accounting or finance. Recruitment of unskilled personnel is rarely difficult.

Skilled personnel, especially those with health care experience are often in short supply. There is a chronic shortage of CFOs. Recruitment should always be national, health-specific knowledge should be highly prized, and the governing board should be directly involved in the CFO selection. Job specifications for CFO of an independently incorporated health care organization tend not to depend upon size. Sustaining qualified professional financial management in small organizations is a severe problem and one that may underlie more mergers and contract management than is recognized. Contract financial management is available through firms providing general management. Auditing firms do not accept responsibility for financial system operations—to do so would destroy their objectivity as auditors—but they do provide substantial ongoing consultation on financial matters to organizations of all sizes.

The Chief Financial Officer

The chief financial officer is accountable for the operation of the finance systems, including the financial management functions, and advise the CEO and the governing board on finance issues. He or she has more access to cash and securities than is typical in commercial corporations, where an employed treasurer assumes the functions of collections, disbursement, and asset control. The hospital treasurer is frequently a trustee who serves principally as chairman of the finance committee. The lack of separation between finance and treasury theoretically increases the risk of defalcation, but convincing evidence of risk is lacking and organizations protect themselves by security bonds and reliance on the external audit.

Training and Skills

Ideally, the CFO should have a master's degree in management or business and be a certified public accountant (CPA). Certification focuses heavily on financial accounting (the issues relating to reporting the position of the firm) and includes practical experience in auditing. It is important to note that certification places little emphasis on two functions that distinguish hospital excellence in finance, control, and financial management. Thus being a CPA is in itself a relatively weak criterion for the job, desirable but not mandatory. Formal education in management is also only desirable, principally because it makes no guarantee of ability and able managers continue to arise without its help. However, it is increasingly likely that a person seriously interested in becoming a CFO will have found an opportunity to earn both a CPA and a master's in business administration.

Experience is more important than formal education or certification. The CFO of a well-run health care organization should have at least 10 years of preparatory experience, which includes exposure to the finance systems of several organizations, familiarity with all functions of the finance system, and demonstrated ability to assist line management in budgeting, cost reporting, and financial planning. This record can be acquired by practice with a public accounting firm on hospital accounts, and deputy experience in a large, well-run health care organization. Evidence of technical skill is important and can be supported both by specimens of work and by references. Evidence of interpersonal skills, particularly the ability to work with people outside the finance department, is also important and can be supported by references. If possible, these should be solicited by telephone or direct interview with non-financial persons familiar with a candidate's work.

Recruitment

Recruitment should always be in national markets, and outside candidates should be considered equally with any promotion from within. Not only does internal promotion foreclose an opportunity to gain fresh perspectives, it increases the risk of defalcation because it concentrates rather than separates responsibility and knowledge. Executive search firms are available to assist in recruitment and selection. Given the importance, technical skill required, and shortage of candidates, use of such firms seems well advised. The larger public accounting firms often assist in finding CFOs and, not surprisingly, are also a major source of supply.

Organization of the Finance System

Internal

The organization of the finance system, like many of its procedures, is dictated by its functions and has been thoroughly codified. Because of the use of separation of activities to protect assets, many aspects of the organization are fixed. The two critical functions, cost control and financial management, require relatively small numbers of people, with the largest numbers of personnel being in various aspects of patient accounting and collections. Figure 8.12 shows a typical organization pattern.

Other structures are possible. Financial management in smaller organizations might be provided by the CFO with an ad hoc team. Figure 8.12 reflects the assignments of information systems, admitting and registration, and materials management (see Chapters 10, 14, and 16). In smaller and more traditional organizations, one or all of these activities might be assigned to the finance system.

Relation of Finance to Line

Almost every part of the organization shown in Figure 8.12 is in direct daily contact with the rest of the hospital, often over sensitive matters. The key to success is maintaining a professional, productive level of exchange. Clear, convenient systems and forms make information gathering as routine as possible, permitting clinical professionals to supply what is necessary at their convenience rather than being interrupted by calls. Continued attention to interdepartmental relations, through orientation and training sessions for finance personnel, also seems helpful. Two fundamentals should be universally understood. First, the accountability hierarchy of general management is responsible for setting, achieving, and departing from the expectations. Second,

Figure 8.12 Organization of the Finance System

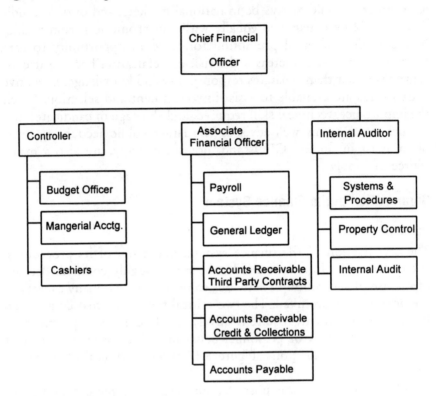

they can carry out this responsibility best in a open atmosphere where information is widely available. The role of finance is to make those statements true.

Role of Finance Committee

In the systems described in this chapter and the planning and marketing chapter, several tasks have been specifically identified for the finance committee of the board:

- Assist in selecting the CFO.
- Periodically review the long-range financial plan and recommend the final version to the full board.
- Approve an annual update of the long-range financial plan.
- Recommend the budget guidelines to the full board: expected surplus from operations, allowable change in total operating cost, and allowable capital investment.
- Recommend pricing policies to the full board.

- Review the proposed annual budget and recommend it to the full board.
- Set the hurdle rate for capital investments.
- Set the final priorities and recommend the capital and new programs budget to the board.
- Receive the monthly report comparing operations to expectations.

In addition, key outside members of the finance committee are usually on the audit committee, where they select and instruct the external auditor and receive the report and management letter. The list makes it clear why membership on the finance committee is time-consuming and intellectually demanding. Members are important at meetings of the full board as well, and there are often overlapping appointments to the planning committee. In addition, the finance committee has routine obligations to approve the hospital's banks and financial contractors, the specific bond or stock offerings, the sale of assets and approval of contracts over predetermined levels, and the approval of officers' salaries and bonuses. Even assuming no turnover in the position of CFO, the list above can easily fill 10 or 11 fast-paced meetings each year.

Poorly run organizations tend to get diverted into narrower, more specific decisions, approving individual purchases, studying current rather than future events, focusing generally on single transactions instead of broad trends. The poorly run finance committee can devote much time to routine obligations, either because they were never integrated properly with the long-range plans and budget or because the committee is uncomfortable dealing with strategic alternatives. The routine obligations are important parts of the system of separation of activity to protect against fraud, but in the well-run organization they take little time. It is evidence of problems if routine actions or current events require debate or contain surprising information.

Measures of Performance

The finance activity can be measured on several of the standard dimensions, but the identification of some parameters, particularly demand and output, is confusing and arbitrary. A practical approach concentrates upon three areas in which finance makes its major contributions to the hospital's success. These are

1. Costs for which finance is directly accountable
2. Collection of revenue and management of liquid assets
3. The quality of information, reporting and consultative services.

Cost Measures

Labor and Contract Services

The finance system has a significant number of employees, consumes much of the computing resource, and often has significant outside contracts for consultation and other services. All of these are costs which should be budgeted, as with any other unit. Accountability can be carried to responsibility centers, as shown in Figure 8.12.

Working Capital Requirements

The funds needed to support operations during the period between provision of service and payment for service represent real resource consumption, although they are not emphasized by the accounting system. Hospitals encounter substantial delays in preparing invoices and receiving payment from third parties, often 12 weeks or more. Although some contracts include advances at regular intervals to offset this lag (*interim payments*), the hospital which minimizes the collection cycle reduces its need for working capital. Inventories are part of working capital; their management is often assigned to materials management units which can be part of plant services (Chapter 16). The lower the inventory, the smaller the cost. Similarly, deferring settlement of short-term obligations such as payroll and accounts payable is financially preferable.

The cost of working capital is the hospital's short-term borrowing rate or earning from investments, whichever is greater. The cost of working capital is not trivial. A medium-sized hospital spending $50 million annually with a 13-week average billing cycle and a four week inventory cycle requires about $15 million in working capital, which will cost about $900,000 per year, the equivalent of 40 full-time employees. Accountability for minimizing the delay is through the CFO to the associate in charge of posting, billing, credit, and collection. It can be further delegated by estimating the delays attributable to each of these groups.

Other Capital Costs

Most health care organizations now borrow funds for various purposes and simultaneously hold long-term investments. The earnings on investments and costs of borrowing are determined in part by the quality of financial planning and financial management. The amounts, timing, and sources of funds determine the costs for a specific project. All of these activities are under the control of the CFO, who should establish and achieve expectations for investment earnings and the cost of capital as part of his or her annual budgets.

Revenue and Asset Management Measures

Operating Revenue Adjustments

The values of revenue adjustments, principally contractual allowances for each third-party contract, bad debts, and charity, can be influenced by effective management. Careful study of third-party contract provisions, billing, and accounting procedures can reveal ways to reduce the allowances. Bad debts can be reduced by more aggressive and more efficient collection policies. Even charity allowances can be limited by careful case review and pursuit of welfare and other third-party coverage.

An expectation should be established for each allowance, and the appropriate RC of the finance group should be held accountable.

Nonoperating Income

Hospitals have a variety of sources of income other than those connected with patient care. Most such income is in rents, dividends, and interest earned, but income from unrelated business is also common. There should be expectations for all major types and sources of nonoperating income, and the chief financial officer should be held accountable for these. Many of these income sources are taxable. Successful management maximizes the return after taxes.

Net Profit from Operations

The expectation for net profit is one of the key elements of the long-range financial plan and is one of the first two short-term expectations set in the annual budget. The CFO, the COO, and the CEO share accountability for meeting it.

Net profit can be volatile, but large well-managed organizations appear to be able to meet expectations most of the time. The net profit figure is dependent on volume, which is well outside the control of the CFO. While some sensitivity to the difficulty of achieving the net profit expectation is in order, the importance of the measure must be recognized. No other statistic so clearly reflects the long-term health of the hospital.

Quality of Financial Planning and Reporting Services

The quality of many of the functions of finance is self-evident or is measured by the output. Quality of the revenue-generating activities, for example, is measured by the adjustment; that of funds management by borrowing costs and interest income. The external audit and the management letter provide qualitative assessment of another large group of finance activities. In two of the five functions, however, the principal product of the system is information, and the quality of the work is not as apparent. These activities are no less critical to success in the long run, however, and there should be expectations for their performance.

Quality of the Financial Plan

Only subjective judgment of the quality of the long-range financial plan is practical. Worse, the people who made the plan are likely to be the ones evaluating it; nonetheless, the importance of periodic review should be obvious. By the time objective tests are available, the organization's existence may be endangered. The following list contains process criteria met by successful organizations:

- The plan is clear, concise, internally consistent, and consistent with the long-range plan.
- Assumptions and their implications are specified.
- Prudent and reasonable sources have been used to develop external trends, and a variety of opinion has been reviewed whenever possible.
- External events requiring modification are unforeseen by competitors as well as this organization.
- The plan is well received by outsiders such as consultants, bond rating agencies, and investment bankers.
- The plan develops contingencies on major, unpredictable future events.

Quality of Patient, Physician, and Third-Party Relations

The finance system has a number of contacts with members of the community and should carry these out in ways that reflect positively upon the hospital. For a great many patients carrying comprehensive health insurance, receiving the final bill can be a positive experience. Even for those who must pay out of pocket, the way in which the charge is presented can make an important difference in the patient's perception. "Guest relations" programs (Chapter 15) are certainly in order for those finance system personnel dealing directly with patients and families. Patient satisfaction surveys usually include questions about finance services.

Many health care organizations now sell accounting and financial management services to physicians. Physician satisfaction will remain a hallmark of the well-managed organization, obviously including satisfaction with the finance system. It is measured by market share and surveys.

Finally, the finance system establishes the image of the hospital in a certain sector of the community, including banks, government agencies, self-insuring employers, and insurance carriers. The well-managed hospital anticipates a reputation of probity, candor, courtesy, and promptness. The CFO and members of his or her staff should anticipate at least informal review of these relationships and should expect to sustain them appropriately.

Quality of Services to Line Managers

The finance system has a clientele for its internal budgeting and reporting activities in the general managers who must use the information. Services to line management are critical to the continuous improvement program. Their criticisms of it should be heeded, particularly when they deal with the accuracy and timeliness of the information. Concerns with conciseness, clarity, and level of specification are also important.

Advice from finance personnel to general managers is also a sensitive matter, and direct assessment of the opinion of general managers about such advice is wise. There is a tendency for finance personnel to enter into the expectation-setting process and the monitoring process beyond what good practice indicates. Consultation and information are likely to be helpful, but intrusion can destroy the motivation for continued improvement, because it erodes the capacity of general managers to set and achieve their own expectations.

Suggested Readings

Berman, H. J., S. F. Kukla, and L. E. Weeks. 1993. *The Financial Management of Hospitals*, 8th ed. Ann Arbor, MI: Health Administration Press.

Gapenski, L. C. 1993. *Understanding Health Care Financial Management: Text, Cases, and Models*. Ann Arbor, MI: AUPHA Press/Health Administration Press.

Hilton, R. W. 1994. *Managerial Accounting*, 2d ed. New York: McGraw-Hill.

Prince, T. R. 1992. *Financial Reporting and Control for Health Care Entities*. Ann Arbor MI: AUPHA Press/Health Administration Press.

Swieringa, R. J., and R. H. Moncur. 1975. *Some Effects of Participative Budgeting on Managerial Behavior*. New York: National Association of Accountants.

Notes

1. P. H. Campbell, J. Hoch, and D. Kouba, 1990, *Physician Compensation: A Guidebook for Community and Migrant Health Centers* (Rockville, MD: U.S. Department of Health and Human Services, Health Resources and Administration, Bureau of Healthcare Delivery Assistance).
2. T. R. Prince, 1992, *Financial Reporting and Cost Control for Health Care Entities* (Ann Arbor, MI: Health Administration Press), 27–146.
3. Ibid., 87–116.

4. R. W. Hilton, 1994, *Managerial Accounting*, 2d ed. (New York: McGraw-Hill), 5.

5. Prince, *Financial Reporting and Cost Control*, 219–88.

6. Ibid., 89–378.

7. Hilton, *Managerial Accounting*, 618–26.

8. B. C. James, 1993, "Implementing Practice Guidelines through Clinical Quality Improvement," *Frontiers of Health Services Management* 10 (Fall): 3–37.

9. J. R. Griffith, D. G. Smith, and J. R. C. Wheeler, 1994, "Continuous Improvement of Strategic Information Systems: Concepts and Issues," *Health Care Management Review* 19 (2): 43–53.

10. James, "Implementing Practice Guidelines," 3–37.

11. Hilton, *Managerial Accounting*, 374–75.

12. Ibid., 502–25.

13. W. O. Cleverley, 1992, *Essentials of Health Care Finance*, 3d ed. (Gaithersburg, MD: Aspen Publishers), 298–310.

14. H. J. Berman, S. F. Kukla, and L. E. Weeks, 1993, *The Financial Management of Hospitals*, 8th ed. (Ann Arbor, MI: Health Administration Press), 385–585.

15. M. A. Abemethy and J. U. Stoelwinder, 1991, "Budget Use, Task Uncertainty, System Goal Orientation and Subunit Performance: A Test of the 'Fit' Hypothesis in Not-For-Profit Hospitals," *Accounting Organizations and Society* 16 (2): 105–20.

16. R. J. Swieringa and R. H. Moncur, 1975, *Some Effects of Participative Budgeting on Managerial Behavior* (New York: National Association of Accountants).

17. J. D. Suver, W. F. Jessee, and W. N. Zelman, 1986, "Financial Management and DRGs," *Hospital & Health Services Administration* 31 (January–February): 75–85; S. A. Finkler, 1985, "Flexible Budget Variance Analysis Extended to Patient Acuity and DRGs," *Health Care Management Review* 10 (4): 21–34.

18. Berman et al., *Financial Management*, 46.

19. Ibid.

20. American Institute of Certified Public Accountants, 1973, *Code of Professional Ethics*, article 101.

21. L. C. Gapenski, 1992, *Understanding Health Care Financial Management* (Ann Arbor, MI: Health Administration Press), 595–634.

22. Ibid., 539–71.

23. Hilton, *Managerial Accounting*, 618–26.

24. R. Cooper and R. S. Kaplan, 1988, "Measure Costs Right: Make the Right Decisions," *Harvard Business Review* 66 (September–October): 25–103.

25. J. S. Coyne, 1985, "Hospital Performance in Multi-institutional Organizations Using Financial Ratios," *Health Care Management Review* 10 (4): 35–55.

26. M. L. Lynn and P. Wertheim, 1993, "Key Financial Ratios Can Foretell Hospital Closures," *Healthcare Financial Management* 47 (November): 66–70.

INFORMATION REQUIREMENTS FOR
THE LEARNING ORGANIZATION

WELL-MANAGED health care organizations pursuing the theory outlined in Chapter 3 study their open systems environment, develop
community-oriented strategies in response, and continuously improve
their ability to deliver on these strategies. They have a strong customer focus, an emphasis on mission and vision, and a commitment
to empowering their operating core. This philosophy leads them to
the activities described so far in this book—a strategically focused
governing board, a flexible, decentralized organization, and a service-
oriented executive and technical support group.

Accomplishing these activities requires decision processes which
solve problems and meet member needs. There are always tasks of
coordination and adaptation to be solved. Resolving competing needs
in ways each member can accept is essential. Solutions must be realistic
and convincing. Well-managed health care organizations rely heavily
on their decision processes, and the processes excel through the use
of quantitative data. Knowledge bases, communications media, and
decision processes are as important as the physical resources; they
distinguish the effective organization from the Tower of Babel.

Purpose of Quantitative Information

The purpose of quantitative information in organizations is to improve
the quality of exchanges between the organization and its external

partners and within the organization between its constituents. Quantitative information allows communication about expectations and performance to be

- Explicit—"High blood pressure" is ambiguous. "Diastolic pressure of 100 mm of mercury" is unambiguous. "High health insurance cost" is ambiguous. "One hundred forty dollars per member per month" is explicit. Removing ambiguity clarifies communication and speeds conclusion of negotiation;

- Precise—"Diastolic pressure of 100 +/− 5 mm mercury" and "$140 per member per month guaranteed" are statements of precision. Precision is only possible with quantitative information. Much scientific and economic advance depends upon precision;

- Efficient—The concept of blood pressure measurement offers a new order of medical control. The graph in Figure 9.1A conveys quantitative information which actually defines the disease of hypertension. A full explanation of Figure 9.1A would be quite lengthy, but any literate person can see the message, "This patient's blood pressure is trending upwards and is already in the dangerous range." Figure 9.1B shows the same graph, but with different dimensions. Its message is, "The cost of our services is trending upward and has already exceeded the amount our customer agreed to pay."

- Timely—Information which is explicit, precise, and efficient can be conveyed quickly. The message reaches the person or group which can do something about it in time for them to act.

Peter Senge has noted the importance of the learning organization, the organization that can meet the steadily changing marketplace, in modern society. He says the learning organization is

> An organization that is continually expanding its capacity to create its future. For such an organization it is not enough merely to survive. "Survival learning" or what is more often termed "adaptive learning" is important—indeed it is necessary. But for a learning organization, "adaptive learning" must be joined by "generative learning," learning that enhances our capacity to create.[1]

Rapid learning, quick response, and close tolerances demand numbers, because words alone are too ambiguous, too inefficient, and too slow.

Purpose of Chapters 9 and 10

This chapter is devoted to a systematic exploration of the use of numbers in health care management. It discusses what they are, where they come from, and how they are analyzed. The chapter which follows describes the information servicing component of the organization, the

Figure 9.1   Efficiency Possible with Quantitative Information

A. Patient's Diastolic Blood Pressure

Patient's diastolic blood pressure by quarter

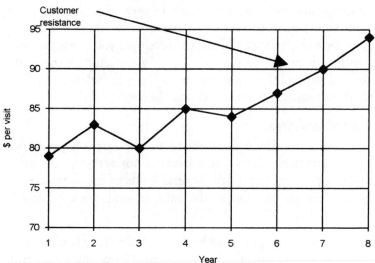

B. Cost of Care per Member per Month

Dollars per visit

design and operation of which collects, archives, and communicates quantitative data. Taken together, the purpose of Chapters 9 and 10 is to describe how the well-managed health care organization gains a competitive advantage from information handling.

Sources of Quantitative Information

The only disadvantage to the use of quantitative information is the cost of collecting the supporting data. Much of this cost is hidden from the accounting system, but it is real. The solution is to make the data collection as efficient as possible, and the keys to efficient data collection are an understanding of data needs, a systematic scheme for collecting data as a routine part of care activities themselves, and an understanding of the levels of precision required.

Data Describing Performance in Organizations

Figure 9.2 shows the dimensions of information required to measure performance of health care activities. They provide a comprehensive description of performance for a responsibility center or a final product. Three of these dimensions, demand, cost, and revenue, are familiar from the accounting system where their measurement originated. They are expanded here from the traditional accounting view, reflecting market issues around the nature of health care as a product or service. The other three are more recent additions, reflecting increased market concerns and improved measurement technology. Conceptually at least, the six dimensions apply to any product or service. A manufacturer or a hairdresser would want to know demand, cost, workers available, sales, quality, and profit, but as the detail develops, the measures become unique to health care. The six are clearly interrelated, often in precise mathematical terms. If all six are managed, the business is likely to succeed; if even one is overlooked, it is likely to fail.

Input-Related Measures

Three measurement dimensions relate to the starting points of the exchange. There must always be a demand for service, raw materials, and people to perform the work. Several kinds of measures are needed for each dimension, to support the various kinds of decisions which must be made.

Demand *Patient management.* In health care, the issue is not simply the existence of a willing buyer. Under managed care, the buyer must be willing, but the service must also be necessary. As described in Chapter 7, sophisticated patient management is promoting cost-effective patient behavior and cost-effective use of services. Demand measures include the number of patients demanding service, in a variety of demographic, economic, and clinical categories or market segments. They include direct and indirect measures of the appropriateness of demand, for example, number of nonurgent emergency visits or number of mothers

Figure 9.2 Dimensions of Health Care Performance

Input-Oriented	Output-Oriented
Demand	**Outputs**
Patient management	Treatments
Clinical management	Productivity
Logistic management	
Cost/Resources	**Quality**
Physical counts	Clinical outcomes
Costs	Patient satisfaction
Resource condition	Access
	Procedural quality
	Structural quality
Human Resources	**Revenue/Constraint**
Supply	Net revenue
Satisfaction	Profit
	Implicit price

presenting at term without prenatal care. They also include measures of promotional efforts to modify these numbers, such as "percent of young women obtaining annual physical visit," or "number of promotional exposures directed at young women."

Clinical management. Much demand for health care services is generated by professionals within the process. It is subject to different management techniques directed at different audiences, but it is measured similarly to patient demand management. "Number of chest films per pneumonia patient" and "number of ultrasound examinations per pregnancy" are examples. "Number of pneumonia patients without chest film" is an example of demand that should have been generated but was not. (The x-ray is indicated in almost all cases.) Such process quality measures can be built into computerized systems as reminders. The process prompts for the x-ray as soon as the diagnosis of pneumonia is entered.

Logistic management. Time is often essential in demand management. Demand must often be expressed in relatively specific periods—per hour or shift, for example. Scheduling systems, staffing levels, and facility loads affect access and output. Other important logistical statistics are expressed in potential units of output. "Maximum visits per week" and "available appointments per day" are examples.

Costs and resources *Physical units* are units of specific production resources, people, supplies, and equipment, paralleling the natural accounts of accounting. Examples are "hours of RN care," "doses of penicillin," and "hours of operating room." Physical quantities are important in managing production processes; staffing decisions and care decisions are made about physical resources, not dollar amounts.

Costs are economic measures of resources. Physical units are multiplied by a market or transfer price to obtain costs. Costs are recorded by natural and general ledger accounts, and expressed as variable, semivariable and fixed; direct and indirect; and average or marginal, as discussed in Chapter 8. A high degree of detail is necessary. Examples are "costs of registered nurse care," "cost of penicillin," and "cost of hotel services".

Resource condition measures are important in some processes. "Percent of rooms out of service for cleaning," "percent of inventory items out of stock," and "percent of laboratory reagents out of date" are examples. Human resources are addressed in a separate category.

Human resources *Supply measures* count numbers of workers available, by skill level. As health care facilities cross-train personnel, counts of workers with specific training and multiple training become important. The supply measure, number of nurses available, is not identical to the cost measure, number paid in a given time period because pay can be flexible, based on actual work done.

Satisfaction measures assess worker and physician satisfaction with all aspects of working conditions. It is important to differentiate among various professions because they have different responses and different supply markets. Physicians may or may not be employees, but they cannot be omitted. Satisfaction affects both retention of current workers and recruitment of future ones.

Output-Related Measures

These dimensions relate to the finished product or service itself. The number of units produced, the efficiency, the quality, and the profitability are all essential.

Outputs *Treatments.* Outputs can be counted as specific services (intermediate products) or episodes of care for individual patients (final products). Although output is closely related to demand, it is important to understand and implement the difference between request for service and delivery of service. Some useful access measures are the ratio of the two: well-baby examinations requested versus examinations performed, for example. In complex organizations, the ratio is not automatically 100 percent.

Productivity. Productivity, or efficiency, measures include any ratio of inputs to outputs, or vice versa. Lab tests/hour worked is a productivity measure. So is length of stay. (It's days of care consumed/patient treated, a measure of resources used divided by the output.) Load and occupancy ratios are productivity measures; they compare the resource used (an output) to the resource available (an input). Bed occupancy (number of patient days of care rendered/number of bed days available) is an example. Convenience and tradition cause some ratios to be inverted. It does not matter because:

$$inputs/outputs = 1/(outputs/inputs)$$

Quality *Clinical outcomes measures* assess the global result of care, usually whether the patient lived or died, got better or not. "Perinatal mortality" and "Hip surgery patients walking after six weeks" are examples. Outcomes are difficult to assess in many situations, such as terminal care. The measures are not sensitive in others, because only very small percentages of patients fail to meet the standard. Finally, outcomes measures are difficult to relate to specific events. For example, if 2 percent of patients fail to walk six weeks after hip surgery, why did they fail? Was it poor surgical technique, poor postoperative care, or factors outside the normal care system, such as a subsequent accident or lack of motivation on the patient's part?

Patient satisfaction measures, whether the patient was pleased with the care received, are a form of outcomes measure. They are distinguished by the patient viewpoint, rather than the professional one which prevails with clinical outcomes.

Access measures reveal whether market demand is met, and how promptly. They are frequently developed from demand and human resources data. "Primary care physicians accepting new patients," "weeks delay for routine physical appointment," and "minutes for cardiac resuscitation team arrival" are examples. Access measures closely resemble logistics management measures; the two should be distinguished to capture real effectiveness of the system

Procedural quality measures are usually ratios of compliance to accepted clinical practice. "Percent of patients with care plans" and "percent of patients asked to file advance directives" are examples.

Structural measures deal with resources present, so that some productivity measures can be used to infer quality or the lack of it. "RN hours/patient day" and "Primary care doctor minutes/visit" are examples. Many are simple yes/no tallies covering safety equipment, sanitation procedures, and the like. Although structural, process, satisfaction, and outcomes measures are presumably interrelated, the difficulties of obtaining quality measures and the different aspects covered lead most institutions to use all forms.

Revenue *Net revenue* the price actually paid by the customer, is the clearest known expression of customer and market desires. It therefore creates the acid test of operations wherever it can be applied.

Profit tests relate directly to the growth and survival of the health care organization. As indicated in Chapter 8, the RC or final product team should expect to earn a profit margin justified from the LRFP by making unit costs less than net revenue. The number of levels where net revenue is directly available and fairly reflects market decisions is dropping rapidly. Under pure capitation, it is available only for the organization as a whole.

Implicit prices construct artificial revenues and profits for those units where true revenue is not available. It remains essential to have some acceptable test of economic performance; in the absence of market revenue a proxy must be constructed. Implicit prices use transfer prices to compare to costs. The approach remains valid where the proxy is related to market realities. An alternative method establishes allowable unit costs for the service under study, using benchmarks or negotiated proportions of an aggregate revenue.

Examples of Performance Measures

These dimensions are measured in different ways in different activities, but they are applicable to almost any level of aggregation, from individual task to health care organization as a whole. Figure 9.3 gives three examples, a single home health visit by a trained health aide (an intermediate product), an inpatient episode for hip replacement (a final product), and a comprehensive HMO provider (an organization). As the dimensions are applied to more aggregate situations, they fit closely with the balanced scorecard approaches being used to report governing board performance, as Figure 9.3 shows.

Data Collection

Performance measures are generated as a part of the work itself. Each activity is recorded, either electronically or on paper, in specified forms which generate the data. With six dimensions for each RC and final product, multiple measures for most dimensions, several dozen important final products and 50 to 100 RCs, the volume of data which must be processed is very large, running thousands of items per day. To fulfill its purposes, information must be accurate. But there is obviously a limit to the amount of resources that can be expended

Figure 9.3 Examples of Performance Measurement

Dimension	Home Health Visit	Hip Replacement	HMO
Demand	Number of visits requested, by type	Number of patients referred for surgery	Number of members, market share
	Time schedule for visits	Appropriateness of referral	Use of telephone triage
Cost/ Resources	Nurse hours	Hospital days	Hospital days
	Supplies cost	Prosthesis cost	Cost of hospitalization
Human resources	Number of nurses cross-trained	Number of orthopedic surgeons	Number of primary care practitioners
	Nurse satisfaction	Surgeon satisfaction	Physician satisfaction
Outputs	Number of visits completed	Number of procedures	Number of member months
	$ per visit	$ per case	$ per member/ month
Quality	Patient satisfaction	Patient satisfaction	Patient satisfaction
	Patient condition	Patient mobility	Number of high-risk births
	% visit protocol met	% care protocol met	Patients with appropriate preventive care
Revenue	Net $ per visit	Net $ per case	Premium $ available for health care
	Profit per visit	Profit per case	Profit per member/month

on data collection. The issue is to design ways of collecting data that are accurate, convenient, and cheap, and the answer is the computer.

Advantages of Automation

Computers contribute to efficient data collection in several ways. These advantages are summarized in Figure 9.4.

- Input can be speeded and controlled by programs which prompt for completeness and audit for consistency. Omissions, spelling, and inconsistencies can be corrected immediately, eliminating errors and confusion. For example, the entry "William Smith, Social Security # 187-27-0887, admitted for pediatric asthma" looks reasonable, but checked against an electronic data base several questions would arise: Is this William G. Smithe, aged 40, Social Security # 187-27-0877? If yes, is pediatric asthma the correct diagnosis, or is it adult asthma? If no, what are the middle initial and age?

- Electronic recovery and communication make it possible to eliminate repeated entry. For example, most patient orders must have at least two means of identifying the patient. Electronic identification substitutes an audit of the request for laborious copying of names and numbers. The laboratory will not receive Smithe's specimen and report it as Smith's.

- Automation can change many patient care decisions from recall to recognition by prompting for the clinically indicated next step. Recognition is faster and more accurate than recall. Expectations translate to check lists and prompts which, in themselves, improve performance. If a specific test or procedure is mandatory for a certain condition, a prompt will appear in the automated ordering sequence whenever the doctor identifies the condition.

- By using agreed upon care plans, a variety of clinical situations can be programmed to prevent accidental error. For example, the following can be prevented by expanding the audit functions to include clinical guidelines:
  - Some accidental misstatements and omissions
  - Inappropriate therapy selections (as with drugs of similar name but different uses)
  - Conflicts with prior orders
  - Absence of supporting diagnostic tests or values
  - Interactions between drugs
  - Failure to obtain consultation or supervision.

- Output can be speeded and organized. When the laboratory does Smithe's tests, the report will be available to the physician immediately, together with the history of Smithe's prior tests. The precision of the laboratory test value and the range of values in a comparable normal population can be added to assist in interpreting the tests.

- Calculations can be made rapidly and cheaply. Smithe's laboratory results can instantaneously update the mean and standard deviation of each test. They can be cross-referenced by his final product, adult asthma. The tests can be entered on his patient ledger and priced, and added to the laboratory daily output statistics.
- An accessible archive is created. The data can be retrieved for Smithe, for the test, for the laboratory, for the insurance intermediary, and for adult asthma. Statistical data bases combine Smithe's data with other in each class.

Major Data Systems

The principal data systems that generate the six dimensions of information are shown in Figure 9.5. Although the groupings can be revised, about 12 systems are necessary to support the information needs of a modern health care organization. The systems can be conveniently grouped into those that emphasize capture of data, those that support the background record keeping and analysis, and those that directly support decisions by caregivers and others in the provider organization. Although considerable amounts of data are still processed manually at some stages of their collection, enormous strides have been made in

Figure 9.4 Contributions of Automated Data Systems

Contribution	Example
1. Rapid, audited input	Automatic check for name, identity, spelling, vital statistics
2. No repeat input	All users access central registration file for patient ID and medical condition
3. Recognition for clinical tasks	Protocol suggests normally indicated treatment, can request either order or explanation before proceeding
4. Verification and cross-check of orders	Drugs checked for patient sensitivity, interactions
5. Prompt result reporting	Instantaneous transmission of diagnostic test findings
6. Statistical and accounting calculations	Charges to date, variance or range of history of laboratory values
7. Accessible archive	Comparison to similar patients, similar procedures

Figure 9.5 Major Data Processing Systems

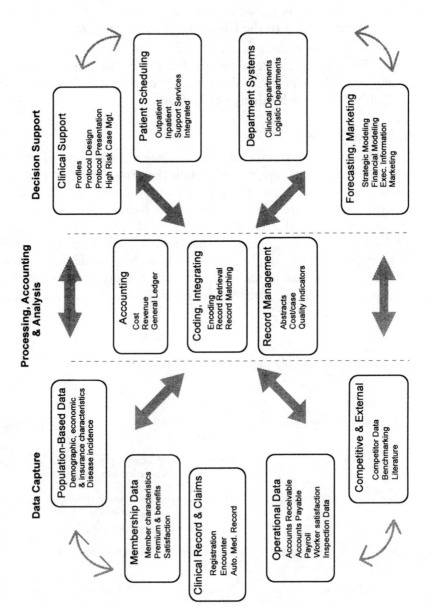

automation in recent years, and even larger ones are likely for the near future. The drawback to computerization is that the systems to do it cost tens or hundreds of millions of dollars and take years to develop. The payback is considerably larger than the investment, however. Even the smallest health care organizations are developing computer capability, and it is unlikely that organizations which do not automate most of each of the twelve principal data systems will survive. The activities and status of each system are as follows.

Data capture

1. *Population assessment systems.* These capture the underlying demographic, economic, and epidemiologic character of the organization's potential market. Current data and trends geographic distributions, age, child-bearing habits, employment, health insurance, disease patterns, and risk factors are used to evaluate population needs, market share, and market opportunities. The data for these systems come from a variety of sources, but purchase of electronic census and related data is spreading rapidly.

2. *Membership systems.* These record details of health insurance coverage, including dependents, and utilization for individual subscribers, and group, benefits, premium, and account status for groups. The records are essential for insurance operations, but also supply data for clinical support activities. The systems are almost completely automated.

3. *Clinical transaction and claims systems.* These record the name, vital statistics and details of care for each patient. They also capture records used for payment of providers and track **censuses**, counts of patients actively using various inpatient facilities. Each patient is assigned a unique lifetime number and the systems include elaborate mechanisms to identify patients quickly and correctly. The data from the systems drive much of the processing and accounting activity and are essential for all the decision support systems on the right side of Figure 9.5. Patient registration, order entry and results reporting are highly automated, and automation is increasing rapidly.

4. *Operational systems.* These record the day-to-day business of the providers, including initial accounting transactions such as payables and payroll. They also record process quality data and worker satisfaction data. The system is essential for provider operation, but it also supports analysis of work processes and worker morale. Many of the accounting transactions are automated, but much of the quality and satisfaction data is manually collected and entered for automated storage and retrieval.

5. *Competitor analysis systems.* These capture data about local competitors and also benchmark and best practice data about similar operations elsewhere. The data come from a wide variety of sources and are frequently estimated or inferred. They are essential for forecasting and marketing activities. The systems are rarely automated.

Processing, accounting, and analysis

6. *Accounting systems.* These perform a variety of accounting and financial calculations, including cost accounting and financial analysis. They include generation of receivables, payables, payrolls employment benefits, and personnel records of skill, age, and cross-training. The general ledger function provides indirect cost data. The information is used by all the decision support activities, including clinical support. The systems are highly automated.

7. *Coding and integrating systems.* These systems allow aggregation of accounting and medical record data by disease, patient characteristic, or site of care. They include the various patient classification systems. They are essential to translate individual patient and provider records to aggregates useful for decision support. The systems are almost completely automated.

8. *Record management systems.* These aggregate individual transactions by patient to form the medical record or history. The medical record itself is a critical part of care management. Aggregated by various patient characteristics of interest through the coding system, the information generated is used in all decision support systems. Record systems are partly automated, and major investments are being made to complete automation. It is likely that all but a few relatively rare transactions will be automated within the next few years.

Decision support

9. *Clinical support systems.* These generate statistical analyses, and profiles which are used to identify patient care improvement opportunities. They also include care protocols and other agreements on clinical procedures and expectations. The systems are largely manual at the present time, but automation will spread with automation of medical record systems.

10. *Patient scheduling systems.* These use historic data on demand and accounting data on availability and cost to schedule patient care transactions. They are partially automated, and growing more sophisticated.

11. *Departmental service and reporting systems.* These govern the internal activities of departments, including many aspects of detailed efficiency and quality control. They include personnel

scheduling, materials management, work processes, quality inspections, and a variety of internal records. Automation varies by department, but specially designed systems are available for the larger clinical departments and most technical and logistic support activities.

12. *Planning and marketing data systems.* These translate data from all other systems to scenarios and forecasts of future events, and are used to evaluate strategies and record strategic decisions. They include financial planning models, models of market development and competitor analysis, and planning data bases for facilities, human resources and information development. Data capture and reporting are increasingly automated through executive information systems. Major strides have been made in the automation of modeling, although the decision processes are supported, rather than directed by the models.

In addition to these sources for routine, ongoing data collection, special nonrecurring studies are also useful. Using research techniques, measurements can be as reliable and valid as desired, within the limits of current technology. Special studies are useful for a variety of purposes, including verifying assumptions about improvement in performance, evaluating new methods or new measures, or collecting very expensive performance measures. Surveys of doctor, patient, and community attitudes, now routine, can be expanded to address particular issues in depth. Processes can be studied in detail, and proposed improvements can be evaluated by special analyses or field trials. Marginal and variable costs can be evaluated in depth. Proposals for new routine measures can be pretested. Investigations of medical and nursing care for specific kinds of cases can be conducted, including formal trials of new methods.

Approaches to Quantification

Only a few health care activities lend themselves easily to measurement. Patients, workers, and dollars come in discrete units and are easily counted. Gender and age and a few other characteristics are easily quantified. Most of the rest of the activities and characteristics do not translate from descriptions to numbers so easily. They are services which often leave no clear trace after they are performed. They tend to continue over long periods of time without discrete stopping points. No two patients or treatments are ever alike; two activities with the same name are quite different when performed on different patients. It is rare to find a single measure of either an activity or an outcome; multiple dimensions must be considered. As a result, quantifying the six dimensions is a matter of continually searching for measures that evolve from crude, almost subjective beginnings. The measures themselves can be understood as estimations which improve in precision as they evolve.

Design and improvement of measures involves scaling, specification of populations, and adjustments to compare diverse populations.

Scaling

The process for translating real activities and characteristics is called scaling. There are four measurement categories, or scales. All are useful, and measurement may evolve through several before reaching the most useful ratio scales. Figure 9.6 summarizes scaling.

1. *Nominal scales.* These identify categories that are useful in accommodating the differences in patients, such as gender, race, or specific diagnoses. Classifications for disease, procedure, and prescription drugs are all nominal scales underpinning health care computerization. The International Classification of Diseases is a nominal scale now used almost universally to describe the illnesses leading to hospitalization. It became the foundation for another famous nominal scale, DRGs. Other nominal scales are useful in differentiating personnel and activities. For example, natural account classifications and aggregates of responsibility centers are nominal scales.

   Nominal scales generate *attributes* measures, that is a binary (yes or no) value for each case. The principal statistic for an attributes measure is the portion passing a certain threshold: portion passing = number yes's/total number examined.

2. *Ordinal scales.* These identify categories that move reliably in a uniform direction, so higher numbers represent consistently different situations from lower ones. (Nominal scales are assigned arbitrarily so that high numbers have no intrinsic meaning.) The five numerical classes of Papanicolaou smears, for example, indicate progressively more serious disease as the numbers get higher. Burns, cancers, respiratory distress, infant distress, and several other clinical characteristics are quantified by ordinal scales. For example, intensive care units use an ordinal scale to determine patient condition and necessity for admission.[2] Individual patients' daily nursing requirements are often assessed with ordinal scales.[3] Satisfaction questionnaires use ordinal scales.

   Ordinal scales are usually treated as attributes measures. Often two or more ordinal categories are grouped together to form the portion passing.

3. *Interval scales.* These are ordinal scales that have uniform values between entries, but an arbitrary end point or starting point. Temperature is an easily recognized interval scale, because two

popular scales, Celsius and Fahrenheit, both have uniform ordinal steps (degrees), but they have two different, equally arbitrary zero points. As a result, it is impossible to make relative comparisons. A fever of 100° F is not 1.4 percent worse than normal; the same condition expressed in Celsius is 37.78° C, 2 percent worse than the Celsius normal of 37.0°. Blood pressure is an interval scale. The starting point, atmospheric pressure, is not only variable, it bears no intrinsic relation to the disease of hypertension. A diastolic pressure of 100 mm mercury is not 25 percent worse than 80 mm mercury.

4. *Ratio scales.* A ratio scale fulfills all the requirements of interval measures but has, in addition, a nonarbitrary zero value. This permits the use of percentages. Height, weight, and percentile standing on comparative distributions are all ratio scales. In accounting, dollars are a ratio scale. Most integer counts, such as discharges, patient-days, and treatments, can be processed as ratio scales, but nominal or ordinal scales must be used to group them into comparable sets.

Ratio scales generate *variables* measures, that is a value can be assigned to the individual measurement. The principal statistics for variables measures are the familiar mean and standard deviation.

There are a variety of mechanisms for translating between scales, but translations can be difficult, costly, and in some important cases, impossible. For example, ordinal, interval, and ratio scales of illness simply do not exist. There are limited ordinal scales for ability to perform activities of daily living, but their meaning outside the specific use for which they were designed is highly speculative.[4] It is clear that patients who cannot handle their own toileting need more nursing care than patients who cannot feed themselves. It is not clear that they are more disabled, and simply false to say they are sicker.

Specification and Adjustment

Most process measures are dependent both upon the process being measured and the characteristics of the population involved. It is important to separate the two; serious errors result if a difference attributable to a population is taken as reflecting a process. One cannot infer anything by comparing the death rates of Utah and Florida without understanding that the Florida population is much older than Utah's. Most diseases and health related events are associated with specific ages, and many are also associated with gender and economic status. Specification and adjustment are used to accommodate differences in the population. Both require the ability to categorize the population into subgroups using nominal scales. The value of the measure and the

Figure 9.6 Scales for Quantifying Information

Scale	Description	Examples	Uses	Limitations
Nominal	Scale without rank or comparability	Men/women; DRGs	Identifying different populations	No comparison between groups, no analysis within group
Ordinal	Ordered scale, intervals not even in size or importance	Patient satisfaction scores, infant Apgar scores	Classifying complex events by desirability or action required	Comparison between groups, no analysis within group
Interval	Even, predictable categories, but no absolute end point	Temperature, blood pressure	Finer classification by desirability or action required	Little advantage over ordinal
Ratio	Ordered scale with even or predictable categories and an absolute end point	Height, percentile standing, dollars	Comparison between and within group, calculation of variance and means	Strongest scale

population subgroup must be available for each individual case. If data are available for a measure y_{ij} in n cases covering m subgroups $j, k, \ldots m$:

Crude rate = Value for n cases

$$\bar{y} = \left(\sum_{i=1}^{n} y_i \right) / n$$

Specific rate for category j = Value for j cases in subgroup j

$$\bar{y}_j = \sum_{j=1}^{j} (y_{ij}) / j$$

Adjusted rate = Value for all cases adjusted to a standard distribution of categories, where

p_j = proportion of the standard population in category j

$$\bar{y}_{adj} = \sum \left(\bar{y}_j(p_j) + \bar{y}_k(p_k) + \ldots + \bar{y}_m(p_m) \right)$$

Figure 9.7 shows the crude, specific, and age-adjusted death rates for Utah and Florida. Are Floridians more likely to die than Utahns, as the crude rates suggest? Yes, they are if they are under 65, but not among Florida's large retired population. And overall, an age-adjusted comparison shows the Florida rate to be 20 percent lower than Utah, not 73 percent higher as the crude rates indicate. Each adjustment requires additional data and calculations, but the misleading character of the crude rate is clearly shown.

Criteria for Selecting Measures

One judges the acceptability of a measure by its value and its cost. Value is indicated by the extent to which the monitor is able to improve performance using the measure. It is usually related to validity, reliability, and timeliness. Costs include the costs of designing the measure, training people in its collection and use, and the cost of data capture, transmission, and storage. Conceptually, both value and cost must be measured against the mission of the organization. If the measure contributes more to achievement than it costs to maintain, it is desirable, but neither values nor costs are easy to measure themselves.

Value

Measures are valuable because they assist the monitor in achieving control. If, for example, a given system for reporting budgeting and

Figure 9.7 Age-Specific, Crude, and Adjusted Rates, Utah versus Florida

Age Category	Utah Deaths	Utah Population	Utah Death Rate	Florida Deaths	Florida Population	Florida Death Rate
0–14	450	538	8.4	2,742	2,412	11.4
15–44	804	789	10.2	11,822	5,595	21.1
45–64	1,446	245	59.0	19,367	2,548	76.0
65–75	2,894	90	321.6	30,618	1,369	223.7
>75	4,624	62	754.8	68,168	1,059	643.7
Sum	10,218	1,742	59.3	122,077	12,983	94.0
Crude death rate			59.3			94.0
Utah death rate standardized to Florida population						113.0

payroll cost allows the monitor to maintain operations while reducing labor costs by $5,000 per year, that is its value. Unfortunately it is rarely possible to isolate the contribution of a specific measure or even a measurement system. The value of information is frequently confounded by other forces causing behavioral change. Market pressures may have pushed the organization to redesign the budget and payroll process. The new process is computerized and much more carefully measured. The new data show the $5,000 improvement in cost and other improvements in quality, but not the relative importance of the three changes. Isolating the contribution of the new measures from the market pressures and the redesigned process is impossible.

The association between value and reliability, validity, and timeliness is similarly complex. Generally speaking, the more reliable, valid, and timely the measure is, the greater its value will be, but there are two important exceptions. First, when a crude measure is introduced it may cause dramatic changes in performance, the so-called sentinel effect. Second, improvements in measures are only useful up to the point at which the monitor can no longer change actual performance.

Cost

The cost of a measurement system is a combination of two elements, first, the resources consumed in obtaining, processing, reporting, and setting expectations for it and second, the costs of incorrect reports. It is convenient to label the first group accounting costs and the second hidden costs. Thoughtful measurement design must always address both.

Accounting costs are frequently buried in other activities. The cost of the data entry to order a test, administer a drug, or take an x-ray are lumped together with other parts of the activity. They can only be identified by special study. Marginal costs of new measures are low, but a systematic expansion of data processing capability may cost tens of millions. It may permit hundreds of additional measurements, making the true cost of each unmeasurable. Not only hardware and software is involved in the expansion cost; measurement definitions, scaling, tests of validity, and training of personnel are all initial investment costs.

Accounting costs tend to increase with improvements in reliability, validity, and timeliness, but automation has greatly reduced accounting costs and simultaneously increased the accuracy and timeliness. The same basic data collection and processing system can be used to generate a large number of accurate measures. Careful attention to system design allows improvements in accuracy and timeliness at modest increase in cost.

Hidden costs occur because of two possible incorrect interpretations of the data. *False negatives* occur when a correctable condition is not reported to the monitor, and, therefore, the monitor achieves less performance than he or she might. *False positives* occur when the measurement system reports a correctable situation when in fact none exists. Both are costly. The first results in sub-optimal performance, and the second leads to costly, disruptive, and futile investigations. Hidden costs decrease with improved reliability, validity, and timeliness.

Reliability

A measure is reliable if repeated application to an identical situation yields the same value. Testing and retesting against the same population, comparison of different observers, and split sample calculations are frequently used to measure reliability. Lack of reliability impairs precision of measurement. Allowance must be made for measurement error. If the goal is 200 units of output, but the reliability of the measure is only plus or minus 10 percent, all values from 180 to 220 must be interpreted as achieving the goal. The cost of achieving a given degree of reliability should be balanced against the ability to translate changes in the measure to value.

Reliability is enhanced by clear definitions, good measuring tools, audits, and training of observers. A measurement that is used routinely is likely to improve in reliability, as observers become accustomed to its use.

Validity

A measure is said to be valid if the reported value is true as defined by the exchange objectives. Validity is measured against a standard understood to be consistent with the objectives. Often an elaborate, expensive measurement system is used to establish the validity of a much cheaper one. The validity of the common desk ruler is traceable through several standards to an optical measurement system used by the National Bureau of Standards. A measure can be perfectly reliable but still invalid. (Using a ruler that is too short, everyone can agree the distance between two points is almost exactly 10 centimeters. A valid ruler would show that it's almost exactly 9 centimeters.)

If an invalid measure is used, energy can be directed toward achieving high scores on that measure rather than achieving the true goals. The result may be a disabling distortion of intended activity. An anecdote may be the best way to illustrate the question of validity. A factory produced nails, and someone wished to improve performance by setting output goals for the employees. So a goal was set at a certain number of nails per hour. After a short time, the goal was exceeded, but the factory was producing mostly tacks. So the goal was changed to a certain number of *pounds* of nails per hour. Again the goal was exceeded, but this time the factory was producing spikes. The moral is that validity of measurements depends upon what the goals are. If one wants a variety of nails, one's measures and expectations must reflect that.

Timeliness

There are two important criteria of timeliness, frequency and delay. Delay is the interval between measurement and report. A measure like payroll costs can be reported with biweekly frequency, and a one week delay. Data do not reach the manager until a week after the period closed. The measurement system that reports too late for the monitor to respond is at best useless and at worst costly, because it generates false positives. (The reported problem may have been corrected by the time the report arrives. In the worst case, further efforts to correct may destabilize the system.) Reports that are too infrequent allow correctable conditions to exist longer than necessary. Reports which come too often waste the monitor's time. There is a finite time attached to a response cycle. Reporting more frequently than once per response cycle is not useful. In some of the complex issues of quality and efficiency, the response cycles are quite long. For example, changing physical facilities may be possible only at intervals of many years. Interim reports on the cost of physical facilities will be of little value. Several dimensions of quality require extensive and careful responses and, as a result, tolerate infrequent measurement.

A Strategy for Information Design

Figure 9.8 summarizes the approximate shapes of values and costs of information improvement over time. Both accounting and hidden costs are included in the cost. The figure assumes that initial costs of false positives are manageable, and sentinel effects are robust. (This is consistent with reported experience. People using new information systems expect false positives and selectively ignore them, and major changes in behavior have been reported just from the introduction of measurements.[5]) It also assumes that continuing investments over time result in improvements in the scope, reliability, validity and timeliness of measures, but that these improvements produce smaller yields. Eventually, then, further investments will cost more than they contribute. A fair estimate—it is only that—of where health care organizations stand is shown. Most observers feel the industry leaders have passed the highest cost initial stages and are on the verge of very high returns.[6]

In such a complex world, where neither costs nor values can be easily assessed, and their relationship to reliability, validity, and timeliness of measures is obscure, it is difficult to justify expenditure on any single measure or even large-scale programs to improve measures. There does seem to be a clear association between good measurement and success, however. Most well-managed organizations inside and outside of health care use measures heavily and are increasing their investment in them. The theory that good management depends on precise, quantitative understanding is compelling and has a number of articulate advocates. (It is inseparable from continuous improvement approaches.)

Well-managed organizations solve this problem by developing a specific information strategy. The strategy has two important elements: a commitment to a continuing investment in information improvement and a plan to move in the directions with the greatest apparent value first. Developing and supporting this strategy is one of the functions of information services, and is discussed in Chapter 10. The commitment of leading organizations is quite strong and specific. It extends over a minimum of five years and amounts to 0.25 to 0.5 percent of their net revenue, or 5 to 10 percent of their net profit.[7] Funds are earmarked in the capital budget for information services, and are thus protected from the general competitive review described in Chapter 8. The information plan is used to justify the overall investment and guide the prioritization of individual projects.

Using Quantitative Information

Information is data processed in ways that help people make decisions. A health care organization can be described as having a certain data

Figure 9.8   Approximation of Costs and Values of Information Investment

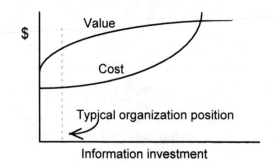

capability, and a certain data improvement strategy, but data themselves are not enough. The effective translation of data to information is as important as the quality of the data themselves. It occurs in three different but related ways, analysis of the past to help identify opportunities for improvement, forecasting to the future to help evaluate competing opportunities, and reporting of current performance to help control.

Analyzing Historic Data

Even a partially automated information system quickly builds up a large archive of data which can be systematically mined to understand processes better. An issue is identified, questions are posed, and the answers to the question suggest the directions fruitful for improvement. Figure 9.9 provides a simple illustration; one way to discover improvement opportunities is to search for specific correctable weaknesses, a "special cause" as opposed to a "common cause" in continuous improvement jargon.[8] Any special causes which are found are pursued with their own Shewhart Plan-Do-Check-Act Cycle.[9] If none is found, a general PDCA strategy may be developed. Pursuing a general strategy will be expensive and futile if a special cause exists. An ongoing dialogue between the operators and the data base, identifying special causes, is part of the improvement process.

Seven Tools of Continuous Quality Improvement

Advocates of continuous improvement have emphasized a set of seven tools for analyzing problems like the satisfaction shortfall.[10] These can be taught directly to operating teams to assist them in improving processes.

1. **Flow process charts** show the steps in a process in the order in which they must be performed, with the criteria and results for various alternatives, or branches. Figure 6.11, the review process for new programs and capital proposals, is an example of a flow process chart.

2. **Fishbone, or cause and effect, diagrams** show relationships between complex flows, and allow the team to identify components, test them as specific causes, and focus their investigation. Figure 9.10 illustrates a fishbone diagram which might analyze causes of low staffing, if the test of patient satisfaction scores showed it to be important.

3. The **scatter diagram** is a graphic device for showing association between two measures. Figure 9.11 shows occupancy, a productivity measure, versus bed size for hospitals in southeast Michigan. The relationship indicated by the diagram can be tested

Figure 9.9 Investigating a Satisfaction Shortfall: Searching for Improvement by Identifying Correctable Weakness

The issue: Patient satisfaction scores have dropped substantially below expectation.

Responses	Analysis	Result
1. Statistically significant?	Test mean and variance of most recent sample against previous samples	Yes—proceed with analysis No—reevaluate need to proceed
2. Related to certain market segments?	Test means of segments	Yes—pursue segment specific strategy No—pursue general strategy
3. Related to certain treatment teams?	Test means of teams	Yes—review with team No—pursue general strategy
4. Related to certain diagnoses?	Test means of diagnoses	Yes—study those diagnoses No—pursue general strategy
5. Related to certain staffing levels	Test association of score with average staffing level at time of treatment	Yes—consider additional staffing No—pursue general strategy

General Strategy

Plan: Develop focus groups of patients and caregivers to identify correctable reasons for low scores.

Do: Devise process changes to address these.

Check: Test changes.

Act: Adopt permanently if improvement results and other dimensions are within acceptable limits.

using regression analysis. In the case of Figure 9.11, the apparent relationship is significant.

4. The **bar chart** is a display of differing values by some useful dimension, such as day of week, operator, site, or patient group. It is useful for revealing special causes that are related to resources,

Figure 9.10 Sample Cause and Effect or Fishbone Diagram

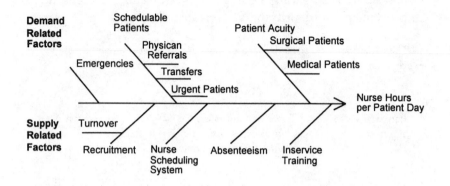

Figure 9.11 Sample Scatter Diagram

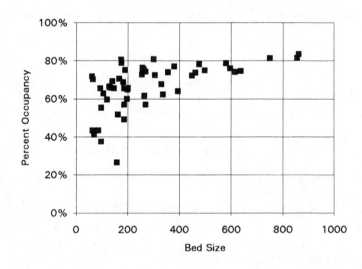

Hospital Occupancy by Bed Size
(Data from southeast Michigan, 1990)

and correctable by process changes, equipment replacement, and personnel training. For example, the bar chart shown in Figure 9.12 shows varying lengths of stay for surgeons doing cholecystectomies. It reflects considerable variation.

Pareto analysis simply examines the components of a problem in terms of their contribution to it. It is a bar chart format, with the items rank ordered on a dependent variable such as cost, profit, or satisfaction. The "Pareto Rule" is that in general a few

Figure 9.12   Sample Bar Chart

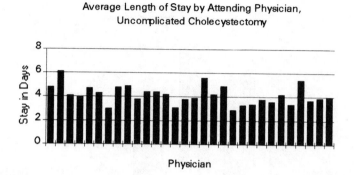

Average Length of Stay by Attending Physician,
Uncomplicated Cholecystectomy

Figure 9.13   Sample Pareto Diagram

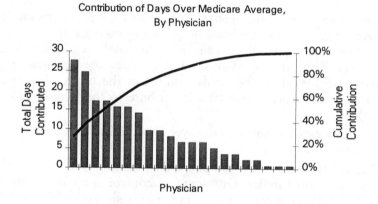

Contribution of Days Over Medicare Average,
By Physician

components will include a large part of the problem. Focusing on the biggest contributors allows the team to find solutions which may not work for every case, but which work well enough overall to be valuable. Figure 9.13 is the same subject as Figure 9.12. The the expected length of stay from Medicare data has been subtracted from the actual lengths of stay for each patient, and the difference has been totaled, to create an excess days per physician statistic. The values are ranked in the table, and predictably, a few physicians contribute to the increased stay.

Figure 9.14 Sample Histogram

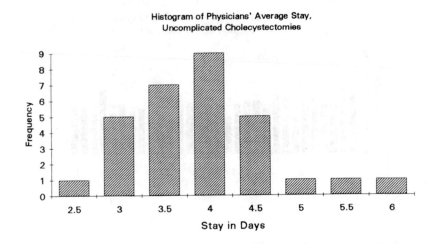

Histogram of Physicians' Average Stay,
Uncomplicated Cholecystectomies

5. The **histogram** is built from the bar chart data. It groups individual values and shows the relative frequency of each group. An example is shown in Figure 9.14, again using the cholecystectomy length of stay. This time, individual patient values were grouped by frequency, yielding the display shown in the figure. The few patients who stay a long time contribute to the long tail to the right.

6. The **run chart** displays data over time and allows a visual perception of trends.

7. The **control chart** is a run chart with the addition of statistical quality control limits. One form of control chart is shown in Figure 9.15. A more complex example is shown in Figure 9.20 below. Figure 9.15 makes quite clear why patient satisfaction is viewed as a problem, and answers the first response from Figure 9.9. The change is significant at a probability greater than 5 percent.

The seven tools can be taught successfully to health care workers and are included in elementary continuous improvement training programs. The statistical analyses and graphics can be prepared with common spreadsheet software.[11] Thus a team pursuing the general strategy to overcome the patient satisfaction shortfall of Figure 9.9 could easily prepare the examples shown here, and the tools would probably help them understand how to improve the care processes and patient satisfaction.

Figure 9.15 Sample Control Chart

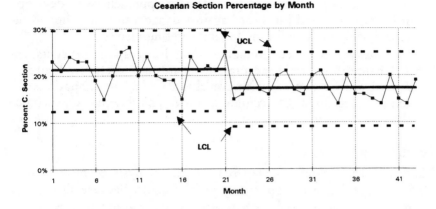

Cesarian Section Percentage by Month

Advanced Analytic Tools

The seven tools may have their greatest value in teaching people how to think analytically. As tools, their utility is soon exhausted. Notably, they do not allow an untrained team to complete any of the statistical analyses listed in Figure 9.9. Easy to use software exists to do the analyses, but an analyst with a knowledge of the data and a graduate degree could answer the questions faster and more reliably. Similarly, they do not address the intricacies of cost analysis. For example, Figure 9.12 assumes that the correct costs have been estimated at each site. Well-managed institutions provide internal consultants who can support and go beyond the seven tools. Their RCs and final product teams at any level can call upon skilled planners, marketers, cost analysts, and management engineers to assist a team at any stage of its efforts. The kinds of analysis they can add include

- *Advanced graphic displays.* These are often helpful in conveying quantitative information and appear constantly in analyses and proposals. A wide variety of graphs are available on common spreadsheet packages. Selection of the proper graph is important, and an experienced analyst can improve the accuracy and efficiency of information transfer.[12]

- *Univariate statistical analysis.* Arithmetic means, standard deviations, and standard errors are applicable to a great many situations, guiding the team to select topics which are likely to be fruitful. Some statistics—for example, low-frequency events—require other tests which are more efficient.

- *Multivariate statistical analysis.* Regression and analysis of variance techniques have expanded dramatically over the past 20 years. A statistician familiar with the different approaches can develop answers faster, and can guard against dangers of using the wrong test or violating conditions for interpreting results.
- *Cost analysis.* Most economic decisions hinge upon unit costs, and as Chapter 8 indicates, accurate estimates are often problematic. A cost analyst familiar with available data and its limitations can produce the most accurate estimate possible in each specific situation.

Forecasting

Many problems require a step beyond the analysis of historic data. **Forecasts** predict future operating environments. Because all management decisions must deal with future events, the use of forecasts is essential. Teams must solve operational problems in the future environment, not the present one.

Demand for service and prices of purchased resources are routinely forecast as part of the budget process. The budget office collaborates with planning and marketing to develop forecasts for the most global demand events, such as new patients, hospital admissions, and outpatient visits, broken down into major market segments. Price forecasting is usually developed by market survey, or from commercial forecasters who sell opinions.

Global demand and demand for many specific care episodes such as DRG can be forecast from institutional history, usually by regression analysis.[13] In addition, commercial data bases allow forecast of demand by episode based on national statistics and population demography. Population itself is measured and forecast for political units by a system of federal and state cooperation.[14] Even smaller geographic area forecasts, such as zip codes, are available from commercial sources. Thus most final product teams have two forecasts for future demand:

Time series regression analysis of the form:

$$\text{Demand} = \beta \text{ (year)} + C \pm \varepsilon$$

Epidemiologic analysis of the form:

$$\text{Demand} = \beta_1 \text{ (population)} + \beta_2 \text{ (age)} + \beta_3 \text{ (sex)} + \beta_4 \text{ (income)} + C \pm \varepsilon$$

Demand for specific intermediate products rendered by RCs is forecast from regression analysis of the historic relation of the service to the global measures. For example, several recent years, data on the number of laboratory tests is regressed against the number of inpatient admissions, clinic visits, and year. A regression model such as

Lab tests $= \beta_1$ (admissions) $+ \beta_2$ (visits) $+ \beta_3$ (year) $+ C \pm \varepsilon$

can be used for the initial forecast, where the forecast year and values for admissions and visits are inserted into the regression equation.

Several regression-based techniques are available to develop the regression models, called *ceteris paribus* forecasts. Further refinements can be introduced. Cyclic variation for seasons or days of the week can be accommodated. The demand can be segmented and forecast by segment at what ever level the data and statistical significance will support. The *ceteris paribus* forecasts can be almost fully automated. Well-managed organizations have sophisticated forecasting systems including several forecasting models and a data base of agreed-upon forecasts of major measures.

Ceteris paribus forecasts are rarely adequate in themselves. Historically based forecasts are impossible when new services are developed because there is no history to use. "Other things being equal" rarely prevails even in existing services. The opinions and evidence from planning and marketing are used to refine the global forecasts. Line operators can adjust forecasts for areas under their authority, based on their judgment. Line operators are recognized to have excellent judgment about short-term forecasts. Planning and marketing personnel can spot variations from the *ceteris paribus* assumption and make adjustments not possible from computerized models.

Benchmarking

Benchmarking is a form of quantitative goal identification establishing the desired forecast, as opposed to the most likely one developed by regression forecasting. A **benchmark** is the best known value for a specific measure, from any source. Benchmarks are obtained by constructing comparative data sets and ranking them. Particularly in cases where price is not available or not relevant, the benchmark can be a powerful tool to guide process improvement. Related to the benchmark is the process used to generate it, called **best practice**. If both are available, a team might decide to emulate best practice, and allowing for implementation delays and learning time, achieve best practice over a few budget cycles. Its forecasts for each cycle would be based upon performance relative to the benchmark.

An example of benchmarking and its use is in infant mortality, a complex problem where American health care does not do well. Nations with better maternal and infant health care are generally below 10 deaths per 1,000 births. The best nations achieve less than five, although they are often small, economically advanced, well educated and ethnically homogeneous populations. Health care organizations in American inner cities have a hard time matching these numbers, and it is known that the problems involved include reducing unwanted pregnancies, eliminating mothers' substance abuse and improving their nutrition, providing early prenatal care, and improving care at birth. Not all of these problems are under the control of the health care system. Collaboration with other social agencies would be required. Additional funding will be necessary, even though the outcome could reduce overall expenditures. An improved process is thus a multiyear project. A typical inner city hospital might face forecasts and benchmarks like the ones shown in Figure 9.16. A deliberate program to improve performance might identify an interim goal of nine, and start programs to achieve it in three years.

Modeling

Models are simplified representations of reality which can be manipulated to test various hypotheses about the future. Real world trials are rarely the best way to begin to evaluate a proposal. Models are easier to adjust and less costly if something goes wrong. The concept of a forecast relates to that of an **exogenous event**, one which is largely outside the control of the line operator. Modeling recognizes that performance depends on both exogenous events and **endogenous events**, those largely within the control of the operator. Models require an **objective function**, that is a quantitative statement of the relationship between events and desired results, and **constraints**, limits on the range of acceptable operating conditions. Typically cost or profit is used as an objective function, and constraints are put on endogenous events representing quality concerns.

A model represents reality for a given set of assumptions and projects the performance on important dimensions. The modeler can then modify the endogenous assumptions and test the relationship between them and performance, eventually finding an optimal performance and accepting or rejecting it for further study. Next, in a process called **sensitivity analysis**, the modeler modifies the exogenous events, usually developing most favorable, expected, and least favorable scenarios. These show the robustness of the proposal and indicate the degree of risk involved. Several forms of models are used by well-managed health care organizations to evaluate proposals.

Deterministic Models

Models which deal with future events as fixed numbers, rather than as random events subject to a predictable variance, are called **deterministic**

Figure 9.16 Forecasts and Benchmarks Compared to Create a Process Improvement Strategy

Problem:

High-risk mothers and babies drive infant mortality rates up. Current rate is 21/1,000.

Benchmarks:

World	Japan	4.6/1,000 births
U.S.	Maine	6.9/1,000 births
Comparable cities		14.2/1,000 births

Strategies	Time to Visible Result	Anticipated Change in Mortality
Encourage prenatal care: Within 3 months, open new care center with focus on teen activities, health care for teen girls	12 months	Year 1: 0% Year 2: 10% Year 3: 20%
Expand use of contraceptives: Offer contraceptives and counseling to teen girls and boys	12 months	Year 1: 0% Year 2: 05% Year 3: 10%
Drug use prevention and education: Work with high schools, police, and social services on drug abatement	24 months	Year 1: 0% Year 2: 0% Year 3: 05%

Budget Expectations

Calculation	Value
Year 1: No change	21/1,000 births
Year 2: Initial value decreased by 5% for reduced pregnancies, 10% for prenatal care	18/1,000 births
Year 3: Initial value decreased by 10% for reduced pregnancies, 20% for prenatal care, 5% for drug abatement	14.4/1,000 births

models. The most common are business plans, but several others are useful in specific situations.

Business plans Business plans are the most universally used model. They describe an operating proposal, identify exogenous and endogenous conditions, and forecast demand, output, revenue, costs, and profit or cost savings over several years. Demand and prices are usually taken as exogenous, and quality concerns are handled as a constraint.

(For example, examining only alternatives which appear likely to give the same or better quality scores.) Business plans are used to justify new programs and capital expenditure, evaluate make or buy alternatives, show returns on improved processes, and estimate break-even conditions and earnings associated with increasing demand. The long-range financial plan is a sophisticated business plan. Scenarios evaluating alternative exogenous and endogenous assumptions are frequently useful for strategy selection.[15]

Business plans assume deterministic conditions, that is they accept the forecasts without error terms or allowance for random variation. They examine alternative exogenous scenarios using sensitivity analysis. Although they are conceptually algebraic models, they are prepared on computer spreadsheets and presented as year-by-year forecasts. The algebra is buried in the spreadsheet design. Spreadsheet capabilities make graphic summaries easy, and they are widely used and expected.

Business plans are not difficult to do. Many line teams will have members who can prepare them. Consultation from technical personnel in planning, marketing, and finance is useful both in the model design and in evaluating the assumptions. The neatness and precision of the spreadsheets and graphs, and concealment of the underlying algebra can be misleading. The key questions about business plans deal with the assumptions, such as the sources of forecasts, the realism of alternative scenarios, time allowances made for implementation and learning, and the operating conditions necessary to reach the performance level used in the analysis. As more complex problems are addressed, the spreadsheets themselves get quite elaborate, and the model builder must have extensive experience.[16]

Other deterministic models   Algebraic models can be developed as such. They show the relationship between exogenous characteristics and desired endogenous ones, such as the relation between demand and staffing, and are useful for illustrating assumptions and gaining improved understanding of operating possibilities.[17]

PERT (project evaluation and review technique) charts are programs for analyzing construction projects and similar sets of complex, time-dependent, interrelated activities. The value of PERT charts lies in their ability to identify critical paths, the sequences and timetables of events that will delay the overall project if they are not met. PERT charting is routine for major construction projects and renovations. It is also useful for complex new program development. Commercial software supports the analysis, but the inputs require substantial knowledge of change processes. PERT charting is generally done by one or two people in the organization who are experienced with it.

A variety of programming models are used in commercial applications, including linear programming and forms of dynamic programming. These models differ from the business plan in their ability to find the optimum set of endogenous conditions. They have found limited use in health care, although linear programming is theoretically applicable to personnel staffing and inventory management. The few applications which have occurred have been incorporated in specific software for departmental operation. A technique called data envelopment analysis allows estimation of optimal operational efficiency in certain multi-dimensional problems.[18] Development of programming models is demanding. Special coursework is essential, along with extensive experience in other modeling forms.

Stochastic Models

Some situations cannot be effectively modeled by deterministic techniques. They are usually those where the exogenous conditions cannot be predicted easily in advance, but still have an important effect on the outcomes. Stochastic means subject to chance variation. **Stochastic models** incorporate chance variation in the analysis and evaluation of the solutions. The traditional example of a stochastic problem is the arrival of women for obstetric delivery. Each event is unpredictable even a few hours in advance, yet it is so important that the health care organization must have adequate staff and facilities to serve the patient when she arrives. A model will be constructed showing how often the staff and facilities will be overtaxed for a given level of average demand. Because the demand is random with wide variation from hour to hour, a deterministic model based on the average demand would be disastrously unsatisfactory.

Figure 9.17 shows the results of a model to determine obstetric birthing rooms and staffing. (The model is simplified to illustrate the issues involved.) On the average, women arriving for delivery will require two rooms and staff groups. Just under 2,200 women deliver each year, and they require on the average about eight hours of service. But because of the stochastic demand, they will keep two rooms and staff occupied most of the time, need a third about 20 percent of the time, a fourth about 10 percent, a fifth less than 5 percent. Only about once a year will six units be required. Quality and patient satisfaction require that some provision be made for the five-and six-unit situations, but because of the cost, the solution will not be to routinely staff for five units, nor to build six units.

Figure 9.17 Stochastic Analysis of Birthing Room Requirements

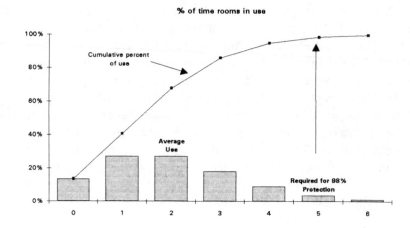

Stochastic models are usually constructed around **Monte Carlo simulation**, computerized test of a model situation by repeated trial. Although advanced spreadsheet software has the capability of doing Monte Carlo simulation, the most important parts of the model are its design and the measurement of the parameters. The birthing room example in Figure 9.17 requires not only forecasts of mean values but reliable distributions of arrival times, service times, and staffing requirements. The final evaluation will weigh probabilities of rare events and the extent to which they violate constraints against the cost of meeting them.

Simulation can also be adapted to expand sensitivity analysis of deterministic models. Exogenous variables must be given realistic distributions of possible values, and the impact of variation can be explored to reveal changes required in endogenous variables and resulting values of the objective function. A range of scenarios, rather than just a few extremes can be evaluated.[19] Advanced software is usually necessary to do this, and is offered by several vendors. These systems allow financial planning in a stochastic mode, and are called **decision support systems (DSS)**. To date, they have found limited application in health care, probably because they require very large, reliable data bases.[20] New program analysis has been reported in a proposed health promotion center[21] and a pharmacy.[22] As health care organizations improve their automated data archives, DSS applications will grow. At least theoretically, a sophisticated DSS model could be used with a process improvement team in real time, allowing the team to experiment with various changes to endogenous events, and see the impact on constraints and objective function almost immediately.[23]

Experimentation

Many improvement possibilities require more than an abstract model evaluation. Relationships between exogenous and endogenous events and final objectives are not always easy to state or even understand. All models are simplifications of reality; one of the most common simplifications is omission of interactions between various events. As a result, real world trials do not always behave as the model indicated. In addition, trials offer opportunities to demonstrate, convince and teach. The model site can be the teaching site to roll out the results to the larger organization. For these reasons, the "check" step of PDCA frequently includes a field trial.[24]

Quantitative information contributes to the field trial in several ways. It allows the improvement team to analyze relationships between various events and design the improvement itself. It supports simple models which rule out unpromising experiments and reveal correctable weaknesses in promising ones. Models also show the kinds of data required for evaluation, and the length of trial necessary to achieve reliable results. They often suggest potential difficulties with the trial or its interpretation; these can be accommodated in design or analysis to strengthen the conclusions.

The most rigorous form of trials are research experiments carefully designed and controlled to yield results appropriate to a large, uncontrolled population or market, such as the United States or all developed countries. They are supported by research funds from large corporations or grants. Design and publication are both subject to rigorous critical review. Many health care organizations participate in alliances or networks formed for the purpose of research. Most clinical research developing and testing new methods of diagnosis and treatment is done this way.

Experiments on operations are more difficult to do at the same level of rigor. Technically, a single organization can represent only itself. Transferability from one organization to another may be limited; indeed the objective may be to develop a unique competitive advantage for a single firm. The question addressed by field trials is whether the change can be made to work effectively for the single organization, a very different question from the clinical trial's "will be effective for a large, uncontrolled population." The level of rigor is only one of the considerations in the trial design. The cost of the trial, including potential dangers to patients or employees, and other benefits such as building consensus or serving as a training site must also be considered. A good field trial is one that

- Presents no increased danger to patients or staff
- Is free of avoidable distortion or bias
- Is conducted over enough patients or events to yield statistically significant results
- Evaluates an improvement worth several times the accounting cost of conducting the trial
- Can be modified in course to yield the greatest possible overall improvement.

These standards are considerably less rigorous than those for formal research. The loss of rigor increases the chance that the result may be due to something other than the experimental modification, and the chance that a second trial will not yield the same results. The so-called **Hawthorne effect** is a frequent issue. A famous series of experiments showed that the fact of experimentation and the attention it drew could improve performance, independent of the experiment itself.[25] Organization field trials often approach the problem of rigor by making allowance for the Hawthorne effect and related risks in judging the results, and by approaching the experiment sequentially. Thus very strong initial results lead to continuation of the trial; weaker ones to consideration of improvements in the proposal; and disappointing ones to discontinuation. If feasible, the continuation can be undertaken on a second site, where pride of authorship is less likely to enhance the results.

A field trial should have the following components:

1. A hypothesis or proposal expressing the relationship between an endogenous event, process, or method, and an objective function, such as "If we change Process A in a certain defined way, we will achieve better outcomes as measured by cost, profit, and quality."
2. Justification from literature or analysis of operational data suggesting that the hypothesis is plausible, that the answer is not obvious, and that a trial is likely to yield improvements worth many times its cost.
3. A method of implementing the change in a real field setting, including site, initial investment in equipment and training, safety factors, and time schedules.
4. A method of measuring the changes in outcomes and any other variables important to the decision.
5. An estimation of the length or size of the trial necessary to demonstrate the improvement.

6. A review of the moral and practical implications for patients and employees involved in the trial.

7. A critical analysis of the reliability, validity, and value of the expected results, including a review of confounding factors which should be considered.

While the steps seem onerous, a field trial involves a disruption of an ongoing process and the danger of doing harm is always present. The steps can be simplified in undemanding situations; operating teams try new approaches constantly as part of their learning. But a trial involving more than a few people in direct personal communication deserves at least a review of all seven items.

Well-managed institutions establish mechanisms facilitating review of field trials. The support includes consultants trained in experimental design and analysis and ad hoc work groups to gain consensus on methods, explore implications, and provide a critical analysis. A **human subjects committee** can contribute unbiased review of potential dangers to patients and employees. It is required by most funding bodies for formal research, but it clearly has a role whenever a process change involves patient care or risks to employees. Similarly, large-scale trials can be given critical review by formal committees from outside the area in question, emulating the research review process.

Monitoring and Controlling

Control, the ability to achieve desired future events, is the essence of all economic activity and the central justification for the organization.[26] Control implies both predictability and uniformity. Variation is a measure of the lack of control; the ideal variation is zero. Monitoring is the measurement of variation. In the real world, of course, variation is always present. The question is whether it is within acceptable bounds. Control is actually achieved by individuals and organizations through a series of human interactions where the quantitative measurement of relevant factors is only a supplement to more powerful and less precise processes. As activities and organizations grow more complex, the role of quantification becomes more central, but it never replaces the underlying human factors.

Continuous improvement theory emphasizes that control is built in, not monitored, and certainly not imposed. Control begins with the design of service and process. The right process, training, tools and supplies, and demand levels lead to control; failures in these cannot be replaced by incentives or statistical systems. A monitoring process, statistical systems, and incentives are necessary to maintain the system after it is designed. Even if it was perfectly designed at the outset, an unmonitored system will deteriorate as a function of environmental changes, wear, and fatigue. Monitoring detects the need for maintenance and the opportunity for improvement.

Cybernetic Systems

The concept of monitoring begins with a **cybernetic system**, the addition of a separate, new activity to a process. A process translates inputs, including demand and resources, to outputs, goods or services sold for revenue and profit. It can be represented as shown in Figure 9.18A. The monitor shown in Figure 9.18B is added to evaluate the performance, identify necessary corrections, and make them. The monitor relies on the same measures of performance as shown in Figure 9.2. The word cybernetic comes from the ancient Greek *cybernos*, or helmsman, the monitor who kept the ship on course. Monitors of some systems are purely mechanical; the thermostat on the heating system is an example. Most human activities are monitored by the person doing them.

Figure 9.18   Cybernetic System

A. Activity Converting Inputs to Outputs

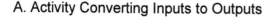

B. Cybernetic System with Monitor

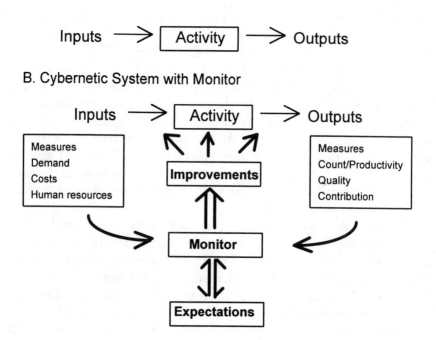

Figure 9.18B applies to any process, from a nurse giving patient care to a complete health care organization. The monitor in direct contact with the process, is called the primary monitor. It is possible to monitor monitors, thus a nest of sequential monitoring functions is established. The accountability hierarchy is such a nest; each level monitors not the underlying activities, but the performance of the level immediately below it. The governing board can be understood as the primary monitor for the organization as a whole.

The monitor, whether it is the nurse, the governing board, or anyone in between, proceeds by comparing the performance information (technically the signal) against the expectation. If the two are not identical, an error signal is generated and the monitor acts upon it. This does not automatically require quantification; the nurse will be working with a wide variety of verbal, visual, and sensory data which is not quantified at all. Quantification is necessary when the direct contact is lost.

As an example of an activity beyond the individual worker, consider a nursing station shown in Figure 9.19. The head nurse is the monitor; nurses and other nursing personnel are the major resources; arriving patients are the demands; and treated patients are the outputs. The budget for a nursing unit will specify quantitative expectations for all six performance dimensions, and measures of achievement will reach the head nurse regularly. (Some will be by direct observation and will not be quantitative.) Head nurses will compare signals to expectations. They will expect no error signals unless unforeseen factors intervene, and in a well-managed institution this expectation will be met the vast majority of the time. The monitor's main effort will turn to identifying issues limiting improvement. Performance will be assured by continuous improvement, not by repair of failures. If the nurse is drawn too frequently into failures, improvements will stop. The failures which do occur should always be studied for ways to eliminate them in the future, by changing the process.

Statistical Quality Control

Because any real system contains a certain amount of variation that cannot be corrected with current technology, the quantitative signals will not exactly match the expectations. Statistical quality control will be necessary to identify variations which are significant, or likely to be correctable.[27] Significant variations can be called special cause variation or error signals. Non-significant variations can be called random variation, common cause variation, or noise. Significance can be tested subjectively or by using standard statistical techniques. An analogous

Figure 9.19 Examples of Monitor Function on a Nursing RC

Dimension	Measures	Possible Improvements
Demand	Number of patients	Patient satisfaction, physician satisfaction, scheduling, case management
Costs	Labor costs	Personnel scheduling, cross-training, new processes
	Supplies costs	New processes, clinical protocols
Human resources	Employee satisfaction	Personnel scheduling, supervisory training, new job requirements
Output/ productivity	Cost per visit or per day	Change processes to reduce variable costs, increase demand to reduce fixed costs
	Cost per member month	Change processes to reduce variable costs, decrease demand, reduce fixed costs by elimination
Quality	Recovery rates	Personnel training, clinical protocols, new processes
	Patient satisfaction	Personnel training, clinical protocols, new processes
	Procedure	Personnel training, clinical protocols, new processes
Contribution	Profit or cost target	Search for improvable inputs, outputs, and processes

process goes on almost subconsciously with directly observed signals. They are judged to be important enough to pursue or not as they are perceived and compared to subjective expectations.

Statistical quality control is now frequently automated and graphically reported.[28] Measures for a specific time period are taken for a sample or for all activity during the period. Each measurement is called a lot, and lots are collected sequentially. Attributes statistics and variables statistics are handled somewhat differently. Values for both the mean and the variance covering sequential time periods can be plotted for variables statistics and control limits established for both, as shown in Figure 9.20. The more common attributes measures can be expressed as a percentage passing (or failing) the threshold for each time period and plotted over time as shown in Figure 9.12. All three of these graphs are control charts. They can be reviewed over time for trends or changes, using statistical techniques to identify the special cause or statistically significant variation.

There are several alternatives and improvements which make the statistical tests more sensitive in specific situations. For further discussion at an elementary level, see Gitlow et al's. *Tools and Methods for the*

Figure 9.20   Process Control Charts for Variables Measures

A. Control Chart for the Mean

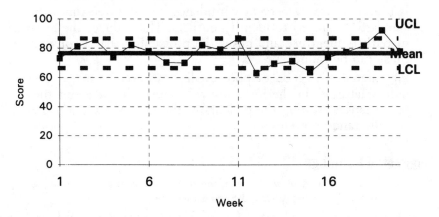

B. Control Chart for Variation

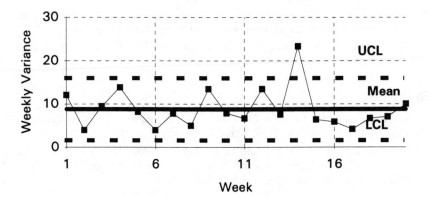

Improvement of Quality, and at an advanced level, Feigenbaum's *Total Quality Control* under Suggested Readings.

Control charts allow monitors to scan large numbers of measures and quickly identify where further improvements are likely. However, there are a number of ways in which the analysis can be misused. Misuse will waste resources, and it may be destructive because it diverts us from important alternatives or results in insupportable accusations and loss of morale. Here are some of the principal problems:

1. The lots must be from the same process. Many uncontrollable events change medical care processes over time, such as changes in the condition of arriving patients. Runs of uncommon patients and other factors affecting the lots must always be ruled out before "outliers" are acknowledged.

2. No inference of good or poor quality can ever be made about a lot until special causes have been identified or ruled out. It is useful to use 99 percent confidence limits (three times the standard deviation) to identify outliers. This reduces the number of outliers identified and raises the probability that a correctable cause can be found.

3. No inference of good or poor quality can ever be made about individual cases in the lot using this approach (or about the practitioners treating the patients in the lot). Many outliers are actually random events.

Suggested Readings

Deming, W. E. 1986. *Out of the Crisis.* Cambridge: Massachusetts Institute of Technology, Center for Advanced Engineering Study.

Feigenbaum, A. V. 1991. *Total Quality Control,* 3d ed. (rev.) New York: McGraw-Hill.

Gitlow, H., and H. S. Gitlow. 1989. *Tools and Methods for the Improvement of Quality.* Homewood, IL: Irwin.

Montgomery, D. C., L. A. Johnson, and J. S. Gardiner. 1990. *Forecasting and Time Series Analysis,* 2d ed. New York: McGraw-Hill.

Remington, R. D., and M. A. Schork. 1985. *Statistics with Applications to the Biological and Health Sciences,* 2d ed. Englewood Cliffs, NJ: Prentice-Hall.

Steers, R. M., and L. W. Porter. 1983. *Motivation and Work Behavior,* 3d ed. New York: McGraw-Hill.

Notes

1. P. M. Senge, 1990, *The Fifth Discipline: The Art and Practice of the Learing Organization* (New York: Doubleday/Currency), 14.

2. W. A. Knause, E. A. Draper, and D. P. Wagner, 1983, "The Use of Intensive Care: New Research Initiatives and their Application for National Health Policy," *Milbank Memorial Fund Quarterly* 61 (Fall): 561–83.

3. R. C. Jelinek, 1969, "An Operational Analysis of the Patient Care Function," *Inquiry* 6 (June): 53–58.

4. B. E. Fries, D. P. Schneider, M. Gavazzi, R. Burke, and E. Cornelius, 1994, "Refining a Case-Mix Measure for Nursing Homes: Resource Utilization Groups," *Medical Care* 32 (July): 668–85).

5. S. G. Martin, 1982, "The Sentinel Effect in Second Opinion Programs," *Employee Benefit Plan Review* 36 (9 February): 24–26.

6. R. Bergman, 1994, "Health Care in a Wired World. Information Management: Experts Zero in on Top Issues," *Hospitals and Health Networks* 68 (20 August): 28–36.

7. J. R. Griffith, V. K. Sahney, and R. A. Mohr, 1995, *Reengineering Health Care: Building on CQI* (Ann Arbor, MI: Health Administration Press).

8. W. E. Deming, 1986, *Out of the Crisis* (Cambridge: Massachusetts Institute of Technology, Center for Advanced Engineering Study,) 309–71.

9. Deming, *Out of the Crisis*, 39.

10. Joint Commission on Accreditation of Healthcare Organizations, 1992, *Six Hospitals in Search of Quality: Striving Towards Improvement* (Oakbrook Terrace, IL: JCAHO), 255–59.

11. D. C. Kibbe and R. P. Scoville, 1993, "Computer Software for Health Care CQI," and "Tutorial: Using Microsoft Excel for Health Care CQI," *Quality Management in Health Care* 1 (Summer): 50–58, and 2 (Fall): 63–71.

12. S. L. Jarvenpaa and G. W. Dickson, 1988, "Graphics and Managerial Decision Making: Research Based Guidelines," *Communications of the ACM* 31 (6): 764–74.

13. T. W. Weiss, C. M. Ashton, and N. P. Wray, 1993, "Forecasting Areawide Hospital Utilization: A Comparison of Five Univariate Time Series Techniques," *Health Services Management Research* 6 (August): 178–90.

14. U.S. Bureau of the Census, *Current Population Reports: Cooperative Program for Federal-State Population Estimates*, Series P-26 (Washington, DC: U.S. Department of Commerce).

15. R. D. Zentner and B. D. Gelb, 1991, "Scenarios: A Planning Tool for Health Care Organizations," *Hospital & Health Services Administration* 36 (Summer): 211–22.

16. P. Kokol, 1990, "Structured Spreadsheet Modeling in Medical Decision Making and Research," *Journal of Medical Systems* 14 (3): 107–17.

17. M. Kim and W. M. Hancock, 1989, "Applications of Staffing, Scheduling and Budgeting Methods to Hospital Ancillary Units," *Journal of Medical Systems* 13 (1): 37–47.

18. Y. L. Huang, 1990, "An Application of Data Envelopment Analysis: Measuring the Relative Performance of Florida General Hospitals," *Journal of Medical Systems* 14 (4): 191–96.

19. L. C. Gapenski, 1990, "Using Monte Carlo Simulation to Make Better Capital Investment Decisions," *Hospital & Health Services Administration* 35 (Summer): 207–19.

20. M. E. Hatcher and C. Connelly, 1988, "A Case Mix Simulation Decision Support System Model for Negotiating Hospital Rates," *Journal of Medical Systems* 12 (6): 341–63.

21. M. E. Hatcher and N. Rao, 1988, "A Simulation Based Decision Support System for a Health Promotion Center," *Journal of Medical Systems* 12 (1): 11–29.

22. A. S. Zaki, 1989, "Developing a DSS for a Distribution Facility: An Application in the Healthcare Industry," *Journal of Medical Systems* 13 (6): 331–46.

23. M. E. Hatcher, 1990, "Uniqueness of Group Decision Support Systems (GDSS) in Medical and Health Applications," *Journal of Medical Systems* 14 (6): 351–34.

24. C. H. Moore, 1994, "Experimental Design in Health Care," *Quality Management In Health Care* 2 (Winter): 13–26.

25. F. J. Roethlisberger and W. J. Dickson, 1939, *Management and the Worker: An Account of a Research Program Conducted by the Western Electric Company, Hawthorne Works, Chicago* (Cambridge, MA: Harvard University Press).

26. A. D. Chandler, 1977, *The Visible Hand: The Managerial Revolution in American Business* (Cambridge, MA: Belknap Press).

27. P. E. Plsek, 1992, "Tutorial: Introduction to Control Charts," *Quality Management in Health Care* 1 (Fall): 65–74.

28. H. Gitlow, S. Gitlow, A. Oppenheim, and R. Oppenheim, 1989, *Tools and Methods for the Improvement of Quality* (Homewood, IL: Irwin), 78–110.

CHAPTER

10

INFORMATION SERVICES

AS CHAPTER 9 shows, automated information services are essential to the successful health care organization. With pressing need for data to improve operations, and the cost of computation falling steadily, the future will bring a rapid expansion of applications. The computer will soon be as ubiquitous as the telephone, a routine part of the work life for all health care workers.

Within a few years, doctors, nurses, and other clinical professions will use electronic systems which suggest a plan of care for each patient based on analysis of both the patient's history and detailed data about specific treatment options. Forecasts of patients' needs will be available to each patient service unit. Electronic systems will prompt completion of the original plan, optimize schedules, order supplies, and demand follow-up of any unexpected occurrence. Complete text and statistical records will be available to establish expectations and monitor performance for all caregivers; the vast data files available will permit great precision in judging the success of both future and past efforts. Within a decade or so, all hospital care will be routinely supported by electronics and scientific analysis more rigorous than that applied to the most intensive care today. Outpatient management will be supported by automated records and communications as well as automated protocols for many diseases and conditions.

In management applications, the strategic, resource allocation, and organizational decisions will be supported by analytic models based on the archived data. New proposals will grow out of analysis of history, will be tested first by computerized models, and will be justified by sophisticated business plans. The improvements themselves will meld the clinical advances with the analytic ones. Heuristic algorithms will allow computers to suggest both clinical and managerial decisions. Human participation in the routine decisions will diminish; their role will shift to understanding the patient and the system itself.

If this vision is correct, health care organizations are only now entering the early phases, and information services are in their infancy. The combination of opportunities from technology and pressure for economical health care suggests that a generation of managers will focus on information services as a central engine of management. Management will have a dual role as development proceeds. First, it must assure that improvements in automation meet the needs of patients and customers. Second, it must guide organization members through the changes as efficiently and humanely as possible.

This chapter surveys the managerial challenges of the information revolution. It postulates a formally accountable information services (IS) activity with broad responsibility for all information- and communication-related support to line management, and it describes: definitions and purpose, functions, organization, and measures of performance.

Definitions and Purpose

Definitions

An **information system** is an automated process of capture, transmission, and recording of information which is permanently accessible to the organization as a whole. Under this definition, not every computer application is part of an information system. An application actually becomes part of an information system when the data are integrated into a permanently and organizationally accessible form. As of the 1990s, most health care organizations have several information systems in finance, plant, and clinical services.

The various information systems must themselves be integrated if they are to provide maximum benefit to management. Much of the following discussion will deal with integrated information systems, defined as follows:

> An **integrated information system** is a set of two or more information systems organized to provide immediate electronic access to information in each.

An example of an integrated system would be one containing both medical records and patient accounting. Integration will occur over several stages of increasing sophistication in accuracy and detail, eventually permitting analysis of all the closed system dimensions discussed in Chapter 9.

As of 1995, health care organizations have pre-systems—that is, automated activity which is not accessible to the organization as a whole, systems, and integrated systems. The migration toward integrated systems has been rapid, but not untroubled. Human, statistical, and technical problems must be solved as applications move from free-standing to system to integration. Information services is the part of the organization that specializes in overcoming these problems. **Information services** is the organization supporting the development and integration of information systems and the supply of information to points of use.

Purpose

Information services is a formal organizational unit created to be accountable for the development of integrated information systems, and for continuous improvement in information availability and use. It provides high visibility to information needs, assures organizationwide access to reliable information, facilitates the integration of systems, and promotes effective use of information. The customers of information services are all the other units of the organization. In general, information services fulfills its purpose by assisting in the selection, design, and operation of information systems.

Functions of Information Services

The information services (IS) department or unit is accountable for five functions, as shown in Figure 10.1. These are functions which if not done impair the organization as a whole. They require a central authority and unique technical knowledge and skills. Maintaining the information services plan is critical to assure compatibility of equipment and software, and also to justify IS strategic expenditures. Assuring the integrity, quality, and security of data is essential. Integrating information capture, communication, and routine concurrent processing is the central technical function, including the network for information transfer and the interfaces between processors necessary to smooth interaction. The archives of data quickly become a unique corporate resource which improves both management and clinical decisions. User training and support is an obligation of all the technical support groups, with emphasis on their area of technical expertise. For IS, the emphasis is on using computer hardware and software efficiently, understanding the archived data, and recognizing computer modeling opportunities.

Maintaining the Information Services Plan

Well-managed health care organizations expend about 3 percent of their operating funds on information services.[1] In the mid-1990s, leading organizations spend 10 to 20 percent of their net profit each year on IS investment. Many organizations were planning to expand their investments.[2] The investment is driven by the conviction that information is an essential resource and managed by an information services plan committing investment levels over several years.

Well-managed health care organizations rely on an information services plan to assure integrated access, establish priorities among competing opportunities, and assure a sufficient level of IS investment. The IS department is responsible for development and implementation of the plan, as shown in Figure 10.2. The plan is incorporated into the

Figure 10.1 Functions of Information Services

Function	Content
Maintain the information services plan	Process which incorporates line views, establishes a prioritized agenda for progress, commits a block of capital funds for several years, and supports an annual review of specific projects
Assure the integrity, quality, and security of data	Activity defining measures and terminology, improving data input, and guarding against inappropriate access or application
Integrate information capture and processing	Operation supporting widespread convenient access to current data, archives, and appropriate software through computers and related equipment
Archive and retrieve data	Activity capturing historic, as opposed to current, data to support management and clinical decisions in forecasting, analysis, and the design of improvements
Train and support users	Program to provide training in the use of automated systems and analytic skills; consulting service to improvement teams to assist in forecasting, analysis, modeling, trials, and improvement design

long-range financial plan, where it acts as a longer-term commitment to information development. The plan which results is implemented as part of the organization's strategic plan.[3] It includes a record of approved information systems proposals, its own capital budget, and an implementation timetable. The planning process includes a procedure for identifying, developing, evaluating, and integrating new or improved information services.[4] Annual improvements in information systems are reviewed against the IS plan, rather than through the capital and new programs budget. Management of implementation is an IS responsibility. IS and the line units share accountability for achieving the intended improvements once the new systems are installed.

Developing and Supporting the Plan

The IS plan should be a general information strategy which specifies the performance requirements for the organization as a whole over the next three to five years and identifies the information services which will be required to achieve these levels.[5] The IS department must monitor technical developments in information processing, the

Figure 10.2 Information Systems Plan Development and Implementation

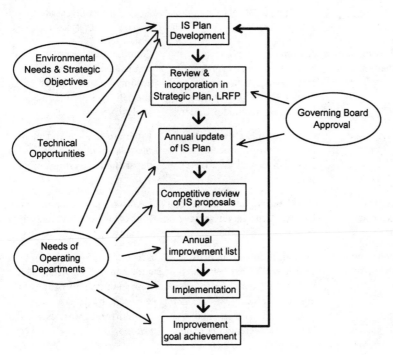

capability of competitors, and the needs of the general environment to identify important trends.[6] As illustrated in Figure 10.3, IS plans cover the following topics:

1. Information goals, the general benefits to be achieved, and the approximate timetable.
2. Major integrated systems to be installed, with specific timetables, costs, financing, and descriptions of capabilities.
3. Central hardware plans, with timetables, costs, and financing.
4. Budget for information needs of individual units, and a procedure for competitive review of unit proposals.

A sound strategy reduces the chance of omitting important areas or of installing systems before they can be translated to real improvements. Strategic selection of priorities is dictated partially by the gains available in each departmental application, and partly by the need for data as a whole. Pharmacy systems, for example, offer opportunities for impressive improvements in unit dose cost and quality of

Figure 10.3 Content of IS Plans

Topic	Large Organization Example	Smaller Organization Example
Information goals	Automatic access to all current patient records, archives of performance measures by RC, routine translation to final product	Complete order entry, major results, clinical abstract, automated budget system, and special project final product analysis
Integrated systems	20 second peak delay, 90% uniform word process, spreadsheet and data base software	Integrate finance and medical records data, integrate existing departmental systems
Central hardware plans	WAN serving all sites, several LANs, client-server archive structure	LAN and phone connection for remote offices, file server for archive
Departmental systems	$100 million 5-year plan allocated 80% to central, 20% to departmental needs; initial reviews by site against established criteria; final review by systemwide panel	$20 million 5-year plan, allocated 50% central, 50% departmental; all proposals reviewed by IS advisory committee, against established criteria

pharmacological services (intermediate product cost and quality). In addition, they generate data on drug cost and use per case which support improvement in the overall efficiency and effectiveness of care of specific diseases (final product cost and quality). An organization which moved too soon to install a pharmacy system might spend money on capability it was currently unable to use, but an organization which moved too slowly could face difficulties controlling final product costs.

A good IS strategic plan has the following characteristics:

1. It identifies essential and desirable applications and rules out those opportunities which are infeasible or problematic in the specific setting. Desirable applications are based on the needs of the organization as a whole, rather than those of individual units. Final priorities incorporate human factors. Work groups that are ready to use technology should receive assistance in reasonable time. Work groups not ready for technology and impeding the organization as a whole are identified for further work by executive management.

2. It indicates the systems to be installed, the order in which they are to be installed, and the expectations to be attained by a combination of systems implementation and process improvement. The plan will address timing, component performance, methods of coordinating and integrating diverse groups and systems, ways of meeting users' needs for training and support, and incentives for acceptance, mastery, and exploitation of the new technology.

3. It minimizes departure from fully tested technology. Emerging information technology moves through three phases— development, initial, or "alpha site" testing, and larger scale, or "beta site" testing, before it is an established, reliable product. Significant costs can be incurred by institutions participating in alpha or beta testing through delays, breakdowns, and reconfigurations even for successful products. Sharply reduced purchase prices and even royalties from future sales are not uncommon for alpha and beta sites. On-site development is deliberately avoided. When essential it is usually a joint venture with a commercial vendor.

4. It recognizes the interactive nature of information systems benefits and contains opportunities for operating units to articulate their own information needs and plans. IS staff assists in development of proposals which are then judged competitively against others, in a manner similar to the new programs and capital budget review.

5. It specifies the benefits to be gained in terms of global measures of organizational performance, and also in terms of specific activity measurements where possible. It specifies the process revisions

necessary to gain the benefits, and the timetable for return on investment. It represents a commitment by IS and executive management to achieve the plan and its benefits.

The joint commitment of IS and line management has a profound effect on information investments. It facilitates individual projects, but it also changes the amount of investment and the forward progress of the organization. The amount invested in the information strategy will depend upon the market pressure to improve cost and quality, the responses selected to meet this pressure, and current information services capability. The strategic questions are the timing and overall amount. Figure 10.4 shows the kinds of costs involved in information system improvement. There is an opportunity cost which mounts with delay. With many health care organizations reporting large-scale investment in information, organizations which do not follow suit risk loss of what could be a vital capability. Implementation of each major system usually takes one to two years; catching up to a competitor with a significant head start may turn out to be impossible. On the other hand, the cost of new technology falls rapidly. Hardware prices fall as much as 50 percent in a year, for example. Finally, there are implementation costs, time and resources consumed in fitting the change to existing systems, training personnel to use the new system, and achieving the anticipated benefits. These are presumably constant over time, but differ between institutions and applications. The proper strategy for an IS plan is to expend the minimum total cost, advancing each year as far as technical and implementation costs permit, and meeting any need with a high-opportunity cost.

The concepts of Figure 10.4 can only be roughly translated to specific situations. The correct balance often depends upon the implementation cost. Organizations that can adapt quickly to new technology and start to generate benefits from it have a clear advantage. They will

Figure 10.4 Factors Determining Information Systems Investment

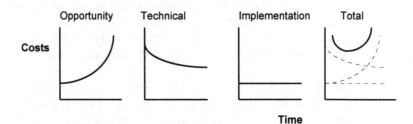

invest less on each project, achieve real benefits from their investments faster, and invest more over time. The organization which finds itself constraining IS investments below the level of its competitors may simply need a more aggressive plan, but it could also need to reduce its implementation costs, improving its operational capability to use information. The latter need must be met by line managers. IS services can help, but they are not likely to be sufficient.

Evaluating Specific Proposals

Information strategies are implemented through proposals for systems improvements. These arise both from IS itself and from other operating units seeking process improvements. Figure 10.5 lists 10 steps in the planning process for specific information services proposals. The steps in Figure 10.5 appear onerous, but it is dangerous to omit them. As is the case with other new program proposals (Chapter 7), well-run organizations seem to make the *preliminary* decisions in steps 1 to 3 quickly, eliminating projects with low value, or which do not support the strategy. They then focus their resources on the reduced set of opportunities, make wise *selection* decisions at steps 4 to 7, and follow through *installation* in steps 8 to 10, assuring that the operational improvements they desired really occur.

The first five steps involve a collaboration between IS and the line units directly affected by a proposal. Together they agree on the system, the benefits, and the vendor. There are often major obstacles. Communication difficulties between the line, which rarely understands data processing technology, and IS, which often has difficulty understanding clinical requirements and processes, must be overcome. Vendors' systems are not directly comparable. Unique features may add substantially to the cost, but eliminating them may require extensive process redesign.

The proposals are usually quite specific as to application, effort, vendor, cost, and implementation timetable, but less clear on benefits. The benefit from an individual information investment is often impossible to calculate. It inevitably involves not only the information system itself, but also the improvements in operations that result. Even if these can be accurately forecast, the problem of allocating the benefits between the line teams which achieve them and the information system that lets them do it is insurmountable. The larger the system, the more difficult the problem becomes. The solution, wherever possible, is to make proposals joint between IS and the line departments involved in implementation. Then both are committed, and the effort to prepare the proposal reveals and solves many of the potential problems.

Figure 10.5 Ten Steps in Information System Improvement

Preliminary: Easy steps that allow many possibilities to be scanned.

1. Identify   Broad search for possible improvements from survey of current capabilities, market pressure, and IS strategy.

Changes should be expected to yield improved control: better mean or smaller variance on one or more performance dimensions, at either intermediate and final product levels.

2. Justify   Demonstrate feasibility of the proposal:
Commercially available pharmacy management system will provide inventory control and drug use data.
Describe necessary process changes:
Dispensing and drug ordering revisions.
Pharmacy Committee revise formulary and prescribing policies.
Quantify anticipated control capabilities:
Inventory costs down at least 20 percent.
Better than 50/50 chance prescribing costs for high-cost drugs can be reduced by 1/3.

3. Value   Estimate the worth of each control improvement:
Inventory reductions $500,000.
Drug usage reductions about $300,000 per year

Selection: Developing detailed proposals and ranking them competitively.

4. Specify   List operating requirements:
Desired features and constraints
Identify and describe available products:
Descriptions for several products
Evaluate each on features, cost, compatibility, expansibility, and maintenance:
May require visits, tests, references, negotiation with vendors

5. Select   Identify the vendors offering acceptable products. This
   Vendor   process is complicated by the fact that both valuation and product specification have several dimensions, and all must be accommodated:
A spreadsheet showing major features and relative advantages of each vendor
Line units and IS must agree on the best vendor, integrating the various advantages and costs:
Further negotiation with vendors is possible
The vendor of choice is selected

Continued

Figure 10.5 Continued

6. Rank   An IS advisory committee of line managers with IS participation
   Projects evaluates all proposals completed through step 5. It must
             incorporate interactions between proposals and rank orders
             them:
                Consensus building techniques, negotiation, and leadership are often essential

7. Select   The advisory committee compares the rank-ordered cost against
   Projects the IS plan and recommends the final list to the governing
             board:
                A rank ordered spreadsheet presents projects, line commitments, timetables, costs, and benefits in summary form

Installation: Installing improvements and assuring actual performance improvement.

8. Plan   The committee develops a sequential plan for installation of all
   Install approved projects, with interim achievements at specified dates:
                Line and IS agreement on installation is important
                Major projects will have a PERT chart and critical path analysis

9. Install IS will monitor installation progress against the plan and will
             report necessary revisions to the advisory committee.

10. Confirm IS and line managers involved will monitor performance
             measures against the value expectations from step 3.
             Opportunities to exceed expectations will be explored.

             Performance will be summarized for the advisory committee.

             IS and line mangers will identify the next round of
             improvements.

Figure 10.5 uses a separate selection process involving an IS advisory committee. The role and structure of the committee is discussed further below. Participating in IS plan development and reviewing specific proposals are the committee's two most important tasks. If IS investments are routed through the new programs and capital budget competition described in Chapter 8, they will often lose out to proposals with faster and more direct results. The committee provides a separate, but similar procedure modified to deal with the difficulty of judging the benefits of information systems and to assure a true joint commitment between IS and the line in the projects selected. The committee must reconcile several conflicting forces. Several units, including IS, will be competing for limited funds. Some units may need encouragement to make necessary process revisions. Agreements must be complete and sincere, but still reached in a timely fashion.

It is likely that success feeds itself. Good strategies, smart selections, and effective installations give the well-run health care organization insights into the next round of information systems improvements. Weaker institutions make inferior strategic choices, belabor the selection process, and fail to capitalize on the installation. They find themselves with reduced choices as the delays and opportunity costs mount.

Assuring the Integrity, Quality, and Security of Data

As massive amounts of information develop and people depend routinely on its use, the importance of uniform definitions, accurate entries, and protection against loss or corruption mount. A well-managed IS assures these characteristics by deliberate programs-controlling measures, data-capture routines, and access to recorded data.

Defining Terminology and Measures

Any term which is used in a quantitative system must have a precise definition, and the definitions must be kept consistent across many different users. Terms like "admission," "patient day," and "unit price" appear straightforward, but in reality require specific, written definitions to avoid inconsistencies which may later prove troublesome (for example, Is a patient kept over night in emergency an "admission"? Is a stay of less than 24 hours one day, and if so, how should it be distinguished from a stay of more than 24 hours but less than 48? Is the price what is billed or what is collected?). The goal is to eliminate cases where two different data sources use the same term for different definitions.

Various units of health care organizations are concerned with the problem of accurate definitions. Accounting has used the audit system and a national panel, the Financial Accounting Standards Board, to assure accurate definitions of public accounts. Over many years, an elaborate system of rules has developed in general use. The American Hospital Association maintains a set of common definitions and statistics which it uses for national reporting.[7]

In clinical areas, medical records administrators and nosologists (specialists in the description and classification of disease) have labored over common medical terms, such as the identification and coding of diagnoses and procedures, for decades. The International Classification of Disease, Version 9, Clinical Modification, (ICD9CM) represents the work of an international panel modified to fit national needs but allows worldwide reporting and comparison of diagnoses and procedures.[8] The DRG system is based on ICD9CM and monitored by insurance intermediaries and the federal Health Care Financing Administration which use it for payment. Similarly, a set of physician and outpatient procedure codes, Current Procedural Terminology (CPT) is maintained by the American Medical Association and serves as the basis for outpatient and physician billing.[9] Various professions and specialties have codes for their activities. The College of American Pathologists maintains codes for laboratory tests.[10] Therapists have formal definitions and codes for their treatments.

In other areas definitions are embedded in business contracts and government regulation. The National Bureau of Standards maintains definitions for common measures of time, energy, temperature, distance, and weight as well as thousands of more specialized technical measures.

The first step in assuring data quality is to compile these definitions and abide by them. But there are so many different sources that problems of conflict and omission are inevitable. Larger health care organizations generally maintain a committee on measurement and definitions which can assure that all relevant national sources have been adopted. It can investigate potential conflicts and ambiguities. Finally, it can define additional measures the institution needs in ways that are acceptable to users and consistent with existing ones. Smaller institutions tend to rely heavily on existing sources, and make modifications by ad hoc study.

In any case, each term which is entered into a common data base or which is used by more than one unit must have a precise definition. With the growth of large scale storage and access devices, the definitions themselves are available directly from computer terminals. Coding systems like ICD9CM, CPT, and DRGs are available in a variety of formats.

Capturing Data

The issues in the capture of information are completeness and accuracy. Missing information not only impairs the quality of various counts, it introduces ambiguities and possible errors. The following steps insure accurate data entry:

1. Direct electronic entry is preferred over written records. A variety of electronic input devices now exist. At worst, they are no less accurate than handwritten records. Subject to even elementary edits, they are substantially more accurate.

2. Automated entry is preferable to human entry. Various card readers, scanners, and devices to retrieve information from electronic archives are superior to their human counterparts. The human interface is both the most expensive and least accurate link in most systems.

3. All important information should be edited and audited at entry to ensure accuracy. Electronic edits can be built into the capture system to eliminate omissions and key stroke errors. Edits generally are based on a single field of information; the field must contain a certain kind of data, such as certain numbers or letters, or selection from a certain list. Audits generally compare two or more fields for consistency; age, gender, and diagnosis are common examples. The extensiveness of edits and audits depends upon the centrality of the information. Key records such as patient registration would be subject to the most rigorous control, possibly including sample audits by a second worker in addition to universal electronic ones.

4. Information should be captured for electronic processing only once. For most applications, retrieval will be less time consuming than re-entry. Some of the savings can be devoted to verifying the retrieved data, as with the use of both names and numbers to retrieve patient records.

For any data capture involving information shared among organization units, IS should advise on the design and maintenance of audits, capture forms or screen specifications, networking, and retrieval capability. In addition, IS has complete responsibility for the management of certain kinds of information, for example

- *Patient registration and placement record.* This information includes descriptions of present, future, and immediate past patients. These are critical to clinical communication, billing, scheduling, and communication with patients and families;

- *Files of patients' unit record numbers.* Patients are usually assigned a unique, lifetime record number that must be retrieved when the patient returns for care, even after a long absence. A special file accesses not only the patient's name and number, but several confirming attributes, such as date of birth, sex, race, and mother's name. Specialized retrieval and entry systems allow sound-oriented searches, searches by portions of the name, or by other attributes. New entries are audited against existing ones to prevent duplication;

- *Patient medical record files.* Medical records are increasingly automated. The medical records management function has moved to be part of IS in many organizations. The files consist of five broad categories, identification and summary material, workup and care plans, orders, order results, and notes. The order file supports the patient ledger. It and identification material are now routinely electronic for inpatient, and outpatient electronic systems are spreading rapidly. Results reporting follows after orders are automated. Clinical protocols permit automation of much of care plans and work-ups. Progress is being made on automation of case summaries and many kinds of notes;[11] and

• *Patient and employee surveys.* Direct querying of patient and family satisfaction is an increasingly important device for marketing and outcomes quality assessment. Patients' attitudes are important elements in the quality of clinical services, particularly nursing and medicine, and also in the quality of plant services, particularly parking and food service. It is believed that positive attitudes can minimize the risk of malpractice suits.[12] Employee and physician attitudes are important to effective recruitment and motivation, and are also surveyed frequently.

To be reliable, surveys must use carefully designed protocols, rigorous sampling routines, and extensive follow-up to reduce nonresponse. Central control over the design and administration of surveys is essential to assure accurate results and interpretation. It should not be used to discourage use of the tool, but rather to assure maximum benefit from it. Control can be lodged either in IS or in units most closely connected to the survey population, such as marketing for patient surveys and human resources for employee surveys.

Other units, particularly planning, finance, and human resources have extensive responsibilities for automated data bases in their areas. IS must assure that these bases are properly accessible and usable with its own.

Maintaining Confidentiality of Information

IS is responsible for designing and maintaining systems to protect files against unauthorized use. Most information about specific patients and some employee records are confidential and need to be protected against unauthorized access. IS must identify the confidentiality requirements and incorporate controls in operations to insure that they are met. These usually take the form of requiring user identification and restricting access to qualified users. Cards, passwords, and voice readers are used for this purpose. Confidentiality is also important in archiving and retrieval. The archive must be protected from inappropriate use and reporting must be constructed in ways that prevent inference about individuals from statistical analyses. Centralized archiving and monitoring of data uses and users protect against these dangers.[13,14] Restrictions on access to small sets of data or certain combinations of data can be built into the archive or the data retrieval system.

The issue of confidentiality is important, but relative. Many health care confidentiality problems are similar to other information sources which are now automated, such as driving records, credit records, and income tax files. The real question is one of the benefits of convenient access versus the risk of damage. Reasonable steps to reduce the risk seem to be all that is required to gain general acceptance. Also, the danger of violating confidentiality is inherent in the information, rather than the way it is processed. Manual systems of handling patient and personnel information were far from foolproof. Just because a great many people are involved in modern health care, a great many people have access to highly personal information. There is little evidence that computers necessarily make the problem worse; properly designed they may reduce the chance of misuse or inappropriate access. Proper design is essential, however. Unprotected electronic files can be accessed quickly, in large numbers, for a variety of improper purposes.

Integrating Information Capture and Processing

To implement an effective plan and provide for data safety and integrity, IS operates a technical service of data communication and processing. The function is to assure that all users have access to data necessary for their operation, and computing capability to use it effectively. With the growth of decentralized computers, the emphasis of the function has shifted from actual data processing on what once were called main frame computers to design and management of data communication systems and control of hardware and software to support integration. The function includes the maintenance of central hardware and software, including communication systems, and the support of departmental hardware and software.

The IS role has moved from data processing to support of integrated systems, where the actual processing occurs in decentralized sites and smaller increments. Figure 10.6 shows the concept of data integration. The major sources of data, discussed in Chapter 9, each access and contribute to each other's needs, and create in the process a data archive.

Implementing the concept of Figure 10.6 requires specific steps to make communications, computing hardware, and computing software compatible. The history of information development makes the task challenging. Different parts of the network shown in Figure 10.6

Figure 10.6 The Concept of an Integrated Data Network

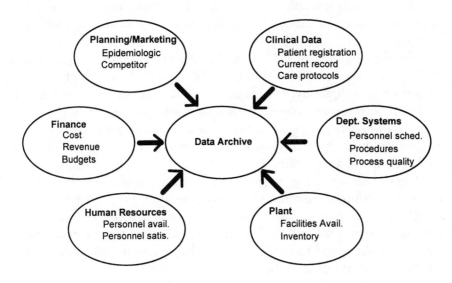

started at different times, with local rather than institutional goals. They tended to choose hardware and software appropriate to their immediate needs. Investment in meeting common needs became feasible and desirable only in the 1990s, with the development of inexpensive personal computers (PCs).

Communications and Centralized Services

The PC makes it possible to meet most people's computational needs with a processor and storage facility on their desks. PCs available today for slightly more than $1,000 can carry out more instructions per second than the largest known machines of a decade ago and store 200 million bytes of data. (That is 60 times the size of this book.) Their widespread use means that the critical task for the organization is no longer to process data or store it; it is to facilitate access and communication.

IS provides for communication by maintaining high-speed links, usually optical fibers, and by operating dedicated hardware and software. These are **local area networks** (LANs) serving individual units within about 1,000 yards of one another, and **wide area networks** (WANs) reaching across cities or around the world. **Client-server** machinery uses centralized processing to reduce data transfer volumes and facilitate translation between alternative data formats used by the competing hardware and operating systems. Most large health care institutions will need all three. They will have LANs serving individual hospitals and clinics, and WANs connecting them together. Centralized processors will maintain shared data bases and do large volume computing.

The development of WANs can be very costly. Several multibillion dollar companies are involved in projects to meet the needs of the "information superhighway," which includes many communications needs of health care organizations. Although some pioneering health care organizations have engaged in joint ventures to develop applications, it appears likely that useful products will be sold as communications packages in the near future.

Central or shared processing units often supplement local user capability. Printers are often shared by several users. Message systems of all kinds are part of centralized hardware and software. Electronic mail is now routine, and the message handling system is maintained by IS. Telephone and facsimile services often share the communication hardware, and are usually the responsibility of IS.

An automatic file backup is usually included in central communications services. Although hardware, software, and operator failures are now rare, it is possible to destroy or lose primary data. The communications system records all data flowing through it, making it possible to reconstruct losses and restore data integrity in most cases. Certain statistical and financial routines require larger central processing capability or other features not commonly found on PCs. Many ISs operate central computers, usually called mainframes, for these purposes. The programming, scheduling, and maintaining of mainframes is an IS responsibility.

Decentralized Hardware and Software

Most of the hardware now used by health care organizations is decentralized and is part of the resources and accountability of operational units. IS supports the hardware management by the following activities:

1. Offering consultative services on hardware requirements and selection, helping users meet their computational needs at minimum cost.
2. Supporting interface hardware for existing systems which cannot easily be integrated without it.
3. Selecting preferred hardware, and negotiating favorable prices by bulk purchase.
4. Providing maintenance service and backup equipment to preferred hardware.

5. Assisting with hardware financing for proposals accepted under the IS plan.

Users are rarely formally limited in their hardware selection. Rather, price and service features are used to make the preferred hardware and software the obvious choice. In certain cases, where the data and hardware compatibility are essential to central needs, IS must negotiate a mutually acceptable solution with the user department. Financial assistance through the IS plan, and the value of purchasing contracts and local maintenance are powerful resources to convince operating units on the virtues of uniformity.

Most software is now purchased from commercial vendors. Even large special-purpose routines like inventory management, payroll and personnel systems, and general ledger systems are available from national vendors, sometimes modified for specific health care use. Much departmental software is available from smaller vendors. IS is responsible for approving any software used in an information system. It must meet the IS plan, be compatible with existing hardware and software wherever necessary, and be supported by the vendor to adopt to changes in hardware and operating requirements over time. (Units can purchase unsupported software for local uses short of formal information systems. IS plan funding and support services are available to convince them not to.)

Departmental Decision Support Systems

It is often possible to identify recurring management decisions that can be computerized on departmental information systems. The systems handle the department record keeping, generate automatic communications such as orders and charges for other systems, maintain current or short-term archives, and undertake elementary modeling of the implications of exogenous conditions such as demand on endogenous parameters such as staffing or supplies orders.

These systems automate management decisions which formerly required substantial time and expert judgment and which were made less consistently by human beings. They become important tools for planning and budgeting as well as aids to day-to-day decision making. An example is the nursing staffing system described in Chapter 13. The system uses counts and severity measures of patient demand with data on the number and skills of nurses to establish staffing. It shows current shortages and overstaffing by unit and shift, and the optimum deployment of available nurses in terms of patient need. A second module suggests staffing levels required for given demand forecasts, estimates employment requirements, and prepares a personnel budget.

A third module translates the available personnel levels into a work schedule which optimizes access to nursing care based on forecasts of volume and severity, and a fourth draws samples, prints questionnaires, and tallies results of process quality inspections. Well-managed hospitals now have departmental information systems in many areas, including clinical support services, nursing, human resources, and plant systems. They perform various tasks, but the following elements are frequently present:

- *Personnel scheduling*, work schedules for individual employees which accommodate patient care needs but are also sensitive to employee desires
- *Patient or activity scheduling*, schedules for the performance of specified work (such as housekeeping or routine maintenance) or for the optimal use of physical facilities (such as beds, operating rooms, and x-ray machinery)
- *Recording and process control*, automated tracking of orders and specimens, preparation of reports and records, and word processing
- *Inventory management*, automated reorder, distribution, and accounting for routine supplies
- *Message capability*, software to permit multiple users of departmental systems to communicate with each other and through networking, with other systems
- *Educational and training programs*, automated prompts on the recommended method or procedure for new personnel or infrequent situations
- *Quality assessment*, measures of process, and outcomes quality obtained by automated sample selection, questionnaire design, and statistical analysis
- *Job assignment and human resources accounting*, provisions for skill profiles of employees and for day-to-day adjustment of actual work to reflect unpredictable variation in demand for personnel

Several examples of these systems are available for a variety of clinical, human resources, and plant services. The central information service has four functions with regard to departmental decision support systems:

1. Assist in the planning, design, installation, and interfacing of the departmental system.
2. Provide the necessary historic and current data from other sources.
3. Maintain data quality of newly input information.
4. Archive the data of general or permanent value.

Archiving and Retrieving Data

A central data archive is a competitive resource which grows in value as it is expanded. Archiving can be an automated byproduct of network communications, and a variety of special-purpose archives can be captured from local applications or acquired from outside sources. Each of the major systems shown in Figure 10.6 generates archives. Some of the more important are

- Archives of clinical activity, compiled from patient records. These permit historical analysis of output, efficiency, and quality, and variation in performance among sites and providers;
- Archives of population, marketing activity, patient satisfaction, and competitor behavior. These support analyses of market needs, promotional activities, and demand;
- Archives of personnel history, skills, and satisfaction. These are essential to determine recruitment needs and to assist in attracting highly qualified workers and physicians; and
- Archives of cost and resource use. These support identification of fixed, variable, and marginal costs and profitability.

These archives are essential for forecasting performance measures, for revealing potential improvements, and for modeling and evaluating them. Many proposals require data from several basic archives.

Other archives can be obtained from national suppliers. Medline, the automated indexing and abstracting service of the National Library of Medicine, is an important example. The archive contains over 8,000,000 references on clinical and health care journal publications, accessible by topic, author, publisher, national origin, language of publication, title, and date. An abstract of up to 250 words is available if provided by the publisher. The archive is current generally to the actual date of publication. A team studying a specific surgical procedure could maintain an up to the minute survey of published literature about it. So could a team studying health care–related issues, such as the organization of clinical services.

Archive Management

Relational retrieval systems make the recovery of information from a single archive quick and easy. However, most relational systems require specific content and format for data entry. Archiving depends upon effective completion of the data integrity function, and often a special step preparing the archive for retrieval. The archive itself must be protected against fire, flood, theft, power interruptions, and sabotage. Retrieval software must be similarly maintained. Often these needs lead to duplication of critical files and the management of updates to duplicates. Larger organizations keep complete duplicate record sets ("backups") in secure locations in another geographic area. Because the archives continue to change, the task of maintaining the backups requires deliberate planning.[15]

Executive Support Systems

The monitoring function of central management is now supported by special-purpose software which allows rapid access to large archives of integrated data. Executive support systems take data from several archives, organize them to parallel accountability and cross-functional team structures, and make them available for either routine or special-purpose reports. The software accesses the archive, selects the measures of interest, and aggregates them to level needed. Board and executive level reports can be prepared routinely every month, assuring consistent definitions and data sources. Graphic presentations are automated, as is table construction and labeling. Either screen, slide, or paper formats are possible. Subroutines make it possible to evaluate deviations from expectations in terms of severity, statistical significance, or duration. In screen versions, the user may "drill down" to identify the source and extent of variation.[16] In addition to performance data, archives like personnel names and addresses, and employment status are routinely accessible.

Archive User Support

The more complicated improvement studies require more than simply the retrieval of specific data. It is necessary to consider whether all possible archives have been included, how to relate data from different archives, and how to deal with omissions and limitations in the data. An archivist expert in archive content, user needs, and retrieval processes greatly amplifies the value of the archives. Linking data from two or more major files is often complicated. Special software may be required. If the link is one that is infrequently used, a program may have to be written specifically to do the job. Even in the best IS there are changes in key definitions and gaps in the data. These weaknesses must be evaluated in relation to the specific questions being asked. For example, a study of a major clinical service such as orthopedics or cardiac surgery might require data from several sources.

- Final product performance integrating cost, revenue, and quality data on the major diagnosis or procedure groups in the service
- Patient satisfaction and market share data by major market segment and diagnosis

- Individual performance and satisfaction variation by provider
- Medline bibliographies on important diagnosis or procedure groups
- Scheduling capabilities of clinical support services involved
- Pricing and vendor data for several expensive supply items
- Epidemiologic trends for national and local data
- Benchmark performance of other provider units.

Most of the information will be retrieved from the archives of the sources generating it. Only the first three topics are likely to be integrated, or to need automated integration, but substantial technical and statistical issues will arise within the first three. The available time period may be different in the clinical and cost data. Is it appropriate to compare or combine the two? Critical definitions may have changed over time. Two new DRGs introduced a year ago divide what once was a single group. Is it better to use the new, or recombine them and gain more history? If there is a loss of some data, can that loss be treated as random, or was it the result of a process that acted systematically upon different segments of interest. A sudden loss of demand may reflect the departure of specific surgeons. Were their case loads similar to everyone else's, or unique? If they were unique, what change does their loss make on the performance statistics? An important part of the archival function is understanding data and computing constraints, devising ways to present the data effectively to users, and making sure the users understand the limitations.

Training and Supporting Users

The training and user support function includes selection and maintenance of general use software, training programs, and consultation and support for specific applications. While the training function is shared among planning, marketing, finance, and IS, the archives and existing software make IS a major contributor.

General Use Software

As shown in Figure 10.7, health care organizations use a variety of commercial software packages throughout the institution. Standardization of these packages is useful because it facilitates communication, supports cross-functional teams, and permits transfer of operators from one application to another. Selection criteria include user acceptability, compatibility, cost, and service. Partly because the vendors tend to be very competitive on compatibility, cost, and service, the decision often hinges on user acceptability. Much of this software is deliberately designed to be user friendly. It contains help facilities, comes with manuals, and incorporates much technical material into background which need not be mastered by the casual user. The goal is to make the technically correct analysis easy to do and easy to understand. Software convenience and clarity encourage the decision makers to make maximal use of the data.

Statistical programs make the analysis more rigorous and more reliable, avoiding false conclusions about reality. Graphic packages permit the prompt generation of colorful displays, which help many people understand the meaning of statistics. Spreadsheet software allows the construction of alternative scenarios and the search for the best solution based upon the improved understanding which comes from

Figure 10.7 General Use Software

Software	Use	Common Trade Names
Word processing	Text entry, formatting, archiving. Allows multiple authors for major reports, subject searches of minutes, etc.	Word WordPerfect
Spreadsheet	Repetitive calculations, graphs, some statistical analysis. Allows multiple versions of business plans, budgets, etc.	123 Quattro Excel
Data base	Uniform entries to data sets, rapid retrieval, sorting. Allows easy segmentation of customer lists, inventories, etc.	Paradox Access FoxPro
Message	Easy posting and retrieval of messages. Allows rapid, recorded communication between many users.	Mail CC:Mail
Calendars	Agendas, schedules, contacts, and future obligations. Allows easy tracking of multiple activities, facilitates planning	Sidekick Advantage On-schedule
Statistical	Advanced analysis of quantitative data. Allows specialized regression and significance testing.	SAS Systat
Graphics	Advanced presentation formatting and graphics. Allows convincing graphics, tables and charts.	Harvard Graphics PowerPoint Persuasion

statistical analysis and graphic display. A central activity of continuous improvement is the search for the optimal set among these numerous alternatives. Spreadsheets allow the decision makers to ask "What if" questions and trace the implications in terms of key performance variables like cost, profit, and quality.

More elaborate software for modeling several financial activities is well developed and is now available commercially. Software for examining alternative pricing decisions and designing future capital debt structures is in widespread use among well-managed institutions. Also emerging is software that addresses marketing-related issues of expansions, acquisitions, and changes in final product profiles. Although the use of financial and statistical modeling requires much expense and effort, it is rapidly becoming standard practice for all decisions at the strategic level.

IS should encourage standardization of this software, select the preferred vendors, arrange purchase and maintenance, and support use with training and consultation. An example is the development of strategies for medical staff recruitment. Word processors, calendars, and message systems are now expected as devices to communicate; they would be used to justify further study and built an improvement team. Statistical and graphic analysis would be used to forecast population trends and patient demand statistics. The potential demand would be organized by primary and specialty care. Spreadsheet software would develop a model showing the impact of alternative locations and specialty mixes on visits, market share, admissions, requirements on clinical services, and revenues. Once the optimum location and specialty mix was determined, the results would be fed to the long-range financial plan to incorporate the impact of these decisions on overall operations.

The IS role includes

- Identifying the preferred vendor or vendors. Large institutions may wish to support more than one vendor. Often institutions which have acquired or merged activities will be forced to support two or more vendors.

- Encouraging adoption of the software. Learning to use new software requires an investment of time and money before the advantages occur. One IS role is to encourage units to make this investment.

- Negotiating price and supplier maintenance. IS can arrange an organizationwide license, and usually can negotiate price advantages and in some cases extended service.

- Providing maintenance and updates. While general use software requires very little maintenance, periodic updates are issued. These must be evaluated, purchased if desirable, and installed, together with whatever training is indicated.

- Supporting the selected software with training and consultation. IS can provide introductory training for new installations and new employees and advanced training for people making extensive applications. Similarly, it can provide assistance when problems arise. These activities are part of the larger training and consultation services discussed below.

Training Programs

Users need training at two levels. New employees or new users need introductory training. Experienced users and people facing unique needs frequently need advanced training. The training should go beyond use of the software to include information about available data and approaches to analysis. The objective is not just familiarity with a tool, it is application of the tool for improved performance. Training should show how the software can be used with the seven tools of CQI, for example. The selection and design of graphs and tables is a useful topic. Advanced training should show appropriate applications of elementary statistics, or address specific issues of recurring concern, such as advanced analysis of control chart statistics.

Training should emphasize the most efficient medium. Formal classroom instruction is one approach, most efficient when the content is relatively clear, human interaction is usually necessary, but the level of interaction is such that one instructor can assist several students. Written and electronic media are far less expensive and allow students to proceed at their own pace, but they lack human interaction. Backing them up with messages and consultation helps assure that the students will remain motivated and make steady progress. Electronic conferences and user groups are popular. They tend to emphasize unique applications requiring considerable human interaction on a one-to-one level.

Consultation

Most large IS offer a help desk which supplements other training activities. The desk is staffed by experts in general software who can help users attempting specific tasks. It is usually accessible electronically and by telephone.

More extensive consultation should also be available, although it can be provided in planning, marketing, or financial management. Although mastery of the general software is included, the subject of the consultation is more problem oriented—ways to accomplish certain analyses, interpreting ambiguous results, improving graphic displays, overcoming limitations in the data.

Management engineering consultation is used by many well-managed organizations. The engineers are trained in analysis of work processes, statistical and financial analysis, development of stochastic and deterministic models, field testing, and design of improved systems. Their skills include most of the areas important to an RC or cross-functional team working on an improvement. They tend to be heavy users of the archived data, and therefore familiar with it and its limitations. Similarly, their training allows them to answer many of the technical questions in statistics and cost accounting.

Organization of Information Services

Well-managed health care organizations have sought centralization, direct accountability to top line officers, and enhanced visibility as a way to promote IS. They use a structure like that shown in Figure 10.8, with central accountability placed high in the organization as a whole. The five functions can be divided several ways but the three part design shown has the advantage of linking similar activities into identifiable roles of roughly equal size and separate skills.

The discussion of the organization includes the roles of the chief information officer and the IS Advisory Committee, the major functions outlined in Figure 10.8, and the use of outside consultants and information service vendors.

Figure 10.8 Organization of Information Services

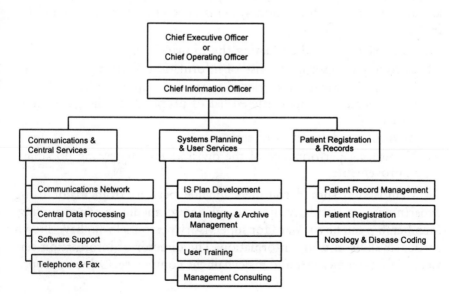

Chief Information Officer

The role of an information executive or chief information officer has emerged with the growth of IS, and has tended to move to a higher level within the organization. Early CIOs were masters of computer technology. The future CIO is likely to need an understanding of the technology and of health care applications. Leadership and negotiating skills will distinguish excellence. Much of the burden of representing information needs in strategic decisions falls upon the CIO. His or her role in many situations will be to convince others of the power of information and encourage them to use it effectively. Success will be accompanied by increased demand, and continued success will require effective service. In larger institutions, the IS itself will include several dozen employees, enough to present a management challenge.

Training for the CIO can come from several routes. Training in computer operations, management engineering, or medical records administration provides a useful beginning, but an advanced degree in management engineering, business, or health administration is valuable. Many CIOs in larger facilities have doctoral level preparation.

Information Services Advisory Committee

A committee of key users of information services is an important adjunct to a well-run department. The committee's purposes include broad representation in the development of systems investment priorities and communication to assure effective systems design and uniform interpretation. On a different level, the committee offers opportunities to increase line participation in important decisions and to encourage acceptance of information systems. The charge to the committee includes:

1. Understanding and evaluating the IS plan
2. Encouraging appropriate use of information services
3. Ranking information services investment opportunities and recommending a rank-ordered list of proposals to the governing board
4. Advising on definitions of terms
5. Monitoring performance of the division and suggesting possible improvements.

Membership should routinely include persons from major using departments, particularly finance, planning, medicine, and nursing. Membership can be a reward for supervisory personnel who have shown particular skills in using information. The director of information services is always a member and may chair the committee. Other appropriate chairpersons would be the chief operating officer, the chief financial officer, or their immediate deputies.

Patient Registration and Records

The volume and importance of clinical data supports a separate activity with an executive who can deal directly with clinical professions. As the traditional medical records activity changes it becomes an inescapable part of an integrated information services. As retrieval technology becomes more widespread, and heuristic use of patient data files more common, the need for combined technical skills in coding, retrieval, statistics, and interpretation will make this a major center of information services.

The patient registration and scheduling functions incorporate the initial contacts between the patient, the attending doctor, and the organization. A critical set of financial, legal, and demographic information is collected which under automated systems is electronically copied thereafter. This information initiates the medical record and is used by all the clinical services as well as the business office. The activities which generate patient registration and records are decentralized to many locations in the institution, but networked computers permit the actual entry to be at the point of service while IS controls the entry screens, data edits, and data quality. The function can be extended to build the overall patient schedule, making it a core part of the hospital's management activity.

The medical records function includes management of record completion and the assignment of diagnostic codes. It is a traditional bottleneck and source of friction between the organization and the physician. Automation and careful attention to the needs of each party have made medical records management a more rewarding opportunity. Because of the irreplaceable value of the clinical archive it remains an important professional function.

Communications and Central Services

The operations group is responsible for the following activities:

- Operation of centralized processing and shared peripherals
- Maintenance of communications hardware
- Management of the physical archive and retrieval software
- Maintenance of personal computer and work station hardware
- Maintenance of all software in common use, including mainframe and supported personal computer programs
- Consultation on planning issues.

As the automated activities have increased in scope, the networked computer system has become more complex and the operational requirements have become more demanding. In particular, order communication requires continuous service of many more remote terminals, with a much lower tolerance of service delays. Shared data such as patient registration information is now required almost instantly through the hospital. The software and hardware for entering it, checking it, and transmitting it are all part of operations. Operations tolerances are very narrow. People now rely on trouble-free computing, and failures can cause massive disruptions.

Systems Planning and User Services

Well-managed organizations are now deliberately stimulating the spread of computer applications by aggressive planning and user service. Most line departments need systematic and extensive assistance to expand automation, and the whole must be coordinated in order to realize important benefits. A well-managed information services unit will have people who devote significant parts of their time to applications planning and implementation. Their activities will include management of the IS plan (Figure 10.2) and assisting line teams to develop information-oriented improvements using the ten-step approach described in Figure 10.5. Although management of the archive is an IS-wide responsibility, the user services unit can be accountable for decisions about data integrity and security. It can coordinate definitions, with input from patient records, accounting, and others.

Training and consultation in using information systems is a natural extension of planning and installation, and it is frequently essential to realization of benefits. Training is important both for new installations and for continued operations. Personnel turnover and systems development make ongoing training essential. Although well-designed software packages now contain training routines designed for the novice user, a local source of advice is important. Interfaces between departmental and central processors are frequently a source of confusion, and these are rarely covered in training material from outside the organization. A good information service orients users to the hospital's system, provides user guides to the interface programs and protocols, gives advice on request, and trains personnel in specific systems when the need emerges.

Management analysis is an internal consulting activity oriented around performance improvement. Management engineers and statisticians in this unit support all forms of improvement studies. They are trained to help managers analyze operating problems and develop work methods. They are equipped to work closely with people from finance, planning, and marketing on large-scale problems. Management analysis requires close collaboration between the technical support activities, and extensive use of the archives.

Familiarity with the archives, the information systems, and the analytic software are important advantages for this group. Their experience with data definitions and processing routines is an added advantage. They should be able to model improvements and design field trials. Many of the existing departmental decision support systems arose from engineering studies and operations research. Conversely, their knowledge of the operating problems makes them valuable contributors to information systems planning. Placing the major analytic capability in IS ties it to a resource valued by the line managers. It gives analysts the opportunity to use computerization as a reward, overcoming perceptions of implied criticism or a threat that often accompany internal consultants.

Use of Outside Contractors

The question of outside contracting for information services is often controversial. On the one hand, there is a well-founded tradition of not allowing a critical service outside the organization itself. On the other, information services is a highly technical area where the expertise of a vendor may be of great value. It pays to understand the opportunities and hazards of outside contracting in order to evaluate the opportunities specifically, rather than by rule-of-thumb.

Several kinds of assistance from outside contractors are available for information services.

1. *Integrated software support.* Computer programs which implement information goals have become increasingly complex, and outside agencies' requirements for data have become more common. These trends make it feasible for commercial companies to develop comprehensive integrated software that is usable in a great many smaller health care organizations. The companies providing the software also maintain it, incorporating changes imposed by outside agencies and technological advances. They sometimes offer customization services as well.

2. *Finance.* Leases and mortgages on hardware are generally available from a variety of outside sources. Software is usually available for purchase or lease from the software vendor. However, there are transaction costs in dealing with several different companies, and in using general institutional debt for information systems.

An outside contractor can consolidate the financing, and offer a comprehensive system on a single lease.

3. *Consultation and planning.* Assistance in selecting hardware and software, analyzing current capabilities, benchmarking, and developing a plan for improvements is available from accounting firms and other consultants.

4. *Facilities management.* Operation of on-site data-processing services under contract is offered by a few companies specializing in health care organization needs. These companies also arrange for financing for the facilities and can be hired for consultation and planning.

5. *Joint developmental ventures.* For those health care organizations in a position to develop new or improved applications, collaboration with an established vendor is highly desirable. The vendor brings experience, extra personnel, capital, and a marketing capability if the development succeeds.

In a complex, rapidly moving technical field, the use of a consultant is often prudent. Consultants can assist materially with the IS plan. Few health care organizations have the expertise to forecast developments in hardware, software, and applications. Both management consulting firms and public accounting firms offer consulting services, as do the firms providing direct information services. There are advantages to each type of company, but the key criterion should be a record of successfully identifying rewarding applications, whether they are in the finance, clinical, or some other system of the hospital.

Integrated software services tend to be selected by smaller hospitals. Relatively complete applications are available at an attractively low price. Flexibility is quite limited, and there is little customizing. Improvements must be selected from among the offerings of the company. The availability of special finance options and alternatives for computer hardware adds to the organization's supply of capital and can help lower the cost of financing generally.

Facilities management of information services has appealed to both large and small organizations. The contracting firm is expected to name a senior data-processing manager with technical skills and knowledge comparable to those of a manager the organization would employ. The on-site manager is supported by the broader experience and specialized knowledge of the contractor's other employees. The skills of the outside group are often useful in information services planning and systems installation. Lower-level employees may work either for the contractor or the health care organization.

A role remains for hospital leadership. The advisory committee would remain in place. The information services plan must become a collaboration between the contractor and the institution. The contractor has no incentive to limit the hospital's choices and usually will profit from an excessive program for improvement. Thus, even with a facilities management contract, hospital governance has the responsibility and the opportunity to select improvements and pace the evolution of the information system. Some well-run organizations hire both service and consulting firms. Although the cost is high, the test of the result is in improved operations. If the information services committee can incorporate the full set of information, balance the competing viewpoints, and devise a more effective program, the cost is justified.

Measures of Performance

Performance measures for IS should cover the full set of six dimensions shown in Figure 9.1. The customers for IS include all the other systems of the organization and some outside clients, but the critical test is the ability to serve clinical departments. Performance expectations are set as they are elsewhere, using a negotiation process centered around the annual budget. Benchmarks, customer needs, and the experience of consultants will be used frequently to set expectations, but as usual, expectations must be set so that they are achieved or exceeded in the vast majority of cases. Monitoring will be important to identify future improvements, to reward the information services committee and information services personnel, and to suggest corrections in the rare cases where expectations are not achieved.

Figure 10.9 shows an array of measures designed to assess the overall contribution, and organized by the major service units of a large IS. Most of these are derived from standard cost accounts, the operating logs detailing automated activities and activities of the director, subordinate units, and the information services committee. Many can be automated and obtained at low cost. Some require special surveys of line managers. Several require a departmental audit. A large number of specific activity measures can be devised to supplement the list in Figure 10.9.

The measures in Figure 10.9 emphasize quality and service more than resources consumed. While resource consumption is important, the central management question for IS is not "How much are we spending?" but " What are we getting for the money?" The outside audit is important. While the JCAHO devotes increasing attention to IS, an annual or biennial audit by a consultant expert could address the full scope of issues and provide a comparison to similar institutions. The audit team would examine centralized operations for the adequacy of service and the appropriateness of software, hardware, and costs.

Figure 10.9 Global Measures of IS Performance

Dimension	IS Unit	Measures
Demand	Communication and central services	Peak load system users
	System plan and user services	Requests for consultation Requests for training
	Patient registration and records	Requests for records Requests for registration
Costs	Communication and central services	Labor and supplies costs by activity Equipment costs by activity Cost of improvements
	System plan and user services	Labor costs by activity
	Patient registration and records	Labor costs
Human resources	All	Employee recruitment and satisfaction
Output and productivity	Communication and central services	Cost per user hour or contact
	System plan and user services	Cost per consultation Cost per trainee hour
	Patient registration and records	Cost per patient
Quality	Communication and central services	Peak access delay User satisfaction Machine failures Timely implementation of improvements
	System plan and user services	Comparative scope of service Trainee satisfaction Line manager satisfaction Audit of archive operation
	Patient registration and records	Record completeness Delay to deliver record Clinical service and finance satisfaction JCAHO audit

Continued

Figure 10.9 Continued

Dimension	IS Unit	Measures
Contribution	Communication and central services	Percent of total expenses
	System plan and user services	Savings attributed to improvement proposals
	Patient registration and records	Percent of total expenses

It would review patient records for completeness, timeliness, and accuracy. It would evaluate the IS plan in the light of achievements of others and the current state of services and archives. It would evaluate both the kinds of training and consultation available and the quality of actual work.

Suggested Readings

Allen, B. 1987. "Make Information Services Pay Its Way." *Harvard Business Review* 65 (January–February): 57–63.

Austin, C. J. 1992. *Information Systems for Health Services Administration*, 4th ed. Ann Arbor, MI: Health Administration Press.

Ferrand, D. J., M. Chokron, and C. M. Lay. 1993. "An Integrated Analytic Framework for Evaluation of Hospital Information Systems Planning." *Medical Care Review* 50 (Fall): 327–66.

Keen, P. G. W. 1985. *Every Manager's Guide to Information Technology*, 2d ed. Cambridge, MA: *Harvard Business School Press*; Symposium on Computer Applications in Medical Care. 1977–current. *Proceedings—Symposium on Computer Applications in Medical Care*. New York: Institute of Electrical and Electronics Engineers.

Worthley, J. A., and P. S. DiSalvio. 1992. *Managing Computers in Health Care: A Guide for Professionals*, 2d ed. Ann Arbor, MI: Health Administration Press.

Notes

1. S. Dorenfest, 1993, *Hospital Information Systems: State of the Art 1992* (Chicago: Dorenfest Associates).
2. G. Levesque, 1994, "1994 HIMSS/Hewlett Packard Leadership Survey Results," *Healthcare Informatics* 11 (July): 8.
3. J. R. Griffith, V. K. Sahney, and R. A. Mohr, 1995, *Reengineering Health Care: Building on CQI* (Ann Arbor, MI: Health Administration Press).
4. D. J. Ferrand, M. Chokron, and C. M. Lay, 1993, "An Integrated Analytic Framework for Evaluation of Hospital Information Systems Planning," *Medical Care Review* 50 (Fall): 327–66.

5. A. L. Lederer and V. Gardiner, 1992, "Strategic Information Systems Planning: The Method/1 Approach," *Information Systems Management* 13 (Summer): 30.

6. D. D. Moriarty, 1992, "Strategic Information Systems Planning for Health Service Providers," *Health Care Management Review* 17 (1): 58–90.

7. American Hospital Association, 1993, *Hospital Statistics, 1993–94 edition* (Chicago: AHA), xiii–xxx.

8. *International Classification of Diseases, 9th Revision, Clinical Modification,* 2d ed., 1980 (Washington, DC: U.S. Department of Health and Human Services, Health Care Financing Administration).

9. *CPT '94 Physicians' Current Procedural Terminology,* 1994 (Chicago: American Medical Association).

10. College of American Pathologists, Committee on Professional Relations, 1977, *Guidelines for Pathologists: Professional Practices* (Skokie, IL: CAP).

11. American Medical Association, 1993, "Users and Uses of Patient Records: Report of the Council on Scientific Affairs," *Archives of Family Medicine* 2 (June): 678–81.

12. R. Penchansky and C. Macnee, 1994, "Initiation of Medical Malpractice Suits: A Conceptualization and Test," *Medical Care* 32 (August): 813–31.

13. B. Wright, 1994, "Health Care and Privacy Law in Electronic Commerce," *Healthcare Financial Management* 48 (January): 66, 68–70.

14. American Medical Association, 1993, "Feasibility of Ensuring Confidentiality and Security of Computer-Based Patient Records," *Archives of Family Medicine* 2 (May): 556–60.

15. R. J. Cox, 1992, *Managing Institutional Archives: Foundational Principles and Practices* (New York: Greenwood Press).

16. T. Franks, 1991, "The Strategic Advantage: Decision Support through Executive Information Systems," *Computers in Healthcare* 12 (January): 36, 39.

Caring: Building the Quality of Clinical Service

IMPROVING QUALITY AND ECONOMY IN PATIENT CARE

Quality and Economy as the Mission of Health Care Organizations

IN THE twenty-first century, the first-line health care organization, whether it is called hospital, health care system, or some other label, will control cost and quality as one of its central functions.[1,2] The marketplace demands no less. The vision, as stated in Chapter 1, responds to that demand:

> the ideal health care organization will provide access for all, sound, comprehensive, and appropriate quality of care, please all its patients, and be affordable to its community. There are inevitable trade-offs between these four dimensions; no real institution will ever achieve the ideal. The well-managed organization must make the trade-offs in a manner that its customers will call satisfactory.

The concept of using the organization to find the trade-offs is not new. It is imbedded in the actions of leading practitioners and managers, and the actions of organizations like the American College of Surgeons and the Joint Commission on Accreditation of Healthcare Organizations. Leading hospitals have been supporting the concept for decades. What is new in the 1990s is a shift to a more universal view of care, incorporating office and outpatient care as well as inpatient, a shift toward more active patient participation, and a broader recognition of the inevitable economic limits. Despite these efforts, it is clear that quality of care,[3,4,5] utilization of services,[6] and patient satisfaction[7] vary between organization structures and physician specialties.

The broad outline of the technology to do the job is also clear. It is based in the continuous improvement approach, and it consists of three components: (1) consensus standards or expectations about the appropriate responses to specific patient symptoms or problems; (2) well-designed processes to provide those responses; and (3) a system to review actual performance and identify future improvements. The consensus and the processes will bear the brunt of the work. Workable components have been tested both in the best-managed community hospitals[8] and leading health maintenance organizations.[9,10,11,12] The role of health care management for the next generation will be to expand and improve consensus development and process design.

The vision must be achieved without resolving the exact definitions of what "quality" and "economy" of health care are. In fact the control systems themselves, and the gap between superior performance and average, stimulate our thinking on these two central characteristics of health care. The two concepts are intertwined. Although it is often useful to think of an ideal quality of care, reality means that quality must always be judged in comparison to economic limits. A starting point on the practical question of building systems to control cost and quality is to accept the consensus definition developed by the Institute of Medicine (IOM):[13]

> **Quality of care:** The degree to which health services for individuals and populations increase the likelihood of desired health outcomes and are consistent with current professional knowledge.

Three other concepts are also required:

> **Appropriate care:** Care for which expected health benefits exceed negative consequences.[14]

> **Efficiency:** Maximization of the quality of a comparable unit of health care delivered for a given unit of health resources used.[15]

It can be inferred that quality care must be appropriate and that both quality and appropriateness are related to efficiency. (Inefficiency reduces benefits for a given level of resources.) But one can be expensive without being wasteful; the cost issue is related to the overall level of health expenditures in the light of the other needs of the community.

> **Economy:** The total level of expenditure for health care, given realistic performance on quality and efficiency and a realistic assessment of available resources.

Abstract or universal answers to the determination of quality and economy are matters which go well beyond the skills and views of physicians and health care professionals, but must at the same time include their insights. (The Institute of Medicine's discussion papers provide a useful summary of the thorny issues involved.[16]) Specific cases are another matter. Despite the complexities, the question of economy and quality are answered every day in every community in the nation. The actions taken, or not taken, for each patient determine the answers.

In well-managed health care organizations, the questions of quality and economy are answered in a manner which strives to optimize the satisfaction of the community at large. Maintaining quality and economy is a process, a continuing effort to come closer to the optimum. It is a central process of the organization. In this respect, control of cost and quality in health care is equivalent to the central processes of many other enterprises. Educational institutions, banks, manufacturers, retailers, and every other enterprise face comparable issues in designing and maintaining their products or services.

Three premises underpin processes to control cost and quality in health care:

- The community at large must establish the desired level of economy. It does so through market decisions, such as the demand for health insurance at various price levels, and political actions such as the governmental budgets for health care programs and institutional budgets for operations and capital. A central function of the governing board is to oversee and build consensus on this complex question.
- Community decisions cannot be intelligently made without extensive input and advice from health care professionals. Although physicians are the leading spokespersons of the professional team because of their superior scientific and technical education, the process must include all clinical activities and the viewpoints of all clinical professionals.
- The control of cost and quality depends upon the entire institutional infrastructure. The five systems (governance, finance, clinical services, human resources, and plant) form the foundation for quality control activities of health care professionals, and the effectiveness of quality control is limited by the effectiveness of these systems.

That is to say, the content of this chapter presumes the other 15 chapters. One cannot achieve the necessary levels of control of cost and quality without a clear mission, governing board review of the medical staff, a well-designed structure for making and implementing decisions, a competent planning function, a sound finance system, and modern information systems. Further, the technology of quality control is built upon an effective medical staff organization, including a recruitment plan that meets competitive economic needs, a process for selection and removal of clinicians based on demonstrated competence, and education to maintain and improve that competence. And finally, no medical staff can achieve acceptable quality in the absence of effective clinical support services, which in turn demand effective human resources and plant support. Conversely, all this can be present, but without an ongoing system to study and improve clinical performance it will not be enough. The well-managed health care organization of the future must achieve clinical effectiveness and mount a comprehensive program of quality improvement.

Plan for the Chapter

This thesis is expanded in the remainder of this chapter, as follows:

- *The clinical quality improvement program:* An overview of the theory which guides medical decision making; implications of the theory; quality improvement of individual patient care decisions—expectations, a system to achieve them, and a formal process of assessment; and program design for continuous improvement—unique aspects of continuous improvement and support structure requirements.

- *Expectation setting:* Definition of clinical expectations; strategies to determine what kinds of expectations should be selected; how many; and who should be involved; and processes of developing expectations which are designed to enhance acceptance and compliance.

- *Monitoring:* Accountability for the program; using the monitor to guide expectation-setting and to indicate areas of process redesign; and guidelines for monitoring individual performance and using rewards and sanctions.

- *Measures and information systems:* Sources of measures for monitoring quality and economy—information processing and display requirements.

The Clinical Quality Improvement Program

A well-managed health care organization which has the infrastructure described in this text will, as a result, have a corps of well-intentioned, well-trained, well-supported clinical personnel. Other things being equal, that corps will deliver good quality. Evidence from well-managed institutions which have studied the problem suggest that the quality can be improved, and the economy is highly variable, unless deliberate action is taken to develop consensus among the caregivers about the many decisions that go into a course of treatment.[17,18] A clinical improvement program is an organized effort to build and implement consensus providing each patient with the optimal level of treatment.[19] To understand such a program, it is wise to begin with an analysis of the care decisions made by individual practitioners about individual patients.

Decision Theory and Case Management

A Simple Decision Theory Model Guiding Clinical Behavior

Conceptually, quality care must be appropriate; care which omits appropriate elements or includes inappropriate elements cannot be of the highest quality. Care is appropriate when the marginal cost of service is exactly equal to the marginal benefit; that is, when the last service ordered contributed more value through improved outcome than it cost, and the next service which might be ordered will contribute less than it costs.[20] Real medical care proceeds in multiple and interacting logical sequences, but each considered step is a simple binary decision, to be answered either yes or no. There are thousands of such decisions, mostly answered no, in a given episode of care. Many considerations recur. That is, a laboratory test may be considered today and again tomorrow. The recurrence is often independent of the decision; whether or not the service was ordered today, it can be reconsidered tomorrow. Each binary decision is reached by the doctor's (or other caregiver's) internal calculus, an amalgam of training and experience. Obviously, given the number of decisions and the difficulty of measuring the costs and benefits, that calculus must be fast, reliable, and robust.

Costs and benefits must usually be evaluated for both possible answers. There are only a few easy decisions, those where one side heavily outweighs the other. For example, immunizations are almost always appropriate. For patients with severe diabetes, insulin is required. For most realistic problems, decisions are more complex, more numerous, and require faster response. When the costs include death or disability and the decisions must be made quickly, the skills of the physician are tested.

Doctors' evaluations center on probabilities, since few things in medicine are certain. Thus, doctors treating patients with pain in the abdomen weigh first the probability that it is self-limiting, knowing that most afflictions, in fact, cure themselves in a few hours or days.

Next, they consider alternative interventions: drugs or surgery for direct treatment versus laboratory tests, imaging, or optical scope for refinement of the diagnosis. Having selected the most promising of these alternatives, the question is, What are the probable outcomes of proceeding and not proceeding and their relative values? The doctors' decision-making processes can be modeled as decision theory, although the actions of real doctors are considerably more complicated than the theory.[21] Taking the most drastic of the interventions, surgery, the possibilities look something like the list in Figure 11.1.

The figure shows that the decision depends upon the probability that patients have appendicitis or a disease treatable with the same surgery and upon the values placed on the costs of surgery and the costs of waiting. The question can be readdressed hourly until the patients either improve or are operated upon. For a given set of symptoms, the surgeon assumes a certain probability of appendicitis and certain values for the costs of doing and not doing surgery. The decision the surgeon faces is not fatal. If patients do not have appendicitis, and no surgery is performed, they will recover (or a new diagnosis can be established). If they do have appendicitis, and no surgery is performed, they will get

Figure 11.1 Decision Tree for Evaluating Surgical Treatment for Appendicitis

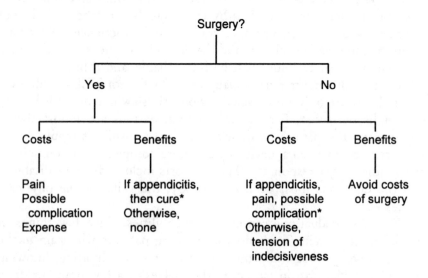

*A few other diseases might also be corrected by the same procedure, with the diagnosis made after surgery is begun.

worse, surgery will be done later, and they will recover. The cost of acting now is weighed against the cost of waiting. As patients' agents, physicians are indifferent to surgery when

Cost of having surgery = Cost of not having surgery

but because surgery will be wasted if the patient does not have appendicitis, the cost of having surgery is

(Probability of not appendicitis) × (Costs of surgery)

and because the question can be revisited later if surgery is not done, the Cost of Not Having Surgery is

(Probability of appendicitis) × (Costs of delay)

If we let

p	= probability of appendicitis at the point of indifference
(1 − p)	= probability not appendicitis
C	= cost of surgery
D	= cost of delay

(C and D will always be less than 0),

then the equation is

$$C(1 - p) = Dp$$

or

$$p = C/(D + C).$$

It may be helpful to assign some arbitrary dollar values to these concepts. Using negative signs for costs, let us assume that surgery is worth minus $5,000, and delay is worth minus $1,000. Then

(Indifference probability of appendicitis) = (−$5,000)/(−$5,000 + −$1,000)
= ($5,000)/($6,000)
= .83

or 5 in 6 chance of appendicitis. The doctor must be 80 percent sure the patient has appendicitis to order surgery. A higher cost of delay and lower cost of intervention would lead to a lower probability of appendicitis required to justify surgery. If the cost of surgery were cut in half, relative to the cost of delay, then the indifference probability would be $2,500/$3,500, or about 70 percent. More surgery would be done, and more of it would be unnecessary, but it would still be optimum care. Conversely, if the costs of surgery were twice as great, the indifference probability would rise to $10,000/$11,000, or 91 percent. Fewer operations would be done, and almost all would be necessary.

Like most models, this one simplifies reality and is not entirely accurate. Few doctors consciously review probabilities in the way the model suggests, and even fewer would attempt to estimate and solve an equation or draw a diagram such as that presented in Figure 11.1. Evidence suggests, however, that even the simple form shown here predicts real behavior. For a very low-cost intervention, say a $5 laboratory test, there is a strong predisposition to do the test. Very high-cost interventions are approached more slowly. Emergencies can be defined as situations in which the cost of delay is very high. In such cases, the mathematics of this simple formula suggest that action be taken on any hint that the patient actually needs the intervention being contemplated. In life-threatening emergencies (essentially situations where delay costs are infinite), that is what occurs.

Use of Decision Theory to Improve Patient Quality of Care

Decision theory suggests three routes to improving the contribution of medicine to health—that is, to improving the quality of care.

1. Increasing the value of intervention:
   a. Finding a new intervention which is more effective
   b. Increasing the variety of cases for which an intervention is appropriate
   c. Improving the discriminatory power of diagnostic tests—that is, the ability to detect whether or not the patient has a certain disease or condition
   d. Improving the results of the intervention—that is, learning to do it better.
2. Reducing the cost of intervention:
   a. Reducing the danger of harm to the patient
   b. Reducing the resources consumed by the intervention
   c. Increasing the variety of cases for which an intervention is appropriate (because many interventions require substantial fixed costs, increases in the volume of an intervention can reduce costs).
   d. Reducing the pain or discomfort associated with an intervention.
3. Reducing the cost of delay:
   a. Speeding or improving the transmission of orders for intervention
   b. Reducing delays between orders and intervention
   c. Reducing conflict between interventions
   d. Reducing intervention failures and repetitions.

Attending physicians improve appropriateness when they make selections that have greater value, achieve the same or greater value with less cost, or reach the correct alternative faster. Clinical support services, including nursing, improve the appropriateness of care when they add a new intervention; increase the effectiveness of an existing one; or reduce the dangers, expenses, or discomfort associated with intervention or delay. The quality assurance program supports better care when it make these actions easier.

Designing Improvements to the Care Process

Any program to improve quality and economy of medical care must match the complexity and sophistication of the care process itself, including the probabilistic character of the decisions. The two major elements of a quality improvement program have been described by Donabedian in two figures. The first, shown in Figure 11.2, recognizes the importance of design and redesign of process. It shows that attention to quality results not only in "alterations of practitioner behavior" but also in changes in the components of the infrastructure— the operational systems, educational activities, and motivational systems of the organization. (Perhaps to emphasize the point, Donabedian does not show a direct line between "Monitoring and Readjustment" and practitioner behavior, although he concedes the relationship is there.[22])

Donabedian's second figure (Figure 11.3) shows the cybernetic monitoring activity, important in clinical systems as it is in others to evaluate changes and guard against unplanned drift. Figure 11.3 expands the steps involved in detecting a change in performance ("Information"), understanding it ("Pattern Analysis"), identifying the specific changes which may improve the result ("Interpretation"), and implementing them ("Corrective Action"). The Corrective Action step can be understood as a new cycle of the process improvement activity shown in Figure 11.2. The activities in Figure 11.3 comprise what was often called quality assurance in the past. Quality improvement, the broader term, encompasses both figures, and the gains tend to come from the process design, rather than the monitoring part.

The Continuous Improvement Approach

The concepts of the combined process improvement and monitoring approach are not new. A number of efforts have been made to implement them, beginning with Codman's efforts before World War I.[23,24] The most successful recent applications in well-managed health

Figure 11.2 Improving Care Processes

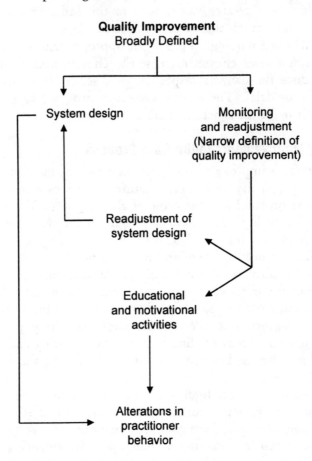

care institutions have emphasized the combined concepts.[25,26] The distinctions between quality assurance and continuous improvement are critical matters of style. Five major elements have been identified:[27]

1. Continuous improvement assumes no upper limit, but rather that any performance of a complex system is improvable. In other words, there is no "good enough." Quality assurance historically emphasized departure from a standard which was accepted as good enough.

2. Continuous improvement tends to explore more broadly for its revisions, deliberately considering not only elements of care

Figure 11.3 The Monitoring Cycle (Traditional Quality Improvement)

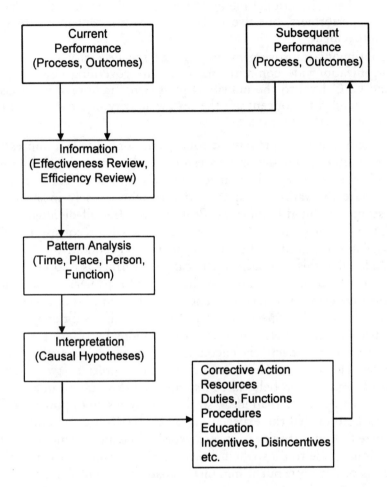

Reproduced with permission from Health Administration Press, © 1991, as it appeared in A. Donabedian's "Reflections on the Effectiveness of Quality Assurance" in *Striving for Quality in Health Care: An Inquiry into Policy and Practice* by R. H. Palmer, A. Donabedian, and G. J. Povar, p. 66.

outside the direct control of the doctor but also the interaction of elements in a complex system. Quality assurance frequently emphasized the identification of individual performance, at the level of the case or the practitioner.

3. Continuous improvement assumes that the customer's perspective is dominant. Traditional quality assurance has tended to focus heavily on professional values, sometimes to the point of ignoring the patient's perceptions.

4. Continuous improvement focuses on the improvement of overall or group performance rather than the identification and correction of outliers. Traditional methods have tended not only to isolate poor performers, but also to focus on punishment more than improvement.

5. Continuous improvement emphasizes the necessity of organizationwide commitment, from the governing board and CEO level to the individual physician. Traditional methods have tended to concentrate the review activity in a narrow set of medical staff committees.

The continuous improvement concept not only has had impressive success in other industries and widespread endorsement in health care, it also is consistent with human relations theory and offers an avenue to integrate the various hospital activities more closely in a patient or customer-oriented framework. Professionals are self-directed under continuous improvement, but their direction is kept consistent with collegial and organizational goals for quality and economy.[28,29]

Underlying this approach to clinical performance is a sophisticated version of the cybernetic model of human and organization behavior. A simple conception of feedback and control assumes that exceptions that do not meet the expectations will be corrected. A subtler approach recognizes that it is better to prevent exceptions by offering positive incentives and prospectively encouraging individuals to modify their behavior. The most sophisticated conception perceives two further truths of organization behavior. First, any real expectation in an organization is always less than ideal, so there is always an opportunity for individuals to exceed the expectation. Second, self-directed employees recognize this opportunity to exceed expectations and are motivated by professional pride to do so. Self-direction not only allows each worker to do his or her best, but it minimizes costly and painful problems of enforcement.

Professional self-direction is a hallmark of the organization as a whole, not just the medical staff. Supportive environments emphasize the value of each worker's contribution to the development of expectations of all kinds. They encourage questions and assure that they are answered. They provide the proper tools to do each job. They have open channels of communication and processes of decision making, so no worker needs to feel excluded. Expectations are routinely achieved. Their achievement proves their practicality and establishes social norms encouraging achievement. Those that are frequently breached are withdrawn for further study. Financial incentives are designed to complement the professional ones.

This level of management capability is often touted, but it is difficult to achieve. Behind the attitudes and the specifics lies a basic technical capability: accounting and laboratory and nursing must be well run in a technical sense; governance must understand the virtues of the environment being built; and so on. Planning and marketing are particularly important: adjusting to a changing external environment without disrupting a supportive corporate environment is difficult. Maximum lead time is often the key.

The health care organizations leading the development of continuous improvement have an underlying commitment to patient care and humanitarian values, as summarized in Figure 11.4.[30]

- Members of the organization understand that their work is on behalf of patients and that excellence will be rewarded.
- Expectations encourage individual judgment to meet particular patient needs and unusual circumstances. They specify situations where judgment is particularly appropriate, and provide a practical procedure to follow when protocols should be overridden.
- Doctors understand that they are privileged to practice the best medicine and to represent their patients' needs vigorously.
- The expectation-setting process emphasizes scientific sources and is approached as a stimulating intellectual challenge. That is, it is approached as a rewarding rather than a burdensome event.
- All workers and managers understand the importance of respect for each individual's contribution, open exchange of information, and prompt response to questions.
- Participation in the development of expectations is widespread. An effort is made to assure that no one is surprised by an unanticipated demand for change.
- The climate encourages change, while also reassuring members of their personal security. Otherwise, anxieties develop and protectionist positions are taken. The major components of reassurance include consistent procedures and processes; well-understood avenues for comment and prompt, sensitive response; avoidance of imposed consensus; and recognition of the importance of dissent.
- Compliance with expectations for the process of management (e.g., scheduling, documentation, timeliness, and courtesy) is accepted as essential. Violations are met with prompt, measured sanctions. For example, the penalty for incomplete medical records, (usually a temporary loss of privileges), is quickly and routinely applied. As a result, well-run organizations have few incomplete records.
- A spirit of fairness and helpfulness characterizes discussion of departures from the expectations about the care itself. The fact

Figure 11.4 Core Values of Leading Continuous Improvement Organizations

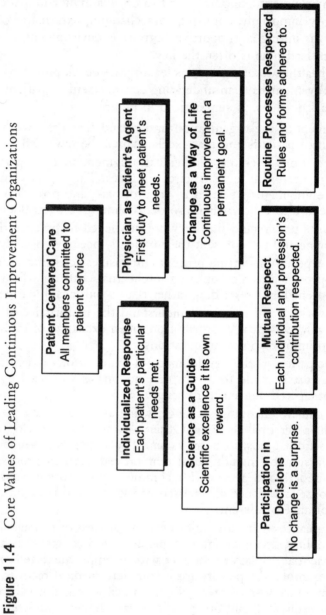

that such departures are rare permits extensive investigation. Sanctions are used reluctantly but predictably in the case of repeated unjustifiable practice.

- The values of the organization are advertised. Recruitment emphasizes the philosophy of the organization so it attracts doctors and employees who are congenial to its orientation.

Role of Clinical Expectations

Medical care activities are not random or haphazard, but rather formalized, often scientific responses to specific patient stimuli. Every time nurses give an injection, they make several specific checks on the site, the drug, skin preparation, and equipment. Every time surgeons start an operation, the anticipated equipment is prepared in advance. Every time patients tell a symptom to doctors, the doctors' responses are predictable for that symptom, considering other information at their command. This predictability is essential to implement quality assurance. It allows the identification of "expectations" in clinical behavior in exactly the same sense as the term is introduced in Chapter 3 and applied in other hospital systems.

Definition of Clinical Expectations

The consensuses reflected in these everyday events constitute **clinical expectations** about the process of care. One can define the term for management purposes by emphasizing its application to the activities of professionals, the recurring nature of the situation addressed, and the need for a consensus rather than an individual professional's opinion or patient's need. **Clinical expectations** are the consensuses reached regarding the correct professional response to specific, recurring situations in patient care.

The primary function of clinical expectations is to make cooperation among different individuals and professions possible. They are necessary to allow any level of sophisticated teamwork to exist in health care. Reflecting this primary function, many clinical expectations are the work of the professions themselves, developed from necessity. Secondarily, they provide the basis for assessing or monitoring clinical performance. Third, they become a convenient statement of contracts with patients and insurers. The courts and the marketplace have reinforced the right of consumers to have their care conform to clinical expectations developed by professionals.

Types of Clinical Expectations

Clinical expectations can be divided into three types, depending upon the level of application. The terminology, **expectation, guideline** or **protocol**, is used interchangeably. **Intermediate product protocols** determine how elements of care, such as drawing a blood sample, interviewing a new patient, or conducting a physical examination, are carried out. The most elementary intermediate product protocols cover small tasks of care such as giving an injection or taking a chest x-ray. Others describe expected set of activities for complex procedures such as surgical operations, rehabilitation programs, or multistep diagnostic activities. They are oriented around the producing departments or units, the traditional accountability hierarchy of the organization. **Care plans** constitute expectations for the care of individual patients; they are normally aggregates of several intermediate product protocols.

Patient management guidelines, or **final product protocols**, define normal care of a common group of patients, such as uncomplicated pregnancies or acute anginal pain. They specify the structural and outcomes quality of service delivered to patients, and they are organized around units of output, treated patients usually classified by disease or condition. Conceptually the two nest; a patient management guideline is comprised of several intermediate products. The formal statement of the expectation at each level represents consensus on the best practice for the typical or uncomplicated patient. Since many patients are not typical, and have complications, part of the professional role is always considering the modification of the expectation to individual patient needs.

Intermediate Product Protocols

Figure 11.5 is an example of an intermediate product protocol showing the process to select, prepare, and administer an intravenous medication. Intermediate protocols are usually established by the profession most directly involved, and they are codified in textbooks for the profession. Modification may be necessary to accommodate the equipment and facilities or the patient population of a specific site. In many cases, the profession involved can accomplish this without assistance. A few applications will require review by other professionals to assure coordination.

Intermediate product protocols exist in large numbers. They determine that the activity will have the desired outcome (the wound dressing will protect the wound, the laboratory value will be correct), and that the record will reveal exactly what was done. Good intermediate product protocols have the following components:

Figure 11.5 Example of an Intermediate Product Protocol

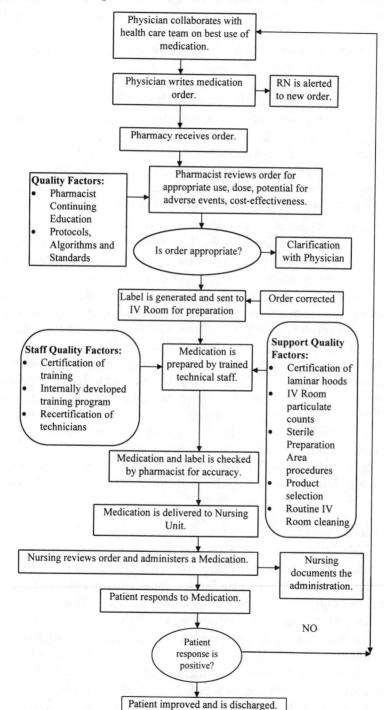

1. *Indication or authorization.* Statement clarifying who may order the procedure and what clinical conditions support its appropriate use.
2. *Counter indications.* Conditions where the procedure must be modified, replaced, or avoided.
3. *Required supplies, equipment, and conditions.* All special requirements and the sources which meet them.
4. *Actions.* Clear, step-by-step statements of what must be done.
5. *Recording.* Instructions for recording the procedure and observation of the patient's reaction.
6. *Follow-up.* Subsequent actions including checks on the patient's response, measures of effectiveness, indications for repeating the procedure, and disposal or clean up of supplies.

Intermediate product protocols tend to be stable over time and between patients and institutions, but they can be modified to improve quality and efficiency. An important source of improvement is eliminating unnecessary or inappropriate procedures by making the indications more restrictive. For example, elaborate diagnostic tests and expensive drugs can reference failure of simpler approaches as indications. Some very expensive procedures can require prior approval or a formal second opinion. The activities themselves can be modified to be safer or less expensive; changes in equipment and supplies often require such adjustments. Follow-up improvements can improve patients' reactions by detecting specific signs or symptoms, and can reduce environmental dangers by improving clean-up. A dramatic example of procedure improvement is the development of automated unit dose drug administration used in inpatient care. The new system has better controls to guard against prescribing the wrong drug, administering the wrong dose, or recording the dose incorrectly. The result is both lower cost and higher quality.[31]

Care Plans

Individualized patient care plans are almost universal. In the most elementary kinds of care, usually for self-limiting diseases, they are not even written. A care plan is developed prospectively, based on the patient's presenting needs or symptoms. The physician or other caregiver reviews the usual options in the light of the patient's condition, selects the most appropriate, and proceeds by ordering the intermediate product. In more complex care, the plan is written. It is often constructed following guidelines or check lists which indicate the actions which might be included. In the case of nursing care plans, there are automated systems to recover and assemble the constituent components.[32] In the most complex cases, the care plan may be a written consensus of professional viewpoints, closely monitored to gain the best possible results while minimizing cost.[33,34] A good plan contains many of the same elements as a protocol.

1. *Indications authorization or assessment.* Justification for ordering or using the protocol. Often includes both an assessment of needs and a statement of clinical goals, such as "restore ability to dress and feed self."

2. *Component activities.* A list, often selected from a more universal set, of activities desired for the patient.

3. *Recording.* A formal routine for recording what was done and reporting it to others caring for the case.

4. *Measures of progress and a time schedule for improvement.* Where possible, measures of improvement should be used, and they should parallel the goals developed in the assessment.

5. *Danger signals and counter indications.* Specific events indicating a need to reconsider the plan.

Final Product Protocols

Final product protocols are an outgrowth of care plans, built around the fact that most patients with similar needs or symptoms will have similar plans and can expect to follow similar courses. They are an expression of consensus about the modal, or most desirable plan of care for the uncomplicated patient. The Institute of Medicine identifies several types for different purposes: "appropriateness guidelines," used to judge insurance benefit coverage; "management criteria sets," used prospectively to guide care; and "care evaluation guidelines," used retrospectively to evaluate care.[35] These distinctions are of limited use in a continuous improvement context. It is clear that the optimal plan of treatment should be the same prospectively and retrospectively, and also that the best way to improve quality and economy is to gain agreement on the plan in advance.

The figure illustrating a final product protocol is shown with its supporting notes in Appendix 11A because of its length and complexity. It describes the optimal care of adult chronic asthma. This relatively commonplace problem can be managed in many patients so that their periodic attacks of breathing difficulty are less frequent and less severe. In addition to being better for the patient, this result is substantially cheaper for the health insurer. Most managed care systems now have protocols for asthma management; the one shown in the figure is from the Harvard Community Health Plan, which has pioneered in protocol development and use. The flow process chart approach is designed to make sure no contingency is overlooked, while at the same time recognizing that overtreatment is costly. The flow chart codifies several decisions like the decision tree described in Figure 11.1. The major branches are for complications (box 5), mild asthma (box 10 and page 2), moderate asthma (box 17 and page 3), and severe asthma (box 24 and page 4).

The thesis of the final product protocol is that it is superior to individual care plans because there are fewer chances for oversights or errors. A patient visiting a primary care practitioner has a right to expect review of the entire list in Appendix 11A. The content will be familiar to a well-trained practitioner; the written protocol is an aid to make sure nothing is overlooked. Recognition, identifying a necessary item from a list, is safer than recall, remembering it without aid. A lengthy list of annotations allows the practitioner to review details at every step, and a bibliography supports detailed review for cases which warrant it. The process of writing and approving the protocol helps remind practitioners of the list, the order of importance, and the desirable therapy at each step. Simply put, a doctor or clinical nurse practitioner using Appendix 11A will make fewer errors of undertreatment, overtreatment, or incorrect treatment. The evidence to date suggests the thesis is correct; few serious disputes about the approach remain.

Figure 11.6 shows a final product protocol for a much more serious condition, cerebrovascular accident, or stroke. Stroke is always treated in the hospital. The result of stroke is frequently paralysis of parts of one side of the body; difficulties with speech, mobility and activities of daily living can result. These impair the patient's functioning; they also add substantially to the cost of care and they can be permanent. Minimizing the results of stroke depends upon prompt initiation of exercise. Although nursing has a major role in stroke care, several professions are involved in the treatment. Their activities must be coordinated to gain quality and economical care.

The first part of the protocol focuses on problem identification, describing the patient's condition in four dimensions of neurological deficit, knowledge deficit, mobility difficulties and problems with eating and nutrition. Below that are eight specific areas of activity which must be coordinated. The columns show the steps which must be taken day by day to reach the optimal conclusion—the patient with an uncomplicated stroke will go home, on the road to an uneventful recovery, at day 5. Although the figure is not written as a flow chart, it could be; each row is essentially a sequential list of what must be done, broken into days.

Figure 11.6 Patient Management Protocol for Cerebrovascular Accident (Stroke)

Time Frame Problems	Day 1 Intermediate Goals	Day 2 Intermediate Goals	Day 3 Intermediate Goals	Day 4 Intermediate Goals	Day 5 Intermediate Goals
1. Neuro Deficit	1. Stable Neuro status	1. Cont.	1. Cont.	1. Cont.	1. No further eval.
2. Knowledge Deficit	2. Pt. &/or family V/U room & unit routines	2. Pt. &/or family V/U neuro deficits	2. Cont.	2. Pt. &/or family D/U safety	2. Cont.
3. Immobility	3. Pt. &/or family V/U restricted activity AROM & PROM	3. Pt. &/or family V/U PT/OT	3. Cont.	3. Pt. &/or family D/U or therapy & appliances	3. Self-care as much as possible
4. Nutrition	4. Prevent aspiration	4. Pt. &/or family V/U or diet	4. Adequate nutrition	4. Cont.	4. Cont.
1. Consults/ Assessments/ Indicators	Dr. H&P Assessment to determine embolic or thrombolytic. Consider ECHO. Consider CRS. Consider Neuro & other consults. Nursing H&P v.s. q4° (Glasgow coma). All to consider swallow eval.	Cont. routine assessments. VS w/neuro's q4° if stable.	Cont. routine assessments. VS w/neuro's q6° if stable. Assess need for home or Nrsg. Home appliances & follow-up	Cont. routine assessments. VS q.i.d.	Cont. routine assessments. VS q.i.d.

Continued

Figure 11.6 Continued

Time Frame Problems	Day 1 Intermediate Goals	Day 2 Intermediate Goals	Day 3 Intermediate Goals	Day 4 Intermediate Goals	Day 5 Intermediate Goals
2. Tests	CT of Brain Carotid - U.S. Doppler Chest X-Ray EKG Consider ECHO Consider MRI CBC w/Diff, MCP, PT, PTT, UA	Daily: Pt, PTT if indicated Follow-up Day 1 lab abnormalities	Consider repeat CT of head for Day 4—order is indicated. Follow-up Day 2 lab abnormalities	CT of head if indicated (could be done as out-patient if necessary). Follow-up Day 3 lab abnormalities	Follow-up Day 4 lab abnormalities
3. Treatments	I&O Medical problems—evaluated and treated. Assess managed deficits. Implement CRS recommendations.	I&O Cont. progressive treatment per CRS team.	I&O Cont. same progressive.	I&O Cont. same progressive.	I&O Cont. same progressive.
4. Meds/IVs	IV to maintain hydration. Medical therapy as necessary.	Maintain hydration. Cont. IV if necessary. Heplock if intake good.	Cont. same.	Cont. same. DC Heplock if still in place.	Cont. same.

5. Nutrition	Cont. medical therapy as ordered. NPO until initial assessment. Step 1 Dysphasia diet (no thin liquid).	Progessive diet per S.T. (Maintenance) and assistant as needed.	Cont. same.	Cont. same.	Cont. same.
6. Activity	PT or Nurse assisted.	Cont. w/Progressive activity per CRS team and Nrsg.	Cont. w/Progression.	Cont. w/Progression. Encouraging self care as much as possible.	Cont. w/Progression. Self-care as much as possible.
7. PT & Family Education/ Counseling	Orient to room, unit & routines. Review Meds. Family education regarding DX, tests, ancillary specialist, physician specialist, disposition options and course of care.	Cont. teaching. Coping w/changes and safety.	Reinforce teaching.	Reinforce teaching. Instruct PT &/or family on appliance, meds, diet and follow-up.	Reinforce teaching. Discharge teaching on follow-up Written instructions for meds., diet, follow-up, activity, appointments given.
8. Discharge Planning	Social Services Psych/Social assessment (Family & care giver assessment)	Cont.	Check w/attending physician re: discharge date & disposition	Written order for anticipated discharge in AM.	Discharge w/Home Health notified or transportation to SNF.

Used with permission of Intermountain Health Care. © 1994.

Stroke is a life threatening diagnosis. Several weeks hospitalization was once routine, and functional recovery was lower because intensive therapy was not started promptly. The approach reflected in the protocol has allowed the stay to be reduced several fold, with an improvement in recovery statistics. As the time involved has gotten shorter, the need for coordination and prior agreement has increased. The extensive array of Day 1 activities involve about 8 different clinical support services. It is noteworthy that rows 7 and 8 relate to emotional and cognitive aspects of recovery from this frightening event, including family needs assessment and education at Day 1. The protocol helps assure that more patients actually receive the optimum, without delays, omissions, or false steps.

Sources and Criteria for Expectations

Guidelines were traditionally established by physician specialties, but they often involve the integration of several professions and specialties. A number of organizations now produce patient guidelines.[36] Clinical expectations at the activity level have commonly been published in textbooks and manuals. Intermediate protocols and patient management guidelines are appearing more commonly in the published literature drawn from comprehensive review of scientific research.[37] For many common applications, the issue is one of review and revision of these published sources. Development de novo is feasible as a starting point, but is probably unwise. The deliberate search for existing alternatives and benchmarks is constructive. It avoids intellectual inbreeding and develops benchmarks. At the same time, critical review is essential. No guideline developed elsewhere should ever be implemented without careful review of the implications of using it in a specific institution. The process of review is essential to build consensus.

The best clinical expectations are scientifically supported. Although a great deal of medicine still lacks scientific support, scientific documentation of diagnostic and treatment alternatives is increasing rapidly. Scientific support establishes three categories of action: mandatory, optional or conditional, and contraindicated. Specific actions relating to prevention, diagnosis, treatment, and maintenance or rehabilitation are categorized based on evidence from the laboratory, review of similar cases, or random-controlled trials. For example, a sophisticated guideline for well-baby care would list as mandatory several specific immunizations for primary prevention. It would list secondary prevention examinations, acceptable ranges for normal behavior for these examinations, and conditional steps to rule out disease suggested by marginal responses to these exams. (Once disease is diagnosed, the baby is no longer "well," and care leaves the domain of the guideline.) It also would identify common concerns of parents and conditional responses to these concerns. Certain actions would also be contraindicated. For example, to make sure the care is economical, an upper limit might be placed on the number of well-baby visits, and the frequency might be reduced as the child matures.

The Institute of Medicine panel noted that the criteria for judging clinical expectations depend on the type of expectation, and on the specific use for the result. Panel members identified 22 attributes of expectations, but agreed on a relatively short list of "key attributes."[38] Obviously, *clarity* leads the list; ambiguous or confusing expectations cannot be helpful. *Validity*, the extent to which the expectation is based upon outcome studies or other scientific sources, is also important, although expectations used solely to screen for further investigation may sacrifice some validity. *Sensitivity*, the ability of the expectation to detect a correctable variation in care, is particularly important in screening, but not so important in patient management criteria.

In addition to these tests, patient management criteria should be *reliable* (uniformly interpreted by different readers), *adaptable* (open to adjustment for a commonly found characteristic of the patient, such as poverty, or of the disease, such as severity), *flexible* (adaptable to individual cases by the practitioner), and widely accepted.

The problem of writing clinical expectations is that little of medicine is *clear* and *valid*, in the Institute of Medicine's terms. Most of what is important is also ambiguous, debatable, or conditional. Expectations that overstate the real limits of clarity and validity create a danger of over specification, of standardizing what should be left conditional. There are two important ways to achieve the flexibility and adaptability the panel is seeking through appropriate wording of the criteria:

1. The expectation can be set separately on smaller, well-defined groups, where the indicated actions are less ambiguous. Patient demographics (age, sex, living conditions) or diseases (type, severity, or comorbidity) can be used to specify alternative treatments. For example, a low-cost antibiotic might be specified for a certain infection, unless the patient has an allergy to it. (This is the panel's concept of *adaptability*.)

   This approach leads to conditional expectations, a branching logic to allow the guidelines to fit a larger set of real patients. Conditional expectations require more data, both for setting the expectation and for monitoring it. As data capture becomes more common and data processing less expensive, conditional expectations become more practical and more commonplace.

2. Rather than specifying alternatives, the expectations can include provisions for the attending physician to justify exceptions. Where there is no scientific consensus on the correct action, any evidence indicating that the doctor is aware of the expectation and is departing from it in good faith is acceptable. (This is the panel's concept of *flexibility*.) The general approach can often be expanded by

- Specifying the optional or conditional possibilities. Continuing the antibiotic example, the guideline might say, "A low-cost antibiotic is the treatment of choice. Expensive antibiotics should be considered if the response is unsatisfactory after two days."

- Establishing a statistical estimate of the frequency of exceptions. For example, the management guideline might state, "Expensive antibiotics have been found necessary in 13 to 18 percent of cases." Applying the guideline becomes impossible in any specific case, but a judgment about performance can be made based on a relatively small number of cases.

Measures and Information Systems for Clinical Performance

An expectation-oriented clinical improvement program increases the value of care by assisting the clinical professions to select and provide the optimal intervention for each patient. The system that supports such a program must process data for four separate purposes:

1. *Prevention*—prompting users to prevent oversight or error, for example using computer assistance to suggest the appropriate action

2. *Monitoring*—identifying compliance with established expectations, and describing and analyzing noncompliance

3. *Expectation design and improvement*—presenting retrospective comparisons that support revision of existing expectations or the formulation of new ones

4. *Education*—providing visual aids which summarize arguments for existing or proposed expectations.

To fulfill the purposes, measures should be available for all the six dimensions, for both intermediate and final product protocols.

Output, contribution, and worker satisfaction present few difficulties unique to clinical applications. Demand for clinical services is complex, but well understood. The concepts discussed in Chapter 9, including marketing and stochastic modeling, apply. The following discussion reviews important issues in the measures of cost, patient acuity, and quality.

Unit Cost Measurement

Clinical continuous improvement relies upon estimates and forecasts of unit costs which are aggregated to final product costs. The measurement goal is to provide the improvement team with a reliable model allowing them to evaluate alternative protocols in terms of cost and quality trade-offs. Cost measures are generally acquired from the accounting system, specifically from the accounts receivable, cost accounting, and budgeting systems. The difficulties lie in identifying true unit cost, and its fixed, variable, and marginal components. It is safe to say that the precise cost, particularly the precise marginal cost, is unattainable. Cost measurement is and will be a matter of approximation.

The problem can be illustrated with a single laboratory test, such as a test for high-density lipids (HDLs) in the blood. The test is important in the management of several kinds of cardiovascular and cerebrovascular disease. It is performed on automated equipment, usually simultaneous with several other tests. The financial accounting system records resources used by natural accounts, (labor, services, and supplies) and responsibility center (hematology laboratory). The estimate for the responsibility center is acceptably accurate. The exact labor and equipment resources devoted to HDLs are problematic. The accounting system is not likely to reveal the amount of labor specifically devoted to HDLs, and the equipment cost cannot be exactly distributed between the various tests done by the same equipment. A study of HDL testing must deal with approximations, and so must final product studies considering the protocol for HDL use. Most important, the real questions (for example, What will be the savings if we reduce HDLs by 30 percent?) involve not today's, but tomorrow's cost, and not the total but the marginal cost.

Several strategies exist to deal with this problem.

1. *Expanding the number of functional accounts and RCs.* The problem is improved if the costs can be aggregated by "automated hematology" rather than by "hematology" or "clinical laboratory."
2. *Using the pareto rule (Chapter 9), and concentrating on the largest components of the final product cost.* While the cost of HDL may

be only crudely measured, one can still determine whether it is an important part of the total care, and whether there are substantial savings to be had. If not, attention is best turned elsewhere.

3. *Routinely identifying the variable elements of natural accounts.* The identification can be subjective, by the RC members, at the time of the budget.[39] One way to estimate the marginal savings from fewer HDLs is to ask the laboratory what would happen in terms of physical resource use, and estimate the marginal cost from that estimate.

4. *Simultaneous effort to reduce the fixed and overhead costs.* It is possible to focus decision making only on marginal costs, ignoring fixed and distributed costs. Unfortunately, fixed and distributed costs are important in the total, so nonclinical teams working on fixed cost reduction are essential.

5. *Use of relative value scales and other adjusters to improve the estimates.* Published studies indicate the relative cost of HDL tests compared to the other output of automated hematology. While these may not be exact in the local situation, they are useful guides. Relative value scales (RVS) exist for laboratory,[40] x-ray,[41] and physician activities.[42]

6. *Amplifying the cost-accounting system with special studies.* If HDLs are important and subjective estimates or RVS are inadequate, work study techniques can establish more precise ones. The level of precision is limited only by the cost of the study.

Patient Acuity

The issue of patient impact on the cost and quality of care is a serious one. Clearly, many elements of the total cost and the eventual outcome are dependent on patient behavior partially or totally outside the control of health care providers. If the patient arrives for care at an advanced stage of illness, the treatment team will be forced to spend more resources, and can expect a less satisfactory result. Examples abound in the areas of pregnancy, hypertension, and the results of alcohol, tobacco, and illegal drugs. An institution which has few of these patients will automatically do better than one which has many. Ideally, one would wish to compare homogeneous populations of like patients. The problem is often raised by caregivers who are concerned that inequitable judgments will be made about their performance.

Considerable effort has been devoted to generalized scales which can adjust for variations in patient condition, usually called **acuity**, or **severity scales**. A number of commercial products are available. Unfortunately, the evidence does not support their routine application. The scales are costly to use and result in modest or no improvement in ability to predict outcomes or costs.[43]

The problem of heterogeneity in patient mix can be dealt with by the following steps.

1. Finely subdividing the complaints, diagnoses, and procedures improves the homogeneity of groups. Often a combination of demographic and clinical characteristics identifies acceptably homogeneous groups. Segregating births by mother's age, presence of prenatal care, and Apgar score is an example. Regression analysis helps identify the important variables to use.

2. Comparing over time, rather than between institutions. While patient characteristics certainly change over time, the differences at a single institution are much less than those between institutions operating in radically different environments, such as inner city or suburban.

3. Selecting external comparisons from similar sites. Results for suburban institutions can be compared to other suburban institutions.

4. Conducting special studies of situations which still show important variations after the first three steps. This is a normal part of the Shewhart cycle, but the improvement team can be alert to the possibility that some exogenous factor is causing the problem they address.

5. Emphasizing continuous improvement rather than identification of error. It is fear of blame, in the form of reduced reputation, loss of income, or potential tort liability that underlies much concern with acuity adjustment. These elements are deliberately de-emphasized in continuous improvement approaches. Many forms of incentive payment actually exaggerate the problem; that is one reason why they are avoided.

Quality and Benefit Measurement

Quality and benefit measures are still not quantified to the degree that accounting costs are. Management-oriented doctors like Codman,[44] MacEachern,[45] Lembcke,[46] and Slee[47] have struggled with the problems of measuring patient care. Their concepts, formalized and extended by Donabedian,[48] have been widely accepted, but until recently data-processing capability has lagged behind them. Even today, measures like HEDIS and the JCAHO Information Management System are only a beginning. Clinical performance measurement will be revised continuously over the next two decades.

Outcomes measures and process measures are more valuable than structural ones, and progress is being made in their definition and automation. (A wide variety of examples and applications is included in the IOM panel report.[49]) Outcomes measures are closer to patient goals, but more remote from the activities that affect the result; process measures are the opposite. It is thus useful to use both, relying on the process measures to identify the specific areas where improvement might occur. As a result, process measures are used more in intermediate product measurement, while outcomes are used mainly in final product or patient management guidelines.

Sources of Quality Measures

The normal sources of quality and benefit measures are as follows:

1. *Routine departmental records and data*, such as laboratory quality control statistics, radiology machine logs, patient schedules, and charge vouchers. These are increasingly automated, but specific plans are needed to ensure retention of detail for historical analysis.

2. *Routine medical records*, which contain patient descriptions, orders, reports, medical notes, nursing notes, outcomes, and dispositions. Notes and most reports are not yet automated.

3. *Sampling surveys*, such as nursing quality audits and patient satisfaction surveys. These are ongoing or periodic and are distinguished from routine data by the fact that they cover less than the full universe of events.

4. *Incidents and noncompliance reports*, such as reports of accidents, equipment failures, and oversights. These are nonrepresentative counts or descriptions. One should not infer that all similar cases are reported.

5. *Special surveys*, which are conducted on a one-time basis. The preferred source, both for cost and accuracy, is always routine records, rather than special surveys. However, many items used in measuring quality are too complex for routine assessment. Measurement costs mount when non–routine sources are used, and the rule that the value of real changes in behavior should exceed the cost of the expectation monitoring system still applies.

Outcomes Measures

Outcomes measures of the quality of the final product usually assess aspects of the patient's condition on discharge or conclusion of an episode of illness or care. The clinical performance measurement system should produce outcomes measures at any level of aggregation, from the individual patient to the entire patient population of the hospital. Most are in the form of counts or rates (counts divided by the total population at risk) and are treated as attributes measures. The available measures include

1. *Counts of negative results or departures from established expectations*, for example, deaths, hospital-acquired infections, complications,

and adverse effects. Unexpected laboratory findings on confirmatory studies such as surgical tissue reports and autopsies also fit this group. It is always possible to state these measures in positive terms, i.e. the number or rate achieving the desired goal. A positive statement is preferable except where the failure rate is very low.

2. *Patient and family satisfaction*, determined through questionnaires covering all aspects of care, and identifying contributions of individual professions or services as clearly as possible.

3. *Placement at termination of care*, whether home, ambulatory care, home care, other hospital, nursing home, or other. The measure is only appropriate when there is a defined end point to the episode of care, such as discharge from the hospital, transfer back to primary care physician, or simply an anniversary in a chronic disease.

4. *Post-discharge course*, which would note any readmission, complication, or deterioration.

5. *Subjective assessment of condition*, for example, cured, improved, stable with reduced function, terminal.

6. *Objective assessment of condition* using various scales of physiological function, such as scales of laboratory values or scales of ability to perform functions of daily living.

Outcomes measures, while useful, present serious difficulties.

- For outpatient care, there is often no clear point at which to assess "outcome," because care is and should be continuous.

- Most patients actually have uneventful care and recovery, and, therefore they escape nearly all the outcomes approaches except patient satisfaction. They have no negative results, and they end the episode at home, fully functioning. (A surprising percentage will achieve this result without clinical intervention.) As a result, outcomes quality assurance focuses on a numerically almost inconsequential minority. Even in the few cases with negative results, the clinical performance implications differ drastically, for example, between cases in which death is inescapable and cases in which total recovery should always occur.

- Disease is frequently a matter of degree, and the contribution of treatment hinges on several factors beyond the specific disease present. For example, hysterectomies, cholecystectomies, spinal fusions, and joint replacements are justified as much by their contribution to the patient's comfort as by the degree of disease present. In medicine, the severity of commonplace problems, such as cerebrovascular accident (stroke) and ischemic heart diseases (heart failure), varies widely but is not reported in the diagnosis itself.

• Subjective measurement of outcomes and tracking of postdischarge course are difficult and expensive to do reliably.

• Patient satisfaction, while relatively easy to assess and quite valid in terms of such marketing factors as compliance and reenrollment, reflects little about the technical quality of care.[50]

• Finally, all outcomes measures share the problem of dependence on factors well beyond the doctor's control. The patient's general physical and emotional condition, affected by genetics and style of life, often makes the difference between successful and unsuccessful treatment.

The implication of these limitations is that outcomes measures are useful mostly as screens to detect possible changes in performance over large populations and long timeframes. Identifying the changes which will result in improvement must rely primarily upon process. The Institute of Medicine describes such measures as "case-finding screens," flags "which identify potential quality of care problems that warrant further investigation."[51]

Process Measures

Process measures should be well documented, easily measured, scientifically noncontroversial, and specific to a homogeneous set of cases. They are relatively easy to formulate, and almost limitless numbers of examples can be found.

Most process measures are counts or percentages of attributes. The attributes process measurement has two components: an expectation reflecting consensus about care (for example, "Patients undergoing surgery with general anesthetic must have a history and physical examination for cardiopulmonary disease recorded"); and counts of exposure and compliance (for example, of the 115 patients who received general anesthetic, 110 had appropriate records). Less commonly, process measures are continuous or variables measures; for example, "Hematocrit for group samples of normal women should have means of 42 percent and standard deviations of 2.5 percent." Variables measures usually arise from diagnostic situations which include continuous measures.

Devising an Appropriate Set of Quality Measures

Given the weaknesses of quality measurement, most situations require a strategy for measurement design. There can be too many measures as well as too few. Each measure adds to the cost, not only by collection but through the risk of a false error signal which leads to fruitless search for improvement. Figure 11.7 reflects a parsimonious reporting strategy which emphasizes selection of measures to avoid both dangers. It includes the following:

1. Patient satisfaction measures are always appropriate. Because of the market implications, statistically significant deteriorations or performance below competitor levels are always cause for investigation.

2. Negative results should also be tracked routinely. Even if the outcomes hardly ever occur, it is important to be able to document this fact, and to guard against unanticipated deterioration. It may not be appropriate to report these statistics except when a statistically significant deviation occurs. Similarly, those events which are somewhat less rare should be reported as success rates, rather than failure rates.

3. Measures of functional status, course, and placement should be included when they appear to reflect correctable problems. Over time, the utility of the measures can be tested. It is related to the actual ability to identify causes and improve performance. Measures which do not lead to improved performance should be dropped.

4. Process measures which appear to be related to outcomes performance and which help identify areas of potential improvement should be included. These also should be validated over time. Measures which fail to meet the dual criterion of improving outcomes and identifying areas of process control are suspect, and should probably be dropped.

Guidelines for Monitoring

The way the measures are used is as important as their design and data collection. Monitoring is a minor part of operational activities; doing the job and planning improvement should take most of the time. Incorrect use of monitors can destroy motivation and a continuous improvement program; energies are diverted to avoiding blame or optimizing personal reward rather than improving performance. Several guidelines support efficient monitoring of individual or small group performance.

- The monitoring process begins with expectation setting, in the sense that any formal expectation must include a way in which it can be monitored. This requirement is a major factor in reducing the monitoring workload because the monitor tests measurable departures from expectations.
- The information system supports the monitoring process. Monitoring can be universal, continuous sampling, intermittent

Figure 11.7 Strategy for Quality and Benefit Measurement

Element	Source	Rule for Inclusion	Comment
Patient/family satisfaction	Survey	Always desirable	Universal patient surveys may be required.
Outcomes failures	Medical record, possibly survey	Only if correctable issues are detected	Report positively if possible. Avoid frustrating recurring negative reports. Some measures reported only if statistically significant.
Functional status & placement	Record. May require special measurement effort	Only if correctable issues are detected	Do not report measures which cannot realistically be improved.
Process measures	Special measurement or analysis	Only if associated with outcomes and correctable issues are detected	Do not report measures which cannot realistically be improved. Do not report process measures which lack clear association with outcomes.

sampling, or ad hoc sampling, depending upon the cost of acquiring data and the value of the potential improvement. It also can be manual or partially or fully automated. Whatever the case, the information system must deliver complete, prompt reports on both achievement and nonachievement.

• Statistical tests are used routinely, and only high-probability deviations are pursued. The anticipated achievement is very high; there will be few error signals to pursue

• Information is reported first to the accountable practitioner or group, who are allowed time to respond before any further action is taken. Each level of the accountability hierarchy and each final product team is allowed time to respond before the next higher level intervenes.

- Clinical chiefs and hospital line managers participate personally in evaluating significant variations, but all other work is done by staff employees or, increasingly, computers.
- Error signals are used in three ways, with heavy emphasis on the first two: To devise educational programs for the staff, to guide systems revisions, including new work methods and equipment and revisions of expectations, and to pursue a program for correction with individual practitioners.
- Individual corrections programs are designed to correct defects rather than to punish.
- Rewards and recognition are provided for exceptional contribution to the mission and vision of the organization as a whole and often for the effort of monitoring itself. Rewards that emphasize individual or single accountability center performance are avoided, because they tend to discourage collaborative effort.

Managing the Clinical Improvement Program

A full-scale program of continuous improvement using clinical expectations is a comprehensive strategy affecting all aspects of management. The expectation-setting debates will eventually involve all clinical services and will become the focal point for policy of all kinds. Clinical expectations will drive the operating budget, the capital budget, and large sections of the planning process. The institution will find its recruitment and staffing decisions, equipment selection, and information systems design heavily influenced by these agreements. The clinical organizational structure will change, putting more emphasis on ad hoc committees that set expectations and reducing the activity of the formal line hierarchy. Its clinical personnel will supervise themselves, and the need for elaborate supervisory mechanisms will diminish.

The governance system must stimulate such far-reaching changes. It does so by establishing a supportive culture; putting the necessary planning, budgeting, and information systems in place, and using its annual environmental assessment exercise to establish the desirability of the approach. As the program continues, these activities themselves expand and are revised, but they continue to be critical infrastructure.

Using Clinical Expectations to Support Self-Direction

The principal benefits of clinical expectations come from the codification of formerly unwritten or unorganized activities, the identification and resolution of differing opinions or approaches, and the education involved in the review process. Beyond that, the protocol is available as a prompt, and as a basis for measuring departures and comparing outcomes. Automation of the protocols, a step just now beginning, will increase their power. It will become easier to implement the norm and to identify reasons for departing from it. The physician's role will focus on two questions: What is the correct protocol for this patient?, and Is there a need to depart from the protocol to accommodate this patient's unique characteristics?

Clinical expectations are not an unmixed blessing, because they raise the danger of regimentation. Clearly, treating every operation or heart attack identically overlooks the reality that each operation and heart attack is different, principally because it occurs to a different person. Thus, another side to the issue of quality and economy has to do with abandoning, modifying, or going beyond the expectations. Doctors and most other professionals not only have rights, but also responsibilities to tailor care to the individual. These are largely defined by the expectations themselves. One may treat *this* heart attack differently, but the very difference in treatment is defined in terms of the expectations for all heart attacks.

To overcome the dangers of regimentation, and to support professional self-direction, individualized patient care plans are emphasized simultaneously with formal expectations. The goal is make the development of the individual plan a professional challenge and a reward in itself. The patient management guideline should become a convenient starting point for the individual care plan. To the extent that this is successful, four things happen:

1. The guideline is widely used and becomes habitual.
2. The several professions can use it to anticipate care events.
3. Doctors can use it as a shorthand or outline to guide their decisions and their communications to others. The individual plan is the exception to the guideline.
4. The individual plans become potential models for revision of management guidelines, documenting departures and results.

The Patient Management Guidelines Program

Patient management guidelines are the most extensive development in clinical expectations, and under the increasing demands for cost and quality control, they constitute a challenge to the success of the conjoint medical staff. The increasing interest in such guidelines that has occurred since 1980 represents another shift in viewpoint about the standardization of medical care and the level of discretion of the individual practitioner. Standardization is being extended rapidly, by patients and health insurance buyers as well as by providers. Expectations now include economy and patient satisfaction as well as pharmacology and physiology. Quality of care expectations, reflected in malpractice decisions, have expanded steadily, with tacit public support and explicit professional endorsement through agencies like the JCAHO. The Medicare payment system establishes an expectation limiting the average cost of hospitalizations in each DRG and designates the hospital as the enforcement vehicle. HMOs enforce a similar discipline via capitation payment and the right of patients to change carriers, doctors, and hospitals annually; HMO providers often rely on specific protocols to attain the required economy and satisfaction. Often, PPOs and related insurance schemes specify their own guidelines, as is the case in preadmission certification or concurrent review of length of stay.

Accountability for Guideline Management

Patient management guidelines specify actions which deliberately constrain doctors' judgments based on their examination of individual patients. As a result, they cannot be isolated from clinical services outside medicine.

The medical executive committee manages the quality assurance program for patient management. Members of the committee who are employed by the hospital frequently bear direct accountability. Management tasks include selecting the agenda, ensuring the acceptability of both the process and its results, monitoring the expectation statements per se, and monitoring the measures of quality and effectiveness of care. The medical executive committee guides the process of expectationsetting. It selects the agenda and appoints major cross-functional teams. Often these teams work sequentially within their area, attacking the most promising diseases or conditions first and proceeding to others as they gain experience. The executive committee also supports the improvement process by encouraging the participation of all the people who are materially affected, setting timelines, and negotiating controversy.

The group charged with developing expectations should deliberately involve all relevant professional skills. Figure 11.8 gives examples of final product development teams. Active roles for nursing and other clinical support services should be formally recognized in committee appointments. Leadership should go to the group or specialty with the central interest. Nursing may lead in the development of many guidelines; it is almost always essential to development and implementation of intermediate product protocols guidelines.[52] Assigning leadership to a single department or division works well for surgery, where there are few territorial disputes; however, in medicine, several specialties treat most common diseases. An interdepartmental committee can review the information, resolve differences, and recommend the expectation to the departments or the medical executive committee.

One alternative to establishing a cross-functional or interdepartmental committee is allowing the central specialty to pursue development of the expectation, but requiring mandatory consultation of other groups with important interests. An opposite alternative allows competing departments deliberate freedom—family practice and oncology may both pursue cancer care expectations. The conflicts which will inevitably arise can be accepted, rather than resolved, if it can be agreed that the two units are justified in using different criteria. One rational possibility is that the patients retained by family practice are not the same as those referred to oncology. Their needs might be viewed as including more holistic care, without intensive intervention. (It is interesting to think about the differences in expectations

Figure 11.8 Representative Final Product Management Teams

Clinical Area	Typical Payment Aggregate or Patient Group	Team Members*	Typical Disease or Treatment Analysis
Trauma	Emergency Department visit, trauma DRGs, trauma cost PMPM**	Emergency physicians, trauma surgeons, pediatricians, health educators	Pediatric and adult trauma care and prevention
Stroke	Stroke DRGs, rehabilitation per diem, stroke cost PMPM	Neurologists, gerontologists, rehabilitation therapists, nurses	Acute and rehabilitation care for cerebrovascular accidents
Obstetrics	Normal delivery DRG, cesarean section DRG, obstetric cost PMPM	Obstetricians, family practitioners, midwives, obstetrical nurses	Prenatal care, normal delivery, cesarean section, postnatal care

*Each team would call in other specialists as indicated.
**PMPM = per member per month.

between the two departments on issues such as indications for referral to hospice care.)

There should be an annual review of progress and selection of new participants, preferably timed to precede the annual budget cycle, because the expectations influence intermediate product volume and cost forecasts. Committee or task force membership and agendas are selected simultaneously with new targets. Good conjoint staff leadership frequently reminds its members that professional self-improvement and the ability to respond to shared economic pressures are the rewards of the quality assurance process. It reinforces this belief in selecting the committee chairs for specific projects. Expected timetables for reports are set at the time of assignment, and foreseeable needs for consultation are also identified.

Expectation setting can be a divisive process. It is the responsibility of the medical executive committee and executive management group to avoid unnecessary conflict by selecting areas in which agreement appears obtainable and by resolving or if necessary, abandoning major controversies. The more frequently an expectation is used, and the greater the risk to the patient, the more time it is appropriate to spend on resolving differences. Many arguments are better abandoned; time changes all perspectives, and in the interim the debate can be ended by allowing alternative management guidelines.

Logic for Selecting Patient Management Guidelines

Management guidelines must be limited to important diseases and conditions, and protocols must be limited to those items most likely to be sources of variation in behavior. Many subjects are easily ruled out. Items on which there is universal agreement do not need to be formalized. Items which have little or no cost and no discernible effect on the outcome are too trivial to formalize. Items on which no consensus can be reached represent unresolved questions that for the present cannot be formalized. The hospital must focus upon those items where substantial value is at stake and substantial variation can be reduced. *Value* in this context is related principally to three factors, patient satisfaction, the maintenance of optimal health, and cost. An item is appropriate for incorporation into hospital patient management guidelines if it reduces variation in a manner that improves the outcome (or benefit) or reduces the resource use (or cost).

Some judgment is necessary to implement these concepts. Well-managed hospitals tend to focus first on variations in benefits, particularly unexpected death, disability, complication, patient dissatisfaction, or risk of malpractice. These concerns are given primacy over dollar expenditures; protocols are selected which minimize the patient's and the hospital's exposure. Although the result may or may not cost less in dollars than the original behavior, the study of quality issues frequently reveals dollar-saving opportunities as a byproduct.

The following four areas may suggest avenues for improvement by developing expectations:

1. *Data on adverse effects, untoward outcomes, incidents, complaints and malpractice*
2. *Patient and family satisfaction survey*
3. *Readmission data or total annual costs of claims per patient.* Provider files are not generally automated to recover this information and may be incomplete. Insurance claims files are a better source.
4. *Clinical literature and the subjective opinion of respected clinicians.* Certain styles of medical practice are clearly more cost-effective than others, and they should certainly prevail in the absence of dissent or contradictory evidence.

High-priority case groups should be studied to identify those with high variability among patients. The range of current performance is a useful measure of variability. The worst performance usually involves only a very small number of cases, and is not often useful in selecting areas for expectation development. The key to the guideline is the difference between the norm, or modal, performance and the best. The most desirable guidelines cause a notable shift in behavior so that the best becomes the norm.

Setting Intermediate Protocols

For the simpler activities, improvements are identified from the professional literature of clinical support professions or from self-study and experimentation. Because the changes are often contained within one responsibility center, they can be implemented as part of the annual budget process. The changes are recorded in procedure manuals, and incorporated into orientation and training routines. Examples abound, including revisions to nursing care procedures, laboratory tests, physical therapy treatments, intravenous drug administration, anesthetic agents, and so forth.

Even at the simplest activity level, it can be necessary to coordinate the changes with final product protocols. Thus it is important to maintain the involvement of the medical specialties most frequently using the activity. Lack of a reliable avenue to evaluate potential improvements stymies many well-intentioned clinical professionals; avenues for improvement exist, but the means of checking them with appropriate medical staff members are lacking or inconvenient. The key to success, then, is an organization where individual professions can relate quickly and professionally to physicians responsible for overall patient management. The physical therapists must have routine access to the orthopedic surgeons, neurosurgeons, and primary care practitioners who refer their cases, the trauma victims, replacement surgery patients, stroke patients, and sufferers from low back pain. The dialogue allows intermediate and final protocols to develop collaterally.

A particularly successful example in many hospitals is the "Formulary and Therapeutics Committee." The committee evaluates specific drugs in terms of their appropriateness to the hospital's case load, the possibilities of lower cost substitutes, and the need to inventory at the hospital. All of these matters fit within the activity level. Well-managed committees go beyond this to the interaction of pharmacy and other clinical services, including special training required for nursing and medicine in administration techniques, contraindications, and symptoms of adverse reactions. The best institutions are investigating the relative value of competing drugs, and specifying their choice in patient management protocols. The decisions of many hospital cardiology staffs to use the less expensive streptokinase rather than transplasminogen activator for acute heart attack care were dramatic examples of the process at its best.[53]

Advanced intermediate protocols involving not single care tasks but sets of interrelated activities will become more commonplace. Surgical care provides several examples. Preoperative care includes obtaining informed consent, instructing the patient, obtaining final diagnostic values from lab and x-ray, completing the preanesthesia examination, and administering preoperative medications. To perform surgery without delay, it must be orchestrated so that each activity occurs at the earliest possible time, and in the proper order. In this example, and in many similar ones, nursing inherits the responsibility for this scheduling. The pre-operative care process requires advance agreement on the tasks and their order among several clinical support and medical professions. Many of these agreements are independent of the patient's specific disease. While the protocols could be incorporated in the final product protocols of each of the several hundred surgical procedures, it is probably easier to develop them around the clinical services, making them intermediate products.

Collateral organization forms are used to develop and implement these protocols. For example, an ad hoc committee might develop the preop care plan for outpatient surgery. It would include surgeons, operating room nurses, surgical care nurses, and representatives from anesthesiology, pathology, and radiology. Implementation of the plan would require formal agreement and acceptance by all these groups. Monitoring would be the direct responsibility of Nursing, but reports of problems would go to the Surgical Committee and the accountability hierarchies for nursing, medicine, and clinical support services.

Suggested Readings

Berwick, D. M. 1990. *Curing Health Care: New Strategies for Quality Improvement—A Report on the National Demonstration Project on Quality Improvement in Health Care*. San Francisco: Jossey-Bass.

Eisenberg, J. 1986. *Doctors' Decisions and the Cost of Medical Care*. Ann Arbor, MI: Health Administration Press.

Goldfield, N., and D. B. Nash, eds. 1995. *Providing Quality Care: Future Challenges*, 2d ed. Ann Arbor, MI: Health Administration Press.

James, B. C. 1993. "Implementing Practice Guidelines through Clinical Quality Improvement," *Frontiers of Health Services Management* 10 (Fall): 3–37, 54–56.

Lohr, K. N., ed. 1990. *Medicare: A Strategy for Quality Assurance*, Volume I. Washington, DC: National Academy Press.

Palmer, R. H., A. Donabedian, and G. J. Povar. 1991. *Striving for Quality in Health Care: An Inquiry into Policy and Practice*. Ann Arbor, MI: Health Administration Press.

Weinstein, M. C., and H. V. Feinberg. 1980. *Clinical Decision Analysis*. New York: Saunders.

Notes

1. R. Stevens, 1989, *In Sickness and In Wealth: American Hospitals in the Twentieth Century* (New York: Basic Books), 351–56.

2. J. A. Chilingerian, 1992, "New Directions for Hospital Strategic Management: The Market for Efficient Care," *Health Care Management Review* 17 (Fall): 73–80.

3. E. B. Keeler, L. V. Rubenstein, K. L. Kahn, D. Draper, E. R. Harrison, M. J. McGinty, W. H. Rogers, and R. H. Brook, 1992, "Hospital Characteristics and Quality of Care," *Journal of the American Medical Association* 268 (7 October): 1709–14.

4. D. G. Safran, A. R. Tarlov, and W. H. Rogers, 1994, "Primary Care Performance in Fee-For-Service and Prepaid Health Care Systems: Results from the Medical Outcomes Study," *Journal of the American Medical Association* 271 (25 May): 1579–86.

5. S. Greenfield, E. C. Nelson, M. Zubkoff, W. Manning, W. Rogers, R. L. Kravitz, A. Keller, A. R. Tarlov, and J. E. Ware, Jr., 1992, "Variations in Resource Utilization Among Medical Specialties and Systems of Care: Results from the Medical Outcomes Study," *Journal of the American Medical Association* 267 (25 March): 1624–30.

6. R. L. Kravitz, S. Greenfield, W. Rogers, W. G. Manning, Jr., M. Zubkoff, E. C. Nelson, A. R. Tarlov, J. E. Ware, Jr., 1992, "Differences in the Mix of Patients among Medical Specialties and Systems of Care: Results from the Medical

Outcomes Study," *Journal of the American Medical Association* 267 (25 March): 1617–23.

7. H. R. Rubin, B. Gandek, W. H. Rogers, M. Kosinski, C. A. McHorney, and J. E. Ware, Jr., 1993, "Patients' Ratings of Outpatient Visits in Different Practice Settings: Results from the Medical Outcomes Study," *Journal of the American Medical Association* 270 (18 August): 835–40.

8. S. M. Shortell, 1991, *Effective Hospital-Physician Relationships* (Ann Arbor, MI: Health Administration Press).

9. W. G. Manning, A. Liebowitz, G. A. Goldberg, W. H. Rogers, and J. P. Newhouse, 1984, "A Controlled Trial of the Effect of Prepaid Group Practice on Use of Service," *New England Journal of Medicine* 310 (7 June): 1505–10.

10. E. Freidson, 1985, "The Reorganization of the Medical Profession," *Medical Care Review* 42 (Spring): 11–36.

11. D. M. Berwick, M. W. Baker, and E. Kramer, 1992, "The State of Quality Management in HMOs," *HMO Practice* 6 (March): 26–32.

12. M. R. Handley and M. E. Stuart, 1994, "An Evidence-Based Approach to Evaluating and Improving Clinical Practice: Guideline Development," *HMO Practice* 8 (1): 10–19.

13. K. N. Lohr, ed., 1990, *Medicare: A Strategy for Quality Assurance*, Volume I (Washington, DC: National Academy Press), 20–25.

14. R. H. Palmer, A. Donabedian, and G. J. Povar, 1991, *Striving for Quality in Health Care: An Inquiry into Policy and Practice* (Ann Arbor, MI: Health Administration Press), 54.

15. Ibid., 55.

16. Lohr, *Medicare*.

17. B. C. James, 1993 , "Implementing Practice Guidelines through Clinical Quality Improvement," *Frontiers of Health Services Management* 10 (Fall): 3–37.

18. P. P. Harteloh and F. W. Verheggen, 1994, "Quality Assurance in Health Care: From a Traditional towards a Modern Approach," *Health Policy* 27 (March): 261–70.

19. P. B. Batalden, E. C. Nelson, and J. S. Roberts, 1994, "Linking Outcomes Measurement to Continual Improvement: The Serial 'V' Way of Thinking about Improving Clinical Care," *Joint Commission Journal On Quality Improvement* 20 (April): 167–80.

20. A. D. Donabedian, J. R. C. Wheeler, and L. Wyszewianski, 1982, "Quality Cost and Health: An Integrative Model," *Medical Care* 20 (October): 975–92.

21. M. C. Weinstein and H. V. Fineberg, 1980, *Clinical Decision Analysis* (New York: Saunders).

22. A. D. Donabedian, "Reflections on the Effectiveness of Quality Assurance," in Palmer, Donabedian, and Povar, *Striving for Quality in Health Care*, 86.

23. E. A. Codman, 1916, *A Study in Hospital Efficiency: The First Five Years* (Boston: Thomas Todd).

24. Donabedian, "Reflections," 86.

25. D. M. Berwick, 1989, "Sounding Board: Continuous Improvement as an Ideal in Health Care," *New England Journal of Medicine* 320 (1): 53–56.

26. M. R. Handley and M. E. Stuart, 1994, "An Evidence-Based Approach to Evaluating and Improving Clinical Practice: Guideline Development," *HMO Practice* 8 (March): 10–19.

27. Lohr, *Medicare*, 62–63.

28. D. Mechanic, 1985, "Physicians and Patients in Transition," *Hastings Center Report* (December): 9–12.

29. B. C. James, 1993, "Implementing Practice Guidelines through Clinical Quality Improvement," *Frontiers of Health Services Management* 10 (Fall): 3–37, 54–56.

30. Shortell, *Effective Hospital-Physician Relationships*, 245–63.

31. C. E. Hynniman, 1991, "Drug Product Distribution Systems and Departmental Operations," *American Journal of Hospital Pharmacy* 48 (October): 524–35.

32. P. Hanisch, S. Honan, and R. Torkelson, 1993, "Quality Improvement Approach to Nursing Care Planning: Implementing Practical Computerized Standards," *Journal for Healthcare Quality* 15 (September–October): 6–13.

33. J. B. Christianson, L. H. Warrick, F. E. Netting, F. G. Williams, W. Read, and J. Murphy, 1991, "Hospital Case Management: Bridging Acute and Long-Term Care," *Health Affairs* 10 (2): 173–84.

34. F. G. Williams, L. H. Warrick, J. B. Christianson, F. E. Netting, 1993, "Critical Factors for Successful Hospital-Based Case Management," *Health Care Management Review* 18 (Winter): 63–70.

35. Lohr, *Medicare*, 304–6.

36. Ibid., 305.

37. P. M. Ellwood, 1988, "Shattuck Lecture—Outcomes Management: A Technology of Patient Experience," *New England Journal of Medicine* 318 (6 June): 1549–56.

38. Lohr, *Medicare*, 320.

39. J. R. Griffith, D. G. Smith, and J. R. C. Wheeler, 1994, "Continuous Improvement of Strategic Information Systems: Concepts and Issues," *Health Care Management Review* 19 (2): 49.

40. P. Raslavicus, 1993, "The Reformation of Medicare and its Effect on Pathology," *American Journal of Clinical Pathology* 99 (April Supplement 1): S12–16.

41. J. M. Moorefield, D. W. MacEwan, and J. H. Sunshine, 1993, "The Radiology Relative Value Scale: Its Development and Implications," *Radiology* 187 (May): 317–26.

42. Health Care Financing Administration, 1991, "Medicare Program: Fee Schedule for Physician Services—HCFA Final Rule," *Federal Register* 56 (25 November): 59502–811.

43. J. W. Thomas and M. Ashcraft, 1989, "Measuring Severity of Illness: A Comparison among Several Methodologies," *Inquiry* 26 (Winter).

44. Codman, *A Study in Hospital Effciency*.

45. M. T. MacEachern, 1938, *Hospital Organization and Management* (Chicago: Physicians Record Co.).

46. P. A. Lembcke, 1967, "Evolution of the Medical Audit," *Journal of the American Medical Association* 199: 543–50.

47. V. N. Slee, 1966, "CPHA Experience in Measuring Quality," Paper presented to the American Public Health Association Program Area Committee on Medical Care Administration, 94th Annual Meeting, San Francisco, November.

48. A. D. Donabedian, 1980, *The Definition of Quality and Approaches to Its Assessment, Volume I* (Ann Arbor, MI: Health Administration Press).

49. M. S. Donaldson and K. N. Lohr, 1990, "A Quality Assurance Sampler: Methods, Data, and Resources," in *Medicare*, Volume II, 140–291.

50. S. Strasser, L. Aharony, and D. Greenberger, 1993, "The Patient Satisfaction Process: Moving toward a Comprehensive Model," *Medical Care Review* 50 (Summer): 219–48.

51. Lohr, *Medicare*, 307–8.

52. K. Zander, 1988 , "Nursing Care Management: Resolving the Paradox," *Nursing Clinics of North America* 23 (3): 503–20.

53. K. L. Lee, R. M. Califf, J. Simes, F. Van de Werf, and E. J. Topol, 1994, "Holding GUSTO Up to the Light: Global Utilization of Streptokinase and Tissue Plasminogen Activator for Occluded Coronary Arteries," *Internal Medicine* 120 (15 May): 876–81, 882–85.

Appendix 11A A Final Product Protocol for the Management of a Common Outpatient Occurrence: Management for Chronic Asthma in Adults*

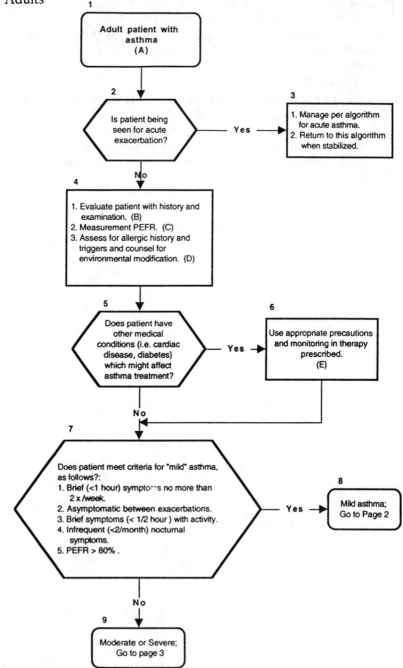

1

Adult patient with asthma
(A)

2

Is patient being seen for acute exacerbation? — **Yes** →

3

1. Manage per algorithm for acute asthma.
2. Return to this algorithm when stabilized.

No

4

1. Evaluate patient with history and examination. (B)
2. Measurement PEFR. (C)
3. Assess for allergic history and triggers and counsel for environmental modification. (D)

5

Does patient have other medical conditions (i.e. cardiac disease, diabetes) which might affect asthma treatment? — **Yes** →

6

Use appropriate precautions and monitoring in therapy prescribed.
(E)

No

7

Does patient meet criteria for "mild" asthma, as follows?:
1. Brief (<1 hour) symptoms no more than 2 x /week.
2. Asymptomatic between exacerbations.
3. Brief symptoms (< 1/2 hour) with activity.
4. Infrequent (<2/month) nocturnal symptoms.
5. PEFR > 80% . — **Yes** →

8

Mild asthma; Go to Page 2

No

9

Moderate or Severe; Go to page 3

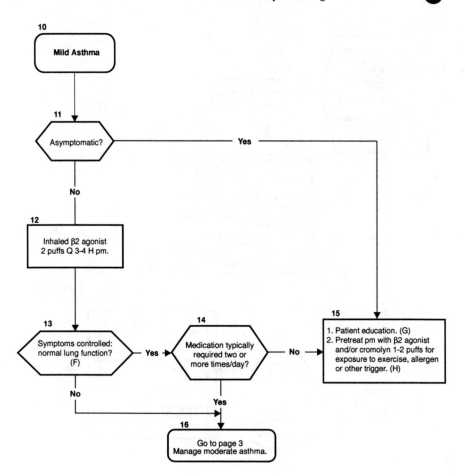

10 Mild Asthma

11 Asymptomatic? — **Yes**

No

12 Inhaled β2 agonist 2 puffs Q 3-4 H pm.

13 Symptoms controlled: normal lung function? (F) — **Yes** — **14** Medication typically required two or more times/day? — **No** — **15** 1. Patient education. (G) 2. Pretreat pm with β2 agonist and/or cromolyn 1-2 puffs for exposure to exercise, allergen or other trigger. (H)

No

Yes

16 Go to page 3 Manage moderate asthma.

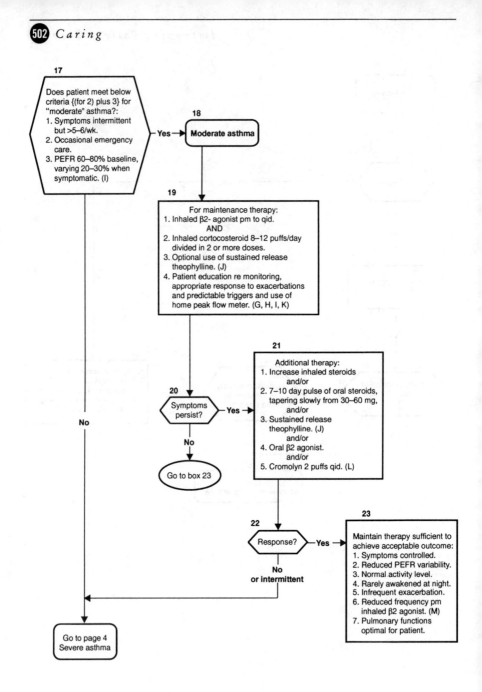

17

Does patient meet below criteria {(for 2) plus 3} for "moderate" asthma?:
1. Symptoms intermittent but >5–6/wk.
2. Occasional emergency care.
3. PEFR 60–80% baseline, varying 20–30% when symptomatic. (I)

—Yes→ **18** **Moderate asthma**

19

For maintenance therapy:
1. Inhaled β2- agonist pm to qid.
   AND
2. Inhaled cortocosteroid 8–12 puffs/day divided in 2 or more doses.
3. Optional use of sustained release theophylline. (J)
4. Patient education re monitoring, appropriate response to exacerbations and predictable triggers and use of home peak flow meter. (G, H, I, K)

20 Symptoms persist? —Yes→

21

Additional therapy:
1. Increase inhaled steroids and/or
2. 7–10 day pulse of oral steroids, tapering slowly from 30–60 mg, and/or
3. Sustained release theophylline. (J) and/or
4. Oral β2 agonist. and/or
5. Cromolyn 2 puffs qid. (L)

20 No

Go to box 23

22 Response? —Yes→

23

Maintain therapy sufficient to achieve acceptable outcome:
1. Symptoms controlled.
2. Reduced PEFR variability.
3. Normal activity level.
4. Rarely awakened at night.
5. Infrequent exacerbation.
6. Reduced frequency pm inhaled β2 agonist. (M)
7. Pulmonary functions optimal for patient.

No or intermittent

No

Go to page 4 Severe asthma

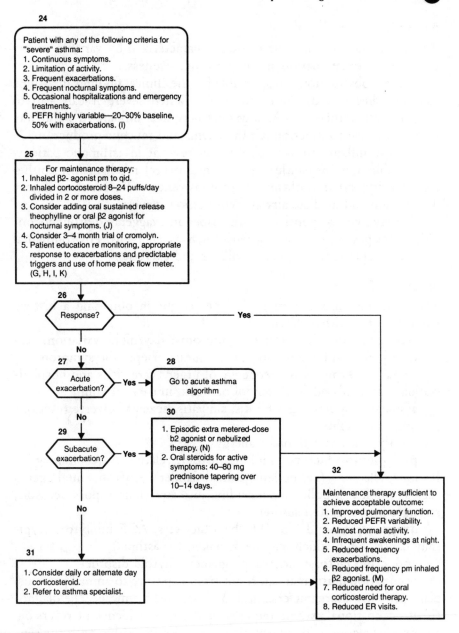

24

Patient with any of the following criteria for "severe" asthma:
1. Continuous symptoms.
2. Limitation of activity.
3. Frequent exacerbations.
4. Frequent nocturnal symptoms.
5. Occasional hospitalizations and emergency treatments.
6. PEFR highly variable—20–30% baseline, 50% with exacerbations. (I)

25

For maintenance therapy:
1. Inhaled β2- agonist pm to qid.
2. Inhaled cortocosteroid 8–24 puffs/day divided in 2 or more doses.
3. Consider adding oral sustained release theophylline or oral β2 agonist for nocturnal symptoms. (J)
4. Consider 3–4 month trial of cromolyn.
5. Patient education re monitoring, appropriate response to exacerbations and predictable triggers and use of home peak flow meter. (G, H, I, K)

26 Response? — Yes

No

27 Acute exacerbation? — Yes → **28** Go to acute asthma algorithm

No

29 Subacute exacerbation? — Yes → **30**
1. Episodic extra metered-dose b2 agonist or nebulized therapy. (N)
2. Oral steroids for active symptoms: 40–80 mg prednisone tapering over 10–14 days.

No

31
1. Consider daily or alternate day corticosteroid.
2. Refer to asthma specialist.

32
Maintenance therapy sufficient to achieve acceptable outcome:
1. Improved pulmonary function.
2. Reduced PEFR variability.
3. Almost normal activity.
4. Infrequent awakenings at night.
5. Reduced frequency exacerbations.
6. Reduced frequency pm inhaled β2 agonist. (M)
7. Reduced need for oral corticosteroid therapy.
8. Reduced ER visits.

Adapted from Expert Panel Report, National Asthma Education Program, NHLBI. Paul Bertozzi, Paul Feiss, Dirk Greineder, Howard Lewine, Nancy Sokol. September 1992.

Annotation A

Asthma in the adult is a lung disease characterized by variable airway obstruction, inflammation and hyperresponsiveness.

Airway obstruction is responsible for the clinical findings in asthma such as wheezing, dyspnea and cough. When severe it can lead to respiratory insufficiency. Airway obstruction is influenced by airway smooth muscle contraction, airway edema and mucous production.

Airway inflammation is chronically present in asthmatic patients and produces abnormalities in bronchial neural mechanisms, epithelial integrity and smooth muscle responsiveness which lead to airway obstruction and mediate airway hyperresponsiveness.

Airway hyperresponsiveness describes an exaggerated bronchoconstrictor response to various agents such as allergens, environmental irritants, respiratory infections, cold air and exercise.

Annotation B

The following information should be sought in obtaining a history from a patient with asthma:

frequency and duration of symptoms: day/night variation, seasonal or perennial exacerbations, continuous or episodic symptoms

impact of symptoms: frequency of urgent care visits and hospitalizations, days missed from school or work, impact on family

associated symptoms: rhinitis, sinusitis, eczema, adverse reactions to foods, GE reflux

family history: asthma or allergy

precipitating factors: smoking history; relation to respiratory infections; allergens (i.e. pollens, animal dander); environmental agents such as smoke, air pollutants including auto emissions, vapors, aerosols, strong odors; ingested sulfites

drugs: aspirin and NSAIDs, beta-blockers, ACE inhibitors (typically cause cough which may be mistaken for asthma)

endocrine factors: menses, pregnancy, thyroid disorders

occupational asthma: can result from exposure to animal proteins, plant proteins, inorganic chemicals and organic chemicals. The diagnosis of occupational asthma requires establishing evidence of reversible airway obstruction and determining a causal relationship with the sensitizing agent. Symptoms may not develop for weeks or even years after initial exposure and may include rhinoconjunctivitis as well as cough, wheeze, dyspnea or chest tightness, initially in the evening or night after work but later often in closer proximity to work. Symptoms may clear over weekends (often a critical clue) but in some cases inflammation is so profound that symptoms subside only after 1–2 weeks away from work. If occupational asthma is suspected objective documentation should be obtained by monitoring frequent peak flow measurements during working and non-working days. Ideally, monitor during 1 week at work, 10 days away from work and then 2 weeks at work, looking for variations in PEFR greater than 20% in relation to work exposure.

The **physical examination** should include a general exam and specifically look for:

evidence of rhinitis or sinusitis
nasal polyps
pulmonary hyperinflation
quality of breath sounds
presence of prolonged expiratory phase
flexural eczema

Annotation C

Peak flow measurement is a simple and important tool in assessing asthma severity and control. An important limitation of PEFR measurement is that it is effort dependent. Proper technique is simple and nose clips are not required. The instrument pointer should be reset to baseline. The patient should stand up, take a deep breath and place the meter in the mouth with lips closed tightly around the mouthpiece, and blow out as hard and fast as possible. It is not necessary to blow out all the way as peak flow is obtained in the first portion of exhalation. Repeat the process two more times and record the best effort.

The recommended frequency of measurement will vary with severity but should include measurements during all office visits, ER and hospitalizations. Nomograms of normal values should be available to physicians (see appendix). Some patients may not be able to achieve normal levels of PEFR and for these patients personal best values should be used as reference points. Typically, values 80–100% of personal best indicate good control, 50–80% of personal best indicate possible exacerbation or poor control, and <50% of personal best signals an acute exacerbation.

Annotation D

Allergies are among the most common and severe exacerbants of asthma and a history to identify the presence of likely allergens (molds, dust-mites, cockroach, animal exposure at home or work, pollens) is particularly important. High humidity conditions that favor development of high concentrations of mold and dust-mite antigen include living in basement rooms, presence of carpeting over a concrete slab, and excessive humidifier use. Wall to wall carpeting, down pillows and comforters, upholstered furniture (particularly if old) may increase dust-mite exposure and forced hot air heat seems to spread the antigen. Patients are often aware that vacuuming, making beds, working in the basement or a closed vacation home, or exposure to animals will increase symptoms of asthma but these questions must be specifically asked. Many patients with pets deny or are unaware that pets increase their symptoms; in general if a patient has *any* symptom or history of allergy, it is prudent to assume that they will be allergic to any furred pet in the home.

Seasonal symptoms may indicate pollen sensitivity (in New England: trees in April and May, grasses in late May and June, ragweed and sage in late August and September) but patients with mold and dust sensitivity often also complain of "spring" and "fall" allergies though these may start earlier and last longer than the classical pollen seasons.

If the history suggests possible allergic triggers patients should be counseled to eliminate or reduce allergen exposure (remove pets, practice dust and mold precautions). Clinical publications on dust and mold avoidance are available in the Centers and should be distributed to patients as needed. However, compliance with allergen avoidance advice is typically poor. If the identity or possible range of involved allergens is not clear (patients with occasional pet symptoms may have a more important dust or roach allergy which is not appreciated) or if patients do not accept the importance of allergen control, referral to allergy may be appropriate. Furthermore, patients with severe allergies may be candidates for allergy immunotherapy and this can be evaluated by an allergist.

Annotation E

Asthma treatment is sometimes complicated by coexistence of other medical conditions such as cardiac disease (i.e., arrhythmias triggered or exacerbated by beta-agonists), pregnancy (possible teratogenic effect of medications) and diabetes (worsening control with prednisone). In general, the risk from uncontrolled asthma and attendant hypoxia is felt to be greater than the risk of asthma treatment, so use of drugs to obtain optimal asthma control is justified. Although medication safety in pregnancy has not been unequivocally proven, hypoxia is likely to represent a much larger danger to the fetus. However, a frank discussion about the potential risk and benefits of these medications with pregnant asthmatics is prudent.

With diabetes or borderline diabetic asthmatics, courses of prednisone require close monitoring of diabetes control by the patient.

Finally, newer recommendations about theophylline levels suggest lower levels (5–15 mcg/ml) have a much higher therapeutic ratio than the former recommended level (10–20). Many commonly used medications (erythromycin, ciprofloxacin, cimetidine) and conditions (congestive heart failure) increase theophylline levels and care should be exercised in prescribing in these situations.

Annotation F

For most patients, "normal lung function" can be assumed with measurement of PEFR > 80%. However, PEFR measures only relatively large airway function. As such it is a useful measure to detect acute asthma exacerbations and to monitor more severe patients who do not easily achieve normal values. Full spirometry (adequately performed with many table-top machines currently available in all HCD health centers) is significantly more sensitive than PEFR because a full forced expiratory maneuver is performed which allows measurement of smaller airway function using FEF 25%–75% and graphically depicts a flow-volume curve. These measurements increase reliability of the objective flow measurements and increase sensitivity. Mild asthma affecting only the small airways can be significantly underdiagnosed if only PEFR is measured.

Spirometry is also a more sensitive measure of reversibility of obstruction with inhaled bronchodilator because FEF 25%–75% is typically more affected than PEFR or FEV1. Consequently, if PEFR measurements with or without bronchodilator are normal but not consistent with the clinical picture, table-top spirometry is indicated.

Hospital-based PFTs, performed in the Pulmonary Function Laboratory, give little more information in typical asthma but may be important if a patient is uncooperative or unmotivated because of availability of more experienced personnel. Lung volume and diffusion capacity measurements also require hospital-based PFTs at present, although these are not usually important in typical asthma patients.

Annotation G

The greater the understanding asthmatics have of their disease the more successful their management will be.

The key educational points patients should feel comfortable with include the following:

1) Knowing their own **warning signs**—increased wheeze, shortness of breath, chest tightness, or cough.

2) Being familiar with what **triggers** an asthma flare for that patient, e.g., viral URI, environment, allergens, exercise, cold, stress and learning how to self-medicate to prevent predictable exacerbations (see Annotation H).

3) For moderate or severe asthma, using a **peak flow meter** and knowing how to interpret the result (see #5 below).

4) Understanding the two major ingredients of asthma: **bronchospasm and inflammation**, and which medications are used for each.

5) Learning how to **self-medicate** to initiate treatment of flares as follows:

   For a **mild** asthma episode (peak flow 70–90% baseline), inhaled bronchodilators should be used regularly for 24–48 hours.

   For a **moderate** exacerbation (peak flow 50–70% baseline) inhaled bronchodilators could be used every 20 minutes for 1 hour. If improved, continue medication every 4 hours for 24–48 hours. If not improved in 2–6 hours after initial treatment, begin or increase corticosteroid inhaler and/or prednisone and contact clinician.

   For a **severe** episode (peak flow <50%) take 4–6 puffs bronchodilator every 10 minutes up to three times, begin or increase prednisone and contact clinician. Seek emergency care if no significant improvement in 30 minutes.

6) Knowing how to correctly use a **metered dose inhaler.** A patient education sheet is included in the appendix, and patient education material on asthma is being revised for distribution in the health centers.

Annotation H

Acute triggers vary among patients but commonly include environmental irritants and allergens, cold air and exercise. Exercise excepted, avoidance of triggers is often the best prophylactic therapy. Beta-agonists generally are the prophylactic treatment of choice, though there will be occasional patients for whom cromolyn is better tolerated or more effective. Some patients experience a late asthmatic response 4–6 hours post exercise. Prophylactic cromolyn may effectively block this while use of pre-exercise beta-agonist rarely does although treatment with an inhaled beta-agonist at the time of symptoms may provide prompt relief.

When exposure to a known trigger occurs inadvertently treatment with a beta-agonist inhaler immediately or at the onset of symptoms is more likely to be effective then if delayed until the asthmatic response is fully developed. A rare asthmatic will have had episodes of acute severe bronchospasm or anaphylaxis. It is often advisable for these individuals to carry an EpiPen or similar device for self-administration of epinephrine should a similar situation occur.

Annotation I

Peak expiratory flow rates (PEFR) correlate with the degree of airway obstruction. Fluctuations in PEFR reflect the degree of airway hyperresponsiveness. The degree of obstruction and hyperresponsiveness usually correlate with the clinical severity of asthma and with medication requirements. Uses of PEFR home measurement designated by the National Asthma Educational Program (NAEP) include:

1) Self-monitoring to increase or decrease treatment.
2) Detect circadian variations that predict instability.
3) Detect decreases that indicate early (possibly asymptomatic) deterioration.
4) Identify triggers of asthma.
5) Report changes in PEFR to physician to help guide treatment changes over the phone.

Optimally measurements should be made daily in the morning and evening, pre and post bronchodilators if these are used. Initial instruction should take place in the office. A diary of results and symptoms should be kept. Published normative values tend to be less a useful guide to the patient's clinical status than is comparison of current PEFR to the patient's personal best PEFR (usually an evening value while symptomatically quiescent, after a period of maximal therapy). The NAEP and others have suggested using a system of PEFR "zones" based on NO (personal best PEFR) to help patients manage their asthma:

e.g., 80–100%: ALL CLEAR: No change in therapy; or if asymptomatic for a prolonged period consider a reduction in medication with continued monitoring.

50–80%: CAUTION: An early exacerbation may be present and an increase in medication may be indicated. If persistent without deterioration the asthma may be suboptimally controlled and maintenance medications may need to be increased.

<50%: ALERT: A bronchodilator should be taken and a clinician should be notified immediately if PEFR does not increase to >50%

It should be noted that there is insufficient data to establish generalizable zones for all patients and, in fact, there is almost certainly individual variability. Over time, however, many patients will come to see that PEFRs in a given range will reliably be associated with progression to clinical deterioration. Particularly in severe asthmatics such data can be useful in timing brief periods of intensive home therapy e.g., steroid tapers, in many cases obviating the need for emergency treatment or hospitalization.

Annotation J

Theophylline has long been used for asthma but recent understanding shows that methylxanthines have only mild to moderate bronchodilator activity. Nevertheless, this can be quite useful for managing some patients, particularly those with frequent variability or nocturnal symptoms not readily controlled with inhaled medication (anti-inflammatory and beta-agonist). Theophylline bronchodilator response is roughly linear with serum concentration, and traditionally levels of 10–20 mcg/ml have been suggested as an optimal compromise between safety and efficacy. Recent data suggest that side-effects and safety are more easily maintained in patients with levels between 5–15 mcg/ml. Since current practice tends to use theophylline as an adjunct to inhaled therapy, not as the mainstay, these lower levels are frequently, adequate.

Sustained release theophylline is a useful way to maintain steady-state levels in the therapeutic range without wide swings or frequent dosing that impairs compliance. Currently, we recommend use of Uniphyl (a "24 hour" preparation) usually administered at dinner time (particularly useful for patients with persistent early morning asthma) with a supplemental dose at breakfast if needed. Many patients do well with 1/3 of daily dose in the AM and 2/3 at dinner. Uniphyl is available only in 400mg tablets that are scored for easy use of 200mg. For more dosing flexibility, Slobid and Theodur are available in many sizes and considered to be 12 hour preparations. These agents are typically dispensed in equally divided doses 2–3 times per day (more frequently in younger patients with faster metabolism, less frequently in older patients or those with slower metabolism). There seems to be relatively little use for faster acting theophyllines as the emphasis for acute therapy has shifted to beta-agonists.

Annotation K

For patients with moderate or severe asthma, potential chronic allergic and non-allergic triggers should be carefully reviewed with the patient. It is especially important to identify patients who may have either overt or latent allergies and are exacerbating their condition by chronic exposure to dust, roaches or pets. While these patients are often unaware of allergy to chronic environmental agents they may often remember allergic reactions on initial exposure if specifically asked. If the evidence of allergy is strong, the patient should be encouraged to avoid the triggering factors (dust, roaches, remove pets from the environment). Allergy referral should be considered to reinforce and corroborate the need for avoidance measures. OFTEN testing may be helpful in some instances to support patient counseling. Platts-Mills has argued that the association of dust, roach and pet allergens with asthma is as strong as the linkage of cigarette smoking with COPD.

The most important chronic non-allergic triggers are chronic sinusitis and GE reflux. Chronic sinusitis may also be associated with allergic rhinitis and allergy. Chronic GE reflux is more common in asthmatics than in the general population so it is necessary to consider this diagnosis in all patients with chronic asthma, and treat appropriately with patient education and and medication as indicated (see algorithm on Management of Dyspepsia).

References

Goodall R et al. Relationship between asthma and gastroesophageal reflux. Thorax 1982; 36:1 16–121.

Platts-Mills TAE et al. Indoor allergens: Do they really cause allergic disease? postgraduate course of the American Academy of Allergy and Immunology. Orlando FL, 1992.

Platts-Mills TAE et al. Dust mite allergens and asthma: Report of a second international workshop. J. All Clin Immunol 1992 (in press).

Annotation L

Cromolyn sodium is an expensive drug with anti-inflammatory properties. Its mechanism of action in vivo remains unknown though it has been attributed to stabilization of mast cells preventing mediator release. Currently it is the most effective nonsteroidal anti-inflammatory drug for asthma and brings with it a long safety record. In general it has played a smaller role in the management of adult asthma than in pediatric treatment. Administered prophylactically, it has been shown to prevent both early and late phase allergen induced airway narrowing and airway narrowing secondary to nonspecific stimuli e.g., cold air, exercise, sulfur dioxide.

Though traditionally thought to have a special role in the treatment of exercise and allergen induced asthma there is in fact no way to reliably predict which patients will respond to therapy with cromolyn. It has no special advantage over beta-agonists prophylactically or inhaled corticosteroids for maintenance therapy when these other medications are effective and well tolerated. Clearly, however, there is a subset (perhaps 5–10%) of adult asthmatics for whom it is more effective then other agents or who derive additional benefit to that obtained from maximal tolerated doses of methyxanthines, beta-agonists and inhaled corticosteroids.

Occasionally chronic therapy with oral steroids can be avoided or a reduction in the steroid dose achieved by the addition of cromolyn. For that reason most patients should optimally have a trial of cromolyn (usually as part of a maximal regimen) if they are requiring daily or frequent therapy with systemic steroids. A 4–6 week trial with objective monitoring of PEFRs and physical exam may be necessary to determine efficacy.

Annotation M

Inhaled beta-agonists have been and remain a mainstay of treatment for symptomatic bronchospasm associated with exacerbations or known triggers. Their chronic regular use has been shown to be effective in the treatment of persistent airway narrowing.

In recent years a number of studies have suggested that asthma morbidity and mortality may be rising. Attention has focussed on the increased use of beta-agonists during the period. Several studies, including a case controlled mortality study (Spitzer) have found an epidemiologic association between regular use of beta-agonist inhalers and increased asthma mortality. One prospective study (Sears) has associated the regular use of inhaled beta-agonists with deterioration in asthma control both as measured by symptom/PEFR diaries and methacholine challenge testing. Postulated mechanisms for this effect were rebound airway hyperresponsiveness and down regulation of beta-receptors.

Against this, a number of prospective studies have failed to demonstrate any alteration in airway hyperresponsiveness with chronic beta-agonist use. In addition, tolerance to the effects of beta-agonists with chronic use has been hard to demonstrate suggesting that significant down regulation of beta-receptors likely does not occur. It is possible that beta-agonists represent a marker for disease, being more frequently prescribed for patients with life threatening asthma while not contributing directly to the frequency or severity of attacks. If beta-agonists do have a causative role, it may be an indirect one such as delaying presentation to the ER until inflammatory airway obstruction due to mucous plugging is more severe. While important to recognize, such an association would not necessarily mandate a change in current prescribing practices.

Certainly more data is needed in the form of large placebo-controlled studies to evaluate the effect of regular versus intermittent treatment with beta-agonists. Currently both chronic and PRN therapy with inhaled beta-agonists are acceptable so long as asthma symptoms are controlled. With the current shift favoring a treatment emphasis on inflammation in asthma many clinicians find that the added control achieved with chronic inhaled corticosteroids allows inhaled beta-agonists to be used on a PRN basis. Increasing reliance on inhaled beta-agonists in an asthma patient may be a marker of worsening disease or an impending severe attack and should trigger an overall reassessment and possible alteration in therapy, usually involving increased efforts to control airway inflammation.

References

Burrows B and Lebowitz MD. The Beta agonists dilemma (editorial). N Engl J Med 1992; 326:560–561.

Crane et al. Prescribed fenoterol and death from asthma in New Zealand; 1981–1983: case controlled study. Lancet 1989; 917–22.

Jackson et al. International trends in Asthma Mortality. 1970–1985, Chest 94:914.

Peet et al, Effect of long term inhaled Salbutmol therapy on the provocation of asthma by histamine. ARRD 1980; 121 :973–78.

Repsher et al. Assessment of tachyphylaxis following prolonged therapy of asthma with inhaled albuterol aerosol. Chest 1984; 85:34.

Sears et al. Regular inhaled beta-agonist treatment in bronchial asthma, Iancet 1990; 336: 1391–96.

Spitzer et al. The use of beta-agonists and the risk of death and near death from asthma. N Engl J Med 1992; 326:501–506.

Annotation N

Home nebulizers may be very helpful in patients who suffer frequent subacute exaceerbations that are unresponsive to metered dose inhalers. It is important, however, that patients recognize that such therapy is not a substitute for initiating other measures, such as initiation or increase in inhaled or oral steroids. Patients need instruction in the mechanical use of the nebulizer (by clinician or pulmonary technician delivering the device) and must be instructed in frequency and dose of medication to use (typically 0.5 cc albuterol solution in 2–3 cc normal saline every 3–4 hours).

Patients with nebulizers should always have peak flow meters and should measure peak flow before and after treatment. If peak flows after treatment do not respond significantly (i.e. return to the patient's "all clear zone", 80–100% of personal best PEFR), or if treatment needs to be repeated more frequently, patients should be told to contact their provider and/or start oral steroids based on a previously arranged protocol.

It is critical that patients be given clear guidelines for nebulizer use so as not to delay initiating more definitive therapy with steroids or antibiiotics. **Patients who regularly need to use a beta-agonist nebulizer are unstable and need more aggressive baseline therapy.**

Bibliography

Comprehensive Review of Asthma Treatment

National Asthma Education Program Expert Panel Report. Guidelines for the Diagnosis and Management of Asthma. J All Clin Immunol 1991; 88 (suppl):425–534.

Barnes PJ. A new approach to the treatment of asthma. N Engl J Med 1989. 321: 1517

Hargreave FE et al. The assessment and treatment of asthma: A conference report. J All Clin Immunol 1990;–85:1098–1111.

Specific Drug Therapy

Blumenthal MN et al. A multicenter evaluation of the clinical benefits of cromolyn sodium aerosol by metered-dose inhaler in the treatment of asthma. J All Clin Immunol 1988. 81:681–687.

Dutoit JI et al. Inhaled corticosteroids reduce the severity of bronchial hyperresponsiveness in asthma but oral theophy line does not. Am Rev Respir Dis 1987. 136:1174–1178.

Newhouse MT and Dolovich MB. Control of asthma by aerosols. N Engl J Med 1986. 315:870–874.

Toogood JH. High-dose inhaled steroid therapy for asthma. J All Clin Immunol 1989. 83:528–536.

THE ORGANIZED MEDICAL STAFF

Models of Medical Staff Organization

DOCTORS HAVE been ascribed magical powers, granted extraordinary privileges and confidences, and expected to assume extra moral obligations since the dawn of human existence. The twentieth century saw a revolution in this social contract. The magical powers have become reality through scientific advance. The privileges and confidences have been divided among many specialists concerned with particular organ systems or methods of treatment. The anticipation of moral obligation has been replaced by the suspicion and retribution of malpractice litigation. Still, the doctor remains the leader of the clinical team, perhaps simply because any venture as complex as modern medicine must have a leader.

Thus at the core of any substantial health care organization is a group of doctors organized into a medical staff. The link between the organization and the physician is symbiotic; without physicians it is impossible to give more than elementary health care, and without health care organizations, most physicians cannot practice modern medicine. There is typically one doctor for every thousand persons or so in the organization's market share. About half are in primary care. The balance of the physicians are in referral or specialty practice. Both groups may be supported by nonmedical practitioners. Larger organizations have several hundred physicians representing a wide variety of specialties and growing numbers of nonmedical practitioners. The economic relationship is also varied. Historically, physicians earned their income from patients' fees, but many are now full- or part-time employees of the health care organization. Employed and fee-for-service doctors work side by side, and individual doctors usually work under both arrangements during their careers. The two forms of economic relationship are likely to continue for the foreseeable future.

The Conjoint Staff Model

Open systems theory suggests that the success of a health care organization is determined by fulfillment of mutually rewarding desires on the part of the marketplace, the owners, and the doctors who participate. This book describes a community-oriented health care organization which is usually locally owned and not-for-profit in structure. The health care organization succeeds because it supplies health care at attractive quality and cost, but also because it offers physicians an economically and professionally rewarding lifestyle. The successful relationship is one of collaboration, a sharing of authority and the risks and rewards of using it well.

The trend in the relationship between community health care organizations and physicians has been and will be toward intensified symbiosis. As market demands increased, the traditional hospital medical staff organization has been strengthened, and the relationship between doctor and organization has been more tightly defined. There are several terms for the emerging relationship. The one used here is **conjoint medical staff**, described by sociologist W. R. Scott.[1] (Shortell identifies his term, "shared authority," as equivalent.[2]) Compared to historical relationships, the conjoint staff participates more actively in all the affairs of the organization. It is more effective in its own peer review. It plays a bigger role in directing the activities of other professional groups. It is a more articulate representative of its members' needs. With greater representation comes greater responsibility. The conjoint staff participates actively in the management of the organization as a whole, including the governance and strategic activities.

Competitors to the Conjoint Model

The conjoint staff arose from traditional community hospital medical staff models, and it competes with two other archetypes, the doctor-owned corporation and the large, multicommunity insurance intermediary.

Traditional Models

The more traditional view of staff purpose, reflected in the medical staff structure of hospitals through the 1980s, tended to emphasize the rights of doctors more than their contributions and their independence more than their shared needs. The structure was limited to institutional practice and assumed that most doctors competed for ambulatory practice in a free market. Traditional hospital medical staff bylaws often failed to reference the community health care needs, eliminated the recruiting purpose, diminished the cost expectation purpose, and ignored the staff role in assuring adequate finance and communications. The medical staff organization which resulted addressed principally issues of professional quality of care and the rights of physicians. An extreme version, and an uncommon one, held that the staff's purpose was to defend physician rights; this had the staff acting more as a union than as a unit of the organization, thereby creating an adversarial relationship with every other exchange partner.

The traditional model reflects three aspects of American society which are no longer true. First, the extreme power developed by physicians relative to other exchange partners was based in large measure upon shortages of physicians which required concessions by others to maintain an adequate supply. There is increasing evidence that these shortages no longer exist.[3] Second, health insurance has expanded to include most acute care in home, office, clinic, and inpatient settings. Health insurance divorces the payment from the individual at the point of service. As a result it must rely on medical staff organizations to control cost and quality in place of individual buyer decisions. Third, the exchange demands of society have substantially increased. A growing portion of the market seeks formal management of care. Payment mechanisms no longer support "reasonable costs," whether by the organization's or the doctor's definition. Concern with quality has increased, and extended to ambulatory and preventive care. Health care organizations are no longer immune from malpractice suits. Racial, religious, and sexual discrimination are no longer publicly acceptable.

These changes spell the end of the traditional model. It will not be a competitor in the twenty-first century. Health care organizations which do not keep up with the transition in their local markets will not survive.

Competing Staff Organization Models

The theory of the conjoint staff makes the assumption that a not-for-profit community organization can succeed by collaborating more effectively with physicians than the two major alternatives shown in Figure 12.1, a for-profit public corporation and a physician-owned corporation. Physician ownership models, represented by organizations like the Mayo Clinic and a small group of other doctor-owned clinics, insure that issues of professional reward and physician participation in decisions will be addressed. Otherwise, they tend to parallel those of the conjoint staff, with only slightly less community participation. The existing physician-owned models have been growing rapidly, but the number of successful examples is increasing only slowly. The public corporation model used by regional and national insurance intermediaries views the doctor as an employee or contractor. Corporate ownership is remote from the local community. The model relies upon the marketplace to define health care needs, without extensive professional input. It does not express a purpose of supporting a rewarding professional life, and it does not involve physician affiliates in the decisions about the organization itself. Given the diversity of America, it is likely all three models will survive for decades to come. Combinations and variations of the prototypes will be tested and some variants may be the most successful of all.

The conjoint staff model's advantage is in blending both of its competitors' capabilities. It can be attractive to customers because it meets health care needs including cost control with a responsive locally owned organization. It can be attractive to physicians because it demonstrates concern for their welfare and deliberately incorporates their professional skill in management and governance process. Its success will depend on two factors; its ability to meet customer demands for price and quality, and its ability to recruit physicians who agree with its mission and vision and are attracted by the opportunity to implement it.

Figure 12.1 Prototypes of Future Health Care Organizations

Type	Usual Corporate Structure	Medical Staff Structure	Example
Community	Not-for-profit	Conjoint	Intermountain Health Care
Doctor-owned	For-profit, limited ownership	Ownership relationship	Mayo Clinic
Public corporation	For-profit, public ownership	Contractor relationship	Aetna

An important competitive advantage of the conjoint staff model is its ability to accommodate multiple forms of patient-physician relationships and physician compensation. Existing forms of health insurance range from giving the patient complete freedom to select a physician and paying a fee, such as in traditional indemnity plans, to deliberately limiting patient choice to panels of employed physicians, such as in Kaiser Permanente. While neither extreme may end up with a major market share, there appears to be deep-seated public demand for almost the full spectrum. Except in the largest metropolitan areas, many specialists will be forced to accept all payment approaches, and some primary care practitioners may choose to do the same. The conjoint staff approach is uniquely suited to a mixed health insurance market. At least theoretically, it can accommodate physicians practicing in any or all modes, and help them collaborate as a team better than competing models.

Another factor in the competition between the three models will be access to capital. Growth itself requires capital. Relatively large amounts of money will be necessary to meet the needs of information systems development, service to physicians, and new medical technology. Corporations that have funds to meet these needs will tend to capture market from those who do not. Presumably, for-profit public corporations have the advantage here, because they can issue stock. But capital access depends on a promising stream of future profits. Any organization which can promise return can raise capital; only the vehicles differ. The conjoint staff starts with the base of capital in not-for-profit community hospitals, and it has an opportunity to grow based on the cash flow of those organizations.

Success for the conjoint model clearly depends on exploiting these advantages. The well-managed health care organization must use its local governance and participative organization, its ability to accommodate a variety of physician compensation arrangements, and its capital generating capability to attract a broad range of customers and a sufficient supply of qualified physicians.

Plan for the Chapter

The remainder of the chapter covers the purposes of the conjoint medical staff and continues with the functions the staff organization must perform, including a description of the privilege relationship, the unique contract that establishes the ground rules for collaboration. The chapter reviews the economic and organizational relationships between physicians and health care organizations, and concludes with a review of measures of medical staff performance.

Purposes

Purposes of the Conjoint Staff

The concept of the conjoint staff organization is to succeed in the marketplaces for patients and physicians by emphasizing similarities, not differences, between customer and provider purposes. Following this line of thought, one may group the purposes of the conjoint medical staff under three headings:

1. The provision of high-quality, cost-effective care to the community
   - to provide the maximum scope of services consistent with community health care needs and economic capability
   - to support a variety of economic arrangements allowing the largest possible market
   - to support a system of recruiting, selecting, and promoting physicians whose capabilities most closely reflect the desires of the community
   - to establish and achieve appropriate expectations governing the cost and quality of patient care
   - to implement peer review of collective and individual performance.
2. The support of rewarding professional life
   - to provide each physician with a competitive livelihood and a satisfying opportunity to practice quality medicine
   - to promote the clinical knowledge and skill of its members
   - to provide equal opportunity for all qualified members of the organization and to assure their rights by due process.
3. The maintenance of the organization itself
   - to maintain communications between members of the organization and decision-making bodies in a manner that promotes full understanding, responsiveness, and fairness in matters affecting the work environment
   - to assure an adequate financial base
   - to aid in the resolution of conflicting desires between its customers, its owners, and its members.

Functions

The conjoint medical staff must complete five major functions to achieve the purposes.

- Medical staff planning and recruitment
- Representation, communication, and resolution of conflicts
- Education of the medical staff and of other clinical services
- Improvement of clinical quality and cost expectations
- Credentialing and privileging of physicians.

These are summarized in Figure 12.2.

Medical Staff Planning and Recruitment

A successful conjoint staff must be properly sized to the community it serves. If it is too large, physician income and professional satisfaction purposes will not be met, quality of care may suffer, and individual doctors may face strong temptations to pursue unnecessary lines of treatment. If it is too small, patients will be unable to get timely service and an adequate choice of practitioners. The solution is to plan the staff size as part of the strategic and long-range planning of the institution. The planning model is an extension of the general epidemiologic planning model from Chapter 6:

$$\begin{Bmatrix} \text{Number of} \\ \text{Physicians} \\ \text{Needed} \end{Bmatrix} = \begin{Bmatrix} \text{Population} \\ \text{at risk} \end{Bmatrix} \times \begin{Bmatrix} \text{Incidence of} \\ \text{disease/procedure} \end{Bmatrix} \div \begin{Bmatrix} \text{Procedures per} \\ \text{physician year} \end{Bmatrix}$$

$$\begin{Bmatrix} \text{Number of} \\ \text{Recruitments} \end{Bmatrix} = \begin{Bmatrix} \text{Number of} \\ \text{physicians} \\ \text{needed} \end{Bmatrix} - \begin{Bmatrix} \text{Number of} \\ \text{physicians} \\ \text{available} \end{Bmatrix}$$

Joint Planning as a Competitive Advantage

Strategic decisions are necessary to establish how and where the need for each specialty will be met. There are two issues underlying the strategic decision, one tending to dominate primary care planning and the other planning for highly specialized services. Both have profound implications for the size and composition of the medical staff.

The first issue is one of meeting expressed patient demand. Access to medical care is highly valued by most people. Customers must be satisfied with primary care availability, selection of practitioners, waiting times, and efficiency. The planning question for primary health care facilities, including doctors' offices, nonphysician practitioners, clinics, and emergency facilities is one of providing sufficient supply to meet customer demand. The well-managed health care organization must monitor demand and satisfaction by market segment, and provide

Figure 12.2 Functions of the Conjoint Staff

Function	Purpose	Activities
Medical staff planning and recruitment	Assure an adequate supply of well-trained physicians	Physician needs planning, recruitment
Representation and communication	Bring medical staff viewpoint to all activities of the organization	Governing board, strategic plans, protocols, organization participation
Education of the medical staff and of other clinical services	Maintain current clinical skills and knowlege for physicians and other clinical professions	Case reviews, continuing education, post-graduate medical education
Improvement of clinical quality and cost expectations	Provide high-quality, cost-effective health care	Design and improvement of clinical care protocols
Review of privileges and credentials	Assure continued effectiveness of individual staff members	Admission of new members, renewal of privileges

sufficient primary care access tailored to each segment. The questions are the number and location of sites, the mix of professionals, and the hours of operation. As Figure 12.3 shows, the patterns of demand are complex, and are influenced by the type of health insurance.

The competitive issues between managed and traditional care relate to influencing patient behavior on the amount and kind of care, and the selection of physician. The health care organization has the opportunity to encourage or discourage demand by promotional techniques. Preventive care, health promotion, and reliance on primary practitioners can be encouraged for managed care patients while traditionally insured patients are left free to seek whatever they desire. This flexible strategy provides continued opportunity for both forms of insurance. By discouraging unnecessary demand, it may offer the best long-run strategy for traditional insurance, whose continued market success may depend upon its ability to curb unjustified use of services.

Primary care physicians have an obvious stake in physician planning decisions. Too many sources of primary care will reduce physician income; too few will cause them to be overworked. The distribution of care between sites and practitioners is partially manageable by marketing techniques and it affects the relative earnings of each group.

Figure 12.3   Complexity of Primary Care Demand

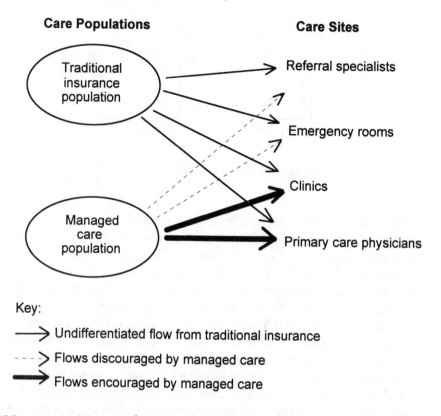

Key:

———> Undifferentiated flow from traditional insurance

- - -> Flows discouraged by managed care

——▶ Flows encouraged by managed care

Nurse practitioners, family practitioners, internists, psychiatrists, obstetricians, pediatricians, and emergency physicians are all prominent primary care providers.

The second issue arises in planning highly specialized services, centering around the existence of sufficient local demand rather than the sufficient supply issues of primary care. In general, highly specialized treatment of disease incurs high fixed costs which must be spread over large populations to be cost effective. Unit cost falls rapidly as volume increases. It is also true that treatment teams caring for higher volumes of patients will have better quality results.[4] As Figure 12.4 shows, for any given treatment there is a declining cost structure and an increasing quality structure. There are also competitive standards for both cost and quality. If these are not met, patients and insurers will select other sources, after allowing for any inconvenience such as travel to a remote site. The standards dictate a critical volume, V_c. A health care organization which operates a specialty below its critical volume faces both losses and poor quality.

Figure 12.4   Critical Volumes for Specialty Services

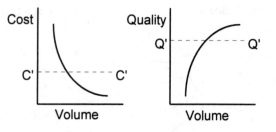

C', Q': Competitive levels

Referral specialists depend upon the organization to supply essential facilities and trained personnel for the procedures, and their own income will depend on the volume of patients. The recruitment plan generates forecasts of average physician income by specialty as a byproduct. Cardiovascular surgery provides a useful example. The need is dependent on the population of the community, its age and health habits. The United States averaged 2,125 operations per million persons in 1991 and the volume of surgery per site is 700 per year.[5] A community of approximately 350,000 persons is necessary to provide average volumes. The institution which cannot attract that much demand faces unit costs higher than the competitive standard. The surgeon who works in that institution faces lower than average income. Both face the problem that outcomes may be below achievable levels because the team does not get enough practice.

The conjoint staff assumption is that a well-managed institution can identify and meet demand more effectively than competing models. Although physicians have unique interests based upon their specialty, they also share general interests in a well-designed system.[6] Referral specialists are interested in the primary care supply because the number of practitioners and the rules for referral directly affect specialist income. Primary care physicians share an interest in the specialist supply because too few referral specialty services means excess patient travel to distant sources, and too many means inferior care and excess cost.

Developing the Physician Needs Plan
Community health care institutions support an employed team and all of the facilities for inpatient care and specialized services like surgery. Institutional support for office practice is growing rapidly. Thus both capital investment in facilities and recruitment of physicians is at stake

in the planning decision. In most cases, the decisions are part of the strategic or long-range plan of the institution. As indicated in Chapter 6, decisions are made first on the question of scope of service, "Should we have a cardiovascular surgery program?" and second on the actual facilities and number of physicians required.

As illustrated in Figure 12.5, the physician recruitment plan is an extension of these decisions. Forecasts of future demand are obtained from the services plan, which extends the strategic plan to specific facility sizes, locations, and dates. Data on output per physician, and the split of demand between specialties (Many procedures are served by more than one specialty.) are obtained from national data bases and local history. Data on the current supply of physicians must be obtained from staff membership files. The starting point should be a record of each doctor's age, specialty, and past activity with the organization. Additional information may be obtained by questionnaire or telephone survey, but direct discussion may still be desirable, not only to clarify intentions but to explore mutually rewarding alternatives. Specialty, age (or graduation from medical school), and level of activity of individual staff members are used to forecast the future supply, and the difference is met by new recruits.

Three problems must be resolved in the physician recruitment planning approach.

1. *Uncertainty about the demand.* The popularity and effectiveness of managed care substantially changes the demand for specific services and specialties.

2. *Uncertainty about the supply.* The activity levels of doctors currently on the staff may change in the future.

3. *Conflicts over the allocation of demand to specialty.* The expectations of one specialty may not coincide with those of others or of the community representatives.

The concept of the conjoint model assumes that these problems will be addressed through discussion, and that the organization and the physicians will share the risks and rewards which result. Furthermore, it assumes that the process of discussion and negotiation is a competitive advantage; communities pursuing the model will reach more realistic strategic plans and will attract better doctors. With the growth of managed care, radical shifts are expected within medicine, with many of the referral specialties facing sharp declines in demand, and some communities facing shortages of primary care practitioners.[7] The consequences of an unmanaged declining demand could be severe. There is evidence that physicians can generate inappropriate demand to

Figure 12.5 Cardiac Surgery as an Example of Combined Strategic, Service, and Physician Planning

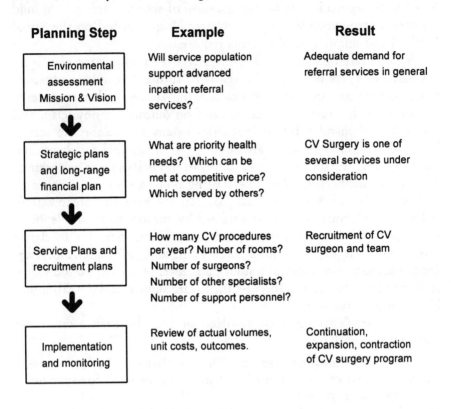

Planning Step	Example	Result
Environmental assessment Mission & Vision	Will service population support advanced inpatient referral services?	Adequate demand for referral services in general
Strategic plans and long-range financial plan	What are priority health needs? Which can be met at competitive price? Which served by others?	CV Surgery is one of several services under consideration
Service Plans and recruitment plans	How many CV procedures per year? Number of rooms? Number of surgeons? Number of other specialists? Number of support personnel?	Recruitment of CV surgeon and team
Implementation and monitoring	Review of actual volumes, unit costs, outcomes.	Continuation, expansion, contraction of CV surgery program

protect incomes,[8] and a deliberate program discouraging further growth and assisting retraining and early retirement is likely to be beneficial to the community as well as the practitioner.

The advantages of conjoint staff planning are summarized in Figure 12.6. Physicians practicing in small groups can rarely afford the data collection and analysis that a health care organization can. The institution benefits by getting physician input and acceptance, reducing the risk of its decisions. As the figure shows, there are opportunities to manipulate both the demand and the supply to gain a smooth transition. Collaborative approaches help identify these, prioritize them, and devise effective solutions.

The final decision on desired specialties and numbers of attending doctors rests with the governing board, as part of the long-range plan. Once these decisions have been made, the well-run organization and its medical staff begin joint recruitment for the desired individuals.

Figure 12.6 Advantages of Conjoint Medical Staff Planning

Advantage	Physician Benefit	Institution Benefit
1. Shared information and cooperative analysis allow more accurate forecasts	See future sooner and more clearly, have more time to react	Improve safety, return, market attractiveness of investments
2. Facility and employee needs integrated with physician needs	Support available when needed	Volumes adequate to keep costs and quality competitive
3. Better management of physician supply	Facilitate potentially painful transitions	Meet community demand for access. Reduce pressure for inappropriate treatment.
4. Better management of insurance contracts	More options for insurance contracts More income stability More market share	Broader array of options for customers More market share

Recruitment as a Joint Activity

Good doctors have their choice of practice locations, and they are actively recruited, even in times of relative surplus. Either doctor groups or health care organizations can recruit on their own; however, the more they recruit jointly, the more successful they are likely to be. This is due in large measure to the complexity of competitive offers. A recruitment offer frequently includes arrangements for office facilities, income guarantees, malpractice coverage, membership in a medical partnership or group, and introductions to referring physicians or available specialists. As HMO or PPO groups become more common, membership in these, too, must be in the recruiting offer. Home financing, club membership, and other social and family issues are frequently important.[9] The organization's buying and financing power is frequently essential to assembling the elements of tangible compensation. At the same time, doctors want to work where their colleagues are friendly, complex offers require early assurance that medical credentials are acceptable, and selecting the right candidate principally involves assessment of clinical skills. These factors require medical staff participation in the recruitment process.

Recruitment has become a relatively well-codified activity, carried out by a search committee representing both the institution and the medical staff. It includes the following components:

- Establishment of criteria for the position and the person sought
- Establishment of compensation and incentives
- Advertising and solicitation of candidates
- Initial selection
- Interviews and visits
- Final selection and negotiation.

Right of the Institution to Deny Privileges

A not-for-profit community health care organization may deny or discontinue the right of a physician to use its facilities and personnel in the care of patients on either of two grounds. The most common is quality, failure to comply with properly established criteria governing quality of care and good character, discussed below as credentialing. The second is economic, that the doctor overtaxes the facilities available for the kinds of care he or she expects to give, or provides a service which is not necessary. Thus a hospital is not obligated to accept a cardiac surgeon if it has no cardiologist, or if it has no cardiopulmonary laboratory, or if it feels it has enough cardiac surgeons already. Similarly, a health maintenance organization or a medical group is not obligated to accept a pediatric hematologist if it routinely refers pediatric hematology, has no laboratory facilities for pediatric hematology, and is satisfied that the existing arrangements are in the best interests of its members. Under certain conditions of declining demand, it might become necessary to reduce the number of specialists on economic grounds.

Medical societies have responded vigorously to the concept of denial of privileges, and have sought legislation called "any willing provider legislation" in several states to prevent it.[10] The intent of the legislation is to assure each practitioner equal opportunity to participate in all insurance forms. Managed care plans must state participation criteria explicitly, and accept all who meet the criteria and wish to participate.

Final Approval of the Medical Staff Plan

Even under any willing provider legislation, it appears that a well-managed health care organization can effectively control the number of providers. Its ability to do so depends upon a carefully designed and implemented plan, as well as an effective credentialling program. The following steps are important.

1. The strategic plan of the institution is firmly based in epidemiologic estimates of need and realistic forecasts of market demand, and is supported by a sound financial plan.
2. The plan is implemented through the services plan which establishes only necessary and cost-effective services.
3. Quality of care issues are addressed through a rigorous program of credentials review and performance review.
4. Participation in managed care plans is separated from privileges to use facilities. All criteria for participation in managed care plans are clearly identified and fairly enforced.
5. The medical staff plan clearly identifies the volumes of work and the number of physicians needed in each specialty, including forecasts of volumes of work under managed care and traditional plans.

These steps have a dual impact. First, they make the economic environment as clear as possible to all practitioners as far in the future as can be seen. Both new and current physicians can use the data to project their own incomes, and can make decisions which are in their own best interest. The organization retains the right to take such actions as are necessary to meet cost-effective community need. It avoids denial of privileges as much as possible, and works deliberately with existing staff to manage declines in volume effectively. It relies on the mission, financial plan, and scope of services to support its economic actions.

Second, the approach allows physicians deliberate choice of relations with insurance intermediaries. Some physicians may opt for a fee-for-service practice and pursue it without participating in managed care. They will know that careful planning has made the facilities costs as low as possible, allowing traditional health insurance to be as competitive as possible on price. Other physicians, presumably the majority, will be able to compete for both managed and traditional patients, and will be willing to accept the additional restraints which managed care imposes.

Success depends upon carrying out all five steps effectively. As Chapter 5 indicates, success will require physician participation in the strategic, financial, and services plans decisions, and as Chapter 6 and Chapter 7 suggest, the technical issues behind these plans must be carefully and thoroughly addressed.

To avoid antitrust issues, physician control over the recruitment plan must be balanced by the extent to which the physicians participate collectively in the risks. Physician advice on the number of specialists for an HMO can be accepted directly; that for practice in a fee-for-service environment should be evaluated more closely by the governing board to assure that it is not unnecessary restraint of trade. It is best if the governing board acts formally on the plan considering the comments of the medical staff as advisory only. Physician members might disqualify themselves because of the potential conflict of interest.

Representation, Communication, and Resolution of Conflicts

Under the theory of the well-managed health care organization described in Chapter 2, the only limits to medical staff participation are the need to keep both the content and the timeliness of the decisions consistent with customer demands and the need to recognize the rights of other provider partners. The conjoint staff model implements the theory by establishing formal physician participation in all decisions, including the mission and vision, resource allocation, implementation, and organization. The most serious limit on participation is likely to be the shortage of physician time. Participation itself takes time away from patient care, and many physicians resent the hours devoted to it even while recognizing its importance.

The goal of physician representation and communication is to assure all staff members that they are empowered to influence decisions affecting their practices. This means not only that physicians are present at critical decisions, but that avenues exist to identify issues, discuss implications, and resolve conflicts. The link between the practitioner and the representative is as important as the representation itself. Success requires a robust communications mechanism which identifies issues promptly, solicits and organizes opinion, and resolves them fairly.[11] Leading institutions deliberately survey physicians about issues important to them; the physician priorities are incorporated in selecting improvement projects.[12] The dual criteria for organization decisions generally, realism and conviction (Chapter 5), apply here as well. Ideally, all physicians should be convinced that they have heard the issue, have had a fair opportunity to be heard about the issue, and that the final decision optimizes market realities, without having had to waste unnecessary time on either step.

Infrastructure of Physician Representation

The formal medical staff bylaws provide the basis for representation. The bylaws specify not simply the rights and obligations of each party, but also the methods by which communication is encouraged and disagreements are resolved. Well-run organizations use such documents as a foundation for the ongoing resolution of issues that arise. The bylaws specify the roles of each office and standing committee of the medical staff. They include provision for ad hoc committee formation. Properly written, they are a set of rights and responsibilities which can reassure staff members about the way decisions are made, and how their voices can be heard. They should emphasize the role of the medical department or section chair to hear, report, and represent the needs of the unit. The organization does not expect that individual doctors will memorize the bylaws, but it prepares useful summaries of the decision processes, and trains medical staff officers about them. When section or department chiefs are familiar with the bylaws, all doctors are close to someone who can explain them.

Well-run organizations use formal approaches to develop consensus on expectations, coordinate activities of the staff, and represent the views of the staff. They use the formal representatives to reconcile differences within the staff (many potential conflicts are between medical specialties) and between the staff and the rest of the organization. The burden on staff members can often be reduced by sensitive design and administration. Doctors can be welcomed to committees, work groups, and task forces where they make a specific contribution and can be excused from meetings where nonmedical issues are addressed. Meetings can be arranged when necessary rather than periodically. Agendas can be developed with an understanding of the need to save time. Advance preparation and distribution of relevant background material make a noticeable difference, as does proper preparation of the chair.

Where communication and trust are supported by a strong formal communication system, informal devices can be used to great advantage. If all staff members are confident that they will know of decisions important to them in time to react and that they have an avenue to make their views known quickly, much time spent in formal communications can be eliminated. In well-run health care organizations, nonmedical managers make a deliberate effort to maintain informal communications with the medical staff. Many successful CEOs and COOs undertake the monitoring function personally. More than one successful CEO says, "I try to stop by the doctors' lounge at least five times a week."[13]

Board Membership for the Medical Staff

The practice of providing seats on the board for the medical staff has become almost universal, and is an important advantage of community-based health care organizations. Exceptions are mainly limited to those institutions whose corporate charters or enabling legislation preclude such participation. In many organizations, doctors are nominated for these seats by the medical staff. Other doctors may also serve on the board, although they are presumably selected for their personal, rather than their professional, abilities. The board majority should remain nonphysicians; rarely do doctors constitute a substantial minority.

These few individuals, representing only a fraction of the specialties, ages, and financial arrangements of the staff as a whole, must fulfill the complex representation needs of all doctors. Like other board members, they are expected to vote for the best interests of the corporation, rather than any short-term advantage to themselves or to the medical staff. They serve the medical staff more by their ability to review decision processes than by advocating specific decisions. Their board membership allows them to make sure the staff's opinions are fully and fairly heard, and conversely to communicate the views of the customer representatives on the board to their colleagues. They are often in a position to resolve disputes by mediation or integration, finding a mutually satisfactory solution that meets all needs better.

Formal Participation in Ongoing Decisions

Because only a few physicians can serve on the governing board, the major substantive representation of medical staff viewpoints and needs is provided by direct and extensive participation in the development of improvements. In well-managed organizations issues are resolved by task forces, work groups, and committees before the final proposal is presented to the board. Figure 12.7 shows the usual means for each of the decision processes discussed in Chapter 5.

Mission, vision and environmental assessment Doctors participate in substantial numbers in the annual review of the environment and any revision of the mission and vision. All members of the medical executive committee are included in the annual review. Doctors who are respected as leaders by their peers, those who are known to represent particular positions, and doctors who are considered as potential officers are also often invited. The review should encourage doctors' comments on the economic impact of the mission and strategic opportunities on members of the medical staff. Participation enhances the factual base for decision making and eliminates unnecessary conflict between the organization and the medical staff over income generating services.

Strategic plan Physicians should participate actively in reviewing the strategic plan. The scope of services of a well-managed health care organization must be designed so that it and its medical staff together can provide quality care and gain a competitive reward for doing so.

Figure 12.7 Physician Representation on Decision Processes

Decision Type	Example	Physician Participation
Mission/vision	Environment assessment strategic plans	Governing board membership Leadership in annual review
Resource allocation	Services plan financial plan	Membership on board planning and finance committees
	Facilities and human resources plans	Representation on committees and consultation for services directly involved
	Physician recruitment plan	Advice from each specialty
	Budgeting	Participation between line units and services particularly involved
	Capital budgeting	Major voice in ranking all clinical equipment Participate in general ranking
Implementation	Personnel selection	Participation on critical search committees
	Process design	Participation by services in all final product protocol development Review of intermediate protocols
Organizational	Information plan	Participation in plan at service level where indicated
	Conflict resolution	Membership in mediation efforts and appeals panels

Medical staff input is essential to finding that balance. Balance among the medical specialties and between medicine and other perspectives is important. Individual specialties automatically become advocates for scientific advances in their areas, overstating the promise of much new technology. Two arguments with strong emotional appeal can be anticipated. They have explicit rational tests which should be met before they are accepted. "Lifesaving" is only applicable to those few conditions where the patient cannot be moved to another facility. To be "essential for recruiting the best people," the item must be available at a visible fraction—say, 20 or 30 percent—of truly competing institutions and in the immediate plans of a majority. Physicians from other specialties are well equipped to mount these challenges.

By the same token, plans and investments which make modest contributions to large groups are sometimes overlooked because they lack persuasive advocates. Doctors in primary care, public health, and preventive medicine can redress this imbalance.

Operating expectations   The medical staff begins contributing to resource allocation by participating in the setting of clinical protocols as described in Chapter 11. Protocols establish the clinical support service resources required for each patient. It is a short jump from them to the service's annual operating budget. The leading indicator for necessary improvements is frequently volume or market share which fails to meet expectations. Medical staff help in analyzing services with unsatisfactory market share is cheap and effective. Doctor or patient concern with quality, access, amenities, or satisfaction is a cause of deteriorating demand. Soliciting doctors' opinions helps both to identify the problems and to stimulate correction of them.

Doctors should participate in the improvement process and the development of the annual budget for clinical support services. The major services have standing committees for this purpose. The pharmacy and therapeutics committee and the operating room committee are examples where many institutions have had success. Similar opportunities exist for the diagnostic and rehabilitation services. Usually the service works closely with only a few specialties, but an outside clinical view may help identify important new perspectives.

Capital and new programs budget   At the capital budgeting level, doctors' most important contribution is their understanding of clinical implications and the economic impacts upon various practicing physicians. Projects where doctors' opinions are irrelevant are rare. All programmatic clinical proposals should include medical review of their scientific merit, demand estimates, procedures and equipment contemplated, likely benefits to patients, risks to patients and staff, and implications for physician income. In cases where the specialty involved may be biased by its economic concerns, independent evaluations may be solicited. Serious disputes on these technical matters are themselves an indicator of project risk and should be presented as such.

The extent of the review can be tailored to the size and scope of the proposal. All important projects should be given independent review by every relevant specialty group. Differences of opinion between specialty groups arising from independent review should be resolved via the medical organization hierarchy. That is, projects advocated by the surgical subspecialties should be collectively ranked by surgeons directly involved, then by surgeons of all kinds, and that ranking should be integrated with similar ones from medicine and other specialties by the medical executive committee. The consensus ranking for all clinical proposals should be integrated into the new programs and capital budget by the planning committee or a specially designated capital budget committee with medical, executive, finance, and board membership.

Marketing and promotional efforts   Doctors can sign individual participation contracts with managed care providers. The contracts specify terms of participation including fee schedules and quality and appropriateness criteria. The conjoint staff allows individual contracting, but it negotiates many contracts collectively for the institution and a group of the staff. This approach allows the group to trade utilization and price, and to accept risk for the total cost of care on either a **common provider entity** or global fee structure (where the institution receives a single payment which it must then distribute to itself and its physician partners) or capitation. The organization's market advantage in these contracts is its ability to assemble an attractive provider panel and to accept risk for managing actual care.

Physician participation is required to permit common provider entity and capitation contracts. The conjoint structure is proving to be an effective way to organize this participation. Conjoint staffs are increasing their ability to act as agents for their members, establishing guidelines and contracting for the group whenever the guidelines are met, without individual review.

Doctors can also be important contributors to promotional efforts aimed directly at patients; they provide a vehicle for reaching the patients and they can suggest appropriate content for promotional material. Conjoint staffs will use the promotional capabilities of the organization for the collective benefit of the doctors, as well as for the organization.

Medical staff plan   As noted above, physicians participate extensively in the preparation of the medical staff plan.

Facilities, information and human resources plans   Physician participation on these detailed plans is also important. Most facility proposals are developed by ad hoc task forces which include substantial representation from interested specialties. Physician participation on the

Information Services Advisory Committee (Chapter 10) is important. All trials of clinical hardware and software should include review of physician user satisfaction.

Medical Staff Leadership

While physicians are notably independent in their professional style, there are recognized informal organizations of physicians and means of detecting physician leaders. Physicians tend to follow the lead of clinicians they respect in clinical matters, and of physicians who gain their respect in other professional matters. Clinical leaders are important in gaining consensus on protocols, credentialing, and other matters relating directly to the cost and quality of patient care. Professional leaders are important in winning support for organizational procedures, budgets, insurance contracts, and services arrangements. Leaders are not difficult to identify. They emerge naturally in informal discussions, and most physicians will simply state their leadership candidates. There is surprising consensus.

Well-managed organizations routinely identify and rely on medical leaders. They form the backbone of the medical staff organization, filling the key positions. A sound program identifies leaders early in their careers and begins assigning activities appropriate to their skills. As the doctors mature, their experience deepens and their assignments become more complex. There is a set of doctors moving through the ranks, toward the critical executive positions, board membership, and committee assignments.

Conflict Resolution

The strategy of conjoint staff management is conflict prevention and amelioration; the intent is to identify potential conflicts in advance, analyze and understand them, and respond in a way that is constructive for all parties. In its most basic sense, the organization is a device for conflict resolution. The open system mechanism assumes customers will want to pay less and providers will want to earn more; it is about bringing the two together. A well-managed institution in fact contains and resolves many issues by pursuing the extensive participation outlined above. But the process is much more contentious than it appears. Substantial conflicts will still arise and painful sacrifices will be involved in settling them.

The conjoint model implies a fundamental change in the doctor's obligation to act as agent for the patient. The conjoint staff model minimizes conflict between the organization and the doctor by deliberately accepting the same obligation. Doctors are less independent because of the partnership. They must affiliate more closely with the institution and carry out agency responsibilities within it. That is, faced with a less than satisfactory service, attending physicians should work with the organization to correct the deficiency. They have a moral obligation to implement the decision processes so that patients are not sacrificed to either their own or the organization's other needs.[14]

A real conflict of interest exists if the organization's advantage diverges from the patients' or doctors'. One common example involves decisions about whether to offer certain services: convenience for certain patients and income for certain doctors will be enhanced, but the community as a whole will benefit more from other services. Those who "lose" to an argument of the general good must content themselves with recognizing their gains as citizens of the larger community, including the knowledge that their future proposals are likely to be judged fairly. Another example is in the application of clinical protocols. What is good for the average patient is rarely ideal for any given patient; the physician has the obligation to modify the protocol appropriately.

At a somewhat less challenging level, conflicts arise between specialties, between clinical support services and physicians, and between individuals. The well-managed health care organization attempts to resolve these as the nation does, by being a society of laws. The following guidelines seem to be helpful.

- The processes for decision making and conflict resolution are respected above the decisions themselves. A strenuous effort is made to follow the processes. This means that the processes themselves must be convenient and flexible to minimize the burden involved. It also means that deliberate circumvention of process is one of the most serious offenses which can occur. Repeated violation of process calls for removal.

- Patient care protocols at all levels encourage professional intervention on behalf of the individual patient. No caregiver should ever feel forced to give or withhold treatment because of the organization's collective position.

- An ethics committee and similar devices exist to evaluate the processes themselves and to assist in individual interpretations. In addition to the usual committee which focuses on clinical issues, there are other bodies with explicit ethical responsibilities, such as committees on human subjects, confidentiality of personal data, sexual harassment, and equal opportunity.

- Conflicts between individuals and groups other than patients are resolved with an emphasis on fairness and long-run benefit. The contribution of each individual to the success of the whole is recognized. Decisions are evaluated on contribution to the good of the whole, more than the power of the advocate. The rules and criteria are consistently applied, giving each individual greater security.

- Appeals mechanisms exist appropriate to the level of the dispute. Ideally, almost any decision can be appealed someplace. A supervisor's decision may be appealed to a higher level of the accountability hierarchy. A capital budget decision may be appealed to the next higher review panel. A credentialling decision may be appealed to the governing board. The appeals mechanism makes a deliberate effort to conduct an unbiased review.

These guidelines are essentially the same as exist for other members of the well-managed organization. Their application to the conjoint staff concept is a deliberate effort to make the organization more attractive to competent and well-intentioned physicians than the competing forms.

Education of the Medical Staff and Other Clinical Services

The organized medical staff of most health care organizations has two educational functions; that of larger organizations has three. All staffs are responsible for promoting the continuing education of their own members and for assisting in the clinical education of other members of the organization. Larger organizations have responsibilities for postgraduate and occasionally undergraduate (i.e., candidates for the M.D. degree) medical education as well.

The interrelation of education with continuous improvement and the development of consensus protocols should not be overlooked. Analysis of past performance, benchmarking, the design of new processes, and the preparation of protocols are educational activities in themselves, affecting all three formal functions. Their educational role is likely to become more central as organizations mature in their use. It is likely that many formal educational programs will arise from needs identified in the continuous improvement process.

Continuing Education for Attending Physicians

Continuing education for doctors is now strongly encouraged as part of licensure and specialty certifications. A variety of educational programs is offered outside the organization; however, these do not substitute for the continued study of the organization's own patients. **Grand rounds** are formal presentations on subjects of direct importance. **Ward** or **clinic rounds** and clinical-pathological, mortality, infection, and adverse effects conferences and committees review actual cases in the hospital.

In well-run organizations, these activities are focused on potential revision of practice relevant to the patient population, that is, on the identification and implementation of improvements in the patient care protocols. Grand rounds can stimulate consideration of new treatment methods. Other conferences can provide collective review of recurring difficulties and can focus educational content on debatable issues. Focusing staff education has a double benefit: it avoids competition with other, more elaborate programs, and it increases consensus about the most acceptable methods. This consensus is essential to using clinical expectations effectively. Using educational approaches helps assure that every doctor fully understands the expectation, develops group pressure to encourage compliance, and, by changing behavior beforehand, eliminates personal confrontations over failures.

Education need not be limited to clinical subjects. Programs to help doctors understand the corporate approach to decision making and to learn specific technologies useful in evaluating various opportunities are also important.

How much to invest in staff education is a difficult judgment. Programs are often expensive to mount, but they are more expensive to attend. The opportunity cost of doctors' time is very high, and educational time must be judged in the context of other demands from family, practice, and, particularly, other medical staff functions. Education from outside sources is often as useful, but availability differs by community. Subjectively, and according to JCAHO philosophy, every doctor should have access to sufficient educational opportunity to keep herself or himself current. This requires, and JCAHO specifies, at least monthly meetings of clinical departments (or, in small hospitals, the entire staff) on educational topics. Attendance is required. Beyond this minimum, it is probably wise to decentralize decisions about staff education to the lowest feasible unit of the staff and to accommodate the programs they suggest when attendance figures indicate cost-effective investments. It is worth noting that large successful organizations like Kaiser-Permanente, Henry Ford Health System, and Intermountain Health Care invest heavily in education. They use their size to assemble programs which might not be cost effective for smaller institutions, but they often make the programs themselves available to others.

Education of Other Organization Members

By tradition, preparation, and law, the doctor is leader of the health care team. With this leadership comes an obligation to educate others, not only other clinical professionals, but also trustees, executives, and other management personnel. A particularly important part of this education deals with new clinical developments. New approaches to care frequently require retraining for personnel at several levels, and doctors should at least specify the content of that education. In addition, trustees and planners rely on the medical staff to identify new opportunities for care, and to make the implications of these clear in terms that promote effective decisions. Many of these educational requirements are met through participation on various committees and day-to-day associations. The needs are closely related to expectation setting, and well-run organizations identify and plan for necessary education in the process of implementing expectations.

Postgraduate Medical Education

Medicine has acknowledged its obligation to train new doctors since Hippocrates. Clinical training of medical students occurs in a limited number of institutions that incorporate such training in their mission. In 1991, about 19 percent of community hospitals offered training positions for **house officers,** licensed doctors pursuing postgraduate education. Many of these sites were in vertically integrated health care organizations, but the majority of training opportunities were in university medical centers.[15]

The content of this education is controlled through certification by individual specialty boards and is coordinated through the AMA. House officers are paid stipends during their training because they provide important direct service, because hospitals feel they are a valuable source of recruits, and because their presence has long been thought to improve overall quality of care. An important benefit to both the community and the attending staff is that house officers are expected to cover patient needs at times when attending doctors are not present. In addition, many of the programs suitable for house officers are appropriate continuing education for attending physicians, and educating house officers is educational in itself.

House officers are generally heavy users of costly services. One avenue for saving costs is the development of better care protocols, emphasizing to the house officer and the attending physician alike legitimate opportunities for economy. Presentation of financial data along with clinical data promotes consideration of the cost-effectiveness of specific diagnoses and treatment steps. Under managed care, economies are translatable to larger profits for the institution. These, in turn, may support a larger or more attractive educational program.

Recent concerns with the relative supply of primary care and referral specialties are likely to lead to extensive revisions of postgraduate training. It is likely that many programs for primary care will be expanded, and that training opportunities will emphasize outpatient as well as inpatient care. Programs for referral specialties seem likely to contract, and to move even more tightly to university centers. The result of these changes may cause a restructuring of inpatient care. The direct patient service may be supplied by physicians employed by the health care organization or the medical group.

Improvement of Clinical Quality and Cost Expectations

The activities of the conjoint medical staff establish consensus on elements of good care which is reflected in all phases of mission setting, planning, physician recruitment, credentialing, and coordination with other clinical professionals. The development of explicit expectations about the quality and cost of care discussed in Chapter 11 has clarified and expanded the medical staff role. Physicians are active participants in teams to establish both final and intermediate protocols.

Most final product protocols are established by a medically dominated committee. Leadership of the committee is usually assigned to the **modal specialists**, the specialists who treat the largest percent of patients with the disease or condition. However, many diseases are treated by several specialties. A good final product panel will include active representation from all the specialties involved in treatment. The **hospital-based specialties**, laboratory, imaging, anesthesia, and emergency care, contribute to care of many diseases. Some conditions are treated by different practitioners depending upon their severity. Obstetrics and newborn care, for example, can be successfully managed by midwives, pediatric nurse practitioners, family practice physicians, obstetricians and pediatricians. A large number of cardiovascular diseases are managed by nurse practitioners, family practice physicians, general internists, cardiologists, and cardiovascular surgeons depending on their severity.

Intermediate protocols are generally the product of a clinical support service or a single medical specialty, but the attending physicians are customers for the product. They order it, and use it in the patient's care. Well-designed intermediate protocols are reviewed by user panels, and the panel's suggestions are incorporated in the improvements. The opportunity to comment on any protocol should be open to all physicians.

Partly because of the complexity of clinical events, but also because protocols are a deliberate consensus-building device, medical staff participation is extensive. It is likely that nearly every staff member is involved in protocol reviews each year. The major medical staff contributions are shown in Figure 12.8. Managing the assignment of specific individuals to committees is an executive job, done by the office of the chief of staff. Review of the decisions by the specialties most directly involved and the medical executive committee should be routine.

Review of Privileges and Credentials

The symbiotic relationship between the organization and its medical staff can be successful only if it delivers a high-quality, cost-effective service. The task of assuring quality and cost-effectiveness in medical practice is assigned to the medical staff. It is implemented by complex and rigorously defined activity, but it is based on a simple premise, that well-trained doctors in a supportive surrounding will provide their patients with excellent care. Each doctor is formally granted the privilege of joining the medical staff and providing treatment within her or his training and experience. In continuous improvement terms, each doctor is empowered to practice good medicine.

Elements of Privilege

The privilege agreement contains the following five elements:

1. *Bylaws.* The governing board and the medical staff, that is, the doctors collectively, establish certain mutually acceptable rules and regulations. These rules define the concepts of privilege, the doctors' relationships to their patients, and the doctors' obligations for peer review. They also define how the medical

Figure 12.8 Major Medical Staff Involvement in Clinical Protocol Development

Type	Leadership	Medical Staff Role
Final product	Modal specialist	Each service involved is represented on team. Protocols are approved by services involved. Protocols can be reviewed by medical executive committee if necessary.
Intermediate	Usually clinical support service	Protocols are reviewed by representatives of relevant specialties. Review by full service if necessary.

staff and the organization make decisions affecting the doctors and how the rule may be amended. Final approval of the bylaws is vested in the governing board.

2. *Privileges.* The governing board on recommendation of the staff extends the privilege of medical staff membership for specific kinds of patient care to each doctor within these rules. Those privileged are called **attending physicians.**

3. *Independent doctor-patient relationship.* Each doctor establishes her or his own relationship to each patient and is expected to pursue diligently the obligations of that relationship.

4. *Peer review.* Doctors receiving privileges are also expected to participate in peer review of the quality of care, both as a reviewer and as a subject of review. The organization can expect that privileges will be curtailed should the clinical performance of the physician fail to meet the expectations of peers.

5. *Representation.* Doctors are expected to participate in the ongoing activities of the organization, including development of consensuses on appropriate care, and assistance to other clinical professions.

The contractual consideration on the part of the organization is access to resources, and that on the part of the doctor is willingness to practice good medicine and accept the obligations indicated in the bylaws. As a contract, privilege is subject to all the legal provisions normally pertaining to business contracts.[16]

Under the bylaws obligations, each doctor is expected to accept both the responsibilities and the rights of management, to not only abide by the rules, but help enforce them and keep them current in a rapidly changing world. Because each accepts this responsibility, only doctors need judge other doctors on medical matters. This concept of peer review is a central element of professional autonomy. It is highly prized by most doctors, and they invest much time and energy in carrying out their obligations.

Flexibility of the Concept of Privilege

The privilege system has robust flexibility. It can cover care in various settings, be tailored to unique geographic needs or special markets, and adapt to any insurance or physician payment system. It accommodates other professionals giving medical care. Among other examples of its flexibility, the system permits but does not require cash and other tangible payments as part of the consideration. Early in this century, doctors contributed substantial unpaid effort to hospitals. The trend since World War II has been toward financially compensating physicians.

Medical leaders are compensated for their time, individual members participate in managed care contracts, and assistance is provided to doctors at various points in their careers as a means of managing the physician supply.

Trends in the Concept of Privilege

The origins of the privileging and peer review system lie in actions taken in the late 1920s by the American College of Surgeons to improve the quality of surgical practice.[17] Its development since has been influenced by legal decisions.[18] In the 1950s, the legal doctrines of charitable and governmental immunity protecting hospitals from suit were overturned. National accreditation recognizing peer review was transferred to the Joint Commission on Accreditation of Hospitals (now Healthcare Organizations) in 1953. The obligation of the institution to assure quality practice by physicians on its staff was substantially strengthened by the Darling decision of 1965, holding the hospital explicitly liable for failure to assure a qualified medical staff.[19]

In the 1970s the courts and legislatures also turned their attention to the rights of individual physicians. Under theories of nondiscrimination and antitrust, the concept of privilege was expanded to include due process, equal opportunity, and the avoidance of restraint of trade. These actions were consistent with major improvements in civil rights and a broadened application of free market concepts in U.S. society generally.

In the 1980s the role of the medical staff was again broadened, this time to incorporate concepts of control of costs as well as quality. Prospective per case payment required that hospitals deliver care through their medical staffs at fixed prices. HMOs and PPOs extended the concept of control of cost beyond the case or hospital stay to the care of the patient over the contract period. Also in the 1980s, the courts required organizations to guard against restriction of trade; the privileging process cannot be used to exclude competing doctors.[20] By 1990, the five elements of the privilege relationship had been defined to include scientific quality, customer responsiveness, nondiscrimination, due process, antitrust, and cost control.

Privilege Review Process

The Joint Commission on Accreditation of Healthcare Organizations now requires that all privileges be granted for specific, limited clinical activity, that they end annually or biennially, and that they be renewed only when there is a consistent record of acceptable quality.[21] As a result, the process of privilege review, that is, **credentialing**, has become an ongoing staff activity with growing impact on the quality and economy of care.

The responsibility for granting and renewing privileges is centered in a committee of the medical staff called the credentials committee. Although the executive office must support the activities of this committee with a variety of records and data, the key evaluations require clinical knowledge and must be made by physicians. The opinion of specialists must be sought when appropriate. Many larger organizations use the credentials committee as a coordinating body, with initial review in the specialty departments. Since the decision to grant privileges has a direct effect on both the organization's and the doctors' income, it must be made under due process and subject to appeal in order to protect the rights of individuals, and it must be recommended to the governing board, which is ultimately responsible for all medical staff appointments. The organization is liable for failure to provide due process, failure to remove incompetent doctors, and failure to establish appropriate standards of practice. The individuals participating in the process are liable for arbitrary, capricious, or discriminatory behavior.[22]

This somewhat ponderous mechanism differs from the usual employment relation between an organization and its members principally in providing more adequate protection to the doctor. The CEO and the management staff, for example, serve at the pleasure of the governing board and can be discharged at any legally constituted meeting for any grounds not discriminatory or libelous. Only civil service, union contracts, and the tenure system of professors provide individuals rights similar to credentialing.

There are seven major elements supporting a well-designed credentialing process:

1. Bylaws provisions
2. Committee membership
3. Standards for review
4. Information and data support
5. Specification of privileges
6. Operation of the credentials committee
7. Provision for impaired physicians.

Bylaws Provisions

The bylaws specify both the processes through which credentialing occurs and the structure which supports those processes. The structure is usually based on the medical and surgical specialties. The process calls for initial review of training, experience, and moral character; extension of privileges for specific procedures or diseases, and subsequent annual or biennial renewal. Most authorities view the medical staff bylaws as the principal source of due process protection for both the individual and the organization. The bylaws establish all procedural elements, including application requirements, timing, review processes, confidentiality, committees and participants, methods of establishing expectations, sources of data, and appeals procedures.

Bylaws are generally developed by the medical staff, with detailed legal review before adoption by the governing board. Regular review and updating of bylaws is important. Once bylaws are approved, the credentials committee must follow them. Failure to do so in one case but not in another is potentially discriminatory. General failure to follow the bylaws is capricious.[23]

Committee Membership

The ideal member of the credentials committee possesses the attributes of a good judge: He or she is patient, consistent, thorough, factual, and considerate. Clearly, clinical knowledge and skill are required, but detailed clinical knowledge is more valuable in expectation setting than in evaluating credentials. Credibility is also important. Committee members should be widely respected within the medical staff.

The usual method of selection—nomination by the departments of the staff and appointment by the medical executive committee—is satisfactory as long as the actions of the committee are prudent and consistent. The governing board's right to reject nominees for cause or to dismiss the committee and seek new nominations under clearly established conditions is a useful protection for the rights of the community and the patients. Appointment by an individual, such as the chief of staff, probably vests too much authority in a single person. Similarly, physicians with other important leadership tasks should not serve simultaneously on the credentials committee, and membership should rotate fairly frequently. The executive office should staff the committee, both to assist in the workload and to assure compliance with the bylaws.

Standards for Granting and Renewing Privileges

Medical quality control is moving to the use of prospectively accepted protocols, as discussed in Chapter 11. These simplify the credentialling review to five questions.

- Did the physician comply with general requirements for continuing education, maintaining certification, and meeting minimum levels of activity?

- Did the physician generally select the correct protocol or plan of care for each patient?
- Did the physician order departures from the protocol appropriate to the individual patients' conditions?
- Did the physician correctly perform the procedures which were his or her direct responsibility?
- Has the physician been involved in activity which directly threatens the safety of patients or colleagues?

The committee seeks evidence that negative answers to these questions are rare and unlikely to be repeated. It grants or renews privileges whenever that evidence is convincing. Only the first and the last are relevant to initial reviews, although references may seek indirect evidence on the other three. The best credentials process limits its review to only these questions. Other issues of quality, patient satisfaction, and cost effectiveness are handled by the quality improvement activities of the medical departments. The credentialing activity is deliberately separated from protocol setting and monitoring to permit fuller exploration of clinical issues in a scientific rather than a judgmental environment. The use of protocols as a referent assures that the physician will not be held to a unique standard, and makes it possible for the committee to evaluate physicians from all specialties. The vast majority of physicians will pass review without difficulty.

Information and Data Support

The record required by the credentials committee has two major components. Initial reviews require the credentials themselves, documents and references testifying to the education, licensure, certification, experience, and character of applicants. The applicant is often charged with collecting the documents, although these must be scrutinized and verified by the organization. Renewals require information on the clinical performance of current staff members. Two groups—medical staff departments or specialties and employees supporting the quality review, utilization review, and risk management processes—monitor clinical activity and prepare reports during the year on serious examples of negative performance.[24] Processes of these groups include opportunities for the physician to review the cases and justify his or her actions. Only those which the review body felt to be questionable are reported to the credentials committee. The executive staff member supporting the committee collects and verifies the factual case from these reports to reduce the burdens upon the committee. His or her role includes soliciting references and verifying educational credentials. In complex cases, the committee may seek additional information, using a formal hearing process to protect the rights of the physician.

Specification of Privileges

It is increasingly common to insist upon full certification in a specialty as a condition of membership, or in the case of young doctors still completing their training, a specific program and timetable for earning certification. Thus the prototype for specification of privileges is that set of activities normally included in the specialty. Well-run organizations have several additional constraints on the specific activities for which privileges are granted:

- *Maintenance of specialty certification.* Many specialties have continuing education requirements.
- *Restrictions based upon the capability of the organization and the supporting medical specialists.* (An individual doctor may be qualified to receive a certain privilege, but the organization may lack the necessary equipment, facilities, and complementary staff.)
- *Maintenance of a minimum number of cases treated annually to ensure that the skills of both the physician and the organization support team remain up-to-date.*
- *For new or expanded privileges, evidence of successful treatment of a number of cases under supervision at an acceptable training facility.*

Two problems arise from excessive reliance on the judgments of specialty boards. First, the issue of quality is not as simple as it first looks. Family practitioners and general internists argue that they can handle a great many uncomplicated cases without referral, while obstetricians, pediatricians, and medical subspecialists argue that their specialized skills are more likely to promote quality. There are two parts to resolving these arguments. The first is correctly identifying the needs of each patient. The identification of the patient's total needs is as important a part of the quality of medical care as the excellence of a specific treatment. It may be wise to sacrifice some elegance in the treatment of a specific disease in order to improve the patient's total medical condition. The higher the value placed on comprehensive care, the stronger the generalists' argument. Many thoughtful analysts believe that comprehensiveness is undervalued in American health care and that the balance has shifted too far toward specialization.

The second problem arising from excessive limitation of privileges is its effect on doctors' incomes. The specialties sometimes conflict with one another or reflect self-interest. A decision to limit all obstetrics to obstetricians and all newborn care to pediatricians transfers income. It may reduce the income of family practitioners and the availability of doctors throughout the community. It also will increase the fees charged per delivery. The traditional fee structure tends to reward procedures more than diagnosis and specialization more than comprehensiveness and continuity. The result has been relatively low incomes for family practitioners, general internists, and pediatricians. The disparity has generated some sensitivity, and an organization which limits privileges to these groups excessively may find itself in an uncompetitive position.

The criteria for limitation of privileges affect the medical recruitment plan and the long-range plan of the organization because they are interrelated with doctors' incomes and hospital support services. As a result, resolving the level of limitation is an important function of the medical executive committee, although specific limitations are usually proposed (and disputed) by the various specialties. Limitations should also be monitored carefully by the executive office, acting on behalf of the board under general policy guidelines in the medical staff bylaws, for compliance with the organization's mission and all aspects of its long-range plan.

Impaired Physicians

The credentials committee faces certain predictable problems, among them the impaired physician. Doctors, like other human beings, can be disabled by age, physical or emotional disease, personal trauma, and substance abuse. The prevalence of these difficulties among practicing physicians is hard to estimate, but it is generally conceded to be between 5 and 15 percent. Thus a medium-sized health care organization could have a dozen doctors either impaired or in danger of impairment at any given time. The response of the credentials committee should be tailored to the kind of problem. Aging and uncorrectable physical disability must force reduction of privileges. Particularly well-managed organizations attempt to provide alternative activities for those who desire them. Alcoholism, abuse of addictive drugs, and depression may be more common among physicians than among the general public. Treatment for depression and substance abuse is clearly indicated, and programs designed especially for doctors can be reached through state medical societies. Arrangements can be made to assist impaired doctors with their practices during the period of recovery, thus assuring that patients receive acceptable care without unduly disrupting the doctor-patient relationship or the doctors' incomes. Larger organizations often have a committee or group set up specifically to deal with this problem. Although it usually keeps affected physicians' identities secret, its activities must be coordinated with those of the credentials committee.

While every reasonable effort at rehabilitation should be made, the credentials committee is ultimately accountable for the suspension or removal of privileges.

Operation of the Credentials Committee

Credentialing activity focuses on the new doctor, whose skills are as yet untested, and on the few who are clearly having difficulty meeting minimum standards. The well-run credentials committee rarely takes negative actions. The better the organization, the stronger the probability that physicians will be reappointed. Credentialing is the final safeguard of medical care quality, and significant numbers of failures are symptomatic of serious difficulties.

The operation of the committee must follow due process. It is wise to assign a trained organization employee, rather than a volunteer committee member, to carry out all procedures under the direction of the chair. Formal procedures for advance notice, agenda, attendance, minutes, and appeal mechanisms are mandatory. Doctors under review should have the opportunity to see the information compiled about them and to comment upon it. Because the committee should function at a secondary level, evaluating the sum of the year's activities rather than actual patient care, the need for new direct testimony is minimized. When it is necessary, the statements should be carefully identified and recorded. The summary of the individual's activities should be compiled in writing and documented. Review of procedures by legal counsel is desirable, and counsel should attend any appeals session. The doctor is also entitled to counsel. The well-managed organization protects committee members and others in the credentialing chain with insurance, legal counsel, and, above all, prevention of lawsuits through the maintenance of due process and sound evidence in support of the committee's decisions.

The actions of the committee may be reviewed by the medical executive committee or referred directly to the board. As noted in Chapter 5, the board is not obligated to accept the committee's actions; rather it is under strong, independent obligations to due process and to protection of the rights of both patients and physicians. In well-run organizations, disputes of credentials committee actions are rare and usually arise from individual appeals rather than board or executive committee disagreements.

The federal Health Care Quality Improvement Act, Title IV of P.L.100-177 of 1986, mandates reporting of loss of credentials or other disciplinary action to a federal information bank. The purpose of the Act is to reduce the chance of an incompetent physician moving to a new location and misrepresenting his or her skills. Specifically the act requires health care organizations

1. To notify the National Practitioner Data Bank of: any physician's or dentist's loss of credentials for any period greater than 30 days; any voluntary surrender of privileges to avoid investigation; any requirement for medical proctoring or supervision imposed as a result of peer review; and any malpractice settlement against any member of the medical staff or "other health practitioner" as defined in the act.
2. To check the information bank prior to initial privileging.

The act also protects any person reporting to or working for a professional review body such as an accredited organization's credentialling committee from legal action by the individual disciplined, by raising the standard of proof.[25]

The act could easily have a negative effect upon the quality of care, because it can discourage disciplinary action where it is indicated. It should not and need not. The well-managed institution can probably avoid this by continuing annual privileges review and using a system of warnings and more frequent direct supervision.

Organization of the Conjoint Staff

Clinical Organization

As the clinical functions of education, clinical improvement, and credentialing have become more complex, the need for a formal accountability hierarchy has become clear, and health care organizations have steadily strengthened a clinical organization hierarchy. As the economic elements, particularly clear in the functions of recruitment and representation, have become more complex, a second formal organization is emerging. Because the conjoint staff model accepts a full range of economic relationships, the two organizations exist side by side. All physicians are members of the clinical organization. Their roles in the economic organization will depend upon their personal economic relationship.

Clinical organizations follow the structure of medical specialties As shown in Figure 12.9, the hierarchy can be subdivided to any level indicated by the size or type of staff. A very large health care organization might have a dozen departments, several divisions under some departments, and sections or even sub-sections under some divisions. Each level would have an appointed leader who is accountable for clinical performance. The leaders of larger units are now paid. The chief of the medical staff (CMS) would normally chair the medical executive committee and have a major role as an executive officer. In large health care organizations the CMS is a full-time salaried position, supported by a staff. The use of formal budgets for the accountability hierarchy is not widespread, but examples exist.[26] As outcomes measures and final product protocols develop, formally negotiated expectations will become more common.

The units of the medical staff review relevant budgets and rank capital budget requests. Many units will participate actively in cross-functional teams. As indicated in Chapter 11, these teams play a major role in setting protocols. The units play prominent roles in education as resident experts in their specialty. In organizations with postgraduate education, the section, division, or department leader is responsible for

Figure 12.9 Clinical Organization Structure of the Medical Staff

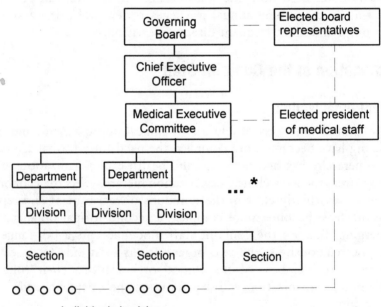

Key:

——————   Board approved appointments

— — —   Elected representation

*   Number of departments, divisions and sections
depends upon size of organization

the quality and effectiveness of the residency program. Many larger organizations have a director of medical education who coordinates all educational activity, particularly postgraduate medical education. The post is usually subordinate to the CMS.

Many conjoint staff organizations also provide for elective representation of the medical staff. Individual members elect a president, who usually sits on the medical executive committee, and other representatives to the governing board.

Economic Relationships in the Conjoint Staff

The economic organization of medical practice itself is in flux, as payment moves from direct to insured fees, negotiated fees, global fees and capitation. Not surprisingly, the transition has generated high levels of anxiety among physicians and an array of entrepreneurial responses by for-profit and not-for-profit organizations. As noted above, the conjoint staff is only one of several contenders, and the models which will emerge as stable competitors in the marketplace are now unclear. There is no reason to rule out community-based not-for-profit organizations from the eventual winners.

Many variations of the possible evolution of the conjoint model are being tried around the country. Observers differ on the classification. Many see the current patterns as evolutionary, with a highly integrated endpoint model.[27] Burns and Thorpe, for example, identify four basic types, culminating in an "Integrated Health Organization" where all physicians are salaried.[28] Both marketplace resistance to managed care and the political difficulties encountered by health care reform in 1994 suggest that this model will not be the sole successful one anytime soon.

The conjoint staff must make a competitive advantage of its ability to accept a full range of individual economic relationships with its physicians. As shown in Figure 12.10, the relationships include one of economic independence, at least in terms of direct linkage, several variants of salaried compensation, and several variants of shared risk or contractual relationships. The problem is to represent this diversity effectively in decisions with shared economic consequences. The solution begins with acceptance of the conjoint organizational model. As described above and summarized in the previous figure, the conjoint staff provides each physician with access to community health care resources and participation in clinical management. It provides the community with reasonable assurances of quality. Three policies permit the development of economic arrangements around the conjoint structure as a core:

1. All physicians affiliated with the organization are compelled to participate in the functions of the conjoint model.
2. All conjoint staff physicians are eligible to participate in other models, providing they meet the particular standards involved.
3. No physician is compelled to participate in anything more than the conjoint organizational model.

Presumably most physicians will seek additional participation, particularly those who have or want the closer economic relations shown in Figure 12.10. The kinds of models, and their relative size will be driven by local markets, and can be expected to differ widely between communities.

As Figure 12.10 shows, closer economic relationships between health care organizations and physicians involve five types of transactions.

1. *Salary arrangements,* permitting the physician to be a full- or part-time employee of a corporation. These options are open under all the economic arrangements including the conjoint model.
2. *Contracts providing office management,* allowing physicians to escape overhead costs and managerial obligations. Almost any office service can be involved, from the facility itself to office employees, supplies, and malpractice insurance. Many forms of contracts are already available under conjoint models.
3. *Joint contracts with insurance intermediaries,* offering physicians increased access or more advantageous terms in managed care markets. These appear to represent the largest dollar volumes in future economic relationships.
4. *Sale of existing practices,* allowing physicians to seek early retirement or liquidate a fee-for-service practice in favor of a salaried one. Practices are also sold by the organization to new physicians.
5. *Joint investment ventures,* offering physicians the opportunity to invest in capital stocks or real property with the anticipation of speculative return and a salable asset. These are the most problematic relationships, raising tax, inurement, and fraud issues which must be carefully avoided. They also present some management problems, as when ownership becomes frozen to a limited group of physicians, or when the value of the asset falls and it becomes illiquid.

The economic organization must facilitate these transactions in ways that forward the mission of the community health care organization, and that meet certain tests for tax exemption, compliance with

Figure 12.10 Financial Relationships between Health Care Organizations and Individual Physicians

Relationship	Type	Example
Independence	Traditional	Physician arranges own payments and contracts
Salaried for clinical services	Employment	Physician spends full or part time providing medical care at site operated by institution, in return for a salary
Salaried for management services	Employment	Physician spends full or part time providing administrative services for the organization, in return for a salary
Purchase of service	Service contract	Physician leases office, personnel services, or information services for an established payment
Joint sales agreement	Preferred provider panels	Physicians and institution agree to participate for separate fees
Global fees	Episode risk sharing	Physicians and institution agree to a fixed price per episode and share risk for appropriate utilization
Shared risk contracts	Capitation risk sharing	Physicians and institution agree to a fixed capitation and share risk for appropriate utilization
Shared ownership	Joint ownership	Physician and institution hold joint ownership in real property
Shared equity	Joint venture	Physicians and institution hold joint ownership in a business venture

NOTE: Many physicians will have several kinds of relationships simultaneously.

antitrust regulations, and avoidance of fraud and abuse.[29] In general, the tax requirements call for avoidance of inurement and are met by maintaining community dominance of the investment and exchanging all goods and services at fair market prices.[30] Antitrust requirements are more important when the organization or its physicians have a dominant market position and are met by sharing risks and rewards between the physicians and the organization and by permitting any qualified physician to participate. Fraud and abuse arise when arrangements are intended to benefit providers at customer expense.[31] In general, they are met by designing programs which are attractive to all insurance approaches, particularly to cost-oriented payment plans such as low-cost HMOs and Medicaid. The complexity and extent of these requirements indicate the need for qualified legal counsel in any specific program.

Two approaches to economic participation models are shown in Figure 12.11. The first (A) envisions a separate organization melding the interests of the community and its physicians. Now called the **physician-hospital organization** (PHO), it has equal or near equal representation of community and physician directors. Assuming that it has the appropriate legal structures and approvals, the PHO can accept insurance risk for the hospital and the physicians, hire physicians, operate support activities, and buy practices. Depending on its charter, it can borrow money and issue stock. By combining these activities, it can operate any kind of facility and even operate as an insurance intermediary. The PHO normally assumes the existence of a physicians' organization for their representation. These are organized around primary and referral practices. Two separate physicians' organizations are possible, but the result would be to give community voices a stronger hand.

The alternative model, shown in Figure 12.11B, is a community-owned foundation which carries out the functions of the PHO and is usually not-for-profit. The foundation operates in parallel with the hospital and has strong physician representation, but without a formal physician organization. Like the PHO, it can implement all the necessary economic arrangements between the organization and the individual physician.

Which model prevails depends upon the initiative of the partners. Foundation-type models prevail where medical staff are unwilling or unable to establish physicians' organizations. Many analysts see a third model as the eventual survivor. It would arise by elevating the foundation or the PHO to the dominant status, where the most central strategic decisions are made. While community forces must dominate to distinguish the model from its competitors, existing examples, such as Virginia Mason Medical Center[32] and Henry Ford Health System have strong physician representation throughout their governance and management decision processes. The governance structure of Virginia Mason shows the careful balance of medical and nonmedical representatives. (Figure 12.12)

Figure 12.11 Models of Physician Organizations

A. The MSO/PHO Approach

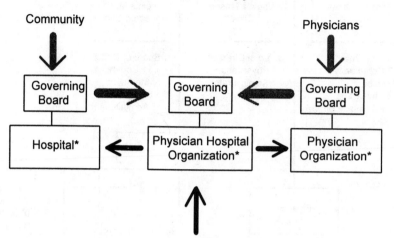

B. The Foundation Approach

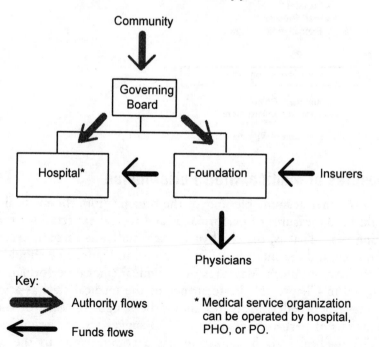

Figure 12.12 Virginia Mason Medical Center Governance Structure

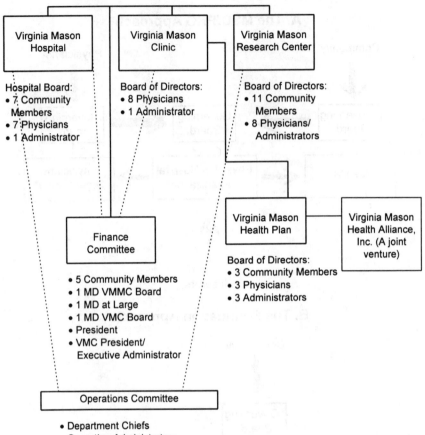

Reprinted with permission of Virginia Mason Medical Center.

Measures of Medical Staff Performance

Like any other accountable unit of the organization, the medical staff should have measures of performance and formal expectations for the coming year. That is, the chief of medical staff, the medical executive committee, and the subordinate units shown in Figure 12.9 should have budgets and monitors. Measures of individual clinical performance are discussed in Chapter 11. Performance of the medical staff as a whole is somewhat broader. Measures should be sought on each of the six dimensions of performance. Figure 12.13 suggests some examples.

The medical staff organization has a commitment to the maximization of appropriate demand which must be measured by market

Figure 12.13   Measures of Medical Staff Performance

Dimension	Measurement Intent	Example
Demand	Response to community demand for care	Market share Available primary care practitioners Appointment delays Out-of-staff referrals Number and variety of payment contracts available
Costs	Costs of physician services and costs of medical staff operations	Physician payments per HMO member per month Labor costs of medical staff management activities
Physician Resources	Recruitment and retention of physicians	Member satisfaction Percent of positions filled with first choice Measures of staff diversity
Output/ Productivity	Conjoint staff and contract management functioning	Enrollment in payment contracts Total treatment costs per member month Cost of payment contracts by contract Labor cost per staff member
Quality	Effectiveness of medical staff management	Patient satisfaction Indexed outcomes quality scores Malpractice settlements Appeals/complaints in member review Member satisfaction with services and representation
Contribution	Global profit or competitiveness measure	Profitability of parent organization Comparison of costs against benchmark

share and access measures. Counts of practices open to new patients and delays for various kinds of scheduled appointments are used. Out-of-staff referrals is a measure of patients selecting the organization but needing services the organization does not provide. While most organizations will refer out very complex cases, the statistic should be monitored, and compared to realistic expectations.

The medical staff is accountable for its own operating cost budget, even though it is only a small part of total operations. Under managed care contracts, the cost of physician services is an important element in competition, measured by the payments made to physicians, per member month. While physicians commonly receive incentives increasing their payment for reducing the total cost of care, the payment should be monitored by specialty to track the community's competitiveness in physician recruitment.

Physician recruitment and retention is central to medical staff organization purpose. Member satisfaction is now routinely monitored. Samples should be adequate to reflect attitudes by several categories of age, and specialty. Success in filling open positions is also important. It is usually monitored for incoming house staff. Measures of staff diversity are important in primary care, where patients seek particular backgrounds, and also in recruitment. With 40 percent of medical classes now female, organizations which do not promote gender diversity will have difficulty recruiting in the future.

Output and productivity measures are important to monitor the efficiency of the staff organizations. The popularity of various contractual arrangements in the eyes of the physicians is important in guiding future arrangements. The cost of care rendered to insured patients cannot be overlooked. It is the main element of premium costs and price competitiveness. The cost of administration of managed care contracts is important in setting the premium. It is often watched by major buyers as an indicator of internal efficiency. It is also important in guiding future arrangements. The cost of medical staff operation per member physician is a measure which can be benchmarked against other organizations.

Quality measures for the medical staff organization should begin with customer or patient satisfaction. Global measure of clinical outcomes have not proven sensitive, but many measures for specific diseases are useful. Aggregating them is difficult, but a useful index can be constructed. Malpractice settlements are a measure of major failures in care. The number of physician complaints or appeals about the medical staff activities and specific satisfaction data reveal trouble spots.

Finally, contribution of the medical staff organization is important, even if difficult to isolate. As an essential component of all care, the medical staff and its members should certainly be accountable for overall profits along with the governing board and the executive. Summary measures of cost, such as the total cost of care, the labor cost of the medical staff organization, and the payment to physicians can be benchmarked against competitors and similar organizations to establish budget guidelines.

Suggested Readings

Coddington, D. C., K. D. Moone, and E. A. Fischer. 1994. *Integrated Health Care: Reorganizing the Physician, Hospital, and Health Plan Relationship*. Englewood, CO: Center for Research in Ambulatory Health Care Administration.

Freidson, E. 1980. *Doctoring Together: A Study of Professional Social Control*. Chicago: University of Chicago Press.

Joint Commission on Accreditation of Healthcare Organizations. *Accreditation Manual for Hospitals*. Chicago: JCAHO.

Lang, D. A. 1991. *Medical Staff Peer Review: A Strategy for Motivation and Performance*. Chicago: American Hospital Publishers.

Luft, H. S., D. W. Garnick, D. H. Mark, and S. J. McPhee. 1990. *Hospital Volume, Physician Volume, and Patient Outcomes: Assessing the Evidence*. Ann Arbor, MI: Health Administration Press.

Rozovsky, F. A. 1994. *Medical Staff Credentialing: A Practical Guide*. Chicago: American Hospital Publishing.

Shortell, S. M. 1991. *Effective Hospital-Physician Relationships*. Ann Arbor, MI: Health Administration Press.

Shortell, S. M., E. M. Morrison, and B. Friedman. 1990. *Strategic Choices for America's Hospitals: Managing Change in Turbulent Times*. San Francisco: Jossey-Bass.

Southwick, A. F. 1988. *The Law of Hospital and Health Care Administration*, 2d ed. Ann Arbor, MI: Health Administration Press, Chapters 14–15, pp. 583–92.

Starr, P. 1982. *The Social Transformation of American Medicine*. New York: Basic Books, 198–232, 420–49.

Notes

1. W. R. Scott, 1982, "Managing Professional Work: Three Models of Control for Health Organizations," *Health Services Research* 17: 213–40.

2. S. M. Shortell, 1990, *Effective Hospital-Physician Relationships* (Ann Arbor, MI: Health Administration Press), 10.

3. J. P. Weiner, 1994, "Forecasting the Effects of Health Reform on U.S. Physician Workforce Requirement: Evidence from HMO Staffing Patterns," *Journal of the American Medical Association* 272 (20 July): 222–30.

4. H. S. Luft, D. W. Garnick, D. H. Mark, and S. J. McPhee, 1990, *Hospital Volume, Physician Volume, and Patient Outcomes: Assessing the Evidence* (Ann Arbor, MI: Health Administration Press).

5. U.S. Bureau of the Census, *1993 Statistical Abstract of the United States*, (Washington, DC: U.S. Government Printing Office), 2, 189.

6. N. B. Fisher, H. L. Smith, D. P. Pasternak, 1993, "Critical Factors in Recruiting Health Maintenance Organization Physicians," *Health Care Management Review* 18 (Winter): 51–61.

7. Weiner, "Forecasting the Effects," 222–30.

8. T. H. Rice and R. J. Labelle, 1989, "Do Physicians Induce Demand for Medical Services?" *Journal of Health Politics, Policy and Law* 14 (3): 587–600.

9. S. T. Valentine, ed., 1990, *Physician Bonding: Developing a Successful Hospital Program* (Rockville, MD: Aspen Publishers).

10. P. R. Leone, 1994, "New Developments in 'Any Willing Provider' Laws," *Healthcare Financial Management* 48 (May): 32, 34–35.

11. Shortell, *Effective Hospital-Physician Relationships*, 10.

12. L. R. Burns and L. R. Beach, 1994, "The Quality Improvement Strategy," *Health Care Management Review* 19 (2): 21–31.

13. Shortell, *Effective Hospital-Physician Relationships*, 79–93.

14. J. R. Griffith, 1993, *Moral Challenges of Health Care Management* (Ann Arbor, MI: Health Administration Press).

15. Association of American Medical Colleges, 1993, *AAMC Databook: Statistical Information Related to Medical Education, January 1993* (Washington, DC: The Association), Table G-4.

16. A. F. Southwick, 1988, *The Law of Hospital and Health Care Administration*, 2d ed. (Ann Arbor, MI: Health Administration Press, 585–622.

17. P. A. Lembcke, 1967, "Evolution of the Medical Audit," *Journal of the American Medical Association* 199: 543–50.

18. Southwick, *The Law*, 589–91.

19. Southwick, *The Law*, 341.

20. B. M. Peters, W. C. Maneval, 1993, "Medical Staff Credentialling: A Prescription for Reducing Anti-Trust Liability," *Law, Medicine, and Health Care* 19 (1–2): 120–33.

21. Joint Commission on Accreditation of Hospitals, 1984, "Standards for Medical Staff-Requirements for Membership and Privileges," in *Accreditation Manual for Hospitals* (Oakbrook Terrace, IL: JCAH), 89.

22. Southwick, *The Law*, 601–22.

23. Southwick, *The Law*, 588, 592–96, 599, 604, 607, 610, 616–17.

24. C. A. Sullivan, 1994, "Competency Assessment and Performance Improvement for Health Care Providers," *Journal for Health Care Quality* 16 (July–August): 14.

25. U.S. Department of Health and Human Services, 1986, *Health Care Quality Improvement Act* (Rockville, MD: DHHS, Health Resources and Services Administration, Division of Quality Assurance and Liability Management), PL 100–177.

26. R. M. Heyssel, J. R. Gaintner, I. W. Kues, M. Jones, and S. H. Lipstein, 1984, "Decentralized Management in a Teaching Hospital" *New England Journal of Medicine* 310 (2): 1477–80.

27. BDC Advisors, 1993, *Physician-Hospital Integration Models* (San Francisco: BDC).

28. L. R. Burns and D. P. Thorpe, 1993, "Trends and Models in Physician-Hospital Organization," *Health Care Management Review* 18 (4): 7–20.

29. Burns and Thorpe, "Trends and Models," 17–18.

30. A. Herman, 1992, "IRS Memorandum Limits Joint Ventures," *Healthcare Financial Management* 49 (8): 51–52.

31. C. MacKelvie, 1990, "Fraud Abuse and Inurement," *Topics in Health Care Financing* 16: 49–57.

32. Burns and Thorpe, "Trends and Models," 15–17.

CHAPTER

13

CLINICAL SUPPORT SERVICES

MODERN HEALTH care is a team activity employing several dozen specialized professionals other than attending physicians in what are called the clinical support services (CSSs). CSSs produce the intermediate products of care. They include activities such as laboratory tests, surgical operations and physical therapy. They also include behavioral and psychological services such as social service, pastoral care, and health education. Most, but not all, CSSs are ordered by an attending physician. They support prevention, diagnosis, treatment, rehabilitation, and daily living and are available to patients at several sites, including outpatient offices, the acute hospital, long-term care facilities, and home. Health care organizations must provide CSSs correctly, promptly, cheaply, and attractively. They must also seek the optimal number and kind of CSSs for each patient. Too many or too few, the wrong CSS, or poor quality CSS will reduce overall quality and increase total cost of care. Optimization of care is often a matter of providing exactly the combination and timing of CSSs required, but it also involves providing each unit of CSS at excellent quality and minimum cost.

Each CSS is supervised by a professional, often a specialist physician. Each has its own technology and procedures discussed extensively in its professional literature. Clinical support services also have a number of common characteristics. This book discusses management of CSSs in light of those common characteristics. This chapter discusses how the well-run health care organization strives to achieve the optimum of CSSs delivery. It is organized around the following topics:

- Definition and purpose
- Functions
- Management and organization
- Measures and information systems.

Definition and Purpose

A clinical support service is (1) a unit organized around one or more medical specialties or clinical professions providing individual patient care on order of an attending physician, or (2) a general community service, such as health education, immunization, and screening, under the general guidance of the medical staff.

Attending physicians order large numbers of CSS as part of the plan for each patient. In addition, health education such as prenatal classes, primary prevention such as immunization programs, disease screening such as urinalysis and blood pressure testing, and behavioral assistance in such areas as smoking cessation and bereavement have all become important in health care organizations. These programs do not require the direct order of an attending physician and are often offered directly to people in the community. Medical staff guidance and support are clearly desirable, however, and the services are part of the CSSs offerings.

Under this definition, nursing is a support service. It is so large and complex, however, that it merits discussion on its own, in Chapter 14. Many observations about support services apply to nursing as well.

The purpose of CSS is to extend the capability of the total health care system by improving quality or reducing cost of each specific service. CSSs are specializations which arose when one person with unique training, skills and equipment could handle one part of the care for many patients better than several people with general skills. Simply put, a CSS comes into existence or continues to exist because it does something better or cheaper than alternatives.

This purpose is intuitively clear, but it contains a hidden complexity. Many of the less elaborate support services can be provided by several professions, and it is often more convenient for the patient to receive them from generalist caregivers. At the same time, CSSs become quite costly if they are not widely used. Most require heavy fixed costs in professional salaries and specialized equipment. Quality of care also often depends upon volume; the more practice the team gets, the better its skills.[1,2] The health care organization must balance the availability of CSSs as it does medical referral specialists (Chapter 12), weighing community desires for convenience against quality and cost. Thus the purpose implies that the profile of services offered must be consistent with the strategic plan. It also implies that the domain of each CSS must be defined by the organization as a whole, trading off the advantages of specialization for those of generalist care.

While a consequence of the purpose is that smaller health care organizations will have fewer CSSs than large ones, most will have several dozen, including critical services such as clinical laboratories, radiology services, pharmacies, electrocardiography services, and operating rooms. A useful classification of the nonnursing CSSs categorizes them broadly into diagnostic, therapeutic, and general community activities. Figure 13.1 shows the types of CSSs all large health care organizations would be likely to have. About 50 separate CSSs are identified.

Functions of Clinical Support Services

A serious illness may require several hundred separate activities from CSSs listed in Figure 13.1. It is obvious that the characteristics of these activities are very different. Yet at one level of abstraction above these differences, similarities emerge. The responsibility center managers of social service and megavoltage therapy, for example, share eight common functions identified in Figure 13.2. Despite the length and complexity of the list, these are functions each unit must perform in order to maintain effectiveness. The distinction between clinical and managerial functions should not be overdrawn. Clinical functions draw more heavily on the CSS's specific professional area, but both are essential.

Technical Quality: Effective and Reliable Completion of Orders

One can construct four important aspects of CSS quality:[3] technical quality, appropriateness, satisfaction, and continuity or integration of care. Although they are interrelated, each is approached by separate means, and each deserves a separate function. Technical quality, a concept essentially analogous to product consistency and service reliability, is the proper starting point; the other three depend upon it. Technical quality is a matter of doing the correct thing for the patient consistently over a wide variety of situations. Technical quality is measured by a variety of process and outcomes indicators, as discussed below. It is achieved by sound procedures, correct equipment and supplies, training, and practice.

Many CSS professionals have formal certification and degrees. The formal education is a major part of technical quality assurance. It includes mastery of relevant theory and supervised practice so that the

Figure 13.1 Clinical Support Services in a Large Health Care Organization

Diagnostic Services	Therapeutic Services	General Community Activities
Cardio-pulmonary	Birthing suite	Immunization and
laboratory	Blood bank	screening programs
Electrocardiology	Emergency service	Cardio-pulmonary
Pulmonary function	Operating suite	resuscitation
Heart catheterization	Anesthesia	training
Clinical laboratory	Surgery	Family planning, pre-
Chemistry	Recovery	natal, parenting and
Hematology	Pharmacy	child care classes
Histopathology	Dispensing	Smoking cessation
Bacteriology and	Intravenous	program
virology	admixture service	Alcoholics anony-
Autopsy and morgue	Pastoral care	mous
Diagnostic Imaging	Psychological	Weight control and
Radiography	counseling	physical fitness
Tomography	Radiation therapy	program
Radioisotope studies	Megavoltage	Respite services
Magnetic resonance	radiation	Nurse consultation
imaging	Therapy	
Ultrasound	Radioisotope	
Other	therapy	**Home Support Services**
Electroencephalography	Rehabilitation services	Organized home care
Electromyography	Physical therapy	Medical equipment
Audiology	Respiratory therapy	Hospice
	Speech pathology	"Lifeline"
	Occupational	Transportation
	therapy	Home meals
	Social services	Homemaker services

student learns the processes, patient indications and contraindications for them, expected outcomes, and the rules governing process design. To reduce costs, many of the actual CSS procedures are performed by aides and technicians who do not have professional training. The staffing of most CSS units consists of one or two levels of professional training, and one or more levels of nonprofessional personnel, allowing each professional to serve a larger volume of patients. Three issues of quality assurance beyond formal education emerge:

- Maintenance of skill for qualified professionals
- Resolution of differences between professionals
- Training and supervision of nonprofessional personnel.

Figure 13.2 Functions of Clinical Support Services

Type	Function	Description	Examples
Clinical	Quality	Provision of technically correct clinical interventions	Outpatient pharmacy: correct drug, dosage, count, and patient instruction.
			Operating room: correct patient preparation, trained staff, equipment.
	Appropriateness	Provision of the most appropriate service for each patient	Outpatient pharmacy: formulary, drug use education and consultation, generic drug substitution.
			Operating room: correct surgical implants and supplies. Capability to do laparascopic and laser substitutes for more invasive procedures.
Managerial	Facility, equipment, and staff planning	Projection of future equipment and facility needs, review of acceptable volumes of demand	Outpatient pharmacy: number and location of sites, hours of operation, staffing required, costs.
			Operating room: number of suites, staffing, inpatient and outpatient demand.
	Amenities and marketing	Additional services for patients and doctors	Outpatient pharmacy: comfortable waiting area, drug usage literature, consultation to patients. Telephone and electronic order systems for doctors, advertising services to doctors and patients.
			Operating room: doctors' lounges, family waiting rooms, advertising services to doctors.
	Patient scheduling	Timely service, integrated with other CSSs	Outpatient pharmacy: limit on patient service delays.
			Operating room: no delay after patient admission; complete lab, x-ray, and anesthesia work-up; on-time start.

Continued

Figure 13.2 Continued

Type	Function	Description	Examples
	Continuous improvement	Monitoring performance measures, benchmarking, and devising process changes to improve.	Outpatient pharmacy: evaluation of new drugs, inventory, packaging, and dispensing methods. Operating room: evaluation of new surgical supplies, techniques, and staffing roles
	Budgeting	Developing expectations for each dimension of performance.	Outpatient pharmacy: implementing new hours of service or staffing. Operating room: implementing new preparation procedures or employee cross-training.
	Human resources management	Recruiting, retaining, and motivating an effective work group	Outpatient pharmacy: pharmacist recruitment, technician training, work group empowerment, worker scheduling. Operating room: nurse recruitment, technician training, work group empowerment, worker scheduling.

Well-managed institutions increasingly rely upon formally developed intermediate product protocols to address these issue. As shown in Chapter 11, Figure 11.5, these are step-by-step procedure statements, preferably developed by continuous improvement teams. The protocols have several advantages. Developing the protocols is an educational exercise for the group. Exploration of variation in performance clarifies the causes and builds consensus. Protocols are excellent classroom aids; they follow accepted training principles of breaking the learning into small parts, and making each action explicit. Protocols make clear the exact demand for supplies and equipment, making it possible to prepare uniform set-ups in advance. They simplify the logistics of complex processes and identify the least-cost alternatives. When written copies or computer screens are used directly, protocols provide recognition rather than recall. Time requirements and error rates are reduced by recognition.

Protocol approaches build in quality by developing and supporting consensus. Monitoring is still important, however, and there are several approaches to measurement:

- *Interim measures of performance*, such as radiation monitors, temperature records, and reagent tests
- *Process inspections*, preferably following explicit protocols and carried out by trained, unbiased observers
- *Record reviews*, including patient medical records and departmental records
- *Counts of repeat tests and unsatisfactory results*
- *Results inspection, or reported values*, such as test averages in the laboratory or inspection of filled prescriptions
- *Accuracy of values on blind, or control, specimens.*

These measures can be developed from either samples or universes, as appropriate, and subjected to statistical analysis (Chapter 9). A well-run CSS identifies a variety of measures of technical quality and uses the least expensive ones on a daily or hourly basis to assure consistent performance, even though the validity of these measures is imperfect. It bolsters this short-term effort with periodic studies introducing greater scope and validity. The frequency and extent of these depends upon the cost of unsatisfactory performance as well as the cost of the studies.

For most applications, the goal of technical quality should be to attain as high a quality as is consistent with the patient benefit. For example, although one wishes to get as many satisfactory x-ray films on the first try as possible, retake has a finite price, the variable cost of another film plus some allowance for patient discomfort and delay. Unsatisfactory exposures can result from improper dose estimation, improper machine calibration, variation in the power supply, or movement by the patient. One would not invest more in improving the protocol than the cost of eliminated retakes. Similarly, one would not make the examination unnecessarily unpleasant by frightening patients into absolute immobility. Satisfactory performance will be something greater than 0.0 percent retakes. The best reported performance, or benchmark, is often used as a guide, but even it must be tested against the cost to achieve it.

Zero-defect goals are appropriate only when failures are life-threatening or cause very high-cost consequences. For example, the blood level of a certain enzyme is used to confirm a heart attack. The test is inexpensive, but expensive treatment is started immediately if the enzyme level is elevated. Delays increase fatality rates.[4] Zero defect is appropriate on a two-sided basis. Understated enzyme values may increase fatalities; overstated values will trigger unnecessary expensive treatment.

Appropriateness

Any CSS indicated but not ordered can reduce quality or add to cost of care. Any CSS ordered unnecessarily adds to the cost and can potentially decrease quality, because there is at least a small risk of negative result attached to each procedure. Much of each final product protocol or individual patient's care plan addresses the correct selection and timing of CSSs. CSS professionals must be expert on the contribution of their services to total patient care.

CSSs contribute to appropriateness of care in four areas, as shown in Figure 13.3. Low technical quality destroys physician confidence in results, resulting in multiple tests or the avoidance of tests that would be used if they were felt to be reliable. High cost discourages appropriate use, especially under managed care. Satisfaction is important to encourage the patient to follow orders, but dissatisfied patients are important to physicians, too. Many satisfaction issues deal with timing and coordination of services. Finally, the CSS is the best source of knowledge about its own services. If it does not share that knowledge with doctors, the orders will be less appropriate. The well-run service participates actively in clinical discussions, provides routine consultation to physicians, and advertises its services and their appropriate use.

Figure 13.3 CSS Contributions to Appropriate Care

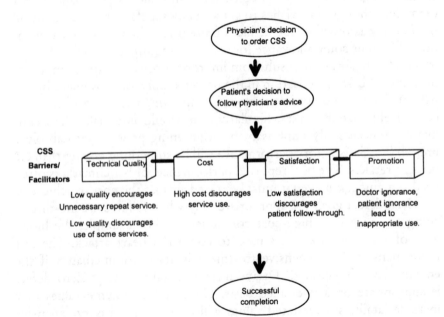

A good CSS unit is one which can document its achievement on technical quality, unit cost, and satisfaction. A better one actively communicates these achievements and promotes its appropriate use. Most physicians have several choices for CSS as well as substitutions among CSSs. Patient satisfaction is critical in gaining patient compliance with treatment.[5,6] The well-managed CSS deliberately advertises its capability and offers helpful advice about the use of its services. The spread of final product protocols has formalized much of this communication. CSSs participate routinely in final product protocol development, advising on the most economical way to gain the benefits available from their service. Similarly, they are available to consult with physicians on individual care plans.

Examples of CSS assistance to physicians are now widespread. Pharmacists develop formularies, indications and guidelines for selecting among drugs, and offer counseling about individual patients.[7,8] Rehabilitation services offer recommended protocols for specific conditions, evaluations of individual patients, and progress reviews.[9,10,11] Diagnostic services provide indications and counterindications for various tests, and consultation about complex cases.[12]

Facilities, Equipment, and Staff Planning

CSS planning involves the size and scope of each service, and the requests for capital equipment necessary to implement service improvements.

Sizing Clinical Support Services

Given the great importance of fixed costs in efficiency, the planning function is crucial. Planning matches the size and scope of each CSS to anticipated demand. It must strive to provide all the services the market can support, but only that level. Services which are missing or too small cause loss of market share to competitors. Those that are too large draw insufficient demand to meet quality and cost standards. CSS planning is based on the epidemiologic planning approach described in Chapter 6. The equation used to size each CSS is:

$$\left\{\begin{array}{c}\text{Demand}\\\text{for a}\\\text{service}\end{array}\right\} = \left\{\begin{array}{c}\text{Population at}\\\text{risk for the}\\\text{service}\end{array}\right\} \times \left\{\begin{array}{c}\text{Incidence}\\\text{rate}\end{array}\right\} \times \left\{\begin{array}{c}\text{Average}\\\text{use per}\\\text{incident}\end{array}\right\} \times \left\{\begin{array}{c}\text{Market}\\\text{share}\end{array}\right\}$$

The equation is usually applied to the proximal demand. That is, for CSS drawing directly from the community, populations are age-specific community censuses, the incidence rate is the occurrence of disease in the general population, and the market share is the institution's anticipated share of the particular market. For example:

$$\left\{\begin{array}{c} \text{Outpatient} \\ \text{pharmacy} \\ \text{demand} \end{array}\right\} = \left\{\begin{array}{c} \text{General} \\ \text{community} \\ \text{population} \end{array}\right\} \times \left\{\begin{array}{c} \text{Outpatient} \\ \text{prescriptions/} \\ \text{person-year} \end{array}\right\}$$

$$\times 1 \times \left\{\begin{array}{c} \text{Organization's} \\ \text{market share} \end{array}\right\}$$

(The average number of scripts per incident is defined as 1.0.)

For CSS demand arising from inpatients, the population is the anticipated number of admissions potentially needing the service (usually counts of specific diseases and conditions), the incidence rate is the percent of patients in the category likely to order the service, and the market share is 1.0.

$$\left\{\begin{array}{c} \text{Inpatient} \\ \text{surgery} \\ \text{demand} \end{array}\right\} = \left\{\begin{array}{c} \text{Inpatient} \\ \text{admissions} \\ \text{per year} \end{array}\right\} \times \left\{\begin{array}{c} \text{Percent of} \\ \text{patients with} \\ \text{surgery} \end{array}\right\} \times \left\{\begin{array}{c} \text{Number of} \\ \text{procedures} \\ \text{/surg. pt.} \end{array}\right\} \times 1$$

The numbers on the right hand side of the equation must be forecast several years into the future. They are usually supplied from the institution's information base. The demand forecast is translated into a business plan for the CSS which provides forecasts of staff requirements by skill level, facility requirements, and costs per unit of demand.

CSS managers are generally trained in their profession, and are not equipped to prepare the forecasts and business plan without help. Planning staff should be available to assist in building the best model and interpreting the forecast. With the radical changes that are occurring in health care today, many CSSs face negative demand trends. It will be necessary to close some services in many health care organizations. The planning process identifies the necessary downsizing, allowing an orderly reduction of resources. Line superiors must assist CSS in meeting the changes. Involving CSS personnel directly in the forecasting process helps them understand the problems which must be faced, but it also improves the accuracy of the forecasts. CSS personnel are the most likely to know of technological changes which may affect the demand.

Preparing New Program and Capital Budget Requests
Technological improvements and revisions in the scope of service require changes in capital equipment. In well-managed organizations, these are developed in advance of the annual budget review and must

compete with other investment opportunities. Managers of clinical support services are responsible for identifying opportunities and developing programmatic capital proposals. The following discussion assumes that the planning process resembles the one described in Chapter 7. It discusses ways in which good CSS managers identify, justify, and defend their proposals.

The professional support service personnel are in the best position to identify all possible service opportunities and to develop proposals for those worthy of detailed consideration. They do this as part of their continuous improvement activities. They must monitor technological developments to identify innovations and obsolescence and respond to shifts in demand for individual services. They must also monitor physician and patient satisfaction, deliberately marketing the CSS and identifying ways in which service can be enhanced by changes in services, hours, and sites. They must also be prepared to reduce or close their service if demand is no longer sufficient to meet cost and quality standards. Expansion was encouraged under the payment systems before competition. As a result, many CSSs are oversized, and deliberate reductions are in order. These reductions may require capital or new programs to facilitate the change.

Proposals are developed in several iterative steps of increasing rigor and complexity. While the CSS can undertake a preliminary evaluation on its own, consultation should be available from the planning-marketing group. Technical assistance will be necessary to prepare most competitive programmatic requests. A competitive proposal addresses all dimensions of performance. The technical issues of forecasting these measures are discussed in Chapter 6. Translating the forecasts into demonstrated benefits is a task for CSS personnel assisted by planning advisors. Most benefits are justified as quality improvements, cost reductions, or competitive improvements. Completely quantitative estimates of benefits are rare. Rather, the justification quantifies as much as is practical, and describes the rest as compellingly as honesty permits. The proposal must then be judged subjectively by review panels. Using a review system which starts by ranking projects in similar departments allows those professionals with the greatest understanding of the proposal the first opportunity to evaluate it.

Quality-related benefits Although many technological advances are described as improvements in outcomes quality, or contribution to patients' health and well-being, the reality is that most proposals involve only convenience and competitive advantage. Benefits must be compared to the treatment alternative with the next lowest cost. A service which supplements another one that is available ten minutes away has a quality value equal to ten minutes' travel, even if the service is lifesaving. (It may have a much higher competitive value.)

If in fact the proposal changes the number of people in the community who will achieve a more favorable outcome, its contribution can be quantified if disease prevalence rates, population reached, and probabilities of success are known:

$$\text{Contribution} = \left\{ \begin{array}{c} \text{Demand for} \\ \text{a service} \end{array} \right\} \times \left\{ \begin{array}{c} \text{Probability that} \\ \text{service will} \\ \text{improve outcome} \end{array} \right\} \times \left\{ \begin{array}{c} \text{Value of} \\ \text{improvement} \end{array} \right\}$$

For example, if a new diagnostic process with a demand of 1,000 tests per year will reduce length of stay by 1 day for one third of those on whom it is used, and a day of stay is worth a marginal cost of $200, the contribution of the process is $67,000 per year:

$$\text{Contribution} = 1,000 \times .333 \times \$200 = \$67,000$$

If the demand is forecast from the epidemiologic planning equation, only the probability of success and the value of the benefit require new information. Precise estimates of value and probability are often impossible, but at least subjective comparisons can be made between competing alternatives. Then the number of people to be helped and as accurate a description of the gain as possible constitute the justification. Descriptions of the benefit and the probabilities of success should be available in the scientific literature. (Clinical proposals not supported in the scientific literature are suspect, except in explicit research situations. Among other problems, managed care plans may deny coverage to questionable services.) Specific benefits can theoretically be scaled by a variety of techniques, including forced choice surveys and Delphi analysis.[13] Years of healthy life restored can also be used to scale benefits, but most new services improve the quality of life rather than extend life itself. Income loss avoided helps evaluate benefits, but it is problematic for retired persons. Because of the difficulties, precise measurement of gain is usually not worth the effort; the proposal must compete on the basis of the verbal description.

Cost-related benefits Because of fixed costs and marketing implications, cost and demand are interrelated. First, CSS costs after adoption of the proposal must be competitive with other sources of the same services. If they are not, the proposal is inadequate to insure long-run survival. The CSS must find a way to deliver services competitively. If they are, a benefit is return on investment, the savings a proposal generates expressed as a return on its capital investment over the years of the life of the project or the capital equipment. In this case, the return each year is the anticipated cost savings. (Return-on-investment calculations are included in most spreadsheet routines.) Care must be taken to estimate all costs and demands accurately, including hidden ones, and to be sure the claims for savings can truly be met. The proposal will be incorporated as an operating budget reduction when it is implemented. The best justification of a cost savings is a prototype for the revised operating budget. (Other issues of cost and revenue estimation are discussed in Chapter 9.)

Some cost improvements occur outside the CSS which must support the service. For example, an improved diagnostic test may reduce drug costs or length of stay. In this case, the cost savings must be traced to the responsibility center where they will occur, and that unit must agree to actual budget changes.

Competitive improvements Competitive improvements are those which improve market share or forestall a loss of market share. Replacing equipment which is critical to continued operations is an obvious, high-priority example. If a modern laboratory must have an automated, multichannel blood chemistry analyzer, and the existing one is no longer reliable, the proposal to replace it will not generate much debate.

A claim that competition has a specific capability that is valued by physicians or patients or claims that a capability will attract market share is a justification for capital investment if it can be shown that the advantage will actually shift market share. The value depends on the magnitude of the shift and the fixed cost involved. The justification requires an estimate of the change in profit. Under traditional fee-for-service accounting this was straightforward. If

$$\left\{ \begin{array}{l} \text{New} \\ \text{output} \end{array} - \begin{array}{l} \text{Old} \\ \text{output} \end{array} \right\} \times \left\{ \text{Price} - \begin{array}{l} \text{Variable cost} \\ \text{per unit} \end{array} \right\} \geq \begin{array}{l} \text{Annualized cost} \\ \text{of improvement} \end{array}$$

then the project was worth detailed evaluation, and the justification was based on the return on investment, calculated from the two terms above and the project life. Under global and captitation payments, the same concept applies, but the left hand, or change in net revenue, term must be calculated for the final products involved or the actual capitation membership. Since only dramatic differences in CSSs are likely to sway people signing up for HMO coverage, most projects must be sold to physician panels who stand to lose or gain income for the total operation of plan. The panel must be convinced subjectively that the improvement is worth the cost.

Other examples are also complicated. The proposal may be a service that has become generally accepted as part of the protocol for a specific disease or procedure. The justification must be based on service for the final product, rather than the operation of the CSS. The budget for the final product protocol becomes the critical document, rather than that of the CSS. If it reflects competitive cost and quality, the proposal is worth further consideration. For example, a special laboratory for in vitro fertilization is a CSS. It can be justified only as a complete service, including evidence of epidemiologic need, evidence of sufficient actual demand, medical staff recruitment, all costs for couples seeking the service, payments allowed by various insurers, and evidence of competitive success rates. The studies to justify the proposal go well beyond the single CSS. As a result, these kinds of proposals are usually considered as strategic, and ad hoc teams are established to evaluate them.

Defending Capital Proposals

The support service manager and the planning-marketing representative are proper advocates of the proposal in the evaluation process. It is their job to prepare the analysis and the justification in the most favorable light. As advocates, they should be prepared to answer questions and make modifications as the proposal progresses. They also must be prepared to accept rejection. By the same token, it is management's obligation to see that their role as advocate is accepted by others; that they do not overstep the bounds of honesty, and that all projects get a fair and judicious hearing.

The procedures supporting annual review of capital and new program opportunities are described in detail in Chapter 7. Well-run organizations emphasize these elements:

- The CSS is clearly responsible for identifying opportunities.
- Planning-marketing assistance is readily available to develop proposals.
- The organization's mission statement is used routinely as the guide to rank new opportunities, makes the preferred direction of growth clear to the CSS, and is kept up to date in changing markets.
- There is medical review and ranking of clinical projects, and support services are fairly represented on the review panel.
- Clinical and nonclinical proposals are judged competitively with one another, in a common review process that includes medical and CSS representation.

Consistency of both process and judgment is the hallmark of success. In most organizations, there is always somebody claiming an urgent need to make exceptions to the review process. A wealthy donor, an unexpected breakdown, a unique technological breakthrough are frequent rationalizations for exceptions. Organizations that yield often to these pleas discover that there are soon enough exceptions to engulf the process. At that point, political influence and persuasive rhetoric become the criteria guiding investments.

One major benefit of consistency is that the dialogue helps the CSS to shape its service to complement others. This contributes, in turn, to an overall market appeal. The feedback to the CSS comes in two ways; through evaluation of its proposals and through participation in the evaluation of others' proposals. Over time, the CSSs learn to identify winning proposals earlier, making the process less onerous.

Managing Amenities and Marketing CSSs

CSSs are in constant contact with both physicians and patients. Their success depends upon maintaining the largest possible volume, and volume in turn depends upon the ability to meet cost and quality standards and the ability to provide prompt, reliable, appropriate, and comfortable service.

Patient and Physician Amenities

Almost all CSS activities, specifically including the eight functions, can also be viewed as promotional or advertising efforts to encourage doctors to select the service over competing alternatives. High quality, counseling on appropriateness, good scheduling, effective planning and budgeting are all aimed at making each CSS optimally attractive to patients and physicians.

Most CSSs have three types of competitors, units of other health care organizations, freestanding services, and doctors offices. Competition with all of these requires maintaining an effective combination of quality, market price, patient amenities, and physician amenities. Patient amenities include scheduling, discussed separately below, and conveniences of access, such as parking, and attractive, comfortable surroundings. These factors are usually assessed by routine patient surveys. Low percentages of dissatisfaction are anticipated and achieved. For laboratories, convenience usually means routine collection of specimens from doctors' offices, so that the patient has no direct contact with the service. It is possible to run most other CSSs with limited waits and with acceptable surroundings. The attitude of CSS workers at all levels is often more important than the physical environment. Many patients are under stress because of their disease or problem. They are grateful for kindness and reassurance and loyal to organizations that provide them. This means that all CSS personnel need training in sensitivity to patient reactions.

Physician amenities include advice and prompt reporting. They also recognize the importance of patient satisfaction with CSSs. Direct electronic communication with physicians' offices is becoming more common. It can be used to verify insurance coverage, assure that the physician's order is complete, communicate special needs, and report promptly and efficiently on results. While these matters can be handled by paper or telephone, paper is slow and costly, and telephone is inefficient and generates no permanent record.

Competition between CSSs and physicians deserves special consideration. Many elementary CSSs can be performed in the physician's office. Doing them there is often cheaper and almost always the most convenient to the patient. The only objection is that quality standards are not met and errors add to the cost of care. Under the conjoint staff concept, health care organizations will negotiate the profile of their CSSs with their physicians in an effort to create an attractive joint offering for patients. The CSSs will emphasize the rarer and more expensive services. The doctor's office will provide any service which meets quality standards and is not cheaper to do at the CSS. Unfortunately, the concept is simpler than the application. An important part of protocol development includes agreement on the site for minor CSSs, and a deliberate effort to eliminate duplication, unreliable results, and unnecessary costs.

Promotion and Sales of CSSs

Most health care organizations find that direct advertising of CSSs is of limited value, because the services must be selected by physicians and because physician services are more important to people selecting health care providers. There are two kinds of exceptions. First, CSSs that do not require a physician's order must be advertised. These include all the general community activities of Figure 13.1. The usual objective of these programs is to encourage preventive behavior. It is important to target promotion to market segments at risk. Promotion is often selective and innovative; the groups most at risk tend to be outside mainstream print and mail marketing. Second, CSSs where the customer has a choice of provider once the physician has made the order can benefit from advertising. Pharmacy and durable medical equipment suppliers are the most common examples. It is considered unethical for physicians to direct patients to a particular supplier unless they have an explicit contractual relationship to do so, such as being employed by the same organization or being in the same HMO. (The ethical issues are one of possible hidden gain or conflict of interest between the patient's needs and the success of a particular supplier, and one of restraint of trade. A physician should not advise patients on cost or convenience trade-offs they are capable of making themselves.) Well-managed organizations respect the ethical problem and avoid placing their physicians in difficult situations. Advertising uses public media, capitalizes on the the organization's relationship to the patient, but does not exploit the physician's relationship.

Promotion of CSSs to physicians and physicians' office staff is important. It tends to emphasize ways of maintaining efficient, high-quality relationships. Newsletters, personal contacts, and service assistants are used. There are ethical constraints; any activity which offers a reward to physicians or their personnel in return for CSS referrals is unethical.

CSSs are increasingly sold as part of integrated contracts with HMOs, PPOs, and self-insured groups. The health care organization must solicit these sales to maintain a cost-effective total volume. Evidence of quality and satisfaction is important to these group buyers, but price is often the determining factor. For those selecting a fee-for-service payment mechanism, most health care organizations offer a variety of discounts in addition to their publicly posted price. Prior to the advent of competition, line managers of clinical service departments were rarely involved in pricing decisions. They now must become sophisticated in cost control and price setting as described in Chapter 8.

Patient Scheduling

Timing of the clinical support services is often critical and rarely irrelevant. Delays reduce quality. Although delay is rarely fatal, it always involves some risk, simply because patients are more susceptible until they recover. The patient seeks prompt attention and rapid recovery. An extra day of illness is a loss of economic productivity. An extra hour in an operating room or intensive care unit, or an extra week in the nursing home adds substantially to cost. Coordination of CSSs is also important. Much of medical care is given in sequence—diagnosis precedes treatment, anesthesia precedes surgery, treatment precedes rehabilitation, et cetera. Interactions between the services abound: certain tests interfere with others, drugs interact, treatments impair organ systems not damaged by the disease itself. The more intense care becomes, the more critical sequencing and timing are. A long list of CSS orders must be completed prior to surgery. Prompt diagnostic services are often required in intensive care, and delays can be as life threatening as inaccurate reports.

Other timing issues are cyclic. Many activities, such as doctors' rounds, occur daily at regular times. Results of routine diagnostic tests are most useful if they are reported in time for rounds, usually about 24 hours after they were ordered. There is little benefit to 12-hour reporting cycles, and reports after 25 hours are no better than reports after 48. Well-run support services determine when and in what order services are needed, measure actual response time, and make an effort to minimize delays that affect the attending doctor and the patient.

Two devices improve the ability of CSSs to meet timing and sequencing needs. Final product protocols and care plans are one. These often help CSSs understand their work load in advance. As soon as a myocardial infarction is diagnosed, a protocol like Figure 11.7 can be invoked The patient's likely needs can be communicated to the CSS who will meet them, even several days hence. Scheduling systems are the other. Obviously, health care needs have different urgency and different predictability. Scheduling systems improve CSSs ability to meet both routine predictable needs and emergencies arising unexpectedly. As they grow in capability, they also improve in ability to coordinate between CSSs. Eventually most patient care episodes will follow automated schedules from the point at which the protocol is selected or the care plan devised. Then the right thing will be done, in the right order, at the right time.

Health care demand can be classified by its urgency and predictability. Services which are both urgent and unpredictable by definition cannot be scheduled. The technical term *stochastic* applies to events that occur at random, that is, totally independent of one another, and that, as a result, are predictable only in the aggregate and with relatively large variation. Efficiency is lower in stochastic and life-threatening situations because resources must be on standby for an unpredictable surge of demand. Delivery suites, for example, rarely average more than 75 percent of capacity, and small ones average much less. Figure 13.4 shows why. Since every mother needs service, and there is no possibility to defer care, a facility capable of serving five births per shift must be built to deliver two babies a shift, or about 2,200 a year. (Even with five rooms, about one mother a month will encounter some crowding.[14]) Similar problems exist with heart attacks and accident victims.

Despite the popular stereotype, most demands made upon the hospital are not stochastic and nondeferrable. Some are quite predictable, such as elective surgical procedures and preventive care generally. Others can safely and comfortably be deferred for several hours or days. If they are scheduled in advance, much greater efficiency can be obtained.

Figure 13.4 Variation in Demand for Obstetrical Delivery Averaging Two Births per Shift

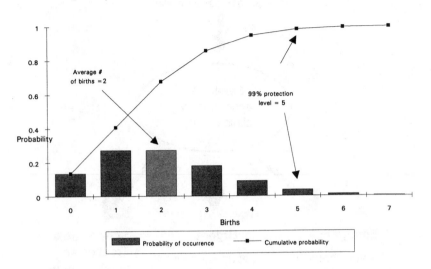

Scheduled care is less prone to error than stochastic care, and it can be managed to the greater convenience of attending doctor and patient. Finally, scheduling permits prospective review of appropriateness. Any question about the desirability of the CSS can be settled during the period before the test occurs.

Scheduling systems work as shown in Figure 13.5. Demand is categorized by priority and is then met with appropriate timeliness. Emergency demand is met when it arises. Deferrable demand is scheduled for a time mutually convenient to the patient and the server. In very sophisticated systems, patients whose treatment could be improved by providing the service ahead of schedule are called in when emergency demand permits. This allows the service to utilize its resources almost fully. The reduction of variation in work load which results from scheduling is converted to lower operating costs.

Scheduling requires an understanding of three major areas: the nature of patient demand, the availability of scheduling resources, and the contribution of stabilized demand to quality and cost.

Analyzing and Predicting Patient Demand

Scheduling models must be based upon specific resources to be used, usually rooms, equipment, or specialized personnel. It is often necessary to consider in several specific demands, scheduling the critical

Figure 13.5 Model of Sophisticated Scheduling Process

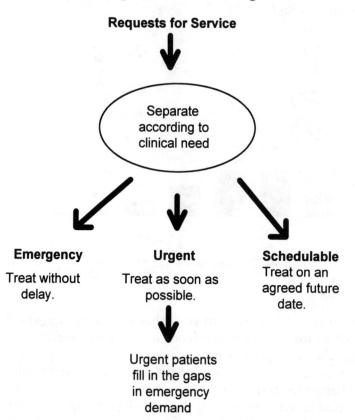

resource for each. A scale of priorities can be developed ranging from "immediate need" to "indefinitely deferrable." In practice, simple scales with three ordinal categories are used. These categories are often called "emergency," "urgent," and "schedulable." The scheduling objective for each category is as follows:

1. *Emergency*—to be treated without delay, despite the loss of efficiency that results. The term *emergency* can be applied to any situation for which first priority service is desirable; it need not be life-threatening. The amount of standby protection will be adjusted downward for less serious priorities. As it is reduced, efficiency will rise. If the emergency category is life-threatening, it is common to accommodate over 99 percent of the anticipated emergency demand at substantial inefficiency, as Figure 13.4 indicated.

2. *Urgent*—to be treated as soon as possible *without* serious impairment of either efficiency or the convenience of others. The

category is appropriate where modest, controlled delay does not impair satisfaction or quality. It thus gets treated as soon as there is no emergency demand. Urgent becomes emergency if demand has not been met within a preestablished time period, or if the patient's condition deteriorates.

3. *Schedulable*—to be treated at a mutually agreed future time. Once agreement is reached, care is delivered as scheduled in virtually every case. It is thus quite predictable for patient, doctor, and service. A subcategory of scheduled patients who are willing to accept an earlier date on short notice can be added. This subcategory actually improves efficiency in some situations, and it is attractive to some patients and doctors.

Uniformity of patient classification can be enhanced by published category definitions, examples, education, audits, and, if necessary, sanctions.

The support services differ in their priority profiles. Physical therapy, for example, is the opposite of the birthing suite shown in Figure 13.4. It has no emergencies and few urgent demands. The largest support service, the clinical laboratory, faces demand in a different sense because it works on specimens rather than patients and often provides several tests upon each specimen. Its emergencies are called *stat* requests (from the Latin *statim*, immediately). It is difficult to define an urgent category. Schedulable is often defined in hours, but it permits substantial efficiencies from batching similar tests.

In addition to the priority categories, it is important to note that demand can vary by time of day, day of week, and season of year. The forecasts for cycles and trends are built into the scheduling system and, in turn, used to establish the required resources and the budget.

Elementary scheduling systems establish an allowance for combined urgent and emergency demand and schedule deferrable demand into the remaining capacity at mutually acceptable dates. They work well in situations where a large fraction of the demand is schedulable. Sophisticated scheduling systems call in patients from the urgent list to fill in gaps in emergency demand, as shown in Figure 13.5.[15] For example, the office scheduling hospital admissions, seeing that fewer emergencies occurred during the night than expected, can summon urgent patients for admission. By doing this, a sophisticated admission scheduling system permits efficiencies of up to 95 percent of bed capacity, while still meeting both emergencies and prior scheduled commitments.[16]

The more sophisticated the scheduling system, the more it costs to operate. Data and processing requirements expand, personnel must be specially trained, and the costs of errors mount. However, well-designed systems are capable of 20 to 30 percent improvements in efficiency of use of fixed resources.[17] They also reduce variation, so labor needs are more stable and more easily predicted. This allows more predictable work schedules for employees and simplifies employee scheduling. Stable work flow reduces errors that result in repeat services. Predictable reporting reduces unnecessary emergencies or stat requests. Finally, they allow both doctors and patients to plan their activities. Except in cases where danger or discomfort is high, a timely, reliable date is preferable to an unpredictable delay.[18]

Sophisticated automated scheduling systems are available for major support services and for admission and occupancy management. These programs keep records, print notices, and provide real-time prompts to scheduling personnel. They automatically monitor cancellations, overloads, work levels, and efficiency. They are integrated with ordering and reporting systems, so that the entire process of obtaining a CSS is automatic from the point of the doctor's decision to order it. Most scheduling systems can also be operated in a simulation mode to analyze the costs and benefits of alternative strategies. Simulation outputs are useful in both short- and long-term planning to evaluate potential improvements in demand categorization, resource availability, and scheduling rules.

Continuous Improvement

CSSs participate actively in cross-functional teams to generate final product protocols and other general improvements in the organization. They must also seek internal improvement opportunities, analyze them, and develop the best for implementation.[19] A key role of the CSS leader or manager is to stimulate specific initiatives which will change processes and generate improvements.[20,21] The initiatives are ongoing, but ideally coordinated with the budget process so that each year's efforts will culminate in measurable improvements in the budget parameters. Many of the improvement opportunities stem from cross-functional agreements, but others stem from a variety of sources, as shown in Figure 13.6. Monitoring the six dimensions of performance can reveal areas for improvement. External data from competitors or benchmarking may reveal an opportunity. New clinical technology means the historic record is no longer relevant. It can mean that an entire new process is required. New equipment, or the opportunity to replace old equipment which has become obsolete, often requires evaluation and detailed planning to get the best results from the new installation.

Figure 13.6 Sources of CSS Improvement Proposals

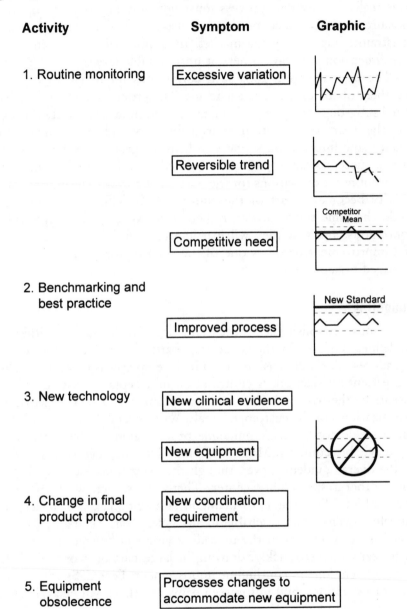

Activity	Symptom	Graphic
1. Routine monitoring	Excessive variation	
	Reversible trend	
	Competitive need	
2. Benchmarking and best practice	Improved process	
3. New technology	New clinical evidence	
	New equipment	
4. Change in final product protocol	New coordination requirement	
5. Equipment obsolecence	Processes changes to accommodate new equipment	

The internal initiatives themselves center on the intermediate product protocols and the equipment. Revisions can improve quality, cost, patient satisfaction, physician satisfaction, or worker satisfaction. In some cases, they can promote an expanded market. The annual budget process and the reliance on six dimensions of measurement keep initiatives realistic. Any new process must not only improve an important measure of performance, but it must also satisfy all other performance constraints imposed by the market. It cannot make improvements in one dimension and leave others at unacceptable levels.

The best managed CSSs seek continuous improvement by using members of the unit as project teams. The group as a whole or designated subgroups study improvement opportunities constantly throughout the year. Consultation is available from planning, marketing, finance, and information services to help the groups develop new processes. Successes can be put on line immediately, but their real impact is to permit new expectations for the next budget cycle. The improvement activity becomes a part of the culture of the CSS. No one expects to do the same thing forever, rather, they expect that change will be continuous, and that they will participate in it. The sense of change and improvement becomes one of the rewards for working in a well-managed organization.

Budgeting

CSSs must establish their needs and negotiate a budget within the guidelines approved by the governing board. The budget should explicitly address all six dimensions, even if the emphasis is on costs, quality, and patient satisfaction. A contribution or acceptable cost guideline is essential; otherwise each CSS tends to optimize its own, rather than the organization's or the customers' goals. With several dozen cost centers, and a single cost increase guideline promulgated by the board, there are inevitable conflicts. Many CSSs may feel they deserve exceptions to the overall guideline, even though the exceptions must come from some other responsibility center. There are several ways to handle the conflicts. The best is to maintain strategic plans which keep the guideline realistic and reachable in any given year. Then a department that has been diligent in the preceding year will be able to formulate next year's budget quickly, drawing in large part on work which has already been done in continuous improvement. Few CSSs will need to ask for exceptions, and unforeseen gains in others will be available to fund justified requests.

Roles of Participants

Well-run organizations have clearly defined management roles for the CSS, the budget manager, and the line supervisor.

The CSS is expected to

- Identify changes in the scope of services and the operating budget arising from the continuous improvement and capital budgeting process
- Review progress in quality, satisfaction, and appropriateness, setting improved expectations for the coming year
- Review the demand forecasts prepared by the budget manager, extending them to the specific levels required in the department and suggesting modifications based upon their knowledge of the local situation
- Propose expectations for staffing, labor productivity, and supplies consistent with forecasts and assumptions about scope, quality, and scheduling
- Identify process changes from current initiatives and show their contribution in specific performance measure
- Identify initiatives that should be developed during the coming year.

The budget manager is expected to

- Assemble historical data on achievement of last year's budget
- Prepare hospitalwide forecasts of major CSS demand measures
- Promulgate the budget guidelines for changes in total expenditures, profit, and capital investment approved by the finance committee of the board (Chapter 8)
- Circulate wage increase guidelines from human resources and supplies price guidelines from materials management
- Assist in calculations and prepare trial budgets until a satisfactory proposal for the board has been reached.

The line superiors of the CSS

- Assure that budget proposals do not endanger quality or satisfaction
- Assist the CSS and encourage steady but realistic improvement
- Coordinate interdepartmental issues that arise from the budgeting process
- Resolve conflicting needs between CSSs
- Evaluate the progress of CSS in order to assist in the distribution of incentives
- Identify interdepartmental opportunities for development during the coming year.

Using the Initiatives to Meet Guidelines

The budget for a given CSS can be complicated by external events related to the service itself. For example, costs of pharmaceuticals have been rising rapidly. A pharmacy might have to pursue a number of initiatives to keep departmental cost increases at a minimum, and even so it might require an exception to the general guideline. Figure 13.7A shows some of the initiatives a pharmacy might support to minimize the impact of drug price increases. The strategy for pharmacy addresses four areas: price and inventory, formulary, final product protocols, and prescribing habits. Initiatives in each area might continue for several years. Figure 13.7B shows a set of initiatives for diagnostic radiology. Although the initiatives are aimed at similar performance measures, the details reflect the differences between these two important CSSs. Each department would count on improvements from the initiatives to meet their next years' budget.

Resolving Shortfalls

Although the well-managed CSS invests heavily in improvement initiatives, it may still have difficulty meeting budget guidelines. In fact, the nature of the shifts occurring in the 1990s implies that some CSSs will grow in size while others shrink. Thus an arbitrary assignment of budget guidelines across the many CSSs will not be effective. Each CSS must defend its own needs, particularly in assuring quality and satisfaction. If acceptable levels on those measures require costs beyond the guideline, quality and satisfaction should get priority. The process of developing the budgets for CSSs must assure that priority. This inevitably means a complex negotiation of conflicting interests between CSSs and usually results in a compromise. The negotiation process has several important characteristics.

- It includes physicians and representatives of the CSSs themselves.
- It follows the accountability hierarchy, beginning with closely related departments and moving to very different ones.
- It assures responsible CSSs of a fair hearing.
- Its goal is the optimization of patient needs as a whole.
- There are at least intangible rewards for CSS managers and personnel who contribute to an effective solution.

If the negotiation is arbitrary, unilateral, or punitive, the CSSs will not be empowered to raise and address initiatives. If it fails to address genuine market needs reflected in the guidelines, performance will fall short of competitive standards. A strong strategic plan is essential. If the strategic plan and the facilities, information, and recruitment plans

Figure 13.7 Improvement Initiatives in Two CSSs

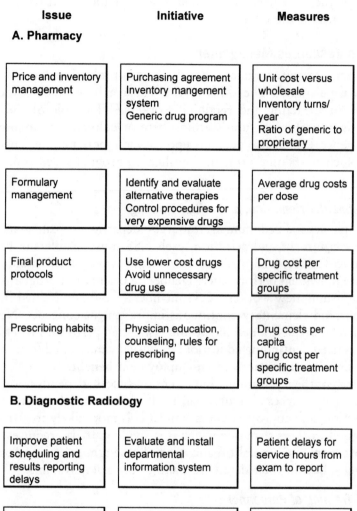

Issue	Initiative	Measures
A. Pharmacy		
Price and inventory management	Purchasing agreement Inventory mangement system Generic drug program	Unit cost versus wholesale Inventory turns/ year Ratio of generic to proprietary
Formulary management	Identify and evaluate alternative therapies Control procedures for very expensive drugs	Average drug costs per dose
Final product protocols	Use lower cost drugs Avoid unnecessary drug use	Drug cost per specific treatment groups
Prescribing habits	Physician education, counseling, rules for prescribing	Drug costs per capita Drug cost per specific treatment groups
B. Diagnostic Radiology		
Improve patient scheduling and results reporting delays	Evaluate and install departmental information system	Patient delays for service hours from exam to report
Reduce retakes	Improve personnel training, intermediate product protocols	Count of retakes
Inappropriate exams	Final product protocols Physician education	Disease-specific exams per patient

derived from it are inadequate, it becomes impossible for the CSSs to reach competitive levels on all six dimensions. Thus if a CSS falls short of its guidelines, the first questions address the strategy of the organization as a whole, and the second questions address the size and scope of the CSS itself. Only then does attention turn to the actual performance of the CSS.

Human Resources Management

CSSs must recruit, train, and motivate both professional and nonprofessional personnel. The skills of the manager have much to do with success in attracting and retaining workers.[22] The role of the group leader is critical in the unit's atmosphere or culture.[23] Maintaining an effective workforce also depends upon several more tangible characteristics, such as training programs, evaluation programs, scheduling, and job security.

Recruitment, Orientation, and Initial Training

Although centralized human resources departments can assist with initial recruitment and selection, each CSS must handle the final selection and attract well-qualified workers, provide specific training, and evaluate individual performance. Deliberate orientation programs assist in establishing new workers. CSS members should be trained in guest relations and elementary continuous improvement concepts. Nonprofessionals must be trained in specific tasks they perform. Professionals in CSSs need continuing education; it is usually purchased from outside professional organizations as an employment benefit.

Much of the recruitment and retention success depends upon actual performance. Success builds upon itself. A unit which meets quality, satisfaction, and appropriateness standards is more likely to attract and keep good workers than one which is struggling. It also requires strong support from the central organization. These armies run not on their stomachs, but on their data bases, and information systems.

Cross-Training of Personnel

Many of the professions have set up licensure or certification requirements for doing specific tasks. These assure customers of trained personnel and provide economic protection for the profession. In other services, prevailing standards of practice have the same effect. The system of public certification or licensure tends to create inflexible job assignments and tasks, not only among the professions themselves but also among their nonprofessional assistants. Highly specialized personnel can sit idle because they are not trained to provide the specific service that is needed.[24]

Cross-training of personnel provides an important opportunity for cost reduction. In the larger CSS, several workers can be trained for infrequent, highly specialized duties, allowing more flexibility and greater efficiency. A given worker can be taught specific tasks originating from several CSSs, and can provide care under the supervision of a physician or nurse. For example, a technician can be trained to perform electrocardiographs, draw blood for laboratory analysis, and take simple x-ray films. Such a cross-trained person would be useful in a moderate sized ambulatory clinic or emergency department. Doctors' offices have long supported generally trained personnel. Larger health care organizations are expanding cross-training. With proper training, protocols, and adequate supervision, the cross-trained individual is as competent as the specialist.

Rewards and Formal Incentives

Extra effort on the part of individuals and groups should always be encouraged, but the methods of doing so are less clear than one might expect. The most powerful compensations are nonmonetary. Recognition, praise, and non-monetary reward are compelling motivators, particularly in a unit where the culture itself supports change and improvement. The sense of a job well done and of belonging to a winning organization are important. CSS leaders and managers play a critical role in recognizing effort and encouraging team members. Many CSSs face grueling emotional and moral pressures related to their work; good leaders often assist with advice, reassurance, and respite opportunities.

Monetary compensation is widely used, but it has recognized drawbacks. Measurement is difficult, "gaming" (maximizing the compensation system rather than the real performance) is a constant danger, and the incentive tends to become expected rather than an opportunity. The incentive can easily create competition between workers or between CSSs which impairs overall mission achievement (Chapter 15). Well-managed CSSs use monetary incentive compensation, but the amount is kept small, the "special effort" character and the contribution to the whole organization are emphasized, and the program supplements strong non-monetary incentives.

Personnel Scheduling

Personnel scheduling systems are important in meeting worker needs as well as maintaining efficient operations.[25] CSS workers are frequently women with child-rearing commitments; flexible hours and part-time assignments are popular and increase recruiting ability. Many CSSs must operate around the clock. Automated personnel scheduling systems improve capacity to handle these needs. They increase ability to cover for absences and provide reasonable advance notice of work assignments. The systems require human management of initial work requests and staffing needs, and final review of schedules. They are often interactive; the manager can revise schedules and choose between computer-generated options.[26]

Job Security

Job security is an important foundation for retaining qualified workers. It stems from effective organizationwide and departmental planning. Technological improvements and changes in efficiency will cause some CSSs to increase and others to decline in size. Competition will require prompt adjustment of the workforce as these changes occur. The better the planning, the longer the lead time for these changes, and the easier the task of recruiting or elimination of jobs. There are six ways to adjust a work force to changes in patient demand:

1. Gain greater output per hour from increased individual effort.
2. Change the number of part-time or temporary employees.
3. Adjust the effective number of full-time employees by using voluntary or involuntary furloughs or increasing overtime.
4. Transfer personnel from assignments with declining volume to those with increasing volume.
5. Use contract, or agency, personnel.
6. Terminate workers or undertake new hiring.

It will be important for most CSSs to systematically use all six. Although the cost of a specific approach depends upon the situation, the higher-numbered responses are generally more expensive for short-term applications. The costs may appear in training, turnover, quality, or other indirect considerations. The use of agency personnel should be a last resort because of the costs, which frequently include losses of quality as well as premium hourly labor costs.

The strategy of the well-managed clinical support service should be to

- Develop long-term forecasts of employment needs and limit permanent employment to the lowest reasonable forecast. These steps will avoid forced terminations and improve morale among permanent workers.
- Develop a cadre of trained part-time or temporary workers. These workers may require a premium over the hourly rate for standby, training time, or similar services, but they will be less costly than agency personnel and more familiar with the hospital's needs and standards of quality.

- Provide systems support and incentives for increased output, particularly when it is necessary to meet short-term fluctuations in demand.
- Use overtime to accommodate short-term increases in demand.
- Cross-train employees in several operations so that jobs can be reassigned without loss of quality.

These strategies will require substantial support from the human resources system, as discussed in Chapter 15. For the larger services, they will also require both personnel and patient scheduling systems to manage the complex logistics.

Management and Organization

The larger CSSs are significant organizations in themselves, providing a substantial management challenge. CSS leaders must combine management and professional skills. The history of CSSs has created a tangle of compensation approaches. The complex technology and the spread to multiple sites convenient for patients, and the need to coordinate between CSS raise challenging organizational questions.

Requirements of CSS Managers

Skill in the profession of the CSS is generally though not always taken as a requirement for the CSS manager. Some services—operating rooms and delivery rooms, for example—use specially trained nurses as their professionals. Pharmacists, physical therapists, occupational therapists, and medical social workers, who traditionally have not held M.D. or nursing degrees, manage another group of support services. Physicians with specialty credentials lead clinical laboratories, radiology and imaging, radiation therapy, anesthesiology, and cardiopulmonary laboratories. Medical leadership is common in emergency rooms. It is growing in rehabilitation services and intensive care units. Physicians certified in physiatry take a special interest in supervising rehabilitation services as a group. Pulmonologists, cardiologists, and neonatologists have assumed leadership roles in intensive care. Many services have both physician and nonphysician professions. Nursing is essential to all inpatient care and has an important role in many outpatient services. There are registered medical technologists, radiographers, respiratory therapists, and nurse anesthetists.

The manager of each support service is usually an experienced leader in the health care profession associated with it. Many CSSs have nonphysician managers subordinate to physician managers with extensive authority over operations. These people are accountable for the eight functions listed above. The range of skills and knowledge reflected in the functions is impressive, from arcane technology to delicate human relations. Not surprisingly, CSS management is a recognized career, challenging, professionally rewarding, and comfortably compensated.

Figure 13.8 illustrates the common alternative structures for the larger CSSs. In CSSs with both physician and nonphysician managers, both managers must share all eight functions. Physicians manage physicians and nonphysicians manage others. Physicians also tend to more strategic and more technical activities. In CSSs with general managers, duties tend to be assigned by function, with the general manager responsible for amenities and marketing, patient scheduling, and human resources management. Quality, appropriateness, planning, continuous improvement, and budgeting should be shared. There is usually an analogous medical staff structure, such as the surgery or cardiology departments, or a specific medical committee, such as the pharmacy and therapeutics committee, to address clinical issues. The general manager model may be applied to either physician or nonphysician led CSSs.

Beyond their professional training, CSS managers need supervisory skills, including personnel selection, management of committees, continuous improvement concepts, data analysis, and participative management styles. Managers of the larger CSSs often have master's degrees in health care management or their specialty. Some have more than one graduate degree. Learning effective management styles requires more than coursework. Well-managed organizations reinforce good practice through line supervisors and consultants from management support services, helping CSS managers to grow more effective over time. Line supervisors can also help by maintaining effective cross-functional teams and supporting an atmosphere of objective inquiry. Not surprisingly, relationships between CSS professions and physicians and even between CSS physicians and attending physicians are a continuing source of friction. CSS managers often need help establishing and maintaining these relationships at an effective level.

Compensation of Support Service Personnel

CSS professionals often command high compensation, and a wide variety of compensation mechanisms have developed over several decades. Method and amount of compensation of hospital-based physician specialists are recurring topics in the management of support services. Although it gets less attention, the subject of compensation for nonmedical professionals leading these services is also important.

Figure 13.8 Models of CSS Management

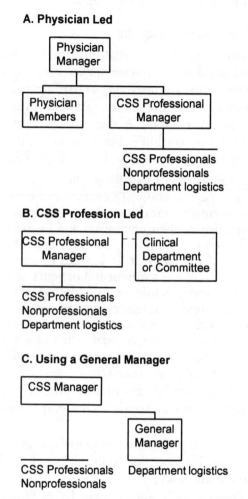

A. Physician Led

B. CSS Profession Led

C. Using a General Manager

Compensation for managers in a bureaucratic organization should meet two general guidelines, and hospital-based physician specialists and support service managers are no exception.

1. Compensation should equal long-run economic opportunities for similar positions elsewhere. That is, the test of compensation is the market. Compensation consistently below market rates will create difficulty in recruiting and retaining professionals. Compensation consistently above market rates will impair the competitive position of the organization.

2. Compensation should encourage professional growth and fulfillment consistent with organizational needs. Incentives to

improve performance in directions consistent with exchange needs are part of a good compensation program.

Compensation for Physician Managers

The historical distinction in compensation contracts was between employment and independent contractor status. Employment compensation from the organization for managing or participating in CSSs is now common. Three-quarters of the pathologists and over half the radiologists have such arrangements.[27] A third category, the joint venture, arose in the 1980s but is now limited in its applicability to CSS.[28] Each of the major forms is quite flexible, with a number of common variants.

1. *Employment.* Employment usually implies regular payment of salary or wages, participation in benefits, and hospital employee status for subordinates. Health care organizations are often liable for the malpractice of their employees and insure them as part of their general coverage. Employee status is not established simply by the wording of the contract; it depends on the locus of specific responsibilities. Employees cannot bill patients or third parties for services covered under employment, although the organization may bill for them under certain circumstances. It is possible for a specialist to be both an employee and a contractor, for different responsibilities. Doctors can be established as a separate class or classes of employees, permitting almost unlimited variation in designing the employment contract.

   a. *Status.* Doctors may be full- or part-time. The employment contract may permit or restrict other employment or private practice.

   b. *Compensation.* Employment compensation can be by either wage or salary. Payment for additional work such as overtime are possible under each.

   c. *Benefits.* Doctors as employees can be included in group retirement, health, accident, and life insurance. Almost any other benefit or perquisite can be specified, sometimes with important tax consequences.

   d. *Incentives.* Compensation can be increased through year-end bonuses for achieving specific or general goals.

   e. *Limitations.* Compensation in the form of equity tends to be more difficult under employment contracts. It is impossible under not-for-profit corporations. This can be a tax disadvantage for the doctor.

2. *Independent contractor.* The contractor arrangement allows the doctor to operate as a business for tax purposes, changing the

rules for deductible expenses. Variants are theoretically even more flexible than under employment. They include arrangements which involve hospital payment to the physician, physician payment to the hospital, and those where there is no monetary transaction between the two.

a. *Fee-for-service.* The specialist and the hospital separately or jointly arrange for payment directly with the patient or the third-party carrier. Such arrangements are not uncommon where the analogy to surgery is strong, such as cardiopulmonary services and radiation therapy. The hospital may compensate for supervisory and teaching services by employment or other contract.

b. *Franchise and lease.* The specialist pays a fee to the hospital, either as rent for the facilities and equipment used or as a franchise for privileges. Franchise and lease arrangements are relatively rare at present. There are barriers to covering the department's operating costs under the physicians' part of Medicare which place the parties at a competitive disadvantage.

c. *Shared revenue.* Historically, CSSs physicians and hospitals developed contracts involving joint billing for services and division of the proceeds. Two versions developed: (1) *percent of gross,* which divides the revenue before deducting the costs of operating the service department and (2) *percent of net,* which divides revenue after deducting departmental expenses.

Compensation of Nonphysician Managers

The compensation of nonmedical managers is not different conceptually from that of physician managers, except employment is by far the usual arrangement. Although many of the nonmedical specialty groups have indicated interest in fee-for-service compensation, the combination of their weaker bargaining power and increasing public concern over the cost of health care has prevented significant growth of any payment method other than salary. Viewed from the perspective of corporate enterprise generally, the use of a nonsalary mechanism is desirable when salaries fail to produce the desired behavior, usually when powerful, specific incentives can be devised. Thus one might contemplate piece rates or productivity bonuses in repetitive, management-defined tasks like pharmacy order fulfillment or laboratory tests. The useful incentives can be achieved through employment contracts rather than fee-for-service arrangements. Fees are becoming less relevant, even within the practice of medicine, as a result of the growth of capitation insurance.

Organization of Clinical Support Services

Clinical support services vary widely in size and activity. The largest is usually the clinical laboratory, which can have over 100 members. The smallest services have only one or two professionals. Large services are usually organized on the basis of their techniques, tools, or modalities. There is an increasing tendency toward cross-training and single-team structure among smaller organizational units, whether a freestanding CSS or part of a larger one. Team collaboration allows greater efficiency, and is preferred unless a clear and cost-effective quality improvement from specialization can be demonstrated. Most CSSs, large and small, provide care in both outpatient and inpatient settings. Organizations must accommodate both geographic and technical differentiation. Figure 13.9 shows a large imaging service, organized by technology and also by setting for the most common services.

The relation of the several CSSs to the organization as a whole presents a serious problem of grouping disparate elements. Each CSS is relatively self-contained. Particularly when it has a complete set of performance measures, a CSS should perform its own services autonomously, but it should participate actively and democratically in cross-functional teams. Guidance from the central organization might be necessary in several areas:

- Relating the CSS goals to the organization's mission and vision, and implementing service plans, budget guidelines, and capital budget priorities
- Assuring adequate technical (planning, marketing, and finance) and logistic (human resources and plant) support
- Recruiting or promoting a leader of the CSS itself

Figure 13.9 Organization of a Large CSS

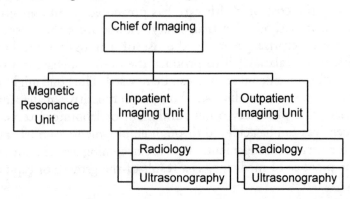

- Resolving conflicts arising from decisions of cross-functional teams or other CSS
- Correcting repeated failure to meet performance goals.

Except in the last item, the contribution of the central organization is supportive, rather than authoritative.

A reasonable accountability hierarchy would place a group manager over several comparable services. Unfortunately, the list in Figure 13.1 represents more than 50 separate cost centers, and common themes to support rational grouping are difficult to find. Figure 13.10 reflects a structure with seven group managers below a vice president. It has three steps between the levels of responsibility center manager and chief operating officer and associates responsibility centers that, for the most part, address related problems and serve the same physician and patient clientele. The three largest CSSs report directly to the vice president. The assignment of responsibility centers to group managers is only occasionally controversial:

- *Cardiopulmonary and electrodiagnostic*—electrocardiology, pulmonary function, heart catheterization, electroencephalography, electromyography, respiratory therapy
- *Radiology and imaging*—radiography, tomography, ultrasound, radioisotope studies, nuclear resonance imaging, megavoltage radiation therapy, radioisotope therapy
- *Surgery, emergency and obstetrics*—operating suite, anesthesia, recovery, emergency service, labor and delivery
- *Social services and health promotion*—social service, pastoral service, clinical psychology, community education, immunization and screening, wellness programs and support group activities
- *Pharmacy*—dispensing and intravenous mixtures
- *Pathology*—clinical laboratory (chemistry, hematology, histopathology, bacteriology, virology), autopsy and morgue, blood bank
- *Rehabilitation and life support*—physical therapy, occupational therapy, speech pathology, home care, durable medical equipment, and long-term care.

The design in Figure 13.10 can obviously be expanded or contracted. There are two other conceptual approaches. One is to associate CSSs with their most common final products, in a product line organization or a matrix. Radiology, pharmacy, and pathology are so widely used that they would remain in a functional organization. The vice president might also remain, to assist in coordinating services which do not easily fit the product line structure. Group manager positions

Figure 13.10 Possible Organization of CSS

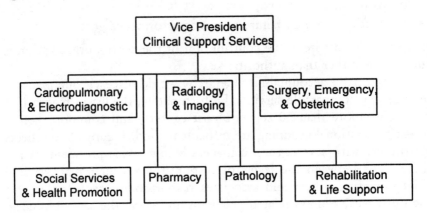

would be abolished. The second approach is to abolish the positions of vice president and all or most group managers, and have all the CSSs report directly to an operating team. The operating team assists in coordinating activities when necessary, and all CSSs can easily get consultative assistance from technical and logistic services. This form requires exceptionally clear objectives, measures of performance, and skill on the part of CSS managers. A few group managers might be designated to support smaller CSSs.

Measures and Information Systems

Measures for demand, quality, and satisfaction, productivity, cost, human resources, and contribution exist for each CSS. Many are the same or similar across all CSSs. Others, particularly demand and process quality, are unique to the service. Figure 13.11 summarizes information available to CSSs. Well-managed organizations are tracking more and more of these measures. Under the continuous improvement concept, realistic and convincing goals are established for the entire set in the budget process. The intent, as discussed in Chapter 9, is to set achievable goals that are consistent with long-run market needs.

Demand and Market Measures

It is important to maintain detailed measures of demand, and also to identify competitors and measure market share.

Measures of the Demand Process
Measures of demand should be maintained in two areas:

Figure 13.11 Measures Available to CSS

Dimension	Measures Routinely Reported	Available in Data Base
Demand	Trends by major services	Referral and payment sources
	Schedule status, delays, and rework	Detail for study of causes
Market share	Share of ambulatory markets	Competitor and services, if available
Competitor information	Services offered by competitors	Detail as available
Outcomes quality	Specific outcomes by case group	Patient, referral source, demographic and disease categories
Incidents and hazards	Adverse event counts, safety surveys	Demographic and disease category
Process quality	Trends by major services	Item, worker, time, patient categories
Patient satisfaction	Trends in overall satisfaction and specifics of service	Time, referral, and patient categories
Physician satisfaction	Trends in overall satisfaction and specifics of service	Physician, referral source, patient categories
Costs	Total, unit, and final product costs for, fixed/variable, direct/indirect; trends	Time, shift, and physical resources; unit costs by service
Human resources	Trends in retention, absenteeism, satisfaction; recruitment records	Worker groups, cross-training, individual records
Contribution	Cost guideline; competitor prices	Final product costs, relative contributions

1. *Level of demand.* These arise from automated scheduling or order entry sources and are reported in counts. They should be reported monthly or weekly, by type of service, referring source, patient category, and pay sources. Historic demand trends for important

service categories should be reported routinely and subject to statistical tests of significance of variation. Statistical histories for specific data groups should be accessible when needed.

2. *Rates of delay and demand failure.* These include times to service routine and stat requests, cancellations by source, delays, and services repeated because of failure or poor results. Automated clinical service systems collect all these measures. Statistically valid comparisons against history or expectations are needed in the larger units. These may require additional software and analysis.

Measures of Market Share

The share of ambulatory markets for each CSS is important. Inpatient markets are determined by the site of hospitalization. The measurement goal is to identify the fraction of ambulatory CSS care provided by each competitor. It is a difficult task, but it can be accomplished by household survey. Surveys of referring physicians frequently provide estimates, and can identify market advantages of competitors, such as location, hours, or parking. The fact that market share is incomplete or crudely measured does not diminish its importance. A crude estimate is superior to no measure at all.

The mix and scope of CSSs are frequently important in marketing the health care organization as a whole as well as maintaining demand for each service. Thus it is useful to survey as formally as possible the services offered by other providers serving the same market. Routine reports might be limited to major changes. Competitor services, prices, and locations are all important for detailed study when indicated.

Quality Measures

Leading CSSs are now using both outcomes and process evaluation of technical quality. Outcomes give an absolute standard, but usually do not reveal actions for correction and are subject to bias from changing patient populations. Process scores identify improvement opportunities but are not always important in outcomes.

Outcomes Quality

Outcomes quality assessment establishes a measurable patient outcome and counts the number of patients achieving it. Global outcomes applying to all patients involve safety, survival, infections, return to work, and similar measures. Their usefulness for CSSs is limited because each CSS contributes only a part of the care leading to the result. Disease- and procedure-specific outcomes are proving more valid and discriminatory. Thus outcomes measures for stroke patients receiving rehabilitation therapies include tests of ambulation, activities of daily living, and speech. The specific tests are unique to the patient; a patient with no ambulatory limitation at admission cannot be counted an ambulation success on discharge. Given reasonable numbers of patients it is still possible to make comparisons over time and against benchmarks. Each test is of the form, "Percent of patients not meeting the goal on admission who met it on discharge," for example, "Percent of patients entering with speech impairment who were discharged without impairment."

There are many areas where no outcome statistic exists. Diagnostic services, for example, are not intended to produce changes. Within therapeutic CSSs it is often hard to specify and measure outcomes. When the outcome occurs, it is not uniquely related to the CSS. Many stroke patients will recover speech function without help, for example. Other services, family, and general environment are important in many outcomes. These difficulties mean that outcomes measures should be used wherever possible as a guide toward absolute performance, but they must be extensively supplemented by process quality and satisfaction measures.

Incidents and Hazards

Closely related to outcomes quality are counts of unexpected adverse events. These are accidents of all kinds, and they occur to patients, visitors, physicians, and employees.

Support services account for significant fractions of the hospital's malpractice, workers' compensation, and general liability. Data on hazards and unexpected events can be compiled monthly, but annual review is more reliable to identify trends and possible improvements. Comparative data are not reliable unless definitions and accounting procedures have been carefully standardized. For most organizations today, historic records are the only useful guides. Case-by-case review may suggest avenues for improvement more often than statistical analysis.

Safety surveys can reveal processes prone to adverse events. These are conducted by government agencies, including the federal Occupational Safety and Health Administration and state Workers' Compensation programs. Insurance companies often offer surveys and private consultants can be engaged.

Process Quality

Process measures of technical quality are generally compliance statistics, that is, attributes counts of acceptance against a priori criteria. Interim product protocols generate many such measures. Often a criterion is established by the profession and is a subjective consensus, for example, "Is the exposure correct on this radiograph?" Occasionally absolute tests are available, as with laboratory blind tests. The measures often cover a diverse array of considerations. If several dozen are evaluated for a single patient, worker, or setting, a score can be constructed and treated as a continuous or variables measure.

Well-run CSSs are implementing the following steps to obtain relatively frequent assessments of process quality:

1. The aspects of the service most clearly contributing to outcomes and satisfaction are identified from procedure statements or interim product protocols. Although these criteria are usually published in the literature of the profession, collective review and local consensus on the items selected are important.

2. A survey instrument reviewing the agreed-upon matters is devised, and surveyors are trained to administer it in an unbiased manner.

3. A sampling strategy is formulated. The strategy identifies how frequently results are needed and at what levels of detail. It specifies a random selection of patients designed to meet the reporting needs at minimum cost. (Consultation with a qualified statistician is usually required.)

4. The strategy is implemented, frequently through automated ordering or scheduling systems, which also support recording, analyzing, and reporting results.

5. Global process quality scores are reported on the shortest horizon consistent with the sample. Data are aggregated over longer periods to reveal information about specific personnel, activity, or patient groups.

Satisfaction Measures

Patient Satisfaction

Customer response to a CSS can be obtained through reliable surveys and should be reported at least annually. The cheapest method is a general, organizationwide survey, with specific questions addressing at least the largest support services.[29] Both in- and outpatients can be contacted after an episode of care. The questions should be sufficiently detailed to identify correctable characteristics. Convenience, timeliness, and attitudes of personnel appear to be the most important concerns. Questions should be constructed from previously published sources, and modified only as necessary for the specific situation.[30] Alternatively, a household survey (drawing a sample of all households in the community, and thus deliberately including patients who use competing sources) can provide information both on satisfaction and on competitor use and weaknesses.

The larger CSSs are used by almost all patients, and therefore can be included in general surveys. These are done by mail or phone, with deliberate efforts to insure high response rates and representative samples. Responses can often be tallied by site, referral source, and other categories of interest.

Smaller CSSs can use questionnaires directed specifically to their patients at or shortly after service. Rather than a random sample, all patients are encouraged to respond, usually to a paper questionnaire. The methodological differences make it difficult to compare the two approaches. Response rates to universal surveys tend to be low, and patients with extreme views may be more likely to respond than those who were simply served according to their expectations. Some CSSs encounter problems resulting from their patient population. Operating room and intensive care patients are often unconscious. Social service clients are often chronically ill, and hospice patients are dying. Special efforts need to be made in these cases to assess satisfaction. Often close relatives are surveyed, rather than or in addition to the patients.

Focus groups can complement or if necessary replace sample surveys. These involve direct meetings with much smaller numbers of CSS users, usually between 10 and 20. The approach trades statistical rigor for more depth of understanding. The loss means that comparisons with earlier data or benchmarks is suspect; the smaller sample and different approach will not yield the same percentage of satisfied patients. The gain is often that ideas for improvement come to light.

Physician Satisfaction

A formal survey of referring physicians' views on support services is desirable annually, at least in larger organizations. The topics are usually reliability and timeliness of response, acceptability to patients, and quality of professional advice and guidance. Well-designed surveys pursue negative responses with follow-up questions and comment opportunities to identify correctable matters. Comparison with results from prior years is useful, and survey questions can address the hospital's standing relative to its competition. ("Rank the five clinical laboratories listed below according to your preference.")

The survey should include all possible users rather than just the group referring routinely. A question indicating frequency of referral can be used to compare results by high and low users. Supplementary information from the viewpoint of the doctor who is already a high user can be obtained from focus groups or direct interviews. Anecdotal and idiosyncratic evidence on physician satisfaction should not be ignored. Those services which provide adequate professional advice and guidance tend to hear of problems and opportunities through that process. The formal mechanisms in such cases simply protect against failure of the informal contact.

Cost and Productivity Measures

The measures for cost and productivity are collected by the accounting system, but the support service manager participates in determining how detailed the data should be. Issues involving the support service include application of accounting definitions and selection of productivity standards (see also Chapter 8).

- *Account center definition.* Supervisors within a support service department should have their own cost and revenue centers. The combination constitutes a responsibility center. Functional account detail for the responsibility center will show labor costs, supplies costs, and so on and revenue by source of payment. Appropriate parts of the budget are similarly segregated, and the supervisors gain the ability to set and meet expectations in which their have participated, a critical component of closed system theory. (Information for more detailed functions or smaller work groups will require special studies.)

- *Labor cost, facility utilization, and total cost productivity benchmarks.* Productivity benchmarks reveal opportunities for improvement after scheduling and forecasting gains have been achieved. Comparative standards are useful in revealing the range of competition and the known limits, but the best expectations always recognize local history.

- *Allowances for variation in demand.* Even under the best of scheduling systems, allowances for unpredictable variation in demand are frequently necessary. Setting these allowances and establishing the cost of them require advice from the support service manager.

- *Flexible budget variance measures.* Flexible budget systems report variances for the demand forecast and labor productivity terms. Most flexible budgets also report any variance in the purchase price of labor, such as might arise from using too high a skill level or excessive overtime. Thus the manager must minimize three variances, price, demand, and quantity of labor. Flexible budget applicability is limited. The approach is effective only when the CSS can accurately forecast output and has the ability to control resource scheduling to affect unit costs. This usually means the ability to schedule personnel. Few CSSs have either the forecasting accuracy or the scheduling flexibility required.

• *Overhead.* Overhead expectations were traditionally reported as fixed costs, but this provides no incentive for economy to either the overhead department or the CSS. Well-run organizations are moving to "sell" as much overhead service as possible to the support services on a transfer price basis (Chapter 8).

Measures of Profit

Measures of profit are determined according to established accounting rules. Once the overhead question is addressed and the support service manager is consulted about the price schedule, a profit expectation can be jointly set. Any departure from it should be traceable to some component: demand, productivity, scheduling, unit costs, overhead, or prices must also depart from expectations. If, and only if, price is competitively set, profit provides a global measure of support service management skill in terms comparable to other support services and the hospital as a whole.

Human Resources

Measures of recruitment, retention, absenteeism, employee cross-training, and employee satisfaction are important. They are generally conducted by central human resources staff. Comparisons can often be made across CSSs. While professional and nonprofessional differences might exist, there is no inherent reason why the reported values for each should be different for different CSSs.

Contribution

Each CSS should understand its contribution to the financial whole, and should operate under a productivity guideline. Market discipline requires that every CSS understand the organization's overall need to earn a profit, and their contribution to that need. The simplest measure is profit under market-determined fees-for-service. Given a market price and a profit requirement, the operating cost of a CSS or any other unit is immediately determinable.

Allowable cost = market price − required profit

Unfortunately the market price term is rarely available. Even in fee-for-service environments, years of distortion under health insurance reimbursement schemes mean that prices paid are anything but market determined. Most CSSs must rely on guidelines apportioned from central measure of market price and profit needs.

Allowable cost = Target constructed
from organizationwide prices and profits

The allowable cost guidelines for CSSs should be realistic and convincing, but that does not mean that every CSS must make the same contribution. Subsidies of some CSSs are desirable, but it is important that the entire organization understands the reasons for and limits of subsidy. Sources of information for establishing the guideline include:

1. *Unit cost history.* Cost per unit of service, by major service group, is available from the accounting and budgeting systems. Comparative data are difficult to find and use. Analysis of fixed and variable cost trends may reveal opportunities and new targets.

2. *Comparative price data.* Prices charged by competitors are easily obtained for health care organizations and independent vendors. While these are not entirely reliable, they should be thoroughly understood and met or bettered in most cases.

3. *Cost per episode.* The measure includes both unit costs and volumes of service. It can be trended over time to indicate the CSS's revenue requirement and contribution to final product efficiency. Publicly available Medicare cost reports permit study of the relative contribution of the CSS to the total for similar hospitals. Shared data services can provide case-specific comparisons.

4. *Charge per episode.* Payments like the Medicare DRG are close to market-determined prices, and can guide cost analysis. Trends and forecasts assist in understanding future operational limits.

5. *Cost (or counts) per member per month.* Contribution of each CSS to capitation premiums for HMO members and costs for PPO customers can be calculated through claims information systems. Counts can be used when unit costs or prices are not available. Claims systems are required because the patient's total use may include several instances and sites of care. The value should be adjusted for age or made specific to the population group most at risk for the service. Availability can be expected to increase in the coming years.

Information Systems

The information needs of many support services are now clear, and the technology is available to deliver them. All the larger CSSs have departmental decision support systems which not only collect the performance measures but also handle appropriate patient scheduling, personnel requirements and scheduling, sampling for quality and satisfaction, cost analysis, and trial budget development. The list of major components of the information system is relatively long, but several components interact, either with each other or with other services. Departmental systems handle all components on an integrated basis, taking advantage of data quality and efficiency.

- *Patient scheduling.* The level of sophistication is tailored to the individual CSS demand. In the future, the scheduling function will be integrated with other CSSs for both inpatients and outpatients so that a patient with several needs can have them met in an orderly and prompt manner. The scheduling component records historical data on demand by category and occupancy or facility use percentages. A forecasting algorithm indicates personnel needs and schedules. The system also reports repeat examinations, cancellations, and delays.

- *Personnel scheduling.* Software recording the personnel available to the department, with data on skills, cost, employment history, and scheduling preferences, accepts short-term demand forecasts and calculates a reasonable schedule of personnel to meet them. Many systems accept individual requests. The schedule is presented to the CSS manager for review and correction and printed in convenient form for each worker. The software is capable of listing overtime, special request and shift assignments for each employee, allowing equitable distribution of these elements.

- *Order processing.* Descriptive data on patients obtained from the scheduling software will be attached to each order for service. When the service is performed, these data will be used to post the patient's account, capture patient characteristics, and to build historical files for protocol development.

- *Results reporting.* Results can be electronically reported to the referring physician. In the diagnostic services, prior tests can be summarized, permitting analysis of trends. Historic results files will also be accessible, leading to improvement of intermediate product protocols.

- *Patient medical accounting.* Summaries of support service activity for episodes of illness will be incorporated in a master clinical abstract file. This file, augmented automatically with billing information, will form the historical resource for patient group protocols.

- *Clinical performance assessment.* An algorithm identifies sample patients for outcomes measures of quality and satisfaction, generates the survey instrument and accepts responses to it efficiently. It prepares summary reports and analysis of trends, calculate statistical significance, and provide early warning of departures from important quality measures.

Suggested Readings

England, B., ed. 1986. *Medical Rehabilitation Services in Health Care Institutions.* Chicago: American Hospital Publishing.

Caring

Folland, S. 1993. *The Economics of Health and Health Care*. New York: Macmillan Publishers.

Patrick, D. L. 1993. *Health Status and Health Policy: Quality of Life in Health Care Evaluation and Resource Allocation*. New York: Oxford University Press.

Snyder, J. R., and D. A. Senhauser, eds. 1989. *Administration and Supervision in Laboratory Medicine*, 2d ed. Philadelphia, PA: Lippincott.

van de Leuv, J. H. 1987. *Management of Emergency Services*. Rockville, MD: Aspen Publishers.

Notes

1. A. B. Flood, W. R. Scott, and W. Ewy, 1984, "Does Practice Make Perfect, Part I: The Relation between Hospital Volume and Outcomes for Selected Diagnostic Categories," *Medical Care* 22 (2): 98–114.

2. H. S. Luft, D. W. Garnick, D. H. Mark, and S. J. McPhee, 1990, *Hospital Volume, Physician Volume, and Patient Outcomes: Assessing the Evidence* (Ann Arbor, MI: Health Administration Press), 102–4.

3. A. Donabedian, 1980, *The Definition of Quality and Approaches to Its Assessment, Vol. I* (Ann Arbor, MI: Health Administration Press).

4. U.S. Department of Health and Human Services, 1993, *Staffing and Equipping Emergency Medical Services Systems: Rapid Identification and Treatment of Myocardial Infarction—National Heart Attack Alert Program* (Bethesda, MD: DHHS, National Institutes of Health, National Heart, Lung, and Blood Institute).

5. W. M. Macharia, G. Leon, B. H. Rowe, B. J. Stephenson, and R. B. Haynes, 1992, "An Overview of Interventions to Improve Compliance with Appointment Keeping for Medical Services," *Journal of the American Medical Association* 267 (1 April): 1813–17.

6. X. M. Huang, 1994, "Patient Attitude towards Waiting in an Outpatient Clinic and its Applications," *Health Services Management Research* 7 (February): 2–8.

7. S. Y. Crawford and C. E. Myers, 1993, "ASHP National Survey of Hospital-Based Pharmaceutical Services—1992," *American Journal of Hospital Pharmacy* 50 (July): 1371–1404.

8. T. L. Skaer, 1993, "Pharmacoeconomic Series, Part 3: Applying Pharmacoeconomic and Quality-of-life Measures to the Formulary Management Process," *Hospital Formulary* 28 (June): 577–84.

9. K. A. Stem and P. Kramer, 1992, "Outcomes Assessment and Program Evaluation: Partners in Intervention Planning for the Educational Environment," *American Journal of Occupational Therapy* 46 (July): 620–24.

10. M. G. Stineman, J. J. Escarce, J. E. Goin, B. B. Hamilton, C. V. Granger, and S. V. Williams, 1994, "A Case-Mix Classification System for Medical Rehabilitation," *Medical Care* 32 (April): 366–79.

11. N. Harada, S. Sofaer, and G. Kominski, 1993, "Functional Status Outcomes in Rehabilitation: Implications for Prospective Payment," *Medical Care* 31 (April): 345–57.

12. B. Portugal, 1993, "Benchmarking Hospital Laboratory Financial and Operational Performance," *Hospital Technology Series* 12 (December): 1–21.

13. D. L. Patrick, 1993, *Health Status and Health Policy: Quality of Life in Health Care Evaluation and Resource Allocation* (New York: Oxford University Press).

14. J. D. Thompson, 1963, "Predicting Requirements for Maternity Facilities," *Hospitals* (16 February).

15. R. H. Edwards, J. E. Clague, J. Barlow, M. Clarke, P. G. Reed, and R. Rada, 1994, "Operations Research Survey and Computer Simulation of Waiting Times in Two Medical Outpatient Clinic Structures," *Health Care Analysis* 2 (May): 164–69.

16. W. M. Hancock and P. F. Walter, 1983, *The ASCS Inpatient Admission Scheduling and Control System* (Ann Arbor, MI: Health Administration Press).

17. W. M. Hancock and M. W. Isken, 1992, "Patient-Scheduling Methodologies," *Journal of the Society for Health Systems* 3 (4): 83–94.

18. A. V. Lewis, J. White, and B. Davis, 1994, "Appointment Access: Planning to Benchmark a Complex Issue," *Joint Commission Journal on Quality Improvement* 20 (May): 285–93.

19. P. B. Batalden, E. C. Nelson, and J. S. Roberts, 1994, "Linking Outcomes Measurement to Continual Improvement: The Serial 'V' Way of Thinking about Improving Clinical Care," *Joint Commission Journal on Quality Improvement* 20 (April): 167–80.

20. T. P. Gibson, 1992, "Continuous Quality Improvement at Work in Radiology," *Radiology Management* 14 (Fall): 48–51.

21. R. T. Preston, 1994, "Patient-Centered Care through Consolidation of Outpatient Services," *Radiology Management* 16 (Winter): 20–22.

22 M. M. Shanahan, 1993, "A Comparative Analysis of Recruitment and Retention of Health Care Professionals," *Health Care Management Review* 18 (Summer): 41–51.

23. C. McDaniel and G. A. Wolf, 1992, "Transformational Leadership in Nursing Service: A Test of Theory," *Journal of Nursing Administration* 22 (February): 60–65.

24. E. Ginzberg, 1990, "Health Personnel: The Challenges Ahead," *Frontiers of Health Services Management* 7 (Winter): 3–20, 21–22, 38.

25. J. Chen and T. W. Yeung, 1993, "Hybrid Expert-System Approach to Nurse Scheduling . . . NURSE-HELP," *Computers in Nursing* 11 (July): 183–90.

26. J. J. Gray, D. McIntire, and H. J. Doller, 1993, "Preferences for Specific Work Schedules: Foundation for an ExpertSystem Scheduling Program," *Computers in Nursing* 11 (May): 115–21.

27. G. Roback, L. Randolph, and B. Seidman, 1982, *Physician Characteristics and Distribution in the U.S.—1981* (Chicago: American Medical Association, Division of Survey and Data Resources).

28. D. B. Higgins and M. L. Hayes, 1993, "Practical Applications of Stark II to Hospital Operations," *Healthcare Financial Management* 47 (December): 76–78, 81, 83–85; J. E. Steiner, Jr., 1993, "Update on Hospital-Physician Relationships under Stark II," *Healthcare Financial Management* 47 (December): 66–68, 70–72, 74–75.

29. M. Zviran, 1992, "Evaluating User Satisfaction in a Hospital Environment: An Exploratory Study," *Health Care Management Review* 17 (Summer): 51–62.

30. S. Strasser and R. M. Davis, 1991, *Measuring Patient Satisfaction for Improved Patient Services* (Ann Arbor, MI: Health Administration Press.

NURSING SERVICES

Definition, Purpose, and Scope of Nursing Services

IN THE health care field, nurses are as ubiquitous as doctors, and about four times more numerous. There is virtually no place that they have not made a contribution Nursing is almost always critical to inpatient care, usually relevant to outpatient care, and central to hospice, home and long-term institutional care. Nurses make major contributions to case management, health promotion and disease prevention. Organizationally, nursing is by far the largest professional employee group. Their contribution is clearly recognized by patients. Most people, when asked to evaluate their inpatient care, speak first not of the doctor, but of the nurse. Furthermore, if they think well of their nursing care, they tend to rate the whole experience, even the bill, more favorably. While the patient's emphasis is in some ways naive, it is not entirely misplaced.

Speculating on the future, the competitive environment suggests a bigger, more influential role for nursing. This chapter addresses this emerging potential of nursing. It assumes that nursing care is defined by patient needs and professional skills rather than in- or outpatient location. It also assumes that the well-run health care organization will be interested in many or all locations for care. Finally, it assumes that well-educated nurses will pursue the broad purpose of homeostasis with professional independence and zeal.

Definition

Defining what nursing service is has proved troublesome to both nurses and non-nurses. In part this may be due to the extraordinary breadth of nursing's contribution. Nursing can be defined by its willingness to undertake almost anything necessary to help the patient return to or sustain independence. The patient need not be sick; nursing services include prevention. The patient need not survive; nursing service is important for the dying. Florence Nightingale saw the nursing role as stretching from emotional support to control of hazards in the environment. She articulated the objective of assisting the patient to **homeostasis**, a state of equilibrium with one's environment, saying in 1859 that nursing is those activities which "put the patient in the best condition for nature to act upon him."[1] This concept prevails in most of the more modern definitions, which add the goal of independence:

> **Nursing** is the provision of physical, emotional, and cognitive services that support or improve the patient's equilibrium with his or her environment and that help the patient gain independence as rapidly as possible.[2]

The definition is limited only by the patient's needs and the services provided by others. As the support services grew to technical and professional maturity over this century, nursing relinquished responsibility for many of them. More remains than has been given away.

Purpose

It is obviously better to prevent loss of equilibrium than to try to regain it. Prevention of illness and promotion of health has always been important in nursing. Nurses' work with individuals and families includes immunization, environmental safety, and disease screening. For the sick patient, the route to homeostasis includes a nursing assessment or diagnosis, the development of an individualized care plan, and the implementation of the plan by specific nursing tasks or tasks requested of other services. Even for the sick patient, preventing the spread of disability is superior to correcting losses. Nurses instruct patients in adapting to disease and disability, speeding their own recovery, and minimizing the risk of further impairment.

The nursing process of diagnosis and response resembles the medical one conceptually, but the details of a nursing care plan seek to complement rather than duplicate a medical protocol. Medicine's focus on technology has stimulated nursing's emphasis on access, mental and emotional considerations, education, motivation, acceptability, and satisfaction. As medicine has become high-tech, nursing has become high-touch.

The purposes of nursing are as follows:

• To promote health, including emotional and social well-being
• To prevent disease and disability

- To provide environmental, physical, cognitive, and emotional support in illness
- To minimize the consequences of disease
- To encourage rehabilitation.

Scope of Nursing Services

Nursing can be classified into two categories, personal nursing services, or what nurses do for patients as individuals such as bedside care, and general nursing services, or what nurses do for people in groups such as educational and public health activities. The first is far larger and historically the center of hospital nursing activities, but the second is important in its own right and is receiving increased attention from health care organizations seeking to maintain community health.

Personal Nursing Service

Personal nursing service encompasses most of the professional activity of nurses and employs about two-thirds of this nation's 1.6 million working nurses.[3] All encounters between nurse and patient have the same purposes and draw on the same professional base, but the site, duration, and clinical character shape the specialization of activity, as shown in Figure 14.1. Nursing sites range from acute inpatient hospitals through ambulatory and chronic care facilities to community and home settings. The encounter can be brief or long-term, and for any of several thousand diseases and conditions represented here by major clinical specialty.

Referring only to the major clinical specialties, there are 9 × 6 × 2, or about 100 potential nursing activities. (A few cells, principally

Figure 14.1 Categories of Personal Nursing Service

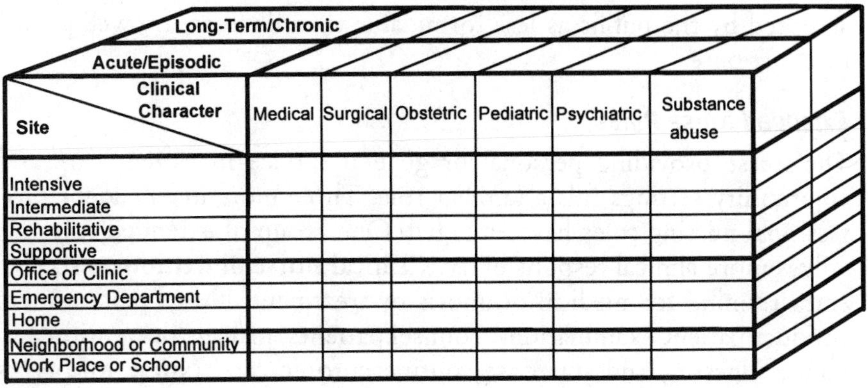

in chronic care, are not realistic.) Historically, most nursing employment has been in acute intensive and intermediate medical and surgical care, the upper and forward sections of Figure 14.1. The movement of nursing is toward prevention and early intervention, reflecting the cost savings that these activities represent. At present, intermediate care is declining and intensive care is relatively stable. Growth is in ambulatory, home, and community sites, and in chronic care. A leading health care organization is likely to have over 80 percent of the services indicated. Its facilities will have about 30 different nursing work assignments. The individuals filling these posts increasingly refer to themselves as specialists, such as home care nurse, intensive care nurse, psychiatric nurse, and so forth. In fact, they use specialized skills and draw upon unique as well as general nursing experience, so organizations would seek related experience when recruiting or promoting them.

General Nursing Services

General nursing services emphasize group activities for disease prevention, as opposed to care of individual patients. The scope of general nursing services is shown in Figure 14.2.

Well-run health care organizations have moved decisively toward collective patient services, not only as a contribution to their public health goals, but also as a way of reducing total cost of care. Smoking, alcohol, and hypertension appear to account for 10 to 20 percent of total health care costs, and these may be reducible through education. Prenatal and neonatal education reduces illness and cost of childbearing and -rearing. Emotional stress within the family, which may lead to spouse and child abuse, can also be reduced by education and counseling. People can be taught to deal effectively with disease and life cycle events in ways which reduce stress, anxiety, and the need for personal medical services. Nurses, because they are knowledgeable, yet accepted by the public as less formidable than doctors, are well placed to contribute.

Extended Nurse Roles

The nurse providing personal or general service in patient care and community settings fills a familiar role. Three more independent professional nursing roles have emerged. One group of extended roles involves more clinical responsibility. **Clinical nurse practitioners** receive extra training for medical diagnosis or treatment. Nurse practitioners conduct patient examinations, counsel patients, manage prevention and minor illnesses, and supervise routine chronic care. **Nurse midwives**

Figure 14.2 Categories of General Nursing Service

Activity	Examples	Benefit
Health Education		
Prenatal and neonatal care	Preparation for pregnancy, delivery, breast feeding	Reduced complications and infant distress
Parenting and child health	Infant care, home safety	Reduced injury and abuse
Child and adolescent development	Nutrition, learning, sexuality	Improved child health and learning performance
Lifestyle and adult health	Menopause, aging parents	Reduced anxiety, fewer office visits
Sexual expression and contraception	Family planning, sexually transmitted diseases	Reduced pregnancy complications, STD incidence
Exercise and fitness	Diet, weight control	Reduced cardiovascular and bone and joint disability
Self-examination and self-care	Breast examination, home medication	Improved survival, fewer office visits
Chemical dependency and substance abuse	Smoking cessation, alcohol use	Reduced serious illness
Prevention		
Primary prevention	Immunizations	Reduced childhood disease and complications
Screening	Hypertension, diabetes	Improved management and reduced complications
Social and home services	Community centers, home health aids	Reduced institutional care needs

handle uncomplicated obstetrics. Both have demonstrated competence equal or superior to that of physicians within these domains. **Nurse anesthetists** are trained to work under general medical supervision.

The second extended role is that of **case manager**. The case manager is a coordinator and overseer who assist other health care professionals in finding the least costly solution at any particular juncture in a lengthy and complex treatment. Patients with permanent or long-term illness or disability develop complex medical and social needs. They often require services from several medical specialties, and social services are necessary to allow them to function at the highest possible level. Nurses, particularly those with postbaccalaureate education and considerable clinical experience, are well positioned to become case managers. Case management is emerging as routine for severe workers' compensation and auto injuries, for AIDS and other chronic diseases, and for many aged persons with multiple diseases and impairments.

The third extended role is in health care organization management. Nurses comprise a significant group of middle management. Some are *nurse clinicians*, specialists in the problems of certain patient groups. Others are general line managers, supervising large staffs and accountable for a broad range of expectations. It is wise to remember that a large nursing floor will involve 50 or more employees and will relate routinely with most clinical support services as well as finance, human resources, and plant services. The nursing department constitutes half the workforce in most hospitals and generates at least half the revenue.

Plan of the Chapter

This chapter describes the functions nursing must perform in a well-managed health care organization, the personnel and organization of nursing departments, the measures of nursing performance, and the information systems it requires.

Nursing Functions

Nursing and the Eight Functions of CSSs

As shown in Figure 14.3, nursing must perform all of the eight CSSs functions. Nursing's emphasis on homeostasis, its commitment to control of the environment, and its central role in the care process have given it a unique profile in six of the eight functions. In quality management, appropriateness management, patient scheduling and continuous improvement, nursing contributes not only to its own services but also to medicine and other CSSs. In budgeting and planning, its heavy dependence on human effort as opposed to equipment and supplies requires an elaborate scheduling and workforce management capability. In human resources management and amenities and marketing management, nursing differs from other CSS mainly in scale, but because nursing is the most visible service to the patient and employs nearly half of the typical health care organization workforce, the scale is impressive.

General nursing, although growing rapidly, is much smaller than personal nursing. Its eight functions tend to resemble those of other CSSs. Marketing is stressed. All the four P's of marketing—product, place, price, and promotion—are important to maximize participation in general nursing's educational and preventive programs.[4]

Direct Patient Services—The Nursing Quality Function

The services nursing provides include:

- An independent diagnosis and plan
- Personal nursing care
- Communication with doctors and support services
- Assistance to the patient's family
- Control of the care environment
- Preventive education
- Case management.

Nursing Diagnosis and Plan

All CSSs are expected to make an assessment of patient needs. Nursing's assessment is particularly encompassing, including many personal and social elements not often emphasized in medicine. These dimensions are important in prevention, management of chronic disease, and building patient satisfaction. The activities comprising the nursing assessment are discussed below, as part of protocols and care plans.

Personal Nursing Care

Nursing's strength lies in the breadth of its services to patients. Figure 14.4 shows the extraordinary scope of nursing care to patients as individuals. Much of this care is managed independently by the nurse, coordinating as necessary with the attending physician and other CSSs. All of it is important. Emotional, educational, and personal care elements contribute to improved outcomes and patient satisfaction.

Family Assistance

Nursing shares with medicine responsibility for communicating with the family or other significant persons in the patient's life. Nursing success in this communication is a critical element of overall patient satisfaction. Generally, the assistance falls into two categories, cognitive and emotional.

The family needs a variety of specific facts, ranging from the name of the responsible nurse to care needs after discharge. Well-run nursing units, including outpatient units, anticipate most of these factual needs and provide educational materials, both verbal and written. The broad

Figure 14.3 Nursing and the Eight CSS Functions

Function	Nursing Implications	Personal Nursing Examples	General Nursing Examples
Quality	Identify and provide personal nursing service	Develop and implement care plan or protocol	Provide accurate, effective teaching and counseling
	Provide care ordered by physician	Administer drugs and treatments	Provide safe, effective screening
	Support and coordinate care provided by other CSSs	Maintain safe care environment	Identify most critical needs and develop attractive programs for them
		Convey CSS orders, specimens, transport patients, and monitor delivery of service	
Appropriateness	Provide timely and complete service	Meet time expectations of protocols	Identify higher-risk, more receptive groups
	Identify and eliminate obstacles to compliance	Instruct patient on preparation, side effects, recovery	Encourage appropriate use of health care services
		Identify patient anxiety, unmet needs, and communicate or correct them	
Facility, equipment, and staff planning	Projection of future personnel and facility needs, review of acceptable volumes of demand	Plan service size, facility requirement, personnel needs	Plan number, locations, and timing of programs
		Monitor employee skill levels and case experience	

Amenities and marketing	Additional services for patients and doctors	Family and visitor support Monitor or participate in food service	Maximize attendance by attention to location, time, and cost and by advertising and promotion Does not apply
Patient scheduling	Timely service, integrated with other CSSs	Maintain protocols and schedules for each patient Coordinate with other CSSs	
Continuous improvement	Monitoring performance measures, benchmarking, and devising process changes to improve	Improve final and intermediate protocols Meet budget guidelines Provide data for medicine, other CSSs	Monitor changing public needs and tastes, revise programs as indicated
Budgeting	Developing expectations for each dimension of performance	Maintain efficient staffing and use of expensive supplies	Maintain revenues or meet unit cost goals
Human resources management	Recruiting, retaining, and motivating an effective work group	Maintain a recruitment plan, training program, incentive program, effective supervision for workers	Recruit and retain effective teachers

Figure 14.4   Scope of Personal Nursing Care

Physical Care of Afflicted Organ Systems

Organ System	Example
Respiration	Postoperative breathing, coughing exercises
Circulation	Ambulation, passive exercise
Digestion and elimination	Dietary consultation, catheterization
Feeding and nutrition	Meal planning, parenteral nutrition
Skin care	Turning, positioning, massage
Bones, joints, and muscles	Ambulation, passive exercise
Sensation	Pain management
Sex and reproduction	Prenatal and newborn care

Emotional Care and Support

Counseling Activity	Example
Reassurance and motivation	Presurgical
Illness related disability and disfigurement	Cancer, AIDS
Grieving and death	Treatment alternatives, bereavement
Supporting general mental health	Stress management
Detection of mental illness and substance abuse	Family support, encouragement of treatment
Psychiatric nursing	Anxiety, depression management

Treatments Ordered by Attending Physician

Treatment	Example
Explicit drug orders	Intra-muscular antibiotic
Judgmental (PRN) drug orders	Pain medication
Other treatments	Wound dressing

Care-Related Teaching

Activity	Example
Self-care	Diabetic insulin, nutrition management
Rehabilitation	Poststroke, posttrauma recovery
Infant care	Breast feeding, safety
Sex and reproduction	Contraception alternatives, avoidance of sexually transmitted disease
Home care	Nursing by family members

Continued

Figure 14.4 Continued

Environmental Control

Activity	Example
Infection control	Isolation procedures
Medical hazard control	Security and sterility of supplies
	Proper disposal of hazardous waste
Narcotics control	Control of narcotics inventory
Patient, staff, visitor safety	Lighting, floor condition, equipment maintenance
	Surveillance of home hazards

outline of the care plan is given to the family, including the anticipated dates of key events such as surgery and discharge. This serves a dual function, relieving anxiety and permitting the family to prepare. Nursing shares with the plant system responsibility for treating visitors hospitably. It must generate incident reports on visitors and floor staff if anything goes wrong.

Illness and hospitalization are anxiety-producing events, and high-quality care strives to minimize the anxiety of both patient and family. The more stressful the event, the more nursing attention to family response is likely to be needed. Terminal illness provides a unique and extreme case, and well-run hospitals are moving systematically to minimize the emotional trauma, guilt, and anxiety associated with the death of relatives. When death is almost certain, this effort frequently centers on the hospice, a blend of home, outpatient, and hospital care designed to make death as emotionally bearable as possible. In less predictable situations, nursing support for the family is as important as nursing support for the patient, for it is the surviving family whose health can be improved.

The key to provision of emotional support to the family is thoughtfully developed protocols which anticipate common problems and provide the staff with solutions. Well-run hospitals are developing protocols for family support in terminal illness and other high-stress events and are incorporating them into in-service education.[5] Such programs include

- Identifying significant personal relationships: evaluating the family structure and recognizing important non-familial relationships
- Identifying family stress: stress-producing medical events and symptoms of stress in family members

- Role of cognitive information in relieving stress
- Specific cognitive requirements for common events
- Professional affect and behavior allaying stress
- Techniques for assisting individuals in stressful situations
- Hospital policies on stress-producing situations, for example: postsurgical notification, terminal care, emergency resuscitation, orders not to resuscitate, and assistance available to family members
- Assistance available to staff
- Dealing with professional guilt and grief.

Prevention and Health Education

Nursing has extensive and important educational responsibilities relating to the consequences of specific diseases and events. It teaches diabetics how to adjust and administer their insulin; heart attack survivors how to regain full activity; hypertensives the importance of their medication; new mothers how to care for and enjoy their babies, how to maintain their own health, and how to avoid unwanted pregnancies; and many other useful programs. If these tasks are well done, future disease is reduced. Under managed care, health care organizations receive direct financial benefits from their successes in this area. Under any insurance, patient, professional, and community satisfaction is improved. Thus expectations for patient education are an essential part of care plans for inpatients and outpatients.

Well-run organizations go beyond the disease-specific teaching in the care plan. They educate the patient about the risk defined by existing disease, sex, age, occupation, and other demographic characteristics. Pursuing the examples above, nursing education might be extended as follows:

- For the diabetic, interaction of diabetes and oral contraceptives, smoking, and use of alcohol
- For the person who has had a heart attack, stress reduction, exercise, and smoking and weight control programs
- For the new mother, child-rearing, immunizations, family relations, avoidance of child abuse, resources available to the family.

All of this is patient-specific education, providing individual patients with information they need at a time when they are most receptive to it. Health care organizations also support general education and counseling to the well population. Programs on smoking cessation, exercise, alcohol abuse, aging, sexuality, and weight control are attractive to the public and may be cost-effective in HMO populations. (Among other virtues, they suggest that self-care is virtuous, cheap, and, if carefully done, effective.) Support groups for stressful events other than disease (divorce, childbirth, job) have become popular following the disease-oriented model (postcolostomy, Alcoholics Anonymous, hemophilia). Nurses can equip themselves professionally to provide educational programs and counseling and to organize and assist support groups.

Environmental Control

Although Florence Nightingale and her followers scrubbed the floors themselves, maintaining a safe and effective institutional or ambulatory environment is now the responsibility of the plant system. Nursing, however, is properly held accountable for reporting any failure of that system and for insisting that it be corrected. The inpatient or outpatient head nurse is responsible to patients, visitors, and staff for general safety, effectiveness, and expected amenities in the floor environment. It is not surprising that nursing is the major source of **incident reports**, written records of untoward events that occur to people as the organization carries out its mission.

In addition to general environmental control, nursing is responsible for clinical aspects of the environment. Certain sites—for example, surgery, premature nursery, and coronary care—have become highly complex. Electronic, mechanical, and chemical environments are created for intensive patient care. They are frequently the responsibility of specially trained and experienced nurse managers. Analogies can be made to quite a different situation, the structured environments of psychiatric care. It is wise to remember that the hospital environment can be a therapy in itself. Hospitalization is occasionally ordered simply to obtain that environment or to escape one that is unsafe or dysfunctional. The head nurse is responsible for maintaining the clinical environment, whatever it might be.

Control of microbial, radiation, and chemical hazards on nursing units is a nursing responsibility. Special techniques for avoiding contamination are part of the clinical procedures of nursing. They often involve other professions and usually require coordinated development. Nursing must enforce these procedures.

Certain addictive drugs, called **controlled substances** or, less formally *narcotics*, are regulated by the federal government. Nursing shares with medicine and pharmacy the reporting and control obligations. Well-run hospitals, recognizing that doctors and nurses have a high risk of addiction, provide preventive and rehabilitative programs.

Protocols and Care Plans—The Nursing Appropriateness Function

Nursing emphasizes the development of an individual care plan based on independent patient assessment, but the plan is increasingly built around disease-specific protocols such as the one shown in Appendix 11A. The nursing care plan documents the needs of each patient and establishes the expectations for nursing procedures and outcomes.[6] The care plan incorporates the discharge plan. It establishes realistic treatment goals and timetables to meet them, ending if possible with the termination of nursing support. The discharge plan is sometimes segregated as a device for coordinating the many professions who must complete their work before the patient can leave. (Even when the discharge planning function is isolated, much of the monitoring and coordinating is assigned to nursing.) The care plan is developed early in the disease episode and is revised as needed. It is more formal in inpatient and long-term outpatient care and is often left unwritten in brief, uncomplicated outpatient encounters. A good care plan strives to do the following:

- Incorporate all care that is cost-effective
- Exclude any care or service which is less than cost-effective
- Anticipate individual variations and prevent complications
- Organize the major events in the hospitalization or disease episode to minimize overall duration
- Identify potential barriers to prompt discharge and plan to investigate and remove them.

Nursing Diagnosis

Each nursing care plan begins with a thorough nursing diagnosis, that is, the identification of actual or potential departures from homeostasis. The nurse evaluates the patient using a paradigm that reflects the scope of personal nursing services (Figure 14.4) and taking into consideration the patient's total set of diseases and disabilities, general physical and emotional condition, and family and social history. Sources of information include observation of the patient, physical examination, patient and family interviews, and the physician's history, physical examination, provisional diagnosis, and diagnostic test and treatment orders. Family views are important, and a description of the patient's home environment is frequently required.

The Plan as Diagnosis Plus Response

The nursing care plan goes beyond the diagnosis to address the correctable departures from homeostasis which have been identified and to prescribe corrections for them. The plan has obvious parallels to the medical patient care plan. It tends to be less specifically related to the disease at hand and more broadly directed to the full needs of the patient. The nursing plan emphasizes physical, emotional, and environmental aspects of treatment as well as disease. Since nursing must deal with side effects and potential complications of treatment, the nurse must be familiar with the medical protocol. If the emotional impact of the disease on patient and family will be severe, the diagnosis should recognize this as an element of comprehensive care and a potential barrier to prompt discharge. Similarly, the plan addresses family and general environmental needs. If the spouse is ill or the apartment has narrow doors, return home may be more difficult.

The nursing plan must be dynamic, tailored as often as necessary to changes in the patient's condition. It must be fully written, because several nurses will be involved in implementing it. Even more than the doctor's protocol, the nursing plan can be significantly aided by computer programs. Models for specific diseases, analogous to the patient group protocols discussed in Chapter 11, can be available on computer as a pattern. Components of the care plan can be assembled from standard nursing intermediate care protocols. Nurses can develop a plan more quickly and with less risk of oversight by modifying a disease model to individual needs. They can control the specific content of several thousand activities by relying on intermediate protocols.

Nursing's Contribution to Economical Care

The nurse's professional skill and judgment contribute substantially to economical care. If the diagnosis is well made and the responses are prompt, much difficulty can be forestalled. The doctor and the nurse ideally collaborate in maintaining or restoring equilibrium, but much of the general observation of the patient is by the nurse. Although the doctor may order any service, a significant amount of care can be given or withheld at the nurse's discretion.

As an illustration, an otherwise well 60-year-old woman with hip joint deterioration will receive a replacement. If all goes well, she will walk that evening and be largely recovered on day seven without further problems. Nursing will avoid the following hazards: circulatory complications from inactivity, respiratory complications from anesthesia, infections at the wound site, imbalances in body chemistry, insecurity and anxiety related to postoperative condition, post discharge complications from poor dietary habits, and drug dependency. Should any of these occur, an expanded course of treatment will be required. The new treatment will introduce new hazards, starting the cycle over. Stay and cost will escalate, and patient satisfaction will deteriorate. Should the patient be older, her systems will be more fragile, and the range of tolerance to nursing error diminishes. If she has an intercurrent disease or complication, nursing needs mount exponentially. Two new groups of hazards must be avoided, one relating to the other disease, the second to interactions between the two. The patient's hip problems create one list; a complication such as diabetes creates a second. Having both creates a third, because surgery profoundly endangers the homeostasis of diabetes.

Coordinating with the Final Product Protocol

The nursing care plan is an extension of the final product protocol. The protocol guides nursing, medicine, and other CSSs towards a common goal such as discharge from the inpatient facility. As final product protocols become more universal, particularly in outpatient care, nursing will be called upon to contribute its skills to protocol design. Nursing care plans will have to be more closely coordinated with the protocols, and nursing will retain the overall monitoring of protocol achievement. Automation will assist in these steps. The inpatient model now only an experimental reality will spread rapidly. An automated protocol, an automated nursing care plan, and automated monitoring will steer most patients on uneventful, minimum cost courses to recovery.

Case Management

Case management is the comprehensive oversight of an individual patient's care from the perspective of long-term cost-effectiveness. It is emerging as an effective device for very complicated patients. It is used primarily with patients at high risk for very expensive care, especially AIDS and trauma patients. Case management begins with a sophisticated care plan, often developed by a multidisciplinary team of caregivers. The plan identifies specific goals, CSS and medical services to meet them, measures of improvement, and timetables. Nurses often manage the cases once the plan has been agreed upon, working to see that the various servers are effectively coordinated.

Case management is also attractive as a way of providing comprehensive but economical long-term care to the aged. The term first arose in experimental HMOs for the aged called social health maintenance organizations (SHMOs). Effective care of the aged must dedicate itself to lengthening and improving biological and emotional life while minimizing lifetime health care expenditures. Although evidence is far from complete, it appears that the best solution is one that guides the patient continuously from late middle age. The case manager maintains a long-term relationship with the patient, one that emphasizes prevention and fitness to the greatest possible extent, treats the deteriorating organ systems thoroughly but economically, provides increasing support as several organ systems begin to fail simultaneously, and arranges the last months of life in response to the patient's own wishes.

Patient and Family Support—The Nursing Amenities and Marketing Function

Nursing's constant contact with patients and their visitors gives it a prime role in amenities and marketing. Nursing's dominance of the satisfaction survey stems from the fact that patients and families see more of nursing than any other CSS and from the supportive design of the nursing role. People expect nursing to be sympathetic and sensitive to human needs. They are vocally grateful when it is, and disappointed when it is not.

Patient care logistics are an important part of both care and amenities. The delivery of drugs, medical supplies, and food usually involves nursing. Drugs for pain relief are frequently prescribed *PRN*, when necessary, at the nurse's discretion. Parenteral fluids present a particularly critical challenge, both to cost and outcome quality. The consequences of error can be life-threatening. Food is important symbolically and emotionally as well as nutritionally. The patient's ability to maintain maximal nutritional status is often important in health education and disease prevention. Nutritional education is done by nurses more often than dietitians.

Nursing has a direct concern with environmental safety for patients and visitors in the institution and in the home. Cleanliness, lighting, state of repair, odors, heating and cooling are part of nursing's concern. Personal safety and security are also part of nursing's general monitoring function. It generally relies on plant services or other CSSs to carry these concerns out in the institutional setting, but it retains responsibility for monitoring both safety and comfort. Nurses are responsible for stopping any unsafe or threatening activity, whether it be caused by an outside agent or an employee or physician.

The amenity and marketing functions are almost automatic in well-managed organizations. They are supported by effective work in plant services and other CSSs, by training for nursing personnel in guest relations, and by executive managers who support the goals of patient and family satisfaction with specific assistance when problems arise and go uncorrected.

Coordinated Care—The Nursing Patient Scheduling Function

Nursing generally coordinates the episode of care, whether it is in an inpatient, outpatient, or home setting. Regardless of the setting, the goal is to organize all elements of care, including nursing care, in the least costly and most patient-satisfactory elapsed time. Patient-related logistics and communications can be grouped into three major functions, initial registration, communication with CSSs, and CSS scheduling and transportation.

Patient Registration

Outpatient registration or inpatient admission is the first clinical contact between the patient and the caregiving team. It establishes the commitment among the doctor, the organization, and the patient, and it is most often made by nursing. Clerical components of the activity are automated. For both inpatients and outpatients, registration originates the medical and financial records and begins patient-related communication. Identification information is obtained, searches are made for record number assignment and existing financial obligation, financial arrangements are established, and appropriate notices and orders are transmitted to interested units of the plant, financial, and clinical systems. Advance scheduling is becoming more common for both inpatient and outpatient care; the predictability is convenient for the patient and aids efficiency and quality for the hospital and the attending doctor. The systems of scheduling used are similar to those described in Chapter 13.

Nursing's goals in the registration process are to meet the patient's emotional, physical, and informational needs as quickly as possible, arrange an orderly plan of treatment, and set the automated communication system in action. In primary care settings the nurse's initial assessment increases the doctor's efficiency by identifying the nature of the complaint, assessing some physical signs, and exploring for factors which may complicate the course of treatment. In the emergency room, nursing evaluation and triage have always been prominent. For inpatients and candidates for major outpatient procedures, several clinical actions occur around the registration or admission. These steps benefit from nursing coordination:

- Important medical orders are now written when the patient is scheduled, before the actual admission. These are transmitted automatically to CSSs, but preparation for preadmission tests often requires patient education by outpatient nursing.

- Patient satisfaction is enhanced by reassurance and explanation early in the care process.

- Discharge planning should begin at or prior to the patient's physical arrival. Some conditions and procedures require prospective review by insurers. Nursing has increasing responsibility for these activities.

- Scheduling of more complex patient care involves a number of choices requiring clinical knowledge. In addition, the location of patients in the hospital affects nurse staffing, quality, and efficiency.

Patient-Related Communication

During the patient's episode of inpatient or outpatient care, it is necessary to maintain a comprehensive, current medical record for the many services participating in diagnosis and treatment. Generally the information must include symptoms and complaints, concurrent disease or complication, working diagnosis, medical orders and nursing plan, of diagnostic orders and results, treatment to date, and the patient's response. The record is increasingly automated. In automated form, it is accessible to all caregivers and is constantly up to date.

The medical records department (Chapter 11) is responsible for the design of the automated medical record as a document, securing the confidentiality of its contents and arranging access among the clinical services. It also manages permanent storage and certain summarizing functions. The attending and house physicians, nursing, and the individual support services are responsible for their own entries into the record.

Under manual record systems, nursing has much more extensive responsibilities Nursing transmits orders to services and receives responses back. The order and response communications are often oral or on temporary papers preceding the final documents. Nursing must secure the confidentiality of the paper record. The significance of nursing's responsibility is often overlooked. In fact, prior to computer assistance, communication of all kinds required about half of the time of inpatient nurses, with patient-related communications consuming the lion's share. Although the process seems simple—order, transmit, respond, file—there are many additional steps. Information from the record frequently must be added to the order. Multiple copies are required for both quality control and billing. Many orders require several steps. Double-checking and error correction multiply the load. Even a simple drug order, "by mouth, four times a day," can trigger a dozen or more communications. The magnitude of the problem is revealed by the numbers. If each patient has ten orders a day and each requires 10 transactions, a 50-patient floor will process 5,000 transactions. Most will be handled by the day shift, at a rate of about one every seven seconds! Similar problems affect scheduling of ambulatory CSSs. There are fewer transactions, but more independent schedules to be coordinated.

Patient Scheduling

Most of the scheduling required to coordinate support service and nursing activity is still done by telephone by clerks. The scheduling must accommodate limitations in the patient's physical condition and competing demands. Most of the services require direct contact with the patient, and many of the services have requirements affecting others, such as being performed before meals or before certain other services. Computerized orders can be scheduled by the computer to improve the efficiency of support service and nursing operation and to minimize the time required of the patient.

The support service departments are rapidly developing their own computerized scheduling systems. Coordination of these into a master schedule for each patient is technically possible and can be expected to emerge piecemeal over the next several years. As it does, nursing's responsibility can shift to active monitoring of the automated process and to more effective preparation for each patient. Substantial reductions in clerical personnel on nursing units appear feasible as the automation of communications and scheduling activities occurs. Quality will be enhanced as oversights and conflicts are eliminated. A reduction in duplicated and spoiled tests and orders can be expected. Prompt fulfillment of scheduled orders also reduces stat requests. Case management can also be improved. The existence of a well-ordered advance schedule, even though it may be only a few hours before the events are to take place, permits prospective review of compliance with the patient group protocol.

Patient Transportation

Nursing is also responsible for the safe transportation of inpatients. Although many outpatients can follow guidance from plant services to reach the various clinical support services, inpatients are frequently impaired by their illness and must be moved by hospital personnel. The task is time-consuming but important to patient satisfaction. Employees who do it are usually unskilled and may be supplied by a unit of plant services (Chapter 15). They should be trained both in guest relations and in handling the medical emergencies which may arise while the patient is in transit.

Staffing—The Nursing Planning and Budgeting Functions

Nursing units like other responsibility centers should prepare long-range plans for major resource requirements and annual budgets covering all six dimensions of effective performance. The process is not different from other CSSs. Because up to 90 percent of nursing costs are labor costs, staffing decisions and personnel scheduling become a critical function in cost control. They are also critical to quality; too few nurses cause the care processes to break down and outcomes to deteriorate. Finally, staffing and scheduling are important in human resources management; nursing personnel appreciate predictable work schedules, choice of time off, and flexible working arrangements that require automated scheduling systems. A three-step staffing, scheduling, and assignment process moves toward progressively shorter time horizons.

1. *Staffing* decisions establish the number of professional, technical, and clerical nursing employees required for each nursing floor or unit. The results of staffing decisions establish scheduling and daily assignment requirements and set the nursing expense budget. Combined with forecasts of patient demand they generate long-range personnel plans.

2. *Scheduling* decisions develop plans for daily availability of personnel and establish the work schedules of individuals over horizons of a few weeks.

3. *Assignment* decisions adjust shift-by-shift variation in personnel requirements of each floor.

Staff Modeling, Planning, and Budgeting

The personnel budget is derived directly from policies implemented in staffing, scheduling, and assignment. Fixed personnel budgets establish expectations for monthly consumption of nursing hours and costs. Flexible budgets use the staffing requirement expectations for each shift and assume that short-term variation in demand will be met by changes in schedule and assignment. Under flexible budgets, some costs vary with census and acuity, although others usually remain fixed.

Well-run organizations now use flexible personnel staffing models for all nursing units. Flexible budgeting must be limited to situations where patient demand varies in a predictable fashion and staffing can actually be adjusted to the changes. (Obstetrics and coronary care are two units in which demand varies but cannot be predicted. Long-term care units often have insignificant variation.) Flexible budgeting for supplies is now routine for all units.

Budgets specify exactly the staff anticipated for each combination of census and acuity. The same computer aids which develop the work assignments generate the forecasts of census and acuity necessary for budgeting. Most computers have simulation features, which allow evaluation of alternative strategies. The labor expense budget is determined almost automatically once the staffing pattern and the forecasts of demand are selected.

Staffing decisions must set both number and kind of staff. Inpatient units particularly operate with several different skill levels (baccalaureate, registered, and practical nurses, nurse aides, and clerks). If the numbers of staff are increased, or the balance is shifted toward higher skill levels, costs will mount. The objective is to find the minimum cost consistent with acceptable levels of quality and patient satisfaction.

Conceptually, a well-designed staffing plan is based upon expectations of what tasks nursing will perform, how frequently these will occur, what indications support them, and what outcomes in quality, efficiency, and economy are anticipated. For example, the following kinds of measures are directly influenced by the staffing decision.

1. Process achievements:
   • Content of nursing care plan
   • Frequency of recurring nursing tasks
   • Frequency of physician order tasks
   • Indications for patient-related tasks
   • Patient education
   • Allowance for inservice education
   • Other measures of quality.
2. Outcomes achievements:
   • Length of stay
   • Readmission rates
   • Patient satisfaction
   • Physician satisfaction.
3. Economy achievements:
   • Nursing cost per patient day
   • Nursing cost per patient admitted.

Decisions about the nurses needed for outpatient care are easy to comprehend and can serve as a model for the vastly more complicated inpatient staffing decisions. For example, a small clinic is staffed Monday through Friday for five identical day shifts with two classes of personnel, licensed practical nurse (LPN) and clerk, a level historically sufficient to provide satisfactory service. This decision sets the budget and establishes the scheduling which must occur. If the staffing is upgraded to one registered nurse (RN) and a clerk, one would expect greater nursing responsibilities and more procedures, such as an increase in patient education. The RN may be able to do telephone triage during and even after clinic hours. His or her telephone conversations will prevent unnecessary office visits, reassure patients, and improve overall care. One would expect the clinic to attract more patients, or to care for them with less hospitalization, or to be more satisfactory to patients and doctors, or in some way to show a measurable improvement for the increased cost.

Inpatient nurse staffing decisions are made for each floor and shift. They establish the number and mix of personnel required for the range of acuity and census that the floor is expected to encounter. Patient requirements are radically different in long-term care, intensive care, the emergency room, and the recovery room. They are also different on different shifts. During a typical year acuity and census on a single unit can vary over a range of 100 percent or more. Staffing decisions are not simple. The process of making them determines the organization within the work group and its capability for undertaking professional responsibilities.

Various team arrangements are now common for most inpatient settings. Team approaches are aimed at reducing costs by substituting less skilled personnel under the supervision of professional nurses.[7] Using either team or primary models, staffing decisions should be developed by nursing management based on careful forecasts of need combined with specific outcomes and process expectations. The staffing problem is an integer problem. It is often impractical to change in increments smaller than eight hours, or one full shift. Thus the desired staff for a nursing unit and shift is usually expressed in a table, such as Figure 14.5. The table keeps staffing between 3.9 and 4.0 hours per patient, and between 40 and 45 percent RN level or better. Shading shows the changes as census varies. Staffing for odd-numbered censuses is the same as preceding even numbers; hours per patient day drops to about 3.9. Given weekends, holidays, and random fluctuation, a typical inpatient unit can be expected to vary over at least this large a range over a year. (The weighting of the census is discussed below.)

The labor budget for the unit is simply the staffing pattern for the average weighted census. The long-range personnel needs can be forecast from a longer-range forecast of the average weighted census.

Figure 14.5 Example of Nurse Staffing Model for Inpatient Floor*

Weighted Patient Census	Head Nurse	BSN Team Leader	RN	LPN	Aide	Clerk	Total Hours	Hours/ Weighted Census	Percent RN
40	8	32	32	16	56	16	160	4.00	45
42	8	32	32	16	64	16	168	4.00	43
44	8	32	32	24	64	16	176	4.00	41
46	8	32	40	24	64	16	184	4.00	43
48	8	32	40	24	64	24	192	4.00	42
50	8	40	40	24	64	24	200	4.00	44
52	8	40	40	24	72	24	208	4.00	42
54	8	40	40	32	72	24	216	4.00	41
56	8	40	48	32	72	24	224	4.00	43
58	8	40	48	40	72	24	232	4.00	41
60	8	40	48	40	80	24	240	4.00	40

*Day shift. Assumes 8 hour increments. Highlights show changes in numbers of personnel by category.

Evaluating Individual Patient Need

The demand for nursing care is a function of two elements, the census, or number of patients, and how sick they are. Sicker patients require more nursing care. There are two approaches to weighting. Acuity is based on an assessment of the patient's condition, which takes into account current acuity and potential complications. Care planning draws upon the time required for individual elements of the care plan. Under either approach, patient needs are expressed as a percent of a standard patient. A patient with twice average needs would count as two standard patients in a weighted census.

Acuity approaches use binary or simple ordinal scales indicating departure from normal function in several physiological and psychological factors known to influence nursing time.[8] Items include therapeutic and diagnostic needs as well as those involving eating, dressing, and elimination; the emotional state; and the amount of observation ordered by the doctor. Scales are now tailored to the clinical area. A patient with a high score requires increased nursing care. Representative acuity variations for obstetrical labor and delivery care are shown in Figure

14.6. When such scales are used, values for each patient are reported by the head nurse. Computerized systems calculate acuity, assign staffing requirements to individual patients, and add up the nursing personnel required on each floor.

Care planning approaches use standard times for care plan elements. As the nurse prepares the patient's care plan in an automated system, the time required for each element is added to the total for the patient. Allowances are made for general care not specified in the plan, and the result is an estimate of the actual time nursing personnel will spend with each patient. It is possible to adjust the calculation to skill level as well. The sum of these hours for the floor can be used directly to generate staffing requirements, or translated to a weighted census value for use in a staffing table like Figure 14.5 by dividing the sum of the hours by the hours required of the standard patient.

The subjective nature of the patient evaluation is an important limitation of weighting schemes. Although acuity assessment is relatively inexpensive, requiring only a few minutes of time per patient, it depends

Figure 14.6 Patient Acuity Variation

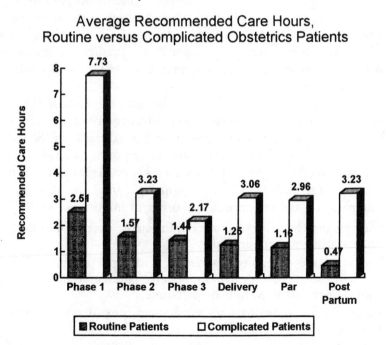

Average Recommended Care Hours, Routine versus Complicated Obstetrics Patients

on human memory, which is fallible and can be distorted by bias. Similarly, the nursing care plan is by definition a subjective evaluation. Elements can be added by the nurse, and each element is likely to produce some gain for the patient. The question of how much the patient and the payment system can afford is far removed from the point of decision. Scores tend to creep upward in an unmonitored system, inflating the nursing staff requirement. Identification and correction of creep is possible, but at added system cost. Audits can control creep. Well-designed computer systems routinely test the means and variances of weighting scores for statistical trend. In addition, protocols represent consensus on appropriateness. While they do not narrow the range of nurse discretion, they do identify the discretionary decisions more clearly.

Scheduling

The staffing plan must be translated to work schedules for specific employees. This step requires a short-range (usually four to eight weeks) forecast of weighted census. For purely stochastic units like obstetrics and coronary care, each shift must be scheduled for the average conditions. On other floors less staff is generally needed on weekends, and needs are often reduced later in the work week. Although most nurses work the traditional 40-hour week, 12-hour shifts are sometimes used instead of 8-hour shifts. Some personnel are part-time, working less than the full number of shifts per week. Predictable absenteeism, holidays, and non-patient care assignments must be accommodated in the schedule.

Nurses must fit their work schedules into the rest of their lives. Predictable schedules or several weeks' advance notice of changes are desired, but nurses also want to request special days off. Scheduling systems which help them do this are an important recruitment and retention device.[9] Computer-aided systems now meet most scheduling and assignment needs.[10] A well-designed program has the following characteristics, listed in approximate order of importance.[11]

- Staffing matches the forecast requirement; overstaffing and understaffing are minimized.
- Personnel are scheduled consistent with their designated specialization, professional competence, and agreed-upon work commitment (that is, full- or part-time).
- Schedules for individuals are maintained four or more weeks in advance.
- Schedules minimize unnecessary transfers between units and shifts.

- Weekends, late shifts, and other less desirable assignments are equitably distributed. ("Equitably" is usually not "equally"; one nurse's preferences are not the same as another's.)
- Personal requests for specific days off are accommodated equally, so long as they are submitted in advance, can be met within cost and quality constraints, and do not exploit other workers.

Assignment

Assignment adjusts staffing on each floor and shift to the best available estimate of immediate need. Given both that the number and acuity of patients can vary, and that staff absenteeism is unpredictable, a given floor and shift will usually be over or under the level provided by the scheduling model. Assignment accommodates this variation by changing the number of personnel on a given floor or unit, or in some cases, by changing the number of patients on a floor or unit.

It is important to note that problems of variability of staff and reliability of measurement are greatly reduced by aggregating individual values by unit. Although individual patients vary three- or fourfold, aggregates of 30 or more patients vary only 20 percent as much, and aggregates of 60 patients only 12 per cent as much. If patient need averages 4 hours per shift and ranges from 1 to 12 hours, a 30-patient aggregate will range only between 2.5 and 3.5 hours per patient. It will be staffed with 15 people, and the range will be plus or minus 3 people. A similar 60-patient aggregate will have 30 people and range less than 4 people. Staff absenteeism will add to this requirement, in both cases.

It is also true that some variation can be handled by the ability of the nursing staff on the floor to work harder. It is clearly understood that workers can sustain peak outputs up to 40 percent higher than the average demand.[12] If the work can be deferred for an hour or two, a fixed staff can expand its output to meet the need. Only emergencies and work which must be done in a constrained period of time actually require extra personnel. Thus larger units significantly reduce the need for assignment changes. They have a lower overall variation and more personnel to reassign internally to meet emergencies.

Using the law of large numbers and the flexibility of workers further reduces the need to assign staff. Staffing flexibility is usually obtained by

- Developing float pools of nurses trained to work at several different locations. Float pool nurses are often given extra compensation recognizing their flexibility.
- Using call-in and agency personnel when needed.

- Assigning overtime to available workers.
- Transferring workers between floors.

Census adjustment is more complex. It combines the patient-scheduling system and the nursing-staffing system to reduce variation in weighted census. Although its greatest application is in outpatient unit management, it offers several possibilities. The patient scheduling system can stabilize both the number and individual needs of the incoming patients. Outpatient visits are usually scheduled as separate events. Inpatient units typically turnover about one-third of their census each day.

- The counts and needs of incoming patients can be coordinated to the staffing level, so that variation in demand is reduced to unpredictable, or stochastic changes.
- Units can be designated for specific ranges of need. For example, the scheduling system assigns the sickest arriving inpatients to intensive care units. This reduces variation on routine care floors, although ICUs themselves are subject to widely fluctuating need for staff.
- In organizations with several similar treatment units, incoming patients can be placed when they arrive to units with surplus staff.

In general the fewer changes at the assignment level, the more efficient the system and the higher the quality is likely to be. The more effective the staffing, personnel scheduling, and patient scheduling, the narrower the range of differences and the less adjustment by assignment. Commercial software offers assignment, acuity, and quality assessment; simulation for budgeting; and basic personnel records in a single package.[13]

The use of float pools, call-ins, and transfers is necessary, but it should be minimized. Float pools are difficult to sustain and generally increase costs. Call-ins from outside pools of temporary employees or agency personnel brought in on contract are even more expensive. At best, the training of agency personnel is outside the hospital's control, and the individuals are less efficient because they are not familiar with their work environment. Transfer of personnel from one location to another within the hospital presents similar difficulties. Most nurses do not like to be transferred, and the problems of cross-training and unfamiliar work stations remain. Quality deteriorates as a result.

Well-run health care organizations now have computer support for staffing, scheduling, census weighting, and assignment. The same software frequently supports quality assessment as well. Combining the software with well-developed nursing procedures, formal nursing care plans and protocols, flexible personnel budgeting, and patient scheduling, they are in a position to specify improvements in cost and quality measures which might result from changes in staffing.[14,15]

Observation—The Nursing Continuous Improvement Function

Nursing's central and nearly continuous contact with the patient places it in a unique informational situation. It has the opportunity to make the most comprehensive assessment of patient needs and progress. It is in the best position to identify oversights, omissions, and failures. It can use this information to monitor not only its own performance, but also that of physicians, CSSs, and plant services, and to identify improvement opportunities for other units as well as its own. In effect, nursing contributes a built-in audit of the medical care process, a focal point for coordinating the final product, and a stimulus for improving its own processes and those of others.[16] A significant part of nursing resources goes to supporting continuous improvement in its own activities and those of other CSSs. Some of these resources are being withdrawn from earlier and less comprehensive monitoring activities, such as utilization review.

Auditing the Medical Care Process

Nursing is the only truly continuous inpatient service. Given that nurses are also frequently in intimate contact with the patient, they are ideally placed to observe and communicate the patient's condition, needs, and response to previous actions. The inpatient nurse is responsible for the following kinds of information.

- Reporting clinical observations to the attending physician and house officers
- Understanding and reporting family-related factors of clinical importance
- Recording drug administration and nursing treatments
- Receiving, coordinating, and transmitting orders for clinical support services
- Preparing patients or specimens for support services
- Knowing patients' locations and receiving them back from support services
- Receiving and transmitting results of reports from support services
- Preparing and forwarding incident reports for any untoward events
- Maintaining the paper medical record
- Recording and storing patients' possessions
- Assisting visitors to the floor.

The outpatient nurse has a similar list. Only details of scheduling, transportation, and reporting, and some elements of family contact differ because of the site of care. Completing this list of information generates nursing's unique perspective on the patient.

Nurses use the information to identify omitted, inconsistent, and incorrect actions, and actions which had unexpected results. They actively monitor the course of care. Although this puts them in a position of criticizing other professionals, they have learned to do this diplomatically and effectively.[17] Nurses catch omitted orders, wrong orders, lost orders, conflicting orders, delayed reports, unexpected reports, lost reports, and unsatisfactory treatments for medicine and most CSSs on a daily basis. They remind, persuade, cajole, and convince others to correct these problems quickly so that they do not escalate. Only rarely do they draw anger or resistance to their efforts.

From a management perspective, two things are important about this ongoing audit. The first is that it is essential to any high-quality system of care, and therefore must be actively supported by management. When nursing cannot get the response it needs from another service, management must investigate and correct. The problem may lie with nursing, with the other service, or both, and the change may involve anything from a revised ordering system to new equipment and processes to a more diplomatic alert. In any case, the cause of any serious failure in this mechanism needs to be identified and fixed. If this system breaks down, quality, cost, and satisfaction will deteriorate rapidly. If it has broken down, the culture of the institution is in a dysfunctional state, and immediate, extensive efforts are required to fix it.

The second issue important to management is that much of this communication represents "rework," the unproductive repetition of something that could and should have gone right the first time. The higher the volume of audit alerts from nursing, the more things have gone wrong and the more resources from nursing or another service will be consumed fixing them. The ideal is that nursing rarely or never detects a failure or omission. Things are so well done the first time that the monitor does not generate alerts, or generates them only rarely, with very complex and unusual cases. The key to the ideal, of course, is well-designed processes.

Improving Intermediate Product Protocols

Nursing is responsible for the continuous improvement of its own care plans and protocols. It is so central to most complex care that it is, a major contributor to final product protocols. Its central position gets it involved with many CSS intermediate protocols.

Nursing has a large number of internal processes and procedures, intermediate care protocols of its own. Leading institutions are computerizing these, allowing nurses the opportunity to recover the procedures quickly and follow written instructions rather than memory. The list of desired procedures can constitute the nursing plan for the patient. Time standards can be attached to these procedures, and totals of planned procedures can be used in place of acuity based estimates to develop staffing needs and cost estimates.[18] It will become important to evaluate the costs and outcomes of the individual procedures. Improvement priorities will be directed to the most numerous and expensive procedures. The improvement questions are, Can this procedure be eliminated? and Can this procedure be done better? The answers to both include evaluation of the cost and outcomes.

Contributing to Final Product and Other Protocols

It is probably impossible to write a final product protocol without active participation by nursing. Nurse specialists have a particular role here, since their specialization makes them expert on particular diseases and conditions.[19] As Figure 14.7 shows, nursing can suggest existing problems (Plan), ways to solve them (Do), and experiments to check new protocols and their comments (Check). Nursing will inevitably implement much of the plan, and monitor implementation of the rest (Act).[20]

Similarly, nursing often has a role in the intermediate products of other CSSs. It should be readily available to consult on new protocol design. Management must see that appropriate consultation occurs and is constructive. Since the interface often involves transfers of responsibility from one unit to another, mediation and consensus building are important.

Quality Assurance and Quality Improvement

Some current functions of nursing are less comprehensive and unfortunately less constructive ways of improving the quality and cost-effectiveness of care. One is utilization review, where nursing verifies the appropriateness of admissions and checks inpatients' progress against expected discharge dates. The negative features of utilization review are serious, and it is unlikely to make a large, permanent improvement in either quality or utilization. It is being replaced by final product protocols. These differ from utilization review in two major ways. First, they are agreements in advance about what must be done, rather than the imposition of an external standard on what has already been done. Second, they deliberately address processes and methods,

Figure 14.7 Nursing Roles in the PDCA Cycle for Final Product Protocols

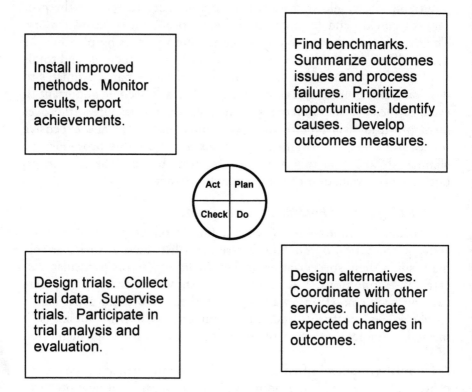

laying out a plan which promotes the right actions, rather than a monitor function which detects allegedly wrong ones.

A more positive and more comprehensive activity with a similar goal is **discharge planning.** Discharge planning, a natural part of the nursing care plan, identifies the expected discharge date at or before admission and coordinates the various services necessary to achieve the target. It is conceptually close to case management but is limited to the hospital episode and lacks the long-term continuing relationship with the patient.

Both of these functions are on their way out. The first is being replaced by protocols. The second is being incorporated in protocols and nursing care plans.

Recruiting and Retaining—The Nursing Human Resources Function

Human contact is the central element of all nursing, and the recruitment, retention, training and motivation of nursing personnel are critical functions. Nursing human resources management is not different from other CSSs; the activities outlined in Chapter 13 apply. There is periodic national concern about shortages of professional nurses.

There is an important need to recruit and retain nurses, particularly the staff RNs who provide most acute inpatient care. A hospital with a patient census of 300 employs about 250 full-time-equivalent staff nurses. Since many of these posts will be filled by part-time personnel, over 300 individual nurses will be employed. The staff nurse job is both physically and emotionally demanding. It tends to be filled by young people who are highly mobile. Compensation is now comparable with similar professional opportunities, such as teaching and pharmacy, although neither of those jobs combines the hours, physical demands, and critical responsibilities of a staff nurse. It is not surprising that staff nurse turnover is high, frequently in excess of 50 percent per year.

Well-managed organizations do not have difficulty recruiting sufficient nursing personnel.[21] They attract new people and retain old ones because they are desirable places to work. An effective nursing culture attracts and keeps qualified personnel, but there appear to be several elements in the culture.[22,23,24,25] They begin with a deliberate effort to reduce turnover and increase work satisfaction.[26,27] Retention is generally cheaper than recruitment. More important, the satisfaction of current staff is quickly sensed by potential recruits, and a reputation as a good place to work is a powerful asset. Most important, there is evidence that nurse satisfaction is related to outcomes measures of patient care quality.[28] Well-run organizations strive for a recruitment and retention advantage over their competition by repeated attention to the following concepts:

Planning

- Human resources planning tracks trends in patient care, translates these to the several levels of nursing skill, accommodates terminations, and identifies recruitment needs well in advance.
- Promotions ladders provide opportunity for advancement. Subsidies are often offered for formal education, and inservice education is available to cross-train personnel.
- Advertising is used to assure recruitment of sufficient personnel. Special efforts are made for undesirable shifts and assignments.
- Job security is used to increase loyalty. Turnover, voluntary retirement, and part-time personnel are used to reduce the work force when necessary.

Operations

- Clarity of roles, procedures, and expectations is used to reduce job stress.

- Effective supervision provides prompt, reasonable response to job-related questions and maintains motivation.[29,30,31]
- Comprehensive, effective nursing care plans and protocols increase the staff nurse's contribution to patient care and make the contribution more visible. Inservice education, floor leadership, and quality monitoring provide skills and guidance to develop and implement a sound care plan.
- Scheduling systems make the work assignments attractive. Hours, scheduling, and work policies designed more for the staff nurse's personal convenience offer a relatively simple, easily promoted attraction.

Compensation

- Base wages and salaries are kept competitive.[32]
- Intangible rewards, chiefly praise and public recognition, reinforce self-respect and collegial recognition of professional achievement.
- Tangible rewards can be used to encourage improved job performance and to undertake less desirable assignments.

The underlying philosophy of this list is that good nursing is its own reward and that the job of nursing management is to provide opportunities to do good nursing. The functions described in the preceding sections, and the systems which implement them efficiently and effectively, are the tools for the job.

Personnel and Organization

Nursing as a profession and as a unit of health care organizations is almost as diverse as medicine. As Figures 14.1 and 14.2 show, the profession contains within it careers reaching from high-tech in the operating room and ICU to high-touch in the home, and include general and public health services that do not involve individual patient care. In addition, there are significant numbers of managerial jobs. The patterns of training and the modes of nursing organization reflect this diversity.

Educational Levels of Nursing Personnel

Formal educational opportunities in nursing, as in most other professions in the United States, have increased since World War II. Unique among the professions, nursing has retained all of its original levels, rather than simply adding years to the training requirement. There are now three professional and four nonprofessional educational levels (Figure 14.8).

Figure 14.8 Educational Levels of Nursing Personnel

Name	Degree or Certificate	Education Required
Nonprofessional Levels		
Nursing aide	None	Only hospital inservice training is required
Licensed practical nursing	LPN	One-year junior college program also called "Licensed Vocational Nurse"
Diploma in nursing	RN	Hospital-based program of three years post-high school, qualifying for RN but not the baccalaureate degree
Associate in nursing	RN, AAN	Junior college-based program of two years qualifying for RN and associate degree. The degree is accepted as partial fulfillment of the baccalaureate
Professional Levels		
Baccalaureate nursing degree	BSN	Four years beyond high school in an accredited college or university are required
Nurse anesthetist	BSN, CNA	One year after the baccalaureate degree is required
Nurse practitioner	BSN, CNP	At least one year after the baccalaureate degree is required
Nurse midwife	BSN, CNM	Less than one year post-baccalaureate
Clinical specialist	MSN	One or two years post-baccalaureate study Fields parallel the major specialties of medicine
Public health nurse	MPH	Two years post-baccalaureate study
Nurse manager	MSN	Two years post-baccalaureate study
Doctor of nursing	PhD	Four or more years post-baccalaureate study

Several attempts to rationalize this structure have led to a career ladder which accommodates repeated return to formal education, via LPN, associate's, bachelor's, master's, and doctoral degrees.[33] The growth of junior colleges has made this career ladder more accessible. Almost all hospitals have abandoned diploma programs in favor of participation in associate and baccalaureate programs. Certification has not kept pace with these developments. Registration, the traditional recognition of professional nursing qualification, is available with as little as two years' study after high school. Well-run health care organizations are specifying BSN degrees for many assignments such as intensive care, team leaders, supervision, and primary nursing. Practical experience as a substitute for formal requirements can be judged on an individual basis.

Trends in Nurse Supply and Recruitment

The number of nurses and the number of students entering RN and BSN programs are both at or near all-time highs.[34] Reports of shortages were widespread in major cities in 1986 and 1987, as they have been periodically for several decades. Despite the recurring public concern about nursing shortages, there has rarely been hard evidence to support the existence of a widespread general shortage. In such a situation, normal markets respond by a rapid increase in wages. Such a response had never been demonstrated for nurses relative to other health care professions, leading economists conclude that alleged shortages were temporary or local phenomena.[35] The 1986–1987 shortage led to widespread increases in nursing compensation, and was probably the first real shortage.

Nursing Organization

Nursing tends to follow a consistent accountability hierarchy in its many sites and specialties. A team led by a staff nurse (sometimes called a primary nurse), constitutes an informal work unit below the responsibility center. The team structure is quite flexible, varying in size and skill levels depending on patient needs, as shown in Figure 14.9. Several geographically adjacent teams comprise a floor or clinic, the usual designation for a responsibility center. The responsibility center manager is usually called head nurse. The hierarchy beyond the responsibility center usually follows clinical specialty lines. Figure 14.10A, shows a medium-sized hospital.

Versions of specialty hierarchies fit most inpatient floors and outpatient units and can be modified to fit home care and nurse-managed CSSs such as operating rooms, delivery rooms, and recovery rooms. Specific policies, procedures, and skills differentiate the various services. Clearly, the procedures for operating rooms are very different from those for outpatient psychiatry, but the structure of teams and accountability hierarchy is the same. The staff nurse for chronic care is usually an LPN; for acute units, an RN or BSN; and for intensive care,

Figure 14.9 Nurse Team Organization

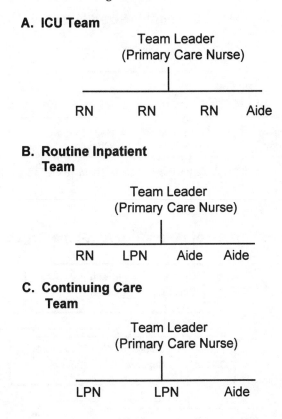

A. ICU Team

Team Leader
(Primary Care Nurse)

RN   RN   RN   Aide

B. Routine Inpatient Team

Team Leader
(Primary Care Nurse)

RN   LPN   Aide   Aide

C. Continuing Care Team

Team Leader
(Primary Care Nurse)

LPN   LPN   Aide

a BSN or MSN. The skill required for outpatient care depends upon the role and can be LPN, RN, BSN, or certified nurse practitioner.

Nurses from all levels are drawn to cross-functional teams to develop final product protocols, work on nursing intermediate protocols, and consult with other CSSs. Matrix structures emerge from close alliance between the nursing and medical organizations. These identify dual accountabilities, and use the matrix and cross-functional teams to gain continuous improvement. Matrices can in turn evolve to product line groups sometimes called triads including a line management person responsible for marketing and logistics.[36] An example tracing just one line of accountability from birthing services to women's services to the executive management team, is shown in Figure 14.10B.

Measures and Information Systems

The growth of automated support for patient scheduling, medical records, care plans and protocols, nurse scheduling, quality assessment,

Figure 14.10 Nursing Accountability Hierarchies

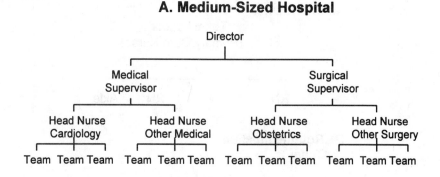

A. Medium-Sized Hospital

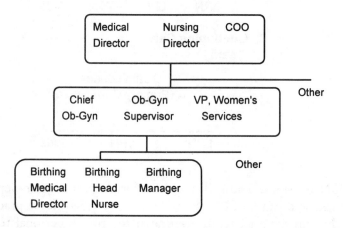

B. Portion of Matrix/Product-Line Organization

and detailed cost accounting has provided a platform for major advances in quality and cost-effectiveness for nursing. It is possible to measure much of what was only conceptual a few years ago, and to use the measures in the routine solution of nursing problems. Both measurement advances and processing advantages have contributed to this development. The discussion which follows summarizes the measures by the usual six dimensions: demand, cost, human resources, output and efficiency, quality, and contribution. Nursing's major data-processing systems are described in terms of their applications.

Measures

Nursing now has a rich opportunity to measure its resource investments, its activities, and its contributions to the steady improvement of hospital performance.[37] The typical responsibility center can set and achieve expectations on all six dimensions. Examples are shown in Figure 14.11. Budgeting sessions for nursing can now easily address the following set of measures at the process level.

- Demand measures such as the average and the variation in demand, delays for scheduled and urgent service, and counts of cancellations or disruptions in the scheduling process. Expectations are set through, and achieved by, patient-scheduling systems.

- Costs by functional account (that is, labor, supplies, and facilities) for both the total dollars per accounting period and, under flexible budgeting, the costs per unit of nursing output. Well-managed nursing units, supported by the full array of computer aids, now find the achievement of cost expectations routine. Summary levels of performance are monitored, and modern payroll, materials management, accounts receivable, and general ledger systems permit the exploration of any level of detail necessary.

- Human resources are routinely monitored through absenteeism and turnover data, and satisfaction surveys. Staffing, scheduling, and assignment systems monitor overtime, understaffed situations, and shift assignments.

- Nursing output is measured in terms of patients treated. Automated systems allow classification by disease or condition and weighting for patient need in both inpatient and outpatient settings. These support precise, stable estimates of efficiency measures such as costs or hours per case, per visit, or per day of care.

- Final product costs are aggregated from unit costs of nursing functions. Functions are recorded by automated patient care plans, protocols, and order entry systems. While precise unit costing remains difficult (Chapter 8), cost estimates for nursing interim products and components of final products are increasingly reliable.

- Outcomes quality is assessed by condition-specific achievement rates such as recovery of mobility and activities of daily living and failure rates, such as infections, or bed sores.

- Patient satisfaction is assessed by survey. Continuous surveying permits monitoring by small nursing units. Questions can address components of satisfaction, such as personal care, reassurance, and patient education.

- Physician satisfaction with nursing is assessed as part of formal surveys of the attending and house staffs. Informal and subjective evaluation of performance is also useful. It should occur at all levels of the accountability hierarchy. Evaluations of nursing supervisors include review of relations with physicians.

Figure 14.11 Nursing Performance Measures

Dimension	Inpatient Examples	Outpatient Examples (Home Care Program)	General Nursing Examples
Demand	Number and acuity of patients, pct. emergencies	Scheduled home visits, delay for visit	Enrollment in programs pct. eligibles attracted
Costs	Labor hours, by pers. class medical supplies	Payroll costs, home supplies, travel costs	Faculty cost, facility cost, promotional cost
Human resources	Satisfaction, turnover vacancies	Satisfaction, turnover vacancies	Satisfaction, turnover vacancies
Output/ productivity	Discharges, cost/discharge, cost/ member month	Visits, visits/patient, patients/visiting nurse, costs/patient month	Number of presentations, attendance, cost/member
Outcomes quality	Return to work, recovery of function, Infections	Daily living scores, hospitalizations, transfers to long-term care	Percentage members smoking, percentage seeking prenatal care, child trauma
Process quality	Percentage complete care plans, medication errors, percentage presurgery pt. education	Percentage visits late or missed, errors in equipment, supplies	Member awareness, curriculum evaluation, facility evaluation
Patient satisfaction	Percentage "very satisfied," number of complaints	Percentage "very satisfied, family satisfaction	Audience evaluation, member satisfaction
Physician satisfaction	Percentage of referring physicians and attending physicians "very satisfied," complaints	Percentage of referring physicians "very satisfied," complaints	Physician awareness, satisfaction, complaints
Contribution	Cost and cost/case limits	Cost/member month limits	Cost/member month limits

- General failure rates, such as incidence reports and nosocomial infections are routinely measured in most settings. The data are used by organizationwide risk management programs and infections control committees.
- Process quality is routinely assessed through inspection of both patients and nursing records. Reliability has been improved by using specific questions to guide the inspection and by developing numerous questions to cover the range of patient needs. Cost and time requirements have been reduced by automation of question selection, sampling procedures, tallying, and analysis.
- Structural measures of quality such as hours per weighted output and percentage of hours by professional personnel are available from staffing and scheduling systems. Occurrences of values below preset minima are the most sensitive indicators. The JCAHO lists a number of other structural standards designed to encourage good nursing practice.[38]
- Contribution or margin remains a difficult concept for nursing. Efforts to establish marketable units of service, such as professional fees for nursing or specific facility charges have run counter to the market trend for more aggregate pricing. Most contribution margins are set on an allowable cost basis. Leading organizations are using both functional cost limits and final product cost limits.[39] Benchmarking remains difficult in many nursing RCs, but is feasible in others.[40]

The rich measurement set depends heavily on information systems. As the systems are installed, obvious avenues of improvement appear and are explored. These are initially at the level of a single process. Integrated and final product opportunities appear later. The process of identifying and addressing these opportunities appears to take several years in most organizations. The best organizations are only now reaching the conclusion of this phase. A third, more rewarding, and more challenging phase is now beginning, where medicine, nursing, and other CSSs collaborate toward a goal of cost-effective care.

Information Systems

Nursing now requires a set of automated systems interlocking with those required elsewhere in the hospital, as discussed in Chapter 10. A summary list may be helpful here.

Patient information systems

- Patient registration (also called admission, discharge, and transfer) records basic registration information, assigns identification number, identifies hospital location of patient, communicates arrival and initial orders, and initiates both patient ledger and patient order file.

- Medical information (also called order entry and results reporting) records physician's and nurse's orders and care plans, transmits orders to support services, receives reports back from support services, supports the patient ledger and prompts recurring nursing tasks. More advanced systems permit tailoring of individual care plans from a patient group protocol and will record nursing progress notes.

- Patient scheduling records classification of demand (usually emergency, urgent, or scheduled) and scheduled future date, if any. Support service scheduling records future support services, resolves conflicts in preparation and transportation needs, and shows availability of service. Advanced systems establish current and future availability of admission opportunities and prompt call in from the urgent list. (Chapter 13)

Managerial support systems

- General accounting and budgeting supports flexible budgeting and cost reporting by physical and dollar units.

- Final product analysis groups clinically similar patient data for cost, quality, and satisfaction according to any of several dimensions such as responsibility center, physician, payment category.

- General patient satisfaction surveys include specific questions on kinds of nursing service and are maintained at frequency that allow analysis at the RC or work group level.

- Physician satisfaction surveys include questions that allow evaluation at the RC or work group level.

- Personnel satisfaction surveys provide evidence of nursing employee morale at RC and job classification.

Nursing management systems

- Staffing and scheduling algorithms support long-range nursing needs, budgets, work schedules, and assignment. They generate structural measures of staffing. Advanced models accept work preferences and special requests.

- Nursing personnel record keeping includes special training and assignment capabilities, work preferences, evaluations, and other data on individual employees.[41]

- Nursing procedure descriptions are instantly accessible, automatically updated nursing procedures. They replace the paper procedural manual and can be used to weight census, construct care plans, and support staffing models.

- Acuity assessment and assignment accepts tallies of patient acuity by floor and shift, and records time series data on acuity scores to provide statistical quality controls to detect significant change in recorded acuity.

- Process quality assessment identifies samples of patients and questions, prints survey questionnaires, accepts responses, and tallies quality scores following preset rules.

Well-managed health care organizations are moving rapidly on this list, and have at least elementary systems in place for most of the list.

Suggested Readings

Charns, M. P., and L. J. S. Tewksbury. 1993. *Collaborative Management in Health Care: Implementing the Integrative Organization*. San Francisco: Jossey-Bass.

Institute of Medicine. 1983. *Nursing and Nursing Education: Public Policies and Private Actions*. Washington, DC: National Academy Press.

Marriner-Tomey, A. 1992. *Guide to Nursing Management*, 4th ed. St. Louis, MO: Mosby-Year Book.

McClure, M., M. Poulin, and M. Sovie. 1982. *Magnet Hospitals: Attraction and Retention of Professional Nurses*. Kansas City, MO: American Nurses Association.

National Commission on Nursing. 1983. *Summary Report and Recommendations* and *Nursing in Transition: Models of Successful Organizational Change*. Chicago: Hospital Research and Educational Trust.

Schroeder, P., ed. 1994. *Improving Quality and Peformance: Concepts, Programs, and Techniques*. St. Louis, MO: Mosby.

Sullivan, E. J., and P. J. Decker, eds. 1992. *Effective Management in Nursing*, 3d ed. Redwood City, CA: Addison-Wesley Nursing.

Notes

1. F. Nightingale, quoted in V. Henderson, 1966, *The Nature of Nursing* (New York: MacMillan), 1.

2. V. Henderson, and G. Nite, 1978, *Principles and Practice of Nursing*, 6th ed. (New York: MacMillan), 1–25.

3. U.S. Department of Health and Human Services, 1990, *The Registered Nurse Population: Findings from the National Sample Survey of Registered Nurses, March 1988* (Hyattsville, MD: Health Resources and Services Administration), 14.

4. V. J. Numinen, D. L. Haas, L. Yaroch, and P. Fralick, 1992, "Building Community-Based Service Systems for Children with Special Needs: The Michigan Locally Based Services Program," *Issues in Comprehensive Pediatric Nursing* 15 (January–March): 17–37.

5. M. M. Seltzer, L. C. Litchfield, L. R. Kapust, J. B. Mayer, 1992, "Professional and Family Collaboration in Case Management: A Hospital-Based Replication of a Community-Based Study," *Social Work in Health Care* 17 (1): 1–22.

6. P. Hanisch, S. Honan, and R. Torkelson, 1993, "Quality Improvement Approach to Nursing Care Planning: Implementing Practical Computerized Standards," *Journal for Healthcare Quality* 15 (September–October): 6–13.

7. F. C. Munson, J. S. Beckman, J. Clinton, C. Kever, and L. Simms, 1980, *Nursing Assignment Patterns, User's Manual* (Ann Arbor, MI: Health Administration Press.

8. C. Y. Phillips, A. Castorr, P. A. Prescott, and K. Soeken, 1992, "Nursing Intensity: Going beyond Patient Classification," *Journal of Nursing Administration* 22 (April): 46–52.

9. J. J. Gray, D. McIntire, and H. J. Doller, 1993, "Preferences for Specific Work Schedules: Foundation for an ExpertSystem Scheduling Program," *Computers in Nursing* 11 (May–June): 115–21.

10. J. Chen and T. W. Yeung, 1993, "Hybrid Expert-System Approach to Nurse Scheduling . . . NURSE-HELP," *Computers in Nursing* 11 (June): 183–90.

11. Medicus Systems Corporation, promotional literature, Evanston, IL.

12. M. W. Isken and W. M. Hancock, 1991, "A Heuristic Approach to Nurse Scheduling in Hospital Units with Nonstationary, Urgent Demand, and a Fixed Staff Size," *Journal of the Society for Health Systems* 2 (2): 24–41.

13. NPAQ, a product of Medicus Systems Corporation, Evanston IL.

14. K. G. Behner, L. F. Fogg, L. C. Fournier, J. T. Frankenbach, and S. B. Robertson, 1990, "Nursing Resource Management: Analyzing the Relationship between Costs and Quality in Staffing Decisions," *Health Care Management Review* 15 (Fall): 63–71.

15. S. F. Hollander, M. Smith, and J. Barron, 1992, "Cost Reductions, Part I: An Operations Improvement Process," *Nursing Economics* 10 (September–October): 325–30, 364; "Part II: An Organizational Culture Perspective," 10 (November–December): 401–5.

16. S. H. Taft, E. L. Minch, and P. K. Jones, 1992, "Strengthening Hospital Nursing: The Planning Process," *Journal of Nursing Administration* Part 1, 22 (May): 51–63; Part 2, 22 (June): 36–46; Part 3, 22 (July): 41–50.

17. E. M. McMahan, K. Hoffman, G. W. McGee, 1994, "Physician-Nurse Relationships in Clinical Settings: A Review and Critique of the Literature, 1966–1992," *Medical Care Review* 51 (Spring): 83–112.

18. P. Hanisch, S. Honan, and R. Torkelson, 1993, "Quality Improvement Approach to Nursing Care Planning: Implementing Practical Computerized Standards," *Journal of Health Care Quality* 15 (September–October): 6–13.

19. E. A. McFadden and M. A. Miller, 1994, "Clinical Nurse Specialist Practice: Facilitators and Barriers," *Clinical Nurse Specialist* 8 (January): 27–33.

20. G. L. Ingersoll, M. T. Bazar, and J. B. Zentner, 1993, "Monitoring Unit-Based Innovations: A Process Evaluation Approach," *Nursing Economics* 11 (May): 137–43.

21. M. L. McClure, M. A. Poulin, M. D. Sovie, and M. A. Wandelt, 1982, *Magnet Hospitals: Attraction and Retention of Professional Nurses* (Kansas City, MO: American Nurses Association).

22. H. Van Ess Coeling and L. M. Simms, 1993, "Facilitating Innovation at the Nursing Unit Level through Cultural Assessment—Part 1: How to Keep Management Decisions from Falling on Deaf Ears," *Journal of Nursing Administration* 23 (April): 46–53; "Part 2: Adapting Management Ideas to the Unit Workgroup," 23 (May): 13–20.

23. C. T. Kovner, G. Hendrickson, J. R. Knickman, and S. A. Finkler, 1993, "Changing the Delivery of Nursing Care: Implementation Issues and Qualitative Findings," *Journal of Nursing Administration* 23 (November): 24–34.

24. J. E. Johnson, L. L. Costa, S. B. Marshall, M. J. Moran, and C. S. Henderson, 1994, "Succession Management: A Model for Developing Nursing Leaders" *Nursing Management* 25 (June): 50–55.

25. M. A. Blegen, C. J. Goode, M. Johnson, M. L. Maas, J. C. McCloskey, and S. A. Moorhead, 1992, "Recognizing Staff Nurse Job Performance and Achievements," *Research in Nursing and Health* 15 (February): 57–66.

26. J. A. Alexander, 1988, "The Effects of Patient Care Unit Organization on Nursing Turnover," *Health Care Management Review* 13 (Spring): 61–72.

27. J. R. Bloom, J. A. Alexander, and S. Flatt, 1988, "Organization Turnover among Registered Nurses: An Exploratory Model," *Health Services Management Research* 1 (November): 156–67.

28. C. S. Weisman and C. A. Nathanson, 1985, "Professional Satisfaction and Client Outcomes," *Medical Care* 23 (October): 1179–92; R. W. Revans, 1964, *Standards for Morale: Cause and Effect in Hospitals* (London: Oxford University Press for Nuffield Provincial Hospitals Trust).

29. L. Chase, 1994, "Nurse Manager Competencies," *Journal of Nursing Administration* 24 (April): 56–64.

30. C. McDaniel and G. A. Wolf, 1992, "Transformational Leadership in Nursing Service: A Test of Theory," *Journal of Nursing Administration* 22 (February): 60–65.

31. J. C. McCloskey, M. Mass, D. G. Huber, A. Kasparek, J. Specht, C. Ramler, C. Watson, M. Blegen, C. Delaney, S. Ellerbe, C. Etscheidt, C. Gongaware, M. Johnson, K. Kelly, P. Mehmert, and J. Clougherty, 1994, "Nursing Management Innovations: A Need for Systematic Evaluation," *Nursing Economics* 12 (January–February): 35–44.

32. M. A. Blegen, C. J. Goode, M. Johnson, M. L. Maas, J. C. McCloskey, and S. A. Moorhead, 1992, "Recognizing Staff Nurse Job Performance and Achievements," *Research in Nursing and Health* 15 (February): 57–66.

33. M. C. Kreider and M. Barry, 1993, "Clinical Ladder Development: Implementing Contract Learning," *Journal of Continuing Education in Nursing* 24 (July-August): 166–69.

34. National League for Nursing, Division of Research, 1993, *National Data Review, 1993* (New York: National League for Nursing Press); *Nursing Opportunities 1993* (Oradell, NJ: Medical Economics).

35. Institute of Medicine, 1983, *Nursing and Nursing Education: Public Policies and Private Actions* (Washington, DC: National Academy Press), 51–88.

36. M. P. Charns and L. J. S. Tewksbury, 1993, *Collaborative Management in Health Care: Implementing the Integrative Organization* (San Francisco: Jossey-Bass).

37. D. G. Huber, C. Delaney, J. Crossley, M. Mehmert, and S. Ellerbe, 1992, "A Nursing Management Minimum Data Set: Significance and Development," *Journal of Nursing Administration* 22 (July): 35–40.

38. Joint Commission on Accreditation of Healthcare Organizations, 1995, *Accreditation Manual for Hospitals* (Oakbrook Terrace, IL: JCAHO).

39. D. G. Anderson, S. F. Hollander, and P. Bastar, 1991, "Customized Productivity Feedback Systems Improve Nursing Performance and Reduce Costs," *Nursing Economics* 9 (September–October): 367–70.

40. J. C. Ziegle and N. K. VanEtten, 1992, "Implementation of a National Nursing Standards Program," *Journal of Nursing Administration* 22 (November): 404.

41. H. A. De Groot, L. Forsey, and V. S. Cleland, 1992, "The Nursing Practice Personnel Data Set: Implications for Professional Practice Systems," *Journal of Nursing Administration* 22 (March): 23–28.

Sustaining: Providing Human Resources and Plant Services

HUMAN RESOURCES SYSTEM

IN 1992, health care organizations had about 6 million employees, reflecting a steady increase throughout the preceding two decades.[1] The number of professions and job categories had also increased. A typical medium-sized health care organization employs persons in over three dozen licensed or certified job classifications, including building trades and stationary engineers as well as clinical professions. Many of the positions are held by part-time personnel. The number of individuals employed is about 30 percent larger than the full-time equivalent (FTE) count.

In addition to employees, the human resources of a health care organization include doctors and others whose services are contracted through arrangements other than employment, and volunteers. The employed health care work force supports a physician group of nearly 500,000 in more than two dozen specialties.[2] Finally, health care organizations also use contract labor services, via long-term management contracts for whole departments and shorter contracts for specific temporary assistance. Long-term contracts are common for house-keeping, food service, and data processing. Among the shorter are consultation contracts with accounting firms and planning firms, as well as shift by shift requests for nurses, clerks, and other hourly workers. In total, a medium-sized health care organization requires over 1,500 persons working at about 1,000 full-time jobs in about 100 different skills.

This group, referred to in earlier chapters as the "members" of the organization, constitutes the most important asset, its human resource.

Regardless of the specific relationship, each member joins the organization in a voluntary exchange transaction. The member is seeking some combination of income, rewarding activity, society, and recognition. The organization is seeking services that support other exchanges. Some aspects of the exchange relationship with members deserve emphasis.

1. The members are absolutely essential to continued operation. Members' motivation and satisfaction directly affect both quality and efficiency. Unusually high motivation can provide a margin of excellence, while a few highly dissatisfied members can temporarily or occasionally disrupt operations.

2. Membership, like the seeking of care, is a free choice for most people. Even those whose skills can be employed only in hospitals usually have some choice of which hospital they will work at and how much work they will seek. Success in attracting and keeping members tends to be self-sustaining; the organization with a satisfied, well-qualified member group attracts more capable and enthusiastic people. The well-run organization markets itself to its members almost as much as it markets itself to its customers.

3. The members represent only about 2 percent of the community served, but because of their close affiliation and their frequent contact with patients, they are unusually influential.

   - As a promotional force, members, both those who come into direct contact with patients and those whose unseen services determine patients' safety and satisfaction, are powerful. What they say and do for patients and visitors will have more influence on competitive standing than any media campaign the organization might contemplate.

   - As an economic force, members are also significant. Health care organizations are always important employers in a community. The medium-sized organization can have a payroll approaching $50 million, including its affiliated physicians and their staffs. Furthermore, about half the payroll represents income from outside the community, largely Social Security payments for Medicare. Finally, most of the employment opportunities are in unskilled and semi-skilled jobs. The economic impact is weighted to lower-middle-class females, a group presenting serious employment problems for many communities.

   - As a political force, members can command increased respect for the health care organization among elected officials of government and labor unions by demonstrating their support of it. While members are only about one-tenth as numerous as patients, their strength can be multiplied when the issue is important enough to motivate their families, as is often the case when substantial numbers of jobs are at stake.

This chapter reviews the purpose of human resources management, the functions which must be performed to sustain an effective workforce, the organization to accomplish the functions, usually called the human resources department, and the measures of success in performing the functions.

Purpose of the Human Resources System

The purpose of the human resources system is to plan, acquire, and maintain the skills, quality, and motivation of members consistent with fulfillment of the health care organization's mission. Since a properly worded mission defines community, service, and cost, this purpose accommodates both the profile of skill levels and the needs for economy defined by the governing board (Chapter 5). Motivation and quality reflect the exchange nature of membership contracts; the human resources system manages all of the monetary transactions and many of the nonmonetary rewards.

This purpose is implemented largely, but not entirely, by the human resources department, a major logistic support unit which provides most human resource functions for nonprofessional employees and a large share of those for professional employees. Doctors and volunteers are least likely to be directly affected by the human resources department, but well-run organizations are increasingly placing key functions of these groups under the department. Even when direct management of the relationships with these groups is assigned elsewhere, it is necessary to coordinate many of the policies. In the well-run organization, the human resources department advises on all human resource issues.

Functions of Human Resource Management

The human resource system must accomplish four functions, as shown in Figure 15.1. Workforce planning tracks the service plan and translates it into specific requirements for each job. These needs are compared to available resources in the membership, and strategies are developed to expand or reduce the category as necessary. Workforce maintenance implements those strategies. Workers are recruited, selected, trained, and encouraged to stay, change, or leave as the plan directs. Compensation is complicated by the need to match market levels for a wide range of jobs, and to provide incentives for achieving the mission. Collective bargaining is important where the workforce is unionized. It is replaced by less formal grievance and mediation procedures in other situations.

Figure 15.1 Functions of Human Resources

Function	Description	Example
Workforce planning	Development of employment needs by job category Comparison with existing workforce and identification of changes	RNs required and available by year Strategy for recruitment, retention, and complement reduction
Workforce maintenance	Advertising, school visits, and other promotion Selection, orientation, and training Record of skill levels and performance Survey of satisfaction and analysis of dissatisfaction Grievance management	RN recruitment program Orientation and continuous improvement education program Satisfaction survey and analysis Personnel record of RNs including special competencies Employee counseling and grievance mediation
Management education	Programs of supervisory training, human relations skills, continuous improvement skills	Head nurse programs in personnel policies, supervision, participation on cross-functional teams
Compensation management	Market surveys of base pay, benefits allowance and incentives Record of hours worked and earnings Maintenance of benefits eligibility, use, and cost	RN pay scales, payment method RN benefit selection, benefit cost, incentives, absenteeism
Collective bargaining	Response to organizing drives, contract negotiation, and administration	Management of RN labor contract if any Record of grievances and disposition
Continuous improvement and budgeting	Analysis of employment markets, benefit trends, and work conditions Development of improvement proposals for general working conditions Development of department budget and budget for fringe benefit costs	Identification of potential shortage situations, of competitive recruitment difficulties Proposals for improvement of benefits or work conditions Human resources department budget and detail for benefits costs budgets

Workforce Planning

Workforce planning allows the organization adequate time to respond to changes in the exchange environment with replacement, increases, or decreases in the numbers of members. The workforce plan is a subsection of the long-range plan. It develops forecasts of the number of persons required in each skill level by year for the length of time covered by the long-range plan. It also projects available human resources including additions and attrition, even to specifying the planned retirement of key individuals.

Development of Plan

The initial proposal for the workforce plan should be developed using forecasts of activity from the services plan. The services plan is developed from the epidemiologic needs of the community and the long-range financial plans (Chapter 6). The workforce plan technically includes, and is always coordinated with, the medical staff plan (Chapter 11). As shown in Figure 15.2, the plan should include

- The anticipated size of the member and employee groups, by skill category, major site, and department
- The schedule of adjustments through recruitment, retraining, attrition, and termination
- Wage and benefit cost forecasts from national projections tailored to local conditions
- Planned changes in employment or compensation policy, such as the development of incentive payments or the increased use of temporary or part-time employees
- Preliminary estimates of the cost of operating the human resources department and fulfilling the plan.

The plan is often prepared by a task force including representatives from human resources, planning, finance, nursing, and one or two other CSSs likely to undergo extensive change. The draft is reviewed by the major medical staff specialties and employer departments, and their concerns are resolved. The revised plan is coordinated with the facilities plan, because the number and location of employees determine the requirements for many plant services. The final package must be consistent with the long-range financial plan. It is recommended to the governing board through the planning committee.

Using the Workforce Plan

The workforce plan must be reviewed annually as part of the environmental assessment, along with other parts of the long-range plan.

Figure 15.2 Illustration of Workforce Plan Content

Category	Current Supply (1995)	Need (FTE) 1996	Need (FTE) 1997	Need (FTE) 1998	Attrition Per Yr.	Recruitment (Reduction) 1996	Recruitment (Reduction) 1997	Recruitment (Reduction) 1998
RN, Inpatient	250 FTE, 300 persons	230	210	200	50	30	30	40
RN, Outpatient	45 FTE, 60 persons	55	60	60	15	25	20	15

RN Strategy

Recruit from three local Associate Degree schools. Advertise in national and state journals. Offer training to facilitate transfer from inpatient to outpatient. Maintain starting salary 10 percent below nearby metropolitan area. Emphasize health, child care, education, and retirement benefits. Encourage LPNs to seek further training.

Costs (1996)

Recruitment/orientation	$1,250/recruit
Personnel records, benefits management, and counseling	$450/employee
Health benefits	$2,400/employee over 20 hours/week
Child care benefits	$100,000 per year*
Social security and medicare	$1,950/FTE
Retirement benefits	$1,500/FTE
Vacation and absenteeism replacements	$900/employee
Training programs	$700/FTE

*Subsidy to Child Care Center. The Center is used by 30 percent of the nurses.

The amended plan and the annual budget guidelines direct the development of even more detailed plans for the coming year. The human resources department works closely with the employing departments to specify individual compensation changes and workforce adjustment. The financial implications of these actions are incorporated into the departmental budgets, which set precise expectations for the number of employees, the number of hours worked, the wage and salary costs, and the benefit costs.

Well-run organizations also use the workforce plan to guide human resources policies. Among these are the timing of recruitment campaigns; guidelines for the use of temporary labor, such as overtime, part-time, and contract labor; and incentive, compensation, and employee benefit design. The plan may be useful in making decisions about new programs and capital, as when the existence of a surplus workforce becomes a resource for expanded services. Even such strategic decisions as mergers or vertical integration can be affected by human resource shortages and surpluses. All of these applications of the plan call for close collaboration with other executives and clinical departments. Collaboration is also desirable on short-term workforce management issues, particularly training, motivation, lost time, and turnover. Improvements in these areas reduce the cost of the human resources department and can be translated into direct gains in productivity and quality by line managers.

The penalty for inadequate workforce planning is loss of the time and flexibility needed to adjust to environmental changes. Many management difficulties are simpler if adequate time is available to deal with them. Inadequate warning causes hasty and disruptive action. Layoffs may be required. Recruitment is hurried and poor selections may be made. Retraining may be incomplete. Each of these actions takes its toll on workers' morale and often directly affects quality and efficiency. Although the effect of each individual case may be modest, it is long lasting and cumulative. The organization which makes repeated hasty and expedient decisions erodes its ability to compete.

Maintenance of the Workforce

Building and maintaining the best possible workforce requires continuing attention to exchange relationships between the organization and its members. The organization cannot remain passive. The best people must be recruited, and they are more likely to remain with an organization that actively meets their personal needs. Investments in recruitment, retention, employee services, and programs for training supervisors in human relations become a part of the intangible benefits as perceived by the employee or member. The additional cost of well-designed programs in these areas is relatively small, but the return is very high.

Recruitment and Selection

Retention of proven members is generally preferable to recruitment, because the risk of dissatisfaction is lower on both sides. However, expansions, changes in services, and employee life cycles result in continuing recruitment needs at all skill levels. Equal opportunity and affirmative action laws, sound medical staff bylaws, and union contracts all require consistency in recruitment practices. A uniform protocol for recruitment establishes policies for the following activities:

1. *Position control.* Documentation of the number of FTE approved, the identity and hours of persons hired for them, and the number of vacancies which exist controls paychecks authorized and approval of recruitment requests, and keeps the workforce at expectations established in the annual budget.

2. *Job description.* Each position must be described in enough detail to identify training, licensure, and experience requirements and to determine compensation. Descriptions are developed by the line, approved and recorded by human resources.

3. *Classification and compensation.* Wage, salary, incentive, and benefit levels must be assigned to each recruited position. These must be kept consistent with other internal positions, collective bargaining contracts, and the external market. Human resources maintains the classification and associates classes with pay scales and incentives.

4. *Job requirements.* The job description is translated to specific skills and knowledge sought with enough precision to permit equitable evaluation of applicants. Human resources assists line managers in making the translation and assessing skills.

5. *Applicant pool priorities and advertising.* Policies covering affirmative action and priority consideration of current and former employees and employees' relatives for job openings. Policies also cover the design, placement, and frequency of media advertising, including use of the organization's own newsletters and publications. Human resources generally develops and administers the policies.

6. *Initial screening.* Screening normally includes review and verification of data on the application. It may or may not include interviews. It includes a brief physical examination and may include drug testing.[3] Particularly for high-volume recruitment, screening takes place in the human resources department so that it will be uniform and inexpensive.

7. *Final selection.* Applicants who pass the initial screening are subjected to more intensive review, usually involving the immediate supervisor of the position and other line personnel. The final selection must be consistent with state and federal equal opportunity and affirmative action requirements and with the job description and requirements. Human resources monitors compliance with these criteria.

8. *Orientation.* New employees need a variety of assistance, ranging from maps showing their work place to counseling on selecting benefit options. They should be given a mentor who can help them fit into their work group. They should learn appropriate information about the organization's mission, services, and policies

to encourage their contribution and to make them spokesmen for the institution in their social group. The mentor is assigned by line personnel, but human resources usually provides the training and counseling.

9. *Probationary review.* Employees begin work with a probationary period, which concludes with a review of performance and usually an offer to join the organization on a long-term basis. Often, increased benefits and other incentives are included in the long-term offer. Line supervisors conduct the probationary review, with advice from human resources.

Modifications of the basic protocol are usually made for professional personnel and for temporary employees. Modifications for temporary employees and volunteers greatly simplify the process in order to reduce cost and delay, while those for professional personnel recognize that recruitment is usually from national or regional labor markets and that future colleagues should undertake most of the recruitment.

For the medical staff and higher supervisory levels, search committees are frequently formed to establish the job description and requirements, encourage qualified applicants, carry out screening and selection, and assist in convincing desirable candidates to accept employment. The human resources department acts as staff for the search committee while assuring that the intent of organization policies has been met. Well-run organizations now use human resources personnel to conduct initial reference checks and to verify licensure status and educational achievement for doctors and other professional personnel. This provides both consistency and a clearer legal record.

Health care organizations are subject to various regulatory and civil restrictions affecting recruitment. Federal regulations regarding equal opportunity require that there be no discrimination on the basis of sex, age, race, creed, national origin, or handicaps that do not incapacitate the individual for the specific job. Those covering affirmative action require special recruitment efforts and priority for equally qualified women, blacks, and persons of Asian and Latin ancestry. (Religious health care organizations may give priority to members of their faith under certain circumstances.) In addition to these constraints, organizations must follow due process, that is, fair, reasonable, and uniform rules, in judging the qualifications of attending physicians. Medical staff appointments are also subject to tests under antitrust laws (Chapter 11). Health care organizations are required to be able to document compliance with these rules and may be subject to civil suits by dissatisfied applicants. Monitoring and documenting compliance with these obligations is a function of the human resources department.

Workplace Diversity

Most health care organizations strive to promote diversity in their workforce.[4] They pursue affirmative action vigorously and make a deliberate effort to represent the ethnic and gender makeup of their community in their medical staff, management group, and workforce.[5] They make a deliberate effort to promote women in management.[6] While this may be driven in part by law or a belief in the need for justice, it is also supported by sound marketing theories. Many people seek health care from caregivers who resemble them. African-American doctors, nurses, and managers are important to African-American patients. Increasing attention to the needs of female workers have clearly influenced the structure of employment benefits and the rules of the workplace.

Workforce Satisfaction and Retention

Health care organizations now routinely survey personnel at all levels to assess general satisfaction with the work environment. The surveys must be carefully worded and administered in ways which protect the worker's anonymity. Special problems which arise from the survey and other monitoring mechanisms are often pursued in focus groups or cross-functional groups. Well-run organizations make an effort to interview persons who are leaving. Their candid comments can be useful to eliminate or correct negative factors in the work environment. They often serve to improve the departing worker's view of the organization as well.

Human resources conducts surveys, interviews, and focus groups, and staffs cross-functional teams working on workplace problems. It analyzes and reports data, and seeks benchmarks to guide line managers. It frequently counsels line managers on individual improvement opportunities.

Policies for promotion, retirement, and voluntary and involuntary termination must be similar in fairness and consistency to those for recruitment. For motivational purposes, they should be designed to make work life as attractive as possible, and they should permit selective retention of the best workers. This means that all collective actions should be planned as far in the future as possible and be announced well ahead of time. Criteria for promotion or dismissal should be clear and equitable, and loyal and able employees should be rewarded by priority in promotion and protection against termination. It also means that all policies are administered uniformly and that there is always a clear route of appeal against actions the employee views as arbitrary. Human resources participates directly in major reductions, designing actions and communications which minimize the impact. It provides counseling and appeals services in individual cases.

Employee Services

Most health care organizations provide personal services to their employees through their human resources department on the theory that such services improve loyalty and morale and, therefore, efficiency and quality. Evidence to support the theory is limited, but the services are often required if competing employers provide them. Specific offerings are often tailored to the employees' responses. Popular programs are allowed to grow, while others are curtailed. Charges are sometimes imposed to defray the costs, but some subsidization is usual. Those commonly found include:

- Health education, health promotion, and access to personal counseling for substance abuse problems. Employee Assistance Programs, formally structured counseling to assist with stress management and alcohol and drug abuse, have been popular in recent years.[7] (Routine personal health services, other than emergency services arising on the job, have largely been replaced by comprehensive health insurance benefits.)
- Infant and child care
- Social events, often recognizing major holidays or corporate events but also used to recognize employee contributions
- Recreational sports
- Credit unions and payroll deduction for various purposes.

One theme of these activities is to build an attitude of caring and mutual support among health care workers, on the theory that a generally caring environment will encourage a caring response to patient and visitor needs.

Occupational Safety and Health

The hospital and some outpatient care sites are moderately dangerous environments for workers. The hospital contains unique or rare hazards, such as repeated exposure to low levels of radioactivity or small quantities of anesthesia gases and increased risk of infection. In practice, however, accident rates are low. Illness and injury arising from hospital work are kept to low levels by constant attention to safety.[8] The organization's dedication to personal and public health encourages this vigilance. For those who might be complacent or forgetful, two laws reinforce its importance. Workers' compensation is governed by state law. Premiums are based on settlements but also on process evidence of attention to safety. The federal Occupational

Safety and Health Act establishes standards for safety in the workplace and supports inspections. Fines are levied for noncompliance.

Much of the direct control of hazards is the responsibility of the clinical and plant departments. Infection control, for example, is an important collaborative effort of housekeeping, facility maintenance, nursing, and medicine to protect the patient. Employee protection in well-run organizations stems from procedures developed for patient safety. The human resources department is usually assigned the following functions:

- Monitoring federal and state regulations and professional literature on occupational safety for areas in which the organization may have hazards
- Identifying the department or group accountable for safety and compliance on each specific risk
- Keeping records and performing risk analysis of general or widespread exposures
- Maintaining records demonstrating compliance and responding to visits and inquiries from official agencies
- Providing or assisting training in and promotion of safe procedures
- Negotiating contracts for workers' compensation insurance, reviewing appropriate language where the insurance is negotiated as part of broader coverage, or managing settlements where the organization self-insures.

Educational Services

Human resources departments provide significant educational opportunities for employees and supervisors. Inservice education is offered on topics where uniformity of understanding is desired.[9] On issues to be handled uniformly among relatively large groups, human resources personnel provide the entire program. Routine offerings are usually less than two hours long, with multiple sessions when more time is needed. Classes are limited in size, and offerings are repeated to provide greater access. Topics include:

- *Orientation*—with a review of the organization's mission, history, major assets, and marketing claims, as well as policies and benefits of employment
- *Work policy changes*—reviews covering the objectives and implications in major changes in compensation, benefits, or work rules
- *Major new programs*—permanent or temporary actions that affect habits and lifestyles of current workers (new buildings, relocations, and construction dislocation are often topics)

- *Retirement planning*—offered to older workers to understand their retirement benefits and also to adjust to retirement lifestyles
- *Out placement*—to assist persons being involuntarily terminated through reductions in workforce
- *Benefits management*—selection of options and procedures for using benefits, including efforts to minimize misuse.

Clinical departments often use their own supervisors or consultants for professional topics, but human resources in larger organizations provides facilities, promotion, and logistic assistance. Human resources can collaborate with governance and finance units on organizationwide concerns such as the annual budget.

Supervisory training and counseling is a particularly important human resources function. Promising workers are identified well before they are promoted and are trained in methods of supervision and effective motivation. Multiple presentations using a variety of approaches and media are used to establish and reinforce basic notions: the use of rewards rather than sanctions, the importance of fairness and candor, the role of the supervisor in responding to workers' questions, and the importance of clear instructions and appropriate work environments. Much of the folklore of American industry runs counter to the realities of sound first-line supervision. Thus even promising personnel need repeated reinforcement of the proper role and style. Cases, role-playing, recordings, films, and individual counseling are helpful in maintaining supervisor's performance.

Guest relations has become a prominent educational offering for human resources departments. These programs use role-playing, games, and group discussion techniques to reinforce attitudes of caring and responsiveness to patients and visitors. Well-run organizations use the guest relations educational programs as part of a comprehensive effort; workers will respond more effectively to customer needs when their own needs are met by responsive supervision, adequate facilities and equipment, and policies which encourage flexibility toward customer needs.

Workforce Reduction

Rapid change in the health care industry has forced many organizations to make substantial involuntary reductions in their workforces. Because job security is an important recruitment and retention incentive, it is imperative that such reductions be handled well. Good practice pursues the following rules:

- Workforce planning is used to foresee reductions as far in advance as possible, allowing natural turnover and retraining to provide much of the reduction.
- Temporary and part-time workers are reduced first.
- Personnel in supernumerary jobs are offered priority for retraining programs and positions arising in needed areas.
- Early retirement programs are used to encourage older (and often more highly compensated) employees to leave voluntarily.
- Terminations are based on seniority or well-understood rules, judiciously applied.

Using this approach has allowed many health care organizations to limit involuntary terminations to a level that does not seriously impair the attractiveness of the organization to others.

Grievance Administration

Well-run health care organizations provide an authority independent of the normal accountability for employees who feel, for whatever reason, that their complaint or question has not been fully answered. Ombudsman-type programs providing an unbiased counselor for concerns of any kind are often offered by larger human resources departments. Personnel in these units are equipped to handle a variety of problems, from health-related issues they refer to employee assistance programs or occupational health services, to complaints about supervision or work conditions, to sexual harassment and discrimination. Most of the approaches are concerns rather than grievances when they are first presented. The function of the office is to settle them fairly and quickly, and if possible identify corrections which will prevent reoccurrence. The office's success depends upon its ability to meet worker needs. It must remain flexible and independent in its orientation, yet its advice must be heeded by management.

A few of the matters presented to ombudsman offices and line officers become formal grievances or complaints. Under collective bargaining, the union contract includes a formal grievance process which is often adversarial in nature, assuming a dispute to be resolved between worker and management. Under nonunion arrangements, a grievance procedure is still necessary.

Good grievance administration begins with sound employment policies, effective education for workers and supervisors, and systems which emphasize rewards over sanctions.[10] Effective supervisory training emphasizes the importance of responding promptly to workers' questions and problems. Good supervisors have substantially fewer grievances than poor ones.

When disagreements arise, they should stimulate the following informal reactions:

- Documentation of issue, location, and positions of the two parties to provide guides to preventive or corrective action
- Credible, unbiased, informal review to identify constructive solutions
- Informal negotiations which encourage flexibility and innovation in seeking a mutually satisfactory solution
- Counseling for the supervisor involved aimed at improvement of future human relations
- Settlement without formal review, either by mutual agreement or by concession on the part of the organization
- Implementation of changes designed to prevent recurrences.

These processes are appropriate in both organized and non-organized environments. They should make the formal review process typically found in union contracts, leading to resolution by an outside arbitrator, unnecessary in the vast majority of cases. Grievances which go to formal review should almost always be decided in management's favor, because a high percentage in the worker's favor encourages more grievances. Even if the concession appears relatively expensive, the organization is better off avoiding review and making an appropriate investment in the prevention of future difficulties.

Management Education

Human resources is responsible for training most line managers in three areas—facts about relevant policies and procedures, skills in human relations and supervision, and tools for budgeting and continuous improvement. The educational program is now often extended to non-supervisory employees as well. Under continuous improvement approaches, more than simply mastery of tools is required. Employees at all levels must think of themselves and the organization as continuously learning.[11] Human Resources has an opportunity to make people comfortable with continuous learning through their programs.

Well-designed programs make learning easier and more pleasant; they encourage people to return for more.

Facts about Policies and Procedures

Effective line supervisors are expected to answer a wide variety of questions from their workers. Many of these will be factual issues about the employment contract and the work environment. Examples are questions about compensation and benefits, incentive programs, and policies on leaves. Supervisory personnel at all levels are expected to know or find answers to these questions. An educational program to support them might include

- Modern theories of human relations and supervision. Learning the supervisor's role, and the importance of sound human relations. Policies and goals for the workforce, including the promotion of diversity and the elimination of sexual harassment.[12]
- In-service courses in major policies, important changes, and how to use the procedure manuals. Leading organizations now have procedures in electronic files which can be quickly searched for the topic. The relevant policy can be quickly printed for the employee, and explained to assure full comprehension.
- Telephone and electronic mail access for specific questions, and personal consultation to the employee or supervisor where indicated.

Skills in Human Relations and Supervision

Few people are naturally good supervisors; most need training and reinforcement to be effective leaders. The actions of supervisors establish an important part of the corporate culture, and affect the success of continuous improvement programs.[13] Human resources assists in the mastery of these skills by providing formal educational programs and counseling assistance. The best formal education emphasizes cases and simulations of common situations where the student can actually practice skills in a supportive environment. Typical topics cover skills in orienting new people, training new skills, motivating workers, answering worker questions, disciplining, and identifying problem workers. Human resources personnel are available to assist supervisors by telephone, e-mail and in person. They also can use employee satisfaction information, grievances, and exit interviews to instigate counseling where indicated.

Tools for Budgeting and Continuous Improvement

Supervisors in continuous improvement programs need a variety of skills to identify opportunities, evaluate them, motivate their personnel, and implement the PDCA cycle. These tools are usually taught in several courses of a day or two each.[14] Budgets and capital budgets have now become complex enough that sessions on how the guidelines are generated, what sorts of improvements and proposals are appropriate, and how to handle the mechanics of preparation and submission are useful. Even the friendliest computer software requires training for many users. Cross-functional teams addressing more complex improvement projects often require ad hoc assistance.

Human resources often organizes these programs using faculty from planning, marketing, finance, and information services. It is important to tie the mechanical skills of budgeting and continuous improvement projects to the human relations skills necessary to sustain motivation.

Compensation

Employee compensation includes direct wages and salaries, cash differentials and premiums, bonuses, retirement pensions, and a substantial number of specific benefits supported by payroll deduction or supplement. Federal law defines employment status and requires withholding of social security and income taxes from the employee and contributions by the employer.[15] Other employment benefits are automatically purchased on behalf of the employee via the payroll mechanism. Compensation constitutes more than half the expenditures of most health care organizations. From the organization's perspective, such a large sum of money must be protected against both fraud and waste. From the employee's perspective, accuracy regarding amount, timing, and benefit coverage should be perfect.

The growing complexity of compensation has been supported by highly sophisticated computer software, with each advance in computer capability soon translated into expanded flexibility of the compensation package. The latest developments in payroll have been increased use of bonuses and incentive compensation, as well as "cafeteria" benefits, which allow more employee choice. Well-run organizations now use payroll programs that process both pay and benefit data for three purposes—payment, monitoring and reporting, and budgeting. This software permits active management of compensation issues in the human resources department through position control, wage and salary administration, benefit administration, and pension administration.

Job Analysis

Compensation programs require a description and classification of each job in the organization. The description should be developed by line personnel, but reviewed by human resources. It outlines the content of the work to be done, specifies the level of training required, and describes any unique features, such as hazards, unusual hours, or particular skills emphasized. It is used to establish recruiting criteria, as a basis for training the worker, and as a basis for classifying the position in a pay category. Human resources advises on the completeness and clarity of the description and on revisions which might make the job easier/or less costly to fill. It then classifies the job in relation to others and establishes a pay scale for it.

Position Control

The organization must protect itself against accidental or fraudulent violation of employment procedures and standards and must assure that only duly employed persons or retirees receive compensation. This is done through a central review of the number of positions created and the persons hired to fill them, called **position control**. Creation of a position generally requires multiple approvals, ending near the level of the chief operating officer. Positions created are monitored by the human resources department to assure compliance with recruitment, promotion, and compensation procedures and to assure that each individual employed is assigned to a unique position. Position control authorization is required before employees can be paid.

It is important to understand the limitation of this activity; it controls the number of people employed rather than the total hours worked. The number of hours worked outside position control accountability is significant. Position control protects only against paying the wrong person, hiring in violation of established policies, and issuing double checks. It does not protect against overspending the labor budget or against errors in hours, rates, or benefit coverage.

Wage and Salary Administration

Most health care organizations operate at least two payrolls and a pension disbursement system. One payroll covers personnel hired on an hourly basis, requiring reporting of actual compensable hours for each pay period, usually two weeks. The other covers salaried, usually supervisory, personnel paid a fixed amount per period, often monthly. Contract workers, such as clinical support service physicians, are often compensated through non-payroll systems. (Benefits, withholding, and payroll deduction are usually omitted from contract compensation, although certain reporting requirements still obtain.)

Wage and salary administration includes the following activities:

- *Verification of compensable hours and compensation due.* This is applicable only to hourly personnel. The accountable department is responsible for the accuracy of hours reported. The task of the human resources department is to verify line authorization, the base rate, and the application of policies establishing differentials.
- *Compensation scales.* The well-run organization strives to be competitive in each position where comparison can be made to other employers and to treat other positions equitably. To achieve

this goal, each position is assigned a compensation grade. These grades establish consistency among similar activities. The human resources department conducts or purchases periodic salary and wage surveys to establish competitive prices for representative grades. At supervisory and professional levels, these surveys cover national and regional markets. For most hourly grades the local market is surveyed.

- *Seniority, merit, and cost-of-living adjustments.* Beginning around World War II wages and salaries were adjusted annually to reflect changes in cost of living and the experience and loyalty reflected by job seniority. Calculating the amount or value of these factors and translating that into compensation at the appropriate time is the task of the human resources department. Well-run health care organizations are rapidly diminishing the importance of these compensation factors. Incentive payments based on the success of the enterprise are replacing the more automatic seniority and cost-of-living raises. Merit raises, increases in the base pay reflecting the individual employee's skill improvements, are difficult to administer objectively[16] and tend to become automatic like seniority increases. They also lack any connection to the performance of the organization and its open systems survival.
- *Incentive adjustments.* The market demand for competitive performance has made tangible reward for individual achievement desirable, and improving information systems have made it possible. As a result, incentive compensation will receive much more attention from well-run organizations in the next few years. The issues involved are discussed below.

Incentive Compensation

A management scheme built on rewards and the search for continued improvement rather than sanctions must develop a system of compensation which supplements personal achievement and professional recognition. Health care organizations have advanced significantly toward this goal,[17] although few reports appear in published literature.

One approach is to recognize that starting wages and salaries should be based solely upon market conditions, but that subsequent adjustments in compensation are most appropriately based on two factors: the employee's unique contribution and shifts in the market that are major enough to require readjustment of the starting rate. In effect, individuals have the opportunity to earn a differential over market by their contribution to organization goals. Certain constraints must be recognized in designing a system of this type:

- The resources available will depend more on the organization's overall performance than on any individual's contribution.

The incentives must recognize this reality, emphasizing overall performance over unit or individual performance.

- The resources available for rewards may be severely limited through factors outside the organization's control.
- Equity and objectivity will be expected in the distribution of the rewards.
- The individual's contribution will be difficult to measure.
- Group rewards attenuate the incentives to individuals. The larger the group, the greater the attenuation.
- The incentive program must avoid becoming a routine or expected part of compensation.

Well-run health care organizations are beginning to experiment with incentive compensation. It is likely that successful designs will have the following characteristics:

- The use of incentive compensation will begin at top executive levels and be extended to lower ranks with experience.
- Annual longevity increases will disappear as incentive pay increases.
- Incentives will be limited by difficulties in measurement and administration, but will eventually reach 25 percent of total compensation or higher.
- Incentives will be related to overall performance but will be awarded to individuals based upon their perceived contribution.
- Assessment of contribution will be retrospective but will be based upon achievement of improvements in expectations set in the preceding budget negotiation.

A bolder scenario is possible under continuous improvement. Where comprehensive measures covering all six dimensions of performance are available, and workers are comfortable with continuous improvement, work groups can set specific expectations and anticipate incentive payment for meeting them. Approaches such as the Scanlon Plan[18] suggest that primary worker groups can effectively set expectations consistent with the needs of the larger organization and that the effort to do so will lead to measurable improvement in achievement. Those gains can then be used in part to reward the workers. Despite a 50-year history, Scanlon plans have worked best where achievements are well defined and work groups are small. It has yet to be proved that the approach can work in complex, multiprofessional organizations with relatively ambiguous goals; however, the time is ripe for experimentation.

Benefits Administration

Many of the social programs of Western nations are related directly or indirectly to work, through programs of payroll taxes, deductions, and entitlements. These programs are fixed in place by a combination of direct legal obligation and tax-related incentives. Nonwage benefits are generally exempt from income tax, providing an automatic gain of at least 12 percent in the benefits that can be purchased for a given amount of after-tax money. Further gains stem from insurance characteristics. Life, health, accident, and disability insurance are substantially less costly when purchased on a group basis.

As a result, health care and other employers in the United States support extensive programs of benefits, which add up to 40 percent beyond salaries and wages to the costs of employment. (The term "fringe benefits" was common until the total cost of these programs made it obsolete.) The exact participation of each employee differs, with major differences depending on full- or part-time status, grade, and seniority. In general, there are five major classes of employee benefits and employer obligations beyond wage compensation:

1. *Payroll taxes and deductions.* The employer is legally obligated to contribute premium taxes to Social Security for pension and Medicare benefits, as well as to collect a portion of the employee's pay for Social Security and withholding on various income taxes. (A few hospitals have special pension programs which substitute for Social Security.) Most employers also collect payroll deductions for union dues, various privileges like parking, and contributions to charities such as the United Fund. Certain funds, such as uninsured health care expenses and child care expenses, can be exempt from income taxes by the use of pretax accounts. While the deductions represent only a small handling cost to the employer, they are an important convenience to the employee.

2. *Vacations, holidays, and sick leave.* Employers pay full-time and permanent employees for legal holidays, additional holidays, vacations, sick leave, and certain other time such as educational leaves, jury duty, and military reserves duty. They grant unpaid leaves for family needs, in accordance with the Family and Medical Leave Act of 1993,[19] and for other purposes as they see fit. As a result, only about 85 percent of the 2,080 hours per year nominally constituting full-time employment is actually worked by hourly workers. The non-worked time becomes a direct cost when the employee must be replaced by part-time workers or by premium pay. It also is an important factor in the cost of full-time versus part-time employees. Part-time positions often do not share in these benefits at all, or share only on a drastically reduced basis. On a per-hour-worked basis, they can be 15 percent less costly as a result.

3. *Voluntary insurance programs.* Health insurance is an almost universal entitlement of full-time employment. Retirement

programs must be funded according to rules similar to those for insurance. Life insurance and travel and accident insurance are also common. Various tax advantages are available for these protections, and they are paid for by combinations of employee and employer contributions. The employer obtains a group rate which is much lower than that offered to individuals. Some employer options for these programs are not technically insurance. They are generally subject to state laws and the federal Employee Retirement Insurance Security Act (ERISA).

Direct employer contributions add about 10 percent to the cost of full-time employees. They are rarely offered to employees working fewer than 20 hours per week and may be graduated to those working between half and full time.

4. *Mandatory insurance.* Employers are obligated to provide workers' compensation for injuries received at work, including both full health care and compensation for lost wages. They are also obligated to provide unemployment insurance, covering a portion of wages for several months following involuntary termination.

5. *Other perquisites.* A wide variety of other benefits of employment can be offered, particularly for higher professional and supervisory grades. These generally are shaped by a combination of tax and job performance considerations. Educational programs, professional society dues, and journal subscriptions are commonly included. Cars, homes, club memberships, and expense accounts are used to assist executives to participate fully in the social life of their community. The theory is that such participation increases the executives' ability to understand community desires and identify influential citizens. Added retirement benefits, actually income deferred for tax purposes, and termination settlements are used to defray the risks of leadership positions.

In managing employment benefits, the human resources department strives to maximize the ratio of gains to expenditure. Four courses of action to achieve this are characteristic of well-run departments; three of them relate to program design and one to program administration:

1. *Program design for competitive impact.* The value of a given benefit is in the eye of the employee, and demographics affect perceived value more than personal tastes do. A married mother might prefer child care to health insurance because her husband's employer already provides health insurance. A single person whose children are grown might prefer retirement benefits to life insurance. Young employees often (perhaps unwisely) prefer cash to deferred or insured benefits. Employee surveys help predict the most attractive design of the benefit package. Flexibility is

becoming more desirable as workers' needs become more diverse. Recent trends have emphasized cafeteria benefits, where each employee can select preset combinations.

2. *Program design for cost-effectiveness.* Several benefits have an insurance characteristic such that actual cost is determined by exposure to claims. Health insurance, accident insurance, and sick benefits are particularly susceptible to cost reduction by benefit design. Health insurance, by far the largest of these costs, is minimized by the use of prospective admission review, copayments, preferred provider arrangements, and capitation. Many health care employers are encouraging participation in their own capitation or preferred provider contracts by increasing the costs borne by employees who choose other plans. Accident insurance premiums are reduced by limiting benefits to larger, more catastrophic events. Duplicate coverage, where the employee and the spouse who is employed elsewhere are both covered by insurance can be eliminated to reduce cost. Costs of sick benefits can be reduced by eliminating coverage for short illnesses, and by requiring certification from a physician early in the episode of coverage.

3. *Program design for tax implications.* Income tax advantages are a major factor in program design. Many advantages, such as the exemption of health insurance premiums, are deliberate legislative policy, while others appear almost accidental. Details are subject to constant adjustment through both legislation and administrative interpretations. As a result, it is necessary to review the benefit program periodically for changing tax implications, both in terms of current offerings and in terms of the desirability of additions or substitutions.

4. *Program administration.* Almost all of the benefits can be administered in ways which minimize their costs. It is necessary to provide actual benefits equitably to all employees; careless review of use may lead to widespread expansion of interpretation and benefit cost. Strict interpretation can be received well by employees if it is prompt, courteous, and accompanied by documentation in the benefit literature initially given employees. Health insurance is probably the most susceptible to poor administration. Careful claims review, enforcement of copay provisions, and coordination of spouse's coverage are known to be cost-effective.

Prevention of insured perils is also fruitful. Absenteeism and on-the-job injuries are reduced by effective supervision. Accidents and health insurance usage are reduced by effective health promotion, particularly in cases of substance abuse.[20] Counseling is also believed to reduce health insurance use. Workers' compensation is reduced by improved safety on the job site and case management of expensive disabilities. Unemployment liability is reduced by better planning and use of attrition for workforce reduction. It is noteworthy that these activities are all affected by human resources management, through employee services, supervisory training, workforce planning, and occupational safety programs.

Pensions and Retirement Administration

Pensions and retirement benefits pose different management problems from other benefits because they are used only after the employee retires. Nonpension benefits are principally health insurance supplementing Medicare. Recent developments have led health care organizations to offer bonuses for early retirement as a way of adjusting the workforce.

Pension design and retirement program management involve questions of benefit design and administration that are directly analogous to those of other insured benefits. Because the benefit is often not used for many years and represents a multidecade commitment when use begins, pensions are funded by cash reserves. As a result, pension issues also include the definition of suitable funding investments, that is, to what extent they should be divided between fixed-dollar returns and those responsive to inflation, and the management of the funds, including investment of them in the organization's own bonds or stock. Finally, pension-related issues include the motivational impact of the design on the tendency of employees to retire.

The pension itself, but not other retirement benefits, is regulated under ERISA. Regulations for ERISA specify the employer's obligation to offer pensions, to contribute to them if offered, to vest those contributions, and to fund pension liabilities through trust arrangements. These regulations leave several elements of a sound pension and retirement policy to the organization:

- The amount of pension supplementing Social Security
- The amount, kind, and design of Medicare supplementation (Capitation and other programs encouraging economical use of benefits will rapidly become more common.)
- Opportunities for additional contribution by employees
- Accounting for unvested liabilities (benefits not paid if the employee leaves the organization before the time required for vesting)
- Funding of unvested pension liabilities
- Use of unvested funds in financing the organization.

- Division of investments between equity and fixed-dollar obligations and selection of those investments
- Incentives to encourage or discourage retirement (Age 65 is an arbitrary and increasingly irrelevant standard. Federal law allows most older workers the right to continue work without a mandatory retirement age.)

Many of these issues can be and frequently are delegated to pension management firms or fund trustees. Others are important parts of a well-planned workforce management program which must be handled by the human resources system. In addition to these financial, technical, and motivational concerns, most organizations accept an obligation to provide retirement counseling, including education to help the employee manage pensions and health insurance benefits.

Retired workers represent large future liabilities. At the time of a female employee's retirement, the organization typically commits itself to pension payments and support of Medicare supplementary health insurance for a period averaging nearly 15 years. ERISA requires a trust fund to support pension payments, and the health insurance supplement payment is represented as a liability on the balance sheet. In past times of high inflation, many hospitals felt obligated to adjust pensions for very old workers, because inflation has eroded their buying power below subsistence levels. Such adjustments are, by definition, not funded.

Although health care organizations are currently using retirement bonuses as a method of workforce reduction, at other times it may pay them to retain older workers. In general, they are more amenable to reduced hours, have reliable work habits, and are less likely to have unpredictable absences.

Economic, Legal, and Social Considerations in Compensation

Employment is an exchange transaction governed primarily by an economic marketplace. Compensation, including benefits, is a major part of the economic agreement. It follows then, that the market is the best and usual source of information on compensation. Health care organizations depart from the market price for labor at their peril: a lower price may not attract enough qualified personnel, and a higher one may waste the owners' funds. Deliberate departure from market prices should be justified by some proven benefit; accidental departure should be minimized. Wage and salary surveys are used to determine market prices. These are often available for purchase, particularly for national markets; however, continuing contact with appropriate markets is one of the important functions of the human resources system.

Legal restrictions are also important. Health care organizations are subject to federal and state laws governing wages, hours, and working conditions. As noted, they are also obligated to follow equal opportunity and affirmative action regulations. The human resources department is usually accountable for compliance with most of these regulations and for instructing others when it is not accountable. It also is generally accountable for all records and documentation in support of compliance.

Social considerations are more complex. Many people who are concerned with health care are also concerned with related issues of a good society, such as the availability of meaningful work for all, the adequacy of low wages and pensions, the equity of payment for equivalent work, and the avoidance of exploitation of minorities or subgroups of the society. These questions are rarely straightforwardly addressed. In particular, efforts to improve compensation are often associated with reductions in the number of jobs available, possibly by reducing the competitiveness of the organization. Well-run organizations tend to do the following:

- Comply with market trends
- Comply with applicable laws and regulations
- Take limited advantage of low-risk ways to increase employment or compensation to disadvantaged groups
- Advocate as an organization more significant redress of these important social problems
- Adopt riskier programs for addressing social problems only as part of an explicit mission implemented through the five-year plan.

This posture makes the organization a passive rather than an active force in resolving social problems related to work. Few health care organizations currently make these issues part of their formal mission.

Collective Bargaining Agreements

Extent and Trends in Collective Bargaining
Health care organizations are subject to both state and federal legislation governing the right of workers to organize a union for their collective representation on economic and other work-related matters. Federal legislation generally supports the existence of unions; state laws vary. As a result of the extension of federal law to hospitals and of the increased availability of funds, hospital organizing drives became more common and more successful around 1970. By 1980, 20 percent of all hospital employees were unionized. The likelihood of

unionization differed significantly by state, with the northeastern states and California most likely, and was far more common in urban areas. The overall percentage unionized held stable throughout the decade, although unionization in general declined.[21]

By 1990, union members were only 15 per cent of the U. S. workforce, down from 25 percent shortly after World War II. Organizing activity in hospitals was down, but hospitals that were organized were more likely to remain organized for several years.[22] Unskilled workers and building trades were the most likely to be organized. Nurses were next most likely; other clinical professionals were rarely organized. Small and declining numbers of house officers were union members.[23] Periodic efforts to organize attending physicians gained little headway.[24]

A 1989 Supreme Court decision is believed to favor the spread of unions. The Court upheld rules by the National Labor Relations Board (NLRB) establishing eight job classes for unionization in all hospitals. The classes are physicians, registered nurses, all professional personnel other than doctors and nurses, technical personnel (including practical nurses and internally trained aides, assistants and technicians), skilled maintenance employees, business office clerical employees, guards, and all other employees. Any organizing vote must gain support of a majority of all the members of a given class.[25] The standardization of groups eliminates a commonplace delaying strategy by hospitals, appealing to the NLRB for an ad hoc definition of the bargaining unit. On the other hand, several of the groups have little in common in terms of their work needs or normal communication. Only guards, business office, and skilled maintenance groups are under the same supervision and have frequent informal contacts. The ruling stimulated interest in unions among most of the groups identified by the ruling, including physicians, and renewed organization efforts by unions.[26,27,28] The efforts did not cause major changes in the overall picture.

For most health care organizations, a position that avoids or diminishes the influence of unions is likely to be consistent with the exchange environment. The organization's relation to unions is actualized through its response to work-related concerns of employees.

Work-Related Employee Concerns

Union organization drives and collective bargaining tend to be strong where employees perceive a substantial advantage to collective representation. This perception is stimulated by evidence of careless, inconsiderate, or inequitable behavior on the part of management in any of the key concerns of the workplace: output expectations, response to workers' questions, working conditions, and pay. It is possible to diminish both the perception of advantage and the real advantage of unionization by consistently good management. Many companies have existed for decades in highly unionized environments without ever having a significant union organization. The first step is to make certain there is little room for complaint about the key concerns of the workplace and no obvious opportunity for improvement. The union then has nothing to offer in return for its dues, and its strength is diminished. The first task of the human resources department in this regard is to achieve high-quality performance on its functions. The second is to assist other systems of the organization to do the same, and the third is to present the organization so that its performance is recognized by workers.

Organization Drives and Responses

Organization drives are regulated by law and have become highly formal activities. The union, the employees, and management all have rights which must be scrupulously observed. The regulatory environment presumes an adversarial proceeding. Under this presumption, management is obligated to present arguments on behalf of independence from the union and to take legal actions which limit the organizers to the framework of the law. If management fails in this duty, the rights of owners and employees who do not wish union representation are not properly protected. Well-run organizations respond to organizing drives by hiring competent counsel specifically to fulfill their adversarial rights and obligations. They act on advice of counsel to the extent that it is consistent with their general strategy of fair and reasonable employee relations.

Negotiations and Contract Administration

Collective bargaining is usually an adversarial procedure, although collaboration with unions can and should occur. The management position should avoid confrontation as much as possible, and seek collaboration. Well-run organizations use experienced bargainers and have counsel available for the more complex formalities. Once again, management is obligated to represent owners and employees who are not represented at the bargaining table. Health care organizations with existing unions pursue a strategy of contract negotiation which attempts to minimize or eliminate dissent. They will accept a strike on issues which depart significantly from the current exchange environment for workers or patients, but as a strategy they avoid strikes whenever possible.

Under certain circumstances, management must pursue contracts which reduce income or employment for union members. Two rules govern such a case: it must apply equally to nonunion workers, and it must be well justified by external forces in the exchange environment.

Contract administration is approached in a similar vein, but the adversarial characteristic of organizing and bargaining should not carry over into the workplace. The objective is to comply fully with the contract but to minimize literal interpretation. Considerable supervisory education is necessary to implement this policy. Supervisors should know the contract and abide by it, but whenever possible their actions should be governed by fundamental concerns of human relations and personnel management. Any distinction between unionized and nonunionized groups should be minimized.

Continuous Improvement and Budgeting

The human resources department is obligated to support continuous improvement in its own unit and throughout the organization, and to prepare a budget for its own activities consistent with collective needs. Its customers are both employees and employing units.

Continuous Improvement

The competitive environment will demand extraordinary efforts to improve human relations. Most health care organizations must make major improvements in labor efficiency and cost. The best will understand that the loyalty, skill, and motivation of the workforce are also critical and that any effort to address the problems of costs must involve increasing the contribution and the compensation of many workers. Pursuing these concepts will improve efficiency while simultaneously making workers more valuable to themselves and to the organization. At the other extreme, badly managed organizations will take hasty, ill-considered actions devastating those persons who are terminated and demoralizing those who remain. The demoralization will generate problems of cost, quality, and attractiveness to patients and qualified professionals.

Continuous improvement of human relations begins with competency in each of the functions of the human resources system, placing special emphasis on workforce planning, compensation management, and management education. It includes information systems for retrieval and analysis of human resources data and measures of performance for the human resources department itself, emphasizing service to other systems and outcomes quality. As shown in Figure 15.3, there are usually several opportunities to expand human resources services. When the indicator directly measures the workforce, as in the employee satisfaction and labor cost illustration in Figure 15.3, the human resources opportunity is clear. Even if the opportunity is in line performance improvement, the possibility exists that motivational issues are involved.

Human resources has extensive obligations to support continuous improvement in other units. These include advising on personnel requirements and recruiting, resetting wage and salary levels, and assisting with training programs. Most important, they include continuous reinforcement of the motivating factors for improvement, particularly empowerment. Empowerment is easily destroyed by authoritarian supervisory practices. Motivation drops quickly when these develop. Human resources must monitor, counsel, and train constantly to support an effective program. Priorities governing which opportunity to pursue are driven by the magnitudes involved, but many opportunities take considerable time to meet.

The internal continuous improvement of human resources is designed to anticipate line needs, and be ready for them as they arise. Improving internal information systems, particularly those associated with workforce planning and management, are examples. Recruitment,

Figure 15.3 Typical External Improvements for Human Resources Services

Indicator	Opportunity	Example
Employee satisfaction variance	Identify special causes and address individually	Improve employee amenities Special training for supervisors with low employee satisfaction
Low-line performance improvement	Support line review of causes	Focus groups on motivation, workplace problems Review of incentive programs
High health insurance costs	Promote more cost-effective program	Revise health benefits or selections Install case management Promote healthy life styles
Labor costs over benchmark	Support orderly employment reduction	Curtail hiring in surplus categories Design and offer early retirement program Start cross-training and retraining programs

benefits, regular and incentive compensation, and outcomes measures of workforce maintenance can be benchmarked against competitors or similar organizations. Programs for special work groups can be redesigned or invented. Because these programs should be anticipatory, there may be no direct measure of need for them. Figure 15.4 gives some common examples.

Budget Development

Human resources is responsible for its own budget covering all six dimensions of performance. Figure 15.5 indicates the management questions to be reviewed in the budget for each dimension.

It is important to establish realistic constraints on cost. The department almost never generates revenue. Its costs and services can sometimes be benchmarked against similar institutions, but one benchmark is the price of outside contracts. It is possible to purchase human resources individual services from commercial vendors. Some companies provide complete workforce management. Thus many of the discussions of appropriate levels of quality and unit cost revolve around competitive sources for equivalent services. It is possible to sell human resources services to line departments on a scheme of transfer pricing (Chapter 8). While this approach may result in economies, it may also unduly dampen demand for services. The costs of inadequate training and counseling to line departments may be unreasonably high. Even so, demands, outputs, and unit costs of specific human resources services are important and should be studied as part of the budget.

Figure 15.4 Typical Internal Improvements for Human Resources Services

Indicator	Opportunity	Example
Potential RN shortage	Expand RN recruitment program	Install expanded part-time RN program, emphasizing retraining, child care, flexible hours
High benefits cost	Redesign benefit package	Cafeteria benefits with elimination of extremely high-cost elements
Low-incentive payments	Redesign incentive pay program	Expand eligibility for incentives, improve measurement of contribution

Figure 15.5 Issues in Human Resources Budget Development

Dimension	Issue
Demand	Adequacy of coverage of training programs, counseling, recruitment assistance
Cost	Comparison of costs with history and similar organizations
Human resources	Satisfaction and performance of department's own employees
Output/efficiency	Comparison of output to demand
	Comparison of cost per hire, cost/employee to competitors and similar organizations
Quality	Employee satisfaction with benefits, training programs, etc.
	Supervisor satisfaction with department
Constraint	Allowable cost for department

Organization and Personnel

Human Resources Management as a Profession

Human resources management emerged as a profession after World War II, in response to the complexities created by union contracts, wage and hour laws, and benefits management. Health care organizations were sheltered from these developments for several years, but as the need arose hospitals moved to establish an identifiable human resources system and to hire specially trained leadership for it. Although there is no public certification for the profession, there is an identifiable curriculum of formal education and a recognizable pattern of professional experience. Health care practitioners have an association, the American Society for Healthcare Human Resources, a unit of the American Hospital Association. Well-run organizations now recruit their human resources director or vice-president from persons with experience in the profession generally and, preferably with experience in health care. Larger organizations often have several professionals. Professional training and experience contribute to mastery of the several areas in which laws, precedents, specialized skills, or unique knowledge define appropriate actions.

Organization of the Human Resources Department

Internal Organization

The human resources department is organized by function, in order to take advantage of the specialized skills applicable to its more time-consuming activities. Figure 15.6 shows a typical accountability hierarchy for a larger organization with labor union contracts. Smaller organizations must accomplish the same functions with fewer people. They do so by combining the responsibility centers shown on the lower row. (Collective bargaining is less common in smaller institutions.)

In very large organizations, human resources tends to be decentralized by work site. While some activities, such as information processing, can be centrally managed, others require frequent contact with employees and supervisors. A central office can monitor planning, support more elaborate educational programs, and maintain uniformity of compensation, benefits, and collective bargaining. Decentralized representatives available in each site concentrate on implementation of these programs and issues of workforce maintenance and continuous improvement. Workforce planning is generally handled by an ad hoc team led by the vice-president for human resources. While various sites must participate as well as various work groups, a centralized approach maximizes the opportunities for promotion and relocation without layoff.

Division of Responsibility with Other Systems

The more controversial organizational problems relate to the division of human resources functions between the department and the line department or unit accountable for the member's costs and output. Whether the human resources department is involved or not, the functions of the human resources system must be performed for all members. Even volunteers require selection and orientation. Although they receive no wages, they are often given some benefits. The question of what benefits they will receive is, of course, a compensation issue. Attending physicians are subject to extensive recruitment and selection and often receive monetary compensation and substantial benefits. By the same token, all members require supervision by and assistance from their accountable line unit. Thus the question of the exact domain of the human resources department is inevitably a matter of judgment.

Well-run organizations have identified the question as one of appropriate joint contribution to the needs of the member. They seek the solution not in the assignment of functions to either the line or

Figure 15.6 Organization of a Large Human Resources Department

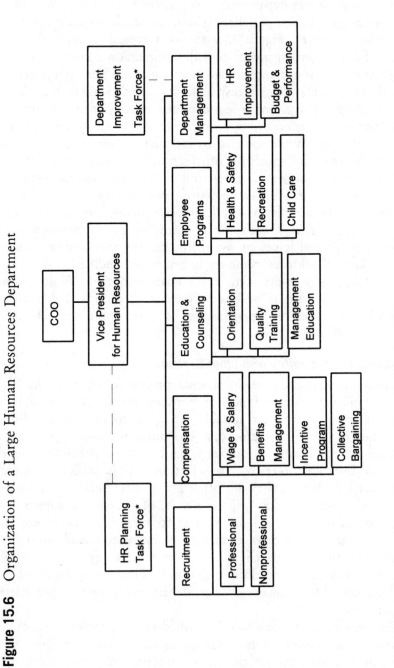

*Task Forces draw on department members and outsiders as indicated. Dashed lines show chairs.

the human resources department, but rather in the identification of the amount and kind of contribution each unit can make in completing each function. This approach recognizes that the goal is to perform each function well for each member of the workforce and that the human resources system must be a collaboration between the department and the line unit involved. In judging the assignment of specific functions, one bears in mind the human resources department's contributions: uniformity, economy, and specialized human resources skills. The line unit's contributions are professional and technical knowledge of the specific tasks.

At present, the major functions tend to be distributed as follows:

1. *Workforce planning.* Line units are generally responsible for short-term forecasts and the relationship between workers and output. Long-term forecasts of output are developed centrally by the governance system. The human resources department is responsible for extending the workforce requirement to the horizon of the long-range plan. These extensions are reviewed by the line units, and discussions of specific adjustments are joint. Governance system members resolve disputes.

2. *Workforce maintenance activities.* These activities include the following:
   - *Recruitment and retention.* Recruitment activities are decentralized to the line units for all supervisory and professional positions, with active participation of the human resources department. Retention is even more decentralized, with participation of the human resources department limited to major workforce reductions and review for compliance with due process and equal opportunity regulations.
   - *Employee services.* These services are centralized.
   - *Grievance administration.* Formal procedures are always centralized. Informal procedures are decentralized, with the human resources department available for advice.
   - *Supervisory training and counseling.* These services are centralized.

3. *Compensation.* Compensation is a centralized service except for three specific contributions from the line units:
   - *Job content and description*
   - *Advice on professional markets and competing offers*
   - *Recommendations for individual merit increases*

4. *Collective bargaining agreements.* These are centralized, but line units have a strong advisory role.

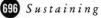

Measures and Information Systems

Quantitative assessment of human resources must address the state and performance of the member group as well as the human resources department. The availability, satisfaction, capability and performance of the workforce are one of the six dimensions of performance for all operating units The human resources department itself must have as comprehensive an information system as an independent consulting company.

Measurement of Human Resource

It is possible to measure many characteristics of the workforce using sophisticated accounting, personnel record keeping, and satisfaction surveys. Precise definitions of the concepts being measured are easily obtained from accounting practice and standard definitions. Figure 15.7 lists many of the commonly used measures for assessing the membership.

Membership assessment is a routine part of the annual environmental assessment. The values for measures in the four dimensions can be compared with benchmarks and comparable organizations and with their own history.

Measurement of the human resources department obviously begins with the measures shown in Figure 15.7. The level of achievement on

Figure 15.7 Measures of the Human Resource

Dimension	Measure
Demand	New hires per year
	Unfilled positions
Costs	Full- and part-time regular hours
	Overtime, differential, and incentive payments
	Benefits costs, by benefit
	Human resources department costs
Output and efficiency	Number of workers
	Cost per worker by categories above
Quality	Skill levels and cross-training
	Employee satisfaction
	Turnover and absenteeism
	Grievances

these measures is an outcomes quality measure for the department; the state of the workforce is its principal product. An additional set of measures is important in assessing the department itself, as shown in Figure 15.8.

Cost measurement of the human resources activity and its components is relatively straightforward. Concerns are sometimes raised about the cost of time spent in human resources activity by nonhuman resources personnel, an amount that would not necessarily be captured by the accounting system. Examples are time spent in training or participating in task forces with a direct human resources goal. These concerns assume that time spent on these activities results in lost production elsewhere. In fact, the premise may be false; the morale or skills improvement resulting from participation may cause production increases rather than decreases.

Figure 15.8 Measures of Human Resources Functional Effectiveness

Dimension	Concept	Representative Measures
Demand	Requests for human resources department service	Requests for training and counseling services Requests for recruitment Number of employees
Cost	Resources consumed in department operation	Department costs by functional account Physical resources used by department
Human resources	The workforce in the department	Satisfaction, turnover, absenteeism within the department
Output/ Efficiency	Counts of the services actually performed by the department Cost/unit of service	Hires, training attendance, paychecks issued Unit costs
Quality	Quality of department services to employees and supervisors	Customer satisfaction with services Process quality measures
Constraint	Market-governed price for human resource services	Price of alternative suppliers Comparison or benchmark values Historic trends

The principle quality measures for the department are satisfaction oriented. Outcomes measures such as workforce evaluation or turnover in general have too many contributing causes. The contribution of human resources is hard to distinguish. The constraint on costs, as discussed in the budget function above, comes from external comparisons or a subjective assessment of what is appropriate. The efficiency measures help guide effective decisions about the level of human resources activity to support.

Information Systems

Structure

The information systems of human resources management are built around seven core files of information, as shown in Figure 15.9. These files record the status of the human resource—personnel counts, qualifications, compensation, and vacancies—and the activity—unit costs, satisfaction, turnover, absenteeism, grievances, and training. Operating policies are implemented through the software that supports the files, and data retrieval generates most activity reports. Only demand and assessment of user satisfaction with the department are missing from Figure 15.9. These are assessed by surveys, and create a separate file. The files themselves and much of the activity to maintain them are fully automated. Data retrieval from the files is automated, and many pieces of information are generated with each payroll cycle.

Ethical Issues

Important ethical questions are raised in connection with the information in these files. The records involved are usually viewed as confidential. At the simplest ethical level, human resources files must be guarded against unauthorized access and misuse.

More serious questions arise when basic concerns have been met. Reduction of dissatisfaction, turnover, absenteeism, grievances, accidents, and illness are socially useful goal of human resources management. It is clearly proper, even desirable, to study variations as measures of supervisory effectiveness that can be improved by systems redesign, counseling and education. Yet actions based upon worker characteristics such as age, sex, or race or records such as illness and grievances can be illegal and are often ethically questionable. Some facts, such as drug test data, are potentially destructive, and the data base cannot be made error free. Some companies have attempted to deny employment opportunities in situations where there was high risk of occupational injury. For example, such an approach would deny employment in operating rooms to female nurses in their childbearing

Figure 15.9 Core Files of the Human Resources Information System

File	Uses
Position Control (List of approved full and part-time positions by location, classification)	Provides a basic check on number and kinds of people employed
Personnel Record (Personal data, training, employment record, hearings record, benefits use)	Provides tax and employment data aggregated for descriptions
Workforce Plan (Record of future positions and expected personnel)	Shows changes needed in workforce
Payroll (Current work hours or status, wage or salary level)	Generates paychecks Provides labor cost accounting
Employee Satisfaction (Results of surveys by location, class)	Assesses employee satisfaction
Training Schedules and Participation (Record of training programs and attendance)	Generates training output statistics and individual records
Benefits Selection and Utilization (Record of employee selection and use of services)	Benefits management and cost control

years, because there are known pregnancy risks related to exposure to anesthesia.

One must note that in almost all cases harm results from the use of information rather than the acquisition of it. In fact, knowledge of age-, sex- and race-related hazards can only be deduced from studies of their specific impact. Thus denial of the value of all or part of the information potential is also unethical—it theoretically causes the organization to do less than it should on behalf of all workers. A sound policy must balance the advantages of investigation against its dangers. These rules help:

- Information access is limited to a necessary minimum group. Those with access are taught the importance of confidentiality and the organization's expectation that individuals' rights will be protected.

- Formal approval must be sought for studies of individual characteristics affecting personnel performance. Often a specific committee including members of the organization's ethics committee reviews each study. Criteria for approval include protection of individual rights, scientific reliability, and evidence of potential benefit.

Actions taken to improve performance are reward- rather than sanction-oriented. Considerable effort is made to find nonrestrictive solutions. (In the operating room example, avoidance of the more dangerous gases would be one such solution improved air handling another, and concentrating use in one location a third. While none of these may be practical, all should be considered before a restrictive employment policy is established.)

When used, sanctions or restrictions offer the individual the greatest possible freedom of choice. The right of the individual to take an informed risk should be respected, although it may not reduce the organization's ultimate liability. (In the operating room example, a nurse may accept employment with a full explanation of the risks as they are currently known. The complex probabilities of pregnancy, stillbirth, and infant deformity clearly depend on her personal lifestyle and intentions. Weighing them would be her moral obligation. Legally, the organization's liability for later injury might be reduced by evidence that full information was supplied about the hazards involved, although such an outcome is not uncertain.)

Use of the Information System for Analysis

The information system described above, plus the normal cost accounting system, can provide most of the measures suggested in Figures 15.7 and 15.8 at negligible cost. Thus expectations can be set each year in the annual budgeting exercise, and reports of achievement can go routinely to sections of the human resources department and to line supervisors.

Special attention will be required to obtain user evaluations. Formal surveys of employees' and line supervisors' perceptions of the department may be infrequent, but they should be conducted often enough to assure that the department recognizes its obligation to be responsive to these groups. The human resources department inescapably has a monopoly on most activity. Thus the surveys of user opinion are an important safety valve as well as a guide to outcomes quality.

Suggested Readings

Carter, C. C. 1994. *Human Resources Management and the Total Quality Imperative.* New York: American Management Association.

Fottler, M. D., S. R. Hernandez, and C. L. Joiner, eds. 1994. *Strategic Management of Human Resources in Health Services Organizations*, 2d ed. Albany, NY: Delmar Publishers.

Jackson, S. E., and associates, eds. 1992. *Diversity in the Workplace: Human Resources Initiatives*. New York: Guilford Press.

Rizzo, A. M., and C. Mendez. 1990. *The Integration of Women in Management: A Guide for Human Resources and Management Development Specialists*. New York: Quorum Books.

U.S. Department of Labor. 1993. *Framework for a Comprehensive Health and Safety Program in the Hospital Environment*. Washington, DC: Occupational Safety and Health Administration, Directorate of Technical Support, Office of Occupational Health Nursing.

Wexley, K. N., and J. Hinrichs, eds. 1991. *Developing Human Resources*. Washington, DC: U.S. Bureau of National Affairs.

Notes

1. U.S. Bureau of the Census, 1993, *Statistical Abstracts of the U.S. 1993*, 113th ed. (Washington, DC: Bureau of the Census), Table 663.

2. J. P. Weiner, 1994, "Forecasting the Effects of Health Reform on U.S. Physician Workforce Requirements: Evidence from HMO Staffing Patterns," *Journal of the American Medical Association* 272 (20 July): 222–30.

3. J. W. Fenton, Jr., and J. L. Kinard, 1993, "A Study of Substance Abuse Testing in Patient Care Facilities," *Health Care Management Review* 18 (Fall): 87–95.

4. S. Cejka, 1993, "The Changing Healthcare Workforce: A Call for Managing Diversity," *Healthcare Executive* 8 (March–April): 20–23.

5. S. E. Jackson and associates, eds., 1992, *Diversity in the Workplace: Human Resources Initiatives* (New York: Guilford Press).

6. A. M. Rizzo and C. Mendez, 1990, *The Integration of Women in Management: A Guide for Human Resources and Management Development Specialists* (New York: Quorum Books).

7. J. C. Howard and D. Szczerbacki, 1988, "Employee Assistance Programs in the Hospital Industry," *Health Care Management Review* 13 (Spring): 73–79.

8. U.S. Department of Labor, 1993, *Framework for a Comprehensive Health and Safety Program in the Hospital Environment* (Washington, DC: Occupational Safety and Health Administration, Directorate of Technical Support, Office of Occupational Health Nursing.

9. K. N. Wexley and J. Hinrich, eds., 1991, *Developing Human Resources* (Washington, DC: Bureau of National Affairs).

10. C. R. McConnell, 1993, "Behavior Improvement: A Two-Track Program for the Correction of Employee Problems," *Health Care Supervisor* 11 (March): 70–80.

11. D. A. Garvin, 1993, "Building a Learning Organization," *Harvard Business Review* 71 (July–August): 78–91.

12. R. K. Robinson, G. M. Franklin, and R. L. Fink, 1993, "Sexual Harassment at Work: Issues and Answers for Health Care Administrators," *Hospital & Health Services Administration* 38 (Summer): 167–80.

13. E. Jansen, D. Eccles, and G. N. Chandler, 1994, "Innovation and Restrictive Conformity among Hospital Employees: Individual Outcomes and Organizational Considerations," *Hospital & Health Services Administration* 39 (Spring): 63–80.

14. C. C. Carter, 1994, *Human Resources Management and the Total Quality Imperative* (New York: American Management Association).

15. W. B. Moore and C. D. Groth, 1993, "Independent Contractors or Employees? Reducing Reclassification Risks," *Healthcare Financial Management* 47 (May): 118, 120–24.

16. M. T. Kane, 1992, "The Assessment of Professional Competence," *Evaluation and the Health Professions* 15 (June): 163–82.

17. A. Barbusca and M. Cleek, 1994, "Measuring Gain-Sharing Dividends in Acute Care Hospitals," *Health Care Management Review* 19 (Winter): 28–33.

18. C. F. Frost, J. H. Wakeley, and R. A. Ruh, 1974, *The Scanlon Plan for Organizational Development: Identity, Participation and Equity* (East Lansing: Michigan State University Press). Also see B. E. G. Moore and T. L. Ross, 1978, *Scanlon Way to Improved Productivity: A Practical Guide* (New York: Wiley Interscience).

19. R. W. Luecke, R. J. Wise, and M. S. List, 1993, "Ramifications of the Family and Medical Leave Act of 1993," *Healthcare Financial Management* 47 (August): 32, 36, 38.

20. J. W. Fenton, Jr., and J. L. Kinard, 1993, "A Study of Substance Abuse Testing in Patient Care Facilities," *Health Care Management Review* 18 (Fall): 87–95.

21. R. Tomsho, 1994, "Mounting Sense of Job Malaise Prompts More Healthcare Workers to Join Unions," *Wall Street Journal* (9 June): B–1.

22. S. C. Simpson and J. Union, 1989, "Election Activity in the Hospital Industry," *Health Care Management Review* 14 (Fall): 21–28.

23. G. J. Bazzoli, 1988, "Changes in Resident Physicians' Collective Bargaining Outcomes as Union Strength Declines," *Medical Care* 26 (March): 263–77.

24. *McGraw-Hill's Washington Report on Medicine & Health*, 1986, 40 (24 February).

25. C. R. Gullett and M. J. Kroll, 1990, "Rule Making and the National Labor Relations Board: Implications for the Health Care Industry," *Health Care Management Review* 15 (Spring): 61–65.

26. D. Burda, 1991, "Service Employees International Union Accelerates Organizing Drives in Wake of Ruling on Bargaining Units," *Modern Healthcare* 21 (13 May): 7; L. Perry, 1991, "$500,000 Added to Nurses' Unionizing Efforts," *Modern Healthcare* 21 (April): 14.

27. M. L. Ile, 1989, "From the Office of the General Counsel, Collective Negotiation and Physician Unions," *Journal of the American Medical Association* 262 (17): 2444.

28. L. V. Sobol and J. O. Hepner, 1990, "Physician Unions: Any Doctor Can Join, But Who Can Bargain Collectively?" *Hospital & Health Services Administration* 35 (Fall): 327–40.

PLANT SYSTEM

THE MODERN health care organization has several different plants and plant-related services. Figure 16.1 shows the major facilities of an integrated health care system. At the simplest level, a number of primary care sites which are deliberately distributed throughout the community provide the usual medical office amenities. These facilities have few needs beyond those of other small service facilities. At the other extreme, the acute hospital provides complete environmental support not only for patients, but for staff and visitors as well. It provides all the services of a large hotel or office building, but with unusual hazards and narrower tolerances. It requires narrower tolerances on temperature, humidity, energy, air quality, cleanliness, and wastes. It has relatively higher volumes of human traffic, particularly during the night hours. Because of its traffic, it has high risks of personal and property safety. It deals with highly specialized equipment, expensive and dangerous supplies, and biological, chemical, and radiologic contaminants.

The plant system must meet all of these needs. It is the second largest system in terms of personnel. Housekeeping and food service often rank just behind the largest clinical departments in employees and costs. Consistent with the plan of the book, this chapter attempts to describe the plant system as it contributes to the other four systems of governance, finance, clinical, and human resources. It emphasizes what the chief operating officer and the heads of the clinical departments expect from plant services. The focus is on:

Figure 16.1 Facility and Supply Characteristics of Integrated Health Systems

Activity	Facility	Nonhealth Counterpart	Special Needs
Primary care	Small office	Small retail store	X-ray machine Drugs and clinical supplies Clinical waste removal
Outpatient specialty care	Medical office building	Shopping mall	Special electrical and radiologic requirements Drugs and clinical supplies Clinical waste removal
Long-term care	Nursing home	Motel	Extra fire safety and disability assistance Drugs and clinical supplies Clinical waste removal Pathogenic organisms Special air handling
Acute and intensive care	Hospital	Hotel	Extra fire safety and disability assistance Drugs and clinical supplies 24-hour security High traffic volumes Dangerous chemicals High-voltage radiology Radioactive products Clinical waste removal Pathogenic organisms Special air handling Emergency power

- The purpose of the plant system
- The functions which must be performed, with attention to the total requirement rather than the part traditionally assigned to plant departments
- The skills and organization required in plant systems
- The measures that show how well the job has been done and areas needing improvement.

There is a substantial library on the components of plant systems which this chapter does not replace. Some of the more general works are cited at the end of the chapter.

Purpose of the Plant System

The plant and the plant services determine in large part what impressions people form about the health care organization. They are thus an important element in promotional activity, not only in regard to patients but also in the recruitment of hospital team members. Beyond the minimum required for safety, the well-managed organization strives to operate a plant system which is reliable, convenient, attractive, and yet economical, because these are the expectations of members and customers.

Smooth, continuous operation of plant services is occasionally a matter of life and death. Several hazards, including fire, chemicals, radiation, infection, and criminal violence, can be life-threatening to employees, visitors, and patients. The well-run organization uses carefully designed, conscientiously maintained programs to reduce these risks to near vanishing.

> The purpose of the plant system is to provide the complete physical environment required for the mission, including all buildings, equipment, and supplies; to protect organization members and visitors against all hazards arising within the health care environment; and to maintain reliable plant services at satisfactory levels of economy, attractiveness, and convenience.

Functions

The numerous activities comprising the plant system can be grouped into seven major categories, as shown in Figure 16.2. It is noteworthy that the physical plant itself is only part of the system. Plant maintenance is obviously essential, but beyond that the plant system deals largely with services providing the environmental requirements for medical care. These range from lawn mowing and snow removal through security guards and signage to the life-support environments of surgery and intensive care. The range and variety of activities constitutes the challenge of managing the system. Everything must be done well: from the smallest primary care office to the inpatient intensive care unit.

Facilities Planning and Space Allocation

Facilities Planning

Plant operation begins with adequate planning for space and fixed equipment and continues through the life cycle of construction, maintenance, renovation, and eventual replacement. Health care plants are

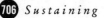

Figure 16.2 Functions of the Plant System

Function	Activities	Examples
Facilities planning	Planning, building, acquiring, and divesting facilities	Facilities plan Construction and renovation management Facilities leasing and purchase Space allocation
Facilities operation	Operation of buildings, utilities, and equipment	Repairs and routine upkeep Heat, air, and power services
Clinical engineering	Purchase, installation, and maintenance of clinical equipment	Magnetic resonance Laser surgery Respirator
Maintenance services	Housekeeping, grounds-keeping, and environmental safety	Cleaning Decorating Snow removal Safety inspections Waste management
Guest services	Support for workers, patients, and visitors	Parking Food service Security services
Supplies services	Materials management	Clinical supplies Drugs X-ray film Anesthesia gases
Continuous improvement and budgeting	Coordination with other systems, service improvement annual budget	Patient transport Cleaning schedules Energy conservation

built for their users, thus plans are often implemented by the development of architectural specifications and the management of construction contracts.

As shown in Figure 16.3, the facilities plan begins with an estimate of the space needs of each service or activity proposed in the services plan. Space needs must be described by location, special requirements, and size. Need is compared to available space, and deficits are met at the lowest cost. Conversion, renovation, acquisition by sale or lease, and new construction are the four major ways of meeting needs. Conversion, the simple reassignment of space from one activity to another, is the least expensive, but so many health care needs require specific locations and requirements that renovation, acquisition, or construction are frequently necessary. The final facilities plan shows the future location of all services and documents the renovation, acquisition, or construction necessary in terms of specific actions, timetables, and costs.

Forecasting Space Requirements

Given a forecast of demand for a service, space requirements are forecast from one of two simple models. Where demand can be scheduled or delayed until service is available:

(1) Facility required = Units of demand/time period
$$\times \text{ space/demand} \times (1/\text{load factor})$$

Figure 16.3 Facilities Planning Process

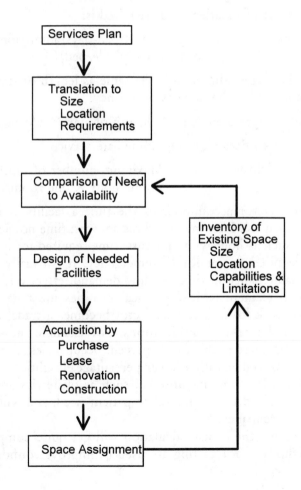

or, where demand must be met without delay (see the discussion of scheduling in Chapter 13):

(2) Facility required = Maximum units of demand in
single time period × space/unit.

The units of demand are the number of patients or services expected in a real time period, the space/unit is the amount of facility required by each patient or service, and the load factor is an allowance for facility idle time. Space per demand is often measured in specific time and facility dimensions, as machine hours/treatment or bed days/patient. Each element must be expressed in the same time period.

For example, for schedulable treatments and admissions, the number of treatment rooms required is:

Treatment rooms = Treatments/week × hours/treatment
× [1/(hours available/room-week)]

and the number of inpatient beds required is:

Beds = Admissions/year × bed-days/admission
× [1/(bed-days available/bed)]

(But since bed days/admission is the same as length of stay, and bed-days available/bed is the same as occupancy:

Beds = Admissions/year × length of stay × 1/occupancy

For stochastic services requiring immediate service:

Number of delivery rooms = Maximum number of mothers
in one hour × one room/mother

The load factor accommodates the time a facility is idle, and is always less than 1.0. Idle time has three sources: time not acceptable to customers, such as holidays and nights; time required for maintenance; and time required as standby for emergency. It is usually possible to schedule maintenance in times of low demand, effectively combining the first two elements. Most physical facilities must have some allowance for peak loads. The load factor becomes a trade-off between occupancy and market considerations. For example, most inpatient beds can be operated in the low 90 percent occupancies, although many are more comfortable with a lower percentage. Facilities where emergency demand is often encountered, such as obstetrics and coronary care, must be sized to accommodate patient need, and will operate at much lower occupancy.

Methods for the actual calculation will get quite complex. Often several methods of forecasting are used to improve confidence in the forecast. For example, surgeries will be categorized by type of room and square feet required. Each type of room will have several sources of demand which are forecast separately. Duration of operations will be studied through industrial engineering techniques. Trade-offs will be required among satisfaction with specific room designs and room locations, and between current efficiency and future flexibility. A room designed for a certain specialty might be highly inefficient for other demand. Trade-offs must also be evaluated between the efficiency of high load factors and the increased customer and member satisfaction and safety of lower levels. A simulation model might be constructed to evaluate trade-offs between various alternatives and establish the optimal load factors.

Renovation, Construction, and Acquisition

Implementing the facilities plan requires a comprehensive program of real estate and building management. The plan indicates the requirements and the way they will be met. These statements must be expanded into specifications and drawings for both space and fixed equipment, and translated to reality by completion of work. Real estate must sometimes be acquired, contracts let, progress maintained, and results inspected and approved before the facility can be occupied. In large projects, several years elapse between approval of the facilities plan and opening day.

Real estate is acquired through sale or lease. Lease approaches were rare in health care until the 1990s, although they are common in other industries. It is possible to lease all or part of a facility, including a single lease for a building and equipment designed and constructed specifically for the health care organization.

Major construction and renovation usually call for extensive outside contracting. The traditional approach is to retain an architect, a construction management firm, and a general contractor. Construction financed directly by public funds, such as that of public hospitals, usually must be contracted via formal competitive bids. Private organizations frequently prefer more flexible arrangements, negotiating contracts with selected vendors. Formal bidding may reduce collusion and fraud; but there is no evidence that it necessarily saves construction costs or total costs, including later maintenance and operation. Recent innovations have reduced the contracts by combining various elements; turnkey construction involves a single contract to deliver the finished facility. Advantages of speed and flexibility are cited, and it is likely that costs can be reduced if the health care organization is well prepared and supervises the process carefully.

Smaller renovation projects are often handled by internal staff. As an interim step, the organization can provide design and construction management, preparing the plans and contracting with specific subcontractors.

All parts of health care facilities are subject to safety and convenience regulations, with patient care areas having the highest standards. Most of the regulations are contained in the **Life Safety Code** and other codes developed by the National Fire Protection Association.[1,2] Licensure, JCAHO, and Medicare certification requirements enforce compliance. Facilities must also comply with federal standards for handicapped access.[3]

These regulations require routine inspection and maintenance. They often dictate important specifications of new construction. They require revision of previously approved construction when a renovation is made to the general area containing conditions no longer in compliance with the current code. They occasionally require renovation specifically to meet changes in the code. The length of time before compliance with current codes becomes mandatory is variable, depending upon the severity of the hazard. The degree of departure from current code is an important factor in renovation and remodeling plans.

Regardless of the size or complexity of the project, any project to change the use of space should be carefully planned in advance and closely managed as it evolves. A sound program includes

1. Review of the space and equipment needs forecast
2. Identification of special needs
3. Trial of alternative layouts, designs, and equipment configurations
4. Development of a written plan and specifications
5. Review of code requirements and plans for compliance
6. Approval of plan and specifications by the operating unit
7. Development of a timetable and PERT chart identifying critical elements of the construction
8. Contracting or formal designation of work crew and accountability
9. Ongoing review of work against specifications and timetable
10. Final review, acceptance, and approval of occupancy.

Space Allocation

The criterion for allocating existing space is conceptually simple. Each space should be used or disposed of in the way which optimizes achievement of the organization's mission. In reality, this criterion is quite difficult to apply. Activities tend to expand to fill the available space. As a result, there are always complaints of shortages of space and an agenda of possible reallocations or expansions. When activities shrink, the space is often difficult to recover and reuse. Space is highly valuable and unique; the third floor is not identical to the first. Space also confers prestige and symbolic rewards; space next to the doctors' lounge is more prestigious than space adjacent to the employment office. As a result, space allocation decisions tend to be strenuously contested.

Well-run organizations address this problem by incorporating space use and facility needs into their long-range planning, developing a facilities plan which translates the service decisions to specific available or needed space. The plan describes necessary additions or reductions in the space inventory. Each unit seeking substantial additional space or renovation must prepare a formal request and gain approval from the space office before submitting a new program or capital proposal following the procedures outlined in Chapter 7. The following guidelines assist in space management:

1. Space management is assigned to a single office which permits occupancy and controls access to space.
2. A key function of the space management office is the preparation of the long-range facilities plan. Planning and marketing staff assist in the preparation. The draft plan is derived from the services plan, and the final version becomes part of the planning package. The facilities plan includes
   - Forecasts of specific commitments for existing and approved space
   - Plans for acquisition of land, buildings, and equipment as indicated
   - Renovation, and refurbishing requirements for existing space
   - Plant revisions indicated by approved new services and technology, the physician recruitment plan, and the human resources plan
   - Plans for new construction.
3. The cost of the facilities plan is incorporated into the long-range financial plan and annual review and approval processes. This step assures a realistic financial plan.
4. Specific space allocation decisions are made as part of the planning process to assure widespread understanding of the decisions.
5. Acquisition, construction, and renovation are implemented by the plant department. Details of interior design are reviewed and approved by units which will be using the space.

Facility Operations

The important components of facilities operations are shown in Figure 16.4. A substantial amount of plant system activity is devoted to

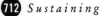

maintaining and replacing the physical plant and its major equipment. Even if most clinical equipment is assigned to clinical engineers, there is a substantial amount of expensive, complex equipment and several buildings to operate. Utilities services for health care institutions are often more demanding than routine. The cost of energy failures is so high that electrical and steam systems are usually built with substantial redundancy.

Maintenance and Repair Services

The objective of maintenance and repair services is to keep the facility and its equipment like new, so that the environment is not consciously identified by patients, visitors, and staff. The goal is achieved by emphasizing prevention. Most equipment requires periodic inspection and adjustment. When the cost of downtime is included, it is usually preferable to fix or replace equipment before it is broken. Well-managed plant systems schedule preventive maintenance for all the mechanical services. A significant fraction of mechanics' time is devoted to preventive maintenance, and adherence to the schedule is one of the measures of the quality of the department's work. Similarly, they inspect plant conditions such as floor and wall coverings, plumbing, roofs, and

Figure 16.4 Facility Operations: Buildings, Utilities, and Equipment

Maintenance and Repair Services	Utilities Services
Plant maintenance and refurbishing	Electrical service
Preventive maintenance	Backup service
Repair of conventional equipment	Emergency generation
Maintenance of nonclinical technical	Cogeneration
equipment	Heating and air conditioning
Vehicles	Routine needs
Laundry machinery	High-pressure steam
Elevators	Special air control problems
Heating, steam, and air conditioning	Communications support
equipment	Telephone, television, and
Other	computer wiring
	Radio communication
	Pneumatic tube systems
	Robot delivery systems
	Patient-related utilities
	Oxygen
	Suction

structural members regularly and schedule repair or replacement as they show deterioration.

The technical requirements dictate that contracts with outside vendors be used to maintain many of the more specialized items. Contracts should weight responsiveness and downtime appropriately and should be for relatively short periods, to permit prompt change of vendor if necessary. One issue is the question of who should initiate and supervise maintenance contracts. Well-run organizations tend to place the responsibility on the line unit using the equipment, if only one unit uses the equipment. The plant department is accountable for equipment in general use, such as elevators, and items is used in several units, such as telephone equipment. It is desirable that the unit using the equipment bear some accountability for the maintenance cost. All the actual contracting is centralized through materials management, which must consult with the accountable units.

The accountable unit is also responsible for initiating requests for replacement. These occur when the equipment is more expensive to maintain than replace, or when new technology offers substantial improvements in operating costs. In the case of critical equipment such as elevators and power supplies, it occurs when the risk of significant downtime reaches critical levels. The risk of significant downtime is highly subjective. Outside consultants are often used to evaluate costly equipment.

Provision of Utilities

Utilities for most outpatient offices are no different from other commercial buildings, but inpatient hospitals operate sophisticated utility systems that provide air, steam, and water at several temperatures and pressures and filter some air to reduce bacterial contamination.[4] They also provide multiple safeguards against failure, because of the extreme consequences. For example, hospitals supply high-pressure steam for sterilizing and laundry equipment. The use of higher pressures requires continuous surveillance by a licensed boiler operator. Operating rooms use specially filtered air, and several sites have unique heat control problems. As a result utilities are more elaborate than those usually found in public buildings.

Electrical systems are particularly complex. Two or three substations are desirable, with feeds approaching the hospital from opposite directions.[5] In addition, the hospital must have on-site generating capability to sustain emergency surgery, respirators, safety lights, and communications. Several areas must switch to the emergency supply automatically, requiring them to be separable from other, less critical uses.[6]

Many hospitals use their heating boilers to generate electrical power, a practice called cogeneration. The hospital's system is integrated with the public utility supplying electricity, and the utility buys any surplus the hospital generates. Alternatively, if the hospital is located close to a generating plant, it may buy steam from the utility, avoiding the cost of maintaining its own boiler.

Several other problems complicate the hospital's utility supply. Most hospitals pipe oxygen and suction to all patient care areas. Many also pipe nitrous oxide to surgical areas. Hospitals generally have a radio paging system and several external two-way radios for use in disasters or when telephone service is interrupted. Telephone service itself is becoming more complicated as it becomes more related to computer communication. Optical fiber networks are now recommended to replace conventional internal telephone wiring. Many hospitals use pneumatic tubes to transport small items such as paper records, drugs, and specimens. A few use automated robot cart systems to transport larger supplies.

Clinical Engineering

Integrated health care organizations require a wide variety of specialized clinical equipment which must be maintained near optimum operating characteristics and repaired or replaced as indicated. Apparatus like ventilators, magnetic resonance imagers, ultrasounds, multichannel chemical analyzers, electronic monitoring equipment, heart and lung pumps, and surgical lasers has become commonplace. The acquisition, maintenance, and replacement of this equipment is often assigned to professionally trained clinical engineers.[7] Their understanding of purposes, mechanics, hazards, and requirements allows them to increase the reliability of the machinery and reduce operating costs.[8,9]

The role of clinical engineering includes the following activities:

- Assisting the user department or group to develop specifications, review competing sources, and select clinical equipment
- Verifying that power, weight, size, and safety requirements are met
- Contracting for maintenance, or arranging training for internal maintenance personnel
- Periodic inspection of equipment for safety and effectiveness
- Developing plans for replacement when necessary .

Maintenance Services

The array of activities involved in housekeeping, grounds-keeping, and environmental control is shown in Figure 16.5.

Figure 16.5 Maintenance Services: Housekeeping, Grounds-Keeping, and Environmental Safety

Housekeeping
Interior decorating
Routine cleaning
    General patient areas
    High-risk patient areas
    Nonpatient areas
Special problem areas
    Odor control
    Sound control

Waste Management
Solid waste removal
Clinical waste removal
Recycling

Grounds-Keeping
Landscaping
Grounds maintenance

Environmental Safety
Physical control of chemical, biological, and radiological hazards
    Contaminant storage
    Contaminant waste removal
    Special cleaning and emergency
        procedures
Facility safety
    Inspection and hazard identification
    Hazard correction

Housekeeping and Grounds-Keeping

In well-run organizations these activities are supported by specialized equipment, training, and supplies. They are conducted to explicit standards of quality and are monitored by inspectors using formal survey methods. These activities also interact with important programs for environmental safety.

Housekeeping and grounds-keeping must maintain campuses in the millions of square feet efficiently at standards assuring bacterial and other hazard control. Some services, such as snow removal and exterior lighting, must be round the clock. Cleaning and landscape services are frequently subcontracted. The most common contracts are for management-level services. The outside firm supplies procedures, training, and supervision; the workers are hourly employees. Large organizations, and those with access to central services for training and development of methods, may be able to justify their own management.

Decorating and landscaping are done with an understanding both of public taste and of the cost of specific materials. Colors, fabrics, and designs are selected both for comfort and durability.[10] The best decorating creates an attractive ambiance, but is made of materials that do not show wear, and are durable, and easy to clean. Careful initial design leads to higher capital costs, but lower operating costs and greater user satisfaction. It is believed to contribute to patient recovery.[11]

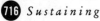

Waste Management

Environmental needs and hazards in clinical wastes have complicated the problem of waste management. Waste disposal must meet increasingly stringent governmental standards protecting the safety of land fills, water supplies, and air. Many cities require segregation of nonclinical wastes to permit recycling. Federal and state laws govern burning and shipment of wastes. A federal law governs handling of clinical wastes.[12] Although evidence that clinical wastes are particularly hazardous outside the institution is lacking, they must receive special handling from source to ultimate disposition.[13]

Within the health care organization, wastes must be handled correctly and efficiently.[14,15] Clinical wastes are a known hazard for hepatitis and AIDS contamination. Systems for waste management must be designed and taught to general housekeeping personnel.[16,17] Interim storage is usually required before shipment to the final site. Health care organizations usually contract for waste removal, but the handler must be certified for clinical wastes and charges more for handling them.

Environmental Safety

There are four basic approaches to control of hazardous materials. These approaches must be coordinated between different units in most health care organizations.

1. *Restricting exposure at the source.* The cheapest way to deal with a specific chemical contaminant is frequently to replace it. Good design and good procedures for cleaning and maintenance often reduce chemical contamination. Many of the chemicals used in health care organizations are selected as part of the clinical diagnosis and treatment, however, so review of the necessity for using dangerous chemicals is often a medical question.

   Restricting exposure to bacteriological contaminants is more difficult, and building design and operation are frequently important in that effort. Air and water handling systems can be made almost completely safe. Special handling is necessary for contaminated wastes. Human vectors in the spread of infection are harder to control, and they include both caregivers and plant personnel. Special gowns and techniques are used to protect workers and to prevent the spread of infection to other patients. Development of comprehensive control systems and monitoring of actual infection rates is a clinical function usually assigned to an infection control committee. It is wise to have at least one plant person on the infection committee. Larger organizations may have persons from plant operations, housekeeping, and central supply services available to consult with the infection committee.

2. *Cleaning and removal.* Construction materials and cleaning methods must reflect the need for bacterial and chemical decontamination. The housekeeping department is usually responsible for cleaning and removing hazardous substances. All horizontal surfaces are major sources of bacterial cross-contamination; in some areas, such as the operating rooms, more extensive attention is needed. There are occasionally special problems of chemical contamination as well, such as from the use of radioactive isotopes.

3. *Attention to exposed patients, visitors, and staff.* Trauma or infection results from exposure to contaminants, which can occur either during patient treatment or afterward, handling or disposing of equipment. Although much public attention has been given to AIDS, hepatitis is actually a more serious threat to hospital workers, and also occurs much more frequently among patients. Health care organizations must provide workers' compensation for any employee injury resulting from exposure. Although workers are entitled to their choice of physician, many organizations use a clinical member of the infection committee to examine any person believed to be injured and to provide care to those who will accept it. Concentrating cases in a single doctor provides continuity and promotes thorough understanding of hospital hazards.

4. *Epidemiological analysis of failures.* Epidemiological studies are an important part of an infection control program. Studies of the incidence of specific illnesses can detect incipient epidemics and may be the only way to reveal certain problems of chemical contamination. The information necessary for epidemiological studies frequently requires the assistance of a physician. The work requires special training in epidemiology. It is often assigned to a member of the infection committee.

Guest Services

Large numbers of patients, visitors, and staff become the guests of health care organizations and require a variety of physical services. People expect to come to a facility; park; find what they want; get certain amenities such as waiting areas, lounges, and possibly food; and leave without even recognizing that they have received service. Those telephoning expect a similarly complete, prompt, and unobtrusive response. The organization's attractiveness is diminished if the services listed in Figure 16.6 are either inadequate or intrusive. The personnel delivering the services are in constant contact with the organization's important constituencies. Their effect upon customer and member satisfaction is almost as great as nursing's.

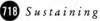

Figure 16.6 Guest Services: Workforce, Patient, and Visitor Support

Security Services
Guards
Employee identification
Facility inspection and monitoring

Food Service
Cafeteria and vending service
Patient food service
Routine patient service
Therapeutic diets

Communication and Transportation Services
Telephone and television service
Messenger service
Tube transport system
Reception and guidance
Signage
Parking
Telephone reception and paging

Guest services frequently involve multiple locations and small work groups, but they require coordinated management and a significant investment in centrally operated support systems. For example, receptionists and security personnel need current knowledge of the location of each inpatient and each special event or activity. Coordinated management of guest services stresses the importance of a satisfactory overall impression. It may also contribute to efficiency by allowing overlapping functions to be eliminated. Relations with housekeeping, security, and plant operations also require coordination.

Reception and Messenger Services

In a large health care organization, several dozen people have reception jobs that involve primarily meeting and guiding the organization's guests. Signs and display of telephone numbers (as in the Yellow Pages) aid efficient routing.

Patients and large physical items must be moved around the organization, and training in guest relations, emergency medical needs, and hospital geography are necessary to do the job well. Larger organizations have circulating vans connecting various sites. These move workers, patients and some supplies promptly and inexpensively. Because requests for transportation are often random and because it is difficult to supervise messengers, there are important efficiencies in pooling messenger needs. Very large organizations may have more than one pool, but smaller ones usually combine all messenger and reception activities under one supervisor.

Security Services

Security services are necessary in most settings to protect employees, visitors, patients, and property. There is a recognized hazard of theft, property destruction, and personal injury to workers and visitors. The hazard is particularly high in urban areas. High-quality security services are preventive. Security involves controlling access to the hospital, monitoring traffic flow, employee identification, and lighting to create an environment both reassuring to guests and discouraging to persons with destructive intentions.[18] Television and emergency call systems amplify the scope of surveillance.[19,20] Employee education is helpful in promoting safe behavior and prompt reporting of questionable events. Special attention must be given high-risk areas such as the emergency room[21] and parking.[22]

Uniformed guards are the final element of a high-quality program, not the initial one. They serve to provide a visible symbol of authority, to respond to questions and concerns, and to provide emergency assistance in those infrequent events which exceed the capability of reception personnel

Security is frequently a contract service, although it obviously must be coordinated with local police and fire service. Municipal units sometimes provide the contract service, particularly in government hospitals. Not-for-profit health care organizations usually do not pay local taxes in support of local fire and police service; as a result, there is often a question about the extent to which taxpayer services should be provided to the hospital. Some states have imposed fees upon not-for-profit organizations to reflect public services provided.

Emergency assistance should normally follow a previously developed security plan. The recurring major hazards of public areas should be addressed in the plan. These include armed and unarmed criminals, political protesters, and the insane; bomb threats, fires, and serious accidents involving damage or release of toxic materials. The security plan for major community disasters is particularly taxing and is part of the hospital disaster plan (Chapter 4).

Food Service

The preparation of hospital food has become a service similar to the food services of hotels, airlines, and resorts, rather than a clinical service. It must be conducted to high standards of quality, beginning with control of bacterial hazards and safety in preparation and distribution. Several foods are ideal media for bacterial growth. Employee hand washing and medical examinations are important to avoid systematic bacterial contamination. Further, careful food handling is necessary to prevent acute food poisoning. Kitchens include an unusual number of burn, fall, and injury hazards. Food service must also provide inexpensive, nutritious, appealing, and tasty meals that encourage good eating habits. It must supply them to remote locations and, either directly or by arrangement with nursing, deliver them to many people who are partially incapacitated.

Hospitals typically offer a choice of entrees, appetizers, and deserts to each patient on census. Patient meals must also be provided to a variety of clinical specifications. Soft, low sodium, and sodium-free diets comprise up to half of all patient meals; however, bulk foods meeting these specifications can be prepared by personnel without clinical training. In addition to patient meals, about an equal number are provided to staff and guests, usually in cafeterias. Visitors and employees expect greater variety, a range of prices, and service at odd hours. Hospitals now generally encourage visitors to eat in the cafeteria once reserved for doctors and employees. In addition, it is common to operate a snack bar or coffee shop and a variety of vending machines offering snack food and soft drinks.

These concerns are relatively easy to meet through sound general procedures. Food service is frequently contracted. Contract food suppliers meet the quality and cost constraints through centralized menu planning, well-developed training programs for workers and managers, and careful attention to work methods. Nutritional education and consultation and the preparation of special diets to meet medical needs is available through the clinical dietetics service. These professional nutritionists have an important advisory role in menu planning, but they have limited contact with the mass feeding operation.

Supplies Services

Health care organizations typically spend nearly 10 percent of their budget for supplies. Like other industries, they use office supplies, foodstuffs, linens and uniforms, fuels, paints, hardware, and cleaning supplies. They also use implants, whole blood, specialized dressings, single-purpose medical tools, and a large variety of drugs. Most supply costs are represented in the following six inventories, which are either large volumes of inexpensive items, like foodstuffs, or relatively small volumes of very expensive items, like implants:

- Surgical supplies and implants
- Anesthesia gases
- Drugs, intravenous solutions, and pharmaceuticals

- Foodstuffs
- Linen
- Dressings, kits, and supplies for patient care.

Improving the Materials Management Function

Materials management concentrates almost all supplies purchases under a single unit of the organization which is responsible for meeting standards of quality and service at a minimum total cost. The materials management function includes the activities shown in Figure 16.7. Many of these items conflict with one another. For example, larger-order quantities save delivery costs but increase warehouse costs, and cheaper distribution systems may increase user dissatisfaction or waste. Thus the problem of materials management is to design systems of acquisition which achieve the lowest overall costs, rather than simply purchasing at the cheapest price.

Specification of supplies is a critical component of materials management. Working with line personnel, materials management personnel strive to standardize similar items, establish criteria for appropriate quality, and eliminate unnecessary purchases. Reducing the number of items purchased reduces the number of orders which must be placed

---

Figure 16.7 Materials Management Activities

Material Selection and Control
Specifications for cost-effective
  supplies
Standardization of items
Reduction in the number of items

Purchasing
Standardized purchasing procedures
Competitive bid
Annual or periodic contracts
Group purchasing contracts

Receipt, Storage and Protection
Reduction of inventory size
Control of shipment size and
  frequency
Reduction of handling
Reduction of damage or theft
Economical warehouse operation

Processing
Elimination of processing by
  purchase or contract
Improved processing methods
Reduced reprocessing or turnaround
  time

Distribution
Elimination or automation of
  ordering
Improved delivery methods
Reduced end user inventories
Reduced wastage and unauthorized
  usage

**Revenue Enhancement and Cost
Accounting**
Uniform records of supplies usage

and the inventories which are required. It may eliminate unnecessarily expensive items. Examination of the application and alternative approaches may lead to improved methods and new supply specifications. Supplies which are processed for reuse are often costly. Use of disposables eliminates much reprocessing. Materials management personnel estimate the cost of disposable and reusable alternatives, and assist in selecting the more cost-effective. The new supply standard is met by contract with a small number of vendors working with professional purchasing personnel rather than end users. Purchasing personnel do not have the authority to change vendors or specifications unilaterally.

Most important, the larger volumes of standardized materials can be controlled more carefully for quality, and used to negotiate lower prices. The purchasing process itself uses longer-term contracting and competitive bidding to reduce prices. Most well-managed organizations now use **group purchasing**, cooperatives which use the collective buying power of several organizations to leverage prices downward. In addition, vendors contribute to the cost of the materials handling system. Automation of inventories, ordering, and billing reduces handling costs. "Just in time" deliveries are calculated to keep inventories at near zero levels. Most major vendors supply just-in-time service, effectively bearing the cost of inventory management as part of their activities rather than the health care organization's.[23] Some large vendors offer comprehensive materials management, providing a complete service at competitive costs.[24]

Significant savings are possible in materials handling systems. These systems receive, inspect, and store supplies, receive and fill orders, and record usage. Routine sampling of received goods assures quality. Centralized storage is protected against theft and damage. Division of duties guards against embezzlement and accounting fraud. Usage records and automated delivery systems reduce or eliminate inventories at the point of use, and are designed to achieve low-cost handling. Materials management includes the design of distribution systems and the maintenance of usage records. Automatic resupply reduces time spent by end users ordering and checking supplies. Some bulk supplies are now delivered by robots to reduce costs.[25] Finally, automated records of supplies use provide data for cost analysis, and in cases where individual payments are made for the supplies, posting of account receivables.

Continuous Improvement and Budgeting

Like all other systems of the health care organization, the plant system must explicitly devote time to improving quality and efficiency of service. Plant systems have undergone substantial revision in recent years. Materials management programs, energy conservation programs, environmental hazard controls, and security services are vastly different from a decade ago. That trend will continue in the decade to come. The cycle of identifying, studying, and improving processes, and incorporating the improvement into the next annual budget, will be a fixture of plant systems management. Much of the improvement activity will involve coordination of services with other units. Much of it will also involve longer-term activities, such as revisions centered around capital replacement.

The Improvement Cycle

The cycle of improvement and budget development and achievement is shown in Figure 16.8. A key function of leadership is to stimulate the cycle. The goal is to have several improvement concepts in process, completing a few each year to meet externally imposed budget standards, so that each year's budget is both acceptable and achievable.

Figure 16.8 Cycle of Continuous Improvement and Budgeting for the Plant System

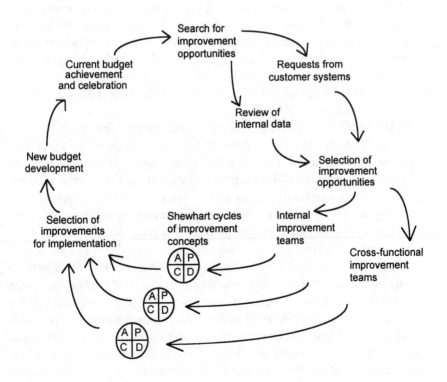

Well-run organizations now hold plant services responsible for meeting market demands for cost and quality. The other systems and their employees join patients and families as explicit customers. Satisfaction of customer requirements, including both price and quality, is the consuming goal. The plant system operates as a service organization for the rest of the world, as a resort hotel might. Like the hotel, it views itself as one of many alternatives where customers could spend their money. Measurement of achievement, revision of methods and equipment, annual expectation setting, training, and reward are the tools for improving service.

Attractive, convenient, comfortable plant services are a competitive asset. Without them, market share may fall. As it does, volume declines, forcing fixed costs per discharge up. Thus final product efficiency may depend more on the quality of plant service than on its intermediate product efficiency. Ingenuity and effort are necessary to avoid reducing quality of plant service under severe cost constraints. Organizations may at times wish to increase plant system costs to gain an advantage in the market.

The well-run organization is moving rapidly toward comprehensive performance measurement which allows direct comparison with alternative sources or desired performance levels. A housekeeping service, for example, can compare its cost to outside contractors' and its customer satisfaction ratings to external benchmarks or internal goals. It conducts process quality review, and can identify variation in its own performance as well as compare itself to industry standards. It surveys its staff, and collects data on absenteeism and turnover which can also be compared to industry standards. (See Measures of Performance below.)

At the same time, the department is evaluated by the other systems of the organization, and is receptive to the needs of those systems. Requests for cross-training, revised scheduling, special cleaning needs are welcomed, and handled as marketing opportunities. Out of the internal review and the requests of the customer systems comes the agenda for improvement. The department pursues that agenda constantly, through internal studies and participation in cross-functional task forces.

Many issues in final product efficiency relate to the coordination of services between clinical services and plant services. New food service systems must coordinate with nursing; patient transportation must adapt to new diagnostic services; new supplies and methods of assembling supplies must be revised for new nursing intermediate product protocols. These improvements are designed by cross-functional teams or by internal teams of clinical services which will require close cooperation by plant systems units. The opportunity to participate on these teams is valuable in two senses. First, the cognitive exchange of information leads to a better result. Second, the participants on the team gain insight into the underlying customer needs. They come away from the process understanding why the improvement was necessary, and more committed to making it work.

Cross-functional team membership is now assigned to the lowest level of personnel capable of addressing the issue. This is often the workers themselves. Food service workers participate on the cross-functional team designing a new food service. (The team will also have membership from nursing, materials management, and clinical nutrition.) The assignment brings a practical perspective not previously available, but more important it demonstrates empowerment to the work group and provides an opportunity to reward work group leadership.

Most improvements are related to changes in work methods rather than better motivation of workers. New methods resulting from cross-functional teams must be explained and sold to plant workers. Internal improvements usually involve changes in equipment and methods. The way in which new methods and equipment are introduced is often critical to their success. The improvement process should follow the Shewhart cycle of Plan-Do-Check-Act (Chapter 2). Improvements from cross-functional teams should be explained, justified, and demonstrated to plant workers as part of their implementation. Alignment—understanding and acceptance—of the plant workers is essential to success; omitting explanation and justification endangers alignment.

Internal improvement teams should be composed mainly of workers. The function of the supervisor is ideally to coach, motivate, and make the opportunity clear. Retraining of workers is often critical to success of the new method. Part of the Check activity involves identifying new methods and learning how to teach them.

The annual budget establishes goals for each dimension of performance for each responsibility center. The next year's goals must meet price and quality standards imposed by the larger organization by implementing improvements developed during the year. An aggressive continuous improvement program should allow most plant units to meet the budget requirements. The new budget should be easily achievable; the challenge should be in finding the improvements for the subsequent year, not in making the proposed budget. Most units should be able to celebrate achieving the current budget as a motivation to work on the next. Failure to improve, or to remain competitive with alternate suppliers, suggests the need to restructure the service or to change suppliers.

Evaluating Long-Term Opportunities

Many opportunities for major improvements in plant services require extensive recapitalization. They involve renovation of large areas or installation of improved equipment and therefore must be integrated with the organization's overall replacement schedule. Opportunities to restructure plant services arise when the organization faces equipment or facility replacement in these areas. Some of these opportunities arise when other systems propose major expansions or renovations. Windows of opportunity arise which close as commitments are made for new facilities and equipment. For example, consider an organization which has operated its own laundry for many years. Its existing equipment is still useful, but aging and already less efficient than current models. As long as the equipment is still serviceable, contract laundry services may not be price competitive, but when the organization faces a major investment to replace that equipment contract services are suddenly more attractive. Similarly, an opportunity to use the existing laundry space for more productive activities changes the desirability of contract services. The alternative use represents an opportunity cost which makes contract service more attractive. The alternative use is also a window; the need will be met in other ways if the laundry site is not promptly evaluated.

Major windows of opportunity are usually two or three years long, covering several budget cycles. They must be identified as part of the facilities plan, evaluated, and accommodated by plant system management. The annual environmental assessment should include review of the facilities and equipment plan and explicit evaluation of opportunities to purchase plant services from outside vendors. The review will require collaboration between facilities planning and space allocation people and the planning unit. The plant system managers must be cognizant of the review and of the basic principle, that any plant service is retained only when it is more effective than an outside contractor. When the decision is made to close a plant service, effective programs to make the necessary conversions require careful planning in themselves.

Personnel Requirements and Organization

Personnel Requirements

Managers and Professional Personnel

There are few widely recognized educational programs in plant management. The professional societies have not offered registration as a qualification for employment, but they do suggest that active membership should be a criterion.[26] As a result, job descriptions depend heavily on prior experience. Contract management firms have extensive on-the-job training and may be the best source of managers.

A bachelor's degree in engineering is generally considered necessary for facility operation managers, particularly if construction responsibilities are included. Some large organizations also employ architects, a profession with both formal education and licensure. Although there are licensure requirements for professional engineers and architects in consultative practice, the requirements do not apply to employment situations. Clinical equipment engineers generally have bachelor's engineering degrees, and specialized programs are available.[27,28]

Materials managers should acquire general business knowledge. Course work in law and business is certainly an asset, but much of the needed knowledge can also be acquired by well-supervised experience. Security managers frequently have active police experience and at least bachelor's degrees in their field. Food service managers have bachelor's degrees, and extensive experience in bulk food preparation.

Several professions are involved in environmental safety. Infection control is often the concern of a medical or nonmedical epidemiologist. Both have formal educational requirements. The physician is frequently privileged in communicable disease and in any case should be subject to routine credentials review. Medical advice on the selection of a nonmedical epidemiologist is highly desirable. Hospitals with high-voltage radiation therapy services usually employ a radiation physicist, who can also assist with radiation safety. Large hospitals employ toxicologists to assist with control of chemical contamination. There is an engineering specialty known as safety engineering. Consultative services in all of these areas are often available through the local public health department.

Employees

The traditional building trades and stationary engineers provide apprenticeships. They are usually licensed by local or state authorities, but licensure is not mandatory for employees under appropriate supervision. Security personnel are frequently former police and may have attended college programs in police work. Job descriptions in these fields normally require the appropriate license or certificate and consider relevant prior experience favorably.

All other employees are recruited as unskilled labor or, in the case of materials management, clerical labor. Even if they have had prior experience, they must be trained on the job in the policies of the hospital. Although the tasks are repetitive, there are clear advantages to the correct use of tools and supplies, and process control is usually important to both efficiency and quality.

Training and Incentives

Cost-effective plant services require both preparation of employees to do the work and incentives for doing it well. The plant system has a variety of training needs for both employees and supervisors. It also requires a system of nonmonetary and monetary incentives to motivate its personnel.

Training Needs

Most plant employees need explicit training in how to do their jobs. As methods and equipment become more sophisticated, a worker who does not fully understand both what must be done and how to do it cannot produce at a competitive level. As a result, sound plant systems programs teach new workers and retrain old ones on an ongoing basis. In addition to job content, purpose, and method, employee training for several plant areas must include guest relations. As participation on improvement teams increases, workers must be trained in continuous improvement fundamentals.

Supervisors need all these skills, including mastery of the work methods. At least one of the contract housekeeping services, Service-Master, insists that all its supervisors including the company president spend a week doing the most menial housekeeping jobs. In addition, supervisors need explicit training in supervision. Conventional wisdom about the supervisory process is quite different from empirically tested models of what supervision should be. The folklore of the boss who gives orders and has special privileges must be replaced with an understanding of a supportive leader who is obligated to find answers to employee questions. Formal education including case studies and role playing establishes the desired model. Constant reinforcement is necessary to keep it in place. Supervisors also need advanced training in continuous improvement and training in budgeting.

These training programs must all be carried out at a high school level, and in many communities they must accommodate several languages. The emphasis is on action, practice, graphics, and only lastly words. The training programs all present important opportunities to build the employee's pride in craftsmanship and loyalty to the organization.

Increasing Incentives and Rewards

If attention is paid to measures, goals, and methods, the gains from reward systems are greatly increased, both for the worker and for the hospital. Three desirable guidelines are that most expectations should be met, rewards for good performance should be frequent and generous, and sanctions should be rare. (Not surprisingly, this is as true for the plant system as for the medical staff.)

The most important incentives are nonmonetary. Pride of achievement is probably the most important. It is supported by prompt reporting of formal measures, well-designed methods, appropriate training, and responsive supervision. Recognition of achievement includes both verbal and nonverbal responses of the supervisor. The amount of recognition should be tailored to the level of achievement: any positive response should be recognized by the supervisor, above average results by coworkers, and extraordinary achievement by the organization at large. The supervisor is critical in pride of achievement and recognition.

Explicit monetary incentives, beyond the basic contract for compensation and employment, appear to play a relatively minor role in motivating workers. For example, they cannot overcome disincentives from poor supplies or inadequate training. Nor do they effectively replace pride of achievement. They are most powerful as supplements to nonmonetary incentives, where even a small payment serves to show the seriousness of management intent. Monetary incentives can be dysfunctional when they encourage unneeded output or disregard of customer wants. They can be defeated by the workers, who can exaggerate supply and equipment problems and create grievances.

Use of Contract Services

Health care organizations have always used contract services extensively. Smaller organizations have relied on building management firms for plant services and a variety of specialized vendors for equipment maintenance. Hospitals traditionally contracted more selectively, usually for specialized equipment like elevators and services like groundskeeping. Major construction usually involves contracts with a planning consultant, an architectural firm, and a builder. It is not surprising, therefore, that, when specific technologies began to emerge for laundry, housekeeping, specialized equipment maintenance, food service, and security, health care organizations turned quickly to contracts which provided inexpensive access to them.

The trend in plant services has been away from ownership and toward contract service for some years, and it is likely to continue. The movement in health care organizations parallels one in industry in general.[29] The following sections review the advantages and disadvantages of contracting, varieties of contract arrangements, and guidelines for successful contracting.

Advantages and Disadvantages to Contracting

The advantage of contracting is access to the contractor's repository of specialized knowledge. A contractor like ServiceMaster, which provides housekeeping and food services to about 2000 health care organizations, quickly acquires an experience base in its areas which exceeds even the largest health care organization's. By specializing in a function and building up experience and activity in that area, the contractor can

1. Develop a cadre of experienced people equipped to solve whatever problems may arise
2. Develop more efficient methods:
   - Specify better tasks, tools, and supplies
   - Train personnel more effectively
   - Develop more precise measures of quality and efficiency
3. Develop and implement software:
   - Improve scheduling
   - Develop quality control
   - Capture and analyze cost and use data
4. Learn more effective ways of motivating personnel
5. Take advantage of larger volumes:
   - Gain lower prices on supplies and equipment
   - Support more cost-effective substitution of capital for labor.

The list is the same set of factors that supports any industrial specialization. Different services have different profiles of specific advantages. In each case, success is proved by growth in the marketplace. Several forms of contracting have met this test.

The disadvantage of contracting is loss of control over quality or price. In an ideal competitive market, a contractor would be forced to match the best competitor on both dimensions, but few markets are ideal. Incomplete or incorrect specification of the desired service may lead to excessive cost or dissatisfaction. The savings may not be passed back to the health care organization. Ineffective supervision of the contract may lead to suboptimal achievement of its terms. Monopoly or ineffective negotiation may leave most of the savings with the supplier. Successful contract suppliers grow and may not be as efficient as they once were. Growth can create personnel shortages, unexpected problems, overcommitment, inflexibility, and loss of motivation.

Thus there is always a point of equilibrium at which contracting and not contracting are equally appealing. The equilibrium is subject to adjustment with changing conditions. It is quite possible that two almost identical organizations will reach opposite conclusions about contracting.

Extent of Contracting

Service contracts vary in scope and duration. The simplest are short-term, task-oriented contracts, such as consulting arrangements or equipment repair contracts. The most complex are long-term commitments for multiple tasks or even for a general purpose. A large-scale construction contract or a contract to operate an entire hospital is an example. Awarding and administering service contracts depends upon their duration, complexity and uniqueness. Simple contracts can be delegated directly to line units, although dollar limits and review by accounting or materials management personnel are used to limit authority. A contract for hospital operation or a major construction project would require governing board action. In between, contracts for managing the entire plant or the major functions shown in Figure 16.2 can be delegated to executive management once initial criteria and procedures are approved by the governing board. Service contracts for the component activities of Figure 16.2 can be effectively assigned to materials management for negotiation and middle management for execution.

The list of actual contracts between health care organizations and service firms is quite long, and growing. The service corporation is usually a for-profit company, and is often a national corporation. Examples include

- Contracts for specified discrete tasks, such as job classification and salary surveys, preventive maintenance, or construction
- Sporadic or infrequent services, such as snow removal, equipment evaluation, or consultation on specific problems
- Contracts for general equipment maintenance or updates
- Contracts for clinical equipment maintenance or updates[30]
- Contracts for continuing services, such as housekeeping, food service, laundry, data processing, and security
- Contracts for complete functions, such as comprehensive materials management services, turnkey construction, or complete facility management.

All forms of contracting seem to have been increasing, but the last four have risen from near zero to a substantial fraction of hospital expenditures. Although exact figures are difficult to obtain, the total is probably 3 to 5 percent of hospital expenditures, approaching $20 billion a year.

Criteria for Successful Contracting

Well-run organizations negotiate contracts in a way that will exploit the advantages and disadvantages to their overall benefit. This is not necessarily to the supplier's disadvantage; the best contracts are frequently those in which both parties win. The following conditions make a successful result more likely:[31]

1. The organization has a full, clear, and realistic understanding of the service desired:
   a. Descriptions of the scope of work are unambiguous.
   b. Systems are in place to measure supplier's performance with regard to demand, output, quality, and cost.
   c. Quantitative expectations on these parameters have been developed from history or benchmarking.
2. There is a competitive market. Several suppliers have records of effective performance in similar situations and demonstrate both interest and capability in the service to be performed.
3. Resources which the health care organization must supply are available:
   a. Facilities and equipment are scheduled for the contractor's use.
   b. Systems for supplying orders and other necessary communications are in place.
   c. Terms, methods, and personnel for contract supervision can be specified.
   d. Programs for the transfer of activity have been developed.
4. The contractor will have a clearly identified manager in the organization who has both skills and rank appropriate to the scope of the contracted work.
5. An initial request for proposals is used to evaluate suppliers and to improve the quality of the specifications:
   a. Invitations include all potentially qualified bidders.
   b. Initial specifications avoid accidental or arbitrary restriction of bidders or of potential gains. The scope of work is pragmatically defined to cover items which are essential to the organization and also achievable by a satisfactory number of bidders.
   c. Suppliers are encouraged to respond with modifications or extensions of the initial specifications; these can be evaluated on their merits.
   d. Further discussion with suppliers can help develop the best possible final specifications.
6. Qualified suppliers are selected from the initial round and asked to submit more detailed proposals, including competitive prices.
   a. Sufficient bidders are invited to the second round to encourage competitive pricing.

b. Format for the final proposal is specified closely enough to permit direct comparison of bids.

c. Opportunity to price alternatives and options separately remains.

d. Contract length is kept to a relatively short period, or termination on short warning is permitted, to provide continuing incentive for achieving the hospital's expectations.

Steps 5 and 6 normally apply only to complex, long-term contracts.

The difficulty with these criteria is that they fail to cover realistic situations in which the organization is justified in seeking a service contract. They say, in effect, that when there are several well-managed suppliers, an organization with a service that is already well managed can negotiate a good contract. While this is true enough, it overlooks situations in which the organization must correct serious weaknesses in plant systems services and situations in which one dominant service contractor has developed an exceptional record. Some issues to consider in those situations are as follows:

• Initial competition can be against the organization's own performance. Renewals present a problem. Either benchmarks must be found, independent consultants used, or the renewal must be subjectively evaluated. The possibility of restoring internal service at a future date should be explicitly evaluated.

• The expertise of the supplier can often be used to strengthen the expectations and establish measures of performance. This can be done either through negotiations, short-term consulting contracts prior to a longer-term commitment, or contracts which specify the development or improvement of performance measures. Contracts for improvement of performance generally contain incentive payments or penalties.

• A poorly run organization or service may have to sacrifice price for quality improvement.

• An organization which assists a new company or pioneers in new areas of contract services should anticipate extra benefits in the form of price reduction or profit sharing on future sales.

Organization of Plant Services

Comprehensive Accountability

Traditionally, larger health care organizations have had chief engineers, purchasing agents, housekeepers, security officers, food service heads, and central supply supervisors with departmental status reporting independently to deputy or chief operating officers. Communications

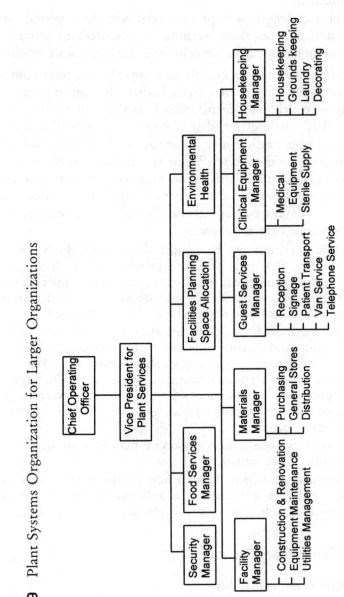

Figure 16.9 Plant Systems Organization for Larger Organizations

services and other support activities tended to be assigned expediently. Comprehensive plant accountability, that is, concentrating plant services under one manager reporting to the COO, seems to have been rare, but it is likely to become more common.

Plant systems organization should be flexible for organization size and extent of outside contracting. Figure 16.9 shows a general model for plant systems organization in a large health care organization. The approach is relatively flat, although the managers on the lower row will have several responsibility centers. Any item on Figure 16.9 can be contracted to an outside firm, including the Vice President for Plant Services.

The assignment of several small activities of Figure 16.9 is debatable.[32] Some or all of guest services and housekeeping can be assigned to facilities operation, for example. Alternatively, guest services and security can be merged. Laundry can be elevated to a manager level, and probably will be if the institution operates its own laundry.

Smaller organizations will be more likely to use contract services. They must still provide the full array of services, and finding specialists in all the areas is expensive and often difficult. In general, the simpler activities such as food service, housekeeping, or security are easier to contract, while the most complicated ones, such as facility operations and materials management, are more difficult. The risk of an unsatisfactory contract rises with the complexity of the assignment. Facility planning and space allocation is the most problematic, and most likely to be retained internally.

The most debatable question appears to be the organizational locus of materials management. Surprisingly, leading materials managers themselves feel that the "importance placed on materials management . . . was related more to who reports to the materials manager than to whom the material manager reports."[33] One option would be to treat the unit as part of finance, but this places product delivery in what is otherwise an information-processing activity, creating few promotional opportunities for the successful manager. The concept of separation of duties to discourage fraud and abuse also militates against the close association of materials control and accounting. A second option would be for the materials manager to report directly to the COO. A third is the hierarchy suggested here, reporting to the manager of plant services, who reports to the COO.

Within the materials management organization itself there seems to be virtue in centralization of authority. The managers surveyed by Holmgren and Wentz saw all plant services except housekeeping, security, and plant operations as their "ideal" domain.[34] They also believed they should control all inventories, including drugs and foodstuffs, although they conceded the need for clinical functions in the dietary and pharmacy departments. Although materials management can easily include supervision of annual contracting for housekeeping and similar services, it seems unlikely that other guest services would be grouped with materials services.

Measures of Performance

Plant services must first be reliable and safe, then satisfactory to hospital members and visitors, and finally efficient. Measures for the closed system parameters are well developed and can usually be transferred easily from industrial sites or between hospitals.

Measures of Output and Demand

Output and demand for plant system services are usually measured identically; output is simply that portion of demand which is filled. Demand is measured differently for each of the functions of the plant system, using various combinations of patient or service requests, specific facility required, and duration, as reflected in the examples shown in Figure 16.10.

To establish resource expectations, it is necessary to forecast demand. This is usually possible by taking the product of service requests times duration for each identified physical resource. Questions of random and cyclic fluctuation are important. The demand forecasts for

Figure 16.10 Examples of Demand Measures for Plant System Functions

Service Request	Incidence Measure	Duration Measure
Surgery cleanup	Number of cases	Minutes/case
Heating/air conditioning	Degree-days	N/A
General housekeeping	Square footage	Minutes/square foot
Specialized housekeeping	Square footage by type	Minutes/square foot by type
Safety inspection	Specific type	Hours/inspection
Meal service	Meals/day by type	N/A
Security and reception	Personnel by location	Hours/day
Supplies	Units by type	N/A

plant systems consist of a large set of numbers arranged to reflect the specific physical resources, the numbers of services requested, and the duration of service. Frequency distributions or ranges by categories of demand are frequently required to set sound resource expectations.

Many activities of the plant system require short-term forecasts, with horizons ranging from hours to months. Efficiency in supply and service processes such as housekeeping, heating, and food service depends upon careful adjustment to variation in demand. Well-run organizations are supplying current estimates of demand for services like these from order entry and nursing scheduling systems. (Several kinds of service are related to patient acuity.) It is likely that, in the future, patient scheduling systems will be used to forecast demand for these services.

Inventory management calls for slightly longer-term forecasts. The key to efficiency and quality of service is accurate forecasts of demand at the most detailed level possible. These forecasts can be used to operate exchange cart deliveries, minimizing out-of-stock items and emergency trips, and to maintain optimum inventory levels and ordering cycles. In well-run organizations, they are prepared from past experience, carefully analyzed for trends, cycles, and random variation. The preparation of these forecasts is normally the obligation of the materials management unit, with guidance from finance and planning. Experienced materials managers can often make useful subjective refinements to statistically prepared forecasts.

Measures of Resource Consumption

Personnel, supplies, and capital resources are all important in plant services. The costs and physical units of all the resources involved should first be accounted to a plant system responsibility center. The plant responsibility center can be held accountable for the total cost of operating the unit, including labor, materials, and capital costs consumed by the unit, as well as purchase price, inventory level, and wastage of inventoried supplies.

Standard cost-accounting practices have some important limitations. Capital costs are accounted at straight-line depreciation of original purchase price, without interest, often resulting in substantial understatement. Inventory costs are rarely adjusted for the value of money invested in inventory. Only the most elaborate cost-accounting systems incorporate all the other costs of maintaining the plant service. A rental concept of capital (that is, the current market cost to rent

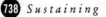

the facility or equipment involved) may be more useful, particularly in deciding whether to continue operating plant system units or to contract services. Similarly, inventory handling costs can include the interest earned on capital rather than the amount invested.

Fixed and Variable Costs

Traditional functional accounting also has inaccuracies because it fails to identify fixed and variable costs. Flexible budgeting and cost-accounting techniques are particularly appropriate for plant units with high variability in demand, such as food service, laundry service, and heating. Fixed cost elements, that is, those not sensitive to changes in demand are budgeted annually and minimized principally through changes in work processes. In the case of variable cost items, including some labor costs and most supplies consumed, the plant responsibility center manager can be held accountable for units used and price, while the line manager is responsible for volume. By identifying the elements of cost variation, one can deal with each as a separate management problem.

When the goods or services are used by another responsibility center, a separate accounting transfers the cost incurred to the user. Transfer pricing (Chapter 8) can be used to distribute the cost to the users. Final product costs representing services actually sold to patients or their insurers are aggregated from user costs, as shown in Figure 16.11. This system permits triple accountability for the costs. The using responsibility center is accountable chiefly for the quantities used. The final product cost can be evaluated by a cross-functional team in the light of competitive prices.

Measures of Human Resources

Well-managed plant systems can retain stable productive workforces despite relatively low wages for most jobs. The secret lies in the quality of training and supervision, and the appropriate use of nonmonetary and monetary incentives. The quality, loyalty, and attitude of the workforce can all be measured. Personnel records show training program completion absenteeism, and disciplinary incidents. Turnover and recruitment statistics show loyalty. (The workers themselves recruit to fill many jobs.) Attitudes are assessed by periodic survey, as they are for other systems.

Measures of Efficiency

Figure 16.11 shows measures for both the intermediate product and final product efficiency. They are identical to the transfer price and

Figure 16.11 Sequence of Cost Accounting and Resource Management

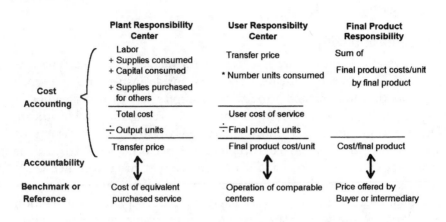

the components of cost per final product. The intermediate product efficiency is expressed as cost (or physical unit of resource) divided by number of such units produced by responsibility center or RC group, for example:

- Energy cost (or BTUs) per square foot of floor space
- Labor cost (or hours) per pound of linen
- Raw food cost (or ounces of food) per meal served
- Materials handling costs (or cubic feet of storage) per pound of supplies purchased.

It is a relatively simple matter to generate these measures for many plant service responsibility centers. Benchmarks and scientific standards for these values are widely available. Labor standards for laundries, kitchens, and the like and cost standards for energy use, construction, renovation, and security are supplied by numerous consultants.

The final product cost of plant services is the amount of the resource consumed to supply a specific episode of care, such as a birth or a surgical procedure to the patient. As shown in Figure 16.11, it is aggregated through user departments.

Some problems become easier with a final product approach. While the intermediate efficiency of certain responsibility centers remains problematic, many final product cost efficiencies, such as security costs per discharge or space management cost per discharge, are easily measured. Most important, it is final product efficiency which meets exchange demands and therefore must be used to guide the expectations for each plant service unit. That is, the true performance requirements for a plant system are set by exchange demands, the price the public is willing to pay for the service. Efforts to understand efficiency require-ments in terms of history or technology rather than willingness to pay can be seriously misleading.

Measures of Quality

Plant systems generally are not lacking for quality measures. The ma-jor sources are users, outside inspectors, inside inspectors, and work records; the number and variety of examples has grown steadily in recent years. The Joint Commission on Accreditation of Healthcare Organizations includes a thorough review of structural measures of plant safety and has moved to emphasize performance statistics for plant services.[35,36] Internal audits of plant systems are recommended.[37] Line managers, particularly in nursing, should be encouraged to report any maintenance failure that is likely to reduce patient satisfaction or safety promptly. Repeated reports on the same problem indicate a major deficiency in quality. Figure 16.12 shows important measures of quality that are available to almost any health care organization.

Process measures are useful in monitoring day-to-day activity. In-spections are critical to laundry, food service, supplies, maintenance,

Figure 16.12 Measures of Quality for Plant Systems

Type	Approaches	Examples
Outcomes	Surveys	Visitor and staff satisfaction
	Incidents counts	Falls, complaints
	User complaints	Cleanliness/repair problems reported by user departments
Process	Raw materials inspection	Compliance to purchase specification
	Service/product inspections	Food preparation, patient food tray, telephone response delay
	Contract compliance	On-time supplies delivery
	Supply failures	Back-ordered items
	Inventory wastage	Losses of supplies
	Schedule failures	Delays in patient transport construction deadlines
	Automated monitoring	Temperature and humidity control
Structure	Plant inspections	Licensure survey
	Equipment inspections	Elevator maintenance
	Worker qualifications	Stationary engineer coverage

and housekeeping. Subjective judgment is usually required, but it is improved by clear statements of process standards for cleanliness, temperature, taste, appearance, and so on. The frequency of inspection is adjusted to the level of performance, and performance is improved by training and methods rather than negative feedback. Work reports, like incident reports, reveal correctable problem areas in plant maintenance and materials management.

Back orders, incomplete work, and delays in filling orders can be reported as incidents or as ratios of days' work outstanding. These are essentially failure statistics, and they need to be classified by severity or importance. Being out of stock, particularly of critical items, can be treated similarly. Many utilities services are now automated, so permanent records exist of environmental conditions. Under automated order systems and electronic accounting of supplies use from exchange carts, out-of-stock items and back orders can be reported automatically as well.

Implicit Prices or Resource Constraints

The plant system, like any other part of the health care organization, must operate in recognition of buyer and patient imposed limits on costs. Thus no measurement system is complete without a market price, an implicit market price, or a carefully constructed constraint on total costs.

Plant services are only rarely sold directly, so that market tests of cost and efficiency are usually impossible. Constraints on costs are derived from two sources: the competitive prices of outside vendors, as shown in Figure 16.11, and the internal needs developed from the budget guidelines. The former are preferable wherever they can be obtained. While plant services must make a fair contribution to overall budget needs, determining what that contribution should be is difficult. Approaches which try to balance the total cost by arbitrary reduction of plant costs are dangerous; the quality of plant services is too visible and too important.

Suggested Readings

Chaff, L. F. 1989. *Safety Guide for Health Care Institutions*, 4th ed. Chicago: American Hospital Publishing.

Chaff, L. F., and U.S. Department of Health and Human Services. 1993. *Guidelines for Construction and Equipment of Hospital and Medical Facilities, 1992–93 ed.* Washington, DC: American Architects Press, with assistance from the U.S. Department of Health and Human Services.

James, P., and T. Noakes, eds. 1994. *Hospital Architecture*. New York: Longman.

Joint Commission on the Accreditation of Healthcare Organizations. 1990. *Emergency Preparedness: When the Disaster Strikes.* Oakbrook Terrace, IL: JCAHO.

Kowalski, J. C. 1990. *Materials Management: Policy and Procedure Manual.* St. Louis, MO: Catholic Health Association.

Malkin, J. 1992. *Hospital Interior Architecture: Creating Healing Environment for Special Patient Populations.* New York: Van Nostrand Reinhold.

Theodore, L. 1990. *Air Pollution Control and Waste Incineration for Hospitals and Other Medical Facilities.* New York: Van Nostrand Reinhold.

Tomasik, K. M. 1989. *Plant, Technology, and Safety Management Handbook: Safety Management, Life Safety Management, Equipment Management, Utilities Management,* 2d ed. Oakbrook Terrace, IL: Joint Commission on Accreditation of Healthcare Organizations.

U.S. Department of Labor. 1993. *Framework for a Comprehensive Health and Safety Program in the Hospital Environment.* Washington, DC: Occupational Safety and Health Administration, Directorate of Technical Support, Office of Occupational Health Nursing.

Wenzel, R. 1987. *Prevention and Control of Nosocomial Infections.* Baltimore, MD: Williams & Wilkins.

Notes

1. National Fire Protection Association, 1981, *Code for Safety to Life from Fire in Buildings and Structures* (Boston: The Association). See also other NFPA publications, such as *Health Care Facilities Handbook*, 3d ed., 1990.

2. L. L. Neibauer, 1990, "Codes Put Greater Emphasis on Life Safety," *Consulting-Specifying Engineer* 7 (April Supplement 2): 18–20, 23.

3. *Federal Register,* 1991, "Americans with Disabilities Act (ADA): Accessibility Guidelines for Buildings and Facilities, Architectural and Transportation Barriers Compliance Board," 56 (26 July): 35408–542.

4. *Healthcare Hazardous Materials Management,* 1994, "Controlling Ambient Biohazards: What You Can't See Can Hurt," 7 (March): 6–8.

5. J. A. Sather, 1990, "Health Care Facilities Demand Reliable Electrical Distribution Systems," *Consulting-Specifying Engineer* 7 (February): 34–39.

6. I. Lazar, 1990, "Standby Power for Critical Areas: Hospitals," *Consulting-Specifying Engineer* 7 (February): 50–55.

7. D. K. Wilder, 1993, "Clinical Engineering Support for the Critical Care Unit," *Critical Care Clinics* 9 (July): 501–9.

8. M. L. Dickerson and M. E. Jackson, 1992, "Technology Management: A Perspective on System Support, Procurement, and Replacement Planning," *Journal of Clinical Engineering* 17 (March–April): 129–36.

9. J. T. Anderson, 1992, "A Risk-Related Preventive Maintenance System," *Journal of Clinical Engineering* 17 (January–February): 65–68.

10. J. Malkin, 1993, "Beyond Interior Design," *Health Facilities Management* 6 (November): 18–22, 24–25.

11. R. S. Ulrich, 1991, "Effects of Interior Design on Wellness: Theory and Recent Scientific Research," *Journal of Health Care Interior Design* 3: 97–109.

12. *Federal Register*, 1992, "Hazardous Waste Management System: Identification and Listing of Hazardous Waste—EPA. Final Rule and Response to Comments," 57 (2 January): 124.

13. J. H. Keene, 1991, "Medical Waste: A Minimal Hazard," *Infection Control and Hospital Epidemiology* 12 (November): 682–85.

14. A. N. Hayne and L. T. Peoples, 1993, "Analysis of an Organization's Waste Stream," *Hospital Material Management Quarterly* 14 (February): 46–55.

15. J. Studnicki, 1992, "The Medical Waste Audit: A Framework for Hospitals to Appraise Options and Financial Implications," *Health Progress* 73 (March): 68–74, 77.

16. P. Hebert, A. Stechman, B. Snyder, and R. Gralla, 1990, "Design and Implementation Issues in Training Staff to do Primary Prevention of HIV in Acute Care Settings," *International Conference on AIDS* 6 (June): 312.

17. J. M. Golden, Jr., 1991, "Safety and Health Compliance for Hazmat: The 'HAZWOPER' (Worker Protection Standards for Hazardous Waste Operations and Emergency Response) Standard," *Journal of Emergency Medical Services* 16 (October): 28–31, 33.

18. *Hospital Security and Safety Management*, 1993, "Special Report—Violence in Hospitals: What Are the Causes? Why Is It Increasing? How Is It Being Confronted?" 13 (January): 5–10.

19. *Hospital Security and Safety Management*, 1993, "Special Report—Update on EAS (Electronic Article Surveillance) Systems: Protecting against Patient Wandering, Infant Abduction, Property Theft," 14 (October): 5–9.

20. *Hospital Security and Safety Management*, 1994, "Special Report—Upgrading Security: Hospitals Opt for New Equipment, New Approaches, Heavy Investments in Additional Patient, Employee Protection," 15 (July): 5–9.

21. G. L. Ellis, D. A. Dehart, C. Black, M. J. Gula, and A. Owens, 1994, "ED Security: A National Telephone Survey," *American Journal of Emergency Medicine* 12 (March): 155–59.

22. *Hospital Security and Safety Management*, 1993, "Special Report—Hospitals and Parking Security: Shoring up a Major Crime Locale," 14 (November): 5–9.

23. G. C. Kim and M. J. Schniederjans, 1993, "Empirical Comparison of Just-in-Time and Stockless Material Management Systems in the Health Care Industry," *Hospital Materiel Management Quarterly* 14 (May): 65–74.

24. J. C. Kowalski, 1991, "Inventory to Go: Can Stockless Deliver Efficiency?" *Healthcare Financial Management* 45 (November): 21–22, 24, 26.

25. P. Cappa, 1994, "Outfitting Your Hospital for the New Wave of Robots," *Journal of Healthcare Materiel Management* 12 (June): 334, 37–38.

26. American Hospital Association, 1974, *Hospital Engineering Handbook* (Chicago: AHA), 20–21; J. H. Holmgren and W. J. Wentz, 1982, *Material Management and Purchasing for the Health Care Facility* (Ann Arbor, MI: Health Administration Press), 243–49.

27. S. M. Majercik, 1991, "The BMET (Biomedical Equipment Technician) Career: Academic Curricula, Hospital Needs, and Employee Perceptions," *Journal of Clinical Engineering* 16 (September–October): 393–402.

28. W. A. Morse, 1992, "Career Opportunities in Clinical Engineering," *Journal of Clinical Engineering* 17 (July–August): 303–11.

29. J. B. Quinn, T. L. Doorley, and P. C. Paquette, 1990, "Beyond Products: Services-Based Strategy," *Harvard Business Review* 68 (March–April): 58–60, 64–66, 68.

30. C. L. Tudor and C. R. Gemmill, 1994, "Third-Party Capital Equipment Management Cuts Costs," *Healthcare Financial Management* 43 (April): 32–36, 38.

31. L. T. McAuley, 1993, "Administrative and Operational Responsibilities in Contract Management," *Topics in Health Care Financing* 20 (Winter): 76–81.

32. M. Frize and M. Shaffer, 1991, "Clinical Engineering in Today's Hospital: Perspectives of the Administrator and the Clinical Engineer," *Hospital & Health Services Administration* 36 (Summer): 285–305.

33. Holmgren and Wentz, *Material Management and Purchasing,* 6.

34. Ibid.

35. O. R. Keil, 1994, "The Joint Commission's Agenda for Change: What Does It Mean for Equipment Managers?" *Biomedical Instrumentation and Technology* 28 (January–February): 14–17.

36. E. Weisman, 1994, "The Agenda for Change: Performance Focus Alters JCAHO's Survey Process," *Health Facilities Management* 7 (January): 16, 18–19; 7 (February): 26, 28–31.

37. L. Duplechan, 1993, "The Internal Environmental Audit: A Practical Plan for Hospitals," *Healthcare Facilities Management Series* (July): 1–24.

GLOSSARY

Accountability. The notion that the organization can rely upon the individual to fulfill a specific, prearranged expectation.

Acuity. A measure of how sick patients are, used to establish nurse staffing needs.

Alliances. Relations between organizations that are entered into primarily for strategic purposes.

American College of Healthcare Executives (ACHE). The leading professional association for health care managers.

American Osteopathic Association (AOA). A voluntary national organization of osteopathic physicians. AOA offers inspection and accreditation services similar to those of the Joint Commission.

Ancillary services. *See* Clinical support services.

Appropriate care. Care for which expected health benefits exceed negative consequences.

Attending physicians. Those doctors having the privilege of using the hospital for patient care.

Bar chart. A display of differing values by some useful dimension, such as day of week, operator, site, or patient group.

Benchmark. The best known value for a specific measure, from any source.

Best practice. A process used to generate a benchmark.

Blue Cross–Blue Shield Plan. A locally managed health insurer participating in the national Blue Cross–Blue Shield Association.

Boundary spanning. Activities through which the organization selects its exchanges looking outward to define what the organization must do to thrive.

Budget guidelines. Desirable levels of key financial indicators established at the start of the budget process by the governing board.

Bureaucratic organization. A form of human endeavor where groups of individuals bring different skills to bear on a single objective in accordance with a formal structure of authority and responsibility.

Business units. Activities for which health care organizations create separate hierarchies. They may include nonhealth care activities, such as health insurance.

Care plans. Expectations for the care of individual patients, normally aggregates of several intermediate product protocols.

Case manager. An individual who coordinates and oversees other health care professionals in finding the most effective method of caring for specific patients.

Cash flow budget. Forecasts of cash income and outgo by period.

Cause and effect diagrams. These show relationships between complex flows and allow teams to identify components, test them as specific causes, and focus their investigation.

Census. Number of patients in a hospital or other inpatient unit.

Centralized structures. Organizations that retain much control in the parent unit.

Certificates of need. Franchises for new services and construction or renovation of hospitals or related facilities, formerly issued by many states.

Charitable organizations. Organizations with tax exempt status distributing funds and other resources for charitable purposes.

Chief executive officer (CEO). The agent of the governing board holding the formal accountability for the entire organization.

Client-servers. Computing machinery that makes it possible for multiple users to be in communication at the same time and facilitates translation between alternative data formats used by the competing hardware and operating systems.

Clinical expectation. A consensus reached on the correct professional response to a specific, recurring situation in patient care.

Clinical nurse practitioner. Nurse with extra training who accepts additional clinical responsibility for medical diagnosis or treatment.

Clinical support service. (1) A unit organized around one or more medical specialties or clinical professions providing individual patient care on order of an attending physician, such as laboratory or physical therapy. (2) A general community service, such as health education, immunization, and screening, under the general guidance of the medical staff.

Clinical system. The part of a health care organization that provides hands-on patient care and monitors it to ensure both quality and effectiveness.

Clinic rounds. Educational review of cases in an outpatient setting or clinic.

Collateral organization. The broad group of organizational activities such as committees, conferences, task forces, and retreats that are established for the purpose of attacking problems crossing several organizational units.

Common provider entity. A single entity willing to accept full payment from an insurance carrier or intermediary for a "bundle" of provider services and distribute it as indicated.

Community. A group of geographically related individuals and organizations sharing some resources. Health care organizations are usually among the shared resources of a community.

Community-focused strategic management. The notion that the organization repeatedly asks itself the questions, What is our community's goal? Why? and How does the organization best serve it? and uses the answers to select among business opportunities.

Community hospital. (1) A hospital offering short-term general and other special services, owned by groups other than the federal government. (2) An institution whose purpose is to provide personal health care in a manner which uses the available resources most effectively for the community's benefit.

Conjoint medical staff. A flexible and pluralistic relationship between doctors and the hospital that assumes increasingly close affiliation. It combines the requirements of a "privileged medical staff" with formal planning for physician recruitment and ongoing participation in operating and strategic decisions.

Constraints. Limits on the range of acceptable operating conditions.

Continuous improvement. A concept of the organization setting expectations that it can and will achieve, but that will be set at a higher level each year.

Control chart. A run chart with the addition of statistical quality control limits.

Controlled substances. Drugs regulated by the federal government, such as narcotics.

Cost budgets. Anticipated volumes of demand or output with emphasis on direct costs controllable by the responsibility center or unit.

Credentialing. The process of privilege review.

Customers. Exchange partners who use the services of the organization and generally compensate the organization for those services (e.g., patients). Also, by extension, other units within the hospital that rely upon a particular unit for service.

Cybernetic system. An organized activity reflecting purposive search: the establishment of goals, measurement of progress, and correction of activity to improve progress.

Decentralized structures. Those that allow much power in subsidiary, as opposed to central units.

Decision support systems (DSS). Information recovery systems that provide rapid retrieval of selected data from multiple files or archives.

Department. A unit of the accountability hierarchy comprised of several responsibility centers, such as "housekeeping department." Also an organization of doctors in a major specialty, as in "obstetrics department."

Deterministic models. Those that deal with future events as fixed numbers, rather than as random events subject to a predictable variance.

Diagnosis-related groups (DRGs). Groups of inpatient discharges with final diagnoses that are similar clinically and in resource consumption; used as a basis of payment by the Medicare program, and as a result, widely accepted by others.

Direct costs. The costs of resources used directly in an activity that can be controlled through the unit accountable for the activity.

Discharge planning. A part of the patient management guidelines and the nursing care plan that identifies the expected discharge date and coordinates the various services necessary to achieve the target.

Diversification. Acquisition of nonhealth care activities, such as residences for the aging, or even commercial activities like laundry services.

Efficiency. (1) The return or output achieved for a given level of input or resources. (2) The ratio of output to input, or input to output.

Employees. Exchange partners compensated by salary and wages.

Empowerment. Achievement of the ability to influence working conditions and service policies; usually applied to lower-level managers and nonmanagerial personnel.

Endogenous events. Those largely within the control of an operator.

Environmental assessment. A corporate activity identifying changes in the environment and the perspectives of others in the community on these changes, with particular attention to those changes affecting customers, competitors, and members of the hospital.

Environmental Protection Agency. Federal and state units which affect health care organizations' interaction with the physical environment.

Equal employment opportunity agencies. Government agencies that monitor the rights of population groups to employment.

Exchange. A mutual or reciprocal transfer that occurs when both parties believe themselves to benefit from it. It results in a relationship between an organization and its environment, such as employment, sales, donations, or purchases.

Exchange partners. Individuals or groups participating in exchanges with the hospital.

Executive. Informally, a manager who participates in the strategic functions of the organization or who supervises several levels of managers.

Exogenous events. Those that are largely outside the control of a line operator.

Expectation. (1) A work goal for an organization unit and its members. (2) A specific statement summarizing agreed-upon dimensions of performance.

Expenditure budgets. Costs anticipated by reporting period, responsibility center, and natural account.

Final product budgets. The cost and revenue for DRGs and capitated costs per member per month.

Final product. A set of clinical services reaching a generally recognized end point in the process of care, such as hospital discharge, or care for an individual for a discrete illness or an extended period of time.

Final product protocol. A consensus expectation detailing the accepted steps to reach a recognized end point in care, such as hospital discharge.

Financial budgets. Expectations of future financial performance composed of income and expense budget, budgeted financial statements, cash flow budget, new programs, and capital budget.

First-line supervisor. *See* Responsibility center manager

Fishbone diagrams. *See* Cause and effect diagrams

Flexible budget. An expenditure budget based on changing variable costs to meet an expectation for a steady unit cost.

Flow process charts. Diagrams showing the sequence of events in a process, frequently used to analyze and improve the process.

Forecasts. Predictions of future operating environments.

Formal organization. One that grants authority over certain activities, is held accountable for certain results, and compensates participants for their effort.

For-profit hospitals. Those owned by private corporations that declare dividends or otherwise distribute profits to individuals. Also called *investor-owned*, they are usually community hospitals.

Frequency. In advertising, the average number of times each person is reached by a specific advertisement.

General ledger transactions. Financial transactions that are internal rather than external exchanges. They often deal with resources that last considerably longer than one budget or financial period.

Governance. The activity of an organization that monitors the outside environment, selects appropriate alternatives, and negotiates the implementation of these alternatives with others inside and outside the organization.

Government regulatory agencies. Agencies with established authority over health care activities—licensing agencies and rate-regulating commissions are examples.

Grand rounds. Didactic presentations on clinical subjects of general interest.

Gross revenue. The sum of all posted charges in a specified time period.

Group purchasing. Alliances that use the collective buying power of several organizations to leverage prices downward.

Guideline. *See* Protocol

Hawthorne effect. The fact that experimentation itself and the attention it draws can improve performance, independent of the experiment itself.

Health maintenance organizations (HMOs). Health insurance plans emphasizing comprehensive care under a single insurance premium and using a variety of devices to control cost and quality.

Histogram. A graphic display grouping individual values that shows the relative frequency of each group.

Homeostasis. In biology a "state of physiological equilibrium produced by a balance of functions and of chemical composition within a organism" and more generally a "tendency toward relatively stable equilibrium between interdependent elements."

Horizontal integration. Integration of organizations providing the same kind of service, such as two hospitals or two clinics.

Hospital-based specialists. Those physicians providing consultative care to attending physicians, such as pathologists, radiologists, and anesthesiologists.

House officers. Licensed doctors pursuing postgraduate education.

Human resources system. The part of a health care organization that recruits and supports the hospital's employees and other workers, such as doctors and volunteers.

Human subjects committee. A committee reviewing research activities for potential dangers to patients.

Implicit profit. The difference between revenues at the transfer price and costs.

Incident report. Written report of an untoward event that raises the possibility of liability of the organization.

Income and expense budget. Expected net income and expenses incurred by the organization as a whole.

Independent physician associations (IPAs). Health maintenance organizations paying their affiliated doctors on a basis other than salary.

Indirect costs. Costs incurred for large aggregates of the organization that cannot be directly attributed to components or responsibility centers. Insurance, debt services, expenses of the executive office, and the operation of central services like parking and security are examples.

Influence. The ability to affect an organization's or an activity's success. Influence is usually gained by controlling a resource.

Influentials. Exchange partners having above-average influence on the affairs of the organization.

Informal organizations. Human behavior where groups of people share information and gratification, make partnerships and friendships, and divide and specialize the work.

Information services. The activity supporting the development and integration of information systems and the supply of information to points of use.

Information system. An automated process of capture, transmission, and recording of information which is permanently accessible to the organization as a whole.

Insurance carrier. An intermediary bearing insurance risk.

Integrated information system. A set of two or more information systems organized to provide immediate electronic access to information in each.

Intermediary. A payment or management agent for health care insurance—e.g., Medicare intermediaries—who pay providers as agents for the U.S. Health Care Financing Administration.

Intermediate product. A procedure that is a part of care, such as a surgical operation.

Intermediate product protocol. A consensus expectation that establishes the normal set of activities and performance for an intermediate product.

Inurement. A dispersal of corporate funds to an individual. Particularly, illegal dispersal of funds of a not-for-profit corporation or dispersal of funds to persons in governance or management.

Inurement rules. Rules that protect against the distribution of assets of a community corporation to individuals or small groups within the community.

Joint Commission on Accreditation of Healthcare Organizations (JCAHO). A national organization of representatives of health care providers: American College of Physicians, American College of Surgeons, American Hospital Association, American Medical Association, and consumer representatives. The JCAHO offers inspection and accreditation on quality of operations to hospitals and other health care organizations.

Licensure. Government approval to perform specified activities.

Life Safety Code. Safety and convenience regulations developed by the National Fire Protection Association.

Line units. Units of the accountability hierarchy directly concerned with the principal product or outcome of the organization. In health care organizations, the clinical units are medicine, nursing, and the clinical support services.

Local area networks (LANs). Computer links that serve individual units within about 1,000 yards of one another.

Long-range planning. The series of resource allocation decisions implementing vision and strategies over several future years.

Long-range plans. Documents that record decisions made, usually in the form of actions or events that are expected to occur at specific future times.

Management by objective (MBO). Agreement in advance between the responsibility center manager and the supercontroller as to the accomplishment, documents, or projects to be completed within the period.

Management letter. Comments of external auditors to the governing board that accompany their audited financial report.

Managerial accounting. A deliberate effort to relate revenue and expenditures to individual services and the activities of responsibility centers.

Marginal costs. Changes in costs attributable to changes in operating conditions, usually volume of demand.

Marketing. (1) In common usage, generally implies sales, promotional, or advertising activity, but in professional texts and journals, it also incorporates the entire set of activities and processes normally ascribed to planning plus those relating to sales and promotion. (2) The deliberate effort to establish fruitful relationships with exchange partners, not just to customers, but to all exchanges, including employees and other community agencies.

Markets. Groups of people seeking to make exchanges of value.

Matrix organizations. Organizations where RCs or middle managers have explicit, permanent dual accountability. Reporting can be developed around any pair of the potential conflict points: geography, time, skill or profession, task or patient.

Media. Press, radio, television, and purchased advertising that provide communications with exchange partners.

Medicaid agency. The state agency handling claims and payments for Medicaid.

Medicaid. Governmental assistance for care of the poor and, occasionally, the near-poor established through the state/federal program included in Public Law 89-97, Title 19.

Medical staff bylaws. A formal statement of the governance procedures of the medical staff.

Medical staff members. Physicians, dentists, psychologists, podiatrists, etc., admitted to practice in the health care organization.

Medical staff organization. The structure that both represents and governs medical staff members.

Medical staff recruitment plan. An element of the long-range plan establishing both the size of the medical staff and the services the hospital will provide.

Medicare intermediary. The private agency handling claims and payments for the federal Medicare programs; often the local Blue Cross–Blue Shield Plan.

Medicare. Social Security health insurance for the aged established by Public Law 89-97, Title 18.

Members. Those people who participate in the hospital's closed system activities. Members are employees, doctors, trustees, other volunteers, and other nonemployed providers of care, chiefly dentists, psychologists, and podiatrists.

Middle managers. Persons with supervisory authority over several responsibility centers, supervised in turn by executives.

Mission. A statement of the good or benefit the health care organization intends to contribute, couched in terms of an identified community, a set of services, and a specific level of cost or finance.

Modal specialists. Those who treat the largest percentage of patients with the disease or condition.

Model. A simplified representation of reality which can be manipulated to test various hypotheses about the future.

Monte Carlo simulation. A computerized test of a stochastic model by repeated trial.

Natural accounts. The kinds of resources purchased, principally labor, supplies, equipment and facilities, and other.

Net revenue. Income actually received as opposed to what is initially requested, equal to gross revenue minus adjustments for bad debts, charity, and discounts to third parties.

Networks. Associations or affiliations among exchange partners with similar interests.

New programs and capital budget. Lists of proposed capital expenditures and new or significantly revised programs, with their implications for the operating and cash budgets by period and responsibility center.

Nominating committee. A standing committee of the governing board usually responsible for nominating board members and officers.

Nurse anesthetist. A Registered Nurse with special training and certification who administers anesthesia.

Nurse midwife. A Registered Nurse with special training and certification who practices uncomplicated obstetrics.

Nurse practitioner. A Registered Nurse with special training and certification providing patient care under the general supervision of a physician.

Nursing. The provision of physical, emotional, and educational services to support or improve patients' equilibrium with their environment and to help the patients regain independence as rapidly as possible.

Objective function. A quantitative statement of the desired results of a process. Used in optimization modeling.

Occupational Safety and Health Administration. Government agency that monitors the health and safety of employees.

Open system. Pattern of relationships and dependencies that connect the organization to its environment.

Operating budget. A forecast of responsibility center costs, aggregate expenditures, and revenue.

Operating system. A process identifying specific expectations of organizational units or activities.

Opportunity cost. The cost of committing a resource and thereby eliminating it from other potential uses or opportunities; they do not appear in accounting records.

Optimization. Allocation of scarce resources to maximize achievement of some good or benefit.

Overhead. *See* Indirect costs

Pareto analysis. A bar chart format, with the items rank-ordered on a dependent variable such as cost, profit, or satisfaction, that examines the components of a problem in terms of their contribution to it.

Patient ledger. Account of the charges rendered to an individual patient.

Patient management guideline. *See* Final product protocol

Peer review. Any review of professional performance by members of the same profession.

Physician-hospital organization (PHO). A formal organization melding the interests of the community hospital and its physicians that has equal or near equal representation of hospital and physician directors.

Plan-Do-Check-Act (PDCA). An approach to problem solving characterized by careful study of the problem (Plan), a proposal for revision (Do), a trial (Check), and implementation (Act).

Planning. The process of making resource allocation decisions about the future, particularly the process of involving organization members and selecting among alternative courses of action.

Plant (operations) system. The part of a health care organization that operates and maintains the physical facilities and equipment.

Position control. A system controlling the number of positions created and identifying specific persons hired to fill them.

Power. Influence that is relative among partners and variable across time and place.

Preferred provider organization (PPO). A health care financing plans that encourage subscribers to seek care from selected hospitals, doctors, and other providers with whom they have established a contract; often an intermediary arrangement with insurance risk remaining with the employer. PPOs may or may not include care management.

Primary care practitioners. Doctors in family practice, general internal medicine, pediatrics, nurse practitioners, and midwives and may also include psychiatrists and emergency care physicians.

Primary monitor. *See* Responsibility center manager

Primary work group. *See* Responsibility center

Privileges. Rights granted annually to physicians and affiliate staff members to perform specified kinds of care in the hospital.

Process. The series of actions or steps that transform inputs to outputs.

Productivity. *See* Efficiency

Professional review organizations (PROs). Organizations led by doctors which do not insure or provide care but which audit the quality of care and the use of insurance benefits for Medicare and other insurers.

Programmatic proposals. Ones for resource allocation usually arising from the units or departments, tending to affect only the nominating department, which are intended for inclusion in the new programs and capital budget.

Prospective Payment System (PPS). A nationally promulgated price structure for Medicare patients.

Protocol. A formal consensus on an appropriate program for diagnosis or treatment. *See* **Intermediate** product protocol and Final product protocol.

Provider. An individual who provides health care services to patients and generally is compensated for the service.

Quality of care. The degree to which health services for individuals and populations increase the likelihood of desired health outcomes and are consistent with current professional knowledge.

Quality. The value or contribution of the output as defined by, or on behalf of, the customer.

Reach. In advertising, an estimate of the number of people who will see or hear a specific advertisement.

Referral specialists. Doctors who see patients referred by primary care doctors.

Relative value scales. Scales expressing the relative value of individual services such as laboratory tests or physician's care activities.

Reserved powers. Those held permanently by the central corporate board in a multi-corporate organization.

Resource allocation decisions. The commitment to expend resources for certain purposes.

Resource dependency. The concept which suggests that organizations depend on their ability to attract resources such as financial support of customers and the efforts of employees.

Responsibility center manager (RCM). The supervisor of a responsibility center, also called a primary monitor or first-line supervisor.

Responsibility center (RC). The smallest formal unit of organizational activity, usually the first level at which a supervisor is formally designated.

Revenue budgets. Expectations of future income.

Run chart. A display of performance data over time to show trends and variation.

Scale. The size and scope of an organization.

Scatter diagram. A graphic device for showing association between two measures.

Scenarios. Various ways to improve the strengths, weaknesses, opportunities, and threats (SWOT) proposed and evaluated against the environmental assessment; alternative perceptions of future actions and performance.

Section. In medical organizations, an organization of members of a given subspeciality.

Segmentation. The deliberate effort to separate markets by their characteristics in order to forecast or modify demand.

Self-perpetuating boards. Governing boards that themselves select new members and successors.

Sensitivity analysis. Analysis of the impact of changed exogenous events, usually developing (in modeling) most favorable, expected, and least favorable scenarios to show the robustness of a proposal and indicate the degree of risk involved.

Service lines. Markets for which health care organizations frequently create separate hierarchies and may include nonhealth care activities, such as health insurance.

Severity scales. Generalized scales that can adjust for variation in patient condition. *See also* Acuity

Shewhart cycle. *See* Plan-Do-Check-Act (PDCA)

Staff units. Units of the accountability hierarchy that serve technical or support activities for the line.

Stakeholders. Those exchange partners whose views are sufficiently important to directly affect the organization's success.

Standard cost. An established expectation for unit cost, usually based on process analysis or best practice.

Stochastic models. Those incorporating chance variation in the analysis and evaluation of the solutions.

Strategic apex. The uppermost levels of a bureaucratic organization concerned principally with functions of governance, planning, and finance.

Strategic opportunities. Opportunities that involve quantum shifts in service capabilities or market share, usually by interaction with competitors, large-scale capital investments, and revisions to several line activities.

Strategic planning. A process reviewing the mission, environmental surveillance, and previous planning decisions used to establish major goals and nonrecurring resource allocation decisions.

Strategic position. Mission, ownership, scope of activity, location, and partners of the organization, in comparison to a market and competitors.

Structural measures. Measures of compliance with static expectations, such as those relating to physical facilities or the formal training of individuals.

Supercontrollers. Managers who supervise responsibility center managers.

Suppliers. Exchange partners for goods and services such as supplies and utilities.

Surveillance. *See* Environmental assessment

Third-party administrators (TPAs). Organizations that process claims and sometimes also control use of benefits for employers who are carrying their own insurance. *See also* Intermediaries

Transfer costs. The costs of maintaining a relationship, including the costs of communication, negotiation, etc.

Transfer price. Imputed revenue for a good or service transferred between two units of the same organization, such as housekeeping services provided to nursing units; where the service is not sold directly to the public, the price is established by complex cost-accounting and comparison against available market information.

Trustees. Members of the governing board of not-for-profit health care organizations. Trustees usually volunteer their time to the health care organization. The title reflects their acceptance of the assets in trust for the community.

Urgent. Demand which may be met within a few days but which cannot be deferred indefinitely.

Vertical integration. The affiliation of organizations providing different kinds of service, such as hospital care, ambulatory care, long-term care, and social services.

Vision statement. An expansion of the mission that expresses values, intentions, philosophy, and organizational self-image.

Volunteers. People who volunteer their time to the health care organization, their only compensation being the satisfaction they achieve from their work.

Ward rounds. Educational review of actual cases in a hospital, or (by extension) a clinic.

Wide area networks (WANs). Computer communication that reaches across cities or around the world.

Working capital. The amount of cash required to support operations for the period of delay in collecting revenue.

INDEX

.

ABOUT THE AUTHOR

John R. Griffith, M.B.A., FACHE, is Andrew Pattullo Collegiate Professor, Department of Health Services Management and Policy, School of Public Health, The University of Michigan, Ann Arbor. A graduate of the Johns Hopkins University and the University of Chicago, he was Director of the Program and Bureau of Hospital Administration at The University of Michigan from 1970 to 1982 and Chair of his department from 1987 to 1991. He was awarded the Gold Medal of the American College of Healthcare Executives in 1992. He has been at the University of Michigan since 1960 and has served as a consultant to numerous private and public organizations. He is the author of numerous publications, including the The *Well-Managed Community Hospital*, which won the ACHE Hamilton Book Award in 1987.